BEING AND DUTY

JACEK JADACKI

BEING AND DUTY

THE CONTRIBUTION OF 20TH-CENTURY POLISH THINKERS TO THE THEORY OF IMPERATIVES AND NORMS

Editing Team:
Piotr Michał Godlewski
Aeddan Shaw

Cover design:
Mariusz Banachowicz

Layout:
Mirosław Krzyszkowski

Typesetting:
Wydawnictwo Profil-Archeo
Magdalena Dzięgielewska

Publikacja dofinansowana przez Uniwersytet Warszawski
ze środków przekazanych przez Fundację na rzecz Nauki Polskiej
w ramach programu *Homing Plus*

ISBN 978-83-7886-017-4

Kraków 2013

Publisher: Copernicus Center Press Sp. z o.o.,
pl. Szczepański 8, 31-011 Kraków,
tel/fax (+48) 12 430 63 00
e-mail: marketing@ccpress.pl;
http://en.ccpress.pl

Printing and binding by *Sowa Sp. z o.o.*

I would like to thank Professor Anna Brożek,
an accomplished specialist in the domain
of the theory of imperatives,
whose constructive criticism
has helped to make this book free
of the many mistakes that might have
otherwise occurred.
I would also like to express my gratitude
to Miss Alicja Chybińska, M.A.,
for her competent linguistic assistance.

Contents

Foreword

The book which the Reader has in front of them is composed of three parts. The first component analyses the creative contribution to the theory of imperatives and norms provided by Polish researchers in the 20th century. The second component summarizes their reflections and considerations. This constitutes the first half of the publication. The third part (and second half) is a compilation of the classic writings of Polish authors of the period and constitutes a practical illustration of the first half.

The following comments are necessary here.

The analysis – included in component one – was made *via* my own examination of the aforementioned intellectuals. Yet everything that I wrote was subsequently critically reviewed and commented upon by Professor Anna Brożek, whom I would sincerely like to thank as her comments prevented many of my mistakes. A certain unified net of ideas is proposed in the analysis. It allows for a comparison between different conceptions within the discussed matter – which were originally referred to under numerous different names.

Part two – the summary – is firstly and foremostly the viewpoints of each researcher presented chronologically (*i.e.* according to the date, when the researcher first spoke on the particular subject). Secondly, special attention is paid to these works which will not be found in component three.

The selection – part three – should provide the Reader with a representative image of Polish thought in the 20th century, within the frames indicated in the publication's title. What matters most are the issues of what is often called "philosophy of language". Texts presenting the original logical systems of imperatives and norms which were published in Poland in the

20th century did not find their way into the selection. One of the main reasons behind this is the fact that a comprehensive presentation of these systems would require the inclusion of the full texts in question. Those texts, usually of considerable, irreducible length, would disrupt the planned size of the book.

1. Preferential situation

The simplest preferential situation – *i.e.* situation of willing – consists in the following:

(1) The person A wants S^1 to occur.

The person A is THE SUBJECT of the act of willing, and S is THE OBJECT of willing (*i.e.* the preferred state of affairs).

The following interrelation occurs:

(2) A wants S to occur – when[2] – if S does not occur, then A will be dissatisfied.

A more complex preferential situation than (1) is the following:

(3) A wants B to cause the occurrence of S.

B is here THE AGENT performing the (object) of willing.

The preference from situation (3) is DIRECTED willing; in fact it is a particular case of situation (1). With directed acts of willing, the agent performing the act might be both the subject of the act or a different person.

Formula (2) might be considered as a definition of "(non-directed) willing".

• The complex of psychological phenomena culminating in the act of willing and leading to the action (*i.e.* the act) was provisionally analysed by Borowski [1923]. He considered the initial phenomenon to be the motives of an activity, or impulses (that is, "impressions, feelings, moods, thoughts, fancies") "judged negatively", and therefore leading towards "liberation"

---

[1] In this work, symbols 'S', 'S_1' and 'S_2' indicate states of affaires stated by some declarative sentences; this manner of symbolization has to prevent using the formulas of the type "the fact that p" (where 'p' is a sentential variable), which contains the word "fact" suggesting unforunately factuality of the suitable state of affair.

[2] Here – and *passim* – "when" means "always and only if".

from them. The motives of an activity were clearly distinguished from its aims – always positive for the performer – that is, from presenting a "certain desired future event". Willing was perceived by Borowski as driving directed from the motive towards the aim, with the underlying conviction that the aim is reachable. In case of different motives and correlated aims – one must make a choice between them, that is between the aims to be realized.

• The term "willing" (or "volition") was thought to be non-definable by Cheliński [1925]. According to him, volitional states are non-analysable and only perceivable when introspecting.

• Znamierowski [1957] presented a more detailed conception of willing – or in his words: driving. Generally speaking, he characterized this psychological phenomenon as follows:

> Driving is, when occurring in accordance with its pattern, tension; it is supposed to trigger a certain movement reaction towards the final state of affairs [1957: 142]. Driving [...] also contains a hidden tendency to change, a movement tendency, as with the physical tension [1957: 130].

Znamierowski distinguished driving from drift – a disposition towards experiencing similar drivings.

There are several constituents of driving, according to Znamierowski:

(a) the perceptive element, an impression part of the preparatory tension;

(b) the psychological impulse, the core of driving;

(c) the scheme of the "movement tract", where driving is realisable (*i.e.* where the aim of driving may be reached).

Drivings differ from one another with regard to the following aspects:

(a) quality (*cf.* hunger, thirst[3] *etc.*);

(b) reason (*cf.* innate or instinctive and acquired drivings);

(c) aim – that is, the point (state of affairs, object of driving) which determines the direction of driving (*cf.* inclination – or appulsion, *i.e.* positive

---

[3] Thirst is here referred to as an equivalent of hunger, but regarding liquids; in Polish the words "thirst" and "desire" are homonyms.

driving towards something, and disgust or repulsion, negative driving away from something);

(d) consciousness regarding the aim (*cf.* conscious and unconscious drivings);

(e) instrumentality (*cf.* independent and dependent drivings, when we drive at something in order to acquire something else).

2. Preferences and impulses, decisions and tendencies

Willing should be differentiated from inclination, resolution, and desire. When speaking about A that:

(1) The person A is inclined towards x.

we speak about a certain inner IMPULSE with its source in a certain disposition.

Naturally:

(2) It is false that (the person A wants S to occur, when the person A is inclined towards S).

Resolution – *i.e.* making A DECISION, an act of volition – is an instant act, contrastively to willing, which is a state that may last for a longer time. The following interrelation occurs:

(3) If the person A at the time T_0 resolved to cause S to occur, then the person A for the time period T, later than the momentary T_0, wants S to occur.

THE TENDENCY (*i.e.* driving) towards something may be understood as somebody's conscious activity towards S. Therefore:

(4) If the person A drives in the time period T towards S to ccur, then the person A in the time period T wants S to occur.

• Modern Polish research on resolutions was first undertaken by Witwicki [1904]. He wrote:

> The aim [...] is to answer the question whether symptoms of will are simple phenomena or whether it is possible to factorize them to psychological components or reduce to simple, known spiritual phenomena, as *e.g.* presentations, feelings and convictions, which are mostly considered to be psychological [1904: 6].

Witwicki offers a suggestion that resolutions are precisely symptoms of will [1904: 8]. There are two conceptions of resolutions as regards their psychological status: idiogenetic and allogenetic. The idiogenetic conception claims that resolutions are irreducible psychological elements. The allogenetic conception reduces them to a combination of other simple spiritual phenomena, or to a specific type of those [1904: 8].

Witwicki supports the second conception, also as regards thirsts:

> Thirsts may be fully factorized down to judgements, presented judgements and feelings. The core of resolutions (the acts of will in a more narrow sense) shall be the judgement concerning one's own [random, independent] activity [1904: 99; *cf.* also 27, 40].

Thirst (particularly the thirst for reaching a certain aim) is a condition for – and not as some may think a component of – resolutions. Another condition for a resolution is for it also "to refer only to those matters that are within our reach, in our opinion" [1904: 37].

Yet not every judgement concerning future events is a resolution.

> Saying: "I will die in a few years due to an illness or by accident" does not express a resolution. Yet saying: "I will cause my own death" is an expression of a resolution [1904: 40].

Witwicki differentiated between such "theoretical judgements", as he called them, and judgements expressing resolutions; he called the latter "practical judgements" [1904: 119].

Resolutions must be also distinguished from evaluating judgements concerning the object of resolutions, *i.e.* the future activity of a given person:

> The resolution is not expressed by the words: "Such an action is beautiful", but by: "So will I act" [1904: 67].

Witwicki justifies his proposals firstly by referring to introspective acts:

At the times of resolutions, non-precedential internal experience deems [...] the judgement on our future activity as a significant element: ["I will act thus and thus"] [1904: 23].

Secondly, resolutions may be classified as a type of judgements because resolutions bear all significant features of judgements, namely:

(a) Resolutions "confirm or reject the reality of an object" [1904: 119]. The content of sentences expressing resolutions, such as:

(1) I resolve to do this and that.

does not add anything to the content of sentences speaking about the future:

(2) I will do this and that.

(b) Resolutions "are true or false" [1904: 119].

A true resolution equals a fulfilled one, a false resolution – an unfulfilled one [1904: 120–121]. At the same time, Witwicki warned against a common mistake: understanding truth as honesty: a true resolution is not the same as a shameful or honest one [1904: 122].

(c) Resolutions "are expressed *via* utterances" [1904: 122]; there are categorical, conditional and arbitrary judgements, as well as resolutions of these three types.

(d) One reaches a resolution "spontaneously" or *via* inference [1904: 122].

(e) Each resolution is marked with a different level of confidence: there are "unwavering" and "faltering" resolutions [1904: 122].

(f) There are actual and potential resolutions [1904: 123].

As Witwicki puts it, the allogenetic conception of resolutions bears far-reaching metaphysical consequences, especially with regard to free will; on the ground of this conception, the question of free will becomes the question of free judgement [1904: 123].

• Now, in contrast to Witwicki, Gabryl [1905/1906] differentiated thirst from, in his words, "mindful" willing (and resolution being its part); the difference still exists even though there are visible similarities. The thirst is spontaneous and may be directed at an unreachable object; if it is realized, it sometimes causes us to lose our inner balance. The mindful willing, contrastively, is reflective ("conscious"), and has only reachable objects; its realization gives us the feeling of "control over ourselves".

Therefore, Gabryl does not perceive the allogenetic conception of will as acceptable.

• Also Borowski [1923] was an opponent of the allogenetic conception of will. He disputes the equation of a person's acts of will with this persons' judgement regarding their future activity.

• Znamierowski also had a different view on the psychological status of a resolution. Znamierowski searched for sources (*i.e.* the foundations) for legal duties [1924] and analysed the relationship between evaluations and norms [1957]; on both occasions, he touched upon the subject of resolutions.

For Znamierowski, the source of a legal duty is the fact which makes the utterance which expresses the legal duty true – and (therefore) which makes it valid as a norm.

Within this understanding, Znamierowski claims that imperatives are the source for any legal duty.

The resolution (*i.e.* decision) was perceived by Znamierowski as a type of settlement (*i.e.* determination); other forms of settlement are for instance an agreement (a joint settlement of a common regulation for an activity, made by several or numerous persons) and a promise [1924: 28 *et seq.*]. The act of settlement may be expressed by verbal and physical means. As Znamierowski wrote:

> It is possible to create a regulation for other people's behaviour, if the physical conditions for activity are first created [...]. [This is] SETTLE-MENT *VIA* CONSTRUCTING PHYSICAL PRODUCTS [1924: 48].

By laying out a road in this and not that way, one makes others to use it precisely as we want it (if they do not want to try a more difficult road which had not yet been laid out).

Such are the characteristic features of resolutions according to Zna-mierowski:

> A norm is settled [...] in relation to the resolution for activity in a cer-tain way, but it is not identical with this resolution. A resolution has AN ACTIVITY OR ACT as its object; the new act of [SETTLEMENT] has the rule

of activity as its object [1924: 27]. [...] [Also], THE RESOLUTION always concerns THE ACTIONS OF THE PERSON MAKING THE RESOLUTION, whereas the SETTLEMENT may as well concern A RULE OF ACTIVITY FOR ANOTHER PERSON – not only the rule of activity of the person making the resolution. When I dictate to someone to act in a certain way – and the dictate [...] is an expression of settlement – then I set out the rule of behaviour foremost for the one who is ordered; I myself am only obliged to approve or not of their actions [1924: 27-28].

    I MAKE A RESOLUTION, when I decide ABOUT MY OWN ACTIVITY, which in my understanding will definitely occur, because the need and opportunity to act will certainly occur [1957: 490]. [...] [I SETTLE, when] I want [...] TO CREATE A NORM of activity, which will conditionally state that "I will do *d*, if *s* occurs". [...] The object of settlement might be not only the activity of MY OWN, but also OF OTHERS [1957: 491].

Settlements of this kind – according to Znamierowski – are not a judgement on our future acts; it is an "autonomous experience" of the choice [1957: 455]: it is "an experience that puts an end to the tangled state of reflection"; reflection is replaced with "the unwavering readiness to act, which will, in some measure, automatically turn into act when the conditions for the act are fulfiled" [1924: 25].

Readiness to act is not equal to a purely intellectual conviction that the resolved act shall take place. This readiness might be only dispositional until the critical moment of the act arrives; if it «becomes real» in the meantime, it will usually be in form of complex experiences – sometimes an unclear emotional intuition, sometimes the beginnings of a deriving, and finally, other times it will be an intellectual conviction that the resolution shall be realized. Alternatively, all these three experiences might become real at the same time.

    The resolution is an act of will, that is: the person making the resolution experiences it consciously and freely; it is not fully determined by this person's former psychological situation [1924: 25].

Znamierowski distinguished the following types of resolutions:

(a) unwavering (*i.e.* steadfast) and wavering;

(b) unconditional and conditional;

(c) concerning a particular act and concerning multiple activity.

The act of will was equated by Znamierowski with the so-called "conscious dart to move" [1957: 418] – that is, a conscious impulse which gradually strengthens the «movement tract» (the predisposition towards a certain activity); the strengthening occurs unconsciously, at first; then the tract reaches the point where it may overcome any resistance of the environment in which the actualisation (*i.e.* growing of driving) goes. The author defines the activity as "an act of will combined with an executive movement" [1957: 419]. "The act" is according to Znamierowski "such an activity and its consequences, which exceeds the boundaries of [the actor's] body and which belongs to the intention of the act of will" [1957: 420]. The first link in the "act's range" is the aforementioned consequence; the next links are the effects of this effect, *etc.* [1957: 420].

Within the act of will, a selection between possible activities occurs [1957: 442]. The selection was described as follows by Znamierowski:

> There is a time when our «I» stands before two possible activities and is supposed to choose; it then understands and feels that none of the pressing drivings is strong enough to lead to activity. The understanding comes from the direct insight into «I»'s experiences, as well as from the two determined factors: movement rush of each driving and resistance that must be overcome for either of activities to occur. The «I» therefore feels it is free, and that its impulse creates something that would not exist without it. Simultaneously, it sees in its unique, indirect way that it is this and not that driving which induces it to support the readiness to move with a decisive impulse. We say therefore that the «I» takes an insight into the MOTIVATIONAL RELATIONSHIP between the driving and the act of will. This relationship is different from a causal relationship: a victorious deriving does not force, but INDUCES to a particular activity [1957: 446].

If the deriving does not meet any resistance, and repeatedly appears in the consciousness, it becomes one of the factors influencing our lifestyle. We say then that we INTEND to do this and that, or in other words: attain this and that by our intentional behaviour [1957: 450].

This thirst was viewed by Znamierowski [1957] as an «incomplete» driving, in particular a driving which lacks the "movement tract" scheme.

Znamierowski believed the basic method of voicing resolutions to be uttering sentences about our future activity:

Usually, THE VERBAL FORM OF THE DECISION is the words: "I WILL DO THIS AND THAT IN A CERTAIN SITUATION s". These words belong to THE DECISION PROCESS itself; they express it in a twofold manner: they reveal that the decision process took place in the consciousness, and they indicate the decision's content [1957: 493].

Additionally, Znamierowski defined the act of «causing» as follows:

A person S is the CAUSER (creator) of his or her work, when the following conditions are fulfiled. S belongs to the system of things U, isolated within the time period from t_0 to t_n; it is so that an event z or trace s will appear in the thing R at the moment t_z, if at an earlier time t_k S behaves in the manner d, or if at a certain moment t_p another event z_p should occur; those events which might in the system U bring independently of each other z or s, may be numerous, but it is so that if one occurred, no other will occur; and in reality the event was that S behaved in the manner d [1957: 532].

• Dąmbska [1938] referred to Witwicki's solution, agreeing that sentences that express resolutions are utterings (true or false) concerning the future.

• Also Ajdukiewicz [1948] writes about the manner of expressing resolutions, and his findings may be, it seems, interpreted as follows: if the sentence Z uttered by the person O expresses judgement on a future act C

by the person O, a judgement which was uttered "on the basis of the experienced act of will" of the person O, and which is the "germ" from which later springs the act C by the person O – this sentence Z expresses a resolution of the person O. Ajdukiewicz [1965: 28] discusses also other attitudes towards a certain state of affairs, namely the reporting, asking, willing (*i.e.* wishing) and dictating attitudes.

3. Verbalization of preferences: imperatives

3.1. The main method of verbalizing one's willings is to formulate imperatives (*i.e.* imperative sentences). The most general form of an imperative is the formula:

(1) Let S occur!

A particular case of imperative (1) is the following imperative:

(2) In conditions W, let the person B cause S to occur!

We might simplify the matter and say that the imperative (2) consists of THE COMMAND "Let!" (or its equivalent) and THE BACKGROUND "in conditions W, the person B cause S to occur".

Formula (2) might yet be treated as a scheme of imperatives in the following, non-synonymous shapes:

(3) IN CONDITIONS W, LET the person B cause S to occur!

(4) In conditions W, LET THE PERSON B cause S to occur!

(5) In conditions W, LET the person B CAUSE S to occur!

The commands would then be correspondingly: "Let in conditions W!", "Let the person B!", and "Let cause S to occur!".[4]

The person who utters the imperative is its SENDER; the person at whom the imperative is directed is its RECEIVER.

It might sometimes be so that the sender is identical with the receiver, but usually they are two different persons. Sometimes the sender is identical with the executor of the will expressed in the imperative, but again – usually it is not so.

---

[4] I am here following Anna Brożek's suggestion that "the commands – as well as questions – are characterised by a certain distinctive part, the matter of the command" [2007: 120].

In case when the receiver of the imperative is identical with the executor of the willing expressed in the imperative, the following formula is one of possible equivalents of imperative (2):

(6) Person B, in conditions W, cause S to occur!

Obviously not one, but more people might be indicated as the executor of the will. We might then create among others the following:

(7) Person B_1 and person B_2, in conditions W, cause S to occur!

If the person B_1 is identical with the sender of the imperative, and the person B_2 with its receiver, formula (3) is shaped as follows:

(8) Person B_2, let us cause S to occur!

3.2. Let us consider these imperatives:

(9) Let the person B cause S to occur!

(10) Do not let person B cause S to occur!

Imperative (9) is A DICTATE, imperative (10) − A PROHIBITION. It is worth noticing that an equivalent of prohibition (10) is the dictate:

(11) Let person B cause not-S to occur!

Therefore, prohibitions are in fact a type of appropriate dictates. We may consider:

(12) The person A prohibits person B from causing S – when – the person A dictates to the person B to cause not-S.

3.3. Imperatives might be divided into ELEMENTARY and MOLECULAR.

A molecular imperative is such an imperative which consists of at least two parts which in themselves are imperatives. An elementary imperative – is an imperative which does not meet this condition.

From the grammatical point of view, molecular imperatives are coördinately compound sentences. Their general structure is as follows:

(13) Let the person B cause S_1 to occur, and let the person C cause S_2 to occur!

If the person B is identical with the person C, imperative (13) might be also formulated thus:

(14) Let the person B cause S_1 and S_2 to occur!

3.4. Some also mention the so-called HYPOTHETICAL imperatives of two kinds – in *casus potentialis* or in *casus realis*:

(15) Let the person B cause S_1 to occur, if S_2 occurs!

(16) Let the person B cause S_1 to occur, since S_2 occurred!

As regards formula (15) – it might be considered an equivalent of formula (2). It is enough to regard conditions W of formula (2) identical with the occurrence of S_2.

As regards formula (16), the occurrence of S_2 is stated therein; it is not, therefore, a condition *sensu stricto* and might be in principle omitted.

3.5. The following interrelation occurs:

(17) If the person A utters the imperative "Let S occur!" then the person A wants S to occur.

As usual with the "experience *vs.* verbalization" relation, the above interrelation applies in typical situations only. It is obvious that to many untypical situations the interrelation (17) would not apply; the simplest of such situations is the one in which the person A by the utterance of an appropriate imperative means to deceive the interlocutors as regards their opinions and willings.

Following the interrelation (17) will is sometimes expressed as follows:

(18) I want S to occur.

(19) I oblige the person B to cause S to occur.

It remains an open question whether the utterance (19) bears the status of a performative.

• Cheliński [1925] believed that the basic method for revealing the willings are utterances of the form: "I want something".

As to imperatives (*resp.* orders), Cheliński distinguished autonomous and heteronymous ones; the division stemmed respectively from whether the sender was identical with the executor of a certain willing or not.

What Cheliński underlined was the difference between the object of willing verbalized in the imperative, and the imperative's aim. It mattered because sometimes the order is given not to make the receiver behave in a certain way, but to "mark" that the sender is the giver of the order (*resp.* codifier).

• According to Dąmbska [1938], in case of the following imperative:

(1) Let the person B cause S_1 to occur, if S_2 occurs!

"we demand the order to be fulfilled [...], only if the state of affairs mentioned in the antecedent is met" [1938: 263].

As Dąmbska put it – the meaning of the imperative conditional clause is the meaning of the consequent sentence determined in a certain mode.

Therefore, this formula might be taken as a paraphrase of imperative (1):

(2) Under the condition that S_2 occurs – let the person B cause S_1 to occur.

These divisions of imperatives are independent of each other: simple and complex, unconditional and conditional. Thus, there are imperatives both simple and unconditional, simple and conditional, and complex and conditional. Dąmbska pointed out that there are also imperatives both complex and unconditional:

(3) Do it, if you love me!

(4) Get out, if you care for your life!

The person uttering them wants to "appeal to emotions" and "make their order more effective" *via* the conditional form of the sentence [1938: 263]. As Dąmbska noticed, the imperative conditional sentences never take the *casus irrealis*. Therefore, it is impossible to say:

(5) S_2 does not occur. [However,] let person B cause S_1 to occur, if S_2 occurred.

• When juxtaposing imperatives – in particular orders – with norms, Ziembiński [1966b] noted that we have usually to do with orders, when the person A induces person B towards a certain action:

(a) being a different person than B;

(b) in presence of person B;

(c) without person B participation;

(e) having "power" over person B (*i.e.* "there is a certain, high level of probability that the settled norm will meet obedience on behalf of the person at whom the order was directed");

(f) "with a certain especially strong accent of suggestion".

• Are imperatives also performatives?

The answer to this question lies in our understanding of both the "imperative" and the "performative".

Performatives were interpreted by Nowak [1968b] in terms of cultural actions (as opposed to natural ones). He believed cultural actions to include, among others, uttering "understood and understandable" statements; performatives would be in this situation cultural actions of a "higher order", constructed over other cultural actions, especially over utterance of other expressions. Additionally, Nowak maintained that:

(a) there are no invalid performatives; if uttering a certain expression is a performative under certain conditions, then if those conditions are not met this utterance simply was not a performative;

(b) thus interpreted performatives – similarly to interrogations, imperatives and norms – do not have any logical value; it is so because respective sentences are not used to stating some states of affairs (what would happen if they were cultural actions of the "first order").

• Grodziński [1980] was convinced that imperativeness and normativity on the one hand, and performativeness on the other are independent from each other. This means that:

(a) imperative sentences are sometimes functioning as performatives, namely when the utterance of a certain order leads to the obligation – it must be performed (such is the case with military orders, court dictates or tax writs);

(b) sometimes what was indicated in (a) does not apply, therefore the utterance of the order does not lead to any obligation (such is the case with orders that the parents give children, or a given person their friends);

(c) performative utterances are sometimes formulated as sentences of duty;

(d) not all sentences of duty are performative utterances.

• Contrary to Nowak, Woleński [1980a] supported the view that performative utterances do bear logical value; they are particularly true when the performative activity they refer to is valid (namely, when the activity actually occurred).

4. Axiological situation. Evaluations

Axiological situations occur when:

(1) *S* is good.

or:

(2) *S* is evil.

They are stated in evaluations, *i.e.* in evaluating sentences.

• Czeżowski [1964] maintained that what matters most in evaluations is the modal functor creating sentences out of one sentence argument; this functor would be similar to this type: "It is necessary that *p*" (*resp.* "What is necessary is that *p*") – namely: "It is good that *p*" (*resp.* "What is good is that *p*") and "It is beautiful that *p*" (*resp.* "What is beautiful is that *p*"). Different existential modes of respective states of affairs would be real referents of these functors.

• Ziembiński [1972a] perceived evaluating statements as one that express or may express approval or disapproval towards a certain state of affairs. According to him, the logical value of evaluating sentences may only be discussed from the axiologically absolutist point of view; in this viewpoint, an axiological system which is not relativized by the evaluating persons exists.

• This position was also maintained by Zieliński & Ziembiński [1988]. Evaluation is "an experience of taking an emotional stance towards certain actual or imagined states of affairs or events – and therefore of approving or disapproving something" [1988: 40–41].

From among the basic evaluations, Zieliński & Ziembiński discerned autonomous and instrumentally grounded (i.e. pragmatic) evaluations; the latter are built from the "intellectual layer" (*i.e.* the presupposition that a certain state of affairs leads to certain results) and the "emotional layer" (*i.e.* the fact that we approve or, contrariwise, disapprove of these results).

Utterances touching upon the subject of evaluations may:

(a) express evaluation (in short: these are evaluating utterances);

(b) describe evaluations;

(c) be descriptive, *i.e.* tinged with evaluation;

(d) state that certain evaluations are in accordance with given evaluation criteria;

(e) subscribe certain qualifications in a non-objective way.

Wanting to comment on (c), they wrote:

> There are certain particular connections between the elements of an evaluating and descriptive utterance; namely, utterances that are in principle descriptive may be formulated with the use of words and phrases of clear emotional tinge. [...] An utterance referring to the same object may be purely descriptive, or approving, or insulting – due to the choice of emotional, positive or negative, words [1988: 50].

The "substantiation of evaluations" is to be understood as, among others, arguments for how the evaluation is "proper, appropriate, and right" [1988: 110]. Zieliński & Ziembiński accentuated the fact that the substantiation of evaluations should not be mistaken for explaining "why did such an evaluation appear in one's consciousness" [1988: 110]. The way in which the evaluation is substantiated depends on the conception of the evaluation itself.

From the point of view of emotivism, evaluations are (psychological) facts which may be "in one way or the other provoked, and when they occur, they may be in one way or the other explained; but they cannot be substantiated in one way or the other" [1988: 111].

In contrast, intuitionism (*i.e.* cognitivism) claims that (moral) evaluations are "a certain act of cognition of what deserves approval or disapproval" [1988: 112]; this act is possible owing to moral sense, *sui generis*.

Also, naturalism maintains that "an evaluating utterance is properly substantiated if one proves that the evaluated state of affairs has certain objective features – with respect to which such states of affairs are praised or criticized" [1988: 113].

> Substantiation "As the object of evaluation O possesses an objective characteristic C, the positive evaluation of O is substantiated" is a satisfactory substantiation only when it had been settled before that all objects bearing characteristic C deserve approval; in fact, this settlement would itself require substantiation, and much more complex.
> Substantiation of evaluating utterances may be based on other, more general justifications. The problem of most general or basic evaluations and their substantiation remains a point of discussion for philosophy [1988: 113-114].

Basic evaluations are substantiated *via* reference to:

(a) authority;

(b) one's own conscience;

(c) evaluations dominating in a certain environment;

(d) evaluations "formulated officially, [...] *e.g.* as constitutional regulations" [1988: 122] (this position is called "legal positivism");

(e) absolute "natural" evaluations, in accordance with the "laws of nature".

> Autonomous basic evaluations occur less often than basic evaluations instrumentally grounded (in the latter, we evaluate a certain state of affairs as one leading to creation or consolidation of another, positive or negative state of affairs. [...] Substantiation of instrumentally grounded evaluations, or challenging such substantiations, consists in verification of certain general statements; what is discussed are statements claiming that in certain circumstances the state of affairs will definitely or with particular probability bring some results non-neutral for us [1988: 117].

This also applies to the situation in which, when substantiating the evaluation, we take into consideration the results brought by the evaluated state of affairs; one considers both immediate and long-term results (and hence the differences between evaluations).

5. Obligational situation

5.1. Let us first consider two notions of obligation *sensu largo*. Suppose that the person A utters a sentence of the following type:

(1) S should occur.

Formula (1) is a formula of obligation – *i.e.* duty – which may be understood as an equivalent of formula (2) or formula (3):

(2) S will probably occur.

(3) It is necessary that S occurs.

Let us differentiate these two cases as duty-probability and duty-necessity.

Duty-probability may be rephrased thus in more detail:

(4) The person A supposes that S will occur.

The person A may have different reasons to think so, among others the fact that this person is certain that the relevant duty-necessity applies. The duty described in formula (1) understood in accordance with formula (2) may be called "PROGNOSTIC duty".

In case of duty-necessity we have:

(5) It is necessary that S_1 occurs – when at the same time:

(a) there is a law stating that S_2 is followed by S_1;

(b) S_2 occurred.

The law mentioned in formula (5) might be a law declaring either a causal relationship, or a semantic relationship. Hence, depending on the relationship, one refers to the CAUSAL or SEMANTIC duty.[5]

---

[5] A particular type of semantic duty is the so-called logical necessity, derivative of semantic relationships between special expressions – namely between logical terms.

It might be so that duty-necessity concerns non-occurrence of a certain state of affairs:

(6) It is necessary that non-S_1 occurs.

whereas:

(7) It is necessary that non-S_1 occurs, when simultaneously:

(a) there is a law stating that non-S_2 is followed by non-S_1;

(b) non-S_2 occurs.

If non-S_1 is the effect of accidental coincidence, the necessity mentioned in formula (7) is TECHNICAL duty. An instance of technical necessity might be: a certain person will not knock an apple down from a 3-meter tall apple tree if a person without a 1.5-meter-long stick cannot knock such an apple down – and this person so happens not to have such a stick[6].

5.2. Obligation *sensu stricto* occurs in a situation where:

(8) In conditions W, the person B should cause that p.

This might be the result of either of these:

(9) The person A obliged the person B to cause that p in conditions W.

(10) In conditions W, the fact that not-p, is evil.

Case (9) is the THETIC duty, case (10) is the AXIOLOGICAL duty. Thetic duty might be reinterpreted thus:

(11) In conditions W, the person B should cause that p – when – if in conditions W, the person B does not cause that p, the person B is threatened with punishment K.

The elements of the situation of thetic duty are as follows: the person A – who is the ADDRESSANT of the obligation; the person B – who is THE ADDRESSEE of the obligation;[7] conditions W – *i.e.* THE CONTEXT of the obligation;

---

[6] It is not always clear whether we deal with technical or *e.g.* causal necessity. Let us consider the sentence: "It is necessary that someone who is right now in Warsaw will not be in New York in 2 hours". There are no planes which would fly from Warsaw to New York in under 2 hours. Here, we do not know whether this fact is a consequence of a law, or a mere "coincidence".

[7] To be more precise, one should speak here about AN INTENTIONAL EXECUTOR of the obligation. The term "addressee of the obligation" is therefore equal here with the term "intentional executor of the obligation".

occurrence of p – *i.e.* OBJECT of the obligation;[8] punishment K, which will be put on the addressee of the obligation, in case they do not cause that p – *i.e.* SANCTION of the obligation.

There are several contexts for obligation, among them:

(a) INTERNAL context (identical to certain internal states of the addressee of the obligation) and EXTERNAL context (identical to certain states of the addressee's surroundings);

(b) QUALITATIVE context (identical to certain qualitatively definite states of affairs) and QUANTITATIVE context, in particular: TEMPORAL (regarding the time when the addressee of the obligation should start fulfilling it) and SPATIAL (referring to the place of fulfilment).[9]

Since the temporal context is so significant here, perhaps formula (9) would be of higher value with an appropriate parameter describing the thetic obligation:

(9) The person A obliged person B to cause that p, in conditions W and in time T.

5.3. Let us compare two situations:

(13) The person B should provide the person C with goods D.

(14) The person C has the right (*i.e.* entitlement) to receive goods D from the person B.

If formula (13) brings about formula (14), we may speak about the INDICATIVE duty of formula 13. If it does not, the duty of formula (13) may be called UNILATERAL duty.

• The relationship between duty and entitlement (*i.e.* claiming one's rights) was analysed by Petrażycki [1907b: 36 *et seq.*]. Petrażycki divided norms into imperative-attributive and (solely) attributive. The imperative-attributive norms are as follows:

(1) If the person A should do this and that, a certain person B has the right to stake out certain claims to A.

---

[8] Parallel to the term "addressee of the obligation" – the "object of the obligation" is an abbreviation for the "intentional object of the obligation".
[9] It is therefore clear that sentence 'p' of formula (11) does not include temporal and spatial parameters. The same pertains to formula (12).

(Solely) attributive norms take the following form:

(2) The person A should do this and that and no person B has [because of that] any right to stake claims to the person A.

According to Petrażycki, moral norms were such "no-claiming" norms; especially the norms of evangelical ethics [1907c].

• Znamierowski [1924] used the term "thetic subject" to describe the addressant of the obligation. He equalled the obligational formula:

(1) The person A obliged person B to cause that p, in conditions W.

with the thetic norm in form of:

(2) In conditions W, the person B performs (*resp.* should perform) an act F.

The act F is of course corresponding with "causing that p", from formula (1). The obligation presented by norm (1) was characterized by Znamierowski as follows:

> If certain conditions have only one possible action assigned, this situation may be called OBLIGATION [1924: 95].

All the acts which clash with action F, *i.e.* actions «contradictory» to action F or hindering action F, are according to Znamierowski acts prohibited by the norm which requires action F.

The object of obligation is in Znamierowski's [1924] and Ziembiński's [1956; 1972a] terms "the range or standardization".[10] If the obligational formula is to be "praxeologically workable", which one must perceive as dictated to or prohibited by this formula are not only actions mentioned *expressis verbis*, but also dictated or prohibited *implicite*. Therefore, if the norm dictates, for instance, the execution of action C, this norm also dictates to execute all the actions which are necessary to achieve C. The above makes the real and actual range of the norm difficult to be settled. It is so since a question arises – may the matter be set out as follows:

(3) If S_1 occurs only when S_2 occurs, and the person B should cause S_1 to occur – then person B should also cause S_2 to occur.

---

[10] More accurately, the object of obligation is here expressed *via* an appropriate norm.

In Znamierowski's opinion, counterexamples may be given which prove that such an interrelation is too strong and unrealistic a demand. In terms of obligation, what we consider are only acts of the person B. However, states of affairs as indicated by 'S_2' in formula (1) may include necessary conditions which are BEYOND person B's control.

Znamierowski [1957] also investigated the relationship between the duty and entitlement. The fact that person A is entitled to something, does not always burden person B with the obligation of ensuring conditions for the execution of this entitlement:

> The feeling of entitlement may be fully disconnected from the feeling of duty. If according to P it is good when A is c_1 ... or c_n, then according to P A may be c_k. The above does not mean any ensuing duty. Since it is good when children spends their time reading, walking or playing, the children have the right to read. But no duty corresponds to this entitlement, especially if the children are alone in a room – and there is no one to take the book away from them. Even Robinson in a desert island could have rights without anyone's correlating obligation [1957: 258–259].

Znamierowski argues that:

> Once the norm N has been constituted by P for P, P has FEELING OF DUTY (ENTITLEMENT) [1957: 496].

• According to Ossowska [1947], different types of duties do not mean that the term "duty" is ambiguous:

> We do not see any perceptible difference in meaning of [...] the word "should" [in different contexts]. The whole utterances including this word are undoubtedly ambiguous, but the word itself is syncategorematic, and only in phrases may it have any definite sense; one will not find its autonomous sense. There is no reason to think that the term "should" when appears in axiological, thetic or teleological norms is

a different "should" each time. If we acknowledged this distinction in axiological norms, the next step would be to further the distinction even more; we would agree that the axiological norm has as many meanings, as there are meanings of the word "good" in evaluations (which are attributed to axiological norms); the above would apply especially if we perceived axiological norms as equal to evaluations [1947: 144].

• The context of the obligation used to be called by Ziembiński [1956] and later by Zieliński & Ziembiński [1988] "the range for the application of the norm".[11] In the authors' opinion, the range for the application of the norm is the class of conditions in which the norm becomes realized; in our case, these conditions, which would put on the person *B* the obligation to cause *S* to occur?

The range of norm (*i.e.* object of obligation) was described by Ziembiński as a class of those future actions of the addressee which are either dictated or prohibited, when the given obligation[12] finds its application. The obligation divides the general class of actions into more specific relevant acts (dictated or prohibited) and indifferent acts (neither dictated nor prohibited).

Even though he did not use these terms specifically, Ziembiński made a clear distinction between internal and external contexts. He would point to the fact that sometimes it is difficult to mark the boundary between these two types of contexts. Ziembiński provides the following as one such problematic obligation:

Each soldier[13] called-up for military service should do this and that.

One may wonder whether being "called-up for military service" is an internal state of the addressee, or rather external factors of the obligation.

What would Ziembiński also notice was the difference between temporal contexts; he noted that there exist obligations which call for immediate execution (*e.g.* obligations expressed in military commands).

---

[11] More accurately, it is here a question of obligation expressed *via* an appropriate norm.
[12] Ziembiński speaks here of the norm – a formula putting an obligation on someone.
[13] Or, what would be better here: "Each citizen".

• Grzybowski [1961] supported the traditional view of jurisprudence: the obligatory situation consists of three parts: hypothesis, disposition and sanction. He interpreted it thus that these parts are respectively:

(a) hypothesis: "[Let us suppose that] S_1 occurs";

(b) disposition: "[If S_1 occurs, then] S_2 should occur";

(c) sanction: " If S_2 does not occur, then] S_3 occurs".

Grzybowski emphasises the fact that implications of (b) and (c) refer to thetic relations (as settled by the lawgiver).

• The thetic, prognostic and analytical meaning of "obligation" was also inquired into by Najder [1971]; he wrote that the term "obligation" may be understood in three ways, often mixed, visible in the following contexts:

(1) The person O should do this and that – therefore, someone requires from the person O that the person O does this and that.

(2) This and that should occur – therefore, someone expects this and that to occur.

(3) The object P should behave in such a way – therefore, it is necessary (or it is an obligation) for the object P (including persons) to behave in such a way.

The term "should" is usually in line of (3) in the so-called postulative definitions:

(4) X should bear the property W.

• The notion of duty might be further analysed when juxtaposed against permission. Zieliński & Ziembiński [1988] reconstructed different understandings of "may" in the so-called permission regulations. Namely, someone may do something, when:

(a) in a given system there is no norm that formulates the prohibition of this act [1988: 75];

(b) the former prohibition of this act was rescinded;

(c) the former range of the norm was narrowed;

(d) "someone obtained competence to act in a conventional way with legal consequences following" [1988: 75];

(e) there is no prohibition regarding usage of a given competence [1988: 76];

(f) the addressee of the norm has suitable "psychophysical" or "economical capabilities" for a given activity.

6. Genesis of the obligation

6.1. The difference between the axiological and thetic duty lies in their respective sources. Let us agree that the source of a given duty causes this duty – *i.e.* that the duty results from the source. Since a given duty is a consequence of its source, the source of a given duty is the reason behind it.[14] Let us consider the most general form of duty:

(1) S should occur.

For axiological duty, the reason for (1) would be the fact that:

(2) Not-S is wrong.

From time to time, instead of reason (2) the following is assumed:

(3) S is right.

This would, however, mean that whatever is right should be realized, which would be too far-reaching an expectation.[15]

The reason behind the axiological duty is sometimes of relational character:

(4) S is more wrong than not-S.

For thetic duty, the reason for (1) would be the fact that:

(5) The person A wants S to occur.

When the thetic obligation assumes the form of:

(6) The person B should cause S to occur.

the reason behind it is:

(7) The person A obliged the person B to cause S.

---

[14] Traditionally speaking, the class of sentences is perceived as the field of relations between cause and result (*resp.* being-the-reason/being-the-consequence). Here, arguments of these relations are states of events to which respective sentences refer. We do not want to decide here what the ontological status of these relations is.

[15] The "too far-reaching" categorical statement is unusually general. Unfortunately, it is not easy to move beyond what is general; unless we clearly state that the considered notion is rejected as utopian.

6.2. As opposed to causal and semantic necessities – behind which there are «hard» laws – if there are reasons for axiological and thetic duties, it absolutely does not «force» these duties.

For necessity, the string:

(8) S is necessary $\Rightarrow S$ occurs.

is characterized by the fact that it is impossible for the first element of the string to occur without the second. In other words:

(9) If S is necessary, S will occur.[16]

We encounter a different situation in these strings:

(10) Not-S is wrong $\Rightarrow S$ should occur $\Rightarrow S$ will occur.

(11) The person A wants the person B to cause S to occur $\Rightarrow$ the person B should cause $S \Rightarrow$ the person B will cause S to occur.

(12) The person A obliged the person B to cause S to occur $\Rightarrow$ the person B should cause S to occur $\Rightarrow$ the person B will cause S to occur.

Here, it is possible for the first and second elements to occur without the third. Namely, S might not occur even though not-S is evil; and the person B may not cause S to occur, even though they had been obliged to do so by the person A. Whether they cause it or not, may sometimes depend on the «force» of the obligation or «force» of other, independent, factors that motivate the person B to cause S to occur;[17] sometimes it depends on whether the obligation of formula (12) does not clash with other duties of the person B.

6.3. Let us consider string (11); let us suppose that the willing of person A really is the reason behind the person B's duty. In such cases we say that the person A is the obligational AUTHORITY for the person B.

---

[16] Let us notice, however, that law – especially one stating a cause-and-effect relationship – is usually a certain idealisation, «eliminating» some (the so-called irrelevant) parameters. What follows is: p is somewhat caused by q – only when q is accompanied by certain additional factors. It is assumed that these factors frequently co-exist with q – and therefore they are omitted. They might be also missing – exceptions apply also to necessity based on laws.

[17] It ought to be noted that there are no clear relationships here. It might be so that someone obliges the person B "strongly" (*e.g.* by a military order) to cause p to occur and the person B does not cause p to occur. It might also happen that someone only asks the person B to cause p to occur, and the request is fulfiled. *Cf.* further.

The authority stems especially from more or less institutionalized regulations.

If the person A is not an obligational authority for person B, yet the person A wants the person B to cause S to occur – the person B might either demand it or ask for it.

Neither THE DEMAND nor THE REQUEST «breed» duty, however.

• Let us consider the sentence:

(1) X should bear the property P.

According to Znamierowski and his terminology [1924], this sentence may bear, for instance, a logical, axiological or thetic duty. Let us signify these type of duty with markers, respectively with 'L', 'A' and 'T'. Thus:

(2) X should$_L$ bear the property P – when – because there is such a property Q that (X bears the property Q, and the property Q is necessarily associated with the property P), X bears also the property P.

The logical duty appears also when we utter the following:

(3) A triangle on a diameter – with one vertex on the circle – should be right-angled [1924: 15].

Now:

(4) X should$_A$ bear the property P – when – it will be better (*resp.* the best) if X bears the property P.

The axiological duty is presumed *e.g.* when:

(5) The weather should be nice tomorrow.[18]

Finally:

(6) X should$_T$ bear the property P – when – [there is a person A, who decided (*resp.* dictated) for X to bear the property P – or when X bearing the property P adheres to "settled norms of behaviour"].

For instance:

(7) The bathwater should be 28° R.

(8) One should register in 24 hours after arrival.

---

[18] A better example here: "John should finally settle down". We usually say that the weather should be nice when «everything» suggests that it will be so.

This [last] sentence means that what should be is simply what adheres to settled norms, a thing or action which belong to the class sectioned off by the act of [...] SETTLEMENT [1924: 12].

The [thetic] norm individuates [...] certain activities and forms a self-contained whole out of them – an «artificially» separated system of activities [1924: 13].

Therefore, the thetic norm of activity is "a rule for incorporating" certain activities into the "system" [1924: 13]: if certain activity is to belong to a certain conventional system of activities, it should be this and that. Outside of this system there is a "freedom zone" [1924: 99].

Znamierowski added also later that:

For the feeling of [thetic] duty to appear, one needs [...] drivings towards a certain state of things *s*, an existential evaluation of this state as well as a complementary evaluation of the state not-*s* and fear of the latter state [1957: 244].

• Cheliński juxtaposed duties settled (by someone) with non-settled ones [1925]. The latter were in his opinion those duties expressed in logical, ethical and aesthetic norms.

Orders and requests – connected by "the will to provoke another person's behaviour *via* influencing their psyche" – are differentiated by the "normative element", which is present in orders and absent from requests; Cheliński defines it as "the norm formed in the mind of the person giving the order, determining the addressee's behaviour". The giver of the order is therefore at the same time codifier: they "dominate" the addressee of the order. The person who requests something expresses "conditional" willing: Do this and that, if you want to do it!

By the way, Cheliński differentiated between orders and demands – the latter did not possess the "normative element".

• Elzenberg maintained [1933] that the notion of DUTY, at least the axiological one, is a primary, «indivisible» notion:

As to [...] the notion „should" used [...] in this basic and uncompro-
mizing meaning taken from ethics and axiology – I believe it is a simple notion; particularly, I do not see any possible interpretation of this
notion in which it would be just an abbreviated description of some
psychological, biological or social facts; it also does not just lyri-
cally EXPRESS certain psychological states, as exclamations do [1933:
11-12].

• Kotarbiński [1934] saw four types of necessity: deterministic, logic,
technical (without actually using this very term) and practical.

The deterministic necessity is according to him characteristic of those
"resolutions and acts following them which are not free [...], because they
result from earlier, unambiguous, causes" [1934: 475]. The logic necessity appears when we deal with such a thesis, "the rejection of which [...]
would lead to contradiction" [1934: 475]. The technical necessity is according to Kotarbiński "effect of obstacles beyond one's strength or skills"
[1934: 474–475]. Finally, the practical necessity is "compulsion to act":
the necessity to choose a certain way in order to avoid unpleasant consequences of a different choice [1934: 475].

Kotarbiński's logical necessity might, it seems, be equated with semantic necessity; the deterministic necessity equals causal duty, and practical necessity – thetic duty.

Among practical necessities (*i.e.* thetic duties), Kotarbiński devotes
particular attention to legal and moral duties.

• Dąmbska [1938] states that there also exist such imperatives which do
not have any corresponding norm, *e.g.*:

(9) Buy two bottles of milk!

What is meant by the norm here is "a general sentence that states one
ought to or ought not to behave in a certain way" [1938: 264].

Sporadically, a given imperative does have such a corresponding norm.
Hence, imperatives such as:

(10) Do not bear false testimony!

and

(11) Wash fruit before you eat it!

are equivalent (of course not logically, as then it would be automatically assumed that they bear logical value *sensu stricto*) to sentences of these types respectively:

(12) One should not bear false testimony.

and

(13) One should wash fruit before eating [1938: 264].

In the second case, the imperative might sometimes conform with the norm; consequently, it also conforms to an appropriate evaluation (or it presupposes it). It might be then "the application of the norm", that is, it "is a part of the activity that aims at realization of the norm"; "for instance, a mother gives her child some fruit and says" [1938: 264]:

(14) Wash them before eating!

Occasionally, the imperative is not in conformity with the norm, and what follows, with an appropriate evaluation; we order someone to "Do not--x", while recognizing the norm "One should do *x*".

• In the beginning [1946], Czeżowski maintained that norms (*i.e.* dictates of behaviour) equal appropriate evaluations (*i.e.* assessments of this behaviour):

(1) It should be so that the person *O* performs an act *C* (*i.e.* performing the act *C* is the duty (*i.e.* obligation) of the person *O*) – when – the act *C* of the person *O* is right [1946].

Czeżowski defined the rightness of an act thus:

(2) An act *C* of the person *O* is right – when – means to, aims and results of the act *C* of the person *O* are good (*i.e.* they have the highest possible value).

He distinguished from among duties [1946] both external and internal duties, while:

(3) Performance of act *C* is an external duty of the person *O* – when – there is such a person (or institution) *R* and such a sanction *S* that the person *O* is subordinate to the person (or institution) *R* (*i.e.* the person (or institution) *R* gives the person *O*, or the obliged person, orders) and performing the act *C* by the person *O* is dictated by the person (or institution) *R* under sanction *S*.

In turn:

(4) The person (or institution) *R* thinks that the act *C* of the person *O* is right – when – there is such a sanction *S* that the person *O* is subordinate to

the person (or institution) R and performing of the act C by the person O is dictated by the person (or institution) R under the sanction S.

Whereas:

(5) Performance of act C is an internal duty of the person O – when – the person O thinks that the act C of the person O is right.

Later in his life, Czeżowski would moderate his viewpoint on relations between evaluations and norms; he may have been wrong to state that the rightness of an act results in a duty to perform it and not the other way round [1964b: 147].

Finally [1964b], Czeżowski's position towards the relationship between norms and evaluations became as follows:

> There exists a common belief [...] that norms are not sentences in the logical sense, since they are not true or false. They do not state or deny that something is or is not; rather, they rule, recommend, dictate or prohibit certain behaviour. I believe that this is not right; the norm itself is not a recommendation or a dictate; for the realization of the norm, *i.e.* acting in accordance with it, a decision is required; it is an additional volitional factor motivated by a norm of one kind or the other. The expression of the decision takes the form of an imperative sentence (often erroneously treated as an equivalent of a norm) directed at the person who is to realize the norm; it might be the giver of the order himself, when dictating himself to behave in a certain way: "Act in this and that way!". The motivational dependence of the dictate on the norm is visible in combinations: "Act in this and that way because one should act like this!" or "Act in this and that way because that is how one acts!". Sometimes, the imperative sentences substitute for norms, *e.g.* in the *Ten Commandments*; they should be then understood as abbreviated expressions, with a default norm as motivation [1964b: 144].

Therefore:

(6) I want the person O to perform the act C [volitional act] because performing this act is the person's O duty [motivating norm]. What follows: Person O, perform the act C [imperative]!

In Czeżowski's opinion [1970] there are two criteria of the duty of an action: teleological and formal.

The teleological criterion of the duty is in fact a more detailed axiological justification. According to this criterion, performance of an act C is an ethic duty if the means to, aims and results of the act C are good:

> Within the teleological [*i.e.* axiological] norm, behaviour is ethical if it aims at realization of moral good. [...] Teleological norms define [...] the obligation *via* what is good: an ethical duty is such a behaviour which aims at maximalisation of moral good [1970: 150].

By contrast, to characterize the ethical duty of an action C by the means of the formal criterion – is to provide a norm that dictates the act C to be performed:

> Within the [...] the formal [*i.e.* deontic] norm, a behaviour is ethical if it follows a moral norm. [...] The formal norm [...] assumed the notion of obligation to be primary; therefore, acting in conformity with the norm we realize moral good [1970: 150].

• Ossowska [1947] analysed the diversity of types of obligation in a detailed manner with regard to their justification.

She juxtaposed the non-normative (one should rather say anormative) sense of the "duty" against the normative (or rather norm-creating) sense [1947: 128–129].

For the anormative sense, Ossowska *explicite* distinguished two types of relation expressed by:

(1) X should bear the property P[19].

Namely, this relationship may be of causal or semantic character – and therefore it would be a causal or semantic necessity:

(2) If conditions W occur, X bears the property P.

(3) If X is a designate of the name N, then X bears the property P.

---

[19] Ossowska uses the phrase "A should be B".

For the normative sense, Ossowska believes the duty to be axiological and thetic – or "advisory", *i.e.* an instruction (see below).

• Tatarkiewicz [1966] was in favour of the position which located the source of all obligations in values. He would express this position by claiming that norms are "implicated" by proper evaluations.

• Zieliński & Ziembiński [1988] wrote:

In jurisprudence, it is easy to confuse descriptive utterances, evaluating utterances and directives – whereas the word "justification" assumes intrinsically different sense for each of these types of expressions [1988: 5].

Therefore, one must make a distinction between holding the sentence to be true, the evaluating utterance to be appropriate (right), the norm to be valid and the performative – to be significant.

Justification of a norm as a valid one might be called "vindicating [this norm]".

What should be distinguished are:

(a) argumentation (convincing others);

(b) justification;

(c) proving.

In jurisprudence, problems may appear when we want to justify the dogmatic statements regarding certain norms called in a given legal system; consequently, we would like to justify also the legal qualification of certain acts; on the other hand, procedures that settle how significant legally are individual facts are also problematic, especially in legal proceedings.

[...] We accept the conception of rigorous differentiation between legal regulations and legal norms; we reject the conception of "permission norms"; we accept the idea of competitive norms as norms which dictate their addressees to behave in a certain way with regard to conventional actions performed by someone authorized to do so by this norm; we accept the derivational (and not the traditional, clarificational) interpretation of legal texts; it all might raise opposition of the traditional position [1988: 10].

According to Zieliński & Ziembiński, a norm of behaviour is settled based on silent factual assumptions:[20]

> If someone rational settles a norm of behaviour dictating somebody's activity, he silently assume that the undertaking of this dictated activity is possible, that there is potential material for the appointed activities, that somebody who is to undertake this action suggested by the norm has proper qualifications, *etc.*; on the other hand, the assumption is also that the norm will find application in the future – chances for someone to bear properties of a general norm addressee and for such conditions to occur in which this person would act according to the norm [1988: 58–59].
>
> In doctor's recommendations, there are no words "If you want to be healthy..." – as the patient's willingness to return to health is something fully understandable [1988: 62–63].

Norms may have – according to Zieliński & Ziembiński [1988] – axiological sources:

> Two matters must be differentiated: first, a general, individual, abstract or concrete norm must be justified *via* certain «good reasons» that speak in favour of validation of this norm, by appropriate evaluations of actions appointed by this norm; second, one must explain whether someone takes a given norm as valid due to experienced evaluations, either approving or disapproving of the behaviour determined by this norm [1988: 150].
>
> The axiological justification for a certain norm is usually based on an important silent assumption that one should do what is good and avoid what is evil; in exceptional cases, it is founded solely on

---

[20] Ziembiński [1977].

such and such evaluation of activities dictated or prohibited by this norm. Usually, approval or disapproval of certain behaviour is related to the state of knowledge about the consequences of given behaviour [1988: 150–151].

Thetic justification is yet another method of providing justification to the norm:

> The simplified traditional model sees settlement of norms by a subject for other subjects, and possibly also for himself, as a manifestation of the settling subject's will [1988: 153–154].
>
> Most generally speaking, an adequate thetic justification of a norm settled by someone would consist in our readiness to show that the addressee of the norm is subordinate to the codifier – who may cause significant evil or refuse what is good; also, we would have to show that the codifier is authorized to settled norms for given addressees in a certain field of behaviour – that is, that they have power (narrowly understood) over the addressees of the norm [1988: 154].

This might happen with or without the addressee's permission. Investigating the authority of the codifier leads to investigation of other people and brings *regressus ad infinitum* [1988: 160].

The norm may be overruled by persons who are or are not competent to do that (*e.g.* in case of a «revolution»). Sometimes, the overruling equals settlement anew norm which does not conform to the former.[21]

The lack of conformity might be of a formal or praxeological character:

> If norms are not conforming formally, in certain cases where both norms find application they appoint such behaviours which may not be performed by the addressees simultaneously. In other words, incompatible norms are norms, which have (at least partially) common area of application and either simultaneously dictate and prohibit

---

[21] Piotrowski [1978], Wróblewski [1984] and Ziembiński [1984].

certain behaviours in a given situation, or appoint actions which cannot be performed with the current state of knowledge (*e.g.* norms that dictate to appear at the same time in different places). The first case describes contradiction of two norms, the second – opposition of two or more norms [1988: 165].

The praxeological non-conformity of norms consists in the fact that realization of one norm fully or significantly thwarts the consequences of realization of the second norm [1988: 166].

Justification of teleological (instrumental) directives has two aspects: intellectual and evaluational:

Justification of teleological directives consists usually, but not exclusively, in stating whether anancastic sentences are true or not; these anancastic sentences declare a relationship between a people's certain behaviour in certain conditions and the consequences of this behaviour in the close or further future [1988: 144].

In the simplest case, the cost of effort invested in the given activity, as well as side effects of this activity are not taken into consideration at all [1988: 145].

Then, the "transmission of information of such a teleological directive" as:

(24) If you want to achieve x, you should do y.

is "basically the same as in the anancastic sentence":

(25) If you do y, x will follow.

However, if the cost of activity and the value of side effects may not be idealistically reduced to zero, and particularly if the teleological directive assumes certain probability factor, clearly we need to find a reference of our justification of the teleological directive to a certain assumed system of values [1988: 146].

The justification for rules of conventional activities (language or terminological rules, game rules *etc.*) is as follows:

The very fact that a person settled such a semantic rule for himself speaks its justification [1988: 143].

An adequate reconstruction of justification methods for dogmatic statements (*i.e.* "statements formulated in various complex disciplines of jurisprudence" [1988: 191]) would require insight into numerous detailed matters; from among those, one would have to explain what the following mean: validity of the norm, overruling of the norm, non-validity of the norm due to *desuetudo*, replacing one norm by another, coding the norm in the regulation, the addressee of the norm, the meaning of a regulation, a regulation modifying the norm, validity of a given norm as a consequence of other norms, praxeological conformity of norms, contradiction of norms, an dictated/indifferent act with regard to the norm *etc.*

To solve these matters, one requires certain validational rules (that allow certain facts to be perceived as law-creating) and exegesis rules (interpretation/decoding, inference and collision).

7. Criteria of factuality of obligation

7.1. Let us consider a situation, in which:

(1) In conditions W, the person B should cause S to occur.[22]

Let us consider these situations, more detailed versions of (1):

(2) The person A obliged the person B to cause S to occur in conditions W.

(3) In time T_0 the person A obliged the person B to cause S to occur in conditions W.

(4) In time T_0 the person A obliged the person B to cause S to occur in conditions W and in time T_1.

In sentence (4) time T_0 is earlier than time T_1. The necessary conditions for the thetic obligation from formulas (1)–(4) to really occur – be FACTUAL – are:

(5) The person A is able to make it so that if in conditions W the person B does not cause S to occur, the person B will meet with evil Z from the person D.

(6) In conditions W, the person B is able to cause S to occur.

(7) S does not occur at time T_0.

(8) S is implementable.

Conditions (5)–(8) are criteria (or presuppositions) of the factuality of obligations (1)–(4). Respectively, we may speak of the following criteria: of AUTHORITY of the addressant (5), and of FULFILLABILITY (6), of NON-PRESENT (7) and of IMPLEMENTABILITY (8) of the object of obligation. The obligation that does not fulfil the criterion of:

(a) authority of the addressant – is a NON-BINDING obligation;

(b) fulfillability of the object – is an UNACCEPTABLE obligation;

(c) non-simultaneity of the object – is an IMPROPER obligation;

---

[22] Here the sentence stating S does not include temporal parameters.

(d) realisability – is an UNSUITABLE obligation.

Let us notice that:

(a) fulfillability of the object results in its implementability – therefore the improper obligation is at the same time unacceptable;

(b) unimplementability of the object leads to its non-existence – therefore, the proper obligation is at the same time improper.

The factuality of an obligation must be differentiated from its SIGNIFICANCE and EFFECTIVENESS. The obligation is namely significant when its contextual conditions occur; let us notice that absolute obligations are always significant. In turn, an obligation is effective when its addressee fulfilled it (see below).

The factuality, significance and effectiveness of an obligation are its objective characteristics. When evaluating an obligation subjectively, what is taken into consideration are the viewpoints of its addressant (accuracy) and addressee (rightness). The evaluation of a given obligation performed by the addressant and the addressee may differ. They might be also incompatible with relevant objective evaluations of this obligation.

The obligation is ACCURATE, when the addressant is sure that it is factual. The imperative is RIGHT, when the addressee is convinced it is right (and as a consequence he has the feeling of respective obligation).

7.2. In cases such as obligation (2) and its derivatives we have:

(9) If the person B does not cause S to occur, the person B is threatened by possible evil Z from the person C.

Let us call the evil Z "the SANCTION of the obligation", and the person C "THE EXECUTOR of the obligation". It might happen that even though the obligation was not effective, its addressee was not sanctioned in any way, because the executors of the obligation do not know that the addressee did not fulfil his obligation – or for some reasons they decided not to execute the sanction. Obviously this does not mean that the obligation does not occur.

The obligational authority might at the same time be the executor of the obligation.

7.3. The factuality – validity – of the obligation should be differentiated from its realization. Let us consider the obligation:

(10) The person A obliged the person B to cause S in conditions W.

THE REALIZATION of obligation (10) might take the form of its implementation, execution or fulfilment.

THE EXECUTION of obligation occurs when the object of the obligation occurred regardless of the manner in which it happened: on its own or due to an action of the obligation's addressee, of somebody else, or autonomously:

(11) Obligation (10) became implemented when S occurred.

Sometimes the person B caused S to occur because he was obliged to do so by the person A, or, as the saying goes, he did it on their own free will. We may then generally say that the obligation was EXECUTED by the person B:

(12) The person B executed the obligation (10), when the person B caused S to occur.

FULFILMENT of the obligation consists in its conscious executing by the addressee:

(13) The person B fulfilled obligation (10), when the person B caused S to occur motivated by (10).

Let us notice that if a given obligation is fulfilled, it is at the same time executed; if it is executed, it had been implemented. The opposite interrelationships do not occur.

• According to Znamierowski's standing, the imperative and particularly the order is settlement of a rule of behaviour for the addressee by the addressant (*i.e.* the giver of the order) [1924: 44]. Znamierowski maintained that for the order to be more than solely "attempt at ordering" [1924: 45], the order must "reach the addressee" [1924: 45].

For the addressee, the most significant matter is whether to submit to a given norm or not. In the first case, the norm will be judged as right, in the second, as wrong.

Znamierowski pointed out that three conditions have to be fulfilled for a given norm to be right from the viewpoint of the addressee; they are the motives for submitting (*i.e.* yielding) to this norm:

(1) the acts dictated by the norm are good;

(2) the creator of the norm is an authority;

(3) the receiver of the norm is under pressure (internal or external) and "complying with the norm is the least evil behaviour" [1924: 37].

> A typically external pressure occurs can be stated in sentences similar to the following: "Either A executes the act c, or because of B the state of affairs s will occur, and it will be worse for A than execution of the act c and its consequences" [1924: 42].

The realization of the abovementioned state of affairs s is the sanction of the norm. Sanction may assume two forms:

(a) punishment – or the means by which the addressant wanted to force the act c;

(b) execution – when it is a realization of the intended consequences of the dictated act c by B in a way that is unpleasant to A.

If the person B is able to impose sanctions on the person A, we say that B has power over A.

• Cheliński [1925] directs the attention of his readers to the fact that the order comes into force only from the moment when all the conditions of its realization are fulfilled; this includes the addressee learning about the order.

He also points out that a necessary condition for an obligational situation to occur – which pertains particularly to an order – is not the existence of the addressee, but the addressant's (the giver of the order) conviction that the addressee exists or may appear. Similarly, another necessary condition is not the addressee being actually informed about the content of the order; the addressant must only drive to inform the addressee about this content.

• The thetic (and more precisely legal) obligation was equalled by Kotarbiński [1934] with the necessity to behave in a certain way; otherwise a sanction may be imposed:

> The legal duty or legal obligation occurs when on the path of temptation there looms evil fate; in other words, walking here means possible punishment [1934: 475–476].

The moral duty is according to Kotarbiński linked to the special sanction: in case of a breach of a moral norm, the punishment is shame of possible contempt of respectful people (hence the pricks of conscience).

• Dąmbska would write about an obligational presupposition to be
fulfiled (or, in more general terms, implemented) without using this specific term; she stated that an imperative, concerning in particular an individual obligation, when formulated "seriously and consciously, is linked
with [the addressant's] conviction that it may be executed" [1938: 264].

In Dąmbska's viewpoint, sometimes the addressee of a given obligation is not capable of realizing the object of obligation; the obligational presupposition of being fulfilled is then not fulfilled; it might be so
because the addressee is obliged by another obligation not to affect the
abovementioned object. This is proven by the fact that sometimes norms
concerning a certain obligation are formulated, even though "one knows
that only in certain conditions or even never will the obligation be realized" [1938: 264].

Dąmbska was also aware that one of the necessary conditions for
the obligation to be effective is its accuracy; in particular, the addressant
must in the given obligational situation be convinced that they have proper
causative power [1938: 265].

• Ossowska [1947: 143], following Moore, distinguishes real obligations (expressed according to her in norms-rules of obligation) from ideal
obligations (expressed in norms-rules of ideals). An instance of the former:

(1) If A should$_1$ be B, then A can be B.

An instance of the latter:

(2) It might be so that: A should$_2$ be B and A cannot be B.

Real obligations might here be called implementable ones, and ideal
obligations – unimplementable ones.

• In Ziembiński's viewpoint [1956: 106 *et seq.*] expressions such as:

(1) You should have gone there.

(2) Caesar should not have crossed the river Rubicon.

are evaluations, and not norms. He believes that an inherent obligational
presupposition is the presupposition of non-present of the object of this obligation. In turn, we do not say:

(3) Stop digesting this food!

(4) You should not contract your pupils in bright light.

Such utterances would signify that we suppose that we have conscious control over the process of own digestion and accommodation reactions of our eyes.

In contrast, a norm pertains in essence to such behaviours of the addressees which are thought to be their (conscious) conduct. On the other hand, imperative (3) might be weakened to such a shape in which it stops breaching the abovementioned presupposition of fulfilment; it is enough to shape it as follows:

(5) Immediately after you consume food that might be poison, force yourself to vomit in order to stop digesting this food!

One should remember that the border between our behaviour understood as ACTION and behaviour which our will does not control is vague. Besides, when formulating a norm one takes into consideration whether the behaviour indicated in the norm might be executed (for any person or particular addressee), or whether the given state of affairs might in any way be realized.

As Ziembiński [1964] and later Zieliński & Ziembiński [1988] pointed out, the expression "valid norm" is ambiguous:

> The expression "the norm is valid" might mean: firstly that the norm is
> in one sense or another socially effective [that is, it is adhered to and
> it "exists"]; secondly – that it is justified, *i.e.* that there are such rea-
> sons (axiological justification, thetic justification) for a given norm to
> be perceived as binding [1988: 142].

Those who argue over the "existence of the norm" should therefore first decide whether they mean the social effectiveness of the norm (whether it is adhered to) or the reasons for it to be followed. It might also be that they argue over the material substrate of the norm, or over the "social fact" – the fact that this substrate affects those who are capable of its appropriate interpretation – or over the probability of sanctions being imposed if the norm is not adhered to [1988: 147–150]. They should also adjust an interpretation of the "change of the norm", "overruling of the valid norm", "settlement of a new norm" [1988: 167].

Ziembiński [1972a] for the imperative:

(1) x, cause S to occur!

and its respective norm:

(2) x should cause S to occur.

indicated the following presuppositions (*i.e.* assumptions which should be true if the imperative is to be "reasonable" and the giver of the order "rational" and not "pathological", *i.e.* aiming for something else than S to become real):[23]

(3) S does not occur now;

(4) S would be the future state of affairs;

(5) S is realizable;

(6) x knows what to do to cause S to occur;

(7) x is capable of causing S to occur, and is capable of causing not-S to occur;

(8) the giver of the order has "power" over x, *i.e.* he might effectively influence x's behaviour;

(9) the giver of the order is in possession of an axiological justification of imperative (1) or norm (2).

• The detailed description of the situation of validity of norm was given by Lang [1962]. The phrase "The norm N is valid" is ambiguous; it may refers to one of the two following situations:

(a) the norm N should (*resp.* must) be obeyed – or one should apply the norm N;

(b) the norm N has a certain value (*resp.* importance, significance).

In the situation (a), this phrase is a norm about norm, and in the situation (b) it is an evaluation concerning norm [1962: 112]. The analysis of the formula (a) and (b) leads Lang to the conclusion that they cannot serve as *definienses* for the phrase "Norm N is valid", because in such a situation the fallacy of *circulus in definiendo* would be imminent. Finally, Lang proposes to define the phrase "Norm N is valid" with the aid of the phrase

---

[23] Let us notice that these presuppositions are not independent.

"The norm *N* belongs to a determined system of law" [1962: 157], whereas the phrase "*x* applies the norm *N*" – with the aid of the phrase "*x* accepts the norm *N* as a criterion of evaluation of his own behaviour" [1962: 169]. We read in Lang:

> The dichotomy "is valid – is not valid" plays in respect to norms the role analogical to the role played by the dichotomy "truth–falsehood" in respect to theoretical judgements (descriptive sentences), which is not suitable for norms. The reason is that normative judgements have not logical value [1962: 188].
>
> Every normative system [...] makes an infinite sequence of norms. Interrupting this sequence in a certain point, accepting a certain norm as a chief norm of the system, being a starting of ending point of the sequence of norms, is always an act arbitrary from the viewpoint of the system and it cannot be justified in the frame of this system – in the language of this system [1962: 197–198].

Lang distinguishes the validity of norms characterized in such a way from their existence (in the principal sense of "existence"). Norm *N* (in this sense) exists – is only that – the norm *N* (as a certain utterance) is formulated by a certain person, but is not necessary a part of a certain system of law [1962: 217–220]. Validity – is also something different from bindingness.

Bindingness concerns the legal act (or verdict) and means:

(a) unimpleadibility of this act (*resp.* verdict) (formal bindingess);

(b) inflexibility of this act (*resp.* verdict) by a change by institutions of the judiciary (material bindingness) [1962: 107–108].

• Ziemba & Ziembiński [1964] enumerated the following understanding of the sentence stating that a norm is valid:

(1) *x* settled the norm *N* and did not overrule the norm *N* (when *x* – are either we in relation to ourselves or someone in relation to other people; it is someone "who has such a social position that norms settled by him are often respected"); this validity is "thetically justified";

(2) according to a certain evaluation, we should act as the norm *N* indicates; this validity is "axiologically justified";

(3) a breach of the norm N is "often enough" negatively responded to in a given community; this validity is "behaviouristically justified".

• A valid (binding) norm, as Zieliński & Ziembiński relate [1988], is either:

(a) a norm which is appropriately justified (vindicated);

or

(b) a socially effective norm – *i.e.* such a norm that "appropriate changes in human behaviour occur because of it, and alternatively also that indicated desired states of affairs might be attained *via* these behaviours", and it is known as well "when the breach of the norm results in sanctions" or when it is, in fact, adhered to [1988: 72].

According to Zieliński & Ziembiński [1988], one should differentiate between the actualization of a given obligation set out by the norm and the concretization of this obligation:

The obligation set out by the norm is actualized when the norm finds application, thus when the last of elements (material and personal) of such a situation, in which the norm's addressee should behave according to the lines of the norm, will occur [1988: 65].

In turn, finding-application must be differentiated from the validity of the norm:

For an obligation [...] to be realized, it must be concertized [1988: 66] [*i.e.* the manner of the realization must be defined].[24]

• From Gizbert-Studnicki's [1983] perspective, the criterion of rationality of a "directive speech act" is that the addressant:

(a) wants the addressee to behave in a way indicated by the directive;

(b) believes that the addressee may behave so;

(c) believes that without the directive being uttered, the addressee would not act in this way.

---

[24] Let us notice that at least some norms might be concreted enough in their initial form.

• A longer list of criteria was compiled by Laskowski [1998], who stated that the "semantics of the imperative mood" assumes the form of "Cause S to occur!" and consists of these features:

(a) the addressant wants S to occur;

(b) the addressant aims at prompting the addressee to cause S to occur;

(c) at the moment when the order is uttered, S is not occurring;

(d) the addressee is capable of causing S to occur;

(e) the addressee knows that (d);

(f) the addressant is "socially superior" towards the addressee (as regards orders; in case of advice – this condition is redundant, in case of requests – the relation is reversed);

(g) causing S to occur is possible;

(h) the addressee is a living creature able to understand the directive.

8. Gradation of obligations

The force of a duty is a derivative of forces of sources of this duty. In case of the axiological duty, its force depends on the place which the object of the duty has in the assumed hierarchy of values. It is especially so that the greater the evil brought by not-S, the stronger the obligation to cause S to occur.

Considering thetic duty – its force depends on: the level of intensity of its addressant's wanting, the level of firmness of the imperative revealing this wanting, and the level of "power" that the addressant has over the addressee.

These factors are independent of each other. We might for instance maximally want for the person B to cause S to occur and formulate the respective imperative maximally firmly – but it is possible that we have at the same time only minimal power over the person B; we might just minimally want the person B to cause S to occur and formulate the respective imperative with least possible firmness – but it is possible simultaneously that we have maximum power over the person B, *etc.*

• Cheliński [1925] referred to the intensity of wanting as "the will's tension", and noticed that the force of this tension is independent of the potential to realize the object of the willing: «wishful thinking» might be much stronger that wanting an act which is rational from this point of view (*i.e.* the object of which is realizable).

• The duty, at least the axiological one, has no types or levels according to Elzenberg [1933]:

Everything indicates that the "duty" [...] [relating to values] has no types. The word "should" has definitely more than one meaning (to be more precise: it is used in numerous different ways), but the word "should" in its axiological sense (the only sense in which the noun "duty" is used) may have variants only when it signifies someone's duty to behave in various ways. Here we might only differentiate between the POTENTIAL duty of performing anything that may make the world more valuable, and on the other hand – the concrete DUTY or VOCATION determined by one's qualification and life situation. But the duty of objects to be such and such does not undergo this differentiation. One lamp may give one type of light, for instance red, another – green light; but we may not say that one object "should" be such and such according to one type of duty, and another should be different according to a different type. The duty does not even have levels; therefore if someone says that one object "should very much", and another only "a little" – both utterances would be faulty [1933: 14].

9. Verbalization of obligations: norms

9.1. For the following to occur:

(1) The person A obliged the person B to cause S to occur

the obligation must be verbalized. Obligations are verbalized by means of imperatives, norms or declarative sentences. They are formed as follows, respectively:

(2) Let the person B cause S to occur!

(3) Let the person B not cause S to occur!

(4) The person B should cause S to occur.

(5) The person B should not cause S to occur.

(6) The person B causes S to occur.

(7) The person B does not cause S to occur.

Sentences (2) and (3) are respectively positive and negative imperatives, sentences (4) and (5) – positive and negative norms, (6) and (7) – positive and negative declarative sentences.

Declaratives, usually in the grammatical present tense, are very often expression of legal obligations;[25] in common speech declaratives used for similar purposes are almost always formulated in the grammatical future tense.

• The main method of expressing (thetic) obligations is A NORM. There are (thetic) norms which do not indicate any addressee of the obligation. Let us consider the norm:

---

[25] For instance, Article 148 of the Penal Code reads: "§1. Who murders a man is subject to imprisonment for no shorter time than 8 years, imprisonment of 25 years or lifelong imprisonment".

(8) Someone should cause *S* to occur.

The norm (8) mentions the obligation to cause *S* to occur – without determining who this obligation is imposed on. In norms with effectively indicated addressees, they are either designated «by name» or *via* an appropriate description. The former are INDIVIDUAL norms, the latter – GENERAL norms.

Among instances of individual norms we find:

(9) The person *B* should cause *S* to occur.

(10) Persons *B*, *C* ... should cause *S* to occur.

General norms have the following form:

(11) Persons bearing the property *W* should cause *S* to occur.

Let us notice that general norms may *de facto* have no addressees (when nobody bears the property *W*), they may have precisely one addressee (when only one person bears the property *W*), they may have more than one addressee or have all people as addressees. In the last case, formula (11) would change into a UNIVERSAL norm:

(12) Everyone should cause *S* to occur.

Let us also notice that each general norm may be paraphrased into an appropriate conditional sentence:

(13) If a person bears the property *W*, he should cause *S* to occur.

9.2. Let us consider the following norm:

(14) In conditions *W*, the person *B* should cause S_1 to occur.

This is a RELATIVE norm in which the existence of the duty is limited to conditions enumerated by the addressant of the duty. The norm is ABSOLUTE when the addressant obliges the addressee to cause S_1 to occur in any conditions.

9.3. Let us suppose that:

(15) To cause S_1 to occur, one needs to cause S_2 to occur.

On this basis, instead of obliging a person to cause S_1 to occur, they may be obliged to cause S_2 to occur with the same result:

(16) The person *A* obliged the person *B* to cause S_2 to occur in conditions *W*.

If we assume (15), formula (14) would be an EFFECTIVE norm, and formula (16) – an INSTRUMENTAL one. We might propose an effectuality hypothesis, according to which each state of affairs (and in particular each change) bring a certain result; then would the differentiation between the effective and instrumental obligations be only relative. For each effective obligation expressed as (14) we might indicate a state of affairs that would turn this obligation into an instrumental one.

Let us consider the following obligations:

(17) The person B should add arsenic to the wine which they will serve to their mother-in-law.

(18) The person B should poison the mother-in-law.

(19) The person B should take their mother's-in-law life.

Here the obligation (17) is instrumental towards obligations (18) and (19), and the obligation (18) is instrumental towards (19). However, also for obligation (17) we might find such obligation towards which (17) would be effective. Such an obligation would be of this form:

(20) The person B should act in this and that way, so that arsenic gets added to the wine which will be served to the mother-in-law.

9.4. We should distinguish the PRODUCTIVE norms from ACTIVE norms. The objective of situation (14) is for the addressee to cause something, therefore the object of the obligation is probably a product. Sometimes, however, it is so that:[26]

(21) The person A obliged the person B to repeatedly cause S to occur.[27]

These situations do not aim at the addressee doing (causing) something, but for him to do something constantly or for some certain time.

9.5. Finally, we should distinguish SINGULAR and MULTIPLIED norms.

A multiplied obligation is such an obligation which has an object in form of another obligation. Therefore, it is expressed thus:

(22) The person A should oblige the person B to cause S to occur.

A singular obligation is the one that does not fulfil this condition.

---

[26] We omit here the context of the obligation as irrelevant.

[27] We should remember here that the negative form of the active norm "The person B should cause S to occur" is for grammatical reasons formed as follows: "The person B should never cause S to occur", and not really "The person B should once not cause S to occur". (In Polish, we have here the opposition between perfective and imperfective verb.)

9.6. Norms and imperatives which express binding, acceptable, proper and suitable, or significant and effective obligations are also described as: "binding", "acceptable", "proper" and "suitable", or "significant" and "effective".

• Twardowski [1905/1906] maintained that all norms, including the ethical ones, are of hypothetical character. In other words, they might always be interpreted as the following formula:

(1) If x want to attain $S - x$ should cause S to occur.

The "scientific" justification of such formulas was seen by Twardowski in norms such as:

(2) If S_1 occurs, then S_1 occurs.

• Znamierowski [1924] juxtaposed imperatives, norms and declaratives, or as he called them – imperative phrases, normative phrases and declarative sentences (declarations); he did that on the basis of their relation to facts:

(a) imperative phrases "plan" certain facts;

(b) normative phrases "indicate" certain facts;

(c) declarative sentences "state" certain facts.

Particularly:

[Imperative] phrases: "Work hard!", "Do not steal!", "Go to sleep at nine!" do not state any existing fact at all, and they only [...] plan and design a certain fact, they present its image at a certain time point with a recommendation what to do [1924: 9]. [...] The imperative sentence is fully understood only in a context: we need to know who says what to whom [1924: 10].

Norms would probably be some linguistic phrases that express a measure and recommendation. [...] A norm is probably a sentence which, when followed by a person, could be presented as his own thought in his conscience; it would also, within his thoughts and during any possible struggle, have its natural context in the complex situation of consideration [1924: 9]. [...] A norm of behaviour [...] should be a sentence requiring no supplement, a sentence of clear and self-sufficient content [1924: 10].

[Declarative sentences such as] "The climate is moderate in Poland" [...] [or] "Snow is white" [...] simply determine certain facts of the reality surrounding us; they state that certain objects of certain properties exist [1924: 9].

Furthermore, he was against reducing norms to orders [1924: 8].

Znamierowski collected different types of "normative phrases" (in particular from the field of law). Firstly, this function is performed by categorical sentences, for instance:

(1) One should shoot when the enemy is 100 steps away.

(2) One should get up in the morning.

(3) I should forgive him his fault [1924: 10].

Secondly, it is performed by hypothetical sentences, *e.g.*:

(4) If someone murders another person with malice aforethought, he will be punished with death.

(5) If someone commits a crime, the state should punish him or her thus [1924: 10].

Formula (5) might be also presented as non-hypothetical:

(6) An offender who did this and that must be punished by the state in this and that way [1924: 10].

These sentences are an indication of "what one should do and what is a duty in certain conditions" [1924: 10].

The general form of categorical norms is the following formula:

(7) The person A should perform the act C.

In turn, hypothetical norms assume the general form:

(8) If conditions W are fulfilled, then the person A should perform the act C.[28]

or logically equal sentences with the words "ought to" and "it is necessary to" [1924: 11].

---

[28] In order not to become entangled in the so-called Chisholm's paradox (the paradox of breaching the norm), we should differentiate between formula (8) and the following: "It should be so that if conditions W are fulfiled, then the person A performs the act C". *Cf.*, in this matter, for instance Brożek & Stelmach [2004].

The relation between the conditions W and the act C is a settled relation (*i.e.* "a scheme of possible motivations"), and not a causal relation [1924: 97]. In such verbalization, the norm will find its application if the antecedent becomes true for somebody.

Znamierowski opposed the idea that each norm is in fact hypothetical:

> It is difficult to agree that all norms must have [...] conditional character. After all, a norm of behaviour is a sentence: "Today I should go to bed at nine", "On July 25th the court should pronounce the verdict" – such individual sentences are also indications of what should be done. Such norms may come into being on their own, after somebody's dictate or settlement regulating a particular case, or they might be a consequence of a general norm being in force; then they are the conclusion to a hypothetical syllogism, in which the *praemissa minor* determines that the conditions enumerated in the antecedent of *praemissa maior* were fulfilled [1924: 10–11].

Finally, Znamierowski acknowledged the following formula to be a verbal expression of duty:

(9) According to P, in the situation S (the only and determined, or in a certain individual situation of the type T, or in any situation of the type T) the state of affairs R (the only and determined, or a certain particular case of the type T, or any of the type T) should (or has the right to) exist [1957: 263].

> The relativizing phrase „according to P" means here: „in the view of an evaluation done by P", or also: "In the view of P's evaluation, P sees (feels) that s should (has the right to, is allowed to) exist" [1957: 263].

Effective obligations are expressed – according to Znamierowski [1957: 501 *et seq.*] – in one of the following ways:

(10) If the situation S occurs, the person B should perform the activity (or respectively: not perform the activity) D.

(11) If the situation *S* occurs, the person *B* performs the activity (or respectively: does not perform the activity) *D*.

The formula that expresses not obligations but entitlements has the following form:

(12) If the situation *S* occurs, the person *B* has the entitlement to perform the activity (or not to perform the activity) *D*.

An example of an instrumental obligation is for instance the following obligation:

(13) When reading, one should keep the book 32 centimetres from the eyes.

It seems that instrumental obligations are according to Znamierowski expressed *via* formulas in such a scheme:

(14) If the person *B* performs the activity *D*, the person *B* should perform (performs or has the entitlement to perform) the activity *D* in a way *M*.

Znamierowski [1957] compiled a list of obligations which may be believed to consist of three obligations (or respectively norms): indicative, constructive and competitive.

Indicative norms state "what should be done in a certain situation" [1957: 501], without indication regarding how to do it. In a different place, Znamierowski calls such obligations "static", as they, as he writes, determine "what should exist in the world of a given feeling or drift" [1957: 344].

Constructive norms state "not that an activity is to be performed, but how it is to be performed" [1957: 504]. They might be, we believe, equalled with norms of behaviour – about which Znamierowski wrote that they are norms "which indicate what activities should (or have the right to) be undertaken" [1957: 344]:

> [The latter] are not limited to stating that this and that should exist, as in static norms – but they prescribe the way in which *via* activity this state of affairs should be reached. [...] The aesthetic feeling will tell us that the painting should be hung over the couch; the culinary taste, that we should add 5% of sugar to our tea [1957: 344].

Competitive norms indicate that "*P* has in the situation *s* the duty or entitlement to make a decision regarding the validity of the norm *N*; this decision might either give, lengthen or remove the binding force of this norm" [1957: 507].

• Cheliński [1925] pointed to the diversification of the "symptoms of the ordering will" – it is expressed *via* gestures, imperatives, norms *etc.*; on the other hand he also noticed how ambiguous these "symptoms" may be, as it is for instance with an imperative which might be used among others "for signifying a request, a demand or advice"; moreover, its subject matter might be signalled by the "tone of the voice" or "facial expression".

• The difference between norms and descriptions (or declaratives) consists according to Kotarbiński [1931] in the fact that "norms dictate, prohibit or permit without claiming anything, and the descriptions do claim certain things".

Kotarbiński noted that the formula:

(1) The person *O* should cause *S* to occur

may be interpreted in the two following ways:

(2) It is recommended that the person *O* causes *S* to occur.

(3) Causing *S* to occur was recommended by someone to the person *O*.

In the case of (2) we mean that certain behaviour was recommended to the person *O*, and in the case of (3) the point is stating that someone issued such a recommendation for the person *O*.

• According to Elzenberg [1935] duties (norms) are drawn by values (evaluations). We may consider:

(1) If the state of affairs *S* is honourable (perfect, noble), then the state of affairs *S* is a DUE state (*i.e.* it should exist or come into existence).

(2) If the state of affairs *S* is a due state, and the person *O* is capable of realizing the state of affairs *S*, then the person *O* has an obligation to realize this state of affairs *S*.

Elzenberg would later [1938] consider the issue of whether it is legitimate to reduce a duty to an order (the legitimacy of imperativism); this should not be confused with reducing a duty to a request. In accordance with imperativism:

(3) The person A should undertake the activity D – when – there is a person B (different from the person A), who ordered (or dictated) the person A to undertake the activity D.

Consequently, in order to learn about our duties, we should acquaint ourselves with appropriate orders (or dictates).

As maintained by Elzenberg, there are three versions of imperativism:

(4) "A sentence that supposedly states a duty [*viz.* an obligational sentence] is simply an order": "You should do this" means as much as „Do this!" [1938: 24].

(5) "You should do this" means as much as "You are dictated so by someone of authority [*e.g.* God]" [1938: 25].

(6) A justification of an obligation to do this and that is an order to do this and that given by a person in authority.

Elzenberg believed that none of these versions of imperativism may hold.

Imperativism from the version (4) needs to be discarded, since orders always concern the future and the person to whom they are directed; obligational sentences may sometimes refer to the past or to persons who do not know about this obligation at all [1938: 24–25]. If imperativism of the version (5) was right, then the sentence "You should do what is dictated by God" would be tautology. Yet in Elzenberg's viewpoint, this sentence is not tautological. In case of imperativism of the version (6) a question arises, why should the giver of the order A be in authority. This question may be answered in three ways: (a) because A always dictates what is right; (b) because A is the best (or most perfect); (c) because A is the strongest. It shows, therefore, that the version (3) is not the final variant of the imperativist conception. It would require further "treatment".

• Wallis-Walfisz [1937] claimed that norms may be expressed in three ways, namely by the means of:

(a) imperative sentences (*e.g.* "Do not kill!");

(b) declarative sentences with characteristic norm-creating functors, such as "one should", "it is necessary", "it is fitting", "it would be polite to..." (*e.g.* „One should meet one's obligations");

(c) declarative sentences without the functors mentioned under (b) (*e.g.* "In a hanged man's house, one does not speak about the rope").

Moreover, formulas of type (c) are ambiguous. They carry one meaning when they describe a certain state of affairs, and another in which they are abbreviations of respective formulas of type (b). For instance, sentence given as example in (c) is an abbreviation for "In a hanged man's house one should not speak about the rope".

Formulas of types (b) and (c) – in the second meaning – are mutually reducible to formulas of type (a), *e.g.*: "Do not kill!" and "It is forbidden to kill" and duty "One should meet one's obligations" and "Meet your obligations!".

Wallis-Walfisz differentiated normative sentences "that always are of general nature" from sentences he called "commissions", "which are of temporary nature and the importance of which ends with its execution". These sentences would correspondingly look like these imperatives:

(1) *x* should cause – in conditions *y* – *S* to occur.

(2) *x* should cause *S* to occur.

The fact whether a given formula is a norm or a commission is – in line with Wallis-Walfisz – not influenced by the fact whether it is directed at a certain (one) *x*, or all *x*'s (belonging to a certain set of more than one element).

• Dąmbska [1938] distinguished from among obligations and, more precisely speaking, imperatives as their verbalizations, individual and general obligations; however, she understood them more broadly: as either limited or unlimited as regards „the given time, place and person" [1938: 265].

• Ossowska [1947] assumed her own, rather reductionist stanza towards obligations. In fact, she proposed to reduce obligations to their verbalizations:

For us, the norm shall not be [...] an ideal living in a separate world of duties, or a „phantasm" or projection, as Petrażycki regarded it. It shall be a certain utterance [1947: 127].

From Ossowska's viewpoint, utterances of duty are synonymous or equal to (perfectionist) evaluations, or they are based on such evaluations [1947: 128–129].

She turns the obligational formulas into schemes, respectively:

(1) This and that should be done.

(2) You should do this and that.

The formula (1) is, according to Ossowska, ambiguous. She provides two acceptable paraphrases:

(3) Everybody should do this and that.

(4) Somebody should do this and that.

On the other hand, the formula (2) may be paraphrased as:

(5) The person B should be doing this and that.

Ossowska [1947: 127] compiled a list of normative expressions, or postulates as Lange would call them; after they were ordered and complemented with missing negative or positive links, the list is as follows:[29]

(6) This and that should be done. / This and that should not be done.

(7) *This and that must be done. / This and that must not be done.

(8) One needs to do this and that. / It is not allowed to do this and that.

(9) This and that is dictated to be done. / It is prohibit to do this and that.

(10) It is x's obligation to do this and that. / *It is x's duty not to do this and that.

(11) Each such and such is obliged to do this and that. / *Each such and such is obliged not to do this and that.

(12) Who does this and that, is subject to such and such punishment. / *Who does not do this and that, is subject to such and such punishment.

(13) *You shall do this and that. / You shall not do this and that.

(14) *Do this and that! / Do not do this and that!

Some norms are found in the imperative or indicative mood, in the present and future tense, with the use of the word "should" or without it [1947: 145].

Each norm is a rule and regulation, but not all regulations are norms (*e.g.* road rules, bridge regulations, kitchen recipes).

Indicative sentences are the form "particularly willingly given to legal regulations, good manner principles or game rules" [1947: 145]. For instance:

---

[29] Formulas added as a supplement to Ossowska's list are marked with an asterisk (*). Incidentally, the list includes a formula expressing the entitlement, here not taken into consideration: Each such and such has the entitlement to this and that.

(15) Who promotes libellous news in press, is subject to such and such punishment.

(16) A napkin is to be put on your knees while eating; you do not tie it under your chin.

(17) Those that play volleyball standing further from the net pass the ball to their partners near the net.

An utterance such as:

(18) The person B has the obligation to do this and that.

is only then descriptive, if it means as much as:

(19) The person B obliged himself to do this and that.

– but it does not constitute a norm then.

As far as the norms uttered *via* conditional sentences are concerned [1947: 146–147]:

(20) If conditions W occur, then the person B should C.

(21) If someone commits such and such a crime, the state should punish him thus and thus.

they contain the word "should" (descriptive antecedent – normative consequent). Whereas:

(22) Do not steal!

means as much as:

(23) If you steal, you will be punished in such and such a way.

which states, "with higher or lower probability, certain future events" [1947: 147].

• With regard to norms uttered in imperative sentences (dictates or prohibitions) [1947: 147–149], Ossowska points out that there had been attempts at reducing legal norms to "orders directed at institutions that are supposed to ensure that these orders are adhered to". This reduction had been criticized by Petrażycki [1907b], Znamierowski [1924] and Elzenberg [1938].

• The fact that the shape of the utterance – the grammatical form or presence of particular functors – does not decide whether it is an imperative, a norm or an evaluation, was underlined by Rudziński [1947]. Particularly, for a given utterance to settle an obligation (or, to be a norm) and not only, for instance, "descriptively state that someone has an obligation towards someone else" (and to be therefore a judgement of the norm) – it must be uttered in an appropriate "social situation".

• Ziembiński maintained [1956] that a model verbalization of the obligation should have all elements of an obligational situation clearly indicated. There are – following Ziembiński [1972a] – three objects that the norm (of behaviour) must indicate:

(a) the addressee of the norm;

(b) circumstances, in which the norm is valid (by the way, if they are not indicated *expressis verbis*, the norm is valid in any circumstances);

(c) behaviour that is the addressee's obligation.

Practically speaking, such utterances are often of an elliptical character. This does not lead to misunderstandings if the elided elements are obvious in the contexts of these utterances. However, sometimes the available context does not stand in favour of a concrete interpretation. Let us consider the following duty:

(1) It should be caused that S occurs.

A more detailed version of formula (1) is *e.g.* the norm:

(2) Every human being should be respected.

Are all humans the addressees of this norm – and if not, what kind of subset are the addressees in?

Ziembiński believes that in the norms one may never omit the object of the obligation. Let us consider the norm:

(3) Something should be done about this.

Contrary to appearances, the norm (3) does indicate an object, namely it obliges to act in ANY way that would do away with „this" which is indicated by the context of the norm (3).

Ziembiński [1966b] commented thus on the three possible methods of expressing the norm – imperative, of duty and (supposedly) descriptive:

(a) the imperative form is imitative; he also pointed out that imperative sentences are used for other different purposes;

(b) the form of duty is ambiguous, *i.e.* either it indicates a way to behave to someone, or it states that someone is bearing a certain duty;

(c) the descriptive form is misleading, *i.e.* it is in fact camouflaged form of duty *sensu stricto*.

Ziembiński [1972a] believed also that the essence of norms, at least of norms of behaviour, is the suggestion (dictating or prohibiting) given to someone about certain ways of behaviour.

Technical directives of the following structure were taken by Ziembiński [1966b] to be a specific type of norms:

(4) If you want S_1 to occur, you should cause S_2 to occur.

These norms are connected with sentences that state interrelationship:

(5) If S_2 occurs, S_1 will also occur.

• Grzybowski [1961] warned against the (legal) norms not being distinguished from imperatives; the former may only refer to the past, the latter – to the future.

• The norm – in Lang's approach – "formulates [...] a rule, or a principle of behaviour", so it is "an utterance of duty, determining most often correlative entitlements and obligations" [1962: 102], usually for the determined subjects. The meaning of the norm is "a pattern of behaviour of duty or entitled human behaviour" [1962: 103].

The norm consists of:

(a) a norm-creating functor of the type "it should (not) be" or "it may be" ("it has right to be" / "it has not right to be") – "with the positive or negative sign";

(b) a pattern of behaviour of the form: "in the conditions W, the person O will behave in the manner Z" [1962: 103].

• Woleński [1966] added a condition to the procedure of rational reduction: if we reduce formula F to formula G, formula G should be "clearer" than formula F. As he thought also that imperatives to which people attempt to reduce norms are, generally speaking, less "clear" than respective norms – he thought that imperativism is of no sense.

• Out of two paraphrases of conditional norms:

(1) If S_1, then it should be that S_2.

(2) It should be so that if S_1, then S_2.

Ziemba & Ziembiński [1964] choose paraphrase (2), *i.e.* the so-called deontological paraphrase, as the most accurate.

• "Normative phrases" are, according to Studnicki [1968], used either in a weak (or referring) way or in a strong (or settling) way.

In the first use, they refer to certain normative state of affairs. In the second use, they perform the settlement function, *i.e.* they settle certain normative states of affairs – or they perform the referring function, *i.e.* they report on those states of affairs; the second function is identical to the one performed by weak normative phrases; the first function proves that the usage of such utterances is arbitrary. Special rules settle whether a given normative expression is used in a strong way.

• Imperativism was thoroughly and critically analysed by Najder [1971]. He analysed two versions of imperativism:

(1) Each evaluating sentence is reducible to a certain imperative sentence.

(2) Each evaluating sentence implies a certain imperative sentence.

According to Najder, the following facts speak, among others, against imperativism in the version (1):

(a) evaluating sentences are grammatically speaking indicative sentences – therefore, they bear logical value as opposed to imperative sentences;

(b) sometimes a person who is ready to approve of a certain evaluation is not ready to submit to an order corresponding to this evaluation, and the other way round;

(c) it would be difficult to settle what kind of orders were standing behind ethical evaluations concerning the past, as well as behind aesthetic evaluations.

Imperativism in version (2) would breach the so-called Hume's guillotine, which states that descriptions are never followed by duty. The fact that imperativists are eager to breach this rule stems from their not noticing that an element of duty hides in their seemingly clearly descriptive premises; it hides for instance in phrases such as "to want something" or "to drive at something". On the other hand, the imperative component is often included into sentences seemingly purely descriptive, and it is more obvious than in evaluating sentences. Someone who says "This is poisonous" suggests the imperative "Do not eat it!" more clearly than someone who utters the evaluating sentence "This does not taste good".

In contrast to imperativists, Najder supports the viewpoint that imperatives are based on evaluations and not the other way round.

• Pelc [1971] would underline the fact that a given expression, for example the word "silence", might, regardless of its grammatical status, retain its meaning even though it is used as an indicative, interrogative or imperative sentence.

• According to Wolter & Lipczyńska [1980b], the function of imperative sentences is to explain to their addressees "how one should or should not behave"; the function of normative sentences is to express "indication of a certain behaviour". Imperative sentences are useful when it comes to verbalizing norms, and also for requests or wishes. In turn, normative sentences must be distinguished from sentences describing norms, which state for example in which conditions is a given norm valid, what kind of addressees it has, *etc.*

Wolter & Lipczyńska divided norms on the basis of at whom they are directed; on the one hand, there exist individual norms (which have one, clearly defined, addressee) and general norms (*i.e.* those which only indicate the criteria the addressee must fulfil); on the other hand, they distinguished common norms (which have more than one addressee), unitary (with precisely one addressee) and empty (*i.e.* norms without any addressees).

Legal norms are often expressed *via* seemingly descriptive sentences, and the norms of social life – *via* rhetorical questions.

• In Świrydowicz's approach [1981], the most general scheme for the normative formula is the following:

(1) When (a) x is A and W, then let (b) x realize B!

In this scheme: 'x' represents individual names of particular persons, 'A' is a general name (or nominal function) of an indicated person, 'B' is a general name (or nominal function for the behaviour of this person, and 'W' – is a sentence (or sentential function) that states that a state of affairs independent of the discussed person occurs; part (a) is the antecedent, part (b) – the consequent of the norm; the functor "when... then..." is a norm-creating functor, with the sentence as its first argument, and the commission as its second argument.

All the variables – therefore variable 'x' and any possible variables standing in 'A', 'B' and 'W' – may be suitably quantified. For example, formula (1) may assume the form:

(2) For any x: when (x remains related *via* the relation R_1 to a certain a) and (for any y: Py), then let x realize that (x will remain in the relation R_2 towards a certain b).

• Gizbert-Studnicki [1983] presented the following as the actually employed methods of verbalizing obligations:

(a) performative ("I order you to do this and that");

(b) imperative ("Do this and that!");

(c) modal ("You should do this and that");

(d) declarative ("I want you to do this and that");

(e) interrogative ("Could you do this and that?");

(f) prognostic ("You will do this and that").

He saw the performative and imperative shapes as clearly declarative; as far as it concerns the others, he claimed that the content of directives thus expressed is determined by the content of these sentences, and the context of the utterance only indicates whether it should be treated as a directive, or as a statement, question or prognosis. This might be explained as follows: utterances of the type (d)–(f) are treated as utterances that have general meaning in a zero context, which may be later described with greater detail; alternatively, sometimes these expressions have one (basic) sense ascribed (respectively: declarative, interrogative or prognostic), which may be later modified by some contexts of the utterances. Gizbert-Studnicki preferred the second interpretation.

All in all, as he noticed, in some situations any declarative sentence may be used to utter a directive.

• Zieliński & Ziembiński [1988] indicate the following types of directive utterances:

(a) norms of behaviour;

(b) technical (teleological, appropriate) directives, which "dictate to do something if one wants or one has to cause a certain state of affairs" [1988: 60];

(c) "rules of sense, which construct certain conventional activities, *e.g.* game rules, linguistic semantic rules, rules of legal proceedings, *etc.*" [1988: 61]; these might also be formulated as terminological directives:

> A norm of behaviour in the essential understanding of this term is an utterance, which directly formulates a dictate or prohibition of a concrete behaviour in concrete circumstances, directed at certain persons [1988: 57].

Additionally – this behaviour is not instinctive, but "depending on the acting person's will" [1988: 58]:

> A norm of behaviour might also mean such expression, which individually or generally, in individually or generally settled circumstances, summons its addressee to realize a concrete act – or an act of a certain type which is abstractly determined and thus possible to be repeated. This is followed by a division of norms into on the one hand individual and general, and on the other – into concrete and abstract [1988: 58].

Zieliński & Ziembiński state clearly that a legal norm should be distinguished from a legal regulation, *i.e.* "the verbalization of a legal norm" [1988: 75]:

> In the numerous branches of law, it is difficult to find such a regulation which would remind us of the model formula of the norm of behaviour. For instance, the Civil Code consists of such regulations in no more than a few percentage points [1988: 74].

In fact, the formulated regulations need decoding and interpretation in order for the form of a legal norm to be attained.

Zieliński & Ziembiński enumerate the following methods for formulation of norms of behaviour:

(a) as an imperative;

(b) as a duty – that "someone in certain circumstances should do something, is supposed to do something, must do something" [1988: 68]; this shape might be categorical or hypothetical;

(c) as an apparent description (which in fact has a default expression preceding the description: "Let it be that...");

(d) as a deontic sentence, *i.e.* a sentence "stating whether a given act is dictated or prohibited" [1988: 70].

> If a norm of behaviour or a technical directive is formulated with the use of the imperative mood, the suggestive sense of this statement is clearly visible ("Close the window!", "If you want quiet, close the window!"). Such an utterance is useful mostly for verbalization of norms settled for their addressee by someone else (or at least with help from someone else), but not so useful with norms that we consider binding only because they dictate to us to do what we also consider right (autonomous norms). [...] An advantage of this [*viz.* imperative] form is the fact that the imperative forcefully shows the directival character of a given utterance, adding particularly strong suggestive character to it. [...] A statement formulated by the means of the imperative might bear the social character of an order; this means it is a powerful settlement of a norm of behaviour without first asking for the addressee's consent; however, it might also seem a request, encouragement, warning, and even humble begging: "Deign not to despise my request!" [1988: 68].
>
> Sometimes one encounters an opinion that the antecedent of the norm might have the character of a descriptive sentence, and the consequent only is a norm in its strict sense; this pertains to hypothetical sentences ["If someone bearing the property A finds himself in conditions B, they should do C"]. This stanza [...] brings uncertainty as to the semiotic character of directive utterances (with such an assumption, the same norm would not be comparable if formulated in categorical and hypothetical structures) [1988: 69].

Statements concerning norms might be both descriptive (*e.g.* referring to its verbal form, origin, legitimacy) and evaluating (*e.g.* stating that the regulation is unclear and ineffective).

Zieliński & Ziembiński also point out that there are other meanings of the "norm":

> (a) a measure or model that some objects should match [...], [*e.g.*] the norm of height, weight, *etc.* – characterizing "normal" objects [1988: 82];
> (b) a description of a model object in a normative regulation; it prohibits manufacturing, or introducing to the market, or using in certain circumstances such objects some properties of which do not correspond to the model [1988: 82].

The last instance is referred to as a technical norm.

In jurisprudence, one might encounter descriptive, evaluating and normative sentences.

Some types of legal sentences include:

(a) dogmatic statements, *i.e.* "statement on certain norms valid in the given legal system, and also on the legal stand of certain acts within the given system" [1988: 85];

(b) "statements concerning the language" [1988: 86];

(c) "statements concerning real aspects of legal phenomena" [1988: 86].

• Opałek [1990] proposed to recognize the following formulas as model normatives, optatives and evaluations:

(1) It is settled as adequate – for *x* to behave in such and such way.

(2) May it be thus and thus.

(3a) The object *S* bears positive/negative value.

(3b) [The fact] that *p* bears positive/negative value.

• Zieliński [1992] listed these methods of indicating obligation:

(a) *via* extraverbal behaviour (*e.g.* by marking the «wanted» path);

(b) *via* extraverbal signs (*e.g.* nautical signal flags);

(c) *via* imperative sentences;

(d) *via* sentences of duty (in the categorical or hypothetical form, mutually translatable, by the way);

(e) *via* modal sentences (with the word "must");

(f) *via* (seemingly) descriptive sentences;

(g) *via* deontic sentences (with words such as "dictated", "prohibited", "allowed", "optional", "indifferent", "obligatory");

(h) via performative sentences (with the initiating word "herewith").

Zieliński maintained the position that the best, and hence most direct, method to verbalize norms is the method (h); others do that in an indirect way, often also performing various different functions which are not easy to distinguish from the normative function.

10. Norms and consultatives, instructions and optatives

10.1. Norms, and sometimes imperatives, verbalize not only (thetic) obligations, but also information that brings advice (or COUNSEL). Let us assume that:

(1) S_2 is the motive of S_1 – when – S_1 occurs, because S_2 occurs.

We have to do with advice in the case of such a motivation:

(2) The person A advises the person B to cause that p – when – the person A obliges the person B to cause that p, because the person A is convinced that [(if p, then q) and (the person B wants that q to occur – and the person B does not know that if p, then q)].

Of course, for the person A, who fulfils the second part of the conjunction from formula (2), to fulfil simultaneously the first one – and thus to advise the person B – it is necessary to have additional motivation, in form of for instance an appropriate imperative from the person B, or the person A's own feeling of caring for the good of the person B.

10.2. Instructions are a specific kind of advice (they include among others doctor's recommendations in medical therapy, culinary recipes, maintenance, production and assembly descriptions of various objects). Let us assume that:

(3) If the person B causes that p to occur, then the person B will attain that q – when – if the person B wants to attain that q, then the person B should cause that p to occur.

With this assumption,[30] the instruction might be expressed as follows:

---

[30] The relation between causing that p to occur and attaining that q is in fact weaker than the assumption (3) would suggest. In particular, for instance recovery is *de facto* only a more or less probable outcome of an intake of medicine.

(4) If the person *B* wants to attain that *q*, then the person *B* should cause that *p* to occur.

Therefore – instructions are expressed by means of conditionally complex imperatives.

10.3. We should differentiate between imperatives and OPTATIVES – *i.e.* utterances shaped thus:

(5) May *S* occur.

We essentially use optatives when we express our volition (*scil.* wish) for a certain state of affairs to occur, regarding the occurrence of which we have no influence, and neither has the person we are speaking to, or the influence is in both cases limited. *Cf. e.g.:*

(6) May not it be so cold next year!

(7) May he manage to catch his train!

Let us, however, notice that such wishes might also be expressed *via* imperatives, as in the following formula:

(8) Person *B*, let the New Year bring you the fulfilment of your dreams!

The *explicite* indicated addressee of this (pseudo-) obligation is in fact an ostensible addressee. Neither the New Year nor the person *B* might be the real addressee, for fundamental reasons.

• Already Twardowski [1901] differentiated between orders and wishes, and both of them (as certain intellectual activities) from sentences expressing them.

• Cheliński [1925] juxtaposed orders, "settling norms obliging one of the parties by the sheer will of the other party", with agreements, "settling norms by unanimous acts of will of both parties".

• Dąmbska [1938: 266] has in turn stated that recommendations are *sensu stricto* not obligations, and in particular not orders.

• Ossowska [1947] wrote in general terms:

The term ["should" has] [...] different hues and sometimes it [...] sounds more imperative, sometimes [...] it is an expression of wishes or advice [1947: 174].

She characterized wishes as follows:

Different ethicists turned their attention to the possibility of treating utterances including the word "should" as psychological sentences. As far as the actual way in which such utterances are used, they are difficult to be ALWAYS read as psychological sentences, although one must admit that they might SOMETIMES assume such meaning. This happens when we want to use them and simply express a certain wish. When we say that studying should be free of charge at all levels, that museums should be open until late evenings so that people who work could use them – we might think that free education and museums open until late might be necessary for a certain social group to be considered as well-organized. In such cases this statement might be perceived as an axiological norm. It might, however, be also an expression of a certain *pium desiderium*, admitting that one wishes it to happen. Sometimes when verbal expressing a wish, we give it a non-personal form in order to strengthen its authority. A child draws lines along a garden path. Another child walks in on a line. "No walking here!" – screams the first child and forcefully pushes the other away. Probably this usage was what was in the minds of those, who claimed that statements with the word "should" are in fact psychological utterances of thirsts of the one uttering them. Indeed, sometimes utterances including the word "should" might be logically interpreted not only as utterances EXPRESSING a certain thirst, or as statements SYNONYMOUS to certain introspective sentences; yet in the light of the above conducted analysis, it seems rather impossible to stretch this interpretation to all cases in which we use the word "should". It is hard to say that someone utters an introspective sentence when he says that a historian should be impartial, that one should attach two photographs to a passport application, or that one should not eat meat in the evening [1947: 144–145].

• Gizbert-Studnicki [1983] recognized as statements included in the "directive discourse" among others: norms, principles, rules, orders, encouragements, wishes, suggestions, proposals, requests, begging, advice, warnings, recommendations, guidelines, hints and admonitions.

• Zieliński & Ziembiński [1988] juxtaposed optative statements, *i.e.* "expressing a wish for a given state of affairs to appear, last or disappear in the future" [1988: 56] with evaluating and directival utterances. Optative statements:

(1) May it be thus and thus.

are foremost formulated when there is even a slight possibility for the wish to be fulfilled [1988: 57].

> If the optative statements are taken to be a stronger form of evaluating utterances, then postulates claiming that this and that should be, without indicating who causes it, might be considered as a weak form of the norm of behaviour; the fact remains however that we do not know to whose behaviour it refers [1988: 57].

It is clearly visible at the comparison of the following optative and postulate:

(2) May the window be clean.

(3) The window should be clean.

> The utterances that are distinctly directive in nature are more or less direct indications of how people should behave in given circumstances [1988: 57].

• Opałek [1974] maintained the position that the so-called directive utterances have special "directive sense" – different from the cognitive (or descriptive) meaning, characteristic of descriptive utterances (or logical sentences), and irreducible to this meaning. The cognitive meaning of an utterance is here equalled with its extension (*i.e.* its logical value) and intension (*i.e.* their assigned judgements). According to Opałek, the difference stems from the fact that descriptive utterances are "reproductive" in character (they bear sense due to a relation with something external); contrastively, directive utterances are "productive" (they create their own sense which may not be analyzed in terms of analogues of extension and intension).

Opałek pointed to a significant pragmatic function of directive utterances: "the ability to influence human behaviour" and ability to express "volitional experiences"; however, both of these also perform an informational function, which must be effective in order for the utterance to perform evocative function (the utterance must be understood to perform the latter).

11. Imperative-normative argumentation

The "logical consequence" in the narrower sense of this term one understands as the relation between the antecedent and consequent of a logically true implication – which is therefore a sentence with tautological scheme, or a scheme of only true sentences.

If a certain sentence 'p' is true, and the sentence 'q' logically follows from the sentence 'p', then the sentence 'q' "inherits" the truth after the sentence 'p'.

"Logical consequence" in this sense does not occur between imperatives, since they do not bear any logical value *sensu stricto*: they are neither true nor false.

However, the sense of "logical consequence" and "logical value", respectively, might be extended so that it would ensure the "inheriting" of properties of imperatives and norms. This applies to all properties taken into consideration when evaluating the willings and duties expressed *via* imperatives and norms.

In the simplest case, for instance, bindingness, acceptability, being-proper and suitability, as well as significance and effectiveness of imperatives or coordinated normative clauses are followed by "consequent" (in the broader sense) respectively bindingness, acceptability, being-proper and suitability, as well as significance and effectiveness of these imperatives and norms.

Such interrelations of the type of consequence are the basis for imperative-normative argumentations. When understanding "argumentation" in this broader sense, one may draw from imperatives and norms other imperatives and norms as conclusions; one may explain or justify them *via* other imperatives and norms, or appropriate declarative sentences.

• Nuckowski [1903] believed obligational sentences (or "practical judgements", as he called them) to carry logical value. He wrote that they state "the duty of being the predicate contained in the subject".

• The first attempts at the construction of imperative logic may be found in Borowski [1924]. Speaking more precisely, they are certain elements of what he called praxeological algebra. Its basic notions are among others: the act, lack of act, abandonment of an act, a reverse, substitute and alternative act towards a given act, being-successful (or unsuccessful) of an act and – what matters most for the theory of imperatives – an acceptable act ("the zone of freedom"), a prohibited and an dictated act (equalled by Borowski with duty).

This provisional system was to be followed by Bautro's system, signalled [1934: 43–44], but finally probably not constructed (or at least not published).

• Znamierowski – both in his [1924] and [1957] work – maintained consequently the position that one may speak about the truth of norms:

Norms [...] are [...] logical sentences, thus: they may be true or false, and may be linked by the relation of consequence [1957: 511].

However, he understood the "truthfulness" in a specific way:
(1) The norm *N* is true – when – the norm *N* is valid.
Znamierowski attached a reservation to this formula:

This does not mean that the term "to be valid" is identical with "to be true". Validity means that the norm as a whole, as an independent object, maintains a relation with an acting subject or subjects; the truthfulness pertains to the relation between the content of the sentence and the state of affairs determined by this content [1924: 15].

"Validity" has a different meaning for axiological and for thetic norms. Thus:

The AXIOLOGICAL norm "*x* should be *a*" or "*P* should perform the act *c*" is valid, [therefore] these sentences are true, when in given conditions w_x or w_p, *x* bearing the property *a*, or performance of the act *c* by *P* is

THE BEST of all possible eventualities. [...] In order to [...] determine
which of the given acts the best alternative is objectively, one should
in fact know and evaluate all their possible consequences. And as the
consequences of an act as a phenomenon deeply linked to the infinite
chain of causes and effects also infinitely go into the future, [...] one
must resign from learning what is ABSOLUTELY the best in given circumstances and settle with determining what is the best in these given
circumstances in HIS UNDERSTANDING [1924: 115–116].

"The given circumstances" also include the actor's knowledge of all the
alternatives. It is different with thetic norms:

A thetic norm [n: "*x* should be a according to an act of settlement [of
will] *s*" or "*P* should perform the act *c* according to an act of settlement *s*"] is valid, [therefore that] sentence is true if this act of settlement [*i.e.* act *s*] has indeed taken place and if the content of this act
[*s*] was indeed identical with the content of the quoted [thetic] norm
[*n*] [1924: 18].

Znamierowski emphasized the fact that the truthfulness of a norm is its
absolute feature:

Sentences that are norms are absolutely and invariably true, just as
any other sentence stating any other state of affairs. They are most
often hypothetical sentences, which in full read as follows: "If conditions *w* are fulfilled, then *P* should this and that". This sentence is
an absolute truth, if it is true at all. Only the application of a given
norm to particular situation of the act depends on the conditions
given in this situation. It is so, because for the consequent of a given
norm to apply in a given situation, the antecedent of this norm must
apply to it, as it settles the conditions of the duty. Existence, realization of a fact may then only settle the application of a particular
norm to a given situation, yet it does not settle whether the norm is
right or not [1924: 17].

The axiological norm depends only on the truthfulness of the sentence which evaluates a value in a commonly valid way – and is of objective, invariable character. [...] Therefore, [...] the axiological norm is at all times true and at all times valid. Its validity is independent from the time condition: morality knows no time limits. [...] [On the other hand] since [...] the moment [...] of [actual settlement of a thetic norm] it is true for each consequent moment that is into infinity. But the validity of the norm does not extend into such infinite time. It is enough that a new decree of will overrules it, or substitutes it with another – and the préstige of its power will disappear [1924: 19]. [...] The thetic norm is valid for a certain time limit; but it is a true sentence on certain time conditions [1924: 20].

[*NB.*] The legislative system aims at the highest possible level of equality between the content of thetic norms and axiological norms [1924: 20–21].

• Kotarbiński [1929] differentiated proper norms from the so-called normative sentences.

Proper norms are "utterances similar to orders, advices, warnings, *etc.*, such as:

(1) Do not kill!

(2) Love thy neighbours!

etc. [1929: 445]. They are neither true nor false [1931]; they may not be justified or falsified (in the sense of proving respectively their truthfulness or falsehood). "They might be only combated or propagated" [1929: 446] (*cf.* also Wallis-Walfisz [1937]).

In turn, normative sentences are sentences of the following type:

(3) For this and that to happen, such and such active behaviour is necessary.

(4) For this and that to happen, such and such active behaviour is enough.

(5) Such and such behaviour would be awful.

(6) To behave so and so in this situation would be honest.

The first two normative sentences are material, the two latter – emotional. Moreover, from among normative sentences we might distinguish general sentences (concerning all possible cases of behaviour) and individual (concerning on certain determined eventual case).

And in turn, normative sentences are in contrast with the proper norms true or false, they might also be justified or falsified.

The following relation occurs between the proper norms and normative sentences: by justifying or falsifying a given normative sentence, we indirectly contribute to the success or failure of a respective proper norm [1929: 446].

Kotarbiński postulated (Sztykgold [1936]) research into the negation "no" ("do not") with an imperative as its argument (*e.g.* in a prohibition "Do not come in"); he excluded treating such negation as sentential negation (of the type of "it is not the case that") with arguments of sentences in the logical sense.

Moreover, Kotarbiński believed that it is necessary to construe a calculus of imperatives [1947]; in terms of such a calculus, one should reconstruct reasonings, in which the premise is the description, and the conclusion is the imperative (*e.g.* "We have rested enough already, so let us go on!"). One should also explain why the reverse structures, *i.e.* with the imperative as the premise, and the description as the conclusion, are felt to be incoherent. Kotarbiński suggested that correct reasoning of the first kind might be ultimately presented as reasonings operating with purely descriptive sentences (*e.g.* "We have rested enough already, so it would be in accordance with the aim of the trip, if we go on").

• According to the general rule of the descriptive paraphrasing of the imperative proposed by Kotarbiński [1966] , the imperative recommending a certain activity to achieve a certain state of affairs has its equivalent in a sentence (in logical sense) stating the purposefulness of this activity for achievement of this state of affairs. Such an approach repeals the so-called paradox of imperative alternative. On the ground of sentential calculus, we have: if p, then p or q. Are we allowed to infer, on such a fundament, the imperative "Put the letter to a post box or burn it!" from the imperative "Put the letter to a post box!"? According to Kotarbiński, "or" in imperative contexts indicates the possibility of free choice between actions recommended by argument of the alternative – in driving towards achieving a determined state of affairs. The paraphrase of the imperative "Put the letter to a post box or burn it!" would be the sentence "Putting the letter to a post box is purposeful for achieving a certain state of affairs or burning the letter is purposeful for achieving a certain state of affairs". Let us assume that the imperative "Put the letter to a post box" recommends a suitable activity for achieving the fact that the letter will be delivered to addressee. If so, it is not true that for achieving the last aim one may choose between putting the letter to a post box and burning it.

• Sztykgold claimed that "so far no one has gathered the theses of formal logic which would find application in norm theory" and that "no one has settled conditions for norm equality" [1936]; he must have overlooked Borowski's attempts. He himself maintained that all the theses of sentential calculus apply to norms, since the norms have their equivalents of the "truth and falsehood criteria", namely the "rightness and wrongness criteria". He would use the relation theory for norms, because he was convinced that the relation of entitlement, significant here, is the reverse of the relation of obligation (*i.e.* the relation of entitlement is definable *via* the relation of lack of obligation, and the relation of obligation – *via* the relation of lack of entitlement).

• Dąmbska adopted a stance on the semantic status of obligational sentences, and she claimed that "accepting or rejecting imperative categorical sentences out of necessity depends on emotional and not cognitive factors" [1938: 265–266].

• Since norms are translatable to imperatives, and the latter are not undergoing qualification with regard to truth and falsehood (understood literally) – also norms have no logical value, claims Wallis-Walfisz [1937].

• Furthermore, Petrażycki [1939] believed that when discussing norms (and evaluations), not the "criterion of concordance with reality" applies, but *e.g.* "the criteria of reasonability and unreasonability, rationality and irrationality, rightness and wrongness".

He divided sentences (and "positions" expressed therein) into, firstly, objective-cognitive, relating (*resp.* describing) what exists, and subjective-relative, in which "we discuss our subjective relation towards something existing or imagined"; he included "critical" sentences (*i.e.* evaluations) and "postulate" sentences (*i.e.* the "requirements") in the latter. Evaluations express emotions directed at something that existed or exists (or is imagined as such); requirements contain emotions directed at (non)realization of something that is not yet there. In Petrażycki's opinion, traditional logic ignored evaluations and requirements, hence it was a "lame" logic. For it to become an adequate theory, it would have to include these too and become a "positional logic", the theory of all sentences (*resp.* positions). One ought to remember that different positions may be expressed in one sentence simultaneously (*e.g.* in the sentence "Goethe, a great German poet, was born in 1749 in Frankfurt on the Main" we encounter the description that "Goethe was born in 1749 in Frankfurt on the Main", and additionally evaluation that "Goethe was a great German poet").

• Similarly, according to Ossowska [1947: 149–153], norms are not judged with the truthfulness/falsity criteria understood in the sense applied to sentences in the logical sense.

The logical value of the norms might consist in their rightness/wrongness. Only and all the valid / concerning everyone norms are right.

Ossowska enumerated the following ways in which norms may be justified [1947: 158–162]:

(1) The norm N is a consequence of a valid norm N^*, which is more general than the norm N.

According to the norm N one should not perform the act C, when according to the norm N^* one should not perform the act C^*, in relation to which the act C is a specification.

For example, one should not poison neighbours, because one should not, in general, take the lives of neighbours (with the assumption that poisoning neighbours takes their lives). One should not steal apples, because one should not steal at all.

This method of verifying may be applied to all kinds of duty. Duty justified thus may be perceived as semantic duty (*scil.* one with semantic reason).

(2) The norm N results from the valid general norm N^* and assumed evaluation O (according to Moore's theory of rights).

Appropriate evaluations read as follows:

(3) If X does not bear the property P, then X is evil X.[31]

or in other versions:

(4) Good X bears the property P.

(5) If X is a good X, then X bears the property P.[32]

(6) X which bears the property P is better than X which does not bear the property P.

According to the norm N one should perform the act C, because according to the norm N^* in each situation one should for instance perform a good, or the best possible act, and according to the evaluation O the act C is good or the best possible.

One should not for instance lie, because it is evil – and one should not do evil things.

This method of verifying finds application at axiological duties.

According to Ossowska:

> A result worthy of mentioning is the possibility that opens with the base in these reasonings, the possibility to recognize any arguments for the norms as arguments implicating evaluations [1947: 142].

Ossowska maintains that there exists asymmetry between the dictates and prohibitions [1947: 161–162].

Proving that the dictated behaviour "does something good to somebody" is not considered a justification for the dictate to "produce well" and "avoid evil" [1947: 161]. The prohibition to "produce evil" is usually justified by proving that the prohibited behaviour hurts somebody:

> This asymmetry is related to the prohibitive character of our morality, which would rather combat evil that produce good; it also leads

---

[31] This example is not the most fortunate formulation of the evaluation in question, since 'X' appears in at least two different functions: the first two occurrences as an individual name (or variable), and the third occurrence – as a general name or a predicate. Therefore we have: If A CERTAIN dog does not have a tail, then THIS dog is a bad (or: is not a good) DOG.

[32] *Cf.* the above note.

to speaking the truth not by recommending its good consequences, but rather *via* reminding about the evil consequences of lying [1947: 161–162].

With the volitional duty, the following justifications for its rightness are possible:

(7) The norm is right, when "it might be derived from previously approved norms or with help of previously approved evaluations and empirical sentences" [1947: 157–158].

(8) The norm N is right when the authority A resolved that the norm N is valid.

(9) The norm N is right for the person O – when – the person O would like the norm N to be valid for everyone (Kant's criterion).[33]

The instrumental obligation (*cf.* further) is verified as follows:

(10) The norm N results from the currently valid norm N^* and a true empirical sentence E.

Thus according to the norm N one should perform the act C, because: (a) according to the norm N^* one should perform the act C^*; (b) according to the (true/accepted) empirical sentence E a condition necessary for the performance of the act C^* is the performance of the act C; (c) if someone wants to realize the given state of affairs, he should realize those states of affairs which are conditions necessary for its realization.

One should for example respect elderly people, because one should respect certain values, which "accumulate" precisely in the elderly.

The condition (c) has two version in Ossowska:

(11) If the person A causes X to bear the property P, then the person A achieves the aim C.

(12) If the person A wants to achieve the aim C, the person A should cause X to bear the property P.

Correspondingly, according to Ossowska, the norms are falsified (*resp.* challenged) as follows [1947: 158–159]:

---

[33] For the evaluation of norms in Ossowska – *cf.* [1947: 162–167].

(13) The norm *N* is followed by the norm *N***, more specific than the norm *N*, but the norm *N*** is not valid.

As Ossowska writes, in here one should point out "concrete cases" in which the given norm should not be adhered to.

For instance, the norm "Do not lie!" is challenged by providing "instances when lies saved somebody's honour or life" [1947: 159].

(14) The norm *N* follows of the valid general norm *N** and the evaluation *O* or the empirical sentence *E*, but the evaluation *O* is not accepted, and the empirical sentence *E* is not true.

This might serve as a basis for falsifying a regulation *via* pointing that it does not serve the purpose it was supposed to serve (American prohibition might be an example here); alternatively, one might point that the regulation has undesired effects (as an example, abandoning a medical therapy because of side effect might be provided).

A particular method of falsifying of the norm is proving that:

(a) this norm is "contradictory" to another valid norm (*e.g.* a norm "It is dictated that *S*" to the norm "It is prohibited that *S*");

(b) this norm dictates to drive to *S* by means that block reaching *S*;

(c) this norm dictates to combat *S* by means that lead towards *S*;

(d) the norm dictates something which, if done universally, would lead to the disappearance of the addressees (*e.g.* universal celibate).

Ossowska adds that when justifying duties (*resp.* norms), one uses also various persuasive arguments, such as: everybody / the authorities adhere to this norm; adhering to this norm is in the best interests of a given person, *etc.*

• Rudziński [1947] perceived the norm's validity or lack-of-validity (treated as a relation between the norm and its addressee) as a feature analogous to the logical value of descriptives. Also the principle of excluded middle would bind in the normative system: if a given norm bears sense, it is valid (in this system) or not.

The logical value *sensu stricto* might be referred to when discussing judgements of norms (*resp.* obligations), in particular, hypothetical judgements of logical relations between the validity of different norms. One might then ask about the logical value of the following sentence, for instance: "If such and such a norm (or set of norms) is valid, one should not do this and that";[34] there is no point in asking about the logical value of the norm "One must not do this and that".

Rudziński underscored the fact that the same norm might be justified in many ways: *via* a reference to the "very value of recommended behaviour", or the "fact that it was settled" by a given provider of the norm.

• It is sometimes said that evaluations are not only the reasons behind the norms, but sometimes norms are equal to evaluations. According to Lande [1948] this viewpoint is faulty. Let us consider the following norm:

(1) The fact that p should occur.

According to the abovementioned viewpoint, formula (1) would be equivalent to the following evaluation:

(2) It is good (or it would be the best), if the fact that p occurs.

This might be agreed upon in certain cases, when the norm of type (1) will be a verbalization of an appropriate teleological regulation, *i.e.* the regulation with a causal regularity behind:

(3) If S_1 occurs, then S_2 occurs. Therefore, if we want S_2 to occur, it is good to cause S_1 to occur.

We sense, however, that such an equivalence does not occur for ethical and legal regulations. It is enough to compare the following formulas:

(4) "If someone hits you on the right cheek, offer the other one, too".

(5) The President of the Commonwealth should summon the Seym if 1/2 of the deputies wish it so.

(6) It would be good if you offer your left cheek to someone who hits you on the right.

(7) It would be good if the President of the Commonwealth summons parliament at the request of 1/2 of the deputies.

The formula (6) attains a theological character which formula (4) lacks, and formula (7) loses the feeling of duty resting on the President of the Commonwealth, present in formula (5).

• A proponent of the viewpoint that the norms (or "normative sentences"), *i.e.* "sentences stating what a human being should do, has the right

---

[34] By the way, Rudziński also noticed that the reverse implication does not occur: "If one should not do this and that, such and such a norm is valid".

to do or might do or not do", do have logical value, similarly to "theoretical sentences" – was Kalinowski [1953]. This viewpoint was for him a starting point for constructing a formalized deductive system of normative sentence-forming functors with two name-forming arguments; examples might be: "x should (not) do y", "x is permitted (not) to do y" and "x might (not) do y".

• According to Ziembiński [1956], the phrase:

(1) The norm N is valid.

has at least three possible meanings. These particular meanings are:

(2) The norm N is valid$_1$ when the norm N has thetic justification in a certain act of settlement (due to an authority or power[35] of the giver of the norm).

(3) The norm N is valid$_2$ when the norm N has axiological justification in a certain evaluation (*i.e.* what the norm dictates is good, and what the norm prohibits is evil).

(4) The norm N is valid$_3$ when the norm N is realized in cases where it finds application.

The following problems might occur here:

What is the relation between the meanings (2)–(4)? In particular, could the validity from (3) be reduced to the validity from (2)?

Let us suppose that a person A realizes the norm "Respect other people!", which supposedly finds application towards all people. Will we say on the basis of (4) that the norm is valid, and if yes, then towards whom, the person A or all people?

Ziembiński [1964] would strongly emphasize the fact that for a given duty many different evaluations may be indicated as justifying reasons; when attributing such and such a reason to someone, we extrapolate, in general, our own preferences, and we additionally suppose that the giver of the norm is a rational, and consistent, person.

• Sztykgod's and Rudziński's research were critically developed by Lang [1960]. He was interested, among others, in the problem of negat-

---

[35] Power towards a person with regard to certain goods is held by someone who may decide whether to provide this person with these goods or deprive them thereof, and thus make them dependant.

ing norms – by the aid of sentential as well as nominal negation. He distinguished negation of norm form negation of the validity of norm. Lang considered negation of the validity of norm as equivalent of sentential negation of norm, claiming that such a negation itself is not a norm. At the same time, Lang [1962] belonged to supporters of the view that norms have not logical value. As he wrote: "It is because norms serve not to describe the reality, but to regulate human behaviour, *i.e.*, in consequence, to actively form the social reality" [1962: 103].

• Czeżowski identified the norm with a sentence stating "the duty of a regulation or a valid rule" [1964b: 144].

According to him, the norms are verbalized *via* sentences of duty of the type (a):

(1) One should behave thus and thus. / One should not behave thus and thus.

(2) It is necessary to behave thus and thus. / One should not behave thus and thus.

(3) One must not behave thus and thus.[36]

or *via* TRUE [1964b: 145] declarative sentences of the type (b):

(4) People behave thus and thus.

(5) Who behave thus and thus, are subject to such and such sanction. The last example is usually a legal norm.

In Czeżowski's viewpoint, normative sentences usually possess logical value. Normative sentences of the type (a) state the duty; normative sentences of the type (b) "state the state of affairs dictated by a norm-giving instance" [1964b: 144]:

A certain external resolution gives such sentences [as (b)] the character of the norm, with the underlying presupposition of the truthfulness. Therefore, such norms are called settling, or thetic, norms. For the legislative norms, pertinent resolutions are resolutions of legislative bodies; for chess or bridge rules the resolutions of inventors and

---

[36] The negation of formula (3), "One is allowed to behave thus and thus", is not an obligation, but an entitlement.

organizers of these games (example: the king moves in chess by one square, in any direction). Such resolutions are of the same character as the so-called axiomatic directives of deductive theories. These directives are metatheoretical sentences; axioms are taken to be true in a given theory so as to construct a certain system of objects with these assumed axioms – which is like the world depicted and described in a given theory, *e.g.* the world of Euclidean or non-Euclidean geometry. Similarly, one could mention the world of chess or bridge combinations formed by appropriate game rules. The resolutions of legislative bodies are directives which introduce sentences that also, just like axioms, create a certain world – the judicial system. In this system, true sentences are legal norms, and also laws in the sense used by for instance theoretical physics to speak about scientific laws; what happens, happens in accordance with these norms, in other words – in the system the norms are adhered to, taxes and payments are levied, crimes are punished, administrative offices issue legal edict [1964b: 145].

• Ziemba & Ziembiński [1964] maintain the position that if deontic logic is to find an application in jurisprudence, it must be a theory of consequences for domain of the norms perceived as sentences, which are devoid of logical value, *i.e.* which are neither true nor false. This theory must not be just a theory that explains how one sentence stating that one norm is valid follows from the other sentence which concerns that the second norm is valid, even though the logic of consequences must somehow refer to such a theory regarding the norms themselves.

Let us assume that the general form of the norms is as follows:

(1) It should be so that p (where the range of variability of 'p' consists of declarative sentences).

The interpretation of consequence in the domain of norms would then be as follows:

(2) The norm "It should be so that p" is followed by the norm "It should be so that q", when 'p' is followed (in particular logically) by 'q'.

To avoid paradoxical consequences in such an interpretation (*e.g.* the so-called Ross's paradox), one should remember about one reservation:

even though a breach to the norm N is followed by a breach to the norm which is the reason behind the norm N – behaviour in accordance with the norm N is not followed by a non-breach to the norm which is the reason behind the norm N.[37]

• Ziembiński [1966b] distinguished, among others, two types of normative consequence: instrumental and axiological:

(a) The norm N_1 is instrumentally followed by the norm N_2, when not-realizing of the norm N_2 is the reason for not-realizing of the norm N_1;

(b) the norm N_1 is axiologically followed by the norm N_2, when the good disturbed by the norm N_2 not being realized is bigger than the good disturbed by the norm N_1 not being realized.

• According to Studnicki [1968], an equivalent to the logical value in the case of "normative expressions" is whether certain normative states of affairs fulfil or do not fulfil these expressions (*i.e.* whether these normative states of affairs occur or do not occur).

• Ziemba [1968] perceived the main function of the deontic logic systems as precizing legal terms and removing "inconsequences in the intuitive usage of some moods of reasoning". A signal for the inadequacy of notions proposed in these systems, against notions used daily in law, are paradoxical theses, *i.e.* theses true for these systems only, and false as interpretations of some common beliefs.

Ziemba [1969], Wolter & Lipczyńska [1980a] see the deontic logic as logic calculi with constants such as "obligatory", "prohibited" and "allowed"; so they do not operate directly on imperatives, but on sentences about imperatives. The particular proposed systems of this logic differ from each other among others about whether the deontic constants are functors of nominal arguments (therefore, whether certain acts are obligatory) or perhaps functors of sentential arguments (therefore, perhaps whether certain states of affairs are obligatory).

The first deontic calculi come from von Wright [1951; 1964] and Kalinowski [1953]. Ziemba thought von Wright's systems to lack a satisfactory interpretation of constants used in these systems and related calculi (*e.g.*

---

[37] The matter is similarly viewed for instance by Brożek & Stelmach [2004].

calculus of acts and changes); also there was no sense of relativization of the truthfulness to "a certain occasion", no notion of the norm breach and of consequence in the domain of norms. Hence he proposed his own interpretations in this domain.

In particular, Ziemba proposed four conditions so as to say that:

(1) The norm N_2 is a consequence of the norm N_1.

namely (in a simplified form):

(2) If someone fulfils the norm N_2, he does not breach the norm N_1.

(3) If someone fulfils the norm N_2, he fulfils the norm N_1.

(4) If someone breaches the norm N_2, he breaches the norm N_1.

(5) Neither someone who performs an act allowed on the ground of the norm N_2, nor someone who performs an act «contradictory» with an allowed act breaches any duty relating to the norm N_1.

Ziemba proposes his own deontic system called "deontic syllogistics", a certain extension to the calculus of quantifiers. Ziemba thinks one of the advantages of his deontic syllogistics to be the fact that the range of variables is constituted by a set of people (and not acts, as in Kalinowski and Hintikka), and that the language of this system allows for formulation of general sentences of this form: "Every X has the obligation to be Y".

Since the "logical consequence" is defined for contexts in which one says that a sentence is perceived to be true because another sentence was perceived to be true, according to Ziemba [1983] there might be no logical consequence between norms (considered as synonyms to respective imperatives). Hence the normative logic exists only so far as it may be reduced to deontic logic.

• According to Najder [1971], the natural course of argumentations including imperatives reads as follows: imperative (imperative sentence) – norm (sentence of duty) – evaluation (evaluating sentence):

x, do this and that! – BECAUSE x should do this and that – BECAUSE this and that is good.

• Kalinowski [1972] carried out a critical and very instructive review of different systems of the logic of imperatives and norms.

Kalinowski [1990], differing here from Ziemba [1983] treats the deontic logic (understood as the logic of the norms) as "the logical basis" for common, everyday legal reasonings. He maintains additionally, that theses of the logic of the norms, just as theses of the classical logic – refer to reality, but to a different aspect of it – namely to certain "normative relationships". Thus the so understood "legal logic" is juxtaposed against the logic of persuasion (*resp.* of convincing) and the "logic" of interpretation of legal texts.

• A statement such as:

(1) It is true that x should cause S to occur.

is, according to Opałek [1974] sensible, when it states one of the two:

(2) The dictate "x should cause S to occur" was given.

(3) The dictate "x should cause S to occur" is reasonable, right or useful.

• Woleński [1980] supported the position that the answer to the question, whether norms have got any logical value, depends on whether we consider the proper norms, or "non-proper", thus these consequent norms:

(a) It should be thus and thus.

(b) It should be thus and thus – on the foundations of a certain normative system.

According to Woleński, "there are rather no doubts about the truthfulness of the latter", but he rejects the notion that the former may have any logical value, as a non-cognitivist. Therefore, the logic of the (proper) norms might not be equalled with the deontic logic, which is primarily concerned with "truthfulness".

Woleński [1982] enumerates permission, dictate, prohibition, obligation (*i.e.* dictate or prohibition) and indifference as basic notions of the deontic logic; he states that the theses of this logic are "sentences on acts, and not on sentences" [1980a]. He would also differentiate between three types of permission:

(a) weak permission (permission$_s$), *i.e.* not-prohibition;

(b) strong (distinct) permission in its normative sense (a notion that Wolański dismisses as unnecessary);

(c) strong (distinct) permission as a permission with a choice (permission$_m$).

Woleński also proposed three versions of the strong permission with a choice:

(1) *A* or *B* is permitted$_m$ minimally, when *A* is indifferent and *B* is indifferent.

(2) *A* or *B* is permitted$_m$ on average, when *A* or *B* are permitted$_m$ and *A* and *B* are permitted$_s$.

(3) *A* or *B* is permitted$_m$ maximally, when *A* and *B* is permitted$_s$, and not-*A* and *B* are permitted$_s$, and *A* and not-*B* are permitted$_s$ and not-*A* and not-*B* are permitted$_s$.

Logical relations between sentences "The act *A* is dictated", "The act *A* is prohibited", "The act *A* is permitted and "The act not-*A* is permitted" might be according to Woleński [1983] represented in a logical square isomorphic towards a square that represents logical relations between categorical sentences. The logic of obligation – as a codification of a non-contradictory normative system – would be an extension of deontic logic based on this square.

To (Kotarbiński's) question on the negation of the norm Woleński answers with a negative: "There is no such thing"; as a consequence, in the normative logic there is no law of excluded middle, because one may not formulate it in this language.

• Wolter & Lipczyńska [1980b] stated that an analogue for the logical value would be for norms their validity/lack-of-validity.

• On the logic of imperatives Zieliński & Ziembiński wrote [1988]:

> The abbreviated expression "drawing conclusions about norms from norms", when fully elaborated on, means [...] that from sentences claiming that a norm N_1 belongs to a system of norms *S*, we may draw a conclusion that a certain norm N_2 also belongs to the system *S* [1988: 212].
>
> Both the premise and the conclusion in the legal reasoning are metalinguistic sentences referring to utterances of different semiotic status – namely, norms [1988: 213].
>
> Admittedly, in the context of connections between norms one speaks also about consequences, but due to the non-sentential character of these statements also the "consequence" assumes in this context a different sense than in relation to sentences. When we speak about the norm N_2 being a consequence of the norm N_1, we usually

think that there is relation between them that consists in the following: realizing the norm N_1 is a sufficient condition to realize the norm N_2, and realizing the norm N_2 is a necessary condition to realize the norm N_1 [1988: 213].

[There are two types of entailment between the norms:] logical and instrumental entailment. The first occurs when the range of application and of standardisation of the norm N_2 falls within the range of application and standardisation of the norm N_1; the second – when the impossibility to realize the norm N_1 without the norm N_2 appears as we state that there is inapplicable cause-and-effect relationship between the acts dictated by these norms [1988: 213].

[There also exist inferential statements], which refer to the relationships between the norms – which are based on an assumption that the lawgiver is guided by a certain coherent system of evaluation, that they are consistent in what and how they are evaluating [1988: 214].

The last instance might bring trouble when settling the hierarchy of preferences of the lawgiver – which is necessary, *i.a.*, by argumentations such as a *maiori ad minus* or a *minori ad maius* [1988: 215].

[The "rules of conflict" we understand as] directive utterances which point to a method of removing or avoiding: (1) a conflict of legal regulations in time (*i.e.* when a regulation issued later is at variance with an earlier regulation which had not been overruled), (2) ostensible coincidence (when ranges of addressees, the circumstances and behaviours set out in at least 2 norm-forming expressions are even partly common after the idiomatic decoding), and (3) real coincidence (when after the process of interpretation is finished and rules of conflict are applied, we still come at conflicting and sometimes radically contradictory or praxeologically incompatible norms) [1988: 223–224].

Zieliński & Ziembiński [1988: 281–283] judge the logic of norms and deontic logic in the following way. The following strategies are used for these matters:

(a) one constructs the deontic logic analogous to the modal logic and assumes that it would to a certain extent convey the structure of legal reasonings;

(b) one constructs the logic of norms *sensu stricto*, and uses it to reconstruct the inferential rules that govern the way in which we hold certain norms to be valid (in a certain system); one tries to retain here as many "existing everyday intuitions" as possible.

The disadvantage of the first strategy is the fact that the level of applicability of the obtained theory to the facts in the field of norms is very much limited. The disadvantage of the second strategy is the fact that it is based on a doubtful assumption that "the notion of a set of valid legal norms equals a very systematic system of legal norms" and on the assumption of the full rationality of the lawgiver.

• Laskowski [1998] recognizes imperative sentences as non-factive ones (*i.e.* they do not state the existence of any determined situations), which demand the listener to perform some actions necessary for the content of these sentences to become true. The condition for their sensibility (the sensibility of an order, a request or a wish) is that the situation which they determine does not exist yet. Deontic (volitional) modality, "signalling the desired action", revealing the "intentions of the speaker", is (in the Polish language) expressed *via*:

(a) the imperative mood;

(b) the lexical means (*cf.* expressions "must", "can", "is allowed to", "needs to", and "let", "may" and "perhaps").

Conclusion

The presented review of research on imperatives and norms done in Poland in the 20th century firstly and foremostly indicates that the research covered practically the whole scope of this theory. Secondly, it shows that the research went in two directions which complemented one other; it aimed at the most precise description possible of the intuitions which drive competent users of imperative and normative expressions (and its derivatives); additionally, it wanted to construct adequate calculi kept in logical check by these intuitions. Research went significantly far in those directions, sometimes along the routes already laid by our own research tradition (most prominently, by the Lvov-Warsaw School tradition), sometimes on routes prepared by thinkers from other countries.

What we discovered was that these two directions were usually parallel, and only crossed at certain points. One of the «external» reasons behind this, theoretically speaking – undesirable, state of affairs was World War II and its consequences of the first half of the 20th century; it broke the continuity of Polish thought. There was also an «internal» reason: unfortunately, the Polish community did not manage to gather and commit themselves to the task of removing – or at least minimizing – a flaw which always looms over such research; I mean here the ambiguity and multitude of terms connected with the given notions. Such chaos has hindered, and continues to hinder, progress in finding explanations to many issues within the theory of imperatives and norms.

I have tried to overcome this unfavourable state of affairs here. However, I am not fully satisfied with the results of my efforts. Nevertheless, I am full of hope that those who decide to follow me might face a slightly easier task. This might be experienced by readers of the "Anthology" which constitutes the remaining part of the book.

Jacek Jadacki

Anthology

Kazimierz Twardowski. Indicatives, interrogatives, imperatives and optatives
[1901: 13–14]

We use SENTENCES when we speak. Normally, sentences consist of several words, for example, "The sun is shining", "A triangle is a geometrical figure", "When are you coming?". At times, however, sentences may consist of just one word, for example: "Coming!", "Quiet!" "Great". A sentence may express an inquiry (*e.g.* "When are you coming?"), an order (*e.g.* "Quiet!"), a wish (*e.g.* "I wish it were sunny tomorrow"), an affirmation (*e.g.* "The sun is shining"), or a negation (*e.g.* "Lvov does not lie on the Vistula river"). A sentence that expresses affirmation or negation is called A STATEMENT. Therefore, every statement is a sentence, but not every sentence is a statement.

Affirmations and negations, which are expressed through statements, are called JUDGEMENTS. A judgement must be clearly distinguished from a statement. A JUDGEMENT is AN INTELLECTUAL ACTION, whereas a statement is an external expression of that action; a judgement is a psychic, spiritual phenomenon, whereas a statement is a physical, sensory phenomenon; a judgement cannot be seen or heard, whereas a statement can be heard (when someone utters it) or seen (when it is written or printed). There is then a relationship between a judgement and a statement reminiscent of the connection between pain (a psychic phenomenon) and an exclamation, which is sensually perceptible evidence of that pain.

One should not forget that there is a fundamental difference between a judgement and a statement, all the more because in natural speech the difference is not observed, as a result of which the same words are used to denote both a judgement and a statement. The words "sentence", "affirmation", and "negation" are examples of such ambiguous terms. Science refrains from ambiguity; therefore, a sentence is always defined in logic as a sequence of words or one word serving to express a judgement, a request, a question, *etc.*, whereas affirmations and negations are understood as psychic phenomena called judgements.

Jan Nuckowski. Practical theses
[1903: 59]

Let us consider [...] the following judgements: "A definition should not be tautological", "Logical classification should be transparent", "Each person should love others as himself", "A student should be diligent", "A soldier should not be a coward", "One should be cautious when experimenting with chlorine or hydrogen"... A vast number of such judgements are issued in everyday life. What kind of judgements are these?

They cannot be counted as modal judgements, since they are not about necessity, nor are they about the reality of form, nor do we want to state possibility, even though we clearly presume it. Neither can we claim these judgements to be individual normal judgements, as the presence or absence of the predicate in the subject, which is an essential feature of such judgements, cannot be ascertained.

Therefore, they can be described either as judgements on judgements, different from modal judgements, or individual judgements, different from individual normal judgements. If they are considered to be individual judgements, then consequently, one can say that the form of these judgements is not the presence of the predicate in the subject, as in normal judgements, but rather THE DUTY OF THE PRESENCE OF THE PREDICATE IN THE SUBJECT. Then these judgements could be distinguished, as practical judgements, from normal judgements, which are THEORETICAL.

Kazimierz Twardowski. Volitional acts
[1904: 203–208]

Within the psychology of desires and volition there is all that is colloquially represented by a whole series of various words, like: "to have a thirst", "to want", "to drive at", "to desire", "to resolve", "to wish", "to intend", "to strive", "to disgust", "to be inclined", "to fancy", *etc.* Let me draw your attention to the abundance of positive expressions, as well as the lack and artificiality of negative expressions: "not want", "to avoid" ["to linger"]. Still, there is no question that this lack only concerns words and names; the item itself definitely exists. Namely, it is in everyone's experience that we may assume two attitudes towards the world which surrounds us, as well as an imagined world, and each of these attitudes is within the general definition of desiring, having thirsts, wanting something. Say there is a dish in front of us, and one of the participants cannot wait to be served; he is famished, and moreover, the dish is his favourite. He desires it, has a thirst for it, wants to eat it. Another participant cannot stand this dish, is disgusted by it and would never eat it, and moreover, the mere sight and smell of the dish is highly unpleasant to him. Therefore he does not want to eat it, avoids it when he can, shuns it. This much is clear. Thus both what we call desire and avoidance reveal a positive and a negative side.

Another remark [...] needs to be made, and a certain characteristic trait added. Any desire, any volition, as was demonstrated, either moves towards or away from something. I want to eat the dish or I do not want to eat it. I want to talk to someone or avoid conversation. I resolve to scold someone or I decide not to deal with him at all. This is the same for all actions and emotional or spiritual states: they concern a given object. This much is obvious. I imagine something, I feel something, I think about something, I am reminded of something, I find something agreeable or disagreeable. Yet, what concerns our desire and our volition has a separate common name, which is not used to describe other objects, that is, objects of other emotional states. We speak of an aim which is in sight when we desire or wish something. What we desire is the aim of our desire; what we want is the aim of our volition; what we resolve is the aim of our resolution. The underlying common character of driving, desire, thirst, volition and resolution is revealed in that notion of an aim. "Towards" something. At the same time, the inadequacy of speech is revealed when the negative aspect is in question: one does not speak of the aim of avoidance, although perhaps it should be mentioned. But this is solely the question of linguistics. [...]

Any judgement can be defined as accepting or denying reality of [a certain] presented object. [...]

Since I accept [reality] or I deny the reality of the presented object, two things may take place. I am either satisfied or dissatisfied with stating the existing state of affairs. In the first case nothing happens, except that I have a thirst that the same situation would continue in the future. Thus there is already thirst. On the other hand, if I am not satisfied with the given state of affairs, then obviously I have a thirst for it to be changed. These cases can be reduced to a common denominator, to one common formula. For instance, I state that there is no such thing as good memory in my case. Good memory [is] the object of my judgement. At the same time, it becomes the object of desire, as it does not exist. What do I desire? I want to have a better memory. Thus again we are dealing with the reality of an object. We can say that the reality of good memory is the content of my desire, or more precisely; creating such reality is. This may be called the aim of desire. [...]

Similarly, we may want something which exists to continue existing. For instance: pleasant coolness. We state pleasant coolness, and thus we accept it as reality. However, this reality concerns the present moment. We have a thirst for it to remain thus in the future. Thus again, we have a thirst for something which is not reality to become reality, namely: lasting, future coolness. As for the positive side of thirst, we can state that it is concerned with the advent of reality, with materializing something whose reality is denied. Similarly, in the case of negative thirst the issue is to subtract, remove the reality of the object whose presence is stated. Thus this issue is analogous to judgements. In the case of judgements, [something] is or is not; here [something] is or is not supposed to be. It is the same in the case of volition and resolution. [...]

One other common feature of symbols of desire and volition can be mentioned here. It derives from the former and is called *nota externa*. From a given mental state, which essentially drives at change the lack of reality into reality, or the other way around, there naturally results the fact that this driving at a change indeed assumes a real, specific form. A natural consequence of any driving, as long as it is not obstructed in its course, is a given action, a series of movements which are supposed to bring about the change or, in the case of trying to withhold a given state, to prevent the change. This comes from the fact that thirst, and even more so: volition, is considered to be a certain kind of force which brings about internal change, and primitive man, or even enlightened man, is prone to express any changes as the image of such mental states. For instance, we say that the air or a certain gas, compressed within a vessel, attempts to burst it, or that any heavy object aims towards the centre of the Earth, or that certain items of underwear «do not want» to fit in the drawer, *etc.* Yet, it is clear that the power of thirst, volition and resolution is mentioned. [...]

Therefore, the actions characterized so far can be given the collective name of symbols or functions of volition in the broadest meaning of the word, where volition is interpreted as the ability to execute mental actions whose vital component is to grant reality to something, or to deduct reality from something, or to retain reality, or to retain the lack of reality.

Władysław Witwicki. Allogenenetic conception of volition
[1904: 119–123]

1. In the critical section of our work we attempted to justify our opinion that resolutions can only be perceived as practical judgements. Based on opinions of various authors, we demonstrated that given properties of resolutions can only be explained against the background of our opinion.

We attempted to present the following sentence: "A resolution is a judgement of our own future activity" as a logical reason for the given results of those attributes of resolutions which we state in our experience. Thus seeking reasons for given results constituted the inversive part of our work.

It results in widening the scope of the concept of judgement rather than broadening its range, since we accept the judgement in Brentano's formulation and we do not add any new feature. We only attempt to show that resolutions should also be included in the range of this concept, since it constitutes a group of phenomena which have not been included in it so far. If the first part were correct, and if our opinion is in fact a sufficient reason for features which are detected in resolutions through observation, then we should also be able to perform the deductive part of the work, as well as derive the concept of resolution from the concept of judgement, and find essential features of judgement in resolutions. If resolutions are judgements, then they should possess those features which differentiate all judgements from the remaining psychic phenomena.

All phenomena which have been included in the range of Brentanian judgements possess two essential features. Firstly, they affirm or negate the reality of an object, secondly, they are true or false.

2. The object of our resolutions is our future activity. Thus the first question occurs: Is it true that resolutions state the reality of my own future activity? We believe it is so, for each act of resolution, without exception. When I resolve in the morning to go to the theatre in the evening, then I do not state anything essential except the fact that my future going to the theatre becomes something real to me, something similar in its being and its reality to traffic in the evening, to the sunset in the city, to all those phenomena and objects which I believe to be true in the future, and on which I issue existential judgements. I begin to relate to my future going to the theatre in the same way as to a number of real phenomena which really await me.

Ehrenfels describes it poetically as weaving a thought object into a chain of subjective reality. We can define it psychologically only as issuing existential judgement about a future phenomenon.

3. Do resolutions ever deny the reality of my future activity? It seems this is so. It happens through negative resolutions. Whoever says: "I will not defend myself", therefore the fact of my own defence ceases to exist in the future, erases itself from the group of real objects and ceases to be a regulatory factor for the individual's conduct, or in scientific phrasing, becomes the object of a negative judgement. In each resolution there is a certain "yes" or "no"; each resolution is either affirmative or negative.

4. The question of the truthfulness or falsity of provisions poses a more difficult problem, since in natural speech one does not use these adjectives to indicate the act of our volition, as is done with judgements. Nevertheless, to be precise, a trace of it can be found in resolutions; namely, we call fallacious such spiritual phenomena which provide us with some re-

ality, while this reality does not exist. So far, the privilege of delivering reality and at the same time the defect of fallibility has only been attributed to judgements.

Affirmative judgements are called fallacious if their subject does not exist. The object of resolutions is future activity. There occurs a question then whether there exist positive resolutions whose objects do not exist, of course in the real future. We believe it is so for all resolutions which were not fulfilled, are not fulfilled or will not be fulfilled in the future. It is also the case for theoretical judgements which concern the future. While formulating such a judgement, a person is convinced about its truthfulness and only learns in the future that the judgement was fallacious. Similarly, when a person formulates a resolution, he creates some future reality, he believes in his future act and only learns in the future that he was deceived; only after the resolution is not realized does he see that he was mistaken in his resolution. Experience provides many examples of such resolutions, the objects of which are never to exist (in spite of the person's good faith). Therefore, the same stigma of fallacy which we found in judgements also is stated in resolutions. True resolutions are all the others, all of those whose objects exist in the future, all of those which will be fulfilled.

Here we encounter an obstacle. The words "true" and "false" have two meanings. They denote certain features of judgements in view of the existence of their objects, but on the other hand they mean respectively "sincere" and "insincere", or "successful" and "unsuccessful". In the second meaning we talk about true resolutions in natural speech and so it is easy to form the objection that the resolution, if it was honest, is always true, regardless of whether it is fulfilled or not. It is indeed so, just like with convictions. If only a conviction occurred, then it was true (sincere), which means that the person truly harboured it and did not only manifest it, though it need not be necessary true in the second meaning, since the person might have been mistaken, all in good faith, just like he is often mistaken in his resolutions, even though he sincerely resolves to do something.

However, the different practice in natural speech should not in any way inhibit us, since we do not intend to introduce to everyday language a phrase concerning fallacious or veritable resolutions. We only wish to state for the sake of science that both resolutions and judgements possess the feature of truthfulness and falsehood.

The only reason it is not mentioned in natural speech is that in real life we care less about the truthfulness of our and other people's resolutions and more about their sincerity and force. Another issue is that the object of a resolution is an activity. Therefore, if it proves to be fallacious, the person feels deficient and talks of failure rather than a mistake. We learned to treat the words "mistake" and "falsity" exclusively as features of theoretical judgements and therefore we are unable to attach them to practical judgements, even though enough reasons occur to use them thus.

5. If the above is true and if resolutions really possess features characteristic exclusively of judgements, then we can include resolutions in the group of judgements and reject the idiogenetic theory of them. Indeed, on closer inspection, one notices in resolutions many secondary features which these phenomena share with judgements. Both ARE EXPRESSED [...] IN STATEMENTS, which are even divided in a similar fashion, since there exist categorical, conditional and alternative resolutions, and if one wishes to make a Kantian division of judgements, then one can easily makes a distinction according to modality and quantity.

EMERGENCE CONDITIONS are also similar for judgements and resolutions. Both require some reflection, some intellectual actions preceeding them, before they come into being in a man, whereas no other occurrence requires inference from which it could emerge. If resolutions were not judgements, it would not explain the fact that sometimes inference is the condition of resolutions. We say: "sometimes", since it might be the case that resolutions emerge spontaneously, without the preceding hesitation period, just as at times some judgements arise without the preceding hesitation and inference.

Even CERTAINTY and PROBABILITY, as well as other judgements, are parts of resolutions. It is sometimes the case that I am absolutely certain of my future activity and then I call my resolution strong, unwavering, unshakable; then again I resolve something and I seem to believe in what the future will bring, but I am not absolutely convinced that in the end the supposed resolution finally will come to pass. I may repeat to myself "I will definitely do this!" but it is not at all a *conceptio clara et distincta* for me;

I cannot vouch for myself. In the latter case we deal with a resolution which is only probable, and therefore, according to the above analysis of probability, it is a judgement with certain features. Therefore, our state [...] should be of incipient thirst rather than a resolution. This is also how we perceive it and how we say it in natural speech: "What is the resolution?" is what we would say about such an internal phenomenon. "The man would like to do it, is willing to do it, has good intentions, noble thirsts, but he has no backbone, he is not firm or self-confident enough".

This feature of certainty and probability is explained through the existence of this mysterious willpower, which is impossible to justify with feelings, and through the fact that even the strongest resolution may be entirely cold and conversely, an act of will undertaken during the turmoil of war may prove to be infirm, unstable, and unreliable.

Lastly, it is worth mentioning that resolutions, as judgements, occur in two forms: *in actu* and *in potentia*. We sometimes issue a resolution in a definite moment and notice this moment of its emergence, but at times its occurrence is imperceptible and then it exists in us in the form of a set of conditions, a readiness to conceive and express a given act of will. Similarly, after a given resolution leaves the realm, our consciousness, we are left with an internal predisposition to perform a given act in our soul. Then we have a certain resolution although we do not realize the fact at that time. All of us have many such resolutions, such as the resolution to finish a job we have begun, or to act according to certain rules in our life, *etc.* This is what forms a man's volition or personality. It is also the case with convictions. They also live in us, hidden *in potentia* and they also organize themselves into a theoretical view of the world and the person's intellectual wealth, just as potential resolutions make up our system of principles and our personality.

6. If this is indeed so, if the analysis of thirsts presented here is right, and reduction of resolutions to judgements is correct, then one class of spiritual phenomena may be left out from our psychological classification. The phenomena of volition do not constitute a separate group, and it is sufficient to describe and classify internal life into the following categories: presentations, judgements and feelings. Obviously, we do not deny a man

his volition, we just notice phenomena in its manifestations which have already been described and named within other groups of spiritual phenomena. This we do according to the rule of *entia non sunt multiplicanda praeter necessitatem.*

Thus we resolve a question which is of great importance in metaphysics as well as in psychology, for if resolutions are judgements, the question of freedom of volition becomes the question of freedom of judgements. This is fully new territory for freedom, one that is fresh and fascinating. This question has not been discussed in this scope and in this light, and it is possible that it does not present itself as obscure and complex as it does against the idiogenetic view. However, this is beyond the scope of our thesis, which is to state and defend a principle.

Franciszek Gabryl. Rationality of acts of will
[1905/1906: 131–134]

Let us compare [...] rational willings with thirsts. It cannot be denied that there is a close relationship between these two psychic phenomena, since each thirst can stimulate volition, and in turn, a willing presupposes a thirst. Nevertheless, these two symptoms cannot be identified with each other, as they differ in their character, objects and the effects they cause.

Considered from the point of view of character, each thirst is something spontaneous, it appears suddenly, is blind in the sense that it precedes rational cognition, does not inquire whether the object of the thirst is worthy or unworthy, or whether it can be achieved or not, but it strives towards satisfaction. On the other hand, a rational willing only appears after shorter or longer reflection, after having considered the object of thirst, after having evaluated the possibility of its realization, after having investigated the means to achieve it. One is passive in the face of thirsts, at least in the initial stage; one is merely an observer, looking on when they appear, or when they fight for priority in satisfaction; one can listen to their calls, their persistent entreaty, but at any point one can direct one's attention away from them by engaging strongly in some other object. On the other hand, through the act of rational willing one abandons the role of a passive witness and actively contributes to the fulfilment of the object of thirst; one initiates an action and takes responsibility for it.

Secondly, thirsts and rational willings differ from each other in their object. [...] Various items can be the object of thirsts; not only one's states but also other people's states, since one may thirst other people to love him, or not to speak ill of him, or not to harm him. Wishing may refer to a variety of times, since one may wish that Hannibal had beaten the Romans, or for the future: that Prussian arrogance will be diminished, or for the present: that the headache will cease, *etc.* One may not only have thirst for possible things but also those of which we are certain in advance will never come true, for instance, a congenitally blind person may wish his sight was restored, or a pauper may wish for great fortune. Do we not make a serious resolution at times about a thing which we consider impossible to fulfil? There is also no doubt that one may even possess simultaneously two opposed thirsts, but one cannot in his right mind want two contradictory or opposite things at the same time. Moreover, the thirst may refer to the aim but not to the means; after all, there are plenty of people who would be glad to have a certain position but without fighting for it, or would like to be saints but without the mortification of one's body and suppression of its desires... If someone wants something reasonably, then he thinks both about the aim and the means leading to this aim.

Finally, when it transforms into effect, thirst may push one out of mental balance and self-control, and conversely, one never masters oneself as well as at the moment when one makes a deliberate decision. [...]

There is no doubt that mind is a necessary component of the willing in the case of rational creatures. Volition must be based on mind: it is the mind that reveals what is good, evaluates impulses and motives of one's activity, presents the *pro* and *contra* arguments for taking the decision; but after all, this theoretical work is not willing, since even when the mind reveals to us what the greatest and best good is at a given moment, we may still neglect to choose this good. *Video meliora proboque, deteriora sequor*: the pagan bard's adage prohibits identifying willing with an action of the mind. Due to a delusion, willing could seem the same as a practical judgement, related to the object of the willing, it bears the name "practical". After all, because the judgement refers to an action which is supposed to happen, it may not transform from a theoretical judgement to an action, nor can it initiate the action. [...] The fact that rational willing is accompanied on the part of the mind, and preceded by a theoretical judgement on the mode of activity, cannot lead to the conclusion that willing and the said act of the mind are the same thing. It is not for the freedom of judgements that some people are rightfully put to prison, since *die Gedanken sind immer zollfrei*, but for committing wrongful acts which originated from volition. A provision on what must be or should be the proper way to act is only a form in which willing is revealed in one's consciousness, and not the willing itself. Therefore it is a long way from conceiving of a resolution to executing it. As the Polish proverb says, the road to hell is paved with good intentions, that is, resolutions.

There has to appear a new connection then between a resolution and its execution. What would it be? According to Ehrenfels and Witwicki, this factor is incipient innervation inside the organs which are used when executing a resolution. [...] There arises a question then whether this incipient innervation can be identified with the act of willing. Let us take a concrete example. Someone looks at an indecent object, no matter if it is live or painted. As a reaction to it, desire occurs, and there then occurs a well-known innervation. However, in the case of a well-mannered, humble man, as soon as the existence of such desire is perceived in the conscience, there also occurs immediately a reflection, which states that giving way to indecent desire is an immoral act, and what follows is arresting the motion and eradicating the desire. Which of these acts revealed effective willing? Probably not the innervation, which was a blind urge to continue to develop the physiological act, and which was blocked by a new impulse. All the same, one cannot say of the mind that the activity which arrested the innervation came from the mind, as it merely has the function of experiencing the object from various points of view; the mind only stated that giving way to indecent desire is an action in contradiction to the norms of morality, and that the activity should be put to an end.

Apparently, a new factor joined the group of various data, a factor distinct from desire, since the modest person's activity was directed against it; a factor distinct from the mind, which is supposed to learn and not act; a factor different from the incipient innervation which was not allowed to develop. We may not know how exactly this factor influences the nervous system, that is, what means were used to block the innervation, which is a different matter. Yet, we cannot deny the existence of this factor in a series of acts presented above. Therefore, if in order for an act which one takes responsibility for to occur it were sufficient to learn whether the act can be fulfilled and how it can be realized, then the allogenetic theory of volition would be right. However, it is obvious to anyone that even if in this case, when a factor like incipient innervation, which stimulates a given organ, enters a series of acts which aim at fulfilment of some act, there is still no act which one could take responsibility for, a free act; what has to appear here, apart from the mind, is a new factor: volition, which makes use of the enlightened mind but is in itself the real doer of the action.

Kazimierz Twardowski. Categorical and hypothetical imperatives
[1905/1906: 135–137]

All ethics which is not biotechnics implies [...] constraint [of an individual in favour of another individuals]. This constraint of one individual by ethical norms is not incidental, but rather an essential issue for ethics. The principal notions in ethics alone indicate this. We speak of ethical orders and prohibitions; we speak of obligation, which is opposed to what we do out of our own inclination and lust; we speak of duty; we speak of what is allowed and what is not allowed, as well as what should be done, *etc.* Let us consider any statute of a society; let us consider school instructions and indications, which also constrain an individual; or the agenda of Parliament sessions, or a notice put next to a railway track saying that trespassing is prohibited, or a notice under the window in a compartment saying: "No leaning out". Some of these regulations contain a sanction: "No speeding on this bridge. Penalty 5 koruns." Also the aim of such regulations is clear. [...] If you do not want to endanger your life, or if you do not want to damage the bridge; if a session is going to take place in the Parliament at all; if the society is to function and achieve its statutory goals, *etc.* [one has to abide by these regulations]. How does it compare to a regulation or prohibition or ethical dictate?

Kant stated the rule that regulations and dictates, that is ethical imperatives, are CATEGORICAL, as opposed to all others, which are HYPOTHETICAL. Rules of hygiene state that one should perform certain actions in order to stay healthy; rules of propriety state that one is not supposed to do certain things (do not pick your nose; greet the elder women first) if one wants to be well liked and not be ill-treated by others. If that is not one's aim, these rules do not concern him; sometimes an additional sanction is needed then, so that the ones who do not feel the inclination to adhere to the rules still obey them out of necessity. These other rules always come with a condition: one is supposed to obey them if some outcome is to be achieved and some other avoided; that is the reason why one obeys them. It is different with ethical imperatives of a CATEGORICAL character. They are absolute dictates, that is, unconditional ones; they are the absolute duty, as Kant expressed it. Thus, if we say, "Do not lie", it is not the same as "Do not lean out". The latter prohibition contains an implicit condition: "If you do not want to be harmed", whereas the former does not contain such a condition, either implicit or explicit. It is as with a child who asks why something is not allowed, and we answer: "Because".

Schopenhauer in his *Fundament der Moral*[38] speaks strongly against the categorical character of ethical rules. He calls unconditional duty *contradictio in adiecto*, and he is right to do it. Unconditional duty is a kind of duty which is not performed in order to achieve some other goal but only in order to fulfil the duty. It seems that Kant was misled by the fact, which was incidentally also unnoticed by Schopenhauer, that there exist people who fulfil a duty for duty's own sake and obligation for obligation's own sake, which is desirable from the ethical point of view. However, it is one thing to fulfil duties in such a way and another to formulate rules, promulgate or issue them. It is still possible in the case of children in the phase

---

[38] *Preisschrift über die Grundlage der Moral* is meant here, which is the second part of the publication *Die beiden Grundprobleme der Ethik* [1841] and is entitled *Über das Fundament der Moral*, and whose significant portion is devoted to the critique of Kant's ethics ("Kritik des von Kant der Ethik gegebenen Fundament").

of their training, but even then we attach a sanction: if you disobey, you will be punished. But in scientific ethics it is quite impossible. Note that scientific ethics does not start with regulations, since first some facts, some laws have to be ascertained, which then give rise to regulations, just as it happens in mechanics, hygiene, *etc.* If mechanics states: the greater the friction during movement, *caeteris paribus*, the greater the force required to maintain the movement, therefore a practical mechanic ascertains that friction has to be reduced. It is not a categorical imperative, it is a conditional one: it comes down to saving power, costs, *etc.* Since it is a common concern, norms deriving from the laws of mechanics are commonly applied. It is also the case with ethics, and the very fact of deriving norms and rules from its laws calls for the norms to be conditional, and not categorical. It results from the logical character of the derivation. For a law to be scientifically grounded, it has to derive from a reasonable judgement. Such a judgement is expressed by a law, which constitutes a connection between two things, facts, or phenomena. For example, "Who sows the wind, will reap the whirlwind"; "If water cools to zero degrees, it begins to freeze"; "Where there is no financial prosperity, art and science will not flourish"; Accelerated heartbeat makes it hard to fall asleep", *etc.* Formulating rules and norms is executed in such a way that one of the facts in a law becomes the goal and the other becomes the means to achieve this goal: "If you want to freeze water, cool it to zero degrees"; "If arts are to flourish, prosperity should be created"; "If you want to fall asleep, avoid accelerating your heartbeat", *etc.* Naturally, wherever the aim is clear and there is no doubt about it, we do not mention it and it takes the form of a categorical norm, an absolute one, for example norms of hygiene such as: Do not abuse alcoholic beverages, Wear clothes appropriate for a given season, Exercies daily; all of them include an aim: to be healthy, and a condition: if you want to be healthy. Thus circumstances present us with another important clue to define ethics.

The first one is in general normative, and is about restraining an individual, and the other one is apparently categorical: it has to be about an aim which imposes itself so strongly that it is not singled out and mentioned; the aim is so powerful that it reveals itself.

Leon Petrażycki. Imperative and imperative-attributive norms
[1907c: 249–253]

The two kinds of obligations characterized above have their equivalents in two kinds of ethical norms, or imperatives.

Some norms settle free obligations towards other people; they require some course of action from us without giving anybody else any rights to claim anything from us; these norms are unilateral, obligatory, claimless, purely imperative. These kinds of norms correspond to some lines of the Gospel:

"But I say to you, do not resist an evil person. If someone strikes you on the right cheek, turn to him the other also. And if someone wants to sue you and take your tunic, let him have your cloak as well", *etc.*

In the psyche of the people who proclaim such ethical rules as well as those who live or lived by them, those norms obviously do not signify that some power was given to the offenders, or do not force anybody to require from the victim that he turn the other cheek, nor do they entitle the person who took a tunic from someone to also take the victim's coat, *etc.*

The same can be said about other norms of truly Christian Evangelical ethics. The spirit of these ethics (which is fundamentally different from, for example, the ethics of the *Old Testament* in this respect), imposes numerous obligations on neighbours towards others, some of which may be difficult to fulfil. However, the other neighbours may not and do not have any claims about executing those obligations. Christian ethics is entirely claimless, therefore if in the Middle Ages or modern times various laws and claims were based on Evangelical dictates (of a religious or social nature), all in good faith, then that is evidence of complete ignorance of the essence of the science.

Norms of the other kind impose obligations on some people while binding the obligations with other people, who simultaneously receive certain rights, claims; some people are obliged to do what other people are then entitled to receive, as it was granted to them by a certain authority (*attributum*). Such norms are called obligation-claim norms, imperative-allocating, imperative-attributive.

Such are the norms which correspond to the following sources:

"Since no one may legally be deprived of what one is entitled to, any loss of property or harm caused to a person obliges one side to pay and gives the other side the right to demand compensation"(*Civil Law,* article 574).

"If one person owes another person a certain sum of money (*а на коем сребро имати*), if there occurs, then, a legal relationship, and that person begins to pay his debt before the assigned time (*до зароку зачнёт сребро отдавать кому виноват*), then he is obliged to pay interest (*ино гостинца дать*), and the other side is entitled to receive interest proportional to the amount of capital, without any deductions (*по щоту ему взять*)" (article 74 of *Judicial Statute of Pskov*).

Norms of the first kind, that is unilateral, strictly imperative and claimsless, will be called MORAL NORMS.

Norms of the second kind, obligation-claim ones, or imperative-attributive, will be called LEGAL NORMS.

The dual, obligation-claim character of legal norms is sometimes reflected in legal language, in utterances which express legal norms, in a very clear form: the content of a given norm is expressed in two sentences; one of them defines the obligations of one side, whereas the second expresses claims, rights of the other side. The structure of the following normative laws may serve as an example: "[...] obliges one side to pay and gives the other side the right to demand compensation", one side is therefore obliged to pay interest and the other is entitled to receive interest, *etc.*

It may be the case that one norm is expressed with two discrete articles in books of legal rules, *e.g.* codes. For example, the opening paragraphs of the second book of the new *German Civil Code* read:

§241. By virtue of debt relation the creditor is entitled to demand from the debtor the execution of a certain provision. The provision may consist in failure to act.

§242. The debtor is obliged to execute the provision in good faith and in accordance with the civil laws.

In colloquial legal language there exist such expressions which express the whole norm, that is, both the obligation on one side (legal liability) and the entitlement on the other (legal asset), in one sentence. For example, a given person has such and such rights and another person is obliged to do so and so for him.

The above mentioned method of constructing legal norms, which consists in simultaneously defining the liability – one side's obligation, as well as the asset – the other side's rights, and assigning one side's obligation to the other side, may be called an obligation-claim norm, or an imperative-attributive norm, or a complete, adequate version of legal norms.

In the field of morality, a complete, adequate version is represented by a unilaterally obligatory, or a unilaterally imperative one, for example: "We are obliged to act in such and such a way", "We ought not to do so and so", *etc.*

Apart from the complete and adequate formulation, or the imperative--attributive one, the following three shortened forms of contracted expressions are accepted and regularly used in the domain of law (unless they cause misunderstandings among listeners or readers):

(1) Summary attributive formulation, which consists in indicating only the legal asset, the claim from one of the sides, without mentioning the other side's obligations, for example: "In the case of failure to fulfil a commitment in a given time, the creditor is entitled to compensation for the losses caused by the delay", "[...] he may demand compensation for the losses", *etc.*

In these cases it is implied that the other side (in the case mentioned above: the debtor, or in the case of his death: his inheritors) is obliged to act accordingly, to provide the required object, *etc.*

(2) Summary imperative, obligatory formulation, which consists in indicating only the legal liability, one side's obligations, without mentioning the other side's rights, for example: "In the case of failure to fulfil a commitment in a given time, the debtor is obliged to compensate the losses".

In these cases it is implied that the other side (in the case mentioned above: the creditor, or in the case of his death: his inheritors) is entitled to receive a provision in their favour, to receive the required object, *etc.*

(3) Neutral, mutual summary form, which consists in indicating impersonally what ought to take place in a given case, without indicating one side's obligation and the other side's rights, for example: "In the case of failure to fulfil a commitment in a given time, the losses ought to be com-

pensated [...]", "The amount of debt is increased by the value of the losses caused", *etc.*

In these cases it is implied that one side is obliged to provide a certain provision in favour of the other side, who, in turn, is entitled to certain rights.

In order to comprehend the substance of legal norms included in sets of acts and other sources of law precisely and completely, one ought to replace the three types of shortened formulations mentioned above with a complete formulation by means of a suitable interpretation; in the case of the shortened attributive formulation, one ought to determine who is obliged to do what, in the case of shortened imperative formulation, one ought to indicate who is entitled to what, in the case of mutual shortened formulation, one ought to introduce a interpretative supplement in both directions. Such an interpretation, or determination of the complete obligation-claim content of the regulation, may prove to be a difficult task, or at least one which requires some additional historical information or information of another kind. For example, in some historical acts of law it is said that in the case of a given crime, like robbery, a given sum of money ought to be paid; if we instruct a contemporary reader, unfamiliar with the law of those times, to explain the norm and present it in its complete, imperative-attributive formulation, he would probably express it so: the robber is obliged to pay a certain amount of money, and the robbed has the right to receive it. However, this interpretation would often be wrong. In the past it was often not only the criminal himself who was responsible for the crime, but also other people bore consequences, such as their relatives, or the inhabitants of the same village, whereas princes could be entitled to receive the assigned amount of money, or the money was divided between a prince and the family of the robbed person, *etc.*

In the domain of morality, in close connection with its unilaterally obligatory character, the way of expressing norms and their interpretation are simpler and more uniform. These norms concern only the ones who are obliged to do something, there is no mention, and cannot be any, of the ones entitled to some claim. It rules out the possibility of the imperative-attributive formulation or the shortened-attributive, claim formulation; what remains is the unilaterally imperative formulation as a complete form and the neutral formulation (not the mutual shortened one as in the domain of law, but the unilateral shortened), which contains exclusively the description of the obligation (*cf.*, for example, statements from the Evangelic Sermon on the Mount).

Marian Borowski. The praxeological situation
[1923: 144–155]

Points which can be enumerated when analyzing the issue of the so--called act can be divided into three larger groups: (1) those belonging to an objective situation which precedes a psychic issue; (2) processes of a mental nature; (3) events determined by these processes, which are something external with respect to the second group. This group includes i.a. all kinds of means and results.

1. The first group is treated here collectively as AN OBJECTIVE INITIAL SITUATION for an act. It includes a man's psycho-physical structure at a given moment, his inherited or acquired dispositions, as well as the state of both physical and social surroundings, norms and ideals which prevail, and finally, this man's attitude to his surroundings. All that makes the surroundings influence a man in some way falls into this category, as well as what conditions a man to be prone to given impulses, and what makes the impulses affect one in a given way, rousing certain inclinations, tendencies and reactions. The objective initial situation can be described in short as the "nature" of the acting subject and its surroundings.

Determinism stresses the importance of these sorts of factors, and therefore so do historical materialism and metaphysical systems, which for various reasons claim that all one's behaviour is predetermined by some transcendental occurrences or one's own acts or the acts of some foreign forces.

2. The internal phase of an act begins with IMPULSES, understood as impressions, feelings, moods, thoughts, images, *etc.*, which emerge in people as a result of internal or external stimuli acting on one's psycho-physical system. The whole of these impulses at a given moment constitutes the initial psychic situation for our behaviour.

3. MOTIVES, that is, impulses which are evaluated as positive or negative. There has to emerge in one the sense or judgement of VALUE, so that the sensations from the outside world, images or thoughts which arise, obtain

the character of motives of activity. Even an unpleasant feeling does not always obtain a character of its own until one adds an "evaluation", that is, realizes that it is something wrong or signifies something wrong and that one should free oneself from this state. [...]

I lean towards a narrower approach to the notion of motive and putting more stress on its emotional, rather than intellectual, character. By motive I understand an evaluated impulse, an impulse which one takes a specific stand on.

Four cases occur here: either the evaluation is positive and may find its expression in a sensation or a judgement: "This impulse has to be retained", or the evaluation is negative and is expressed as "This impulse has to be discarded", or the impulse is deemed neutral, or finally, it is impossible to evaluate it and therefore there is some confusion as to its meaning or value.

The matter of differentiating between the notion of motive and the notion of aim is unclear in the sources. Motives belong to the emotional sphere, whereas aims belong to the intellectual sphere. Motives concern the present and aims concern the future states of affairs. An aim is what we drive at and what we are going to create; a motive is the reason why we create a given state of affairs. An aim is always evaluated positively, whereas an impulse, or at least an impulse to active behaviour, is usually a negative value. Feeling the need to activity and causing a change in an existing state of affairs has a negative value and prepares us to attempt to free ourselves from it. When one lights an unfamiliar brand of cigarette, there comes an impulse in the form of a negative taste sensation. There follows a negative evaluation expressed in, for instance, the exclamation: "Horrible!" which constitutes the motive of my behaviour. An aim would usually be a project of freeing oneself from this value, or a thought about atonement the experienced need in some way, for example, the thought of discarding the cigarette.

Also the act of refraining from activity is motivated by a negative evaluation of thoughts on the change of the situation. If in some cases active behaviour seems to be induced by an impulse which had been appraised positively, then we always manage to discover an additional negative impulse, for instance, the thought that without our active behaviour the present positive situation may change. Then our aim is to secure the existing state of affairs and avoid the impending change. The positive impulse itself may only become a motive of passive behaviour. Such behaviour is caused by an impulse which has been evaluated as neutral or an impulse whose value we are not certain of yet.

With respect to the act of will, a motive and an aim differ from each other in that the occurrence of a motive is not dependent on will, as it is an instinctive reaction of the type of feeling or emotion. Volition does not determine the quality and power of motives, nor does it administer sanctions to motives, but only to a presentation of a given aim.

We speak of the conflict of motives rather than of the conflict of aims. Only tendencies can fight with each other, whereas presentations and aims cannot, even if they are contradictory.

The circumstances which deem the frequent mistake between aims and motives easier to understand are the following. Each aim in turn highlights the motives, for example, by way of contrast. The evaluation of the present situation seems negative against the background of thought on ideas; it is often the case that thought makes the situation, which had been evaluated as positive, appear negative. The second cause for confusing aims and motives is that presentations of aims, presentations of means, courses and consequences of activity in turn play the role of secondary motives. Moreover, a very loosely formulated aim is indeed already contained within a motive itself. If a motive is described as inclining towards avoiding evil and retaining well-being, then this can be seen as the main aim of one's behaviour. After all, the term "aim" is not used in such broad meaning. An aim is something which determines the direction and manner of one's reactions more EXACTLY. The evaluation of impulse alone does not suffice to execute the act. It can only cause anxiety or even some aimless motor discharge. Therefore, obviously those who use the term "motive" to describe whatever can be understood as a kind of act also necessarily regard aims as motivational complexes.

Even more contentious than the idea of motive is the basic notion of values. Here only one remark will suffice. From the point of view of psychology, the most appropriate theory is expressed in the old expression: "*Bonum est id, quod appetitur*". A value presents itself as a correlate of driving. In particular, that which one wishes to continue or to occur has positive value and that which one has thirsts to be rid of has negative value. (The scholastic formula which describes "an object" in general as *id, cui correspondet intellectus* is analogous.) Pleasure is a value only when one desires it, and pain is something wrong only when it causes one to drive to remove it. Neutral things cannot have any value.

4. AN AIM, which may be described as A PRESENTATION of the future state of affairs, and therefore, of one's certain behaviour on the one hand, or as a result of this behaviour on the other. However, regarding an aim directly as some desired FUTURE EVENT, rather than a presentation of a future event and the present mental experience, is closer to the common meaning of the word "aim". According to this view, the aim is an object which, although it does not really exist, is going to realize. It is what one imagines rather than a presentation, that is, a spiritual matter which makes one realize the aim at a given moment. These two manners of perceiving aims entail ascribing a causal structure or a teleological structure to aims. Only the current experience can become the efficient cause which determines one's future behaviour. Yet, if by aim we understand the future objective state of affairs, then it determines one's behaviour as a standard *causa finalis*.

We speak of closer or direct aim and indirect or further aims, or even ultimate ones. For instance, an ultimate aim for one could be to acquire wealth, whereas a subordinate aim would be to receive a message, a closer aim – to send a letter, a direct aim – to write a letter. By focused people, the whole of their aims is put in strict hierarchy. In the case of unfocussed people, the system of aim is oligarchic or even disorganized and it contains aims which are internally incompatible.

With performing an act based on habit or routine comes the awareness of further aims only. Conversely, instinctive actions or the ones performed under hypnotic suggestion bring with them the awareness of direct aims only.

5. Motive and aim are two pillars which support the arch of the special mental phenomena called DESIRE, WILLINGNESS, THIRST. The greater the difference between the value of a present impulse and the value of the aim, the greater the intensity of driving. One always drives from something at

something else. If the longed-for object is unachievable, the driving takes the form of "regret", which may concern past, present or future events. If valuable occurrences which are independent from one seem uncertain, one experiences „hope", or "anxiety".

All kinds of driving are of highly individualized character. They are not some kind of passive reception, perception, ascertaining of something given and finished, but they concern what should be, what is supposed to be, what is needed, and they are the prototype of physical notions of dynamics. Just as a difference of potentials is necessary for a physical change, so mental stress constitutes the source of one's act.

Drivings take on a strictly individualistic character in psychology. They are "mine" in a greater degree than perceptions or judgements. One usually becomes aware of one's own "self" when one thirsts something, whereas in receptive states the idea of a separate, uniform self fades from awareness. [...]

6. In order for a driving to develop into act, rather than remain a mere liking or wish, there has to appear A CONVICTION THAT THE AIM CAN BE ACHIEVED THROUGH ONE'S BEHAVIOUR.

This is why one remembers the causal sequence which had so far induced the thirsted aim. At the same time, one goes to further causes, where the source of the latter may lie in one's own actions, for instance, in gestures. As long as one can find such actions which may give rise to a causal sequence whose effect is the realization of the aim, one can claim that this aim is achievable. The fact that something is achievable as a result of one's certain behaviour is referred to as one's "ability", "power", "force", or "might". [...]

7. CHOICE is made when more achievable aims arise. Then one has to decide to behave in one of the presented ways and cannot avoid this choice, as also the lack of decision entails some kind of behaviour.

The mechanism of decision-making in a complicated situation is one of the most vital issues in life. Therefore, when one reflects upon one's behaviour, reads psychological novels or watches court procedures, one becomes aware of how the mechanism operates. Comparative evaluation of secondary motives, presented future situations and presented emotional reactions is especially challenging. There may occur certain illusions in evaluations; for instance, it is known that a presentation of future pain has less motivational power than a *caeteris paribus* presentation of future pleasure. One is subject to the illusion of perspective when evaluating values which were not directly given. It is both common knowledge and experience derived from experiments that the motive which one considers at the end is privileged. A correction of such illusions is the role of upbringing, ethics and life wisdom. It is reduced to the artificial reinforcement of general, further motives as opposed to closer, actual ones.

In order to find and assess all the pros and cons of a given aim in a particular case, one resorts in life to various methods. [...] Generally, taking decisions is easier for people who possess a number of constant motives of invariable force, or for people with little imagination and poor value judgement.

8. Between the proper clash of motives and RESOLUTION or DECISION there is usually a break of various length, which is characterized by the sense of anticipation, hesitation and procrastination. During this break, the flow of thoughts and images is blocked, the breath is held and tension occurs in the chest, head, neck and fingers. At the moment of making the choice, the sense of anticipation and doubt is replaced by the sense of certainty, muscle tension is released and deep breath reappears. [...] Another important consequence of taking a decision is "mental attitude", when the idea of the aim enters one's consciousness and thoughts on other ideas, incompatible with the chosen one or extraneous with respect to it, are obstructed.

After all, choosing, that is, making a decision, [...] does not differ in intensity. It has nothing to do with what we call weak or strong will. It can be compared to turning on a switch. Hence the temptation to treat decision as a kind of JUDGEMENT (according to Prof. Witwicki, a judgement on one's future behaviour[39]) just as a judgement is made as a result of theoretical consideration, as with mathematical exercise.

Yet, is it not true that the act of choosing should be differentiated from a resolution, which is the proper act of will? One might think so if the act of

---

[39] Witwicki [1904]. [...]

choosing were a simple, objective stating of some motives' superiority over others, and therefore a sort of a judgement. However, the act of decision is of an emotional, subjective character, and even often accompanied by the sense of total freedom and arbitrariness. One's "self" does not only outbalance the vote in the case when pros and cons are equal, but, as many claim, it also takes decisions autocratically, and motives serve the function of advice and inducement. The act of taking a decision consists in weighing the motives of one's self against each other. It is not until the result is realized and the effects of one's behaviour are predicted that it can assume the form of a judgement: "Then I will act thusly".

As far as acts of will are concerned, one's self and the awareness of one's integrity plays an important role, though one difficult to describe. It is related to the necessity of determining one's actions unambiguously. In order to achieve something, one has to coordinate one's behaviour. As long as one remains in the intellectual sphere, one may tolerate various contradictories and forget about integrity, represented by one's "self". However, upon moving into the sphere of activity, one has to remove all contradictories, as they may stall all organized and consistent, and therefore effective action, and appear as a homogenous, integral self.

9. An aim which has been decided upon and determined is called an intentional aim or, in short, A DESIGN or A PROJECT. This phase is visible when there occurs a break in time between the decision and the beginning of execution or when the execution is prolonged in time. Then we speak of declaring a design and confirming a design. A person's will may be described as persistent and strong on the basis of his ability to retain his design and keeping it in mind by frequently reminding himself of it.

10. If the aim is not directly attainable, one needs TO DEVELOP A PLAN. [...]

11. MENTAL EXECUTIVE ACT. One of its varieties is referred to as an innervative act. An impulse may be positive, when it introduces new readiness or reinforces some preexisting motor tendencies, or negative, when it suppresses the existing tendencies. Moreover, we can distinguish a motor impulse from an impulse which only concerns the mental sphere, for example when it comes to performing some mental work (task), or a change in the affectional mood, as well as noticing or remembering something.

Another kind of an executive act is A simple PERMISSION, agreeing to something, tolerating something or giving in to an existing tendency. As the results of the psychological analysis reveal (described below), this other kind of an executive act actually seems the basic one, whereas what is called an impulse is an automatic update of one chosen tendency when other tendencies are blocked. Therefore one may only speak of the physiological matter of innervation, rather than an impulse as a psychic act.

However, the matters of innervation sometimes affect one's conscious self. It takes place when a decision is changed or withdrawn after the execution began. Then either the intended activity is stalled or it is left in its initial phase, or there occurs some other modification. Such reactions are easily distinguished from resolute and firm reactions both in everyday life and in psychological laboratories. Our consciousness registers this "struggle of impulses" as a specific sensation, affectionally unpleasant, and also in the form of specific kinaesthetic and cenesthetic sensations. Yet, this does not prove that physiological acts of innervation as such possess an equivalent of one's consciousness.

Sometimes executive acts are also perceived when the resolution is executed under the condition that a certain period of time passes or that a certain requirement is met, or if a decision was alternative. This situation often occurs during laboratory experimentation on the phenomena of volition and hence the objection that the experimenter does not reach primary acts of will and only researches secondary matters. This is because the person experimented upon decides in advance to react as instructed by the experimenter and only awaits a sign in order to react in one of the previously decided ways. These mental secondary volitional acts are not remade, but weaker, decisions. They probably only consist in realizing what one's initial decision had been and remembering that the time has come, or the circumstance has occurred which was the necessary condition for the execution. In any case, they can be described as mental executive acts and can take on the term: impulse, instead of an innervation act, which is a matter of automatics and physiology rather than an impulse.

The third group of instants of action is of more external character. These constitute means, work and execution of the work.

12. One of the means is THE PERSONAL BEHAVIOUR of the perpetrator, guided by the idea of an aim and the adopted plan. Physical or psychic actions, called labour or personal work, can be mentioned here. Among these activities we can distinguish initial actions, intermediary actions and the so-called final touches.

How does one's will induce one's body movements?

The question is not how "the soul" affects "the body" metaphysically, but what the mechanics are of such very commonplace phenomena, as uttering any word or response to someone's greeting. One's will is able to strike the right keys of motor centres and put in motion a whole complex of necessary muscles. [...]

Formerly we settled for the explanation of this process in terms of association between a reconstructive image of the desired result and a reconstructive image of the movement which previously led to this result. However, our images of movement are very inaccurate and superficial, not to mention the fact that we do not usually have the sufficient understanding of anatomy and physiology of human body.

We would sooner speak of the idea-motor connection, that is, the link between the image of a result with the proper motor process itself (rather than an image of this process). In childhood one performs certain spontaneous movements and then perceives their results; in later years what prevails is that first one imagines a certain result and this image in turn entails a proper movement. In 90% of one's daily actions this relationship is direct and automatic. An act of will occurs relatively rarely, namely, when one considers incompatible aims. What follows is hesitation and the need to decide which aim's motor tendency should be stalled, and which one should surrender to or even reinforce. Such an idea-motor theory of how the will of movement works finds confirmation in experiments. These show that the main factor in voluntary actions, both physical and psychic, is "perseveration" of the image of the aim in one's conscious and focussing one's attention on it. This way ONLY one image can develop a body movement connected to it. Even if we consider accurate imitation of executing of movement or position which had been demonstrated, the kinaesthetic image of one's own future movement tends to be in the way, as it is by far less expressive than the visual image.

Among voluntary psychic actions the phenomena of sensory attention should be mentioned first. They are the most basic manifestations of will at work, which is all about retaining in one's consciousness a certain framework image and protecting it from interfering foreign influence. This framework image is only the ground for this image in the case of pure OBSERVATIONAL attention. One focuses his attention on a screen in order to notice things which are supposed to appear on it. A different kind of attention is SEARCHING attention. Then, apart from retaining the ground for impression in one's consciousness, one also retains the special framework representation and seeks sensory complement. This happens when, for instance, one observes a crowd of people in order to find friends in it or only one particular person, like one's brother.

Voluntary mental actions, like solving certain intellectual tasks or consciously trying to remember something, reveal a similar mechanism. On the one hand, one retains in his consciousness the elements which constitute a starting point, and on the other, one retains a framework, schematic images of the aim. One strives to render the update of the greatest number of associations (which are independent of one's will) possible, pick out adequate associations and assemble the framework which was initially provided.

Observation of everyday life confirms the above view. In order to ensure that one's resolution is effective, one often repeats it to himself a few times, or generally, arranges matters in such a way that the resolution is often remembered, and avoids situations and thoughts which would lead one astray. Also in theoretical psychology attention has long been turned towards the privileged character of these images whose subject is an aim. Some psychologists [...] openly identify the act of will with an intense, emotionally tinted, image of an objective.

Having assumed that influence of will both upon movements of the body and mental processes happens through perseveration of certain images and enabling them to develop processes connected to the images freely, let us ask further: what is the very mechanism of maintaining certain images in the centre of consciousness? I believe the following holds true. The immediate effect of taking a decision is preoccupation with the chosen idea of an objective, and therefore removal of all other, foreign or incompatible ideas. Almost all psychic phenomena facilitate their own repetition. Owing to this disposition, secondary volitional acts are facilitated. They may be relatively weak, not enough to retain or resume, after a break, the idea which had once been decided upon and therefore held a privileged position in one's mind.

Marian Borowski. Praxeological logic
[1924: 59 – 60]

One may attempt to formulate the relationships between acts in a symbolic fashion. Let us mark:

an act – as p;

another act – as r;

lack of act p and an act consisting of neglecting act p – as p^0;

an act inverse[40] to p – as p';

succeeding of the act p, its practical value, its acceptability in a given practical system – as 1;

not succeeding, lack of practical sense, a prohibited act – as 0;

a group of acts – as their symbols written next to each other;

replacementability[41] and alternativeness[42] of acts – as the plus sign;

consequence connection (duty, obligation)[43] – as the logical symbol of entailment;

---

[40] "If two acts, following each other in sequence, remain in such relationship that the latter abolishes what the former achieved and therefore returns to the initial state of affairs, we speak of the INVERSE relationships. The result of a set of acts, inverse in relation to each other, does not differ from the result of neglecting both or simple lack of them. Acts of this kind, if done simultaneously, are called ANTAGONISTIC or COMPENSATIONAL" [1924; 54] [my footnote – JJ] .

[41] "If two acts can bring the same effect so that one can be replaced with the other and realize a given state of affairs in various ways, depending on the choice, then we speak of SUBSTITUTE acts" [1924: 52] [my footnote – JJ].

[42] "If we choose between acts, not as between various means leading to the same work but as between separate wholes together with inherent aims, we speak of ALTERNATIVE acts" [1924: 53] [my footnote – JJ] .

[43] "Actions affect each other, and not only when they accidentally occur together. The connection may be deeper and consist of one act leading to the other. Some acts generate others; they constitute a starting point and impulse. This relationship is called a CONSEQUENCE of acts. [...] Consequence is often called DUTY, COMMITMENT or OBLIGATION" [1924: 55] [my footnote – JJ].

"is practically the same", "does not differ in practice" – as the symbol of equation;

"means the same as", "is called" – as the symbol of equivalence;

the whole of the situation – by including it in brackets;

a negation of the above relationships – as a comma at the top of a bracket which includes elements of a relationship.

We obtain:

$(pp') = p^0$ – a unit of an act and another act which is the inverse of the former does not differ from the lack of act p or neglecting it.

$(pp^0) = 0$ – a unit of an act and neglecting it does not fulfil any of them and does not have any practical value.

$p^{00} = p$ – neglecting to neglect is the same as fulfilling act p.

$p'' = p$ – fulfilling the inverse of the inverse of act p is the same as fulfilling act p.

$(p = p^0) = 0$, $(p = p') = 0$ – an act which does not differ from neglecting it or its inversion does not have practical value.

$(p^0 = (p = 0))$ – the lack or neglecting of act p does not differ from a situation where fulfilling act p has no meaning, in which, for example, act p remains an attempt only, without result.

A similar situation, where the consequence of act p is its compensation[44] or failure, is expressed in the following formulas:

$(p < p^0) = O.$

$(p < p') = O.$

Conversely:

$(p < p^0)' = O.$

expresses permissible acts, that is the so-called sphere of freedom.

Further:

$(p + r) \equiv (p^0 < r)$ – these two acts are alternatives in the situation where at least one of them should be fulfilled.

$(p < r) \equiv (p^0 + r)$ – conversely, the situation in which act p obliges one to fulfil act r has the same meaning as the situation in which there is a choice

---

[44] *Cf.* footnote 40 [my footnote – JJ].

between neglecting p or fulfilling r, for instance, either neglect to borrow or to give a deposit.

$(p < r) \equiv (pr^0 = O)$ – act r is a consequence of p if the unit of act p and neglecting act r is devoid of practical meaning, for instance, if one made extensive preparations for some act and does not take that act, then this unit does not make sense. Similarly, if one takes some articles from a shop *cum animo sibi habendi*, but does not pay what is due, then *de iure* one does not become the owner, but *de facto* the articles or *quod mihi interest* will be taken away. One cannot speak of obligation, when there is no sanction at all.

Formula $(p < r) \equiv (r^0 < p^0)$ generally expresses situations like: failing to pay for articles obliges one to neglect to take ownership of it. Let us omit the question whether the relationship of praxeological consequence is mutual, and therefore, also the question if every obligation comes with an entitlement to something and if every entitlement to something comes with someone's obligation. Let me then propose a general formulation of a relation of entitlement to obligation:

$p \equiv (p < p^0)'(p < r)$ – act p is called entitlement if it is a permissible act (that is, belonging to the sphere of freedom) and if it obliges to the action r; for instance, one is entitled to demand the return of his debt when the demand is not a prohibited act and, at the same time, is an act which obliges someone to pay the debt. Similarly, the law of ownership is expressed as a person's freedom to dispose of an object, and at the same time, other people's obligation not to interfere with it.

We speak of a praxeological unit when the fulfilment of one of the acts does not entail an obligation to neglect the other:

$(pr) \equiv (p < r^0)'$.

Similarly:

$(pr)' \equiv (p^0 + r^0)$ – we may not speak of the link of two actions in the situation where one has the choice of neglecting at least one of them. At the same time, fulfilment of both acts simultaneously is permissible when neglecting one of them is not an alternative:

$(pr)' \equiv (p^0 + r^0)'$.

The rule of syllogism:

$$[(p < r)\,(r < s)] < (p < s).$$

finds easy interpretation in praxeology. Similarly, *modus ponens* and *modus tollens*:

$$(p < r)\,p < r.$$
$$(p < r)\,r^0 < p^0.$$

if taking the goods obliged one to pay within some practical system, then if one paid, he would have to pick up the goods, and if one did not pay, he would have to refrain from picking them up.

Finally, analogously to one of the rules of apagogical reasoning:

$$[p^0 < (r < r^0)] < p$$ – if neglecting act p entails some practical null as a consequence, then the act should be performed. Indeed, one tries to avoid fruitless acts. Given the choice of fulfilling act p or act r, when one is aware that act r will not have a practical meaning, one should fulfil act p:

$$(p + r)\,(r < 0) < p.$$

This formula may be used to express the aforementioned basic maxim of our praxis.[45]

The above remark on "praxeological algebra" is of temporary character and does not claim to be as exact as the *formularium* of logical algebra. In any case, the present attempt may uncover plenty of ambiguities which still lie in praxeological concepts, and is an invitation to create the rules of transformation of equations, and therefore, to create "a moral calculation".

Stanisław Cheliński. Types of imperatives
[1925: 94 – 99, 102 – 115]

Obliging norms always refer to [...] some subject; in other words, they always oblige someone to do something. There are some among them[46] which oblige because someone SETTLED them with his act of will and there are also some which do not possess that feature. Examples of unsettled norms are norms of logic, ethics and aesthetics; sentences which state that

---

[45] "ACT IN SUCH A WAY THAT YOU ACHIEVE THE GREATEST AMOUNT OF INTENDED RESULTS" [1924: 58] [my footnote – JJ].
[46] Somló [1917: 58 *et seq.*].

one should not contradict himself in thought or that people should be honest cannot be justified by someone having made the decision to give these resolutions binding force.[47] An example of a settled norm would be a statement that the children in family X should go to bed at 9 p.m. because the father of the family said so.[48]

Will is an element of spiritual life of a kind, which is distinguished as a separate entity in internal experience by our though. The above sentence obviously is not a definition; will cannot be defined, just as the colour white cannot be defined. One can only indicate where and in which conditions such phenomena are available. Such indication is, for example, the fact that will is what we mean when we utter the judgement: "I want this". For instance, in the judgement: "I want to go to the garden" there is an indication as to the following psychic experiences: (1) the image of "me"; (2) the image of the garden; (3) the image of the activity of "my" walking in a more or less specified direction; what remains is something which does not succumb to analysis, which one nevertheless recognizes infallibly and distinguishes as something separate, which is indicated by the word "want". Apart from that, one should assume the presence of other elements, which are not mentioned in the content of the above judgement, namely, some affectional states which prompt the mentioned resolution. Let us disregard the question of whether the element of pure willing ever appears in one's psychic life as separate from affectional and cognitive elements. What matters for the theory of norms is only conscious will, combined with images or concepts which determine its direction; it is not solely "wanting" but "wanting something" that is a feature of settling a norm. In the acts of will which are the concern of the theory of norms, an element of pure willing is actually only an abstract of certain concrete experiences in which we always additionally distinguish intellectual and emotional elements.[49] This is not to say that the

---

[47] It is obviously different from the point of view of the so-called heteronomic ethics. Among unsettled norms one may mention a separate case of norms based on custom, especially norms of customary laws, which are in many ways similar to settled norms.
[48] This division partly corresponds to Znamierowski's division of thetic and axiological norms [1924: 15 *et seq.*].
[49] The latter will not concern us here.

element of pure willing is not something which really exists in these experiences; it is real as one's thought necessarily distinguishes it from the psychic reality given to us. The element of pure willing in turn leaves an imprint on the whole psychic event which we call the act of will. Affectional elements constitute motives of will, intellectual elements determine its direction, but the element of willing and the role it plays here constitutes a feature which distinguishes this category of psychic events from other spiritual phenomena. From normative point of view, the element of willing plays a special role; the element is specifically connected to the notion of duty.

This very element of pure willing[50] is what I shall call will, and those experiences which consist of connecting willing to the image (or concept) of the object and the subject of the willing person shall be called acts of will; this is stated in judgements of the following pattern: "I want something". The reference to the self as well as the THING I want may be more or less conscious. Only a combination of these three elements constitutes an event which can be described as "an act of will". An act is understood as a subject's action and only when we connect willing with our "self" in our conscious, and we undertake the willing as OUR action, OUR willing. Wherever this situation does not occur, where willing is connected only with an image of the object of willing (for example, when a baby reaches for a toy), then we should probably speak of the process of willing taking place inside a person rather than somebody's willing.[51]

One kind of acts of will are those in which the object of willing is not only some desired state of affairs but also realizing that state of activity of the subject of the willing, for instance: "I want to go to the garden", "I want to sew a button on", *etc.* These are PURPOSEFUL acts of will. By aim I mean any state of affairs which one wants to realize, which does not only include ultimate aims but also states which one wills to cause as means leading to this aim. Another kind of acts of will are ones in which the subject DOES NOT DRIVE to bring about the desired state of affairs due to the inability to realize it, or for other reasons (for example, desiring that

---

[50] *Cf.* Sigwart [1879] and Petrażycki [1905: 165 *et seq.*].
[51] *Cf.* Sigwart [1879] and Reinach [1913: 21].

a tragic event from his past had not taken place: the partitions of Poland, the death of a beloved person, *etc.*). This is the half-facetiously called in natural speech "wishful thinking". Experiences of this kind are very common and notable for experiencing great discrepancy between "self" and "non-self". The well-known concept of the ideal as something practically unattainable applies here. Reducing the term "will" to purposeful acts of will only (or even to acts of will which correspond to the movements to one's body), which is not uncommon in the field, is not consistent with the data coming from one's inner experience. One may "want" something very strongly and at the same time be aware that any activities leading to realizing the object of willing is futile. "Willing" in this case does not differ from "willing" in purposeful acts. What is more, "wishful thinking" may be infinitely more powerful than willing in a purposeful act (compare the thirst to avoid certain death to the acts of will which accompany a set of motions in everyday activities, like getting dressed or washing up).[52]

A subgroup of purposeful acts of will can be distinguished which concern some people. For example, if one asks somebody a question, then by uttering certain words one addresses the person in order to obtain an answer. By asking a question, one does not only want to obtain an answer but also wants to ask the question, that is, perform an action which concerns another person. One's action is an object of that will, and it concerns the person asked. Therefore, the person asking is the active part (the subject of the activity), whereas the person asked is the passive part (the object of the activity). Experiences of this sort could therefore be called bilateral events. Bilateral events usually consist in (intended or realized) affecting the other side's psyche (question, announcement, request, *etc.*) or affecting the other person physically (strike). However, there are certain bilateral events which are not concerned with affecting the other side in any way, for example, when one wants to get to know a person, one observes him, watches his movements and gestures, commits his words to memory when he does not realize it; or when one bequeaths his property to someone. [...]

---

[52] *Cf.* Petrażycki [1905: 165 *et seq.*].

A bilateral event may consist in an action happening only on one side; such a bilateral event shall be called A UNILATERAL ACTION. A typical example is a question: one side is merely a subject here, and the other side is exclusively the object of the action. However, if an answer follows the said question, then a complex event, called conversation, occurs. Answering is the action performed by the person asked, which concerns the person asking and is induced by the question; the passive side becomes the active side and vice versa, the active side becomes passive. The nature of an answer is that it is dependent on the question. Bilateral events of this kind, composed of both sides' activities connected to each other, can even be called BILATERAL ACTIONS.

Settling an obliging norm consists in SOMEONE creating a norm which binds SOMEBODY, and doing so as an act of his will. Therefore it is always an activity which concerns another person, that is, a bilateral experience. Settling a norm which binds one of the sides through the other side's will is an ORDER; settling a norm though concordant acts of will of both sides, that is, a bilateral action, constitutes AN AGREEMENT.

In general, any act of will which settles an obliging norm can be called OBLIGING WILL. [...]

An order is a unilateral settlement of an obliging norm.[53] The term indicates two crucial and fundamental features of an order: settlement of a norm and unilateralism. The former is *genus proximum*, the latter is *differentia specifica* of an order.

Having conducted the division of obliging norms into settled and non--settled, we already stated that the defining attribute of the former is their dependence on specific acts of will (or a unit of them), whereas the defining feature of the latter is lack of such dependence. The ethical norm: "All people should be honest" does not in the least base its binding power on the fact that someone resolved it at some point; the same also applies to a logical

---

[53] *Cf.* Znamierowski [1924: 43]: "An order is nothing else but a special variety of settlement". Bierling [1894: 27] adds the following passing remark in a footnote: "Der Austruck 'Befehl' ist immer nur zulässig wo auf die blosse einseitige Normsetzung des Befehlenden hin Gehorsam vom Adressaten erwartet wird; Vertransnormem sind niemals Befehle". [...] A definition of a norm – [1894: 29].

norm which orders one to avoid contradiction in thinking. In the nature
of an ordering norm, settled by the father of the family, which dictates to
the children to go to bed at 9 p.m., lies dependence on the father's specific
act of will. If someone faked the father's order, the above commanding
norm would certainly have its binding power in the children's consciousness, but as soon as the lie came out, it would not only cease to "be obliging" in the children's consciousness but it would also be regarded as delusory and as having never even been obliging. It will not mean repealing
the norm but mere ascertaining its absence. The same is true if a law was
declared in the *Dziennik Ustaw* [*Law Gazette*] which would later turn out
to have not been declared by the Seym; obviously, it would be commonly
accepted that no obliging norms had been stated. Here arises a question of
what the relationship is between a norm and a specific psychological experience, namely, an act of will. First of all, let us note that a settled norm
is AN ABSTRACT OF THE SPECIFIC EVENT WHICH IS SETTLING A NORM.[54] The ordering norm: children should go to bed at 9 p.m., is an abstract from the
event where the father behaved in a specific manner in a particular time
and place: he uttered the words or used other signs which corresponded
to his internal experiences. This psycho-physical event also contains the
thought which constitutes the ordering norm mentioned above. THE RELA-
TIONSHIP OF THE NORM ITSELF TO SETTLING THE NORM IS therefore A RELATION-
SHIP OF A PART TO THE WHOLE. A settled norm, conceived with no connection
to the settling event, loses its meaning altogether. The sentence: "Children
should go to bed at 9 p.m." is not in itself an ordering norm and from the
look of it we do not learn anything about the norm's derivation or of the
nature of its obliging force (for instance, it could be a proposal coming
from reflections on hygiene and education). In that case, we are dealing
(as opposed to a similar ordering norm) with two disparate norms, just as
the norm of civil law: "*Pacta sunt servanda*" is entirely different from an
ethical norm of the same content. The former is closely connected with
a specific historical event, namely, an act of will of specific persons who

---

[54] As for the relation of norm to normative events in general, see Petrażycki [1907a:
II. 326].

are introducing civil law in a given territory; from the point of view of the latter norm, this event is completely irrelevant [...]

An order directed to a person other than the order giver himself I call a heteronomous order. The notion of order is usually limited to a heteronomous order only, [...] which is incorrect [...]. The aim of a heteronomous order is usually the addressee's behaviour, more of less specified in the order. The image (or concept) of the addressee's behaviour must therefore have its place in the order giver's consciousness; this is not to say that in the consciousness of the order giver there has to be necessarily the CONTENT of this behaviour. It may be described by indicating all essential features (for example: "Bring me a glass of water!"), but it may also be only OUTLINED with the aid of indelible elements of behaviour of the addressee (for example, "Do what X asks of you!").[55] The addressee's behaviour is the object of the order giver's purposeful act of will; the consciousness of that fact includes what is expressed in this sentence: "I want X to do it (or not to do some other thing)". In order to achieve this aim, the order giver has to influence the addressee's psyche in such a way that the knowledge of the settled norm enters the addressee's consciousness. As the order giver and the addressee are two different persons, it may take place only by inducing certain physical events (movement, uttering of words) which are symbolic of the order giver's inner experiences. Thus informing the addressee about a norm created in the order giver's mind, a norm which determines the addressee's behaviour, which is supposed to influence his psyche through making its uncompromising character known (usually, under the threat of some punishment), which in turn puts the order giver's behaviour in the category of duty, or finally, through both of the above.

The relation of various elements of a heteronomous order in its typical, classical form is as follows. Firstly, there is aspiration to induce an event which consists in the other person behaving in a certain way. Let us call it the UTILITARIAN element of an order. The normative element is only a means

---

[55] It follows that the view which denies a law the features of an order because the content of the law is indeed usually unclear to the people who exercise legislative authority, is unfounded. However, the following sentence can also be an order: "I resolve that what is written there will be an obliging norm for the relevant people".

to an aim; the order giver determines his stand with the aid of category of duty; he resolves to acknowledge that the addressee should do something (or not do it), as he believes in this way he will achieve his aim more easily, more surely and better, or he will only be able to achieve it with the help of this means. Despite this subordinate, instrumental function of the normative element, it is not a necessary component of an order, as it is not the aim that is the characteristic feature of purposeful events; inducing the other person's behaviour by affecting his mind is also present in a request. A characteristic feature of an order is the said normative element (apart from unilaterally); these two features make an order a kind of means to achieve the aim which consists in somebody's behaviour.

It is often the case that the normative element is only faintly present in the consciousness of the order giver, who is mostly concerned with the practical outcome of the order, for example, when an employer tells a servant to bring him a glass of water, he does not usually expressly consider settling a norm in order to achieve this aim. However, he does realize in some degree that his act of will is in some way connected to "should" for the servant. Strictly speaking, he wants a norm as such, but it remains relatively unclear in his consciousness. The normative element will only appear in full force in case the servant does not fulfil the order.

Another case is when the addressee's behaviour is only an incidental aim of an order. Here the order giver is mostly concerned with confirming his position as a norm giver and emphasizing his superiority, *etc.* A settled (and revealed) norm predominantly serves this very purpose. Then the normative element obviously comes to the fore. Finally, in some cases both utilitarian and normative elements may have a strong presence in the consciousness of the order giver, and both the addressee's behaviour and the emphasizing of the order giver's position are equally important aims.

There are also rare cases where the aim of the order is not its object (that is, the addressee's behaviour described in the order), but the mere fact of emphasizing the order giver's position. For instance, a commander of a mutinous squad issues an order while nursing no hope of it being executed by his subordinates. In this case the addressee's behaviour is not the aim of the order, even though it is its object, as only that can become an aim which one hopes can be realized. There may even be no discordance here between will and manifestation of will ("I realize you will not comply but I order you nevertheless"). The aim is only to confirm one's position as a superior who does not negotiate with rebels, and this is the sole reason why he settles a norm obliging his subordinates and informs them about it. Although there occur discrepancies between the object and the aim of an order, still, from the nature of an order it follows that USUALLY the aim of an order is its object (the addressee's behaviour). Settling an obliging norm, not to channel other people's will accordingly but for other, secondary aims, may occur only when there are some special grounds for it. This occurs when incidental effects which are tied to the occurrence of an order become so significant to the order giver that he issues the order to achieve these incidental results despite his disbelief in the order being realized. It may even be the case that the order giver does not want the order to be executed. In the example of the commander of a mutinous squad it was shown that although he does not strive for his subordinates to behave in the way determined by the order, he still truly wants it. Although the aim of the order issued by him differs from its object (his subordinates' behaviour), it is in perfect accordance with it. There are cases where those in power do not refrain from using the unethical means of provocation; for instance, they issue an order which is designed to cause outrage and lead people to rebellion, which will in turn give opportunity for heavy persecution; such events took place in the period of partitions of Poland. Here an order is issued specifically so that it is not fulfilled; the addressees' obedience (and therefore realizing the object of the order) is exactly what the order giver does not want.

Let us proceed to consider the other crucial feature of an order, namely, UNILATERALITY. As opposed to an agreement which consists in cooperation on both sides, an order is an action of one side only. The passive side, or the addressee of the order, does not take part in the order itself, and is merely an element of the order giver's consciousness, an element which in a way determined the direction of an order, its "address" and nothing more. It follows that the addressee of the order may not even exist at the time of issuing the order. However, the order may be directed at a person who will be born in future and able to understand the order. After all, each existing statute of law will also apply to the people who had not yet been born at the time of issuing it (unless obviously it is repealed before). Even if the addressee does not even exist at the time in which the order is to be valid for him (for example, when one takes a tree for a man in the darkness and tells it to step aside), the occurrence still has all the characteristics of an order. This is because an order is only the order giver's behaviour and an occurrence of this kind also consists in another person's behaviour which bears all characteristics of an order.

Insomuch as the existence of an addressee is not necessary, it is obviously necessary that the order giver has THE CONVICTION that the addressee either exists or at least can exist in the presence or in the future. A heteronomous order is directed at another person; the order can be issued conditionally, in case an addressee exists or will exist, but in this case in the order giver's consciousness it is directed at someone who exists, but only as long as this person exists or will exist. The addressee of an order must be indicated in a manner which lets it be distinguished from those who the order does not concern. In the cases where the order giver turns to the addressee directly, the latter can often be marked out by the order giver physical posture (his face or his voice may be directed at the addressee, *etc.*), which is also the case for a greater number of addressees (for example, a crowd). In these cases an addressee is determined either through his name and surname or some general characteristics. Naturally, this occurs in the cases when the order is directed at an undetermined number of persons (for example, enlisting all men of a certain age); here enumerating all recruits according to their individual features is impossible.

Because a heteronomous order is an act of will of the subject which settles a norm for another person, a norm which obliges the person, therefore it results that an order has to contain the striving to inform the addressee. He is always, as Reinach claims, "vernehmungwedürftig", directed at the addressee. It is not in the least about REALIZING the announcement but about DRIVING to inform others. "When I issue an order to my servant", says Somló,[56] "it will remain an order even if he does not hear it as a result of his

---

[56] Somló [1917: 199].

absent-mindedness". After all, not hearing an order does not mean that there had been no tendency of informing the addressee.

A heteronomous order which was not communicated to the addressee would contain an internal contradiction. If one does not know an order, one cannot obey it and comply with it (another thing is that one may act in accordance with it by chance). From the point of view of what we called a utilitarian element of an order, the necessity to notify the addressee does not pose any problems. If one wants to induce the wanted behaviour from the addressee through an order, then one obviously has to introduce the order into his consciousness. One may not strive for an aim with the help of determined means and at the same time not want to use this means. To issue an order and not notify the addressee would be similar to attempting to write a letter with a pen, without using the pen. Thus, the source of the necessity to notify the addressee is a logical axiom of contradiction.

As we already know, the utilitarian element is not an essential feature of an order; however, it does determine the function of this event in human life in the vast majority of cases. There is a group of orders whose aim is only to confirm the order giver's position rather than to make the addressee behave in a certain way. Still, also in those cases the necessity to notify the addressee is apparent to everyone. In our example of a commander who issues an order to his subordinates, aware that it will not be executed (and even displaying his awareness), it is clear that he still has to make the order known to the addresses and that if he failed to do it, they would not at all be obliged to fulfil the order.

The source of absolute necessity to notify addresses about a heteronomous order is the connection between this element and two crucial elements of an order (unilaterality and settlement of a norm). The connection is the normative axiom: "*Impossibilium nulla obligatio*".

The principle which states that only those can be obliged who CAN perform the obligation bears the characteristics of absolute obviousness in our consciousness. It is clear to all that no one can have the obligation to change the sequence of seasons, or to build a house in a minute, or other things of this kind. A norm settled by one person for another comes into being because of a concrete event and if the addressee is not aware of it, he is also unaware of the settled norm, or the obligation imposed on him, and therefore cannot fulfil it. Naturally, he can act in accordance with the norm by chance, by performing an action which in principle will be equivalent to the action of fulfilling the obligation, but it will not in fact constitute fulfilling the obligation. If a servant who had not heard his employer's order to bring him a glass of water still did it on his own initiative, then we cannot speak of fulfilling the obligation which resulted from the order, since there is no act of obedience in relation to the ordering norm; one cannot be obeying an order which one did not know about. THIS IS WHY FROM THE POSITION OF AN ORDERING NORM ONLY THOSE ARE OBLIGED WHO KNOW ABOUT THE ORDER.[57] If we believe that, for example, an absent-minded student who had not heard his teacher's order to write a composition fails his obligation if he does not write it. This is not because we apply the above ordering norm in this case, but because we are reasoning from the position of another norm, which imposes on the student an obligation to listen to what the teacher is saying. It is obviously not the case if we assume that the student was utterly unable to pay attention or to hear the order at all.

Thus, from the point of view of the order giver himself, from the position of the ordering norm which he had settled, the addressee comes under the obligation no sooner than at the moment of learning about the order. Admittedly, the relevant action of the order giver will remain an order regardless of this circumstance, but the addressee's obligation resulting from the order is dependent on the action. As we know, the nature of an obligation is to refer the norm to a subject. However, the norm can be of hypothetical character; referring it to the subject may depend on a new circumstance arising. The order: "Bring X a glass of water if he asks you to!" obliges the addressee under the condition that X issues a request. The norm is already settled and the addressee notified, but he is not obliged yet nor will he ever be. From the point of view of the normative axiom: "*Impossibilium nulla obligatio*", an ordering norm always has to bear the condition: "if the addressee learns about it", and it is in order to fulfil this condition that the order giver has to drive to notify the addressee of the order. If the addressee

---

[57] *Cf.* Binding [1877: 60].

does not learn about the order due to his own failings, then another norm is used which dictates to him to learn more and pay attention to the manifestations of will of the order giver, but this responsibility will result from a different norm altogether.

The principle that an order only obliges those who know about it is not in contradiction with the unilaterality of an order. An order is an action performed only by the order giver, but this action has to incorporate a driving to notify the addressee, since it is necessary to achieve the aim, which is always (not always, exclusively) the addressee's obligation. If the aim is not achieved, the order ceases to be an order. This also applies to other unilateral activities (request, demand, question, *etc.*).

It results from the above that the order giver has to be certain that the addressee is able to learn about the order; only if there is no such possibility does the order stand in contradiction to the mentioned normative axiom. Moreover, the action of ordering always contains an element of making the order known to the addressee, or in other words, enables him to learn about the order. A manifestation of will which states the order definitely contains this element, and, at the same time, it signifies that the order giver believes there is a possibility to notify the addressee. Yet, if actual will does not contain the drive to notify, there occurs a contradiction between a manifestation of will and actual will. Still, it will be an actual order; one should keep in mind that although driving to notify the addressee is a necessary element of an order, this is not to say that the lack of the said element deprives the relevant event of the features of an order. There are only two essential and principal features of an order: unilaterality and settling an obliging norm. A combination of these elements with the normative axiom: *"Impossibilium nulla obligatio"* creates a LOGICAL (and ethical) necessity to notify the addressee about the order. If the order giver did not in fact drive to achieve this aim, he is in contradiction with the principle whose rightness he himself accepts. Still he retains some elements of the order in his activity. This is why this activity is an order, one that is absurd and unfair, but one which remains an order nevertheless. The logical and ethical necessity of notifying the addressee about the order is always obvious to the order giver. The best proof of it is the fact that even when the order giver is convinced it is impossible to notify the addressee, on the outside he behaves as if it was still possible.

The renowned issue of *iuris ignorantiae* does not in the least concern the question of whether a law is an order (considering that those obliged by it in some cases cannot certainly know about it). The issue is whether in these cases a law is a rational and just order. Since legal knowledge is obviously only available to specialists, then the honour of the legislator can be saved in another way: by ascertaining that a law cannot be an order, even though the opposite seems apparent.

We cannot debate the vast issue of order in law here. An exhaustive study of this matter would require a systematic review of all legislature from the point of view of the questions: (a) who is the order giver, (b) who is the addressee, (c) how is the addressee notified and what is the value of this method from the point of view of the aim it serves, (d) which norms are the basis for judging as guilty an addressee who did not learn the content of the law, although it was possible. Only such research would lead to answering the question of whether addressees of a legislator's orders are truly able to learn about these orders. In any case, it seems one cannot debate this issue from the point of view which states that all inhabitants of a given country are always the addressees of legal orders, and that the manner in which laws are proclaimed has no value in terms of actual notification of the addressees.

We can already state in advance that the research will reveal that many laws will not deserve to be called rational and just orders (let me just mention some cases of putting a law or a regulation into effect on the day of its proclamation). If nothing else, the fact that laws are usually obeyed to some degree proves that notifying addressees is not a great obstacle, considering the immensity of laws in operation present-day state. Clearly, it is impossible even for a most learned lawyer to learn all of them, and even more so for the vast majority of people with no access to the study of law.

As we stated before, the settlement of an obliging norm is not equivalent to obliging the addressee. A norm takes effect at the moment when the addressee learns about it. Moreover, whenever fulfilling an order is dependent on another condition, the addressee becomes obliged only after this additional condition has been fulfilled (let us also include here the cases mentioned before in which an addressee does not yet exist at the time of issuing the order). Finally, an order may dictate for an obligation to be executed starting from some established time. If the father of a family tells the children at noon to go to bed at 9 p.m., then until that time the children do not have an obligation resulting from the order. In all of the above cases, there is an interval between issuing an order and its coming into force.

The time interval between settling a norm and obliging the addressee may therefore be a necessity which results from the content of a given order (and the conditions for notifying the addressee). However, if these special circumstances do not occur, such an interval would be unfounded and even absurd. If A is supposed to issue an order to B in a letter, it is clear that between the moment of settling the norm and the moment of emergence of the addressee's obligation some time has to elapse. Yet, what is the sense of such an break if the employer gives his servant employee an oral order to bring him a glass of water? Why would the employer first settle a norm in his consciousness and only then notify the servant of the fact? Evidently, this is not the case. MANIFESTATION OF WILL OF THE ORDER GIVER IS NOT NOTIFYING THE ADDRESSEE ABOUT WHAT HAD HAPPENED BUT EXTERNALIZING THE PROCESS OF SETTLING A NORM, WHICH TAKES PLACE SIMULTANEOUSLY IN THE CONSCIOUSNESS OF THE ORDER GIVER. "I order you" does not mean "I am notifying you that I have settled a norm which obliges you", but rather: "Be informed that I am now SETTLING a norm which obliges you!". Naturally, the order giver has been keeping the content of the norm in his consciousness in the form of an outline when he decides to settle it, but he settles it and adds "want" or "should" to the preconceived content at the same time as he externalizes his act of will. This is the state of affairs which is meant by ISSUING an order. Issuing an order before the moment of obliging the addressee, a time break between manifestation of the order giver's will and this moment, is rational and often necessary, but settling a heteronomous ordering norm before the said manifestation of will would make no sense (not to mention that even then it would be an order). The addressee of an order may be obliged AFTER the order giver's will manifests itself, but he cannot be obliged BEFORE the manifestation of will, according to the principle: "*Impossibilium nulla obligatio*". Settling a norm at a different time than the moment the order giver's will was manifested would be contradictory to the natural course of events.

A heteronomous ordering norm is directed at the outside world and may play a role in it before it takes effect or even if it never does (for example, when the condition is not fulfilled). Therefore settling the norm before the moment of obligation is quite natural, but settling it before externalizing it would be contradictory to the nature of a heteronomous order.

Symptoms of order giving will assume various forms. Under some conditions an order can even be issued through a gesture; if words are used, the form is most commonly imperative, which cannot be considered as a linguistic equivalent of an order, as this form is also used to indicate a request, a demand or advice. The words: "Bring me a glass of water!" could just as well be a request as an order. The meaning is often determined by the tone of voice or facial expression. It is relatively uncommon that an order is issued in the form of a sentence which clearly states that someone should do something or not do something.

The element of unilaterality distinguishes an order and an agreement, whereas the element of settling a norm clearly distinguishes an order from other unilateral acts of will, in particular requests and demands. A DEMAND, just as an order, is an act of will directed at another person; the aim is also the addressee's behaviour and the means to achieve it; the means leading to this aim is affecting the addressee's will through notifying him of the demander's act of will. However, there is no such thing as settling a norm here; the demander does not 'impose' any obligations on the addressee. Admittedly, a demand may have a great normative meaning, but it is as a condition for the validity of a norm rather than its settling. The idea that the person who one directs the demand at should fulfil it is never included in the demand as such; whenever it accompanies a demand, it is only an expression of the fact that the demand is a condition for implementing a norm, its validity, a condition of the same kind as, for example, *Insula in flumine nata* is a condition for application of the said norm of civil law, which does not imply that this natural phenomenon contains any normative elements.

A demand may be justified in a norm (for instance, a plaintiff's demand in a civil court case) and then it is usually connected with declaring the addressee's obligations, which is limited to explicating the content of a norm and the logical connection between the content and a demand, and does not include settling a norm, as in the case of orders. Still, there are cases where a demand is not based on any norm, or is even contradictory to all existing norms in the consciousness of the demander. Such a state of affairs occurs, for instance, in the case of blackmail and robbery. There is no question of any obligation on the part of the victim, neither in the consciousness of the person blackmailing by threatening to reveal some secret, nor anyone else. Similarly, in the case of a robbery, the robber DEMANDS money from a victim, threatening to kill him, but does not order, since even from the point of view of the demander there is no question of OBLIGATION to hand money over on the part of the victim.

Another group of cases where the difference between a demand and an order is particularly vivid is characterized by the demand being based on a norm which obliges the demander but does not oblige the addressee, or even contradicts what the demander considers the other side's obligation. For instance, a commander of an army which besieges an enemy's stronghold demands that its commander surrender immediately, otherwise he will destroy the stronghold together with its crew. In this case, the demander fulfils his obligation, stated in the norm dictating him to take the most effective military action possible in order for his country's victory. He is not in the least concerned with the will of the addressee of the demand (the commander of the stronghold), but this is intuitive as the stronghold commander's obligation is to defend it, against the demander's will. In some cases, fulfilling the demand would even result in invoking feelings of disrespect on the part of the demander. Conversely, in the case where the same commander issues a law obliging the citizens of a besieged city after having conquered it. Then it would be called an order, or settling an obliging norm, and those who will not obey will become rebels who neglect their obligations (whether it is only from the point of view the order giver is another thing).

A REQUEST differs from a demand in that it is conditional in character. The condition is the fact that the addressee wants the same thing as the person requesting. The above condition clearly does not concern the act of will of the person requesting as such, as he wants the request to be fulfilled regardless of the addressee's view; it is not the act of will of the person requesting that is conditioned but rather fulfilling the request by the addressee. "I want you to do this if you will (and not: I want you to do this if you also want the same thing)", is the form which expresses the essence of a request. The person requesting does not restrict the addressee's will in any way; he wants to influence it but does not restrain it in any way; from the point of view of the person requesting, the request does not hinder the addressee's freedom of choice whether or not to fulfil it.[58] Whereas a demander does not take into account the addressee's freedom; he wants the addressee to fulfil the demand whether he likes it or not.

Thus unilaterality is a common feature of orders, demands and requests; what distinguishes demands and requests from orders is the lack of the settlement of a norm. It is not in conflict with the fact that both a request and a demand can become a condition for the application of norms. We mentioned it before in the context of a demand; the same applies to a request. There are requests whose fulfilment is dictated by a norm, but the norm is never settled in a request.

A common feature of an order and a demand, contrary to request, is inexorability, which can be defined as not respecting the addressee's will. A demand, as well as a command, is in its nature an attack on the addressee's freedom, whether effective or not. This (intended) restriction of the addressee's will in an order is a derivative of unilaterality and settling a norm; if one declares a norm which obliges the addressee through one's own act of will, one does not take into account the direction of addressee's free will. Conversely, in the case of a demand, inexorability is an essential feature; the active party simply declares that their will prevents the passive party's will from being realized in determined direction and demands compliance to the requestor's will.

Although in natural speech, and even in legislation, the notions of order and demand are not properly differentiated, and it is at times hard to decide whether a given manifestation of will is an order or a demand, it would be wrong to claim there is no such distinction in real life. If a

---

[58] *Cf.* Somló [1917: 195].

clerk demands from his superiors the payment of his salary on time, or a taxpayer demands settling his tax on a level no higher than the law provides, or a soldier demands to be released from the army after the period of military service, it is recognized as quite natural. If these same people came forward with an order of the same content, they would be ridiculed. This is because one will does not receive higher rank than another in a demand, therefore even within a hierarchy, subordinates issue demands towards their superiors. The essence of an order, on the other hand, is putting one individual above another; when one creates a norm through their own act of will, one emphatically elevates oneself above the addressee. To order someone is to ascribe to one's will the ability to determine what the addressee should do, regardless of the content of the latter's will. An order giver regards the addressee's will as a passive tool of his will rather than a human will equal to his. Therefore certain inexorability, or one might say: brutality, lies in the nature of an order, and it is worth noting that, apart from the army and monastic life, all other spheres of social life are characterized by driving to conceal orders under a pretence of other events. Within civil service (perhaps with the exception of judicial system) everything is necessarily based on orders issued by superiors, but using this word would often be treated as manifestation of bad manners; the superior does not order his subordinate; he "asks" him, or at most "instructs" him. This very symptom occurs in the family, at school and for hired labourers. Only the army is exempt from such tendencies; on the contrary, this manner of organizing life within a group highlights the importance of order; the subordinates' unquestioning obedience to the will of the superiors is in fact as necessary as in many other domains of social life, but in the army this necessity is more evident, and the consequences of loosening the rigor more severe and immediate.

Naturally, in accordance with the most essential features of human nature, one should pose the question of why one man assumes a position of that sort towards another; what empowers the order giver to claim that his will is the source of what others should do. However, this issue does not fall within the scope of the present paper, since justification is not an essential feature of an order. When an order giver fails to justify his

standpoint (*Sic volo, sic iubeo, stat pro ratione voluntas*), we are still dealing with an order, as well as when the order giver invokes a higher authority or an settled norm (for instance, an ethical norm which dictates children to be obedient to their parents), or finally, an agreement under which
one person undertakes to be obedient in some respect (contractor agreements). Yet, orders which the order giver does not even attempt to justify
are a rare occurrence.

The issue of justifying an order is closely connected to the issue of justifying state authority; this problem played an important part in the history
of the Theory of State, and is still relevant now. Authority (in the objective sense) is a relation of subordinating the will of some people to the will
of others, either factual or normative. In the actual sense, authority occurs
wherever the will of one person (or a group of persons) unilaterally determines actual behaviour of other persons; no normative elements may occur in this relationship (for instance, a bandit who terrorizes people living
in a given area has actual power); this kind of "power" clearly needs no justification. Normative subordination occurs when one person should obey
another from the point of view of a norm. An order is a kind of unilateral
settlement of such norm, which is why any ordering relationship is a relationship of power,[59] and not the other way around. Still, such a norm settled
by an order giver is not enough. He may want to rely on some other, higher
norm, possibly also accepted by the addressee of the order; hence attempts
to justify an order. State authority is in its essence a complex of ordering relationships, where ordering norms are usually realized by the addressees; in
the SUBJECTIVE sense, state authority is the authorization to order resulting
from a norm (if only from the ordering norm of that authority). Therefore
the question of why a citizen should obey certain people (the monarch, the
government, the parliament, the majority of people, *etc.*), in other words,

---

[59] Znamierowski [1924: 43] is right only insofar as he claims that an order may only
be issued by a person who has power. Undoubtedly, a person who issues an order appears as authority to the addressee on the power of this act. However, the order may be
treated as unfounded, or even as absurd pretence for power from any other viewpoint
(for instance: a student ordering a teacher to give him a good grade). Still, a student
DEMANDING this same outcome from a teacher could be perfectly reasonable and valid
is some circumstances.

why the authority of some people is legitimate, what its "source" is, is nothing more than the issue of justifying certain orders. Historically, the most important attempts to justify those orders are: the idea of God's order, the idea of social contract, and the idea of the will of the nation.

Tadeusz Kotarbiński. Norms and normative theses
[1929: 445 – 446, 448 – 449]

Misunderstandings often arise [...] around the topic of norms, just as in the case of evaluations, since the word "norm" signifies both proper norms and normative sentences. The former are understood as utterances in the form of order, advice, warning, *etc.*, such as: "Do not kill!", "Love thy enemy!", *etc.* Proper norms, fundamentally and intrinsically, do not belong to the realm of science, as they are not true or false, and not even declarative sentences at all. It is then impossible neither to verify in the sense of showing their truthfulness nor to falsify them in the sense of showing their falsity. One can only overcome or propagate them. It is different in the case of normative sentences, that is sentences such as: "In order for such and such event to occur, it is necessary to behave actively in a given way", or "In order for such and such event to occur, it is enough to behave actively in a given way", *etc.*, or: "Such and such activity would be abominable", "It would be fair to act in such a way in this situation", *etc.* Normative sentences are declarative sentences; some of them are true, others are false; one can prove or disprove them scientifically in many cases. This way one may contribute to the success or failure of a proper norm. While proving the following normative sentence: "In order to prevent a child from catching smallpox, it is enough to vaccinate it", one contributes to the success of the proper norm: "Vaccinate against smallpox" in the circle of people who care about their children's health. Let us notice that normative sentences are evaluations of a kind, namely, evaluations of possible acts. They concern acts which were not performed, but which are going to be performed or not performed, depending on one's decision. Whether we call a sentence of this kind an evaluation or a norm (in the sense of normative sentence) in a given case, generally depends on a more precise direction of interest. That is, if we focus on the considered action and we are interested in what consequences it leads to, then we will sooner use the term 'evaluation' in respect to a thesis stating whether the action would be enough to achieve something or if it would be necessary to achieve something; whereas if we care more about a given aim and we consider what could lead to it, then we are more willing to call this type of thesis a norm (in the sense of normative sentence). The above is true for materiel evaluations; as for emotional evaluations of possible actions, there is little visible hesitation in recognizing evaluations in such norms. Normative sentences can be divided into MATERIEL (see the first two examples of normative sentences above) and EMOTIONAL (see the latter two examples). We can also distinguish between general and individual ones. The former concern all examples of possible behaviour of a given kind; the latter concern a certain possible example. [...]

Normative sentences face [...] the objection [of not being scientific sentences]. This is justified by the claim that they do not state how things really are but how they should be, how things ought to go. On the other hand, advocates of counting [...] the discussed disciplines [that is, normative fields] into science could at least attempt to partly replicate the following content. Evaluations, even emotional ones, are true or false sentences, then if we rightly assess, accurately appraise something as "beautiful", "disgraceful", *etc.*, or in particular, if we evaluate something rightly (that is, we think about it rightly, with conviction), then we learn about it in a way. As for norms (or more precisely: normative sentences), it is true that in a sense they do not say: "this is so". However, it is only true for those meanings of words which require the same comment about various non-normative sentences which belong to the field of mechanics, physics, physiology or other sciences. In the fields of science mentioned above it is proclaimed that "If so and so happens, so and so will happen" or "In order for so and so to exist, so and so has to exist first" or " So and so is enough to cause so and so to happen", *etc.* Here are some examples: "If two spheres of identical mass, completely resilient, running along the collision line with equal speed, collide, then they will rebound in opposite directions with the same speed", "In order for frozen water to reach a temperature above zero degrees, some amount of heat has to be used for its melting", "A viper bite is enough to induce symptoms of serious illness", All of these sentences proclaim, in a sense, that "if this is (was, will be, would be) true, then that is (was, will be, would be) true also", rather than "it is so and so", as they are hypothetical sentences rather than categorical ones. Among such sentences we can distinguish sentences concerning possible matters, which proclaim that "if it was so and so in the future, then it would be so and so in the future (earlier, at the same time, or later)", *etc.*, or proclaiming that "if it is so and so then it will be so and so (earlier, at the same time, or later)", *etc.* Moreover, in a certain supplementary sense, they do not proclaim that "it is so and so" since they refer to the future. Normative sentences are some among those conditional sentences referring to the future, and they "are not concerned with what is", only in the two indicated meanings of the expression. This alone would not be enough to reject them from the group of scientific sentences. Normative sentences stand out among the above mentioned sentences only in one aspect: one of the parts of a normative sentence is always a description of a possible action. Less importantly, the one who proclaims the norm usually considers the activity to be EXECUTABLE, and usually, which is also irrelevant here, the second part of a normative sentence takes the form of a description of something which the proclaiming person wished for himself or another person. The following is an example of a normative sentence: "Criminals should be overpowered in order to retain public safety" (in other words: "If public safety is retained, then criminals have been previously overpowered"), or the sentence: "It is enough to take care of a dog to win its affection" (in other words: "If someone takes care of a dog, he will win its affection"). In the first sentence the possible action took on the role of a necessary condition and the remaining part ("safety will be retained", "he will win the dog's affection") represents something which the proclaiming person probably wishes for himself or another person.

EMOTIONAL NORMATIVE SENTENCES constitute a special kind of normative sentences, as it is possible to represent them in the form of "If a given person does so and so (in a special case: "If I do so and so"), his deed will be fine (despicable, noble, dishonourable...)". Here a description of a possible action appears as an antecedent of conditional sentence and the consequent is in the form of emotional evaluation. As a consequence of this argument, it becomes understandable what the actual meaning of the thesis is which claims that normative sentences say "what should be" or "what should be according to our intentions". If we say so, then it is claimed that normative sentences concern possible actions, or they concern that which is needed to do something which is described in the form of an emotional evaluation. It is therefore clear that talking about "what should be", *etc.*, or in other words: "what should be the state of affairs", *etc.*, does not cease to be identical with talking about "what the state of affairs is" in some regard.

Tadeusz Kotarbiński. Classification of norms
[1931: 410–415]

Prolegomena [*do nauki o państwie* [*to the study of state*] by Czesław Znamierowski] [1930] leave the reader in doubt [...] as to the character of the distinction between norms and descriptions declared in the principle. The distinction would be clear and decisive if one insisted on the norms to dictate, prohibit or permit while claiming nothing, and descriptions claim; therefore, norms are not logical sentences, so they do not fall under the distinction of true or false. In that case there would be a norm in the following regulation: "Let John go to the post office every day!". Saying "John should go to the post office every day" would only be a replacement for the former sentence; an illusion of a logical sentence. However, I doubt that these are the Author's intentions, [...] even though He considers the utterance: "Let so and so be the case!" to be a verbal expression of an intention to action, or the content of creative *fiat* [1930: 67] [...]. After all, He must allow the entailment from norms and entailment of norms, understood in the logical sense, if he supposes that "by the power of logic" [1930: 174], since whoever reaches the shore in his boat should moor it in an assigned place, and because Peter reached the shore, he should moor his boat in an assigned place [1930: 173, 174]. He also writes: "... it will become true that: "B should do d"" [1930: 220]. Moreover, at times his statements suggest that he identifies

the meaning of saying "Should do so and so" with saying "Do so and so!".
Here is an example: "Sentence «Take (you should take) the first left» was
for *P* the directive of his activity" [1930: 8, also 20, 52].

Consolidation of all which was stated about validity of norms in *Pro-legomena* requires a lot of effort on the part of the reader. The topic is mentioned in many places and for many reasons. Here, the large index may prove
helpful, although it is not without gaps (*e.g.* under "order" there does not appear an important entry from p. 118, verse 15, which seems to contain a definition of an order), and slightly whimsical, as is the use of sparse print, since,
for example, some entries appear under "application of norms" and others appear under "norm application". Therefore, with the help of the index, among
other things, and a bunch of quotations gathered from it and also from outside the index, we can figure out that the author uses the words: "exist" (about
norms), "oblige" and "should" in the meanings which take getting used to. We
read, among other fragments, "Existence, that is obligation of norm"... [1930:
18]. We should then keep in mind that it is not "existence" in the ontological sense; that "norm exists" does not mean simply "something is a norm" in
the Author's language, instead, it means that the norm obliges. Here appear
some questions without explicit answers: according to the Author of *Prolegomena,* do norms exist in the ontological sense or are they only spoken of as
if they existed, and if they exist in the ontological sense, then do they exist in
the world of perceptible things (if the norms were to be inscriptions or a set of
movements) or in some sham world of ideal objects (if they were to be content symbolized in inscriptions or another set of signs). The manner in which
the Author expresses his thoughts may lead the reader to think that the latter
is true, which is not exactly to the liking of the author of the present paper.
Later we learn that a person may settle a norm which, in spite of this, does not
oblige (that is, when he demands an executable act) [1930: 32]. The conclusion may then be drawn that in this case the norm does not exist, although it
has been settled, since in order for it to obliged, or to exist, it is necessary that
the intended act be executable. Therefore, settlement is not a sufficient condition for obligation [1930: 59].

The settlement of norms which advocate unexecutable, self-contradictory acts is not thwarted by the so-called "principle of contradiction"

which was coined somewhat hastily, since the term has other established meanings in logic as well as in the psychology of judgement. The principle of contradiction in norms postulates that no one can settle a norm if they are aware during the settlement that the norm demands self-contradictory action [1930: 27, 28]. Further explanation [1930: 32] does not leave any doubt as to the awareness of the Author of the limited value of the rule of contradiction, especially in the light of the fact that the rule does not prevent from settling such norms in the case of a self-contradiction concealed from the settling person. After all, we read further to discover an expression, which is clearly too bold for the above mentioned reasons: "... one cannot settle obligation concerning impossible acts" [1930: 54], one may add: "consciously" or "effectively". However, settlement is not the necessary condition for validity, since for example when a norm is settled, a derived, though unsettled, "norm of general prohibition" begins to apply ([1930: 34, 35, 183]; in the proof [1930: 34] there is a defect through the introduction of unjustified simultaneousness), contrasting a moral norm with a settled norm [1930: 98] leads to the assumption that some unsettled, and therefore moral, norms oblige.

The word "should" is used in a very general role here, certainly not limited to the domain of moral dictates or social rules, as an element of an issue of norm which advocates a given act, even if the norm is settled by an individual to himself [1930: *e.g.* 8, 14]. There arises in this background a question connected with the phrase: "... the product of the settlement is that the following will become true: "*B* should do *d*"" [1930: 220)]. The question is whether the Author agrees that: if it is true that *p*, then *p* (and therefore, if it is true that *B* should do *d*, then *B* should do *d*). If so, then the following consequences may arise: (1) When the father tells his son to leave the room and the mother tells him to stay, the son should leave and the son should not leave, therefore the son should act contradictorily. This generally applies to norms which are mutually contradictory, despite the presented reasoning on a contrary tendency [1930: 59], deceptively suggestive thanks to the comparison with activity of magnets which neutralize each other. (2) If a barbarian, for example John, settled a norm that the Author's work should be burnt, the Author would have to draw the conclusion of a norm on burning his work from stating the fact of this settlement taking place. He would have to argue thus: John settled that *Prolegomena* should be burnt (p), and if John settled that *Prolegomena* should be burnt (p), then it is true that *Prolegomena* should be burnt ($p < q$), then it is true that *Prolegomena* should be burnt (q by virtue of the form of inference called "modes ponendo ponens"); and if it is true that *Prolegomena* should be burnt, then *Prolegomena* should be burnt ($q < r$), and therefore *Prolegomena* should be burnt (r, with the same method). In general, if anyone settled anything, the author himself would have to recommend what the person had settled as a consequence of acknowledging the fact of settling. A possible solution would be to note the ambiguity of the phrase: "B should do d" which may recommend that person B does act d or just state that the act was recommended. In the quoted fragment from p. 220 the Author probably uses the word "should" in the latter meaning, although he generally uses it in the former meaning throughout his book. As we noticed, He may not be aware of this difference.

Two fundamentally different definitions of the term "isolated norm" are opposed here: (1) "...if an isolated individual does not possess any other norm except the very norm N" [1930: 25]; (2) "... if, after we substitute definite values with variable norms included in the formula, then we obtain the following form of a norm: "P willed it that P settled that P should (can) c"" [1930: 98]. Clearly, two different meanings of "isolation" are meant here: in the first case, it is the isolation of a given norm from other norms for this person, and in the second case, it is the isolation from interference on the part of the settling person, excluding the addressee. It is the reader's task to figure out that the same term is used in two different functions (which should have been distinguished by adding relativizing complements).

The classification of norms from the point of view of logical forms [1930: 169 *et seq*.] proves incomplete, even if only the differences in quantification according to persons and conditions are taken into consideration. For example, the following norm does not fit in the classification: "Some (at least one, a certain...) soldier from the 2nd regiment should deliver a report to one of the nearest posts one dark night". (Certain A should perform one of the actions from the kind c in one case of the occurrence of conditions w), since only the cases of individual or universal treatment of 'A' and 'w' were taken into consideration (single A, single w; single A, each w; each A, single w; each A, each w), whereas the cases of individual treatment of 'A' or 'w' were omitted, which amounts to five cases in total, not mentioning three analogous possible combinations with 'c'.

Jerzy Sztykgold. Negation of a norm
[1936]

1.1. Normative theories of law aspire to be theories of sentences which express duty and not to be formal logic. They seek specific methods and, as a result, they do not go beyond this search and definition of law. The psychological theory of ethics does not deal with norms. So far, no one has gathered all formal logic applicable to norms; no one has settled the conditions for equivalence of norms. Psychologists are not even certain whether only one formulation of an ethical experience or several equivalent norms correspond to the said experience in our speech. They are also not certain whether, on the other hand, for each formulation of normative content there exists an equivalent in the form of a discrete, specific ethical experience, or whether there exist such ethical norms that our mind does not update in a manner specific to ethical judgements.

1.2. Both the normative and the psychological theories of law deal exclusively with judgements (logical or psychological) expressing rights and responsibilities, and overlook those judgements in the definitions of law where the lack of rights or the lack of responsibilities is detected. Still, theses of these theories are also valid in relation to the latter judgements.

1.3. It should be determined which theses of logistics, which is a settled study of phrases, apply to sentences which express rights and responsibilities, the lack of rights and the lack of responsibilities.

2.1. Criteria of validity or non-validity, which are closely connected to the criteria of truth and falsity, apply to norms.

2.2. Therefore all theses of sentential calculus also apply to norms.

3. From the point of view of the calculus of relative sentences, one may express the following thesis on the relation between rights and responsibilities: there are such couples of manners of behaviour wherein the relation of

rights to one of them is equivalent to the lack of responsibilities towards the other, and conversely: the relation of responsibilities towards one of them is equivalent to the lack of rights to the other. For instance: the relation "*A* is obliged to tell the truth" is equivalent to the relation "*A* has no right to lie". How are these couples of manners of behaviour characterized? I CLAIM THAT THE EQUIVALENCE IS FULFILLED FOR THOSE MANNER OF BEHAVIOUR WHERE ONE IS THE INVERSE OF THE OTHER. What I understand as inverse behaviour is such behaviour which complements first behaviour to its nearest precedent class, to its *genus proximum*. For instance, "lying" is inverse to "telling the truth". The closest precedent class to "telling the truth" is "uttering sentences". Within "uttering sentences", all that is not "telling the truth" is its inverse: "lying". A formulated law allows for the formulation of the relation of entitlement through the lack of obligation and the relation of obligation through the lack of entitlement.

4.1. The above law is adequate to a category of relations which is wider than just the relation of rights and responsibilities. It is also valid for relations of the POSSIBILITY and NECESSITY (if only teleological) of certain behaviour. For instance, the relation "*A* must walk faster if he wants to be on time" is equivalent to the relation "*A* cannot walk more slowly or at the same pace if he wants to make it". One cannot create an adequate logistic "pure theory of law", but one may utter logistic judgements relevant for legal theory.

4.2. For the psychological theory of ethics, what results from the above considerations is that for a certain ethical experience there exist at least two equivalent projections – formulations in the domain of speech – and therefore attempting to identify a discrete and specific experience for every conceivable norm is a systematic error and may not bring satisfactory results.

Discussion:

Witold Steinberg. A mirror image is a real object, not an ideal one, even though one cannot touch it. If an ethical norm is a sentence which contains the words: "is entitled", or "is obliged", then in the case of inexclusive "or" a paradox becomes possible in which the same action is at the same time entitled and obliged. However, an obligatory action cannot be entitled in the same system of a norm. One should distinguish sentences which state the lack of obligation in a descriptive manner from sentences which express the lack of obligation in a normative manner.

Walter Auerbach. The general intention of the paper resemble Meinong's ideas (relation of omission) and his disciple Mally's (inference system for deontics in *Grundgesetze des Sollens*). Whether one recognizes "the relation of obligation" as triple, depends on the ethical standpoint; in some ethical standpoints it would be considered as a ternary relation.

Tadeusz Kotarbiński. I do not sense any material objections to the speaker's reflections on the types of utterances discussed by him. Still, I believe these are self-evident uses of laws known from formal logic which concern sentential negation and nominal negation. However, it would be interesting to consider the relation of logical negations to those negations which constitute a part of prohibitions (for instance: "Do not come in!"), as neither the whole prohibition nor its part which follows the negation are either true or false sentences, whereas logical sentential negation produces a true or false whole (and is often attached to such sentences).

The speaker's response:

1. There are norms which determine certain behaviour, both entitlement and obligation, for instance: entitlement to vote is in some countries simultaneously an obligation.

2. I consider the relation of entitlement to obligation to be triple and I believe this view is independent of the ethical standpoint, but rather it is based on the rule of examining whole utterances instead of incomplete utterances.

3. In the present paper, the speaker only intended to collect those logical theses which are applicable to expressions as sentence-creating functors "is entitled" and "is obliged", without dealing with expressions of different types.

Mieczysław Wallis-Walfisz. Normative phrases

[1937: 434–437]

[1.] Norms and normative sentences

One needs to distinguish between evaluating sentences [*propositions de valeur*], which express evaluations, and normative sentences [*phrases normatives*] – commandments [*commandements*], dictates and prohibitions, regulations, rules, postulates, general directions which express norms, that is judgements of whether someone should or should not act in a given way.

Norms and their utterances, that is normative sentences, are of general nature, contrary to commissions [*ordres*], which have an *ad hoc* character and which are no longer valid when they have been executed. The piece of advice: "Take an umbrella!" is not a normative sentence, whereas a Chinese wise man's saying "Always take an umbrella, even if the weather is fine" is one. The statement: "Peter should go for a walk" is not a normative sentence, but it will become one if we say: "Peter should go for a walk every day".

Normative sentences may concern everybody, for example: "One should tell the truth"; they may only concern members of a specific group of people, for example: "A Muslim should not drink wine"; or even just one person, for example: "Peter should go for a walk every day". Normative sentences also belong to that last category, since a given person creates them for himself, for example: "Play the piano every day!", "Do not smoke!". However, these sentences are of a general nature just in themselves.

[2.] Normative sentences from the grammar-logical point of view

Normative sentences can be divided into three groups with respect to the grammar-logical perspective.

I. Normative sentences which take the form of imperative sentences,[60] for example: "Love thy neighbour", "Keep smiling!", "You shall not kill", "Let the plot focus on one day and place and attract the viewer's attention from beginning till end" (Boileau).

II. Normative sentences which take the form of indicative sentences which contain expressions such as: "one should", "one must", "it is proper", *etc.*, for example: "Each person should be treated as an aim in himself" (Kant), "One should keep their commitments", "*Nil desperandum*".

III. Normative sentences which take the form of indicative sentences which do not contain expressions such as: "one should", "one must", "it

---

[60] Through "imperative sentences" I understand such sentences whose predicates are either in an imperative mood or a form similar to it.

IS PROPER", *ETC.*, for example: "During a tennis game one hits the first ball diagonally towards the smaller rectangle", "One does not hunt partridge in May", "One does not talk of rope in the house of a hanged man".

Sentences which belong to group III, which do not contain expressions like: "one should", "one must", *etc.*, seem to be propositions at first glance, and they are indeed if we accept them as being strictly descriptive. If someone writing a description of a tennis game states, "During a tennis game one hits the first ball diagonally towards the smaller rectangle", or if someone describing hunting traditions in a given country states, "One does not hunt partridge in May", they produce true propositions. However, if we are to use these sentences to express norms, these sentences are only contractions where elements like "one should", "one must", *etc.* are implied. Then the sentence: "During a tennis game one hits the first ball diagonally towards the smaller rectangle", means: "During a tennis game one should hit the first ball diagonally towards the smaller rectangle", whereas the sentence: "One does not hunt partridge in May", really means: "One must not hunt partridge in May".

This way, normative sentences can be reduced to three types from the grammar-logical point of view: imperative sentences and those which do or do not contain expressions like: "one should", "one must", *etc.*

It seems that every sentence of the first type can be transformed into an equivalent sentence of the second type and vice versa. The sentence: "You shall not kill" is equivalent to the sentence "You must not kill", and the sentence: "Let us keep unity of time, place and plot in a drama" is equivalent to: "One has to keep unity of time, place and plot in a drama". It also works the other way; the sentence: "Each person should be treated as an aim in himself" is equivalent to the sentence: "Treat each person as an aim in himself"; "One must fulfil commitments" means the same as "Fulfil your commitments!".

There arises a question of which of these transformations is more beneficial for us from the theoretical point of view: transforming imperative sentences into those which contain expressions like: "one should", "one must", *etc.* or transforming sentences which contain expressions like: "one should", "one must", *etc.* into imperative sentences.

There are two arguments in favour of the latter solution:

(1) Expressions such as "one should", "one must", *etc.* are ambiguous. Therefore eliminating them or refraining from their use is beneficial.

(2) The logical structure of imperative sentences is clearer that the logical structure of sentences which contain expressions like: "one should", "one must", *etc.* It seems one can transform any normative sentence into a corresponding imperative sentence. Imperative sentences do not undergo evaluation according to their truth value and are not propositions. Therefore, normative sentences also do not undergo evaluation according to their truth value and are not propositions.

[3.] Normative sentences and evaluating sentences

At the base of each normative sentence there is an evaluating sentence. For example, the base of the commandment, "You shall not kill" is an evaluating sentence, "Killing is a sin", or, "Killing is immoral", or, "Killing is a crime". The base of the principle: "Let us keep unity of time, place and plot in every drama" is an evaluating sentence: "A drama in which unity of time, place and plot are kept is beautiful".

However, can we go [fluently] from evaluating sentences to normative sentences superstructured over them, or from true or false sentences to those which do not undergo such an evaluation, or from propositions to non--declarative sentences? Most scholars would deny such a possibility, since they believe that normative sentences cannot be proved or exposed as false; they can only be either propagated or overpowered. Yet, this issue will not be considered here.

Izydora Dąmbska. Imperatives and relativized norms
[1938: 242–243, 263–266]

Researchers of conditional sentences usually limit their analysis to conditional UTTERANCES, that is sentences in the logical sense, which are either true or false. Some even define a conditional sentence as a sentence which expresses A hypothetical JUDGEMENT. This sort of description seems too narrow, since there exist sentences structured in a similar way as conditional utterances, which express questions, orders, wishes, requests, resolutions, *etc.* Among those, only the sentences which express resolutions can be counted as utterances, both because of their morphological structure and because resolutions can be considered as a kind of judgements about the future. Sentences which express resolutions are true or false; this feature is a property of utterances. Yet, sentences remain which express requests, orders and questions. Are these conditional sentences?

Seemingly, the following reasoning speaks to the contrary: a characteristic feature of a conditional sentence is that its meaning is not the meaning of the condition clause or the consequence clause, but rather something different that is based on these meanings. Moreover, the meaning of the whole conditional sentence falls in the same logical category as the meaning of the parts considered separately, regardless of their role in a conditional sentence. These conditions are fulfilled only by conditional utterances, and not by sentences. In a way, the meaning of those sentences is the determined meaning of the second part of the conditional sentence (question, order, request) and moreover, the meaning of the whole conditional belongs to a different logical category than the meaning of the antecedent in itself. One could say that the sentences concerned are interrogatives, imperatives, *etc.*, but the question or order they express are in some way determined by whatever is expressed by this segment of a sentence which is in the form of an antecedent of a conditional utterance. However, the fact that some element of sentence of the type 'n' (in this case: the antecedent of a conditional sentence) occurs in a different combination (in this case: together with an imperative, an interrogative, *etc.*) does not result in other combinations also becoming sentences of the type 'n'.

The above reasoning would perhaps be convincing if not for a certain freedom in accepting both premises, that is, assuming it is important in the case of conditional sentences that the meaning of the whole sentence is not the meaning of the antecedent or the consequent, but rather something different from either, which is based on those meanings, and also that the meaning of the whole conditional sentence belongs to the same logical category as the meaning of both of the parts considered separately. The conditions fulfilled by conditional utterances do not have to be necessary for all conditional sentences. Anyway, the first argument is only valid for a specific interpretation of conditional utterances. For example, it would not be important for a person who claims, according to Pfänder, that the meaning of a conditional utterance is the meaning of the restricted consequence clause. Pfänder's interpretation does not seem right here; still, for the reasons cited above, the argumentation leading to identifying the scope "conditional sentence" with the scope "conditional utterance" can probably be rightfully rejected.

Admittedly, one could accept arbitrarily the definition of the term "conditional sentence" which would define the specific scope of it. However, there is concern that in that case one would encounter significant difficulties in the analysis of these interrogatives, imperatives, *etc.* Morphologically, they undoubtedly belong to the same category of sentences as conditional utterances, and some common features can also be detected in their semantic aspect.

Therefore, I believe the notion of a conditional sentence should be expanded so that it encompasses utterances as well as interrogative, imperative and optative sentences. Until now, the analysis was restricted to conditional utterance, without taking into consideration other types of conditional sentence, which can be explained by the fact that the people dealing with it were almost exclusively logicians, who are primarily interested in sentences which are true or false, that is utterances. Still, some of them took on a secondary interest in the form of conditional sentences which are not utterances (and so for example Rostohar mentions an interrogative conditional sentence). The present paper will deal with interrogative and imperative conditional sentences in more detail, but first conditional utterances will undergo analysis: their morphological and semantic structure as well as their relation to other utterances. [...]

Imperative conditional sentences express a relativized order or a relativized norm. The relativization of an order or a norm in a conditional sentence consists in demanding the fulfilment of an order or we believe that one can only behave in a certain way as long as there occurs the state of affairs mentioned in the antecedent. For example, "If someone is quick-tempered, do not give him any hot food!",[61] [...] "If any of you wants to be my

---

[61] The quotation comes from Rey's *Zwierciadło* [Mirror] [my footnote – JJ].

follower, you must turn from your selfish ways, take up your cross daily, and follow me!"[62] [...], *etc.* It is clear in these examples that the question is not to ban hot food altogether or to deny oneself completely; the prohibition and the dictate is relativized to specific conditions. Seemingly, examples like the ones below speak to the contrary: "Do it if you love me!", "Get out if you want to live!", *etc.* Anyone uttering such sentences does not mean by them that something has to be done in the occurrence of such and such conditions, but rather wants to make his command more effective through a kind of emotional appeal. His command is absolute and not conditional. How to reconcile this fact with what had been previously stated? It seems that we can resort to Marty's hypothesis about "internal speech". The intentions of the one uttering a sentence are not always consistent with the actual meaning of this sentence. What is more, as the expression is used more often to represent some other, "unofficial", content, the unofficial content becomes the meaning. Yet, a person unfamiliar with phrases such as "Get out if you want to live!" may experience the actual meaning of the sentence and accept the order as a conditioned order.

One the other hand, do non-relativized orders and norms – absolute orders and norms – exist? Is not the fact that an activity that should be performed or neglected in order to achieve a goal is a part of the notion of an order and a norm? Even if this were true, there is no doubt that in natural speech imperative sentences do not include this common relativization. When an officer orders in front of his detachment: "Present arms!" he does not imagine any relativization of this order, he does not think that the soldiers should present arms in order to fulfil the requirements contained in the military regulations or military salutes. Neither do his soldiers. Neither does anybody else who takes into consideration the natural meaning of the sentence. Therefore, even if one's standpoint is not to acknowledge absolute norms and orders, the difference between a conditional and a categorical imperative sentence remains clear. The difference can be expressed by claiming that a conditional imperative sentence expresses an order or a norm which concerns an activity relativized to the

---

[62] The quotation comes form *The Gospel of St. Luke* [my footnote – JJ].

state of affairs indicated by the conditional phrase in the intention of the giver of the order.

We noted that an imperative sentence expresses an order or a norm. Then what is the difference between an order and a norm? It seems that there are several of them. A norm is a general sentence stating that one should or should not behave in a certain way. If an imperative sentence expresses a norm, then it is equivalent in meaning to a sentence in the form: "One should x" or "One should not x", where the range of the variable x is constituted by names of various courses of behaviour. For example, the sentences: "Do not bear false witness!", "Wash fruit before eating!", *etc.* are equivalent to the sentences: "One should not bear false witness", "You should wash fruit before eating", *etc.* Each norm assumes an evaluation of value. The sentence in the form: "One should x" states implicitly that "x is right", and the sentence in the form of "One should not x" presupposes that "x is wrong".

An order does not necessarily have to be general. In fact, it is often individual, limited to a given time, place and person. An order may but does not have to be compatible with a norm. An order compatible with a norm may be an application of the latter. Then it is incorporated into the activity directed at realization of a norm, for example, when a mother gives fruit to a child and says: "Wash it before eating!". An order may also be incompatible with a norm. A person may believe that "one should x" but order "not-x", for example, when someone who recognizes the norm "Do not kill!" hires a thug and tells him to kill an inconvenient adversary. Thus orders, contrary to norms, do not have to be compatible with evaluations or even presuppose them. There may be order which does not correspond to any norm, whether compatible or incompatible with them, for example, when a boy is sent to the shop and told: "Buy two rolls!".

Moreover, there is a certain difference between an order and a norm connected with the empirical conditions of their formulation. An order, issued in earnest and consciously, is connected with predicting the possibility of its fulfilment. Therefore, conditional imperative sentences which express orders do not occur in *casus irrealis*, as it would be absurd to demand the execution of an action in the presence of a certain condition and to claim at the same time that this condition will not occur. And so, conditional sentences which express orders usually occur in *casus realis* or, less often, *potentialis*. Norms behave otherwise. One can formulate norms which are certain not to be realized in some conditions or even never. Such orders cannot be issued in earnest. Very many ethical norms should probably be counted as practically infeasible. For example, the norm "Do not kill!" taken literally is impracticable. Everyone kills constantly through the very fact of living, eating, breathing. One does not necessarily kill other people, but one does kill plants and animals. We may assume that the norm was wrongly formulated as it is too general. We may also agree that the norm is right but it is infeasible. We may believe that taking life is wrong in itself and therefore one should never kill, with the awareness that killing is inevitable, because such is the organization of the world of nature which humans are a part of. We may recognize the rightness of a theoretically feasible norm and be unable to issue an order to such effect in some cases, because of the lack of competence to order or because of impending sanctions, or because of the lack of proper conditions to use the norm on the part of the addressee. (For example: the inability to issue an order introducing in life some legitimate hygienic norms in a certain environment if the norms are contradictory to religious regulations operating in this environment.)

Being able to distinguish a norm from an order is of great importance in legislation. The inapplicability of many legal norms is revealed only after the implementing regulation has been issued and attempts have been made to issue orders which exert these norms. The ability to issue feasible orders which enforce a norm is a test of its applicability.

The question arises whether imperative sentences which express norms are imperative sentences only morphologically, while syntactically they are utterances, since they are synonymous to sentences in the form: "One should *x*" or "One should not *x*". If sentences in this form are true or false, then imperative sentences which express norms of behaviour should belong to utterances. Perhaps even imperative sentences which express orders and not norms could be classified as utterances. After all, the person who orders, claims something and the person who prohibits, denies something in somebody else's future activity, considers the activity as ones that are supposed to occur or not, and feels empowered to be a partial cause of these future activity. Yet it seems that in the case of orders and categorical norms, even when they are formulated as declarative sentences, they cannot be treated as equal to utterances. Sentences in which it is stated that "One should *x*" or "One should not *x*" are not resolvable in the same sense as sentences like: "*x* exists", or "*x* does not exist", "*x* is such and such", "*x* is not such and such" are resolvable. Accepting or rejecting categorical imperative sentences necessarily depends on emotional factors and not cognitive factors. But perhaps it is different in the case of conditional imperative sentences? For example, "If there is an epidemic of Foot and Mouth disease in the area, you must not sell cattle", or "If you see someone being bullied, help him". Also in these cases the situation is not much different. This is how much one knows and is able to justify: "If there is an epidemic of Foot and Mouth disease in the area, selling cattle may cause the disease to spread", and "If you see someone being bullied, you can sometimes prevent it by coming forward and acting". But cognitive methods of dispute cannot be used for the sentences which claim that one must not sell cattle in given conditions and that in some conditions one should help. One kind of conditional imperative sentence seems to be an exception, namely, sentences in the form: "If one wants to achieve the aim *x*, one should perform the activity *y*". To exemplify: "If you want to prevent the spread of Foot and Mouth disease, do not sell cattle during an epidemic", "If you do not want to tolerate harm, help those who are being bullied". However, these sentences can hardly be considered as imperative, in the proper meaning of the word. Their content is stating that performing activity *y* is a means to an aim *x* as well as the obvious rule that one has to use some resources in order to achieve an aim. These are not orders or norms in the meaning discussed above. If the content of these sentences included the statement that one should prevent Foot and Mouth disease from spreading or that tolerating harm is wrong, these sentences would take on an emotional character, as mentioned before, and would differ considerably from statements. Therefore it seems that both morphological and semantic properties of imperative conditional sentences indicate that these sentences should be treated as a class different from the class of conditional statements.

Henryk Elzenberg. Imperativism
[1938: 23–28]

A polemic paper with solely negative conclusions is only relevant as long as it opposes a widespread and influential theory. The following remarks do not strictly fulfil this condition; the attack is directed against a fairly general tendency rather than a set and definitive view. However, these theoretical tendencies, not specified into doctrine yet, often have far-reaching practical consequences which cannot leave a moralist indifferent. It is for the reader to decide whether this is the case here and whether the discussed issue is worth raising.

There is a tendency in the theory of obligation which could be called IM-PERATIVISTIC and which, in its purely speculative form, consists of attempting to realize either the NOTION of obligation through the notion of order, or the FACT of obligation through the fact of order; or taking a more normative angle, one could claim, FIRSTLY, that the content of all our obligations is identical to the content of certain orders which were actually issued; and SECONDLY, a derivative claim, though crucial for practice, that in order to learn our obligations it is appropriate to get acquainted with the orders which were actually issued. This is an ethical view which many political and interpersonal systems have relied on to a greater or lesser extent; those systems which aimed to base the whole social order on the principle of pure obedience; as we are aware, those systems are revived now with great force. Therefore, our abstract discussion may prove to be significant in the area of the most substantial and direct reality: since to deny the premises of imperativism is to deprive many contemporary political systems of their philosophical base, which may well not concern the system's advocates in the domain of act, but which will certainly concern a theorist if the base presents essential value.

Naturally, the notion of order does not only appear in ethics advocating heteronomy; in contemporary times it played the most significant role in a decidedly autonomic system. Therefore, one might be tempted to deem acceptable the theoretical standpoint which would be imperativistic in the scope of the ethics of autonomy. However, it seems that it would be a mistake (and let us omit the reasoning leading to it, as it would not fit in these pages); in fact, an autonomist mentioning an ethical order or dictate uses the term in a purely figurative sense. Also in Kant's work, one should speak not of the NOTION of an order, but rather – without any pejorative intentions – of A certain PHRASEOLOGY of an order, that is, of a certain repertory of figurative phrases drawn from this field, which screen the notion which is essentially different and insufficiently precised. Let us then assume that imperativism makes sense only in heteronomical ethics, and we will attempt to discuss it only in this area; an order under discussion here will therefore invariably come from the outside.

The way we have defined it, the imperativistic tendency may probably be expressed through THREE different theoretical views. These views are clearly mutually exclusive, although all three can be subsumed under the general theory of imperativism mentioned before, which seems very flexible. In other words, it is possible to create three concepts inconsistent with one another, from among which a relativist is forced to choose and which he must not merge or combine. This fact should be stressed as an imperativist may actually be content with such imperceptible sneaking from one of these views to the second or the third one, and such sneaking may at times give his reasoning the appearance of strength. However, if the distinction between these three separate conceptions is drawn and the incompatibility firmly settled, then disproving an imperativist's arguments in favour of either of the three views seems feasible, if not easy.

Here are the three theories in question, with a proper critical commentary for each of them.

The first one consists of the following assertion: a sentence supposedly stating an obligation is simply an order which has lost its imperative character in the process of being put into words. "You should do it" would mean the same as "Do it!" according to this theory, where "Do it!" should be understood clearly and distinctly as an order rather than a request or an appeal. This view may seem right in some circumstances, which we will not go into, nor will we consider the flaw it contains even then; instead, we will just state that the thesis is definitely wrong if considered as a general one. For it is in the nature of an order that it concerns future behaviour and, directly or indirectly, refers to the person who is expected by a giver of an order to behave in a given way; whereas obligational sentences (let us thus name the sentences stating obligation for short) do not always fulfil these conditions. On the contrary: without even changing the meaning of the word „should", they often state an obligation in the future or an obligation of a person who will never even learn about the relevant sentence being uttered; sometimes both of these occur. In any of these cases, the obligational sentence cannot be a verbal formulation of an order, which is enough to recognize this theory as faulty.

Here is another imperativistic view (second of the three which should be discussed by us), which does not fall under our objection and refers to the mentioned cases equally well as the other ones: it consists of a statement that an obligational judgement is in fact a judgement stating an order, whereas an obligational sentence is merely a variation in the verbal formulation of this judgement. The simplest form of this thesis would be one according to which the assumption would be that the relevant order can be issued by anybody, such that "you should" simply means the same as "you are dictated to". However, we will not deal with this variant of the theory. In the case of two mutually contradicory orders concerning the same situation, it would lead to the statement that in this situation given behaviour and its opposite are equally valid; and that would make the notion of obligation a relative concept and deprive it of any applicability in practice. Although this consequence is relativistic in theory and devoid of obligation in practice, it does not correspond to the imperativists' intentions which we formulated initially. This thesis only takes on its imperativistic meaning in the following form: obligational judgements are judgements which state the orders of a privileged giver of an order. This privileged giver of an order could be a more or less hypostatic "society" of some sociological ethics, or the state, or some extraordinary individual (a sage, a prophet, a messiah, a political leader, or the chosen one raised above the rest of mankind in one way or another), or even God. The latter would lead to an especially simple and clear concept which will provide us with a particularly convenient example in our discussion. Therefore, an obligational judgement means stating God's order: the sentences "You should" and "I should" would be equivalent to the sentences: "God commands you" and "God commands me". How would such a kind of thesis keep its appearance of rightness? Surely through the ability to state with some degree of probability that, from a psychological point of view, a believer in God cannot think "God tells me to" and at the same time not think "I should", as these are inseparable convictions in his mind. However, the psychological inseparability of these two thoughts, even if it were stated and well settled, does not entail identical content; in order to explain the inseparability, it suffices if in the eyes of a believer the sentence "God tells me to" constitutes the reason of the sentence "I should" and if the relation of the reason and the consequence is recognized by him in an instantaneous act of thought each time. The question of the alleged synonymy of the two thoughts still remains open then. Can it be settled in the negative sense? For the author of the present remarks, it certainly can. Personally, I can only state most categorically that when confronting the thought "I should" on the one hand with the thought "God tells me to" on the other hand (or any other thought of the same kind, where God is replaced by any other giver of an order), I can see quite clearly that the contents of these two thoughts are different. On his side, an imperativist must claim the contrary, and in further consequence he will also have to claim that the sentence: "You should do what God tells you to do" is pure tautology and simply means: "God tells you to do what God tells you to do". Would any imperativist be prepared to accept this consequence? It seems quite improbable. And in case it were otherwise, it would be equal to stating that also the other theory under consideration was deemed unacceptable by common consent.

This leaves us with the third, and last, conception, which seems more elusive than the first two. Its most natural formulation would probably read like this: any obligation is always formed by an order; or: whenever one should do something, it is BECAUSE it was dictated. Just like in the previous conception, and for the same reason, we will not take into consideration the variant in which anyone's order would constitute the justification of an obligation. Also here, only a privileged giver of an order is taken into consideration. One would say then: "You should because God dictates so", "You should because the State dictates that it is so", *etc.* This conception is impervious to attempts to disprove it in the way the two other conceptions can be disproven. Certain complications and intricacies are concealed in it, so we must analyze it further in order to reveal them.

The starting point of the mentioned analysis would be the notion of the privileged giver of an order mentioned before, but not discussed yet. Whenever I speak of such privilege, I am obliged to justify it, that is, answer the question of WHY it is God's or the State's orders which create obligations, whereas orders from other givers of orders do not create them. Depending on the answer, the discussed thesis may assume various forms. Again, there are probably three possible answers. The first one: behaviour ordered by a privileged giver of an order *X* has the character of duty, because *X* always orders what is right. The second: it has this character because *X* is the best or the most perfect of all the ones who may issue any order. The third: it is because *X* is the most powerful.

Critical analysis of these answers leads to the following conclusions:

(1) The first answer is clearly devoid of an imperativistic character.

(2) The second one:

(a) either it is reduced to the first one in a circuitous way;

(b) or, in a different interpretation, it is also only seemingly imperativistic.

(3) The third one:

(a) either comes to the second interpretation (b);

(b) or it is not in fact a theory of duty;

(c) or again, in a different interpretation, it is not imperativistic.

As a result, in all of these cases but one, imperativism is lost in analysis, and in one remaining case, the theory of duty itself is lost.

Here is the summary of the arguments connected with all these points.

(1) AN EVER-RIGHT ORDER. In this hypothesis it is not the order that creates duty, but rather the rightness of the dictated thing. Duty would remain even if there was no order.

(2) PERFECTION. Those who rely on a higher value or the perfection of the giver of an order in their answer should be asked the question of why,

then, we should always do what the best or the most perfect person orders. Two answers are possible here:

(a) Because the most perfect person can only order that which is right. This way we come back to the answer which had been deemed non-imperativistic.

(b) Because the most perfect person deserves love, respect and worship; because our obligation is to manifest these emotions and one way to express these emotions is to meet his will. In other words: all our particular obligations are justified through the general obligation of expressing those emotions; the obligation itself is definitive and presented as self-evident. The answer to that is the following: this conception is a CULT conception; whether it concerns God or a human giver of an order, obedience of orders is perceived as an element of a cult. Yet, this is not an imperativistic conception. It is not contained in the formula according to which "duty is created through order", since what creates duty is only the will or wish of the Perfect One, regardless whether this will or this wish were manifested in the order. If the order is indeed ISSUED, it does not have the role OF AN ORDER, but rather of one of the possible means to manifest the said wish or will. However, other means are no worse for this purpose; for example: God's will may be learned through mystic intuition, the "will" of a society can be known through contact with public opinion, the will of an individual authority figure can be learned through psychological observation. Thus, the conception under discussion at present also does not fit into the general formula, according to which being acquainted with certain orders is the only method of learning our obligations.

(3) POWER. This time it is claimed that the privileged giver of an order is the most powerful one. Again, if we ask why that is, we may receive one of the following three answers:

(a) Because power is a part of perfection or rather it is perfection itself, so that the most perfect one is at the same time the most powerful one. Here we return to conception (2), with one difference: the decisive feature of perfection is specified this time.

(b) Because the most powerful one, having the ability to punish us in the case of our refusal, evokes the feelings of fear, submission, and other similar feelings, which as a whole constitute what we would call "the sense of duty": this theory is common but it is also psychologically inaccurate. However, it is not for us to discuss, since it is a genetic theory of the SENSE of duty rather than a theory of DUTY itself.

(c) Because the most powerful one has the ability to punish us, that is, inflict certain pain on us, our accepted, anyway, obligation is to avoid pain. Also here, there is no imperativism. Here the obligation of doing what we were told does not result from the order itself but from the application of a more general rule, that is, the hedonistic rule in its negative form ("avoid pain"). Pain inflicted on us as a punishment should be avoided to no greater or lesser degree than any other pain. Therefore, it is not true that an order always creates duty or that duty can only be learned through learning certain orders.

Thus, whereas it seems that the first two imperativistic conceptions should be rejected as being clearly WRONG, it is not exactly the case with the third one. We distinguished several various conceptions within it, which were not discussed from the point of view of their truthfulness or falsity, but we ascertained that none of them constitute a truly imperativistic theory of duty, and that seemingly imperativistic terminology stands in the way of a completely different reality. One somewhat «idealistic» viewpoint, one or two cult conceptions, one psychological theory of the sense of duty, and finally, a specific application of simply hedonistic ethics: this is what was revealed when the appearances of imperativism were dispelled, having proved to be purely verbal. It was not insignificant to be able to state this if you realize that purely verbal doctrines and those which fall apart under analysis tend to have extraordinary power of suggestion in practice.

Leon Petrażycki. Positional logic
[1939: 17–19, 21–23]

In my lectures on the psychological essence of judgements I spoke of two types of judgements and sentences (1) objective-cognitive and (2) subjective-relational.

The first type, objective-cognitive, is about the study of what there is, regardless of whether we like this or not, regardless of what we want and what we believe we should aim for, *etc.*

The second type, subjective-relational (subjective-relative) is concerned with our subjective relationship to what exists or is imagined – our liking, fancy, praise; or antipathy, repulsion, rebuke; or our wish to eliminate or create something, aims we strive for, rules of behaviour, *etc.* […].

There are two kinds of subjective-relational judgements and sentences: (1) judgements and sentences which express positive or negative (emotional) attitude towards an existing thing or something which is imagined as existing or realized (praise or criticism in the general sense) – such judgements or sentences can be called critical (for instance: "This world is horrible", "This person is likeable, unpleasant", "This act is shameful, bad or good, noble"); (2) judgements or sentences which express willingness, demands, requirements for something to occur or not occur, happen or not happen, especially judgements and sentences concerning how one should behave in a given situation or if one should behave at all. Such judgements and sentences can be called postulative.

In objective-cognitive judgements there occur specific objective-cognitive emotions which state the current state of affairs, the existence or non--existence of something, *etc.* In subjective-relational judgements there occur various other emotions.[63] In postulative judgements those emotions, whether attractive or repulsive, aim to realize or not-realize something, they act *ante factum*; in critical judgements these emotions concern something which had happened or come into existence (or imagined as existing), they act *ante factum*; they accept what exists as something good (attractive emotions), or they protest against it (repulsive emotions). […]

THE CRITERIA OF COMPATIBILITY WITH REALITY, TRUTHFULNESS, OR INCOMPATIBILITY, FALSITY, IS ONLY APPLIED TO OBJECTIVE-COGNITIVE JUDGEMENTS (POSITIONS). As for subjective-relational judgements, various criteria can be applied, depending on the specific character of relevant judgements, for

---

[63] The author characterizes them in *The Introduction to the Theory of Law and Morality. Foundations of Emotional Psychology* [1905]. [...]

instance, the criteria of rationality and irrationality, rightness and wrongness, *etc.*, but the criteria of compatibility or incompatibility with reality, truthfulness or falsity, does not find application here, as the concern here is not the study of reality but other matters altogether.

The distinction between objective-cognitive and subjective-relational sentences and judgements, as well as the distinction between critical and postulative within subjective-relational ones are distinctions unknown to contemporary studies, proposed by me. Especially in the case of logic, subjective-relational judgements (as well as the corresponding notions and reasoning) are ignored altogether. Whenever there is a mention of judgements, only objective-cognitive judgements are taken into account, and accordingly, other sciences are built on this basis. The task of logic is considered to be the creation of supervision in the domain of the search for truth; the logical criteria is considered to be the criteria of truthfulness or falsity; the feature common to all judgements is considered to be the feature which consists in their truthfulness or falsity. Studies such as that of the principle of contradiction or the law of the excluded middle, which can only be of significance in the domain of objective-cognitive judgements (as only they are concerned with the truthfulness or falsity of corresponding judgements) are taught as studies of all judgements, *etc.*[64]

However, such limitations of logic to the scope of objective cognition cannot be accepted. In real life as well as in science, what matters alongside objective-cognitive thinking is subjective-relational thinking, both critical and postulative.

Thinking directed at explaining how one should behave in given cases is of particularly great importance in practical life. In the domain of science, this corresponds to practical skills through which one develops general rules of conduct, various practical sciences, like medicine, hygiene, pedagogical studies, political studies; practical legal studies and others.

[64] However, one cannot claim that such limitations of the class of objective-cognitive judgements, disregarding subjective-relational judgements, *etc.*, is something logicians are aware of, not to mention being able to justify. This is more the case of unconscious historical adaptation of logic to the main type of suppositions and objective-cognitive thought dating back to the time of Aristotle.

Critical thinking is also of great importance in human life: criticism of people's behaviour or personality, of governments states, criticism of social systems […].

IT RESULTS FROM THE ABOVE THAT THE STUDY OF CONTEMPORARY LOGIC IS LAME TO VARIOUS DEGREES. ALL OF CONTEMPORARY LOGIC IS MONSTROUSLY LAME AS IT ONLY INCLUDES JUDGEMENTS AND SENTENCES AND NOT ALL POSITIONS; HOWEVER, A SIGNIFICANT PORTION OF CONTEMPORARY LOGIC IS LAME TO AN EVEN HIGHER DEGREE, AS APART FROM THE ABOVE IT ONLY INCLUDES OBJECTIVE-COGNITIVE THINKING, WHEREAS IT SHOULD ALSO INCLUDE SUBJECTIVE-RELATIONAL THINKING.

Judgements and sentences in the subjective-relational domain do not constitute a category fit for constructing proper logical studies, like judgements and sentences in the objective-cognitive domain.

Here one should achieve proper elementary logical sizes, which are contained in a judgement or a sentence in significant numbers, or which may also be contained within items other than judgements and sentences. Such elementary logical sizes, ELEMENTARY POSTULATES OR CRITICAL RELATIONS, can also be called SUBJECTIVE POSITIONS, as opposed to objective-cognitive positions.

Thus: (1) one subjective-relational judgement or sentence may contain more than one subjective positions, for instance: "One should not do any business or maintain social relationships with such an evil and despicable man as *N*", "Let us stay here longer, I want to look at this magnificent view!" (there are four positions in these judgements or sentences: two critical ones and two postulative ones); (2) subjective positions are not only found in subjective judgements or sentences but also in various other experiences, utterances and other manifestations of mental experiences.

In particular, objective judgements and sentences often contain subjective positions, for instance: "Goethe, the great German poet, was born in 1749 in Frankfurt on the Main". (The word "great" signifies evaluation and introduces a critical position.) "I hope the patient gets well". (Three positions: first is psychological, second is a prognosis, third is a subjective-positive emotion.) Similarly, the sentence: "I worry the patient may die" contains three analogous positions.

Besides, such judgements or sentences where there are some combinations of objective and subjective positions should not be qualified as objective or subjective judgements according to a prevailing element from the point of view of positional logic, but rather as MIXED JUDGEMENTS OR SENTENCES, partly objective and partly subjective.

Among other things, the very fact of the existence of mixed judgements and sentences indicates that the category "judgement" or "sentence" is unable to build logic, therefore it is necessary to go further in the logical analysis and accept the category of position as the basic category of logic. […]

The lectures on emotions showed that all kinds of emotions play a crucial part in our inner life as well as our external behaviour. Emotions play a leading role and study is a subordinate medium.[65] At every turn of our lives we experience various emotions which are attractive or repulsive towards various perceived or imagined objects; we experience various emotional drivings, desires, wishes; we choose appropriate means to realize them, *etc.* Subjective-relational positions are included in corresponding experiences. In the vast majority of cases, such experiences occur without corresponding judgements. Similarly, in the objective-cognitive domain corresponding judgements are experienced when we prepare A VERBAL FORMULATION of our subjective-relational views or if we imagine ourselves speaking or writing. There are also many more subjective positions included in our inner experiences than corresponding judgements.

Both in the subjective-relational domain and the objective-cognitive domain, in order to examine the principle of adequacy one should take into consideration, apart from positions included in judgements and other inner experiences, also the positions which are included in sentences and other external manifestations of internal experiences, whether genuine or not. […] Subjective positions may be included in sentences and all other utterances, including questions. For instance: "Have the perpetrators of the horrible crime from Krakowskie Przedmieście[66] been found?".

---

[65] *Cf.* [1905: 406–409].
[66] One of the main streets in the city of Warsaw [my footnote – JJ].

Moreover, they can also be included in all other manifestations of emotional relation.

The category of positions should be the basic and central category of logic, constructed according to the principle of adequacy. This entails broadening the subject and the scope of logic considerably, as if transforming logic from a tiny shack to a grand palace.

In connection to this reform, a reform of the system of logic is required (a general section and two special, adequate ones). [...]

However [...], logic should not only be adequately constructed but should also instruct others how adequate studies and adequate positions should be constructed as well as how to avoid the mistake of inadequacy. [...] In order to reform the content (and partly also the scope) of logic, one should distinguish various species and subspecies of positions, objective and relational, and in general, conduct a detailed classification of positions and reform the system of logic accordingly in the direction of constructing various special studies for various categories of positions, objective and subjective.

Thus, both in objective-cognitive logic and subjective-relational logic further divisions will occur.

Tadeusz Czeżowski. Intentions and evaluations
[1946: 157–161]

[1.] Through a provision the object of a driving becomes an AIM [...] of actions. Only that which we value as a positive value and which we consider to be a good can be an aim. Socrates claimed that each person naturally drives at what he considers to be good, and it suffices to know what is truly good in order to be virtuous; this meaning is ascribed to Socrates' adage: "Virtue is knowledge". However, not all values can become aims; only those which we consider to be achievable. The choice of aims [...] is based on an evaluation of values, where closer aims are evaluated as relative values, and dependent on the value of further aims. However, the justification of an aim does not rest only on settling its value. It is necessary to show that it can be achieved and, if its value is a relative value, that is, dependent on the value of a further aim, to show that it is the proper means of achieving the mentioned further aim. For example: if someone sets for himself the aim of graduating from medical studies, then apparently he sees the value of this aim in the fact that a doctor helps the afflicted, therefore the justification of this aim seems sufficient if we assume that the aim really has the value we ascribe to it, that it is achievable (that is, the candidate is in possession of sufficient financial resources as well as aptitude in order to graduate), and that the doctor-to-be is indeed able to help those who suffer (and does not refrain from medical practice and does not try to use his knowledge to harm patients, *etc.*).

ULTIMATE AIMS of behaviour are justified through manifesting their absolute value and their feasibility. At the same time, these two factors determine the choice of the ultimate aim. Given the choice between two values differing in their degree of being ultimate aims of behaviour, provided that both are achievable to an equal degree, the one which is of greater value is chosen. Yet, if the choice is between two values of the same degree, then the more achievable one is chosen. For example, if someone considers graduating from university his ultimate aim and is given the choice of studying in a technical college or technical university, then he will choose the university; however, if he definitely can meet the requirements of a technical college, but the chance of graduating from a technical university is slim, then he will settle for a college.

Various people take on various aims for their behaviour, whether close, further, or ultimate, guided by evaluations of relative and absolute values. Still, evaluations can be true or false; therefore, if someone sets himself an aim on the basis of an false evaluation of its value, his behaviour will be improper as they would drive at achieving an aim which should not have been chosen. This concerns ultimate aims in particular, as relative value of close aims depends on the absolute value of the former. It is not only the value of the ultimate aim which determines behaviour; what should be taken into consideration is also the value of means used to achieve the aim and the value of its result. Sometimes an ultimate aim which is right in itself is nevertheless rejected if dishonourable means have to be used to achieve it (there is no approval for the principle: the end justifies the means), or if it could entail negative results. Behaviour whose ultimate aim, together with its results and all that is necessary to achieve it, has the greatest value in comparison with all other manners of behaviour available to us, is called RIGHT behaviour. Right behaviour is A DUTY and therefore AN OBLIGATION. If one should do something, it means that this action is right. Sentences which state which behaviour is a duty are called NORMS or DICTATES of behaviour. These sentences prescribe a certain behaviour, demand it or dictate it, in order to give priority to this behaviour which is right. Dictates, such as: [that] everyone should be a useful member of a society, or: [that] a soldier should be prepared to die for his homeland, or: [that] everyone should behave in such a way that truth wins over falsity, state that whoever acts in such a way that he is a useful member of a society, or whoever dies for his homeland, or whoever contributes to truth winning over falsity, behaves rightly. Norms, duties and evaluations of values are connected to each other in such a way that norms indicate as duties only those courses of behaviour which are right, that is, those whose means and aims together with their results have the greatest possible value.

Certain behaviour may then be described as duty, either through indicating the aims which determine them as right, or in such a way that we determine the given behaviour as the object of a norm. The first way to indicate duty is called determining through the TELEOLOGICAL criterion, and the other way is called determining through the FORMAL criterion (from Greek, teleological: concerning aims; formal: taking into account the behaviour's conformity with the norm, rather than the content of the norm). There are various theories which attempt to determine which behaviour is a duty, among them, perfectionism and eudaimonism, both mentioned before [...]; perfectionism recognizes as right that behaviour which makes one more perfect, whereas eudaimonism recognizes as right the behaviour which contributes to making humanity happy to the greatest degree. Both theories define duty through the teleological criterion. Defining duty through the formal criterion is included in the following principle formulated by Kant: "Act only according to that maxim whereby you can, at the same time, will that it should become a universal law". A norm, rather than an aim, is indicated here: Right behaviour is behaviour which may serve as an example for all people. Creating such theories, justifying them and reviewing them all fall under the branch of philosophy called "normative ethics".

In everyday life, the term "OBLIGATION" may often be understood conversely. Obligation in the colloquial meaning can be called "EXTERNAL". An example of an external obligation is going to school for a student or studying for classes. External obligation is behaviour dictated by a person or institution which one is subordinate to, where the dictate contains A SANCTION (RIGOUR) of negative effects for those who would attempt to evade the obligation. Examples of sanctions at school are bad grades, negative evaluations of behaviour, reprimands and penalties. An external obligation, for those who are bound by it, is behaviour evaluated as right behaviour by the giver of an order, whereas an obligation based on my own judgement is AN INTERNAL OBLIGATION. When evaluations of the giver of an order and the person bound by the obligation are not compatible, internal, obligations do not coincide with external obligations, and we perceive the external obligations as imposed on us and we perform them under duress of sanction. On the other hand, there often comes a time when we would like the kind of behaviour we perceive as intrinsic obligation to apply to other people as external obligation as well, for example, social or religious reformers strive to impose their ideals on others in the form of a universally obligating norms. Legislators and all those who settle external obligations for others always ought to be guided by the principle of issuing "JUST" dictates, that is, ones based on solid evaluation of the rightness of the dictated behaviour, since such warrants will also be accepted as internal obligations by the bound. The notion of obligation was developed by ancient philosophers from the stoic school of philosophy. Stoics believed that the world is governed by Providence which is an intelligent guiding force. Wise are those who understand the dictates of Providence, guess his aims and are able to properly evaluate their value. Then they will accept as internal obligation to resign to the inevitable adversity of fate designed by Providence, they will overcome the sensation of its inevitability, they will achieve true freedom and happiness associated with it.

[2.] Striving to achieve a certain aims, as long as it has not been achieved yet, one experiences a negative value emotion, which is usually unpleasant. This emotion is tied to the conviction that the object we value and therefore have elected as our aim is not there. For example, let us assume that the aim of my behaviour is to compensate for certain harm done to someone; I experience unpleasantness as long as this aim is not achieved. However, the moment the aim is stated as achieved, the negative value emotion transforms into a pleasant positive value emotion, which is often accompanied by additional satisfaction drawn from succeeding, victory, and overcoming obstacles in one's way. It might seem (as it is often said) that, when one attempts to reach any aim, the most important issue would be the said value emotions, and that this is the sole reason why one accomplishes any good deeds – in order to free oneself from the unpleasant negative value emotions and to experience the pleasant positive value emotions; therefore, any aims of our behaviour only serve the purpose of removing unpleasantness and achieving pleasure.

Such an interpretation does not summarize the issue well enough, as it was stated before that the objectives of one's behaviour are not the emotions of value, but rather the subjects of these emotions. Indeed, one often strives to avoid unpleasantness and achieve pleasure, since these are also objects of emotions of value, but then one often clearly sets them as aims and selects appropriate means to achieve them. This is the case with, for example, attempting to free myself from pangs of conscience and finally performing the task which I am supposed to perform, even though I do not care for it. Yet, when I do value something which is not solely pleasure, for example, writing an important letter, and that is what I select as the aim of my behaviour, and the pleasure accompanying having written the letter is only a circumstance which accompanies achieving the aim, then one must distinguish it from the proper aim in order to realize what all the agents of my behaviour are.

One also has to distinguish INCENTIVES or MOTIVES of a resolution, thanks to which one settles the aim of behaviour, from the aim itself. Incentives, or motives, of a resolution are all those psychic phenomena which appear as the background of psychic dispositions causing the object to be capable of making resolutions, and constituting sufficient conditions for the resolution. Two elements can then be distinguished in a resolution: wanting and conviction, and so incentives of a resolution are at the same time incentives of both these elements together. Therefore the motives could be the emotions of value together with the representation of their object (the aim of behaviour) and a resolution which constitutes the basis of an emotion, as well as motives of a conviction about one's own future behaviour, which can all be psychic phenomena of different kinds. [...]

The view according to which motives of behaviour fully determine a resolution as their cause, provided the motives occur against the appropriate psychic dispositions, is called ETHICAL DETERMINISM; the view is an application of the general principle of determinism to human behaviour. [...] The opposite view, called ETHICAL INDETERMINISM, assumes that dispositions of the subject and motives, that is, psychic phenomena which determine a resolution, are not the only factors which determine a resolution; another factor is the subject's active attitude, called free will, which ought not to be understood as a disposition or a psychic phenomenon. If this attitude is varied in any two cases, then the resolutions will come out differently, despite the compatibility of dispositions and motives.

Ethical determinism resembles associationism [...], since it assumes that dispositions and motives of a resolution determine that resolution just as, according to associationism, associative dispositions and motives determine the flow of thought. Similarly, ethical indeterminism is closer to the view opposed to associationism, which assumes that the mind regulates active thinking with unrestricted attention, regardless of various associations which come up. Free will and unrestricted attention [...] are analogous ATTITUDES of the subject (rather than psychic dispositions or phenomena, which occur as motives), making a choice from among the possibilities which motives suggest. Ethical determinism and associationism are known as MECHANISTIC views in psychology, whereas indeterminism and the view which recognizes active thinking regulated by unrestricted attention, contrary to associationism, are counted among VOLUNTARISTIC views.

Tadeusz Czeżowski. Types of intentions
[1946: 201–203]

Contrary to disinterested aesthetic emotions, emotions of value are of utmost importance to behaviour. Emotions of value arise in connection with the stating of the existence or non-existence of the subject of the emotion;

they in turn become motives of experiences which are active in character, which push one towards behaviour leading to the realization or preservation of valuable objects and the removal of that which is evaluated negatively. One attempts to create surroundings which would be enjoyable and correspond to one's tastes; one strives to remove objects of distress; one shuns the company of unpleasant individuals. The experiences under discussion make the fourth major set of psychic phenomena, the remaining three constituting presentations, convictions and emotions. They bear the general name of DRIVINGS, which encompasses several variants: thirst, desires, willings and resolutions. All drivings share a common characteristic factor, which is called aspirational. We recognize it as a part of our internal experience, but we are unable to analyze and describe it, as we only view it as something elementary.

Drivings are characterized through their QUALITY and INTENSITY. We distinguish two, mutually exclusive, qualities of drivings: POSITIVE DRIVING towards an object and NEGATIVE DRIVING away from an object. They are expressed in affirmative and negative sentences like: I desire, want this and do not want that, or: I drive towards this and avoid that. We drive towards objects of positive value and we avoid objects which we evaluate negatively.

The INTENSITY of driving depends on the intensity of the emotion which is the motive of the driving, that is, on the degree of pleasure or unpleasantness contained in the emotion. The greater the pleasure it leads to, or the greater the unpleasantness it avoids, the more powerful the driving. However, the intensity of a driving is not directly linked to the extent to which the object of a driving is valuable, such that driving for a higher value may be weaker that driving for a lower value if the degree of pleasure in the second case is greater than in the first case:

> ...*Video meliora, proboque,*
> *Deteriora sequor...*

(I see the better and acknowledge it but I follow the worse) according to the sentence of Latin poet (Ovid, *Metamorphoses*, VII, 20).

Drivings are also divided into two groups according to their FIRMNESS, which defines their attitude towards the object of a driving and to one's behaviour. NON-RESOLUTE DRIVINGS fall into the first category. They arise in us regardless of our conviction about whether the object of the driving is achievable. These are, more or less precise and settled, THIRST and DESIRE; one jas a thirst that all people love each other, or one desires many forbidden things, even if it is clear that achieving this is impossible. Therefore, such experiences do not affect one's behaviour directly, since one does not attempt to achieve something one does not consider to be achievable. In order to express such experiences, the conditional mood is used: "I would like to", "I would wish", together with an implicit clause: "if it were possible". RESOLUTE and definite DRIVINGS fall into the second category; they are expressed in such phrases as: "I will go to the theatre" (rather than "I would like to go to the theatre") or "I resolve that I will act so and so". These drivings control behaviour, as they emerge when their object is considered to be not only valuable, but also achievable, and thus they lead to behaviour aiming to achieve the object in such a way that the drivings become motives of belief about one's own future behaviour in this area. These convictions are expressed in the phrases cited above. The experiences which contain resolute driving, based on the conviction about the feasibility of a valuable object, together with the conviction that one will act in such a way that brings this object, are called ACTS OF WILL or RESOLUTIONS. Dispositions which are the source of resolutions are called WILL. All normal people have it, just like they have dispositions to imagine, perceive, remember, *etc.* In the abnormal cases of people who are psychically or neurologically ill, the lack of will may be disclosed, which is called ABULIA: a person without will is unable to make a resolution, even though all necessary conditions are given.

Tadeusz Kotarbiński. Evaluations, norms, imperatives
[1947: 200–202]

While attempting to eradicate the thesis that the requirements of logic and the specifics of legal thought are disparate, we have no intention to negate certain apparent shortcomings of logic, in its present stage of development, as compared with the requirements of legal thought. Logic only revolves around declarative sentences or propositional functions whose substitutes are such sentences. What is of equal importance is that the notions of truthfulness and falsity used in logic were probably constructed only in connection with the analysis of sentences which do not express the subject's emotional attitude towards the described reality. Yet, a lawyer is constantly forced to deal with EVALUATIONS of this kind (that is right, that is fair, that is unjust, *etc.*); with norms which claim that one should not act so and so, but one is obliged to act another way in a given set of circumstances; with IMPERATIVES, and finally, with formulations of various decisions, regulations, verdicts, *etc.* Some of these issues have just come into logicians' scope of interest as the question of the possibility of counting imperatives. Interestingly, certain combinations of imperatives and declarative sentences are possible. The following combinations seem sensible, and even justified: "We had enough rest; let us walk on", where the imperative is a conclusion in a way. Yet, if an imperative is used as a premise, incoherent nonsense arises ("Let us walk on, so everything is fine!").

In the current state of research it would be wise to attempt to extract from a given issue, formulated with the help of emotional evaluations, norms, imperatives, *etc.*, content which can be expressed with a combination of declarative sentences only, not tinged with emotions. As experiments revealed, probably all that bears the marks of proving with connection to emotional evaluations, norms, imperatives, *etc.*, can become independent of the specifics of such utterances tinged with emotion. For instance, the issue of whether it is just to pay women less than men for the same work, which is tinged with emotion in view of the emotional element contained in the word "just", could probably be reduced to an issue devoid of this term, which can be resolved in the following way: if the principle of equal pay to all is conditioned only by the dependence of the amount of wages exclusively to the work done, then it also contains the condition of independence of the amount of wages from the worker's gender. The justification of the phrase: "We had enough rest, let us walk on", is contained in the justification of the following utterance: "We had enough rest, then we would act accordingly with the aim of this trip if we walked on".

In any case, there are plenty of unresolved cases for logic, which arise from the distinctive character of humanist thought in general, and legal thought in particular. Logic and jurisprudence could then be creative inspirations for each other, which opens up a splendid prospect of cooperation.

Maria Ossowska. Norms and imperatives
[1947: 145–149]

Our discussion of norms thus far was focused on the analysis of utterances which contain the word "should", though with the reservation that utterances which are commonly perceived as norms can be formulated without the aid of the word mentioned, and that, on the other hand, not every utterance which contains it can be considered a norm. In other words, the use of the word "should" is neither a necessary nor a sufficient condition to recognize an utterance which contains it as a norm.

As we recall, norms are commonly given an entirely different form, namely, the form of declarative sentences, the form of conditional sentences or the form of imperative sentences. All of these forms still have to be considered in order to decide whether we are dealing with something new. The three forms mentioned above stand out particularly well as the object of analysis, since previous discussions connected to them contained some misunderstandings, which should be repealed here.

"Who spreads defamatory news in the press, shall be punished in such and such a way", "A napkin should be put on one's knees when eating, rather than tied under one's chin", "Those who play volleyball on the positions away from the net, pass the ball to those members of the team who play near the net" – these are examples of formulations which are often used to create regulations of law, rules of savoir vivre or rules of a game. Norms formulated in such a way have the appearance of purely descriptive utterances, therefore this form is often chosen by those who would like to give the uttered norms the appearance of factuality, as well as give the branch of research which use the norms the appearance of science. Sadly, contrary to appearances, those utterances are not descriptive.[67] For instance, the first one is not an empirical generalization, as it would seem, and nobody would

---

[67] Compare Wallis-Walfisz [1937].

attempt to justify this utterance by proving that whenever someone spread defamatory news in the press, he would be punished in a given way. It is also the case with the two remaining utterances. Also here, there is an implied "should" or a similar expression, therefore it is delusory to think that if one formulates a regulation or rules of a game in the indicative mode, one becomes more scientific than when they use words like "should" and other, similar words. Naturally, the formulation of norms in the form of utterances such as "X is obliged to do so and so" or in the form of utterances in the future tense, also seems more scientific. In utterances of the type: "X is obliged to do so and so" the non-descriptive factor is disguised in the expression: "is obliged to", unless "is obliged to" means the same as "he committed to". But then the utterance, while turning into a descriptive sentence, ceases to be a norm.

As we mentioned before, there have been various attempts to give norms the form of conditional sentences. Some researchers formulate certain ethical norms in the form: "If conditions W occur, then X should say C", which does not free us from the word "should" in the consequent, so that not much is gained from the transition, apart from the duly emphasized point that any "should" applies only in certain conditions which are implicitly regarded as satisfied. The attempt to give legal norm the character of conditional sentences in the form: "If someone commits a given crime, the state should punish him in a given way",[68] as far as the formal structure of a norm goes, does not bring anything new either. This proposal could only apply in some fields of the law; moreover, it should be treated as a postulate to formulate future codes of law, rather than an attempt to interpret the content of the existing legal norms.

Apart from these conditional sentences which are of a mixed character (descriptive antecedent and normative consequent), there also exist norms which have the appearance of conditional sentences devoid of any semblance to a normative element. In view of proposals of this kind,

---

[68] The latter formulation is supposedly perceived by Kelsen as the only proper formulation of a norm (*cf.* Znamierowski [1924: 8] and relative footnotes on p. 138). Elsewhere in the same book, Znamierowski ascribes to Kelsen a form which is not synonymous, namely: "If someone kills deliberately, he will receive a death sentence".

instead of "Do not steal!" there would be a conditional sentence which concerns the future, of the form: "If you steal, you will be punished in a certain way". If we interpret this utterance in the same way as the utterance of the type: "If you insert a coin into the machine, it will produce a ticket", then in this interpretation nobody would consider this sentence to be synonymous with the utterance: "Do not steal!" while legal or ethical norms would become utterances which state certain future events with greater or lesser probability.

Finally, let us add a few words on identifying the norms which contain the word "should" with someone's orders. This issue is represented in vast, though theoretically not very productive, literature. Whether norms are orders or not has been argued, but also, in the case of the above being resolved as true, who was supposed to order something to whom has also been argued.[69]

Identifying norms with orders can only be taken literally in one case, that is, when one claims that the norm and the corresponding order are synonymous utterances. Naturally, this view cannot be held in relation to all kinds of norms. There is a difference between the utterance "Divorce should not exist" and a ban on divorce. The former can be deemed right, and the

---

[69] Here we recall, among others, Ihering's classic theory, which perceives legal norms as orders directed at institutions which are to supervise the execution of orders, as well as Petrażycki's criticism concerning this theory and his criticism of identifying norms with orders in general [...] [1907a: § 23] [...]. Also Znamierowski and Elzenberg speak against identifying norms with orders. The former accomplishes that in the much cited book [1924], in which he does not consider as a norm the order issued by someone, for example, an order directed at soldiers: "If the enemy approaches within 100 steps, shoot". On the other hand, the verbal representation of the thought which emerged in the minds of the soldiers, that is: "We should shoot now", is a norm in his view [1924: 9 – 10]. Elzenberg considers the relationship between norms and commands in the work entitled *Duty and order* [1938] [...]. Imperativistic tendencies which consist in attempting to understand the NOTION of duty through the notion of order or to understand the FACT of duty through the fact of order, find their expression in three discrete views, according to the author: (1) in one of them it is claimed that utterances which allegedly stating duty are in fact orders, (2) in the second one it is claimed that a judgement on a duty is in fact a judgement stating a given order, (3) in the third one it is believed that each duty always creates an order. The first two theories appear to be false, whereas the third one is differentiated in detailed analysis, but none of these versions justifies the tendencies which the author called imperativistic.

latter can be deemed wrong, that is, not leading to a desired state of affairs formulated in the relevant norm. As we may recall, there were among axiological norms, some norms which refer to an object, which cannot be ordered to do anything after all, and among norms which apply to behaviour, such norms may be found that apply to the past and which cannot really be considered as orders for that reason.[70] Moreover, teleological norms are not fit to be interpreted either.

The answer to the question of whether norms are synonymous to orders calls for further specification as to what is understood by order. Let us assume for now, in order to simplify matters, that an order is always a certain utterance (although clearly a gesture like pointing at the door can also be interpreted as an order). Is it enough, in order to recognize an utterance as an order, for the utterance to be structured in a certain way, for example, to contain a mood which we call imperative, or is it sufficient, regardless of its structure, for it to express someone's imperative volition, together with a threat of repression consequences, even if the person we are addressing will never hear us? In the structural view of the issue, only utterances of the type: "Do not steal!" could be orders, and moreover, they would remain orders even if one did not wish to express any of the above mentioned experiences through them (mentioned with no claim for the psychological characteristics to be anything more than provisional, and quoted here only to illustrate the point). In the psychological conception of order, any utterance with a specific expressive function can be an order, such as the question: "Where is my hat?" aimed at a servant and uttered in an impatient and imperious manner by a master in a hurry to go out.

Finally, a conception of order which is a fusion of the former two can be imagined. According to that third possibility, the necessary and sufficient conditions for an utterance to be recognized as an order are both its structure and its expressive function.

Let us take another look at identifying orders with norms in light of these distinctions. If an order is supposed to characterize a certain kind of utterance, then clearly not all norms are orders, since utterances which people

---

[70] *Cf.* Elzenberg's article quoted in the previous footnote.

consider to be norms rarely use the imperative mood. It is also out of the question for norms to be identified with psychologically characterized orders. Therefore, the issue seems to have been resolved both for the second and the third conception of order.

In fact, identifying orders with norms should not be taken literally. Whoever claims that each norm is practically an order, uses a certain *façon de parler* to state the following possible connections between a norm and an order:

(1) It could be stated a certain genetic correlation between the former and the latter, which consists in the idea that the existence of an order is a necessary condition to create a relevant norm, or in other words, that each norm assumes the preexistence of someone's order. According to this view, the norm: "One should not lie" would not exist if someone had not forbidden to lie, which is perhaps a defendable view in the field of legal norms, as norms with a perceptible genesis, but harder to defend in the field of moral norms or rules of good behaviour.

(2) It could be stated a certain "logical", if not genetic, correlation between a norm and an order, so that whenever someone questions the norm, not wanting to accept it or hear it, we invoke the fact of the existence of a corresponding order for its supporting. Thus some individuals attempt to maintain moral norms, by invoking God's orders. The order constitutes what is sometimes called the source of bindingness of a norm.

(3) Finally, treating norms as orders can take place because of their psychological effects. One may maintain that psychic reactions to norms and to orders are the same. Therefore, according to this view, one reacts to a norm directed at him with the same sensation as when one hears an order, that is, he experiences some kind of compulsion. This issue, as any psychological issue, can only be decided through observation or experimentation.[71]

As for connections between orders and norms, understood according to the two latter points, the situation is different for various kinds of norms. Lawyers, whose concern is obviously legal norms, have at their

[71] *Ibidem.*

disposal more data to search for the source of the bindingness of norms in one's orders than those who were influenced by moral norms, which, as we mentioned before, are not manifestly connected to any order, at least when the norms concern things and not human behaviour. The lack of connection between teleological norms and orders does not require further comment.

Taking into consideration the content, a norm seems the closest to an order when the order belongs to no one, but then the order practically ceases to be an order, at least when it is supposed to be characterized by some expressive function. It also ceases to be an order in terms of psychological effects, as for reacting to an utterance as if it was an order, one has to be aware of who the giver of the order is and whether the giver of an order has some grounds to order us, whether he is authorized to do so, and whether he has the ability to exert punishment in the case of our insubordination.[72]

Maria Ossowska. Evaluation of norms
[1947: 162–167]

As we discussed at some point, to deny norms truth value does not necessarily entail denying them any logical value. It is a fact that norms can be justified in a similar way to how the truthfulness of logical sentences is proven; it is also true that there exist certain conditions of their formulation which reinforce their reliability. These facts induce to ascribe certain logical value to norms; this value will be henceforth called rightness or wrongness of norms in order to distinguish them from the logical value of logical sentences. Let us speak some more of the mentioned rightness or wrongness.

There are two common ways of describing the rightness of norms: in one meaning it is understood as similar to the truthfulness of logical sentences, understood as a property of an utterance in view of its relation to reality or in view of its relation to other utterances which had previously been accepted. In the other meaning, when we speak of right or wrong rules, regulations or norms, we identify the validity of a certain utterance with its purposefulness.

---

[72] Compare Znamierowski [1924].

However, it does not seem to be a pragmatic interpretation of the previous conception of rightness, but rather a variety of this conception.

Whoever claims that the condition for the rightness of a norm is that the experience which led to its formulation were *als richtig charakterisiert* [...], or that the condition for the rightness of a norm, or rather, the criteria for its rightness, is experiencing a certain sensation in relation to it, called a sense of duty, that person understands the rightness of norms similarly to the truthfulness of logical sentences.

Whoever claims that the regulation prohibiting the use of alcohol in the United States was wrong, uses the conception of rightness according to which "wrong" means "purposeless".[73] This kind of wrongness of certain rules, norms or regulations is spoken of in the following two cases:

(1) When they are unable to state the purpose which might have driven the person who formulated or issued the regulations. For example, if a regulation was issued in which all the people who wear glasses should sit in separate compartments on the train, we would deem this regulation wrong, unjustified and silly, as we would be unable to guess what its purpose was in the mind of the person who issued this regulation, or what kind of connection he could have detected between wearing glasses and the necessity of staying in isolation.

(2) Sometimes we understand the motives which the person who formulated a given regulation had in mind and we accept its purpose, but we do not believe that the regulation will serve its purpose; in other words: we do not believe that obeying the regulation will lead to the realization of the result which was desired.

Although we understand what drove the author of the norm, and although we accept the fact that the norm is not purposeful in the sense that obeying it leads to the aim which was intended at the norm's formulation, we can still perceive this norm as wrong and still oppose it on the grounds of the conception of rightness assimilating this rightness with its truthfulness.

---

[73] Purposefulness or purposelessness of a norm is to constitute its logical value, according to Löhrich [1937].

In the case of an old regulation formerly in effect in the United States, which ordered black Christians in the southern states to pray in separate churches, it is possible to state the aim of this regulation and to decide that the regulation had a purpose. However, if we do not accept this aim, we can oppose it, referring to the fact that there exists a contradiction between it and the laws of the religion to which the churches are devoted. We may not accept the aims which a given norm realizes, while simultaneously accepting it that the norm really realizes what it was intended to realize; at the same time, as in the case of the American prohibition, it may happen that we accept the aim of those who issued a given regulation, but we oppose the regulation because it serves the purpose of the aim badly. As we support the notion that there should be as few divorce cases as possible, we may at the same time oppose a regulation which introduces extreme impediments in getting a divorce, based on the idea that the statistics in the countries where divorce is permitted exhibit a lower number of divorce cases. A regulation based on a right norm (in this case, a norm which says that there should be no divorce) may therefore be deemed wrong in the sense of "not purposeful". Both notions of rightness require some relativization, though each requires it for different reasons. A norm is right in the first sense in view of certain factual relationships between actions which the norm advocates and a state which it is aiming for. Therefore one of the important conditions of uttering a right norm in the second sense is familiarity with certain factual relationships. Thus, we may speak of greater or lesser competence in this field and of people who are more or less authorized to formulate commissions or regulations. Factual knowledge is also necessary to prove the rightness of norms in the first sense, when norms are justified with the help of other norms and empirical sentences. Apart from that, norms which concern behaviour also require certain factual knowledge, as the formulation of norms which set certain models, not only for people but also for objects, requires [...] certain factual competence. One of the conditions of uttering valid norms is therefore the possession of certain factual knowledge, just as its possession is the condition of uttering true empirical sentences. This is not the only analogy between the conditions of truthfulness of empirical sentences and the conditions of rightness of norms. Both empirical sentences and norms arouse distrust when one's emotions influence their formulation. To put it more precisely, some emotions do, since there exist emotions, like the love of truth, antipathy towards irresponsible cliché, work in favour of the rightness of one's utterances, which is important to note for those who view emotions as a factor which in principle works for irrationality. In fact, the point is to formulate norms in such a way that is consistent with one's thirsts and interests. Revisionists of the so-called bourgeois ethics undermine our trust in some of its norms by revealing that they served well the interests of those who propagated them, for example, an image of a faithful servant serves the interests of employers. Norms which regulated the relationship between parents and children served the interests of parents, whereas norms which dictated respect and obedience served the purposes of the elders.

We had discussed the issue of how to understand the notions of right norm and purposeful norm. Let us then comment briefly on the predicate "rational" with respect to norms, advice, and regulations. After all, in the ethics of the turn of 19th century the idea of rationalizing ethical rules was still in use. Why was it so?

The word "rational" used in an utterance of the type mentioned above reveals analogous ambiguity as in the case of the word "right". Therefore, a norm which had been justified by other, previously accepted norms is often called a rational norm. A norm which states that an insult to one's honour should cause one to challenge the offender to a duel is considered irrational, since it clashes with a previously approved norm which states that only the perpetrator should atone for his deed, since during a duel both the perpetrator and the victim are at risk. In turn, this norm clashes with a commonly approved norm that punishment should be proportional to the offense, whereas during a duel the punishment depends on pure chance and it may well be that one pays with his own life for a minor offense. Here both the rationality of a norm and its rightness is a certain property of a norm in view of its relationship to other, previously accepted norms. However, we do not only speak of the rationality of a given norm or its rightness in the context of its relationship to other norms, but also in view of the aims it is formulated for. An irrational norm, or an irrational regulation, is equivalent to a norm which commits something which does not serve the purpose of realization of what the person issuing the norm wished to realize. In order to use rational norms in the first sense, it is necessary to learn about relationships between them and set them in order. This way the postulate of using norms which are rational in this sense led to attempts at systematizing ethical sentences, whereas the notion of a system or plan in theoretical proceedings had long been connected with the notion of rationality. At times, Hobbes' ethics was classified as rationalistic, mostly if not entirely, as some semblance of a system can be detected in it.[74]

Yet, those who worked on rationalizing ethical norms are not primarily concerned with those two conceptions of rationality, which require relativization. They are concerned with freeing ethical rules from all magical elements; from regulations deriving from religion, which do not prevent anyone from being harmed nor are they of any advantage to anyone; from the pressure of tradition which is not justified in any way except that it is tradition. The dictate of non-eating meat of certain animals is irrational in this understanding if the dictate is nourished by the conviction that the animal is impure (the conception of purity and impurity is clearly a typically magical conception). The same prohibition is considered to be rational when it proves to be caused by concern about the health of the addressees of the norm rather than the alleged impurity of the animal (controversy over the issue of the ban on eating pork by Jews).

In the name of thus understood rationality some authors questioned the sanctity of virginity, which has obviously exercised great influence over the norms which regulate sexual morality of some peoples, especially those peoples which have been under the influence of the Christian religion. As Hobhouse writes in the book entitled *Morals in Evolution* [1906], marriage is treated as abolition of a kind of taboo. An unmarried woman who violates the prohibition is strongly condemned. At the same time, "in nine cases out of ten the condemnation is not really of moral nature, that is condemnation based on a rational opinion on her personality and good and evil potential,

---

[74] Compare a compilation of various meanings of the word "rational" in Weber [1920: 266].

but rather a magical condemnation, which ascribes to her some evil feature acquired irreversibly through violating the prohibition, as a result of which she becomes like spoiled goods on the social market", writes Hobhouse. Just as all magical features are contagious, so is the feature acquired through violating a prohibition, therefore all respectable women move away from the contaminated one.

Let us consider how the word "rational" is used in our example. Condemning the woman would be rational if her act clearly harmed somebody else or built a predisposition to commit such acts. Since losing one's virginity does not harm anybody else and does not change any trait of one's personality (one may add, except for the effects caused by the awareness of having done something which will be condemned by a given circle of people), then condemning the act is not a rational moral condemnation; it is a magical anachronism. This is how we attempt to reconstruct the author's idea. We took the liberty of quoting it, because it seems very characteristic to all those who would wish to rationalize ethical norms.

Many sanctified evaluations and norms underwent revision in the last fifty years in the name of rationalization, understood as eliminating from ethics the norms forbidding things which do not violate the harmony of human relations, or the norms prescribing things which do not contribute to enhance someone's happiness, or even those which sometimes contribute to reducing someone's happiness. This view influenced and changed people's outlook on sexual deviations; this view is also shared by those who fight for birth control in the name of eradicating unnecessary suffering; it is also shared by those who would like to eliminate punishment in the sense of a tool for revenge ad replace it by punishment as correctional instrument. From this point of view came the questioning of the rationality of our attitude to suicide, since this attitude was regulated by religious considerations rather than only by the hygiene of coexistence.

A norm or an evaluation would be rational or irrational in this understanding depending on whether it was valid or not, in view of some specific assumptions. One only needs to look through numerous publications of that period, which argue for what is called RATIONAL GOOD or *art moral rationnel*, in order to find out that for them rational is what can be derived from its assumptions and irrational is what cannot be derived from its assumptions or what clashes with them.

These remarks on how the rationality of moral norms was understood do not exhaust all the threads around the matter. Namely, there are some norms which seem particularly "rational" to people for different reasons than mentioned before. For instance, it seems that the rationality of the norm which states that a client who came into an office first should be served first is obvious. Similarly, a norm which states that if there is not enough of an essential commodity to serve everyone, then it should not be sold in unlimited amounts to the first client; it should be sold in limited amounts to all or at least the greatest number of clients possible. In a line, people fight about who was first but they never question the rule of first come, first served. "It is dictated by logic itself", is what we hear in such cases. The same "logic" makes us refrain from the idea that someone other than the perpetrator was to atone for his deed. This is why the notion of justice, which all the above situations apply to, was tied to the notion of consequence. For instance, L. Chwistek linked these two in a paper presented in the Third Polish Philosophical Congress. In the paper, the notion of social justice is linked to the rule of consequence formulated by the speaker: "One should behave in the same manner in identical situations".[75]

What is this about? Are we dealing with an appeal to those [supposedly neutral] intellectual values [...] as well as "reducing" the so-called moral values to intellectual values? Are we dealing with greater popularity of the latter in the sense that whatever is foolish is more indisputable than that which is morally wrong? An issue is revealed here which we will not attempt to resolve at this point. Indeed, we feel there is a difference between a norm of the type: "One should not bully the weak" or "Love thy neighbour", and a norm which states that one should receive higher wages for more work (obviously, if the work is of the same quality). Perhaps the difference lies in the fact that the first two norms are supported only by moral evaluations, whereas in the case of the latter norm and similar norms one can STILL argue that putting the matter differently would be UNREASONABLE.

---

[75] *Cf.* Chwistek [1936: 494].

Norms which contain this kind of double foundation would have reasons to aspire to supreme norms, since they are particularly obvious. Unfortunately, distinguishing them from norms based on a moral evaluation proves to be wavering. For instance, it is uncertain whether it is "logic" which makes us blame someone for something he did involuntarily, or if it is only our moral sense.

Aleksander Witold Rudziński. Norms and declaratives
[1947: 5–18]

1. Norms and judgements stating obligation

Let us start from familiar matters. Distinguishing judgements from norms and juxtaposing them is commonly accepted in research.[76] "It is snowing here" is a description of a fact, a judgement on something which exists; "Love thy neighbour as yourself!" is a norm about something which should be, which does not passively reflect, is not an image of the existing state of affairs. Hence the commonly accepted conclusion: norms cannot be true or false; the dichotomy of truth and falsehood never applies to them the way it applies to judgements.[77]

For the purpose of our considerations it should be noted briefly that norms (ethical, that is moral, and legal, as only these will be considered) are understood as utterances which are a verbal expression of ethical emotion and whose content is settlement of an obligation (or obligations) in a given social environment.[78] Therefore, an utterance which states descriptively that

---

[76] For instance: Bierling [1883: 271]; Kaufmann [1922: 31]. Jevons [1870: 48] supposes that interrogatives, imperatives, sentences expressing wish, *etc.* can probably be reduced to declaratives; if that does not occur, however, he denies them a place in logic.
[77] This view was formulated by Aristotle (*Categories*, cap. 4). Among contemporaries, the following firmly support it: Ross [1933: 435], also Bierling [1883: 281] and Kaufmann [1922: 31, 34–35 and 70]. Rand [1936: 438] draws attention to the impossibility of verifying some kinds of judgements, *e.g.* general judgements, judgements which form parts of fairy tales, romances, *etc.*
[78] Various meanings of the word "norm" are mentioned by Spiegelberg [1935: 64 – 67]. I do not accept any of them. It is good to know there are researchers who reject the view according to which rules or principles exist at all in law and morality: Cardozo [1921: 126] [...]. "Naive faith in the authority of rules" is ascribed to the Freudian father

an obligation towards another person is incumbent is not a norm. Then how can one distinguish a norm from a description?[79] The phrasing itself, the tone, the text or other symbols of an utterance provide no certainty in this matter. Even if expressions such as: "should", "is obliged", "is authorized", "is entitled", "is allowed", "is not allowed", *etc.*, are found in an utterance, it is still unclear whether this is a description, stating something "existing" or a requirement, a demand for something to occur, a permission, or settlement an obligation, *etc.* It is only after we research the social context where the utterance took place that we can determine what we are dealing with. Apart from the symbols of the utterance and the content conventionally attached to it in a given environment, we also have to take into account the social situation of the person uttering, that is, his attitude towards the environment and vice versa, the environment's relation to him, as well as the intention expressed in the utterance, as well as the emotional experiences of the person uttering.

Thus, both a judgement which states descriptively the occurrence of an obligation (a judgement on a norm) and a norm settling it can occur in the same verbal (symbolic) formulation.

Let us consider the question of whether the verification of a judgement stating the existence of an obligation occurs in the same way as for any other theoretical judgement. It is assumed that the verification of a standard perceptive (experimental) judgement is conducted through referencing the content of the judgement to its designates, that is, to the object which it is stating about, and therefore to perceptive data which emerge on contact with a given object in the first place. Yet, if we "state the existence of

---

complex which, after having lost the naive faith in the father's infallibility, settles for a replacement idea of the Law (Frank [1931: 18]) [...]. It is necessary to distinguish an utterance as a social process from an utterance as a creation (*cf.* Adler [1931: 103] [...]), as this prevents psycho-sociological reflections from being confused with logical ones, though one should keep in mind that one cannot properly understand the sense of utterances as creations without having examined the social environment in which they occur. Regarding utterances in isolation from the environment leads us astray in the deraction of verbosy. In addition, Kaufmann [1922: 89, remark. 1] seriously and emphatically claims that the sense of norms is not connected to the existence of people!!!
[79] The words "description", "descriptive", are used also in the meaning of "statement", "stating".

an obligation", the matter gets more complex, as the obligation alone is not a perceptible object.[80]

Therefore, if we confirm the existence of obligation in a judgement, there is no question of a regular comparison of the judgement's content with perceptions. Admittedly, in the case of a positive regulation we may state whether the regulation has been issued by a given person or authority. The verification of such a judgement seems *prima facie* similar to the verification of a perceptual judgement.[81] Although I cannot personally check the content of the judgement on the existence of obligation, I can research whether there occurred a normative fact which the obligation is based on.

---

[80] It consists of a multi-argument (3–4 arguments), and therefore complex and specific, relationship between elements of a varied ontological structure: (1) someone obliged, therefore: a person; (2) the activity or behaviour, therefore: a dynamic element, a process, proceedings, which on its part constitutes a relationship; (3) usually, though not always, someone entitled, therefore: a person again; and finally (4) a norm, that is, an utterance with a given content. The last segment (the norm) probably has to be included also in the relation stating an obligation, since the following expressions are not meaningless: "By violating his obligation to perform the activity, the defendant *ipso facto* violated article... of the code of law...". Therefore, it seems that in researching the structure of obligation, one should not neglect the norm itself, whose content is to state just this obligation. This is visible in the case of obligations introduced through positive norms, but may seem questionable in reference to intuitive obligations, since there a norm as an utterance takes second place to emotionally tinged valuation of activities. In spite of this, one cannot do without a norm (verbal expression of emotions) when constructing the said obligation. As it turns out on analysis of the notion of obligation, judgements which "state" descriptively the existence of obligations are judgements on norms which settled and introduced a given obligation, and therefore are derivative kinds of judgements which cannot be equated with descriptive-perceptual judgements. [...] Profound differences in the ontological character between the elements of the relation of obligation certainly do not prevent the whole from creating a logically correct relationships. *Cf.* Carnap [1929: 30–31]. Kaufmann seems to consider obligation as a two-argument relation [1922: 82–83]. Ross presents a valuable analysis of experiencing an obligation from the point of view of contemporary psychology [1933: 429–430].

[81] To keep matters simple, I omit further conditions necessary to fulfil in order for a supposition on the "existence" of an obligation to be considered as verified within a given system, and therefore, the fulfilment of the facts described in the antecedent of a norm (regular perceptual suppositions) and the normative evaluation of whether a given person or authority is authorized to issue the researched regulation which introduces the «stated» obligation, in accordance with a given system, and whether the norms on the manner of issuing such regulations has been fulfilled.

Judgements on the existence of intuitive obligations are verified based on more general intuitive norms, or by proving that within a given system they logically follow from norms, based on the system's assumptions and directives of behaviour. Naturally, the chief norm(s) of a given intuitive system cannot be justified, and they have to be accepted as self-evident chief assumptions within a given system. When verifying judgements on intuitive obligations discussed here, one comes across logical operations (reasoning), where both judgements on norms and norms themselves occur. The simplest example, without the deductive reasoning, is as follows. General norm: "Love your neighbour as you love yourself!". Derivative norm: "Feed the starving, give drink to the thirsty!". Obligational judgement, and thus, judgement on a norm: "There is an obligation to feed the hungry".

It clearly results from the above brief analysis that it is vital to distinguish intuitive norms from positive ones, also in the logical-normative field. The above example illustrates a well-known fact that the same normative content, and so *prima facie* the same norm, can be intuitive in some cases, when one does not refer to any specific social "normative fact", that is, the act of its settlement, in order to justify its validity, but rather to the worth of the recommended behaviour in the last resort. In other cases, the norm can be positive, when its binding power is derived from the fact of its settlement by, *e.g.*, God or the gospel.[82]

Apart from the judgement stating the existence of an obligation, another kind of judgements on norms, that is, judgements stating the validity of a given norm "Norm Y is valid", will be considered further. One encounters such judgements frequently in the work of lawyers and in arguments of scholarly dogmatists.

2. Truth and falsehood in the normative area

A paradoxical issue was touched upon in the title. There immediately arises a suspicion that we are dealing with a misunderstanding or even nonsense. After all, legal norms are neither true nor false, they are at most right

---

[82] Lande [1925b: 280 – 281]; Ehrlich [1913: 133] [speaks] against this view and claims that the same wording of a norm may consist of different content in different domains of ethics.

or wrong, just or unjust, socially useful or harmful, backward or progressive, just as physical phenomena are not morally right or wrong; they go "beyond good and evil". Still, the problem included in the title makes perfect sense, albeit not as simple as the above objections.

Norms do not fall under the dichotomy of truth and falsehood as it is commonly thought. "Bring my coat!" uttered to a servant cannot be true or false, just as the law of gravity does not fall under ethical evaluation. If I say: "John said to Blaise: "Bring my coat!"" then obviously this sentence is not a norm any more but a judgement on a norm, and as a judgement, it can be faulty or truth.

Is validity or non-validity of a norm an analogous feature to the truth or falsehood of judgements? If so, it would have to be a relation. This is indeed the case. Generally speaking, truth is a judgement's relation to reality (facts), whereas validity is relation of norm to people (addresses). Let us not go into details about the kind of relation that is present, respectively, in the first and second case, or the important issue of a clear distinction between the validity of a norm and an obligation settled through this same norm. [...]

For the discussed analogy between truth and validity it does not suffice to state that both are relations. Validity would have to fulfil a complete alternative analogous to truth. In a given specific case, a judgement may or may not be true or false, but it cannot be true and false at the same time. It also has to possess one of these features, unless it is nonsensical.[83] Is the same true for norms? Admittedly, within a given «system», a given norm applies or does not apply in relation to the chief norms (assumptions) of the given «system» and the directives of transformations possible within it, and therefore, accepted methods of interpretation, transformation and regulations on settlement norms accepted within this "system".[84]

---

[83] Naturally, in the field of deductive research the same judgement may be true within the same deductive system, with respect to the data of the assumption and the directives of transformations, and false in the presence of other premises and directives. Within the scope of empirical science, the relativization of truth and falsehood of perceptual judgements is limited to the theoretical interpretation of direct sensory data.

[84] It is worth noting that «systems» of present positive state legislation as well as positive religious rights contain regulations which originated in various times and social conditions, impossible to compare, and they contain incompatible, or even conflicting

The third possibility is the occurrence of a (normative) nonsense instead of a norm. Such an utterance as: "The star 3 Geuze should pay 8,000 złotys to The Polish State Treasury" cannot reasonably be deemed as valid or invalid.

Therefore, validity or non-validity of norms *prima facie* reveals analogous features to the truth and falsehood of judgements.

It would seem that thus both fields are separated completely and the function of the functor of truth and falsehood is fulfilled by the functor of validity or non-validity on the side of norms. However, the case is not that simple, in spite of what some prominent logicians may imagine.[85]

Here arises the issue of whether one can transform norms into logically equivalent, if not synonymous, judgements and conduct reasoning on them, thus eliminating norms from the scope of logical considerations.

Let us consider this issue with the example: "The obligation of citizens of a country is to defend their land from military invasion". It is unclear whether we want to say that someone imposed this obligation on the citizens at some point or that they adopted it recently or long ago, or if we claim that citizens SHOULD defend their country, according to our belief.

In the first case, our statement should be complemented in the following way: "According to the law of military duty dated... *Polish Code of Law* No... par. ..., each citizen is obliged to defend his country by joining the army". Undoubtedly, we are certain of this view's rightness on uttering it, we strongly experience the relevant legal emotion, we feel that each citizen SHOULD defend his country, and the country has the right to demand it from the citizens that they bravely fulfil their duty. However, it may be the case that the whole matter is considered coolly, purely theoretically, contemplating only whether such an obligation really «exists» or not, and the moment we find a relevant regulation, we are satisfied with stating that it

---

data. It is only when dogmatists, that is learned lawyers and theologians, work on aligning them that a «scientific» legal system of a given country, or the ethics of a given confession, is built. *Cf.* Lande [1925a: 70]. Therefore, one should always distinguish between a «system» of regulations which are valid positively (norms) and a system which constitutes its «scientific» description (judgements on norms).

[85] Wilkosz [1925: 48–48]; Sztykgold [1936: 493].

legally «exists» indeed. The point of approval, of experiencing a legal emotion fades and moves to the background. The question is whether it entirely disappears in psychological sense in our emotions and whether we can assume that it can be omitted in theoretical discussion on this subject.

First, another example: "One should not torture animals". We experience this norm emotionally, perhaps we even feel that animals have the right to demand from us kind treatment, but we do not refer to any normative facts, that is, the fact that God dictated it, or the lawgiver did, or the teacher, or mother. It may be expressed in a slightly more theoretical manner: "People are obliged to refrain from torturing animals", but this does not change the matter significantly. What remains is the distinct residue of a negative emotional evaluation of torturing animals, or a repulsive legal emotion, as Petrażycki would put it.

Some may obstinately claim that it can be expressed in the following way: "There is an obligation not to torture animals", and then no emotion is experienced. Perhaps. But this is not about what is experienced by the person uttering certain words or expressions with understanding, as emotions may be considerably weakened or even imperceptible in introspection, as a result of dulled sensitivity caused by experiencing the same norm often in the same actual conditions. The focus has to be moved to the criteria which determine whether the uttered content is appropriate or not. Then it occurs that the willingness to learn whether such an obligation exists or not resulted in encountering either an intuitive emotional experience, or a social fact that someone demands such behaviour from us. Then we also encounter, among other things, ethical emotion, on the side of the other person rather than ours, when the obligation exists.

Let us return to the point. The utterance: "There is an obligation not to torture animals" cannot be justified in any other way besides the following: because tormenting animals is wrong, unworthy of a human being, a despicable overuse of human advantage, *etc.*, if the obligation is not based on any normative fact. Clearly, we refer to the ethical EVALUATIONS of a given behaviour which is contrary to the obligation being justified.

However, if we quote any normative fact in order to justify the existence of the above obligation, for instance: "because the *Polish Code of Law,*

No..., par. ... banned torturing animals", then the whole situation changes significantly. The fact is objectively stable and the norm gains an objective basis. It is unimportant in the above situation that one experiences a weak ethical emotion or does not have any emotional experience at all when uttering the whole phrase: "There is an obligation not to torture animals on the basis of the *Polish Code of Law*, No..., par. ...". In a way, the utterance can be tested by itself, since, as we mentioned before, one could state the normative fact which was discussed. An utterance or another specific social fact, the so-called conclusive fact, that is one which leads to a conclusion that this fact indicates a norm of a specific content, or settles it in a way according to the rules (directives) of a given normative system, can also be a normative fact. This way one is able to research whether the content of the norm in question is included in the normative fact, and whether the content will indeed be found implicitly in some way or explicitly, then it can be assumed that the justification of the existence of an obligation is at least partly successful. There always remains the question of whether a normative fact as such possesses a normative quality, whether it is consistent with the more basic norms of a given system, not to mention the fact that the norm expressed in it can be questioned on the basis of norms from other systems of the same kind (for instance, other legal or foreign norms) or norms of an entirely different kind, for instance, moral norms. This does not undermine the stressed difference between norms which are justified through referring to the valuations themselves and norms which are motivated through indicating normative facts.[86]

This approach should be rejected in order to decide that the very fact of a given norm being ethically experienced by the person uttering it or any other person is a justification of its validity, since this reasoning leads to claiming that all judgements uttered with conviction are therefore true. The quantitative criterion, that is, research of the quantity of people in a given social group or in general who perceive a given ethical view as right and

---

[86] Let us entirely disregard another way of justifying norms which consists in referring to the usefulness of the proscribed activity, since although this way plays a crucial role it has played in social life for ages, it belongs to the pedagogical sphere rather than the normative-ethical sphere.

who experience a relevant ethical emotion, is worthless, not because other people's psyche is not directly accessible to us but because the criterion does not at all work as an argument to justify the validity of intuitive norms.

One might try the view which states that a norm is valid when (1) a vast (what?) majority of people act according to it in a vast (what?) majority of cases, and (2) a majority (what?) experiences it as a moral or legal emotion. Alternatively, the same idea with a modification: (1) as above and (2) when a majority (what?) of the actual ruling class experiences... *etc.* Here a discrepancy between the normative approach (justifying the validity of norms) and the research of the actual social processes is revealed. The above view will have to be rejected for normative purposes, not because of the difficulty in establishing facts in (1) and (2), but rather because it does not explain why we are prone to accept an activity as contrary to moral or legal obligations, even if they occur constantly, or why there are some social classes which condemn as immoral or contrary to the (natural, right) law certain commonly performed actions which had been regarded as obligatory.

Let us then stick to the following: Intuitive norms can be replaced with hypothetical judgements on norms of the type: "If one should love one's neighbour, then one should feed the hungry".

Positive norms can be replaced with judgements on themselves (judgements on norms) when they are verbally formulated in a way which encompasses the relevant normative fact, and then this kind of utterance can be treated as a theoretical judgement stating a certain «factual state».

What would play the role of the factual state? Let us discuss the latest example: "There is an obligation not to torture animals on the basis of the *Polish Code of Law*, No..., par. ...". We assume we stated with our own eyes that the said law actually resolves that one must not torture animals. What of it? Do we have the right to separate the norm "One must not torture animals" and deem it proven? No; we can only assume a statement of the following kind: "If the Law No..., par. ... is valid, then also the norm: "One must not torture animals" is valid". No more, no less than that.

As shown in the above discussion, stating the validity of a norm is done in an entirely different (normative-dogmatic) way than stating the facts. Still, this way we settle relationships between the validity of norms and the validity of normative facts (sources), which are of a factual character as purely logical relationships of entailment.

As we established, it is possible to replace norms with obligational judgements or judgements on norms through settling in a definition how the existence of obligation and the validity of a norm should be understood. Still, those very definitions,[87] which the mentioned replacement depends on, cannot be formulated in such a way that stating the existence of an obligation and settling the validity of a norm is possible in the same manner as stating regular facts of theoretical sciences or daily life is possible (a normative verification of sorts).

Therefore, only logical relationships between the validity of one norm and the validity of another can be settled, and only this kind of judgements on norms are testable, or true or false in the purely theoretical sense. However, stating single, separate, and therefore absolute, obligations is impossible through theory.

The replacement of norms with judgements on the existence of obligations is therefore possible with the above reservations; only conditional (hypothetical) relationships between norms or obligations are stated. In spite of that, it is impossible to entirely eliminate norms from the scope of the discussion of them and replace them with judgements, as chief norms of intuitive systems have to retain their form of norms, just as in positive systems norms on settling norms do not allow such transformations into judgements.

In the above discussion, utterances of the following kind were used again and again [...]: "There is an obligation for person A to perform (or neglect) action x" and testing this kind of utterance was considered, among other things. Judgements of this kind are indirectly judgements on norm, and directly: obligational judgements, and therefore something derived from norm and genetically dependent on it. Expressions of the kind: "There is such and such an obligation for person A" seem acceptable and reasonable, since we do not decide in them about the existence of person A or any other subject of this kind, which would ontologically meet with certain familiar difficulties (the ontological proof of the existence of God), but we speak of

---

[87] *Cf.* below.

a certain description as meant by B. Russell,[88] that is, the only such thing introduced by the relevant norm (the obligation of behaving in a specific manner).

Another thing to consider is the kind of utterances as follows: "Regulation *Y* is valid". This is undoubtedly A JUDGEMENT ON NORM, so the question of its verification arises again. We predicate a given norm to be valid. This predication can be true or false. How do we state it? The problem is analogous to the issue of the existence of obligations [...]. This is simply because an obligation settled by a given norm "exists" only when the norm is valid.

A judgement settling whether a given intuitive norm is valid will therefore be true when we can deduce it from the overriding intuitive norm(s) within the system, whereas a judgement concerning a positive norm will be – when the norm is proven to have been settled correctly by an authorized person or authority within a given system. Also in this case, full removal of norms is unattainable, as there remain at least the chief intuitive norms, as well as norms on imposing positive regulations.

Another question to be considered is whether the judgement on a norm obtained through replacement is logically equivalent to the norm which it arose from. "The regulation: "One must not bake white bread" is valid" is a judgement on a norm. "One must not bake white bread" is a norm. Logical equivalence of sentences *p* and *q* lies in the fact that sentence *q* follows from sentence *p* but also sentence *p* follows from sentence *q*.[89] How is it in our case? From the fact that the regulation: "One must not bake white bread" is valid it results that such bread must not be baked, but not the other way around. From the norm: "One should not bake white bread" it does not at all result that the norm is valid; therefore, a judgement on the norm does not result from here. Thus, there is no logical equivalence between them.

The case of obligations judgements is analogous. "There is (*scil.* according to norm *X*) an obligation to be cruel towards «enemies»" is an obli-

---

[88] Whitehead & Russell [1910: 30 – 32, 173]; Russell [1924: 174 and next]; Carnap [1929: 15 – 16]; Kotarbiński [1929: 237 – 238].
[89] Kotarbiński [1929: 173]; Sleszyński [1925: 132].

gational judgement, and therefore, a judgement on the relevant norm (intuitive or positive). The fact that the above obligation exists entails that "One should be cruel towards «enemies»" but the fact that "One should be cruel towards «enemies»" does NOT entail that there existed such an obligation, since this norm may not be valid in a given system. Thus, there is no logical equivalence between obligational judgements and the relevant norms.

Let us briefly sum up the outcome of the above chapter:

(1) In the normative domain, truth and falsehood do not refer to norms, since these may be valid or not, but rather to judgements on norms.

(2) Among judgements on norms, we discussed two types which are of particular importance to normative discussions, that is: (a) judgements on the existence of obligations and (b) judgements stating the validity of a given norm.

(3) Judgements on the existence of obligations are a special kind of judgements on norms, as a relevant norm settling the given obligation is included in the relation of obligation.

(4) Norms can be replaced with relevant judgements on norms, either of the type (a) (judgements on the existence of obligations), or of the type (b) (judgements on the validity of a given norm), as a result of which these kinds of judgements on norms can be used in the processes of reasoning, as regular judgements.

(5) Yet, the verification of such judgements on norms occurs in a different manner than in the case of theoretical judgements, namely, a specific normative manner, that is, through referring to normative facts and basic norms of a given system as well as directives of transformation adopted in them, if we consider positive norms, and only to basic norms and directives of transformation if we consider intuitive norms.

(6) Only hypothetical judgements are testable; those which state a conditional relationship between the validity of norms, or between the existence of obligations, or between the validity of normative facts and the validity of norms.

(7) From the real judgement on a norm [and therefore (a) from the fact that a given obligation exists, or (b) from the fact that a given norm is valid], a given norm results, that is, its disposition (content), but not the other way

around. Thus, there does not occur a logical equivalence between a norm
and a judgement on the given norm.

Kazimierz Ajdukiewicz. Volitional acts

[1948: 204 – 209]

John, who has been a chain smoker, decides that smoking has a negative effect on his health and quits. It is not easy for him: he is INCLINED TO
light a cigarette, he wants one badly; nonetheless, he does not smoke because he WANTS not to smoke. Someone has a lot of work which he cannot
cope with if he does not stay up late and work. Therefore, he sits by his desk
and works late, even though he is INCLINED TO work anymore. Still, he does
not stop working, as he WANTS to work.

These situations exemplify two types of drivings, one of which is described with the phrase: "be inclined", and the other: "want". Already the
verbal form of these phrases indicates that there is a significant difference
between the two types of drivings. Namely, the first type is represented in
sentences like "I am inclined" and in the other type is used in sentences
like: "I want", where the name of the person experiencing the driving is the
subject. The difference in verbal formulation aptly reflects the difference in
the way we experience these two types of drivings. Whenever one's driving
assumes such a form that one would express it through "be inclined", this
driving presents itself as a passive state, a state which has been imposed,
rather than a spontaneous act of my own «self». When a person tired with
his work feels logy and sleepy, but manages to overcome these feelings and
forces himself to continue working through an act of willpower, he realizes that the tendency to stop working comes from his own body, whereas
what he experiences as the core of his personality opposes this tendency and
overcomes it. Similarly, a person who decides to quit smoking experiences
a strong temptation to succumb to the addiction. In this situation the temptation, which is a kind of a driving, is experienced as something which does
not come from the inside, and is not experienced as one's own activity, but
rather as a force which acts upon the person from the outside. Conversely,
the drivings expressed through the phrase "I want" are experienced as one's

own, spontaneous acts, rather than passive states. The point from which the driving derives is the very self, the deepest core of my consciousness.

All of these drivings whose nature is of a passive state, a state which has been imposed, rather than a spontaneous act of the core of one's consciousness, will be called PASSIVE DRIVINGS. Those drivings which are experienced as one's own spontaneous act, as a driving caused by the person, will be called SPONTANEOUS DRIVINGS or PROPER ACTS OF WILL.

What one is inclined to do, that is, one's passive driving, can be perceived as wrong, which means that one would have the aim of his driving not implemented rather than implemented. For example, a person who is aware that cigarettes are harmful "is inclined" to smoke but he realizes that it would be better if he did not smoke. On the other hand, a spontaneous act of will is always connected to the approval of its aim and with the sense of rightness of the driving contained in it. When one is inclined to smoke but does not want to smoke, then while experiencing the latter driving one experiences it with a sense of rightness. This sense of rightness, or approving of a certain driving and regarding its aim worthy of existence, is inseparable from proper acts of will as well as characteristic of them. AN ACT OF WILL IS ALWAYS AN APPROVED DRIVING. This approval, this accepting the experienced driving as right, this applause to a given driving decides that accepting this driving as one's one and this approval distinguishes it from passive drivings, which one does experience however not as one's own drivings but as imposed ones.

As we look for examples of passive drivings, we find them mostly in our thirsts, that is, those drivings which stem from emotions. When one is thirsty and is inclined to drink something, one experiences a certain driving, which certainly has a trait of a passive driving. This does not mean that the aim of one's driving cannot be an aim of an act of will at the same time. That may take place when one is not only thirsty but also one wants to drink, that is, when one sympathizes with the passive driving in a way, when one inwardly accepts it as belonging to oneself. When, for example, an ill person is thirsty but does not know whether perhaps the water is not recommended in his state, then he experiences a passive state of thirst but has not granted it his approval yet. However, when the doctor tells him that drinking water is recommended in his state, then a spontaneous act of will is added to his up to now passive thirst. Therefore, acts of will do not necessarily have to stand in opposition to passive drivings, as it was the case in the examples used in the introduction but may be in line with them.

Passive drivings and acts of will can both be transformed into acts. A thirsty person is usually pushed to action by passive thirst only. In such cases it does not usually come to the proper act of will, to granting approval to the experienced driving, to internal sympathizing with it. Similarly, a person who is tired with a long hike: when he reaches his destination, he sits down or lies down, even though no internal approval for satisfying this driving occurred inside him. Also, a person who impulsively and «without hesitation» comes to the aid of a neighbour who is in sudden danger; a sudden feeling and a thirst connected to it is immediately turned into act. We speak of such actions induced directly by feelings and thirsts as actions induced by an impulse. They still belong to activities conscious of their aim, but are on the border of reflexive actions.

However, in many cases one's acts derive from acts of will. Let us consider the emergence of an act of will which leads to act. One contemplates, for example, about what to do with a certain sum of money which one has at his disposal. The person really is inclined to buy a new radio for that money, but knows that the money will be needed to buy more important things later. He does not know what to do yet. However, at some point an act of will takes place. He will deposit the money in the bank! From that moment on, the person knows what he will do. His future activity which up until that point was not known to him, is perfectly clear to him now. The act of will which took place is experienced as a creative act which decided one's future course of activity, or created the core of the course of activity at that moment. One also draws assurance out of this act of will that one is going to deposit the money in the bank; the act also provides an insight into what he is going to do. Such an act of will is called a resolution. A RESOLUTION IS THEREFORE AN ACT OF WILL WHICH AIMS TO FULFIL A CERTAIN AIM THROUGH ITS OWN ACTIVITY, AND FROM WHICH ONE DRAWS THE CONVICTION THAT THE ACTIVITY WHICH DRIVES AT THIS AIM WILL TAKE PLACE. If a person decides that after passing the high school exams he will become an engineer, then from the moment the resolution occurred he knows that he will act in such a way that he may achieve the aim of obtaining an engineer degree. He did not know that before he undertook the resolution but now he does, but he does not learn it from experience or from others. He derives his certainty from the act of his resolution.

It may sometimes be the case that the object of an act of will is not necessarily one's activity directed at a certain aim, but the fact that one will decide to perform an activity provided certain conditions are fulfilled, which at that point one is not sure will happen. In such cases this activity is not called a resolved activity; it is called AN INTENDED ACTIVITY. For instance, I say I am going to go to the seaside this holiday when I want to state that I resoved on doing it provided some conditions, which I am not mentioning, are fulfilled. A design is then a conditional resolution to act.

Resolutions are uttered disclosed to others in sentences which state one's future activity. When I disclose my resolutions to others, I say, for instance: "I am going to hang the new painting on the wall", "I am going away in a month", "I am going to buy myself a motorbike", *etc.* Resolutions are then expressed in the same way judgements on one's future activity are expressed. Yet, resolutions are not at all identical with judgements on one's future activity. If it were so, then at the moment when Oedipus learned from the oracle that he will kill his father and marry his mother, and, trusting the oracle, believed in his future terrible acts, he would have to resolve them. Someone who, having made a confession, is full of remorse and good designs, but realizes that he will yet commit many more sins, would therefore have to resolve to sin more, since he believes he will sin some more in the future. A sentence which expresses a judgement on one's future activity is an expression of a resolution only as long as the judgement is issued on the basis of the experienced act of will, and if, at the moment of issuing a judgement on one's future activty, one feels that at that moment a core has been created by my act of will, a core of my future activity, a core, which did not exist until the act of will occured.

The scope of the aims which one may resolve to realize through one's activity is limited, as it is impossible to resolve to act towards realizing an aim whose unavailability one is convinced about. Thus, one cannot resolve to lift oneself or to move the Alps to Poland. Admittedly, one can resolve things which are impossible to accomplish, but only when one at least supposes (wrongly) they are achievable. It is not the case with thirsts. One may have a thirst for both things which are considered possible and things which are considered impossible. However, in order to resolve something one has to believe that it is achievable. This is the reason why people who have little faith in themselves have low capacity for possible resolutions. For that reason, it often happens that people who do not believe in themselves have weak capacity for making resolutions and therefore for creative acts of will. The lack of faith in one's own strength may become the source of real, and not only imaginary, weakness. Hence a guideline: one should sooner commit the sin of overconfidence than be unduly humble ("Look before your leap").

Activities which are expected as a result of resolutions (as well as designs) may be expected immediately after the resolution has been made or in some further, specified or unspecified, future. Depending on that we can say that the resolution concerns activity, which take place immediately after it or more remote in time. If the resolution concerns an activity which is remote in time, then it may prove effective, that is, it may lead to the resolved activity, even if one is not aware of it at the time the action is executed. A resolution creates a disposition to react with the intended action to the relevant stimuli, where the scope of the effective stimula can be wider or narrower. Someone who resolves to send a letter to a friend will react with the action of putting the letter in the mailbox if he sees one; an action which realizes the aim of the resolution as its result. It may also be the case that the resolution of putting the letter in the mailbox is taken under the influence of the sight of a person going out, who will definitely walk past a mailbox, and triggers the reaction of handing the letter to the person and asking him to put it in the mailbox. The disposition created by a resolution lasts only until we achieve some knowledge that the activity which is supposed to realize the aim of the driving took place, that is: only until the resolution is fulfilled; thus, if one puts the letter in the mailbox or asks someone else to do it for him, the sight of a mailbox will not trigger the reaction which had occurred while the mentioned disposition still lasted.

A specific stimulus which should automatically (that is, without a new act of will) trigger an activity which would in turn realize the aim of the resolution may not trigger the activity even if the resolution has not been executed. However, it is often the case that one resolves to put a letter in the mailbox, walks past a few mailboxes and still returns home with the letter in his pocket. We say of such cases that we forgot about the resolved act. It often happens to absent-minded – "forgetful" as one jokingly calls them – people. Experimental research shows that one cannot prevent forgetting the act even if the resolution is of great strength. Strongly resolved acts are forgotten equally easily to poorly resolved ones. The ease with which we forget depends on whether our actions are driven by only one, previously undertaken, resolution, or by a greater number of them. Acts stemming from one superior resolution constitute an organic whole where executing one part automatically transfers us to another; similarly, by singing a melody, singing one sound out of this melody transfer us for singing the next one. It is hard to play on a piano simultaneously two melodies which do not constitute an organic whole, and similarly, it is difficult to execute two processes of actions at the same time if they depend on two unconnected resolutions. If one is aiming for only one main task which requires a series of actions in a given time, then one has the greatest chance to remember all of these actions.

Resolutions may not be fulfilled also when they are breached or changed before relevant activity takes place. A change of a resolution consists in withdrawing it and replacing with another resolution, both being mutually exclusive. A breach of resolution occurs when there occur so strong desires whose aims exclude the aims of the resolution that they prevails over the resolution and prevents it from being realized.

Finally, a resolution might not be fulfilled when external conditions necessary to achieve the aim do not occur, and therefore, against expectations, the resolved action turns out to be impossible to accomplish.

Jerzy Lande. Normative and teleological rules
[1948: 275 – 276, 278 – 281]

We mentioned the equivalence between evaluating sentences and practical sentences. Let us then attempt to transform practical sentences of various types into evaluating ones.

We shall start with teleological rules and take as an example several recommendations for photographic techniques from *Handbook of Photography* by T. Barzykowski and J. Jaroszyński [1928: 111–112]. In the chapter on developing film we read:

> While developing one SHOULD continuously rock the tray in order to accelerate the reaction and spread it evenly on the whole surface of the plate. At the beginning of developing one SHOULD NOT bring the plate to the source of light as even red light affects the emulsion and may cause it to fog over. It would be BEST to cover the tray with a piece of cardboard or keep it away from the lamp.

The first two rules are stated in practical language, whereas the third one is put in the language of good and contains the word "best" ("the best possible"), which is a favourite with some philosophers under Brentano's influence.[90] The words stressed in the first two sentences can be replaced by "it is right" and "it is wrong". Then the whole paragraph will be translated to the language of good and in this case, since its teleological character is conspicuous, it will not lose its expressiveness. Therefore, it seems that teleological systems can be transformed this way to a certain extent.

The outcome of the attempt will be much worse in the case of ethical rules. Let us consider the moral rules of the gospel:

> If someone strikes you on the right cheek, turn to him the other also. And if someone wants to sue you and take your tunic, let him have your cloak as well.

This version is entirely practical, normative. Let us replace the imperatives with evaluating expressions: "It will be good if you turn... (let him have...)" or "You will do well if you turn... (let him have...)". Then the les-

---

[90] According to W. Tatarkiewicz [1919: 139 *et seq.*], "the best act", or "the best possible", is "a right act", and the rightness constitutes a criterion of morality. Therefore, it seems the rule of covering the tray with a piece of cardboard shifts the issue from the domain of photographic techniques to the domain of morality.

son will lose its character and become a riddle: the authoritative, "categorical" dictate of obligation disappears and what remains is an undefined evaluation which suggests a teleological interpretation. Why will it be good to turn the other cheek? Perhaps to amuse the attacker or to evoke pity in him?

The case of legal ethics is even harder. Let us consider paragraph 3 of article 25 of the *Constitution*, of 17 March 1921:

> The President of The Republic of Poland may convene the Parliament for a special session at any time at his discretion, which should be done within two weeks of being demanded by 1/3 of all the MPs.

As opposed to unilateral obligations of morality, we are dealing here with obligations of one subject, which at the same time settle entitlement (commitments) of the other subject. The President's entitlement to call a special session corresponds to the MPs' obligation to meet in session and to the entitlement of 1/3 of the MPs to demand such a session to be called, as well as the President's obligation to fulfil this demand. As we established before, the obligation ("should be done") cannot reasonably be replaced with the expressions: "well", "right", not to speak of the entitlement ("may", "has the right to")! Shall we call this act neutral, since it is neither dictated nor prohibited? No, the entitlement contains a kind of authorization, empowerment, or a specific approval which is paired on the other end with the obligation to comply. The language of values has to surrender in the face of a legal norm. [...]

Recipes, regulations of photography or any engineering technology, army strategy and tactics, medicine and hygiene, handbooks of all technical sport rules, pedagogy, politics and many others contain abundant material of teleological rules. Commandments of the Church and God, codes of honour, game rules for sport and other domains (not technical ones but the ones stating obligations and entitlements of the competitors), rules of social behaviour, legal regulations and codes of law provide us with a rich source of fundamental, normative regulations. Some of these domains, like technology, medicine, or law, generated rich literature which is logically arranged into systems which emphasize the character of the relevant regulations, their logic and cognitive basis. [...]

Let us first work on the TELEOLOGICAL evaluation. We already know the photographic instruction: "While developing one should continuously rock the tray in order to accelerate the reaction"; or it can be expressed in the formula: "If you want to accelerate the reaction, rock the tray". It is a model example. Ossowska's example is equally good: "In order to cause ether to boil in a test-tube the temperature should be so and so". Here we recommend (approve) a course of action as a means to achieve a specific aim. From the point of view of psychology, we are aware of images of two states of affairs: (1) our behaviour, which we desire because we want to achieve something through it, (2) some state of affairs which we also desire. It seems that Ossowska [1946: 280; 1947: 111 *et seq*.], Ingarden [1948], Kotarbiński [1929: 445–446] and many others rightly claim (yet without mentioning the term "causality") that we justify such regulations by referring to causation. A theoretical sentence states that the cause "heating a test-tube to temperature T" results in the "boiling of ether"; on which the practical regulation is based: "If we want to achieve the aim: "boiling of ether", we should subject the test-tube to temperature T" (or an evaluating sentence: "Heating the test-tube to temperature T is the proper way to produce the result of ether boiling").[91]

---

[91] In a conversation we once held, Petrażycki questioned the dependence of a teleological sentence on a causal sentence which I settled in one of my works. Unfortunately, we were interrupted before I heard the justification. Only while reading *New Foundations of Logic* did I happen on a probable explanation. According to the author, logic is a teleological science; its task is to formulate the rules of producing and justifying the relevant positions and criticizing the faulty positions and justifications (Petrażycki [1939]). The rules of logic are probably not based on any causative sentences; they are based on some theoretically stated ideal relationships. If this is so, and it may be so also in the case of some other domains of ideal teleology, then the thesis of the dependence of teleological sentences on theoretical causal sentences would only be adequate in terms of real means and aims. Since the present paper only takes into account real teleologies, the issue of their dependence on causal sentences is not probably faultily formulated. Obviously, Petrażycki's view of logic as a practical science concerns logic drafted by him, or according to him, logic the way it should be. Speaking of contemporary logic, he mentions its theoretical character which researchers attempt to grant it, which he considers to be a misunderstanding; he characterizes «traditional» logic as a medley, although it is hard to infer from the short and incoherent content of the notes whether he means contemporary or earlier logic. All these matters seem to me as worthy of the interest of our logicians.

Apparently, any teleological rule is justified in the relevant causal sentence when a norm can only be justified by basing it on a higher norm of this same system, and the hierarchic ladder ends sooner or later, leading to a void, where advocates have to support the case with "axioms". This possibility to base teleological instructions on theoretical, experimentally testable theses gives the relationship of means to the aim an empirically testable character and gives an objective quality to the relevant domains. Therefore, as opposed to norms with their "hard", "categorical" character, we tend to refer to them as "advice" or "reasonable advice". The teleological postulate is always given in the conditional form ("if you want..."), so in a way it is presumed that someone may not want it. In accordance with that, the value of teleological behaviour does not usually arouse enthusiasm or another emotion; instead, the reasoning is cool and matter-of-fact: "If we want this or that, we should act so and so". However, this issue should not be perceived in a way such that teleological experience is always emotionally cooler than fundamental, nor that evaluation is focused exclusively on the aim, whereas the image of behaviour-means does not arouse enthusiasm. We may be pulled in the first direction when we consider: "If you want A, do B", "If you wish A', do B'''". Then both instructions are treated unemotionally. However, when the aim: "I want A, I do not want A'''" has been chosen, immediately both the aim and the means become "valuable", that is, become emotionally tinged. The second hypothesis often comes to one's mind, but it is enough to listen to two skiers discuss two types of grease which serve the same purpose, or two photographers discuss the choice of developer, in order to realize that the evaluating emotion is also connected with the fancy of means and, as it encounters resistance, it increases its force; that is the use of "the prevention method" recommended by Petrażycki in order to increase the force of emotion which is more elusive.

The case of FUNDAMENTAL evaluations is different. Here we recommend or reject certain behaviour "as such", "in itself". A lie may be recommended as the proper means to achieve an aim in life, even if we are not Machiavelli's princes; however, at the thought of telling a lie we immediately think: "No, that is not allowed, it is wrong to lie". Whoever rejects lying in fear of a sanction in the afterlife, like eternal damnation, or a social sanction, like imprisonment, being put in a corner by one's mother, or embarrassment, he is guided by teleological motives. An "honest" person, a "gentleman", that is a man who is of strong fundamental disposition, rejects lying "on principle", regardless of the consequences; he rejects lying as a wrong, improper, vulgar act in itself.

Jerzy Kalinowski. The grammatical structure of normative sentences
[1953: 113 – 117]

Sentences which have the logical value of truth, falsehood or intermediate, between true and false, can be divided with respect to what they express into theoretical sentences and normative sentences. Theoretical sentences are sentences which predicate on reality the way it is or is not, which give an overview of it; thus the name (from Θεωρεω – I view). Aristotle divided these sentences further into sentences *de inesse* and sentences *de modo*, as they were later called. [...] Normative sentences are sentences which predicate on how a person should, has a right to, can or cannot act; they take their name from the fact that they express norms of behaviour.

So far, almost exclusively, theoretical sentences have been researched. At its beginnings as well as throughout its history up until the period of great popularity nowadays, logic has been shaped in relation to theoretical sentences and sciences which consist of them. Meanwhile, in the period of fundamental transformations which the world is undergoing at present, normative sciences and skills, which are ordered sets of justified normative sentences, are gaining importance. The statements within these fields list either the rules of human behaviour or the rules of producing various works by people. Therefore research on the logical basis of normative sciences is significant and momentous, as it leads to settling logical statements which are the basis for rules of reasoning characteristic to the study of controlling activity.

The theory of normative sentences presented in this work is an attempt to formulate a formalized deductive system of certain logical statements which can be specifically interpreted by normative sentences – in light of the specific construction of the latter. We will fulfil this task in two stages.

Firstly, we will build a certain formalized deductive system of certain sentence-forming connectives with two nominal arguments, which we will mark as K_1. Theses of system K_1 are the basis of formulating one group of rules of reasoning characteristic to normative study. Moreover, together with specific theses of sentential calculus and calculus of propositional functions, they constitute a portion of the auxiliary theses of the second formalized deductive system, which we will denote as K_2. [...] The theses of system K_2 are the basis for formulating the second group of rules of reasoning characteristic to normative study. Thus, the theses of both of the interlocked systems constitute the logical basis of normative study, or in short: the logic of normative sentences. [...]

Before attempting to execute the task of the formalization of the logical basis of normative study, let us determine in brief the grammatical and logical structure of a normative sentence and the relevant logical propositional function. [...]

From the grammatical point of view, as normative sentences we will regard grammatical predicative sentences which, according to the grammar of the Polish language, or analogous rules of grammar in other languages, are equivalent to sentences created with the aid of the following expressions:

> "... should do..."
> "... has the right (is allowed) to do..." } personally or impersonally
> " ... can (may) do..."

We will continue to only speak of normative sentences created with the aid of the above expressions.

As for gender form, the remarks on normative sentences created with verbs in the third form singular of Present Tense refer *mutatis mutandis* to sentences created with the same verbs in another gender form, another grammatical number and a different tense.

The expression: "...has the right to do..." is adopted in the meaning it has in the sentence: "If John should clean up, then John has the right to clean up", whereas the expression: "...can do..." is used in the meaning it has in the sentence: "If Stanley can sell his property (that is, "execute the sale of his property"), then Stanley may not sell his property". An analogous expression: "...is allowed to do..." has the meaning like in the following sentence: "If it is allowed to stockpile, then it is allowed not to stockpile".

The infinitive "do" may be preceded by NEGATION OF INFINITIVE: "not". Taking this into account, we can settle three further kinds of normative sentences created with the following expressions:

"...should not do...";

"...has the right (is allowed) not to do...";

"...can (may) not do...".

Negation of infinitive ("not") is given such meaning that in the sentence: "Steve should not make noise" is equivalent to the sentence: "Steve should make not-noise". As we can see, it is not only the infinitive "do/ make" that can be preceded with negation of infinitive, but also the NOMINAL NEGATION.[92] This negation is a specific «TRIVALENT» complement of the name. For that reason we shall call it the mark of COUNTERACTION. The mark of counteraction, that is, action opposite to a given action, can be characterized by matrix analogous to the trivalent propositional matrix.

What does the trivalent character of the mark of counteraction consist in? Let us assume that a set of activities whose names in sentences regarded as normative can be items closer to the infinitive "do" are divided into three subsets: POSITIVE, NEGATIVE and NEUTRAL activities. Let us not go into discussing the criterion and meaning of evaluations which settle positive, negative or neutral value of each human activity. We will assume that a positive activity is one that should be executed; a neutral activity is one that can be executed or not executed; and a negative action is one that should not be executed. We are not attempting to determine whether a positive activity is positive because it should be executed or if it should be executed because it is positive.

---

[92] Nominal negation in the meaning of regular divalent complement of a name can also be the element preceding the name of the subject of the activity (*e.g.* "not-Steve"). Negation can be used in practical sentences in many other ways, which were mentioned as examples in a discussion by prof. T. Kotarbiński: "John can do so that not *f(x)*, ... not so that *f(x)*, ... so that *f*(not-*x*)" *etc.* The scope of the present work does not include the analysis of logical statements which express relationships between normative sentences, because of other negations, like the negation of the infinitive "do", or negation of the name of an activity, or negation of a whole sentence [...].

If an activity is represented by the symbol of name variable α, the positive value of an activity is 1*, the neutral value of an activity is ½*, the negative value of an activity is 0*, and counteractivity is N, then we will be able to characterize them in the following matrix, analogous to the matrix of trivalent sentential negation.

α	Na
1*	0*
1/2*	1/2*
0*	1*

The whole normative sentence can be preceded by a bivalent propositional negation. Since a normative sentence expresses the thought that a subject of activity is in a (normative) relationship of duty of doing, duty of not doing, possibility of doing, possibility of not doing or possibility of doing and not doing in terms of an activity, the negation of a normative sentence may be regarded as equivalent to the complement of the relation (symbolically: it is not true that Rxy only if NOT-Rxy). Therefore, further in this work we will not use the concept of propositional negation, but instead, we will use the concept of NEGATION OF FUNCTOR which, together with functor variable or functor constant, creates a relational complex variable or functor constant of the complement of the relation.

Before you know it, the analysis of the grammatical structure of normative sentences turns into a discussion of their logical structure. To continue the logical analysis thus commenced, we will conduct a comparison of normative sentences and modal sentences.

A comparison of these performed by J. Nuckowski in *Basic Logic for Secondary Schools* [1903], although it was undertaken in order to stress the distinctness of normative sentences, made the author consider putting forward a hypothesis concerning the analogous character of normative sentences and modal sentences. The hypothesis was confirmed by the fact that the theses of both systems analyzed in the present work can be interpreted both through modal and normative sentences. However, it is worth noting here that not all logical claims which are interpretable through modal sentences can thus be interpreted through normative sentences (*e.g.* the logic of normative sentences does not contain equivalents for the laws of conversion of modal sentences, just as in syllogistics of normative sentences there are only syllogisms whose major premise and conclusion are normative sentences, whereas minor premise is always a theoretical sentence *de inesse*).

Czesław Znamierowski. *Fiat*
[1957: 416 – 429, 560]

Fluid accumulated in a pipette does not drip at first, as it adheres to the glass more strongly than it is attracted to the ground. However, at some point the amount of the fluid increases such that THE RESISTANCE from the viscosity is overcome and a drop breaks off the glass. Some imperceptible increase provides the fluid with AN IMPULSE TO MOVE: the drop falls. As soon as the ultimate amount is gathered, there arises in the fluid A SUDDEN MOVEMENT.

This is also the case with the movement of living creatures. Muscle, as inert mass, resists movement. Apart from that, every kind of movement, even best designed, is counteracted by an inhibiting impulse. It is not in the best interest of a living creature to respond to an impulse hastily. Thus the inhibiting impulse controls the motor reaction and allows it only when the tension reaches a certain degree. The final increase of tension is the motor impulse which is followed by a sudden movement.

Many such impulses and movements are not even registered by the consciousness. For instance, we are not aware of the movement of the heart, intestines, stomach, or iris. Sometimes we receive a report of a change which had already taken place, but we do not perceive the motor impulse. A muscle "starts up" like a train which, if driven by a skilled driver, begins to move so smoothly that it is imperceptible to the passengers who notice the movement only after a while. It is often so in the case of REFLEXES.

The consciousness is also unaware of a motor impulse when an image of movement or an image of an object are enough to cause movement. When

I look at somebody who is yawning, I will start yawning myself. When I am distracted by conversation, I may look at a bunch of grapes and pluck one. The movement originated from an event which took place in my conscious mind; therefore, the image of grapes is the initial link in the chain of events which ends with picking a grape. However, my conscious mind was not aware of the initial event, as it did not presuppose the motor impulse. It must have missed the surging motor tension which achieved its aim without encountering resistance or drawing attention to itself. The whole motor issue developed outside the consciousness or on the edge of it, and it would be a difficult task for memory to recreate its course. In any case, the motor impulse was not registered in the consciousness: the hand just reached for the grape.

Such peripheral driving may face EXTERNAL RESISTANCE. Let us say that I pull a grape but this is not enough to detach it. This is when the consciousness comes to assist and surveys the situation like an appraiser: thus the consciousness clearly realizes the driving which had already begun to fulfil its aim. First of all, the consciousness recognizes the SITUATION in which the movement was and is supposed to occur, that is, the part of the environment where the aim of the driving is to be realized, and the position of one's body in this "area". At the same time, it looks into the content of the driving being realized and learns its AIM, as well as the IMAGE OF THE MOVEMENT which is supposed to lead to the aim, and which requires an additional impulse in the face of resistance. The consciousness finds in the developing driving a CONNECTION ready for the future MOVEMENT TOWARDS THE AIM. The movement was chosen to match the aim unconsciously, thanks to the fact that there are ready movement tracts in the nervous system. In a simple example, the consciousness does not investigate or evaluate the aim or the choice of means, but rather it accepts the driving, concurs with it and reinforces it with a new impulse, which overcomes the resistance and leads to movement.

It is a specific experience for the consciousness to opt for this driving. Here the consciousness seems to tell its driving: "Let whatever you wish occur". Therefore, we may determine it with the Latin "FIAT". Since this simple spell comes to the aid of an already formulated driving and gives the impression that in it the emerging movement is liberated from the bonds of the resistance it encounters, then the "fiat" can be regarded as A CONSCIOUS

SUDDEN MOVEMENT, that is, an event which initiated the movement. It is colloquially called AN ACT OF WILL.

The conscious mind feels that it sets the body in motion, as the driving clearly presents the scheme and the aim of the movement. The image of this movement and its aim makes the CONTENT OF THE ACT OF WILL, or its INTENTION. This intention is a plan of the movement and what shall be achieved through it, where the consciousness determines and predicts in advance a certain course of events. Here I provide my "fiat" so that my hand picks a grape. Therefore, I can see the movement of my hand and the picked grape in my hand. The fact that the movement and its outcome is predicted and calculated in advance is what is meant when we speak of the movement being INTENTIONAL and that the effect is achieved intentionally.

After an act of will, the movement designated by it occurs so quickly that one can say it occurs immediately. It's AN EXECUTIVE MOVEMENT, as it accomplishes what the intention of the act of will had planned. The act of will together with the executive movement are called ACTIVITY. This term encompasses a specific set of events in the soul and in the body. What is characteristic for most activities is that they are of dual nature: on the one hand, they belong to the realm of the consciousness, on the other – to the acts of the body.

One could say that activity is also composed of another, third phase, wherein the course of action returns to the consciousness. Namely, the executive movement makes itself felt through muscle, joint and tendon impressions; together they form THE PERCEPTION OF MOVEMENT. The conscious mind learns through perception that the body has executed its plan which had been crystallized in the act of will. It may also compare its plan to its execution; thus the perception of movement becomes a supervisory agent.

The consciousness is not only interested in the movement executed because of it but also in the effect which the movement was undertaken for. In most cases the effect lies BEYOND THE BODY, in the outside environment. Picking a grape from a bunch takes place beyond the skin, and therefore outside of the body. Since activity reaches only up to the boundary of the skin, then picking a grape does not constitute activity. However, the line of causative range clearly connects it with activity, whereas the intention of the act of will includes this effect even more conspicuously, as the link in the causal chain which activity is taken for. Activity, together with the effect which extends beyond the body, which the intention of an act of will encompasses, is called an ACT. This term consists of ACTIVITY and CHANGES IN THE ENVIRONMENT, which lead to the state of affairs designated in the intention. In our example, the series of changes is very short, since detaching a grape immediately follows tugging it. However, it may be the case that a chain is very long, for instance, when a telegraph operator pushes a button and causes the mechanism to move in a distant telegraphic machine. This chain of results is a measure of THE SCOPE OF AN ACT.

If the scope is small, the consciousness promptly registers the effect of the act. THE mentioned PERCEPTION OF THE EFFECT is the controlling factor in activity, as it helps determine whether our "fiat" has led to the state of affairs which the intuition anticipated. The driving is extinguished and appeased only when the consciousness registers that the aim has been achieved. The cycle of activity and act closes and the accomplished matter is filed for record in the consciousness.

This is the operating scheme in the simplest case. However, it is usually the case that activity is more complex in all its stages. [...]

The act of will, both as a choice and executive experience, has A FORMAL FUNCTION, as it is the ultimate mediator between the drivings which precede it. The act of will encounters thirsts and interests in the conscious itself. [...] THE SELECTION OF MATERIAL does not derive from the act of will itself. Still, it is A CREATIVE ACT, since it materializes what was only possible or near realizing.

Wiesław Lang. The consequences of negating the norm
[1960: 57–62]

Negation of normative sentences, just as negation of descriptive sentences, can be SENTENTIAL NEGATION or NOMINAL NEGATION.[93] However, the logical consequences and directives of both forms of negation of normative sentences are different from the directives and consequences of negation of descriptive sentences.

---

[93] Ajdukiewicz [1955:73–78].

Sentential negation of a norm consists in negating a normative utterance in the form: "It is not true that the owner of real estate should pay a wealth tax" or "It does not occur that the owner of real estate should pay a wealth tax". A sentential negation (or negation of predicate) of a norm consists in inserting the symbol of negation before the predicate of a normative sentence in the form of: "The owner of real estate should not pay a wealth tax".

Both forms of negation occur [...] in the bivalent logic of sentences; within this logic, sentential and nominal negations are equivalent only in certain types of sentences, whereas the equivalence does not occur in other types.

In the logic of normative sentences, apart from the rules of equivalence in operation in the logic of theoretical sentences, there occur additional rules which are not used in the bivalent logic of theoretical sentences. In order to settle the logical consequences of negation of the validity of a norm one has to investigate the specific rules of equivalence of two forms of negation within normative sentences. According to the conception of a legal norm assumed in the present paper, a legal norm can also be expressed in the form of two sentences: a sentence on obligation and a sentence on entitlement. One also has to consider the logical consequences of sentential and nominal negation of both of these sentences and settle rules of equivalence which occur between the negation of a norm and the negation of sentences on obligation and entitlement (negation of legal relationship).[94]

Let us begin with the last issue, namely, the problem of the negation of sentences on obligation and entitlement.

(1) (a) Sentential negation of a sentence on entitlement provides: the obligation to execute the opposite activity, entitlement to execute the opposite activity accessorily connected with this obligation, or an extra-legal sphere.[95] (b) Nominal negation of a sentence on obligation provides: enti-

---

[94] Rudziński [1947: 35–37].

[95] This is based on the conception presented in the paper I wrote together with A. Delorme [Lang & Delorme 1957], according to which the entitlement to execute a given obligation is always connected with the given obligation within a working legal system. The content of this entitlement does not extend beyond the content of obligation (it is equivalent to obligation in subject), which is why it is not usually taken into consideration. Rather, this kind of "accessorial entitlement" is a kind of "permission" within a legal system to execute given activity accepted as obligatory within this

tlement to execute an opposite activity or one in accordance with the content of the negated obligation, or an extra-legal sphere, but it does not provide the obligation to execute the opposite activity.

(2) Nominal negation of a sentence on entitlement and a sentence on obligation provides the same results, with one significant difference: nominal negation of sentences on entitlement and obligation NEVER PROVIDES AN EXTRA-LEGAL SPHERE.

The above theses can be supported by simple examples:

Ad (1).

(a) "*A* has the right to demand the return of money from *B*."

Sentential negation: "It does not occur that *A* has the right to demand the return of money from *B*".

Consequences: I. *A* has the obligation not to demand the return of money from *B* and obviously also has the entitlement to do it. II. *A*'s demanding or lack of demanding the return of money from *B* legally has zero value, and thus this kind of *A*'s behaviour towards *B* is not legally regulated or is legally neutral.

(b) "*B* has the obligation to return the money to *A*."

Sentential negation: "It does not occur that *B* has the obligation to return the money to *A*".

Consequences: I. "*B* has the right to return or not to return the money to *A*." II. "*A*'s returning or not returning the money to *B* legally has zero value, and thus this kind of *B*'s behaviour towards *A* is not legally regulated or is legally neutral."

Contrary to expectations, situations I and II are not identical. In situation I – *A* has the obligation to "abolish" *B*'s activities which consist in returning or not returning the money. He has the obligation not to demand the return of the money and the obligation to "abolish" *B*'s behaviour connected with attempts to return the money. This behaviour is legal and *A* is obliged to "abolish" it (*e.g.* he may not consider these activities as an unlawful attack).

---

system, rather than entitlement in the meaning of freedom and possibility of choice of given activities.

In situation II no obligation of *A* towards *B* can be constructed, as there is no entitlement of *A* towards *B*. The relationship of *A* to *B* remains an EX-TRA-LEGAL relationship in this case, whereas in situation I the relationship was LEGAL.

Ad (2).

(a) "*A* has the right to demand the return of the money from *B*."

Nominal negation: "*A* has no right to demand the return of the money from *B*".

Consequences: "*A* has the obligation not to demand the return of the money from *B* and obviously also has the entitlement to behave thusly".

(b) "*B* has the obligation to return the money to *A*."

Nominal negation: "*B* does not have the obligation to return the money to *A*".

Consequences: "*B* has the right to return or not to return the money to *A*".

"*A* is obliged to abolish *B*'s behaviour connected with the realization of his entitlement to return or not to return the money to *A*."

As results from the above analysis, sentential and nominal negation of sentences on entitlement and obligation are not equivalent.

Let us now in turn proceed to the analysis of the negation of a norm as a normative sentence about the logical connective "should".

(1) A sentential negation of a norm of the type "It does not occur that *A* should return the money to *B*" settles an utterance which, as Rudziński proves, is not a norm.[96] As a normative utterance, a sentential negation of a norm is an internally incompatible utterance, since the utterance means in the above example: "*A* may or may not return the money to *B* or *A* should return the money to *B*". Only the last part of the utterance, after the word "or", is a norm, but the whole expression does not have a definite normative sense, nor is it a norm as a whole. This is because there occurs a contradiction between the first part which expresses the state "without obligation" and the second part which introduces an opposite obligation.[97]

---

[96] Rudziński [1947:29–30].
[97] Rudziński [1947: 29].

A sentential negation of a norm is equivalent to a sentential negation of sentences on entitlement and obligation. A sentential negation of these sentences always leads to an alternative of the normative sphere and the extra-normative (extra-legal) sphere. This concerns negation of both obligation and entitlement. Both a sentential negation of entitlement and one of obligation result in utterances which are not norms and are not equivalent to norms.

(2) A nominal negation of a norm of the type: "*A* should not return the money to *B*" leads to a negative normative utterance, that is, a norm which is contradictory to the negated norm.

A nominal negation of a norm is only equivalent to a nominal negation of entitlement, but it is not equivalent to a nominal negation of obligation, as a negation of obligation does not lead to obligation with contradictory content (an opposite obligation). Such an obligation has to be settled with a separate norm.[98]

The statement that sentential negation of a norm does not settle a normative utterance, whereas only a nominal negation of a normative utterance settles a norm (with negative content), justified in detail by Rudziński, mostly explains the relationships of equivalence presented before.

Thus a sentential negation and a nominal negation of a norm obviously do not lead to equivalent sentences. At the same time, equivalence does not occur between a sentential and nominal negation of sentences on entitlement and obligation.

However, these rules only concern norms of the same degree, whereas rules of equivalence are entirely different in relationships between norms of varying degrees, an issue which has gone largely unnoticed in publications on the logic of norms. Namely, THERE MAY BE EQUIVALENCE BETWEEN A NOMINAL NEGATION OF A NORM OF THE SECOND DEGREE AND A SENTENTIAL NEGATION OF A NORM OF THE FIRST DEGREE. This statement is fundamental to the issue of the negation of the validity of norms discussed here.

As I mentioned before, repealing the power of a norm is a normative negation of a norm, which constitutes A NORM WITH NEGATIVE CONTENT: a norm which formulates the prohibition to use a given objective norm (here

---

[98] Rudziński [1947: 30–36].

the object of the obligation is a lack of activity). Such a norm, as a norm of the second degree, is a nominal negation of an equivalent norm of the second degree which formulates the prohibition to use a given objective norm. Thus repealing the binding power of a norm means issuing a categorical norm of a higher degree which settles a nominal negation of a categorical norm of the second degree, equivalent to the expression: "Norm N is valid". Thus a negation of the validity of a norm means settling a norm of the second degree which is the relationship of logical contradiction with the norm "One should apply norm N" (negation of "One should not apply norm N").

The negation of the validity of a norm leads to infinital consequences. Negating the validity of a norm assumes accepting the validity of a norm which is contradictory with a norm of the second degree which is equivalent to the phrase "is valid". Thus, "negative verification" of the validity of a norm results in *regressus ad infinitum*, just as "positive verification" does.

Thus a normative negation of a norm of the second degree results in the equivalent sentential negation of an objective norm.

A normative negation of a norm of the second degree equivalent to the expression "Norm N is valid" is "One should not apply norm N". This means that no behaviour of other addressees should be evaluated on the basis of the norm N. The obligation of lack of activity results from a negative norm of the second degree and is directed only at the addressees of a norm of the second degree. On the other hand, negating a norm of the second degree, equivalent to the phrase "is valid", does not settle a prohibition, nor does it abolish the obligation to behave according to the content of the objective norm for the addressees of this norm. Logically speaking, no consequences for the addressees of the objective norm result from the negation of a norm of the second degree which rule on the application of the norm, since they also are not addressees of a norm of the second degree anyway. However, pragmatically speaking, in legal practice, negation of a norm of the second degree equivalent to the phrase "is valid" also means freeing the addressees of the objective norm from the obligation of behaving according to this norm. In legal practice, a legal norm whose validity has been negated «ceases to exist» for its addressees. Thus negation of validity practically means abolishing entitlement and obligation which result from the norm which has been hitherto valid, and therefore: «abolishment» of the norm itself. «Abolishment of a norm» is a sentential negation ("Norm N does not occur").

Thus the negation of validity of a norm is equivalent to the sentential negation of an objective norm. This is a pragmatic rule of legal language; nevertheless, we can accept it as a rule of logic of legal norms within such language whose semantic directives are based on pragmatics. In my opinion, directives of the logic of legal norms should be based on the pragmatic use of the law. Only then will they be practically useful. As we know from previous considerations, a sentential negation of a norm is not a norm. Thus a negation of the validity of a norm, as equivalent to a negation of a valid norm, results in a sphere in the scope of an objective norm which is not normatively regulated by norms. Naturally, it is not regulated by norms which have been hitherto valid.

As is evident from the above discussion, a negation of the validity of a norm is a fairly complicated matter. This is because a negation of the validity of a norm has various consequences in various «normative spheres». The results of our analysis differ greatly from the theses encountered in relevant texts in the same field,[99] and they also differ significantly from the results Rudziński reaches in *From the Logic of Norms* [1947] as a result of in-depth analysis. Rudziński does not differentiate between the two issues: the issue of a negation of norm and the issue of a negation of the validity of a norm, and thus he does not take into consideration the complex issue of a normative negation whose logical consequences primarily depend on the degree of the negated norm. A negation of a norm of the first degree obviously leads to a different result than a negation of a norm of the second degree.

Accepting the fact that the phrase "Norm N is valid" is equivalent to a categorical norm of the second degree, which determines the use of the objective norm, seems to lead to a more correct solution of the issue of negation of a norm and negation of the validity of a norm, and to discover the logical results of these negations in the normative sphere.

---

[99] See Sztykgold [1936].

Stefan Grzybowski. Normative relation
[1961: 20–21, 23–28, 31, 80–82, 98–99, 120–121]

Research of the essence and structure of a legal norm traditionally and commonly reveals three components (elements, parts): hypothesis, disposition and sanction. [...] These three elements are taken into consideration both in the case of the concept of the ternary construction of a norm and in the case of only recognizing binary structure, and thus recognizing the existence of primary and secondary norms (sanctioning and sanctioned) or "double" norms, [...] or even in the case of proceeding to the four-part construction of a norm, since the existence of two hypotheses is then visible, that is, the hypothesis of disposition and the hypothesis of sanction. [...]

Hypothesis will be understood as determining (describing) a certain factual situation, imagined and expressed in a generalized and abstract manner (this will be the ground for the concept of legal facts or legal occurrence), which induces the normative (never other than normative) effect, which will then be determined in a disposition. Thus a hypothesis contains generalized and abstract possible actual situations in an undetermined and unlimited number. Admittedly, it is sometimes the case that the amount of situations in a given, specific hypothesis seems limited, sometimes to the extent that it might denote only one unique situation, not in the least imagined. [...] Determining the formal scheme of a hypothesis will be proper also if its realization is unique and unrepeatable, [...] if a specific situation is realized (even in a unique manner) just before issuing a legal norm or determining a normative utterance, [...] or if the realization is impossible, and also when individual components of the realization (*e.g.* subjects or objects) are individualized in advance. [...]

Disposition defines the normative (and none other than normative) effect of a factual situation, generalized in the hypothesis. As it is usually said, a realized factual situation which is a legal occurrence has «legal effects», that is, to put it in a traditional way, the emergence, alteration or termination of a legal relationship. [...]

Thus, a disposition contains the normative evaluation [...] of an imagined, generalized, abstract factual situation. If there occurs a certain factual situation p, then NORMATIVELY it is evaluated as situation q. The term "normatively" is used in order to stress the fact that situation q does not at all result LOGICALLY from situation p, but that the relationship between the two situations is settled by us, and that the relationship consists in a disparate, actual and normative, evaluation of the same situation. [...] In this sense the symbol $p > q$ can be used. However, the expression "normatively" also means that situation q is determined in the scheme of obligation. Therefore the symbol q indicates that there SHOULD occur a situation which is determined as αq. Let us imagine the situation: if someone harmed another person and acknowledges his guilt (*cf.* art. 134.), then the factual situation p is evaluated normatively as situation q; the person is obliged to compensate the loss (the situation αq should occur). In this example, q denotes: "He is obliged to compensate the loss". However, transition to the so called sanctions does not assume: "and if he was not obliged to compensate the loss", but rather: "and if the loss was not compensated", or: "and if he did not compensate the loss". Therefore we switch from a normative situation determined by q to a factual situation, contradictory to the one which was postulated by q. The situation postulated by q is marked as αq, whereas the situation contradictory to the postulated one is marked as αq'.

Thus one can now repeat, in detachment from the terms used in the course of study on the structure of a legal norm, that a disposition determines the normative (and none other than normative) effect of an imagined factual situation generalized in a hypothesis. [...]

In the course of study on the structure of a legal norm A SANCTION was generally understood as the specification of the normative effects of a disposition not being implemented. [...] The enumeration of effects of violating a norm for the subject [...] or the effects in case of failing to comply with the rules of behaviour, [...] are in fact supposed to mean the same, and whereas the expression may seemingly be more precise, it is also highly inadequate to the theme of our research and impedes proper evaluation of the term.

Treating a sanction as an effect of violating a norm or failing to comply with the rules of behaviour would only be proper in the case of reducing the issue to sociological analysis. [...]

However, if we proceed for the scope of sociological analysis to the field of researching the structure of a legal norm [...], and especially the field of researching the formal structure of a normative utterance which is of more interest to us, we will immediately see that it is not an easy task to deny the existence of the question of what the effects of «failing to implement» a disposition are. Sanction, which defines the mentioned effects, is at least a regular consequence in the structure of a legal norm, [...] whereas in the structure of a normative utterance, it is a necessary consequence of a hypothetical character of an utterance as well as obligatory character of a disposition. If these elements were of a declarative character, there may not have been room for sanctions. However, since the first two elements of a normative utterance are of a hypothetical-obligatory character, and since it has been settled that a disposition states situation q which indicates that a factual situation αq should occur, as explained above, one has to predict "failing to realize" the situation, "failing to implement" the sanction, and thus the factual situation $\alpha q'$. Situation q is, after all, a normative evaluation of situation p, but an evaluation expressed in the form of obligation. Let us remember that situation q consists in the fact that there should occur a factual situation αq. However, the situation αq may not occur, that is, it does not result that it WILL OCCUR from the fact that it SHOULD occur. It is only in this sense that we can speak of the failure to implement a disposition, remembering that it only concerns the failure to implement (realize) a factual situation which should have occurred according to the disposition.

This state of affairs raises the question of what exactly are the effects of failing to realize a factual situation, indicated by a disposition, and thus the utterance on this matter cannot be treated separately from the utterance involving a hypothesis and a disposition. We can only proceed from the disposition, assuming that the factual situation shown in the disposition has not been implemented, to some further element (segment) of the whole normative utterance, and therefore, to use the terminology created when researching the structure of a legal norm, proceed to sanction. Whether the term "sanction" is relevant in our argument may and probably should be doubted. [...]

How are we then to formulate the effects of failing to implement the factual situation αq indicated in the disposition, that is, the effect of the situation αq' not occurring? Here follows a normative evaluation of the situation. Let us ascribe the symbol r to the evaluation. A formal scheme of a normative utterance is therefore as follows: if p (hypothesis) occurs, then q (disposition) follows normatively, and if αq does not occur (if αq' occurs), then r follows normatively. With the aid of the symbols used by logicians (we will return to certain serious reservations which should be raised [...]), let us present our scheme beginning with the following two relations:

$p < q$.

$\alpha q' < r$.

where:

p denotes the utterance of a hypothesis (an imagined and generalized factual situation);

q denotes the utterance of a disposition (a normative evaluation of a factual situation uttered in the obligatory form: there should occur an actual situation αq);

$\alpha q'$ denotes a situation contrary to the situation determined by the disposition;

r denotes a normative evaluation of the situation $\alpha q'$. [...]

To manifest the structural connection between the relations more clearly [...], [the chain scheme can take on] the following form:

$(p < q) \ o \ (\alpha q' < r) \ \infty$.

where the symbol o together with the symbol $<$ denotes: "and if". The symbol o is used here in order to highlight the word "and", in order to avoid symbols which denote the familiar functors in formal logic, especially the functor "and", as it is too early to make decisions in this matter. However, it should be noted that there is no ground for assuming any functor known to logic. Likewise, the symbol $<$ does not denote implication here. [...]

One other element was occasionally noted in the structure of a legal norm, an element of a special nature. J. Lande called it "positive foundation":

> Each positive norm possesses, apart from a disposition (and a hypothesis if it is a hypothetical norm), one other element, which is usually placed at its very beginning. It contains a reference to those positive facts (rules, regulations, customs, court practice, precedents, *etc.*), whence the norm draws its binding force. Such an element of a norm is called the positive foundation, and the fact mentioned in it – a normative fact [...].[100]

Therefore, "in order to state the binding force of a given norm", as J. Lande continues, the positive foundation should be mentioned, for instance: " Under article 134 of the *Code of Law*, whoever...", *etc.*[101] A similar approach was previously presented by A.W. Rudziński, except he was also concerned with obtaining "an objective foundation", that is, an utterance which would state the existence of a legal obligation.[102] [...]

From the very beginning of our considerations, we have been heading towards taking a firm stand which would grasp the structure of each normative utterance in the scheme:

$$(p < q) \; o \; (\alpha q' < r) \; \infty$$

and thus deny the existence of normative utterances without any of the elements included in the scheme. [...] If, when reading the texts of a law and looking at the expressions and phrases included in them, we appear to be missing any of the elements, then the only reason for it would be that the element is "hidden". [...]

First of all, we ought to refuse to rely on a simple prohibition. Some "categorical norms" would also be imperatives, as T. Kotarbiński would

---

[100] Lande [1956: 10 *et seq.*].

[101] Lande [1956: 11].

[102] For instance, the utterance: "One should not torment animals", which is experienced only on an emotional level (as wrong, unethical, *etc.*), in combination with an utterance based on a prohibition stemming from a normative fact (article... of the statute..., *Code of Law*, number..., par. ...), where our emotional experience is irrelevant; *cf.* Rudziński [1947: 11 *et seq.*].

put it.[103] Besides, what would we do with an utterance in the following scheme:

$$(q!) \; o \; (\alpha q' < r).$$

where $q!$ would denote the mentioned imperative or prohibition, if we were faced with norms which *retro agunt*? After all, imperatives can only refer to the future. Normative utterances (and norms) can be directed "at the past", which does not make them evaluations, as L. Petrażycki and H. Kelsen claim. [...] Besides, the utterance: "Do not kill!" has a completely different structure and sense than the utterance: "You should not have killed", which is a moral evaluation, directed at facts in the past which really took place. [...]

It is necessary to reject the scheme which is derived from a simple and general imperative, also because some crimes can be committed only by people who belong to certain categories, rather than everyone. [...]

Examining chosen logical relationships in combination with the relation contained in a normative utterance, and thus «a normative relationship», we intentionally sought not to stress one particular feature of this relationship, even though it kept coming up. Unlike in the case of logical relationships, a normative utterance $p < q$, together with its occurrence, «creates» the mentioned q, which does not exist beyond it, and it randomly and arbitrarily settles a certain relationship between p and q, a relationship which is not – in the logical sense – any kind of relationship between sentences. In other words, there would and could not be any relationship between p and q if it was not SETTLED by an utterance which contained the mentioned p and q. The same can be said about the relationship $\alpha q' < r$ and further relationships as well as the relationship between those relationships. Relationships in a normative utterance are therefore settled arbitrarily, and are therefore THETIC relationships. [...]

Thetic relationships are a structural trait of utterances which express legal norms, but also any normative utterance, that is, any utterance of normative structure, [...] both sensible and devoid of sense, in the common sense of the word. Anyone who harmed another person is obliged to repair the damage; anyone with a heart defect should go to the doctor; any-

---

[103] Kotarbiński [1947: 201].

one hiking in a group should not separate from it; one should not kill song-birds; one should be polite towards other people; honour your father and mother!; it is forbidden to consume beef; one should assail people one en-counters in a secluded place; anyone who harms other people should rob them; anyone who stains a book should get drunk; anyone who inflicts on himself a wound which leaves a scar comes of age; blonde people and people under three years old are eligible for election – here is a handful of utterances which can be reduced to the formula $p < q$ and which (regard-less of their foundation being a legal, religious or social norm, and regard-less of whether they are moral or sensible) possess a structure based on a thetic relationship.

As we mentioned before, there is no other explanation than settlement for the appearance of element p and the relationship $p < q$ in our utterance, as well as the appearance of r and the relationship $\alpha q'$, and in fact, also the tran-sition from q to $\alpha q'$ and from r to $\alpha r'$. Neither in the formation of q or r, $\alpha q'$ or $\alpha r'$, nor in settling thetic relationships are we bound to or limited by any external, objective facts. The point is only formal liberty, used when a for-mal scheme of the structure of a normative utterance is created. Practical aims obviously prevent the excessive saturation of arguments with examples of nonsensical utterances, or even those kinds of utterances whose founda-tions are not legal norms which are or were in operation. Stating the formal liberty in a limited scope of research themes does not affect the importance of all factors which induce the lawgiver to choose a norm of a given con-tent. In this field the choice is not unlimited.

In order to avoid misunderstanding when stating the thetic character of the relationships included in a normative utterance, especially in view of the symbols used, one should complete the structural scheme of a normative ut-terance, which should then assume the following form: [...]

$$T\,[(p < q)\ o\ (\alpha q' < r)\ \infty].$$

where T at the front denotes the thetic-normative character of the whole ut-terance together with the relationships included in it. Thus the symbol T plays a similar role to that previously ascribed to the symbol N used in or-der to mark the normative character of an utterance, rather than the formal--logical character, which can be marked with the symbol L. Since T indicates a distinct character of the connections in a normative utterance, it can only be omitted when there are no grounds to fear misunderstanding in the scope of the argument, nor is there useless search for formal-logical relationship in the utterance.

The thetic character of a normative utterance, and especially the thetic character of relationships contained in this utterance, consists in the thetic nature of entailment. The structure of an utterance is based on thetic entailment, even more, on linked multilevel entailment. Thus we say: q when p, and r when $\alpha q'$, *etc.* [...]

Relationships contained in a normative utterance are not formal-logical relationships, or even logical ones, in the broad sense of the word. In particular, one ought to refuse to identify the normative relationship with relationships of equivalence, identity, conjunction, implication, logical entailment *sensu stricto*, causation and inferential entailment. The normative relationship is A THETIC RELATIONSHIP, settled by the utterance which contains it itself, and was settled at the moment of the birth of the utterance.

Tadeusz Czeżowski. Modalities
[1964a: 108–109]

Terms such as "beautiful" or "good" fundamentally differ from terms like "round", "colourful", "loud", *etc.*, and instead they belong to the same group as "existing" ("factual"), "necessary", "possible", *etc.*, which are called "transcendentals" in philosophical terminology, that is, terms which lie beyond the scope of categories, or proper predicates, such as "round" or "colourful", as they do not form complex predicates, nor do they, so to say, determine the terms. Categorial predicates correspond to the elements of the contents of representations, images or concepts; transcendentals are not representable, however, they can be detected in modal sentences of various kinds. Existence is determined in sentences of the kind "it is true that...", and similarly, other transcendentals are determined in sentences: "it is necessary that...", "it is good that...", "it is beautiful that...", *etc.* The adjectives "true", "beautiful" and "good" are morphologically similar to predicates, but are not them syntactically, as they are the equivalents of the logical connectives mentioned above; however, the expressions such as "it is round that...", *etc.*, formed analogously to predicates, would be clumsy.

Thus unrepresentable expressions, such as existence or truthfulness, necessity and possibility, beauty, moral value or goodness, although they are not features of objects, they are inherent to objects as expressions detectable in modal sentences. [...] Contrary to features, or accidents in Latin terminology, they are called *modi entis*, that is, manners of objects' existence. The relationship between features and manners of being is that each feature is ascribed to its object according to a certain *modus*, in some manner: either factual, or necessary, or possible, or in a way that is beautiful or good, *etc.*

Zdzisław Ziemba & Zygmunt Ziembiński. Calculus of norms
[1964]

1. In 1951 an article by the renowned Scandinavian logician, G.H. von Wright, entitled "Deontic Logic" [1951], was published in the *Mind* quarterly [...]. It was an attempt to compile and systematize normative sentences. Although others have attempted it before,[104] those earlier formulations were imperfect from the formal point of view. Since that time, the term "deontic logic" has permanently joined the scope of vocabulary used in logic, and the number of works devoted to this relatively new branch of logic is on the rise. However, the base for creating deontic calculations is, among other things, a certain assumption which questions the possibility of using the achieved results in, for instance, legal practice. Von Wright himself recognized it after having published the article mentioned above, when he wrote on deontic logic:

> This, however, has to be continued with far greater subtlety than it was in my first work. [...] From the philosophical point of view, this work seems unsatisfactory to me. This is mostly so because it treats norms as a kind of judgements, which can be true or false. I believe this is a mistake. Deontic logic is philosophically significant partly because

---

[104] A critical review of previous concepts of logic of norms is presented by Weinberger [1958a].

norms and evaluations, although removed/distant from the realm of truth, are after all the subject of logical laws. This discloses, so to say, greater scope of logic in comparison with truth.[105]

Therefore, while not denying the worth of work done in the scope of deontic logic, one has to admit that the manner in which the issue of logical relationships between norms has been dealt with has pushed aside an issue important to the theory of law and legal practice: the issue of logical relationships between norms, understood in such a way that they are neither true nor false.

The development of deontic logic may be of great importance to legal science, even though not all expectations of lawyers in the field are justified.

Lawyers are interested in deontic logic for three reasons. Firstly, some of them seem to hold a false belief that it is possible to organize a country's legal norms into a system built *more geometrico*, where some «chief» norms in consequence «result in» all the detailed norms. Secondly, lawyers are interested in justifying legal subsumption, that is, a process which usually consists in «inferring» a norm for a specific individual case from a norm formulated generally; such a process is the ground for judging, issuing an administrative decision, *etc.* Thirdly – and this point raises the largest number of open problems – jurisprudence is in need of a general theory of entailment of norms, a theory which would go beyond a simple subsumption process.

It seems an explanation is due in connection with the latter issue. There is a need to define a certain relationship between norms; a relationship which one would be tempted to call entailment of norms, whereas in fact the subject in question is the relationship between SENTENCES ON VALIDITY OF NORMS. The relationship of entailment which occurs between norms should possess such qualities that, on the basis of the statement that norm N_2 results from norm N_1, one could REASONABLY accept the sentence: "If norm N_1 is valid, then norm N_2 is valid".

Validity of a norm is a certain state of affairs, an occurrence. However, even lawyers dispute what the state of affairs should be for us to state that

---

[105] Wright [1957: VII].

a given norm is valid. It is sometimes said that "Norm N is valid" simply means as much as "Norm N was settled and not withdrawn by someone with a social position such that norms settled by him in a given field are respected frequently enough" (besides, we ascribe to ourselves the competence to settle norms which concern our own actions). At other times it is said that "Norm N is valid" means the same as "In view of a given person's evaluation, we should act according to norm N". In the first case, the justification for the validity of a norm is thetic, in the other, it is axiological, regardless of the subtle differences connected with this distinction.[106] Let us only note that accepting a norm as valid may have a twofold explanation, for example, when we encounter a homonymous legal and moral norm. In both cases, there is a visible tendency to accept as valid, apart from a given norm, also its unspecified "consequences", which is of interest here. Other meanings are ascribed to the expression "Norm N is valid", for instance, in some social circles breaking the norm N always or at least often enough meets with a negative reaction on the part of the environment. However, it seems that such behaviourist interpretation of the expression "Norm N is valid" would be radically different from the preexistent colloquial meaning.

As a result, the first obstacle which appears when formulating the "entailment" relationship between norms is the ambiguity of the term "valid" itself. However, let us suppose one of the actually used interpretations of the expression "Norm N is valid" was chosen in order to examine the relationship between norms called "entailment". The task of formulating entailment relationships between norms can be understood as follows: first to settle the relationships between the validity of norms, putting them in statements:

(1) If norm N_1 is valid, then norm N_2 is valid.

and then to formulate statements accordingly:

(2) Norm N_2 results from norm N_1.

The point of departure for the formulation of statements in the form of (2) should probably be those statements in the form of (1) which express general relationships between validity of norms. The generalization would consist in the fact that names of schemes of norms instead of names of

---

[106] For more on the subject see: Ziembiński [1963].

norms themselves would appear in the place of letters 'N_1' and 'N_2' in statements in the form of (1), for instance:

(1a) If the norm "x should do A and B" is valid, then the norm "x should do A" is valid.

Accepting such a statement would give rise to claiming that

(2a) The norm "x should do A" results from the norm "x should do A and B".

Setting aside the issue of clarifying the idea presented above (especially the issue of connective "if... then..." in statements in the form of (1)), one may formulate the following remark: settling entailment relationships between norms would be a SECONDARY issue compared to settling the relationships between validity of norms. In some cases, like the one which is used in example (1a), logical relationships determine the fact that the validity of one norm cannot be recognized by negating the validity of another. Yet, statements on a relationship between the validity of norms usually seem to be empirical generalizations which concern social facts, namely, FACTS OF VALIDITY of norms. Therefore the "logic of norms" would actually appear to be an empirical theory, possible to formulate only as far as the relationships concerning the validity of specific norms were determined without any doubt.

This take on the matter would probably disappoint lawyers, as they expect something opposite. Since they often doubt whether a specific norm N_2 is valid when the norm N_1 is valid, they would like to see these doubts removed by the theory of «entailment» of norms from norms. In other words, they expect that logicians, exclusively through logical means, will be able to prove the very claim that norm N_2 is valid since norm N_1 is valid, and norm N_2 is in a specific relationship to norm N_1. However, this is not possible. As it was mentioned before, statements in the form of (1) are not logical statements. One cannot derive a sentence on a relationship between the validity of certain norms from a sentence which states the occurrence of a certain relationship between norms exclusively through logical means.

It seems that the procedure in the issue of «entailment of norms» should be different. It is for THE LAWYER, not for THE LOGICIAN, to DECIDE what norms he regards as valid. In particular, he should decide which norms, apart from those expressly announced in the relevant published legal records he would like to regard as valid. For a reasonable lawyer, this decision will be shaped by specific teleological considerations. Then, following this decision one may construct such a definition of entailment of a norm from a norm that it fulfils the condition:

(3) If norm N_2 results from norm N_1, then: if norm N_1 is valid, then norm N_2 is valid.

Therefore, the problem does not lie in finding any relationship between norms, calling it entailment and then proving that the condition (3) is fulfilled in the presence of a preexisting notion of the validity of a norm. The problem is to consciously ACCEPT such an interpretation of the expression "Norm N is valid", and such an understanding of the notion of entailment between norms, that accepting norm N_2 as valid is purposeful and useful, when it had been accepted that norm N_1 is valid and norm N_2 results from norm N_1. In other words, accepting the postulate (3), with a specific interpretation of the term "results from", is to be the result of a decision as to how the expression "Norm N is valid" is understood.

Some may be daunted by the element of «convention» in such an interpretation of the issue. However, it should be remembered that consequences may be useful or not, purposeful or not. The problem is that ideas as to how to interpret the expression "Norm N_2 results from norm N_1" and accordingly, ideas on how to interpret the expression "Norm N is valid" so that condition (3) is fulfilled, should be accompanied with justifications which consist in proving that it is useful to accept norm N_2 as valid when norm N_1 is valid, and norm N_2 results (in a way) from norm N_1. However, clearly in the case of discrepancies on what is useful and what is not, various interpretations of the expression "Norm N_2 results from norm N_1" can be proposed, and following that, various interpretations of the expression "Norm N is valid", in accordance with condition (3). If two lawyers chose (influenced by different views on what is useful and what is not) different relationships between norms as entailment, and accordingly, various notions of entailment in such a way that condition (3) is fulfilled, then the dispute between them on whether norm N_2 is valid when norm N_1 is valid will be a verbal dispute. Since their interpretation of the expression "Norm N is valid" differs, no proof that one of them «is wrong» in accepting norm N_2 as valid will be possible. At most, they can dispute whether accepting norm N_2 as valid is useful when norm N_1 is accepted as valid. Accepting one notion of entailment between norms, and respectively, one notion of validity of legal norms which fulfil condition (3) is a matter of DECISION, which can either be adopted through convention, or forced.

2. For the sake of further discussion we will formulate norms as follows:

(4) It should be that Z,

where 'Z' is replaced by a specific sentence which describes the specific behaviour of a person designated individually or generally. This manner of notation of norms will facilitate the formulation of issues of interest to us.

One of the possible interpretations of the term "results from" in postulate (3) is the following:[107]

(5) The norm "It should be that Z_2," results from the norm "It should be that Z_1," if and only if the sentence 'Z_2' results from the sentence 'Z_1'.

The interpretation of the defining expression: "'Z_2' results from the sentence 'Z_1'" may of course be various in definition (5); for instance, one might mean logical entailment and accordingly, speak of logical entailment of norms. For instance, from the norm:

"It should be that for every x, if x is A or B, then x makes C".
there entails (logically) the norm:

"It should be that for every x, if x is A, then x makes C".

Thus defined relationship of entailment for norms (at least partly consistent with intuitions) possesses a certain specific quality: the falsity of sentence 'Z' is equivalent to lack of fulfilment (violation) of the norm "It should be that Z". In consequence, one of the features of the relationship of entailment for norms described above is the following: when the norm N_2 results from the norm N_1 and the norm N_2 is unfulfilled, then also the norm N_1 is unfulfilled. This is so because from the norm "It should be that N_1," there entails the norm "It should be that Z_2," if and only if from the sentence 'N_1' there

---

[107] *Cf.* Hofstadter & McKinsey [1939: 452].

entails the sentence 'Z_2'. Therefore, if the sentence 'Z_2' is false (the norm N_2 is unfulfilled), then also the sentence 'Z_1' must be false. (The norm N_2 is unfulfilled.) In other words, the fulfilment of the norm N_1 (that is, the truthfulness of the sentence 'Z_1') causes the norm N_2 to also be fulfilled (that is, the sentence 'Z_2' is true). Therefore, the proposal of interpretation of entailment of norms in the manner mentioned above, and accordingly, the proposal of such interpretation of the expression "Norm N is valid" that condition (3) is fulfilled, seems purposeful. A refusal to accept the norm N_2 as valid when the norm entails (in the presented sense) from the valid norm N_1 and accordingly, accepting as allowed a behaviour which violates norm N_2 would result in accepting as allowed a behaviour which violates the valid norm N_1.

At this point we should consider an objection against the presented description of entailment for norms which is based on the so called A. Ross's paradox.[108] According to the presented description of entailment for norms, from the norm:

(6) "It should be that for every x, if x is A, then x makes B"
there (logically) entails the norm:

(7) "It should be that for every x, if x is A, then x makes B or x makes C"
and on the basis of the postulate (3) it should be assumed that when the norm (6) is valid, then also the norm (7) is valid.

Thus, for instance, from the norm:

(6a) "It should be that for every x, y, z, if x did harm y to person z, then x repairs harm y to person z"
there entails the norm:

(7a) "It should be that for every x, y, z, if x did harm y to person z, then x repairs harm y to person z or x kills person z"

If, following the definition (5) of entailment of norms such an interpretation of the expression "Norm N is valid" is assumed that condition (3) is fulfilled, one is forced to assume that if a norm in the form of (6), for instance norm (6a), is valid, then also norm in the form of (7), for instance norm (7a), is valid. Yet, accepting norm (7) as valid may lead to the conclusion that x, who is A, is given the choice between performing act B

---

[108] *Cf.* Weinberger [1958a: 77–78].

and performing act *C*. However, accepting a norm as valid does not repeal the validity of norm (6). When *x*, who is *A*, does *C*, but does not do *B*, he admittedly acts according to norm (7), but he violates norm (6). Therefore *x*, who is *A*, cannot simultaneously behave according to norms (6) and (7), not performing act *B*. However, if apart from norms in the form of (6) and (7) another norm is valid which prohibits *x* who is *A* from doing *C*, or performing act *C* together with performing act *B* is impossible, the behaviour determined by norm (7) which does not violate the mentioned other norm or norm (6) can only consist in performing act *B*. But if performing act *C* is not prohibited to *x*, who is *A*, by a valid norm, then performing act *C* together with action *B* does not after all violate any valid norm, and as norm (7) was realized by act *B*, act *C* is also not dictated.

Therefore we should pay attention to a property of the relationship of entailment for norms, namely, that VIOLATION of a norm of entailment entails VIOLATION of a norm which the former one results from, but acting according to a norm of entailment does not determine compatibility of this behaviour with the norm which the former one results from. Thus we obtain a practical guideline that in order to behave according to all valid norms, it does not suffice to know the consequences of explicitly settled norms and act accordingly, but one should also know all valid norms. It is the same in the case when one regards as valid only these norms which were explicitly settled. Familiarity with some of the norms and abiding by them does not necessarily mean that none of the other valid norms will be violated.

Let us assume, for instance, that apart from norms (6a) and (7a) the following norm is valid:

(8) "It should be that every *x* refrains from killing a person"

Killing a person in a situation in which the killer did some harm would indeed be in accordance with norm (7a), but it would violate norm (8). Therefore, in order to behave in accordance with norm (7a) when one does some harm, and not to violate norm (8), there is no other choice but to repair the harm.

3. Following these explanations, let us analyze the following tasks which are set by lawyers to logicians in the field in question.

3.1. The first task, that is, the task which consists in organizing the legal norms of a given country into a system resembling a geometrical one is obviously unfeasible. H. Kelsen noted[109] that legal norms of a contemporary constitutional state form a system as long as in the case of retaining the rules of the legislative process, each act of settling a norm by a competent body obliges one to abide by the new norm, on the basis of a dictate of obedience (norm-creating competence) included in a norm of a higher order. However, they do not form a system of norms in the sense that norms of regular laws result from what constitutional norms proclaim, or ordinances result from laws, *etc.*, if only because the lawgiver, even if he is endowed with absolute consistency (and a contemporary "lawgiver" is a fictional person), does not settle a whole set of norms for a given state at the same time. What happens instead is that fragments of the set of valid norms are changed piece by piece, whereas knowledge and evaluations which induce the lawgiver to settle other norms undergo changes of various degree. Even in the field of morality, where instructions are less technical and more general, the reconstruction of moral systems by deducing it from several main principles is usually a somewhat doctrinarian undertaking.

3.2. The second task set by lawyers is feasible. It seems that the process of subsumption, provided we accept the assumptions mentioned before, is based on the entailment of an individual norm from a general norm, such that it can be accepted as logical entailment. If the following norm is valid:

(9) It should be that every x who is A does C.

then, by the accepted assumption, the following norm is valid as well:

(10) It should be that x_1 who is A does C.

It is logically impossible that the indication of the first norm is fulfilled and simultaneously, the indication of the second norm is not fulfilled, so that norm (10) is violated without violating norm (9). The inference scheme in this case can be called a NORMATIVE *dictum de omni*.

In the practice of legal subsumption, features ascribed to subject x would break down to many examples of situations. If the following norm

---

[109] Kelsen [1945: 110 *et seq.*].

is valid: "It should be that every x with given personal characteristics, at any time t which belongs to a given period, in any place m which belongs to the area, in any circumstances s which belong to a given general definition, does C (behaves in the manner of C)", then the following norm is valid as well: "It should be that x_1 in the moment t_1, in the place m_1, in the circumstances s_1, does C".

Naturally, subsumption may also consist in accepting a norm in which only one of the elements of the general norm is individually specified or replaced with a general term subordinate to the given one.

In contrast, the process of subsumption, which is based exclusively on logical knowledge, lets us present some examples of inference on the validity of norms based on such entailment of norms that one has to refer to knowledge beyond logic. This is true for accepting as valid prohibitions or dictates instrumental in relation to the basic norm accepted as valid.[110] Then we refer to the knowledge on causal relationships.

Let us assume that one cannot realize the state of affairs R without having done C; in other words, from the sentence "x realizes through his activity the state of affairs R" there (extra-logically) entails the sentence "x does C". Then, respectively, from the norm:

"It should be that x realizes the state of affairs R through his actions" there entails (extra-logically) the norm:

"It should be that x does C"

There are practical difficulties connected with the issue of great variety of laws in terms of drafting. The possibility of formalizing the relationships of entailment of norms from norms assumes previous unification of the structure of the norms so that they are written in such a form that the relevant statements on entailment can be formulated unambiguously, whereas the lawgiver's actual utterances, that is legislation, rarely assume the form "It should be that x does C", or more colloquially, introduce the norm-creating operator inside the utterance: "x should do C". The law-

---

[110] In legal language this is (wrongly!) called "inference from aim to means", or "rules of general prohibition" to do something which would prevent from fulfilling the norm, or "a general duty" to do everything that is necessary in order to fulfil the indications of a norm.

giver is using various abbreviated forms; for instance, instead of settling a norm in the form of the utterance: "Every citizen, except the owner of the object, should refrain from interacting with the object", he can put it in a shorter form: "The owner is entitled to use the object, excluding other people". Regulations state that someone is entitled to authority, powers, claims, *etc.* One has to be closely acquainted with the language in order to be able to reword the regulations using the language of norms which indicate to given subjects the duty to do something. As in the case of colloquial speech, one encounters ambiguous expressions; for instance, the expression "be entitled" usually has different meanings in the domain of constitutional law and in the domain of civil law, and even there the expression has several meanings. Therefore, reasoning of lawyers on the validity of a norm on the validity of other norms is preceded by an interpretive procedure which rewords regulations into norms. In this procedure, not only the linguistic context of the utterance is taken into account, but also the situational context of it.

This has significant practical consequences, for instance, a regulation which states that one cannot walk on the grass can be interpreted as simply: "It should be that a citizen does not walk on the grass", or: "Every citizen should not walk on the grass". However, taking into account the situational context of the utterance and analyzing the intentions of the codifier more closely, one may interpret the regulation as: "Every citizen should refrain from damaging the lawns, at least to a degree which is caused by damaging through walking on it", and then, knowing that digging ditches, storing bricks, *etc.*, damages lawns to at least the same degree as walking on them, one may deduce through subsumption that the norm "It should be that a citizen does not dig ditches in the lawn or store bricks on it, *etc.*" is valid.

This kind of well or badly justified conjectures as to what states of affairs a lawgiver wanted to achieve by formulating regulations published in some codex of law as well as the process of subsumption both lead to lawyers using such methods of reasoning as *argumenta a fortiori, a simili,* or *a contrario,* in order to conclude that an individual norm in question is valid. Naturally, a lawgiver's, or competent official interpreters', response stating that the reasoning as to the intentions of the lawgiver's intentions was inappropriate causes thusly obtained conclusion to be rejected.

3.3. As for the general theory of entailment of norms from norms, it seems that it can be constructed. However, it is not deontic logic as hitherto understood.

We assumed that a norm is understood as an utterance which directly indicates to someone the duty to execute a given act, an utterance which suggests certain behaviour. It seems that in the systems of deontic logic, it is not logical relationships between norms that are examined, but rather relationships between sentences which characterize given acts in view of their relationship to a given norm, and therefore, sentences which state that, in view of a given norm, a certain act is dictated, forbidden, allowed, *etc.* Naturally, just as stating that a given norm is valid is not equivalent to the norm itself (which as a norm does not state anything), it is also not equivalent to a norm to state that a given act is dictated by the norm.

If we assume the following symbols and terminology:

Nncx = in view of norm *n* act *c* is dictated to $x =_{df}$ norm *n* dictates to *x* act *c*.

Zncx = in view of norm *n* act *c* is forbidden to $x =_{df}$ norm *n* indicates to *x* to refrain from *c* or to perform such an act which would be impossible after performing *c*.

Dncx = in view of norm *n* act *c* is allowed to $x =_{df} \sim Zncx$.

Fncx = in view of norm *n* act *c* is facultative for $x =_{df} \sim Nncx$.

Incx = in view of norm *n* act *c* is indifferent to $x =_{df} Dncx \vee Fncx$.

Oncx = in view of norm *n* act *c* is the subject of obligation for *x* $=_{df} Nncx \wedge Zncx$.

then it is easy to see that the relationships between values of these sentences about person *x*'s act in view of norm *n*, which can be described in the form of the following hexagon:[111]

---

[111] This idea was presented in Conte's work [1962: 4].

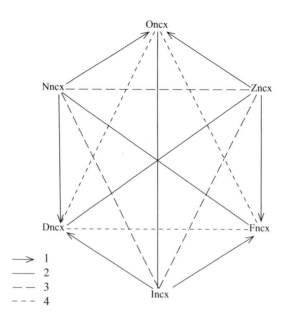

1 – entailment, *2* – contradiction, *3* – opposition, *4* – subopposition

These relationships are intuitive for lawyers, therefore misunderstandings arise only when, for instance, *Dncx, Fncx* and *Incx* are not clearly differentiated, as in the practical application of modal logic, where it is difficult to decide if unilateral or bilateral possibility is concerned. Moreover, as it was mentioned before, the actual basic lexicon of a lawgiver does not only consist of expressions like '*N*', '*Z*', '*O*', '*D*', '*F*', '*I*', but also expressions such as: "is the subject of norm-giving competence", "is the subject of claim", and so on, and therefore lawyers' interest in relationships between sentences which characterize acts in view of their relationship to a given norm greatly extend beyond what deontic logic has dealt with, as at this point its lexicon is too modest from this point of view.

3.4. Taking advantage of the achievements of deontic logic in legislation entails the necessity to standardize the present approach to norm in these two disciplines. Previous attempts to build deontic logic were characterized with a common tendency to present the structure of a norm as an utterance consisting of a norm-creating operator complemented with the name of the act, for instance: "It should be that: if it is raining, the janitor closes the windows". Lawyers tend to put norms into schemes in the form of a conditional sentence, which states that if given circumstances concerning the addressee, the time, the place and other elements of the situation ("hypothesis") occur, the addressee should behave in a given way ("disposition"), for instance: "If it rains, the janitor should close the windows". In the structural manner of formulating a norm used by lawyers the description of the circumstances of undertaking the act was placed in front of the norm-creating expression "should" introduced to the consequent of the conditional sentence. This creates the appearance of the antecedent of such a conditional sentence being a sentence in the logical sense, and only the consequent being a norm. In order to avoid such an appearance, it would be advisable to use the "deontological" scheme of formulating norms.[112] It is also worth adding that there is a dispute among lawyers as to how to formulate the structure of a norm in general.[113]

4. To conclude, it must be noted that the concerns of deontic logic and the concerns of lawyers coincide only in part, and that the approach to many of the discussed issues differ greatly, which may lead to wasted effort as research progresses. It is necessary to interest logicians with the practice of legal reasoning from norms about norms, since so far lawyers either undertake mostly unsuccessful attempts to resolve these issues, or they approve "the art

---

[112] Moreover, the scheme used by lawyers enables misunderstandings connected to confusing CONDITIONAL DUTY, for instance: "If you want to achieve A, you should do B" or "If Z decrees so, you should do C", and UNCONDITIONAL DUTY TO DO SOMETHING IN A SPECIFIC SITUATION, for instance: "If the state of affairs R occurs, you should do C". The janitor's duty to close the windows is not caused by the rain but, for instance, by settling this norm for him by the headmaster. The norm is valid for the janitor from the moment of its settlement, but it dictates to him to take a given act in specific, and not all, circumstances, and is applied only when it rains.

[113] For those familiar with legal language, we should explain that we do not mean the so called "ternary scheme of a legal norm" ("hypothesis", "disposition", "sanction"), which completely obscures the issue of the structure of legal norms for the older generation of lawyers, but rather the dispute over the structure of a sanctioned norm or a sanctioning norm. There are ongoing disputes as to what belongs to "hypothesis" and what belongs to the "disposition" of a norm, as well as what the difference is between norms expressed as conditional sentences and those expressed "categorically". In order to demonstrate the idleness of those disputes it suffices to quote the following formulations of the same norm, implicitly general: (1) "A firefighter should extinguish fire", (2) "If a fire arises, then whoever is a firefighter should extinguish the fire", (3) "If a fire arises and someone is a firefighter, that person should extinguish the fire", (4) "If a flame arises and the flame is considered undesirable and someone is a firefighter, then this person should extinguish the flame", *etc.*

of legal thought" which cannot be described in precisely formulated canons. There is also concern that in some cases it would be harder to use clearly formulated, but extremely intricate canons than be certain that one mastered "the art of legal thought".[114]

Zygmunt Ziembiński. Consistency in the domain of norms
[1964: 241–245]

One often hears statements in colloquial speech that a norm results from another norm: for instance, from the fact that A_1 should do C_1 there entails that A_2 should do C_2. There are some obvious examples, like the entailment of a detailed norm from a more general norm: if someone is obliged to maintain his ascendants who have found themselves in hardship, then he is obliged to maintain his great-grandfathers who need such help. Even if we omit examples of such kind, there is usually no doubt that since every person who changes the place of residence should report the fact to the adequate office, the workers in this office should accept the submitted check-in form; also, if someone should be particularly careful about his health, that person should avoid sleeping on a damp meadow, *etc*. The issue of the entailment of norms from norms is of great significance in legislation, where it is commonly recognized that only some norms are directly expressed in the regulations of law, whereas others result from the former.

Without going into the linguistic character of norms, we may assume a provisional definition that norm N_1 entails norm N_2 if and only if it is impossible that norm N_1 is valid and at the same time norm N_2 is not valid in a given situation, that is, if it is impossible that the sentence on the validity of norm N_1 is true and the sentence on the validity of norm N_2 is false. Only at this point do serious complications in the issue arise, as the notion

---

[114] Having written the present article, we had the opportunity to read the book by G.H. v. Wright: *Norm and Action* [1963a]. In the book, G.H. v. Wright conducts a thorough critique of his own previous conceptions of deontic logic and formulates new conceptions, which mostly veer towards the postulates put forward in the present article. It seems to us that the manner of interpretation of "entailment of norm from norm" introduced by G.H. v. Wright in his new book with the aid of a comprehensive assortment of conceptual apparatus generally corresponds to the proposals of the present article.

of the validity of norms comes into play. This notion cannot be explained without referring to facts which are within the field of interest of psychology and sociology.

The expression "Norm N is a valid norm" always requires relativization. Norms are valid according to the position of specific people.[115] It may be the case that person P believes that A should do C, since person P is experiencing or is disposed to experience an evaluation, either accepting C's activity in itself or, more commonly, accepting the effects of C's activity known to person P. In order to avoid misunderstanding, let us add that what is meant here is a global evaluation of C's activity, which is to be executed by a person who is in a properly specified situation, where the activity is considered feasible, and the "costs" of executing this activity (effort, undesirable side effects) are taken into account in the global evaluation. Then we can say that, according to person P's standpoint the norm which dictates activity C is valid for person A as an axiological norm.

However, in some cases P believes that A should do C because a person R settled a norm which states that A should do just that, but according to P the said R is in such social position compared to A that A should do everything that R settled in a given domain. Then we say that, according to person P's standpoint, person A is bound by a norm settled by R which dictates activity C as a thetic norm. In some cases, P, R and A can be the same person. However, person A may not even be aware that a given norm binds him, which often happens when P is a lawyer and R a specific governing body in the country. Norms recognized as thetically valid may also be axiologically valid.

It is possible to envisage a situation in which every person asked is inclined to accept that A should do C, whereas it is nonsensical to say that some norm of someone's behaviour is simply valid, without referring to an entity which would regard the norm as valid.

---

[115] Naturally, we can say that a given norm is valid "from a specific standpoint", leaving aside the person who takes this standpoint. However, ultimately we always have to refer to (someone's) evaluations or to the fact of someone having recognized the person as an authority who is competent to settle valid norms. We lack the space to critique some oversimplistic standpoints which are sometimes assumed as a starting point for deontic logic.

Clearly the issue of the entailment of one sentence from another is not only an issue of a relationship of implication between their logical values, but also an issue of some logical or extra-logical relationships which the juxta-position of the two sentences describes. Saying that whenever it rains, there are clouds present, we express a certain regularity of meteorological nature; saying that if no S is P, then no P is S, we express a certain logical regularity. Therefore a question arises what kind of regularities we state when we say that from the sentence on the validity of norm N_1 there entails the sentence on the validity of norm N_2. From what had been stated so far we can infer that the issue of the entailment of norms from norms treated as axiological norms is connected to the issue of certain regularities, or tendencies, observable in our mental life in the domain of experiencing evaluations. Although the dis-pute on human nature is inconclusive, we can agree that people in their eval-uations, especially when formulating global evaluations is concerned, are not usually fully consistent, even though they attempt to be consistent.

How should we interpret consistency in evaluations? If someone evalu-ates that it is good to help every member of his family in misfortune, and at the same time does not evaluate positively the help which he is supposed to provide for his brother, alone in sickness, then he is incompatible, because in one specific case his evaluation is different from what should be expected on the basis of the evaluation formulated in a common fashion, that is, refer-ring to common behaviour of a given kind. It is incompatible for someone to appreciate the advantages of having electricity and at the same time not to appreciate the need for the maintenance of the whole of the wiring sys-tem, and not to evaluate positively the necessary conditions for the present state of affairs to last. If someone evaluates that he values health above all else and does not disapprove of drinking excessive amounts of alcohol al-though he is aware that it will be detrimental to his health, then we say that he is incompatible, as he changes the hierarchy of evaluations he had as-sumed for a specific case. A person consistent in his evaluations would be one who continues to evaluate facts according to the hierarchy of values he has assumed, taking into account the relationships of these facts with oth-ers, which constitute a necessary condition for the former, as well as these facts for which the former constitute a sufficient condition.

However, we have to be aware that such a definition only seems precise. After all, we know very well that such hierarchies of values that produce systems of evaluation which are, in a sense, «complete» and «consistent» do not exist is anyone's mind, and even if it were possible to formulate a consistent system of principles to evaluate facts from a certain point of view, then this task in reference to global evaluations, which «summarize» various points of view, would probably be unfeasible. It seems that we tend to formulate a few general principles, which will clash in some specific cases, and the evaluations actually formulated in individual cases are often of a strongly casuistic character. We should also remember that the assumptions of someone's system of evaluation are not usually static, and that changes and deviations from the principles which had been assumed are most often made in the face of a specific situation rather than beforehand, in advance, on the basis of reflection on various situations possible in the future.

On having voiced these crucial objections which indicate the great intricacy of the issue which should be investigated further, let us return to the issue of the entailment of norms from norms treated as axiological norms. If we say that from the fact that norm N_1 is valid according to P in view of his evaluations O_1 and knowledge W, there entails that norm N_2 is valid according to P, which if we assume P's high enough «degree of consequence» probably means that we expect with high probability that since P makes evaluations O_1 and possesses knowledge W, which justify norm N_1 in his eyes, then he also makes evaluations O_2 which justify norm N_2 on the basis of knowledge W. Through knowledge W we understand a collection of sentences regarded by P as true and, for the sake of simplicity, also a collection of deductive conclusions which P could derive from these sentences.

This complex issue usually becomes even more complicated because we usually hear from P only utterances which state that the norm of behaviour N_1 is valid, or simply, utterances where A should do C, which only let us infer indirectly about what evaluations he makes and what knowledge he possesses. If some P living among us states that A should stop a child who is going to run across the road right in front of a car, then we can infer various evaluations motivating P's standpoint: that it would be wrong if any child died; that it would be wrong if any Pole or any other person died hit by a car, which *P* regards as certain or at least highly probable at that moment; that it would be wrong if any car accident happened in that time and place, because then he, *P*, would have to go to court as a witness; that it would be wrong if such a pretty car was damaged as a result of it swerving, which according to *P*'s knowledge would be necessary to avoid hitting the child; that it would be wrong if the nice lady who is driving got upset, *etc.* The issue is clearer if we know about many norms which are valid as axiological norms according to *P*, as then if some evaluations are repeated within default justifications of many norms, the supposition that *P* does in fact make such evaluations gains firmer grounds.

However, when attempting to infer the evaluations of others which justify norms presented as valid, first of all we are inclined to imagine the other person *P's* view as in the image and likeness of our own. This is not without grounds if person *P* and we belong to the same cultural circles where similar living conditions shape similar evaluations and similar hierarchies of values, and also if person *P* and we are "normal" individuals from a specific point of view, that is for example, ones who are not tired of living, who try to avoid pain if possible, who care about their health, safety and personal freedom. The environment passes, among other things, certain patterns of evaluations, which may be useless in modern times if they grew out of different social conditions, but which carry a binding burden of tradition with them.

Guessing someone's evaluations, one may expect that the person evaluating will globally approve of what in a given situation will generate the greatest achievable good on a given «scale» of evaluation, and the least unavoidable evil, and that he will not approve of any evil means to achieve the approved state of affairs, *etc.* We can generally count on the approval of whatever is approved by unquestioned tradition and unshakable authority. This is exactly why there is no doubt in practice that if according to *P* norm N_1 is valid as an axiological norm, then according to the said *P* norm N_2 is also valid.

In turn, an explanation is due as to what is meant by the statement that if N_1 is valid as a thetic norm, then norm N_2 is valid as well (for instance, when a citizen has a legal obligation to report his change of residence to the appropriate office, and the office is obliged to accept the report). If in this case we speak of the entailment of norms from norms treated as thetic norms, it is because we assume that the norms are axiological norms in character from the point of view of an accepted codifier, and that the codifier is a reasonable person who acts purposefully, and settling norms is not only an act of manifesting his strength, or manifesting power for the sheer pleasure of issuing orders. If such people could be found who would be prone to following Napoléon's orders issued from the lunatic asylum, they would probably be unable to find any grounds for reasoning on the validity of other norms from the fact of settling a certain norm by such a "ruler". But if a lunatic really took the throne, the case would probably look different: compliant legislators would probably discern a certain system of evaluations in the ravings of the ruler, the less clear and numerous the better from this point of view. Whatever the lawyers dealing with the theory of interpretation and logical expansion of norms write in their papers, there is not even a hypothetical mention of the lawgiver acting unwisely and aimlessly. Most reasonable intentions are usually ascribed to the lawgiver, which are usually the intentions of an interpreter, the result of it being that the so called «objective» theories of interpretation become, as some claim, specifically subjective theories.[116]

Since the lawgiver settled the obligation to state one's place of residence, then apparently he anticipated some benefits coming from controlling the flow of people, and therefore he would disapprove of an official denying to accept a properly fulfilled statement of residence when a citizen submits it according to the obligation. After all, the issue here is not merely to test the citizens' obedience, or the obligation to take a bow in front of the governor's hat, as there are some substantive aims to achieve.

Yet, if a norm contains a conclusion which cannot be justified axiologically except that it would be wrong if the case was not concluded somehow, one way or another, then nothing results from such a norm. If judge *A* should examine cases written in a repertory written under odd numbers and judge *B* should examine cases written under even numbers on the orders of

---

[116] *Cf.* Ross [1958: 142–143].

the head of the department who aimed to divide the work between them in some manner, and he based his decision on a coin toss: «heads» or «tails», then such norms in themselves do not allow for any further conclusions.

To support the thesis that this is the common understanding of the entailment of norms from norms, one may mention the fact that those legal directives of entailment of norms from norms which extend beyond the obvious acceptance of the entailment of a more specific norm from a more general one are based in an apparent or covert way on the presumed will of "a reasonable and consistent legislator".

Kazimierz Ajdukiewicz. Propositional positions
[1965: 38]

What all judgements, both issued and only preconceived, have in common is a response of a reporting character to a given state of affairs. However, other responses than a reporting one towards the state of affairs are also possible.

The response could also be interrogative, wishing, or dictating one. In the thought which I express in the words "John is going on holiday" I refer to the given state of affairs in a reporting manner. In the thought articulated as "Is John going on holiday?" I refer to the same state of affairs interrogatively; in the thought expressed as "I wish John would go on holiday!" I refer to it wishfully; in the thought expressed in the utterance "Let John go on holiday!" I refer to it in a dictating manner. The distinction between declarative, interrogative, optative, or imperative sentences corresponds to the distinction between the mentioned various manners of referring in thought to the states of affairs.

In particular, an expression will be called a declarative sentence (or a sentence in the logical sense) in its given meaning if in this particular meaning the expression expresses a judgement, that is, a thought which refers to a given state of affairs in a reporting manner. Similarly, an expression will be called an interrogative sentence in its given meaning if in this particular meaning the expression expresses a question, that is, a thought which refers to a given state of affairs in an interrogative manner. [...] Optative sentences and imperative sentences can be defined analogously.

Tadeusz Kotarbiński. The logic of imperatives
[1966]

Logicians are often concerned with the question of whether it is possible (and if so, how it is possible) to prove imperatives, for example: "Do not drink water from a ditch!". It is seemingly very simple. Such advice is justified by referring to the fact that there are plenty of pathogenic germs in ditch water; for instance, one can say: "It is easy to catch an infection when you drink ditch water, so never drink ditch water!". Thus we attached our own imperative to a given true statement with the help of the word "so" and thus implicated that it constitutes a conclusion derived from a certain argument. Here certain doubts arise. After all, the relationship of a sequence derived from the argument is a relationship of entailment, and entailment occurs only between elements belonging to the realm of truth and falsehood, or between schemes from which such elements are obtained through substituting them with variable symbols which are parts of these schemes. However, the imperative mentioned (or in this case, so to say: «prohibitive») is neither true nor false, precisely because it is an imperative. Both of these qualities are foreign notions for imperatives, just like for instance the attribute of «legibility» is foreign for birds or hats. Therefore can one speak sensibly of imperatives entailing from anything and of proving them with the help of logical arguments? Is it therefore not a mistake to use the word "so" in the above example and in all similar examples?

I believe we are not forced to assume such a limitation. The only issue is to realize that there is a wider choice of possible conclusive conjunctions which can be used rationally ("so", "thus", "therefore", "*ergo*", *etc.*) and others used in logic ("if – then", "and", "or", "yet", *etc.*), which are used reasonably in complex utterances which do not only encompass declarative sentences which undergo evaluation regarding their truthfulness, but also other sentences, for instance imperative sentences.

A number of methodologists are concerned with similar potential problems in reasoning with the use of norms, where the following utterances are given as examples of norms: "Each newcomer should register", "Smoking is not allowed during session", or "A man's house is his castle". At the same time it is assumed that norms, like imperatives, are neither true nor false, which leads to qualm and trouble at the attempts to connect them with conjunctions whose sense is determined by referring to the truthfulness or falsity of the connected sentences, for instance: the conjunction "and" produces a true whole if and only if both sentences connected with it are true, and the conjunction "or" produces a false whole if and only if both sentences connected with it are false. Some lecturers of scholarly logic are surprised and concerned with the idea of denying norms their value of truthfulness or falsity. Upon asking the reason for it, they obtain the following answer: any true sentence is either analytical, that is: true by virtue of the meaning and sequence of its components, or empirical, where only such a sentence is empirical which gives a direct account of an observation, or can be justified by virtue of observations. As was mentioned above, norms are neither analytical nor empirical, and therefore they are not true; on the other hand, they are not false either, since the attempt to refute any norm by demonstrating analytically or empirically the truthfulness of its negation is also bound to fail. However, not everyone is satisfied with an answer of this kind. The proponents of the truthfulness or falsity of norms are of the opinion that the above view limits the criteria of truthfulness and falsity unfoundedly. Is it not the case, they say, that a newcomer should register? If he should, then it is true that he should, otherwise it is false that he should register. Also the question of whether it is or is not allowed to smoke during session is resolved by demonstration that, for instance, those who claimed that smoking is not allowed were right, and therefore believed rightly, and those who insisted that smoking is allowed were wrong, or believed wrongly. Perhaps after consideration it can be demonstrated that justifications refer to certain experience, or certain observations, except perhaps they are observations concerning qualities which are not emotionally indifferent, or concerning things which someone wants or demands. The dispute over this issue continues. I do not intend to develop arguments in favour of the party in the dispute whose arguments seem more convincing to me, which is the side of the proponents of the truthfulness or falsity of norms which are not imperatives, which is precisely the type of norms in question. However, I will assume that the only kind of utterances in question which may not be suitable to be used in logical argumentation (although there seem to exist examples of their use) are imperatives, and only those norms belong to the set of incriminated utterances which are intended to be imperatives themselves, even if they are not expressed in the imperative mood. I will only be concerned with the question of imperatives in the present discussion, which has to be stated at the very outset in order to counter the prevalent course among authors concerned with the main issue mentioned at the beginning. The dominating idea is to combine all utterances called *Soll-Sätze* in German, or *fiat* in English (or rather in Latin, genetically) and deal with them jointly, regardless of whether they are imperative in character or if they proclaim duty in a non-imperative manner, *etc.*

Let us therefore establish the meaning of the term "imperative": by imperative I mean any utterance which does not undergo evaluation from the point of view of its truthfulness or falsity, but which recommends certain activity. With this interpretation, it is clear that a recommendation can be more or less firm, can be a mere suggestion, a prompt, or pressure, or can be directed at a specific addressee or a group of addressees, or at anyone, or at unspecified persons, or it can refer to someone who is being addressed, or to the third person, or to the speaker himself; it can recommend a clearly specified action or only a type of actions; it can be expressed with the use of particles like: "may", "let", in the form of the imperative mood, but also in the form of the declarative mood, in sentences which appear to be ascertaining utterances. The imperative mood or an utterance with the particle: "let" are the most significant here, while others act as their substitutes. Here are some examples: "May God send us rain", "Let all the locks be secured", "Let us go home!", "Let the wind be ever at your back", "You shall finish the paper by tomorrow", "Пошли!" (Russian for "Let us go!").

Finally, all these explanations and reservations should be followed by the formulation of the main idea of the present paper. I would like to make a trial version of a certain way to make sure that an argument is rational, with the use of imperatives. This method will be demonstrated mainly in simple examples. "There are a lot of pathogens in ditches, so do dot drink ditch water!" This is rational, because the argument: "There are a lot of pathogens in ditches, so refraining from drinking ditch water is advisable in order to remain healthy" is valid. The rationality of the argument with an imperative conclusion is recognized by the validity of the argument in which the imperative was replaced with a declarative sentence which undergoes evaluation as to its truthfulness or falsity. In our case, the sentence ascertains the purposefulness of the activity recommended by the imperative. Another example: "If it snows, skiing conditions will be good; if skiing conditions are good, we will go to the mountains", and therefore: "If it snows, we will go to the mountains". Everything is in order as the argument remains valid after replacing the imperative with a statement that going to the mountains is purposeful in view of the assumed designs. Another one: "Let us defend ourselves or flee, but fleeing will do us no good, therefore let us defend ourselves!". This makes sense as well in view of the validity of the argument: "Defence would be purposeful or flight would be purposeful, but fleeing would do us no good, therefore defence would be purposeful". On the other hand, the following argument would be faulty: "Do not open tap A and tap B simultaneously!" and therefore "Do not open tap A and do not open tap B, since from the fact that it would not be purposeful to open both taps simultaneously there does not entail that it would not be purposeful to open tap A and it would not be purposeful to open tap B".

Generally, every imperative has the aim it serves, which is not usually directly manifested but is only visible in context; in order to recognize whether given reasoning with the use of imperative is valid, it suffices to replace the imperative which recommends a given activity with a sentence which states the purposefulness of a given activity from the point of view of the function of the imperative. Figuratively speaking, if an imperative which recommends activity A is marked as '$!A$' and the set of sentences which create the reasoning with the use of imperatives is marked as '$f(!A)$', then the validity of the reasoning is investigated sufficiently if '$!A$' is replaced with the sentence "A is purposeful", meaning purposefulness in relation to the function of the imperative in a given example.

The question is how to handle negative recommendations according to the above instruction. The answer is clear as long as a negative recommendation ("Do not do A!", *etc.*) is always understood as equivalent to a positive recommendation towards an action which consists in refraining from executing the action mentioned in the negative recommendation ("Refrain from *A*!", *etc.*). "Driver, if the road is icy, do not accelerate to 100 kilometres per hour!" means the same as "Driver, if the road is icy, refrain from accelerating to 100 kilometres per hour!" which can be investigated satisfactorily by testing whether the fact that a driver refrains from driving at 100 kilometres per hour on an icy road would be purposeful (naturally, from the point of view of attempting to drive without an accident).

If the sense of the presented general directive is clear, let us now test it in examples which are deemed controversial in the logic of imperatives and norms. How does it work in the case of conjunctions? Is the following reasoning correct? "Let John close the door and let Peter open the window" and therefore "Let John close the door". It seems so. Sometimes derivation of a specific recommendation from the conjunction of recommendations is questioned based on the idea that by issuing a conjunction of recommendations one recommends the execution of a given action on the condition of executing another one, and by issuing a single recommendation one recommends executing an action without the need to fulfil that condition. The objection would be right if recommending something without mentioning the conditions meant the same as recommending something regardless of the conditions. Well, the thing is that: if opening the window by John was purposeful activity and closing the door by Peter was purposeful activity, then opening the window by John would be purposeful activity (naturally, in view of the intention of the person issuing the recommendations). This is directly based on the tautology: $p \land q \to p$.

What about alternative? Here the dispute is more heated. "Put the letter into the mailbox!" One may derive the following recommendation from that recommendation: "Put the letter into the mailbox or burn it!". Is this derivation right or wrong? Let us apply the proposed criterion. We obtain: "If putting the letter into the mailbox were a purposeful action, then putting the letter into the mailbox would be a purposeful action or burning the letter would be a purposeful action". In view of such a *dictum* some would say this reasoning is absurd as a notoriously wrong conclusion is derived from a clearly right premise. After all, can we assume that the executor of the action can choose between one of the two: either put the letter into the mailbox or burn the letter, and will always choose the purposeful action from the point of view of the designs of the person who gave him the letter? Others defend this reasoning, simply regarding it as a direct example of use of the following tautology in sentential calculus: $p \rightarrow p \vee p$. In my opinion, everything becomes clear when we realize the deceptive ambiguity of the word "or". If it means the same as the symbol of alternative in sentential calculus, then the reasoning based on that sentential calculus is correct, but its sense ceases to be paradoxical. This is because stating that "putting the letter into the mailbox would be the purposeful action or burning the letter would be the purposeful action" does not say anything about the fact that the person executing the action has freedom of choice and that it is true that his action will be purposeful from the point of view of the designs of the principal both if he puts the letter into the mailbox and if he burns it; this utterance only informs us that there is a true utterance within the two parts connected with the word "or", and nothing else (and what it states is not at all strange as we know that the first part is true). On the other hand, if the word "or" is interpreted differently, when it informs of the possibility of reasonable choice one of the two possibilities, the reasoning mentioned above immediately collapses, as it ceases to be an application of the scheme: $p \rightarrow p \vee q$, where the symbol 'v' is equivalent to the former, initially discussed "or" and does not imply any supposed freedom of choice of any of the parts of the alternative.

Hitherto everything seems to be going smoothly, but a willing seeker of problems could present us with the following task: examine the following reasoning according to the proposed criterion: "If let the room be heated, then it will not be too cold". Before addressing this issue, I have to make a belated declaration, as it would have been better suited at the beginning. Namely, we are not going to test nonsense occurring as a result of confusing semiotic categories. For instance, the outpour of words: "If and/or p let q if" is not suitable to be tested, as it is simply hodgepodge. The only question is whether the example with the heated room and similarly built examples are semiotic nonsense. This issue is worth further consideration.

At first, one is certainly inclined to disregard such structures. There is an opinion that nonsense occurs whenever an imperative attempts to take the place of the antecedent in a conditional sentence. "If p, then let q!" sounds reasonable, whereas "If let p, then q" generally does not. Supposedly, there may occur other forms of construction of utterances where a certain contribution of an imperative results in nonsense, which frees the person asked from attempts to vindicate a given enunciation according to the proposed criterion. This view is juxtaposed with another, according to which one may sensibly insert an imperative in place of a sentence which undergoes evaluation as to its truthfulness or falsity in any example. Only some cases result in a stylistic dissonance which cannot be identified with semiotic nonsense. It would be dissonant if one called the violin a musical machine instead of a musical instrument, or if a washing machine was called a washing instrument, although "machine" and "instrument" (let us assume) mean the same and thus: although both dissonant names can be used sensibly to describe both of the discussed items. It is similar with forms of verbs and the particles which accompany them. "If work hard and you will get rich" sounds dissonant, but no one will dare call the utterance "Work hard and you will get rich!" dissonant, although it seems that they express the same idea: that hard work makes one rich and people should be encouraged to work by referring to this relation. If so, then also the previous example holds true, since it is equivalent to the utterance in the form which is devoid of dissonance: "Let the room be heated and it will not be too cold", and there will emerge the obligation to test it according to the proposed criterion.

I will not attempt to devote any space in this paper to the issue of which side of this argument is right: whether those who repeal certain structures in which nonsense emerged from a sensible whole by replacing a logical sentence with an imperative, or those who do not see nonsense in any case of such sort. It is sufficient to resolve to only test such utterances which are not semiotic nonsense. Let me just add that I am inclined to see dissonance only where there occur at least some appearances of nonsense. The main reason for it is that although "If let p, then let q" sounds wrong, "Let p, then q" sounds quite sensible, even though it probably includes the former in its intention.

However, since we raised the question of the applicability of the imperative, I would like to take a stand on several issues discussed within this topic. Some authors allow for connecting the particle "let" with descriptions of other events rather than activated by discussing an utterance of the following kind: "Let there be frost!". I will not deal with such utterances in the present paper, which is not to say that I question their sensibility. In my understanding, a recommendation always concerns some activity. Apart from recommendations, one can utter so called "wishful thinking". However, let me restrict my discussion to recommendations. Another issue is whether one can include in the imperative a whole which includes the conditions for activity, of the type: '$p \rightarrow A$', rather than a certain activity. Thus, the whole '$!(p \rightarrow A)$' rather than the whole '$p \rightarrow !A$'. I see no reason not to. Here is an example: "Since we are ready to respond, let us do the following: if they attack us, we will respond". According to the proposed criterion, a testing utterance would be: "Since we are ready, then it would be purposeful to behave in the following manner: if they attack us, we will respond". Another issue of interest is whether it is possible to sensibly refer a recommendation to the whole of activities given in a conjunctive description or given in an alternative description rather than to refer it to a specific activity, and thus, if one can sensibly issue recommendations in the form of: '$!(A \wedge B)$' or recommendations in the form of: '$!(A \vee B)$'. In both cases, there is no problem with operating such wholes, or with using the proposed criterion of validity of arguments derived from the use of such wholes.

I submit the proposed directive after having acquainted myself with the content of the publications [...],[117] which deal with the more recent attempts to construct logic of imperatives, which do not seem to state clearly an idea for how to resolve the fundamental question. Admittedly, they mention procedures which are similar to some extent, yet are rightly rejected. The common ground is that in order to vindicate the imperative reasoning, imperatives are replaced with sentences which undergo evaluation as to their truthfulness. However, all sentences which replace imperatives prove to be unsuitable for the intended aim. Here are some examples. The following reasoning is considered: "Keep all your commitments, and this is your commitment, so keep this commitment". In order to justify it, imperatives are replaced with sentences stating their fulfilment, thus obtaining a faulty argument in this case, although the initial imperative reasoning is necessarily true: "You keep all your com-

---

[117] See Weinberger [1958], [1960], [1964b]; Wright [1963a]; Kalinowski [1963].

mitments, and this is your commitment, so you keep this commitment". What if the individual we are addressing does not keep all his commitments? Then the conclusion is not justified by a statement which is incompatible with reality, although the conclusive imperative is justified by the imperative which performed the function of the premise of the imperative. The following idea is also no better: let us replace the imperative '!A' with a sentence stating that someone demands action A to be executed. Thus we obtain the following argument: "Someone demands that you keep all your commitments, and this is your commitment, and therefore someone demands that you keep this commitment". The critique proceeds analogously.[118] Another failed solution for our question is replacing the imperative '!A' with the statement "I want action A to be executed".[119] Does the utterance "If there is a gas leak, put on your mask!" become justified when it is the case that "if there is a gas leak, I want you to put on your mask"?

When browsing through the mentioned sources in order to state whether an idea similar to the main concept of the present paper was expressed I find information on Reichenbach's statement, where he ascertains that "sometimes an imperative can be considered as implication between the desired aim and the activity". Yet, his example of an imperative is the following: "You have to put on your coat", which seems to prove that he treats sentences of duty *etc.* as imperatives. However, I do not count the quoted sentence as an imperative since, according to Reichenbach, it was supposed to be interpreted as: "If you do not want to get cold, you have to put on your coat".[120] Here I attempt to draw a sharp line between imperatives and sentences of duty, norms, *etc.* and only deal with imperatives, and I refer the proposed directive to all imperative reasoning rather than just some.

*

I must add that after having written this article I came across a discussion on the topic of imperatives and reasoning using imperatives between H.N. Castañeda and L. Bergström.[121] Castañeda considers similar reasoning as vin-

---

[118] See Weinberger [1958a: 43–50].
[119] See Weinberger [1958a: 70].
[120] See Weinberger [1958a: 72].
[121] See Bergström [1962] and Castañeda [1962].

dicated if the action demanded in the imperative is purposeful from the point of view of both the person issuing the imperative and the addressee of the imperative, where purposefulness is interpreted as at least not interfering with the intention. He understands imperative as the correct answer to the question: "What am I (are we) supposed to do?" or "How am I (are we) supposed to do it?".[121] In spite of certain differences between the conceptions and the wording, the convergence of Castañeda's standpoint with that of the author of the present article is apparent. Thus, unable to rejoice putting forward a fresh idea, I find consolation in the fact that if a thesis becomes apparent to several researchers simultaneously, it is only in its favour.

Władysław Tatarkiewicz. Normative implications
[1966: 297]

Ethical sentences usually assume the form of norms, regulations, dictates, or recommendations. However, every norm, regulation, dictate, or recommendation implies some kind of a judgement; namely, an evaluating judgement, which evaluates an object or an action positively or negatively, as good or bad, right or wrong. If kindness and honesty are recommended, it is because they are evaluated positively and regarded as good, worth striving for and implementing in one's life.

Jan Woleński. Reduction of norms to imperatives
[1966: 4, 7]

Reduction of the meaning of norms to the meaning of other utterances assumes that the meaning of the latter does not pose any problems. The following versions of reductionism can be distinguished: (1) reduction of norms to descriptive sentences; (2) reduction of norms to evaluations; (3) reduction of norms to evaluations and descriptive sentences (the so called hybrid conception of the meaning of norms); (4) reduction of norms to orders (the imperativistic concept). [...]

The last of the enumerated conceptions of reductionism is imperativism. The motto of this conception is the following statement: "The content of all our duties is identical with the content of certain actually issued orders".[122] The imperativistic view is widespread in the positivistic theories of law and in the heteronomical approach to morality. It is therefore a consequence of common views on the nature of law or morality and in this sense the methodological status of this conception is similar to the status of the conception which describes norms as sentences on the objective realm of duties. Regardless of the analysis of the framework of imperativism, the conclusion seems to be that the notion of a command is as unclear as the notion of an order, therefore little is gained through attempts to explain the meaning of a norm by referring to orders. It seems that the opposite approach, which consists in reducing orders to norms, is proper. Therefore O. Weinberger is right in stating that: "An order as a derivative notion emerges as a special case of a normative sentence".[123]

Zygmunt Ziembiński. Verbalization of norms
[1966b: 54–57]

[...] How can norms be verbalized regardless of their kind, namely: legal, moral, social, aesthetic, and other forms? We distinguish the following verbal forms of a norm:

(1) the "imperative" form;

(2) the form "of duty";

and

(3) other, seemingly descriptive forms of a norm.

Ad (1). There is a widespread view, particularly among logicians, that the fundamental way to verbalize a norm is to use an imperative utterance, that is, an utterance which contains a verb in its imperative form. It seems this is not exactly the case, as an imperative utterance is not the most common way of verbalizing a norm (at least this is not so in the field of legal norms), and besides, not every norm can be verbalized in the form of an imperative utterance. An utterance in the imperative mood is

---

[122] Elzenberg [1938: 3].
[123] Weinberger [1958a: 1].

not only used to verbalize norms of the kind which are within the scope of jurisprudence.

It is quite important to distinguish an order as a certain social fact from an imperative utterance as a specific form of expression. AN ORDER is a social fact which consists in someone settling a certain norm of behaviour for someone else, without his participation. Naturally, a reasonable person usually takes such activity only when there exists a relevant social situation, that is, when there are grounds to believe that for some reason he has power over the person for whom he settles the norm (that is, if it is probable to a high enough degree that the settled norm will be respected by the person the order was directed at).

However, the act of settling a norm for another person does not necessarily have to be verbalized in the form of an utterance which contains a verb in the imperative form. The imperative mood is typically used when someone settles a norm for another person or persons with them present, and the act of settling the norm is connected to a particularly strong accent of suggestiveness. This particular suggestiveness of the imperative mood makes it suitable for use also in those situations where no ordering in the common meaning of the word occurs: in order to express strong encouragement, an earnest begging or request, where it is indicated how one should act, but not in a domineering manner. "Have mercy, spare my life!", "Buy only As soap!" are imperative utterances which would not be considered as expressing a social act of order in the common meaning of the word. Besides, the use of the imperative mood can simply be a way to express one's emotional state, for instance in proposals such as: "Go to hell!" or "Get lost!". Therefore using the imperative mood is socially unacceptable in some cases, although the suggestive character of the utterance formulated in this mood is particularly pronounced.

It is worth noting that the imperative mood does not normally take on the form of the first person singular, although, which is of less interest to lawyers, norms of behaviour can be settled for oneself. Therefore, not every norm can be verbalized in the imperative form. Similarly, the person for singular and plural of the imperative mood is only expressed through replacement forms ("Niech da", "Let him give", *etc.*), which is connected to the fact that the imperative mood is normally used when addressing another person or people directly.

The legislator does not use the imperative mood as settling norms does not usually take place in the presence of the addressees who would immediately take activity dictated in the norm. At most, the imperative mood can be encountered in political manifestos, in preambles to statutes of particular political significance, rather than in regular legislature.

Ad (2). In handbooks on the theory of law and other theoretical discussions on the meaning and structure of norms, the most common formulation of norms is in the form "OF DUTY", that is, with phrases like "should" or equivalent. Naturally, in certain cases there may arise an interpretive dispute over whether the word "should" was used in the sense of directive, as an indication of a given manner of behaviour to someone, or in order to describe the social fact that in some (or other) sense the person mentioned in the norm is obliged to comply with its instructions. As will be discussed later on, logicians sometimes address norms in this form, the only difference being that instead of using the form "x should do (not do) C" they are inclined to use the phrase of duty at the beginning: "It should be that x does (or does not do) C".

Ad (3). Apart from "imperative" form and form "of duty" of verbalizing a norm, where it is directly stated who should do what, we also use such utterances which, literally speaking, would be sentences which characterize a given person's act from the point of view of the validity of a certain norm, or characterize the situation of a given person from the point of view of a given norm.[124] In colloquial speech, as well as in legal language, utterances in the following form are used interchangeably: "x should do C", "C is x's obligation", "x is obliged to do C", "action C is dictated to x", "act C is x's obligation", *etc.* If one pays close attention to the wording, it is easy to see that the first of these utterances indicates clearly what x should do, whereas the remaining utterances state that in view of the validity of a given norm, there arose for x a given situation. If we say that someone has the obligation to act in a certain manner, or that someone is obliged

---

[124] For appropriate remarks on the subject – *cf.* Wróblewski [1959: 21–27].

to do or prohibited from doing something, it basically requires a complement in the form of indicating a norm which dictates or prohibits this act. However, it seems obvious that when the legislator uses the expression "is obliged", the function of the expression is not to formulate a description of the situation which the addressee of the norm found himself in, but rather to verbalize the norm, similarly to the form "of duty" or "imperative" form.

It is also commonly known that a legislator often settles norms of behaviour such a form that they sound like descriptions of acts whose fulfilment is the subject of the norm's indications. "The Parliament adopts the budget of the country yearly (art. 19, act 2 of the *Constitution of People's Republic of Poland*) means as much as: "The Parliament should adopt the budget of the country yearly". The expressions included in the law: "The testator is responsible for...", "Whoever kills a person shall be punished..." are indications of the duty to give compensation, or the duty to punish a criminal, rather than descriptions of, for instance, court proceedings.

Clearly, the more indirectly expressed an utterance is which indicates to someone what he should do, the more opportunities it presents for misunderstanding its character, whether normative or descriptive.

Zygmunt Ziembiński. Technical directives
[1966b: 74–76]

We stated that a norm of behaviour was an utterance in a given language, which indicates to someone directly what he should do in a given situation or how to behave in certain circumstances. The reason why he should act a given way is the issue of justifying the validity of a given norm [...]. However, the issue of justifying a norm in a certain way is not essentially connected to the meaning of the norm. The meaning of the norm: "If someone harms another person through his own fault, he should compensate it" is essentially the same, regardless of whether the norm has a legal, moral or religious justification; in any case, it expresses the dictate to compensate the harm (although it cannot be ruled out that from the point of view of various legal, moral or religious systems, the notions of "harm" and "compensation" can be interpreted somewhat differently). Within a given system of norms it would be an absolute, "categorical" dictate, rather than one dependent on the volition of the addressee who chooses the aims of his activity; not a «hypothetical» dictate.

For the sake of comparison, let us analyze the meaning of the utterance: "If one wants to obtain a train ticket, one should insert a 2 złoty coin into the machine". Is this sort of utterance a norm of behaviour, an indication of how the person standing in front of the machine should act? If so, then at any rate, we are dealing with a specific kind of norms.

This utterance does give an indication, but it is a conditional indication, for those who would like to obtain a ticket. This utterance is obviously tied to the sentence in the logical sense, which states the relationship between inserting a 2 złoty coin into the machine and a ticket falling out of it. The sentence provides the basis for the formulation of the appropriate indication, just as the sentence: "Whenever one flips the switch in this installation, the light will turn off" constitutes the basis for the formulation of the indication: "If one wants to turn off the light, one should flip the switch". If one does not want to purchase a ticket, or turn off the light, then the utterances cited above do not indicate any specific behaviour for them.

Utterances in the form of: "If one wants A, one should do C" again bring the possibility of a twofold interpretation. If such an utterance is interpreted exclusively as stating a necessary relationship between activity and its effects (an anancastic sentence[125]), then it can be predicated whether it is true or false that flipping a given switch causes a given light to turn off. If this utterance is to be treated as a norm of behaviour for someone who wants to turn off the light, then it can be debated whether this is the indication for the best method of turning the light off, or whether, for instance, there is a different method to turn the light off. If someone wants to turn off the light in such a way that prevents it from being turned on again, he should destroy the whole installation. If he wants to turn off the light so that he is the only person who can turn it back on, he should break the circuit in an imperceptible, but easy to fix, way. If he wants to turn the light off and leave the installation in such a state that it enables others to use it, he should do it the usual way, by flipping the switch.

---

[125] *Cf.* Wright [1963a: 10].

In brief, this interpretation raises the issue of the justification of the norm rather than determining the logical value of the sentence.

Utterances which indicate how one should behave in order to achieve a given state of affairs will be called TELEOLOGICAL DIRECTIVES, or technical directives. For those who would like to achieve this state of affairs through their own or somebody else's activity, the technical directive becomes the basis for settling an (absolute) norm of behaviour. For those who have not yet made the decision to strive for that state of affairs to come into being which realizing the directive will lead to, it has the character of a conditional indication, still dependent on the choice of one or another course of driving.

One should differentiate between, for instance, a legally valid norm: "If someone harms another person through a fault of their own, they should compensate for the harm" and a technical directive: "If someone wants to avoid conflict with his environment, he should compensate for harm done by him". The first one indicates to the addressee what he definitely has to do as dictated by the legislator if a given social situation occurs, whereas the second one indicates what one should do if he wants to achieve a given aim (that is, avoid conflict and disapproval of his environment) upon emergence of a given situation.

Naturally, as for the legal norms valid for citizens, one could also take the stance that they are teleological directives from the point of view of an observer of social issues, and they indicate the proper course of action in order to avoid sanctions in the form of punishment or execution on the part of the state. Still, disregarding other fallacies of this view, one should keep in mind that lawyers are used to speaking of legal norms from «within» the system, that is, on the assumption of the absolute validity of norms, assuming that indications of the norms, or at least *ius cogens* forming them, are binding regardless of the views of their addressees.

Zygmunt Ziembiński. Instrumental and axiological consequence
[1966b: 237–243]

[1.] If the impossibility of realizing norm N_1 in the case of the failure to realize norm N_2 is connected to the fact that there are relevant causal relationships between these two facts, the relationship of these norms could be called INSTRUMENTAL ENTAILMENT of norm N_2 from norm N_1. Therefore, if a lawgiver settled a norm which dictates to someone to realize a given state of affairs, then in accordance with the terminological convention one may assume that from that norm there entail instrumentally: firstly, a norm which prescribes doing all that is a necessary condition for causing that state of affairs, and secondly, a norm which dictates doing anything which is causally a sufficient condition for the mentioned state of affairs not to occur. It can be assumed that each valid dictating norm is coupled with a whole set of norms determined by:

(1) THE DIRECTIVE OF INSTRUMENTAL DICTATE to do all that is necessary to cause a given state of affairs to occur,
as well as

(2) THE DIRECTIVE OF INSTRUMENTAL PROHIBITION to do all that is sufficient for the given state of affairs not to occur.

Respectively, if there is a norm which prohibits realizing a given state of affairs, then all that is necessary to avoid the occurrence of that state of affairs is dictated, and all that is sufficient to cause that state to occur is prohibited.

Accepting the directive of instrumental dictate and the directive of instrumental prohibition is inevitable in jurisprudence, as otherwise, when settling a dictate to realize a given state of affairs, one would additionally have to settle norms as to all the actions which may be necessary in order to realize that state of affairs by the norm's addressee, which would be practically unenforceable. Obviously, the lawgiver may, for instance, prohibit doing something which is a necessary condition to realize the previous dictate, but this is either a form of repealing the dictate, or it leads to a «logical gap». In concentration camps the prisoners were ordered to wear a cap which had been thrown over the fence, but then the aim of the dictate was not to direct someone's activity, but rather to find a pretext to murder a prisoner.

When analyzing the instrumental entailment of norms from norms one should keep in mind that for these purposes the entailment occurs under the assumption that there are some causal relationships between the addressee's activities and the state of affairs which is indicated to be realized by the norm. Therefore if the following norm is valid: "One should not cause a fire" and it is true that "Throwing a cigarette end onto a pile of dry straw causes a fire", then the following norm is valid: "One should not throw cigarette ends onto a pile of dry straw". The latter norm is valid in view of the validity of the former one, and it is valid even for those who are not aware of the causal relationship between throwing a cigarette end and a fire. Naturally, the issue of the unawareness of the causal relationship extends beyond the scope of interest of logic.[126]

The discussed directives of instrumental dictate or prohibition can not only be referred to the act of the person who the basic norm concerns, but also to acts of other people, causally connected to the acts of the given person. One should mention THE DIRECTIVE OF SOCIAL INSTRUMENTAL PROHIBITION which states that if norm N_1 which dictates to person x to do C is valid, then (in the lack of explicit adverse reservations of the lawgiver), norm N_2 which prohibits all other people from doing anything which would prevent person x from doing act C is also valid. Respectively, it is assumed that, if person x is not allowed to do C, then other people must not force him to execute the act.[127]

At the same time, if someone is prohibited from preventing a specific person from realizing a given state of affairs, then that person is also prohibited from preventing him from activity necessary to realize this state of affairs. Therefore, if someone is allowed (strong permission) to enter a neighbour's plot in order to pick the fruit hanging from his trees, then he is also allowed to bring a ladder if it is necessary to pick the fruit.

---

[126] In the legal tradition, the schemes of reasoning from norms on norms based on settling causal relationships between states of affairs indicated by norms to be realized are described as reasonings "from aim to means". This terminology is faulty in so far as in order to achieve a given state of affairs (the «aim» of the activity) one may undertake as means such activities which are useful in order to achieve a given aim only in that person's imagination, for instance, when a superstitious person destroys an image of his opponent, considering this to be a means to achieve a given aim. Traditional formulations are easy to criticize; for instance, the formulation of the directive: "Whoever is prohibited from achieving the aim, he is also prohibited from activity leading to this aim". International law prohibits waging bacteriological war, although research of epidemics, necessary both as the means to the sinister aim and to realize humanitarian aims, like fighting [preventing] epidemy, is not prohibited. One should not confuse the subjective connection of the means and the aim in someone's mind with an objective relationship between a given state of affairs and the necessary or sufficient conditions to cause the state. [...]

[127] The situation this directive is referring to cannot be confused with the situation where the law formulates "a strong permission": "x may not do C".

Inferential directives based on instrumental entailment of norms should be regarded as infallible directives in a sense. It is impossible for the lawgiver or interpreter to reject them in the sense that it would lead to great incompatibilities in the construction of the legal system. [...]

[2.] Apart from reasoning based on the previously settled entailment of norms from norms, one may encounter in legal practice reasoning which is only based on the assumptions that the lawgiver always has a certain system of evaluations in mind while settling legal norms. In view of this assumption, in the situations which are not mentioned in the regulations settled by this lawgiver, in some cases one should accept as valid such a norm of behaviour which could be justified axiologically in evaluations which justify norms which are undoubtedly verbalized in the regulation, according to the interpreter's conjecture. Naturally, conclusions drawn in this manner are often very controversial.

An example of reasoning of this kind is reasoning from the analogy of the law (*analogia iuris*). Reasoning from the analogy of the law is something different from reasoning from the analogy of a regulation (*analogia legis*), although the terminology in this issue is very varied. In the case of *analogiae legis*, it is simply a subsumption of a certain factual state under a regulation interpreted in such a way that it is assumed it does not only refer to the explicitly stated situation, but also to a situation which is substantially similar to it in the eyes of the interpreter. On the other hand, reasoning from the analogy of the law consists in settling basic evaluations which guide the lawgiver's decisions in creating the norms for a given area of behaviour, as well as in accepting as valid a norm which is axiologically justified in these basic evaluations, as opposed to a situation without clear norms. This type of reasoning is sometimes applied when, for instance, there arises a need to find the principle of resolving conflicts of interests not predicted by the lawgiver. This is also how various «legal principles», in one of many meanings of this term, are formulated.

Reasoning of the type discussed here can be based on conjecture as to the hierarchy of evaluations assumed by lawgivers. If in order to achieve a given state of affairs the lawgiver settles a norm which imposes on the addressee obligations regarded as more oppressive, then one should reason that a norm which imposes less oppressive obligations in this area is also valid "as decided by the lawgiver". If the lawgiver granted someone freedom to act in a broader scope, granting them "a strong permission" (prohibiting others from interfering), then it should be accepted that this freedom is also granted in some, respectively narrower, scope. A summary formulation of this directive of reasoning is as follows: "If one is dictated to do more, he is dictated to do less, and if one is allowed to do more, he is allowed to do less" (*argumentum a maiori ad minus*). If one is obliged to deliver crops to a town, then he is all the more obliged to deliver them to the mobile purchasing centre in his village. If one is allowed to cut down a tree, then he is also allowed to cut one of its branches. At the same time, one should expect that when the lawgiver prohibits some actions, regarding them as violations of a good which is valued by him, he is all the more inclined to prohibit such activities which violate the good to a greater degree: "If one is prohibited from doing less, then he is prohibited from doing more" (*argumentum a minori ad maius*). If one is not allowed to dig in such a way that the act may threaten to cause the neighbouring building to collapse (article 147 of the *Code of Civil Law*), then he definitely is not allowed to dig directly under the foundations of the neighbouring building.

Naturally, the expressions "more" and "less" in both of these directives are not only unclear semantically, but also refer to some unspecified system of evaluations (what is more and what is less oppressive; what violates somebody's good to a greater, or lesser, degree). This in turn provides greater freedom in selecting various default premises of this kind of reasoning. A clerk may believe that it is easier for a farmer to transport his crops to a mobile purchasing centre, whereas the farmer may consider it easier to transport them to the town, where the warehouse is open at certain hours, and it is more inconvenient to wait for the irregular service of the purchaser at home.

Reasoning along the lines of *argumentum a maiori ad minus* and *argumentum ad minori ad maius* (described jointly as arguments *a fortiori*, although even here the terminology is irresolute) can be formulated in such a way that they will be reduced to regarding as valid the more detailed norm on the basis of regarding as valid the more general norm, one which was interpreted on the basis of the regulations, presupposing the lawgiver's intentions. For instance, if the regulation: "One must not walk on the grass in city gardens" is interpreted as a norm: "Everyone should refrain from damaging the grass to a degree caused by walking on it or to a greater degree", then assuming the enthymeme that storing bricks on the lawn damages the grass to a greater degree than walking on it the conclusion that one should not store bricks on the grass logically entails from these premises. Except that it follows from the norm which was only loosely derived from the regulation formulated in this area. Therefore, instead of precarious reasoning, a considerable degree of freedom of interpretation of the regulation is encountered in this approach to the discussed "arguments".[128]

In the reasoning discussed above, accepting a different conclusion in the discussed case would not lead to an inevitable incompatibility of the derived norm with norms previously accepted as valid, although it would be unexpected, provided that norms of a given legal system are axiologically justified in some consistent system of evaluations.

When referring to the notion of the "will", "design", "aim", or "intention" of the lawgiver in this kind of reasoning, one has to be aware that now it is usually a fictional person, and hence, his "will", "aim", *etc.* are also fictional. "The lawgiver's will" is a certain legal construct, a product of legal doctrine which dictates to one to attribute to the legislating group as a whole certain uniform evaluations, drivings and semantic intentions of the expressions used. This way the legal doctrine constructs for itself such an emperor which it would like to serve.

Upon realizing the character of the phenomenon, it does not seem that the use of the expression "the lawgiver's will" as a shortcut could lead to any particularly troublesome consequences.

Leszek Nowak. Evaluation of performatives
[1968b: 148, 151–156]

The issue of performatives has hitherto only been discussed by linguistic philosophers, who have treated it with the lack of attention paid to conceptual precision which is so characteristic of them. Thus, for those who do not profess the assumptions of linguistic philosophy, works of

---

[128] *Cf.* Ziemba [1957: 274].

these philosophers may only provide, admittedly very interesting, initial intuitions. [...]

In every culture certain rules are assumed, and these shall be called RULES OF CULTURAL INTERPRETATION, which settle when someone who performs a certain natural activity can therefore be described as performing a certain cultural action. Thus, these rules settle the conditions necessary to turn a certain natural activity into a cultural action. [...] Generally speaking, the rules of cultural interpretation have the following form: if person X performs in time t a natural activity Z, then he performs a cultural action C if and only if he fulfils in time t conditions W. [...]

Since giving (with understanding) any language utterances is a cultural action, then obviously one cannot describe performative utterances as utterances of the kind for which the act of their formulation is a cultural action. In this approach, any utterance is a performative utterance. Therefore, we are forced to look for another criterion which would distinguish performative utterances from any other utterance.

Let us compare the following two rules of cultural interpretation: (1) If X took off his hat upon seeing Y, then X greeted Y if and only if X and Y are acquaintances or at least X knows Y, as well as (2) If X tells Y "Let me invite you home to lunch!" then X invites Y to lunch if and only if X is the host of the house or acts upon commissions of the host of the house. The difference between the rules consists in the fact that in the antecedent of rule (2) there is a reservation that person X performs a cultural action, namely, formulates the utterance: "Let me invite you home to lunch!". Yet, the action of inviting itself is not at all equivalent to giving this utterance, since the person formulating it invites only when he fulfils the conditions provided in the rule (2), namely, if he is the host of the home which the invitation concerns or he is authorized by the host. At the same time, only giving (with understanding) the discussed utterance is a cultural action regardless of who and in what circumstances is giving the utterance. Therefore, the action of inviting somebody to lunch is in some measure «superstructured» over the cultural action of giving the utterance: "Let me invite you home to lunch!". Therefore, in order to perform the cultural action of inviting someone to lunch, first one has to perform a cultural action which consists in formulating a language utterance. The action of inviting someone to lunch is therefore an action of a higher order than the action which consists in delivering a linguistic utterance. A cultural action of the first order is such an action which does not require performing any other cultural action, but necessarily requires performing a natural activity. [...]

From the definition of a notion of cultural action it follows that performatives cannot be invalid. For instance, let us consider if the utterance: "I will give you my neighbour's car" is a performative utterance. According to the conception presented in the present work, giving this utterance is only a first-order cultural action, just as giving any other language utterance. However, giving this utterance is not an action of donation, as the following rule is assumed in our culture: If X tells Y: "I will give you x", then X gives Y an object if and only if X is the owner of this object.

Let us now consider the question of the logical value of performative utterances.

It is sometimes assumed that a performative utterance is such an utterance for which the act of its formulation causes a certain state of affairs to occur which makes it true.[129] From this definition it follows that every performative utterance is a sentence in the logical sense. This conception seems inadequate, not only because it is hard to grasp the exact sense meant by the authors who adhere to this view when they speak of causing a state of affairs which makes a performative true, but also because it leads to questionable solutions for a series of semantic issues. For instance, legal norms or military orders are certainly performative utterances; after all, the fact of settling legal norms by the State authority or issuing an order by a superior to a soldier of a lower rank, are cultural actions in the understanding adopted in the present work, and at that, actions of higher order. Therefore, the discussed definition leads to the conclusion that legal norms and imperatives have a logical value. Similarly, a teacher directing questions at a student at an exam is not performing a cultural action of the first order consisting in formulating an interrogative utterance, but rather performing an action of

---

[129] Hedenius [1963: 117]. Similar intuitions lie in the basis of the so called lalic implication: sentence p lalically implies sentence q when the very use of p suffices to accept truthfulness of sentence q. *Cf.* Castañeda [1957: 89 *et seq.*].

formulating an exam task for a student, and therefore performing a cultural action of the second order. Thus at least some questions, for instance, exam questions, are performative utterances. The discussed conception would also lead to the conclusion that these questions are sentences in the logical sense. If we accepted this conception, we would be forced to reach the precarious conclusions that both legal norms and imperatives, as well as some questions have a logical value.

The discussed view is countered by the opposite view which states that performative utterances as utterances-acts cannot be either true or false. Their function is to perform something other than to tell the truth or falsehood.[130]

It is easy to see that the definition of the notion of a performative utterance adopted in the present work does not favour any of these views, as the notion of the performative is defined without any reservations as to the structure and semantic feature of the utterances described as performative.

Franciszek Studnicki. The semantic function of norms
[1968: 195–198]

Normative expressions belong to a specific category of expressions *n*, different from category *z*, where sentences belong. The difference is manifested, among other things, in the fact that such expressions perform different semantic functions from the ones performed by sentences. In particular, the semantic function of sentences consists in reporting such states of affairs which could be the subject of descriptive analysis,[131] whereas normative expressions may perform either one or two semantic functions, depending on whether they are used in the manner which we will call weak (or referring), or in the manner which we will call strong (or settling). Neither of these functions coincides with the semantic function performed by sentences.

---

[130] Austin [1961b: 223]; Black [1963: 219].
[131] On the difference between descriptive analysis and normative analysis, *cf.* Studnicki [1967: 121 *et seq.*].

In the case of weak (referring) use, the semantic function of normative expressions consists in reporting a given states of affairs, However, the states of affairs have to be different from the ones the sentences may report. The states of affairs mentioned here consist in the fact that certain kinds (categories) of behaviour are not dictated, prohibited, or facultative in view of a specific normative order, for instance, in view of a specific legal order. The terms "dictated" and "prohibited" are used here in the meaning which coincides with their colloquial meaning. By the state of affairs consisting in the fact that a certain kind (a certain category) of behaviour B is facultative we mean a state of affairs consisting in the fact that behaving in the manner B, as well as behaving in the manner non-B is allowed.[132]

The described states of affairs, that is, states of affairs which consist in the fact that certain kinds (categories) of behaviour are dictated or prohibited, or facultative in view of a specific normative order, will be called "normative states of affairs".

On the other hand, in the case of strong (settling) use, normative expressions simultaneously perform two semantic functions. The first one, which shall be called settling, consists in the fact that they settle the normative states of affairs described above. The other one, which shall be called referring, consists in the fact that they report such states of affairs. This function coincides with the semantic function performed by normative expressions used in the weak manner.

Identifying the settling function of normative expressions used in the strong manner reflects the arbitrariness of such use. In particular, the arbitrariness consists in the fact that, if certain conditions are fulfilled, the normative expression used in the described manner creates a certain specific state of affairs which had not existed before such use.[133]

---

[132] The term "facultative" is used in the meaning distinct from how it is used by Z. Ziemba and Z. Ziembiński in their paper [1964: p. 111 *et seq.*]. In these authors' approach, the term "facultative" means as much as the term "not dictated". According to them, a facultative act is therefore also a prohibited action. *Cf.* also Ziembiński [1966b: 101 *et seq.*].

[133] This approach is inspired by the theory which ascribes to certain utterances the character of the so called performative utterances; *cf.* Austin [1962: 6 *et seq.*]. In Polish sources, the issue of performative utterances (or ones that fulfil performative functions) is discussed by Ziembiński [1966b: 26 *et seq.*].

Whether one can assume that a certain normative expression is used in the weak manner or that it is used in the strong manner is determined by the semantic rules of the language this expression belongs to. Specifically, the character in which the expression is used, and thus, semantic functions which it performs in a given case, depend on the circumstances in which such a use occurred. For instance, certain expressions are treated as being used in the strong manner, and therefore as performing the settling function besides the reffering function, in the case when their use constitutes an implementation of a certain procedure, for instance, the procedure of adopting a law, concluding an agreement or issuing verdicts.

In the states of affairs which were previously described as normative, only certain kinds (categories) of behaviour, distinguished through the expressions mentioned before, are entitled to the qualification of "being dictated", "being prohibited", and "being facultative". One may also speak of the occurrence of certain normative states of affairs which consist in the fact that certain kinds (categories) of behaviour are not, in view of a certain normative order, prescribed, prohibited or facultative, when no one has hitherto behaved in such a manner that the behaviour belonged to one of the kinds (that is, one of the categories) of behaviour distinguished by these expressions, and regardless of whether someone behaves in this manner in the future. For instance, one can speak of the occurrence of a normative state of affairs which consists of the fact that entering a specific street is prohibited when no one has entered the street yet, and regardless of whether someone enters it in the future.

Although normative expressions are not entitled to value of truth or falsehood, one can still speak of certain states of affairs fulfilling such expressions. What is usually understood as fulfilling a norm is the relationship between the norm and such a state of affairs in which what the norm obliges to, or what the norm allows, is fulfilled. However, let us use a different notion of fulfilment in reference to normative expressions, one that refers to the notion of fulfilment used in logical semantics. In particular, fulfilment will be understood here as the relationship between a language expression fit for acceptance or rejection and such a state of affairs where the expression should be accepted according to the rules of the language.

Language expressions which are fit for acceptance or rejection are, among others, normative sentences and expressions. A specific example of the relationship of fulfilment is the relationship between a sentence and such a state of affairs described by it that this sentence is true. Such a relationship is described as a relationship of truthfulness. In order to emphasize the fact that the relationship of truthfulness is a special case of the relationship of fulfilment we shall call it the relationship of P-fulfilment, or in short: P-fulfilment. Another special case of the relationship of fulfilment is the relationship between a normative expression and such a state of affairs where the expression should be accepted. Such a relationship shall be called the relationship of N-fulfilment, or in short: N-fulfilment.

The state of affairs which fulfils a language expression fit for acceptance or rejection can only be the state of affairs which the expression describes. Let us for instance consider the expression (normative phrase) in the form: "Pedestrians walking in a column are obliged to walk on the right side of the road...". The state of affairs which fulfils (N-fulfils) this expression can only be the state of affairs described by the expression, that is, the state of affairs which consists in the fact that pedestrians walking in a column are obliged to walk on the right side of the road. However, this does not include the state of affairs which consists in the fact that pedestrians walking in a column walk on the right side of the road, since the expression in question does not state that pedestrians walking in a column walk on the right side of the road.

Clearly, only normative states of affairs can be the states of affairs which fulfil (N-fulfil) normative expressions.

Zdzisław Ziemba. Paradoxes of deontic logic
[1968: 49, 55 – 56]

The meaning of primary terms, for instance: "It is obligatory that", is settled arbitrarily in deontic logic, that is, by assuming a proper decision as to terminology. However, this does not mean it is unlike the meaning of this expression in the colloquial language. The question arises of what one is supposed to go by when selecting the axioms of deontic logic, and in consequence, in assuming various relationships between deontic sentences. One may reason thusly: deontic sentences are an important instrument of regulating people's behaviour. Since the manner in which it is stated that such sentences are true is not clearly defined, therefore it is important to impose certain limitations concerning the manner in which such sentences are used which would, for instance, make it impossible to accept simultaneously two sentences: 'Op' and '$O\sim p$' as true. It would be disadvantageous for a citizen if the manner of understanding the expression "It is obligatory that" made true both sentences "It is obligatory that p" and "It is obligatory that not-p", since that would put one in a situation where, whatever he does, he cannot fulfil the obligation.

Still, it may also turn out that the language of deontic logic is constructed in such a way that specific colloquial sentences are impossible to translate into the language of deontic logic, that is, it proves impossible to express in the other language what we can express in colloquial language. Outwardly, it may seem that specific formulas of deontic logic are such a translation; but the statements obtained in deontic logic prove this wrong. There occur "paradoxical" statements, which are clearly false if certain deontic formulas are treated as a translation of certain utterances from the colloquial language, that is, as a different way to record what is stated in one's utterances. Then the language of given deontic logic proves insufficient and it becomes necessary to seek a more perfect language through which one would be able to express what we utter on everyday basis, except in different words. This is where various systems of deontic logic come from, systems which are increasingly richer in vocabulary, systems which aim at taking into account the richness of the language which is used every day. [...]

In conclusion, we should consider the benefits coming from practising deontic logic. It may be used as a tool of critical analysis of the encountered reasoning conducted with the use of deontic sentences. Moreover, research in the field of deontic logic concerns the mutual definability of deontic terms. This research also reveals various incompatibilities in the intuitive application of certain manners of reasoning. It seems that from perfectly «obvious» assumptions there result entirely obscure consequences which force us to revise the starting point. Therefore, building deontic logic is, among other things, specifying legal language,[134] whose accuracy leaves much to be desired, contrary to popular belief. In this situation, the results of research in the scope of deontic logic cannot pass unnoticed by a theorist of law, but probably also by a practitioner of law.

Zdzisław Ziemba. Interpretation of deontic logic
[1969: 5, 48, 53 –55, 57– 60, 65 – 66, 77–78, 81– 82, 87, 112]

We call deontic logic the kind of logical calculus where the language contains deontic constants: "obligatory", "prohibited", "allowed", *etc.* Dynamic development of this logic dates back to 1951, that is, from the time of the publication of the article "Deontic Logic" by G.H. v. Wright. After that time, there occurred many other papers which presented various kinds of deontic calculus.

The weak side of deontic logic is its interpretation. One of such issues which still pose various difficulties is the formalization of deontic sentences, that is, sentences which state the possession of an obligation, issuing a prohibition or permission. There may be doubt as to whether deontic sentences are supposed to state that ACTS are obligatory (allowed, prohibited), or to state that STATES OF AFFAIRS are obligatory (allowed, prohibited). Accordingly, it is also discussed whether deontic constants are functors of a nominal or sentential argument. The issues are resolved in various ways. When presenting various deontic calculi, the authors never, or hardly ever, explain the meaning of deontic constants. In consequence, it is not entirely clear why they choose this axiom system of deontic calculus and no other. Finally, one ought to mention the difficulties facing deontic logic which result from the occurrence in calculi «paradoxical» statements, when the former shows that deontic constants (contrary to their authors' intentions) have different meanings than equivalent expressions in colloquial language. [...]

[J. Kalinowski's K_1 and K_2 system] is actually one of the first deontic calculi; it was proclaimed in 1953, that is, shortly after the OS system was

---

[134] This view was formulated by Ziembiński in [1966a].

proclaimed by v. Wright.[135] However, the author does not quote v. Wright and, as one might expect, v. Wright's system was neither a model nor the object of comparison for Kalinowski. [...]

In his book entitled *Norm and Action*, G.H. v. Wright, an exceptionally ingenious author as it comes to constructing ever new deontic calculi, presented a deontic logic which is specifically «conjugated» to the logic of norms.[136]

According to v. Wright, utterances of duty can be understood in two ways: either as norms-directives (prescriptions) which are not logical sentences, or as statements of duty (normative statements), with the aid of which the existence of a given norm is ascertained. Accordingly, one may distinguish between the logic of norms, whose statements concern specific relationships between the set of norms X and norm N, which is called the entailment of a norm from a set of norms, from deontic logic, whose statements concern sentences of duty. Deontic logic «reproduces» the logic of norms in the sense that, if norm N entails from the set of norms X, then the implication in the form:

$$z(N_1) \wedge ... \wedge z(N_k) \to z(N).$$

is a statement of deontic logic, where '$z(N_i)$' is a sentence of duty which states the existence of the norm N_i, whereas the set of norms X contains all, and only, norms $N_1, ..., N_k$. [...]

The author does not go into details concerning what exactly is a norm. G.H. v. Wright belongs to the Anglo-Saxon school of thought which differentiates between a "proposition" and a "sentence". The same proposition can be expressed through various, and diversiform, sentences. The same proposition corresponds to two synonymous sentences.

Similarly, the author distinguishes between a norm and its formulation, that is, a specific utterance [1963a: 93–94]. He does not necessarily discuss the relationship between a norm and its verbal formulation. However, he does state that if a norm is a commission (and it is one of the kinds of norms he distinguishes), then its promulgation, that is verbalization, which con-

---

[135] Kalinowski [1953].
[136] Wright [1963a].

tains given data (what is demanded, from whom and in what circumstances, or respectively, allowed) is necessary for a norm to exist. The advantage of such terminology is that it allows for stating that whether a given utterance is or is not a formulation of a norm does not depend on its construction, but rather on whether it expresses a norm. Moreover, sentences of duty interpreted as sentences which state the existence of a norm, are not metalinguistic sentences.

The presented logic of norms concerns such utterances which perform the function of dictates, prohibitions and permissions, utterances which are still called commissions. They are proclaimed by a given norm-giving authority and directed at given subjects. The norm-giving authority proclaims them because he wants their addressees to perform a given action. These utterances may take the form of an order, but it is not necessary. In any case, they are neither true nor false. As it was mentioned before, diversiform utterances fulfil these conditions. However, the logic of norms has to use a specific formal structure in order to describe the relationships of entailment between norms precisely. Formalization of commissions must differentiate between dictates, prohibitions and permissions, and must take into account that they are commissions to perform specific acts. Relationships between norms assume the occurrence of specific relationships between acts. Some of the acts are ones which cause certain changes in the outside world. Again, some relationships between acts occur because certain relationships between the changes occur. Such an approach requires developing a language fit for describing changes, and only then a language which describes the acts which cause the changes, and finally, the language of commissions to perform the actions which cause changes in the outside world. Therefore, the settlement of the logic of norms is preceded by building the logic of changes and the logic of acts. Sentential calculus is used in this process. [...]

Roughly speaking, the considered changes are events which consist in the disappearance of an existing state of affairs at some point and the appearance of another. For the sake of convenience, change is a name given to events which consist in a given state of affairs existing until a given moment and continuing to exist, as well as events which consist in a given state of affairs not existing until a given moment and continuing not to exist. The author introduces certain symbols which represent the utterances on changes. In particular, he introduces the letter 'T' and places variables 'p' and 'q' on its right and left side, or combinations of such variables connected by conjunctions written analogously, like conjunctions of negation, logical conjunction and alternative from the sentential calculus, for instance:

pTq.

$\sim pTp$.

$(p \lor q)T(r \lor \sim s)$.

Variables 'p', 'q' ... shall be called variables of calculus of changes.

The interpretation of the expression 'pTq' poses certain difficulties. On the one hand, it is said of it that it represents an utterance which describes an abstract event. The event consists in a transformation of the state of affairs described with the expression 'p' into a state of affairs described with the expression 'q', where these states of affairs are successive, that is, the state of affairs q occurs at the moment the state of affairs p ends. However, both of these states of affairs are abstract rather than concrete, and therefore reproducible. Thus, letters 'p', 'q', ... are not propositional variables. They are variables which replace utterances which are described by the author as expressing general, true or false propositions IN CERTAIN CASES. The sentence "It is raining" is quoted as an example here. It is meant to be true in one case and false in another. However, we learn little in such cases. V. Wright refrains from specifying the concept and only states that they cannot be identified with "points" in time and space. These cases are more of "temporal-spatial locations" [1963a: 23]. Respectively, when 'p' is the expression "This window is closed", 'q' is the expression "This window is open", then the expression 'pTq' can be read as "The world in which this window is closed changes into the world in which this window is open" [1963a: 28–29]. This utterance is not a logical sentence which describes only one unique change, but rather, it is an utterance similar to the utterance "It is raining", except the latter is true in some cases, and the utterance in the form of 'pTq' is true in two successive cases.

Such a presentation of the problem is highly unsatisfactory. Speaking of true utterances in a specific case is unclear when one knows next to nothing about these cases. However, there seems to exist such an interpretation of the expression 'pTq' where speaking of occasions becomes redundant, and v. Wright's calculus of change does not require any modifications.

Let us return to the utterance "It is raining". Instead of saying that it is true in a specific case and false in another, one would rather say that it is considered to be an abbreviation of the propositional function "In the place x and in the moment t it is raining", where this propositional function takes on the value of truth, or the value of falsehood, with various values for the variables x, t. Respectively, the expression in the form of 'pTq' can be interpreted in such a way that it becomes a propositional function. For instance, an utterance quoted by the author as an example can be understood as an abbreviation of a propositional function "This window is closed up until the moment t, and from the moment t the window is open". Such an utterance is true if the first of the described states of affairs existed for some period of time which preceded the moment t and the other state of affairs existed for any period of time beginning from the moment t. The symbol 'T' is then read as "...from the moment t and from the moment t ...". The expression 'pTq' is then a conjunction of sentences but the expressions appearing in place of the variables p, q are not sentences, but rather expressions which, together with the phrase "until the moment t", or respectively, with the phrase "from the moment t" create a sentence. Admittedly, they can contain variables, but they are never propositional functions, for instance: "The window in the place x is closed". [...]

The logic of acts formulates statements which concern activities which cause changes in the world as well as neglecting to cause such changes. In order to describe these two kinds of acts two functors are introduced: d, f, which denote, respectively: activity and negligence. The expression: 'd', *resp.* 'f', can be placed in front of any T-expression. One can distinguish ATOMIC d-f-expressions, that is, expressions created by adding one of the two functors d, f in front of the (atomic or molecular) T-expression, for instance: $d[(p \lor q)T(r \lor s)]$. Among atomic T-expressions one may distinguish ELEMENTARY d-f-expressions, created by adding one of the d-f-functors in front of the elementary T-expression, for instance: $f(\sim pTp)$. Atomic d-f-expressions may be connected with conjunctions of sentential calculus into complex (molecular) d-f-expressions. All the mentioned types of expressions are called in short "d-f-expressions" [1963a: 56 *et seq.*].

Here arises another issue connected with their understanding. Let us consider an elementary d-f-expression:

$d(\sim pTp)$.

The author claims that the expression is a schematization of an utterance which describes action [1963a: 42]. He proposes an example: if p is the utterance "This door is open", then the expression '$d(\sim pTp)$' also represents the utterance "This door is being opened" [1963a: 43]. The author's intention is that the formulation '$d(\sim pTp)$' is obviously a schematization of true or false utterances IN SOME CASES. Also, the author uses the phrase "act $d(\sim pTp)$" as if the symbol '$d(\sim pTp)$' represented the NAME of an abstract act. Then attributing logical values to d-f-expressions, as the author does, is incoherent. Such formalization is unclear. As a matter of fact, the content of the statements on calculus of acts is unknown. The issue is worth organizing all the more that d-f-expressions appear as parts of expressions of the logic of norms. Consequently, we propose the following organization of the symbols of action calculus. Since logical value is supposed to be ascribed to expressions represented by d-f-expressions, they must be interpreted as propositional functions. In particular, the expression '$d(\sim pTp)$' will be interpreted here as an abbreviation of the propositional function:

x makes it that $\sim p$, until the moment t, and p after the moment t.

where the variable 'x' includes the set of human individuals. This can be stressed by using the symbol 'dx' instead of the letter 'd'. However, taking into consideration the assumptions of the calculus of acts, the same variable 'x' should be added to all d-f-expressions, so in order to simplify the formulations we will avoid it.

By assuming the relevant definitions one might cause each d-f-expression, interpreted as a propositional function, to be translatable into an expression in the form of:

x in the moment t fulfils act C.

where 'C' is an atomic or complex d-f-expression, understood as one that represents the name of an abstract act. Such translation would justify speaking of tautological and equivalent acts, of negation, alternative and conjunction of acts. Therefore, in order to shorten the argument, sometimes the act $d(\sim pTp)$ will be mentioned in the meaning of person x's act which consists in causing the change $\sim pTp$. Strictly speaking, the expression '$d(\sim pTp)$' is not the name of an abstract act, but rather a propositional function which takes on the value of truth or falsehood for specific values of variables 'p', 't,' x'.

Let us now explain the sense of elementary d-f-expressions.

The expression '$d(\sim pTp)$' should be read as "x causes it that $\sim p$ until the moment t, and p after the moment t". The author stipulates that such an act is realized only when the change $\sim pTp$ does not occur "spontaneously" [1963a: 43]. The condition for the realization of such an act is that p, until the moment t, and WOULD BE p until the moment t if not for a relevant activity. This meagre explanation requires some elaboration. The issue is clearly that person x does not cause the change $\sim pTp$ when it occurs without this person's suitable participation. However, saying that the conceivable happening of the change $\sim pT\sim p$ is the condition for the realization of the act which consists in causing the change $\sim pTp$ presents some trouble. If two persons x, y are prepared to make the same change $\sim pTp$ and one of them, for instance, person x, causes this change, then it is hard to say whether the change $\sim pT\sim p$ would take place if not for the activity on the part of person x, since person y was prepared to cause the change $\sim pTp$. In this situation one must say that the person x did not make the change $\sim pTp$, as the condition for the action's realization was not fulfilled. Moreover, if person x did not make the change $\sim pTp$, and instead, person y does it, then it can be stated that person x neglected making the change as well as neglected to prevent the change from occurring; therefore, it is true that:

$f(\sim pTp) \vee f(\sim pT\sim p)$.

which, again, is contradictory to the assumptions of the calculus of acts [...].

The easiest way out of the situation consists in assuming that person x is the only one who is prepared to, or is able to, cause a given change. This assumption can be justified by the fact that two people can never cause a given change in the same moment. Therefore, one can say that the condition under which the expression: '$d(\sim pTp)$' is true is that the change $\sim pT\sim p$ would occur if person x was passive. The possible change $\sim pT\sim p$ shall be called THE CONDITION OF REALIZATION of an act which consists in it that $d(\sim pTp)$.

The expression '$d(pTp)$' can be read as "x causes it that p until the moment t and p from the moment t". It is a description of an activity which consists in sustaining the existence of a given state of affairs which would vanish without the activity. The possible change $\sim pT\sim p$ which would occur in the case of person x's passivity is called THE CONDITION OF REALIZATION of an activity which consists in it that $d(pTp)$.

The expressions '$d(pT\sim p)$' and '$d(\sim pT\sim p)$' are interpreted analogously. The changes pTp and $\sim pTp$ are respectively THE CONDITIONS OF REALIZATION of these activities.

V. Wright understands negligence in a specific manner [1963a: 43 *et seq.*]. Neglecting to cause a specific change by person x is not merely not causing the change by person x. Relying on colloquial speech, the author assumes that neglecting to do something occurs only when there is a possibility of doing the thing. The expression: '$f(\sim pTp)$', which shall be read as "x neglected to cause it that $\sim p$ until the moment t, and p after the moment t", is therefore true only when the conditions to cause the change $\sim pTp$ are fulfilled, but person x is not causing the change to occur. Still, the condition to cause the change $\sim pTp$ is that it be p until the moment t, and moreover, in the case of person x's negligence, also $\sim p$ from the moment t. In consequence, THE NECESSARY CONDITION TO PERFORM the act $f(\sim pTp)$ is that the change $\sim pT\sim p$ occurs.

Respectively, '$f(pTp)$' is read as "x neglected to cause p until the moment t and from the moment t". THE CONDITION OF REALIZATION of such an act is the occurrence of the change $pT\sim p$. In other words, neglecting to cause the change pTp occurs only when there is p until the moment t and $\sim p$ from the moment t. Thus, it is negligence to sustain the existence of a given state of affairs.

Respectively, THE CONDITION OF REALIZATION of the act $f(\sim pT\sim p)$ is the change $\sim pTp$.

There is a certain difference between the conditions of the realization of an activity described with an expression of the type 'd' and an expression of the type 'f'. In the first case, the changes called the conditions of realization are POSSIBLE changes, that is, they would occur if not for person x's activity.

In the case of negligence to cause a change to occur, the changes called conditions of realization do in fact take place, but with the reservation that nobody except person x has the ability, or intends to, cause such a change. [...]

In the language of the logic of norms there occur O-P-expressions, that is, ones which are formed by adding one of the functors O, P in front of a d-f-expression. Thus, the following are O-P-expressions:

$Od(pT\sim p)$.

$P[d(pTp) \wedge f(\sim qTq)]$.

An O-P-expression constructed from an elementary d-f-expression is called an ELEMENTARY O-P-EXPRESSION. Since O-P-expressions do not represent logical sentences, they are not meant to be joined with conjunctions. O-P-formulas express norms which are commissions. The interpretation of O-P-expressions requires a few words of commentary.

We learn from the author that O-expressions represent expressions of duty, that is, ones which claim that a certain activity should be undertaken. P-expressions represent expressions which state that certain activity is allowed. The former are called dictates, the latter: permissions. The author does not prejudge the matter of whether P-expressions can be defined with O-expressions [1963a: 92]. Although he enumerates various meanings of the expression "be allowed", in the end he does not take any stand on the question of meaning of P-expressions, except that in his logic of norms he accepts certain relationships between O-expressions and P-expressions.

V. Wright supports his explanation of the meaning of O-expressions with an example [1963a: 74]: when 'p' means that the door is closed, and 'q' means that the window is open, then the expression:

$O[d(\sim pTp) \wedge f(qT\sim q)]$.

is a schematization of the dictate to close the door and leave the window open.

However, the assumptions of logic of changes and the logic of acts used in the logic of norms cause it that a d-f-expression has to be interpreted accordingly. In particular, as was mentioned above, the expression '$d(\sim pTp)$' is read as: "Person x causes it that $\sim p$ until the moment t and p from the moment t". In consequence, '$Od(\sim pTp)$' must be treated as a symbol which represents a dictate of performing a given change in a given moment t issued towards person x. Respectively, Pd($\sim p$Tp) is treated as a symbol which represents a norm which allows a given person x to perform a given change in a given moment t. Naturally, person x is able to cause the change $\sim p$Tp to occur when the conditions for the realization of the act d($\sim p$Tp) occur, and especially if there is $\sim p$ until the moment t and it would be p from the moment t if not for person x's activity. The change $\sim p$T$\sim p$, which is the condition for the realization of the act d($\sim p$Tp), is called the CONDITION OF APPLICATION of the norm Od($\sim p$Tp). Generally speaking: if a d-f-expression, which is the content of a given O-P-expression, is in the regular positive form, then the conditions for the realization of the act described with this d-f-expression are simultaneously THE CONDITIONS OF APPLICATION of the norm represented by a given O-P-expression.

A central concept in v. Wright's logic of norms is the notion of the entailment of a norm from a set of norms. (For the sake of simplicity, if a set of norms is a one-piece set, we will speak of the entailment of a norm from a norm.) The notion of entailment is particularly interesting since norms, or more precisely: verbal formulations of norms, are not understood here as sentences in the logical sense. The logic of norms formulates this notion for O-P-expressions; however, it can also be used with norms represented by these expressions. Therefore we will still speak of norms at times, rather than O-P-expressions which represent these norms.

The respective steps leading to specifying the notion of the entailment of a norm from a set of norms are sequentially built definitions of:

(1) a contradictory norm;

(2) a contradictory set of norms;

(3) a negation of a norm;

(4) a norm which is absolutely incompatible with a given set of norms. [...]

There arises the question of what should be the consequences of the fact that a norm N entails from set of norms X.

The author [v. Wright] argues [1963a: 156–158] that if a creator of norms cannot dictate a given action without causing a contradiction to previously settled norms, then in fact he allows for the norm's negligence. If he cannot prohibit a given action without causing a contradiction to previously settled norms, then in fact he allows for it. If he cannot allow, then in fact he prohibited it. If he cannot allow for its negligence without causing a contradiction to previously settled norms, then in fact he dictated performing the action. The author stresses further on that a codifier who decides to punish those who do not comply with the norms issued by him cannot remain indifferent towards disobedience of norms which clearly entail from the settled norms. The author reminds that in light of his definition of the entailment of a norm from a set of norms the statement that a given dictate entails from a set of norms means that it is not logically possible to execute a prohibited action without disobeying some dictate or breaking a previously settled prohibition. Therefore, if a codifier reveals his interest in whether his addressees obeyed the dictates and prohibitions settled by him by punishing the disobedient, therefore he manifests his concern that the addressees obey the norms which entail from explicitly settled norms. Prescriptions, prohibitions and permissions which entail from an explicitly established set of norms are as «wanted» by the codifier as those which belong to the set of explicitly settled norms. According to v. Wright, norms which entail from a set of explicitly settled norms also necessarily belong to this set even if they are not promulgated; their promulgation is implied in the promulgation of the explicitly settled norms.

This much we learn from the author. These theses are undoubtedly right, but they require further explanation. The author is right that behaviour which is incompatible with an O-norm which entails from a specific set of norms X is a violation of some O-norm from this set. However, we need to settle precisely what the violation (failure to fulfil) a given norm consists in. The issue is all the more worth an explanation as it seems that the author never clarifies the notion of violating a norm. Another issue is the notion of the schemes of norms which do not contain the symbol which represents the norm's addressee. […]

These remarks entitle us to draw the conclusion that the statement that a given norm entails, in v. Wright's sense, from the set of explicitly settled norms, is not very significant from the point of view of the choice of the way of behaviour. If someone wants to act so that he does not violate any explicitly settled norm, he still has to make himself acquainted with the content of all of these norms. From the point of view of using information, it seems that if a given norm entails from a set of explicitly settled norms, then the relationship of entailment of a norm from a set of norms ought to fulfil the following conditions:

(1) No behaviour which realizes an act dictated by an O-norm, which entails from a set of norms X, violates any O-norm which belongs to this set.

(2) All behaviour which is a realization of an act dictated by an O-norm, which entails from the set of norms X, is behaviour which realizes an act dictated by an O-norm which belongs to X.

(3) Each violation of an O-norm which entails from a set of norms X is a violation of an O-norm belonging to X.

(4) Neither the finalization of the act described in the content of a P-norm which entails from the set X, nor the realization of the act described by an internal negation of the content of the P-norm, violate any O- norm which belongs to the set X.

V. Wright's relationship of entailment only fulfils the third condition.

It is worth noting that the content of the norm N_2, which entails, in v. Wright's sense, from the norm N_1, originates in the following way: either through writing content identical to the content of the norm N_1, or through adding a specific conjunction of elementary d-f-expressions which possess the same condition for realization as any conjunction of elementary d-f-expression in the norm N_2, or through adding more than one such conjunction. There is a limit to the use of the relationships of entailment to norms whose content is expressed through T-expressions, and in consequence the considered notion only concerns commissions of performing a relevant change in a given moment. Such commissions are orders to perform a single action in a precisely defined moment. It seems that orders to perform a specific action in a given time interval are more common.

There is one weak link in the construct of the notion of entailment of a norm from a set of norms X. The notion of entailment can only be applied to a set of norms such that their content is in a regular perfect form and is uniform. Therefore, either the notion of entailment is not applicable to other sets of norms, or one has to assume that a particular norm, which belongs to any set of norms, can be replaced by one whose content is a perfect, positive form of the content of the replaced norm, and moreover, all d-f-expressions which occur as the content of the norms in the set can be standardized, again, by replacing certain norms with others. Then one can expand the notion of entailment to include any set of norms, assuming that norm N entails from a set of norms if and only if, after having replaced the norms from the set X and thus creating a set of norms X', norm N entails, in the sense presented by v. Wright, from the set X'. However, then it is necessary to prove that also in this case, a violation of a norm N which entails from the set of norms X is a violation of a norm from the set X, which the author does not do. [...]

The construction of the logic of deontic sentences is based on the assumption that O-P-expressions can be interpreted twofold: as commissions which are neither true nor false and as deontic sentences whose truthfulness depends on the existence of a relevant norm [1963a: 105–106]. The existence of a norm depends on performing the act of promulgation of a norm and on the occurrence of a specific relationship between the codifier and the subject who the commission is directed at [1963a: 116–118]. The existence of a norm is an existence in time, that is, a norm may cease to exist when the mentioned relationship between the codifier and a given subject ceases to occur. During its period of existence the norm is valid (is in force).

Therefore it seems one can say in short that O-P-sentences are true if a given norm is valid. The trouble is that since a given norm is valid in time, then the truthfulness of O-P-sentences is also truthfulness in time (probably, as v. Wright would say, it is the truthfulness of a sentence in SOME CASE, a case which lasts in a given period of time). If O-P-sentences were utterances which state PRESENT validity of norms, there would be no doubt as to their truthfulness. Without having decided on the matter, v. Wright builds deontic logic which concerns O-P-sentences. The general assumption of this logic is that the claims of the logic "map" logical properties of norms [1963a: 143]. It seems like the issue is that from O-P$_1$-sentences there entails, according to the statements of deontic logic, an O-P$_2$-sentence, if the norm O-P$_2$ entails from the norm O-P$_1$. Thus, the silent assumption behind the implied tautology of deontic logic is that when a given norm N_1 is valid and the norm N_2 entails from it, then also the norm N_2 is valid. [...]

Our deontic calculus [...] is called deontic syllogistics. [...] Deontic syllogistics is a calculus superstructured over the calculus of predicates with quantifiers. [...]

Let us note that deontic syllogistics, despite the great simplicity of its language, is a better tool to formalize normative reasoning than other deontic calculi, as one can formulate general utterances in its language, such as "Every X is obliged to be Y", "No X is obliged to be Y", *etc.* Quantifiers bind variables which include the set of human individuals rather than variables which include the set of individual actions, as in Hintikka's or Kalinowski's systems. Therefore this solution seems better.

Deontic syllogistics can be interpreted in a manner which reveals the relationship between the truthfulness of a sentence on obligation and the existence of a given dictate in a set of dictates, to which deontic sentences are relativised; additionally, this interpretation does not require the set of dictates to be closed in any specific manner. Thus, it is not necessary to settle the relationship of "entailment" for dictates, as v. Wright did in the system presented in *Norm and Action*. This solution seems to be closer to natural language.

Zdzisław Najder. Imperativism
[1971: 100–117]

[1.] Imperativism (also called "prescriptivism") can be considered as a kind of emotivism. [...] Stevenson sometimes interprets the emotional influence of an evaluating judgement with the possible influence of an order or instigation.[137] However, since the present work is not of historical character, but rather systematic, and because the methodological and logical issues of imperativism differ greatly from the issues of emotivism in the narrower sense, we will discuss separately the arguments of those who identify evaluating judgements with imperative sentences (radical imperativists), from those who claim that evaluating judgements are a kind of dictating sentences or imply imperative or normative sentences (moderate imperativists).

---

[137] Stevenson [1944: 21] [...]. *"This is good* means I approve of this: do so as well."

The radical standpoint tends to be supported solely in the heat of discussion. Carnap's formulation is the most concise: "In fact, an evaluating utterance is only a command [*scil.* order] presented in a misleading visual form".[138] It seems obvious that such a statement is not defensible. More contemporary imperativists, the most renowned and influential of whom is Richard M. Hare, proclaim a more moderate thesis: logical analysis of an evaluating judgement reveals the existence of an order or a norm as its basic and characteristic ingredient. "We are therefore clearly entitled to say that the moral judgement entails the imperative"[139].

The views of moderate imperativists can be interpreted twofold: (1) The essence of evaluation is dictating; evaluating judgements are a kind of normative-imperative sentences. (2) Evaluating judgements imply normative-imperative sentences. Let us in turn consider the two possible interpretations.

[2.] "The language of the moral is one sort of prescriptive language [*scil.* language of dictates]",[140] writes Hare in the first paragraph of his book. Later on he explains that interpreting any evaluation as other than dictating is a misunderstanding.[141] Hare considers his theory to be true on the principle of definition;[142] however, it is our right to inquire whether the decision to assume such a definition is methodologically justified.

It raises various reservations. Let us start with reservations of a logical nature. Evaluating judgements are, at least in their grammatical form, declarative sentences. Dictates, norms and recommendations do not belong to this category. W. Dubislav has proven that there is a sharp logical divide between declarative and imperative sentences.[143] The theory claiming that they belong to the same logical or semantic category (since Hare uses the notion of prescriptive or commendatory [*scil.* imperative] meaning) is defendable only on the basis of the claim that they perform the same functions. Such a functional identity could prevail over structural differences.

---

[138] Carnap [1935: 16].
[139] Hare [1952: 172].
[140] Hare [1952: 11].
[141] Hare [1952: 171–172].
[142] Hare [1952: 164].
[143] Dubislav [1937].

Do evaluating judgements perform the same functions as dictates and norms? Indeed, the principles of value seem to perform the function of general norms of behaviour at times. "Killing a person is an evil act" can perform the function of a dictate "Do not kill!" or a norm "You should not kill". (We shall discuss the reasons for the exchangeability of function further, par. 4.) However, people usually react differently to utterances of the kind "John is a good person" and to utterances like "Do as John does!". The reaction to "It is bad to do *A*" is different from the reaction to "Do not do *A*!". One may accept the principle of value or an evaluating judgement and still have doubts as to a recommendation which is apparently analogous to it. One may also accept as right a statement which is a part of a theoretical system of evaluation, and simultaneously reject as unjustified the dictate or recommendation of a person whose authority one does not accept. (However, if one resolves to obey the dictate because one trusts the person who issues it, it does not necessarily have to be connected to the theoretical settlement of this dictate.) Finally, let us note that the content of the dictate, as one which is usually more practical, is at the same time more concrete than the content of an "analogous" evaluating judgement. Let us compare, for instance, "It is good to get up early" and "Get up early!" or *"Dulce et decorum est pro patria mori"* and "It is sweet and fitting to die for your country!".

Considering evaluating judgements as a kind of imperative or normative sentences results in a rather unsettling and unpleasant image of human relationships. It is a world filled with the bustle of a crowd of obtrusive despots and barkers, peopled solely with individuals who actively strive to influence the behaviour of their neighbour, a world of dictates, objections and obedience. This image does not seem realistic, since most people intuitively feel the difference between answers to the question: "How do I evaluate act *B*?" and the question: "What shall I do in the situation when act *B* is possible?". Moreover, as Kurt Baier rightly remarks, even the question: "How should I act?" is often asked "not in order to receive an order, but rather to obtain advice. We ask for knowledge, judgement or experience rather than authority."[144]

---

[144] Baier [1958: 56].

Two kinds of evaluating judgements pose a particularly difficult problem for the followers of imperativism: evaluations which concern the past and aesthetic evaluations.

When one evaluates the behaviour of Cyrus and Cambyses on the basis of information presented by Herodotus, do the issued evaluating judgements in fact contain any dictates or recommendations? One regards Cyrus as a good ruler although one would certainly not want people who rule to act as he does. However, one's supposition is not simply «quoting» a supposition of Cyrus's contemporaries; specific criteria based on a historical perspective are used when evaluating the Persian king; different from ones used to evaluate 18th- or 19th-century monarchs.

However, let us assume for a moment that we accept Hare's theory and understand the judgement: "Cyrus was a good monarch" as one containing a moral dictate. (According to Hare, if a judgement does not contain a dictate, it is not evaluating.)

The said dictate, probably directed at present and future rulers, would recommend to them behaviour similar to Cyrus's behaviour. Yet, such a dictate would only make sense if, when issuing it, we would be able to imagine a present or future situation in which someone could act exactly as Cyrus. Such an interpretation of a judgement seems precarious at best, as it is perfectly possible to discuss Cyrus's and Cambyses's behaviour in moral categories, using the criteria of honesty and benevolence which correspond to their historical times and situation. Evaluating judgements which result from such a discussion will not "in any way correspond to anyone's manner of behaviour", although according to Hare, such a practical correspondence is a necessary condition for moral considerations.[145]

If one wishes to apply the imperativistic set of notions to the analysis of aesthetic evaluating judgements, there immediately arises a tough problem: what is actually dictated and to whom? When we read that "Mozart was an excellent composer", or that "*Et in Arcadia ego* is a beautiful painting", is one supposed to understand these judgements as recommendations for composers and painters, or for listeners and viewers? The first option is suggested by

---

[145] Hare [1963: 90].

the analogy with ethical judgements, which are to be interpreted as dictating something to people who find themselves in situations analogous to the position of a person who is evaluated in a given judgement. However, it seems so absurd ("Compose like Mozart!" or "Paint like Poussin!") that it has to be discarded at the beginning. The other option seems no more promising, since what is in fact recommended? Is it aesthetic pleasure or perhaps something different? Who (and why this person?) is supposed to draw pleasure of some kind from listening to *Cosi fan tutte* or looking at Poussin's canvas? Should our pleasure be equal to that of their contemporaries? Imperativism does not answer these questions.

[3.] Let us now consider the second interpretation of imperativism: evaluating judgements imply normative sentences. Here we need to consider (only very superficially, taking into account the scope of this work) the issue of the logic of imperative and normative sentences, and sentences of duty.

Hare and other imperativists, as well as critics of imperativism, do not draw a definite line between imperative sentences ("Do *a*!"), normative sentences ("One should do *a*") and sentences of duty ("You should do *a*"). By assuming that dictating is an indispensable element of evaluating, they put evaluating judgements on the same level as imperative sentences and present examples accordingly. Yet, when discussing the thesis which states that evaluating judgements imply practical instructions, they tend to give examples in the form of sentences of duty. Despite the resulting lack of clarity, one may agree that such a presentation of the issues reveals their most vital aspect. Let us then discuss the possible relationship between sentences of the type: "*a* is good" and "You should do *a*".

The word "should" [Polish "powinien"] (which is characteristic; it does not have an infinitive form in Polish or English) has three meanings:

(1) It may refer to requirements we would like someone to meet: "You should come here at once";

(2) It may refer to something we expect of someone or something: "The bus should come soon";

(3) It may refer to someone's obligation or to the conditions an object must fulfil: "A shop assistant should make change"; "A tire should have a well maintained tread".

The threefold meaning is not unique to Polish, as it also exists in English (ought to, should), and German (*sollen*). Regrettably, the meanings are rarely divided, and especially meanings (1) and (3) are notoriously confused. It leads to the suggestion that the content of the meaning (3) is reduced to the content of the meaning (1): duty in the sense of obligation is based on duty in the sense of requirement, for instance: "John should (is obliged to) go to Cracow, because John should (is required to) go to Cracow".

Whatever the understanding of the word "should", the statement that an evaluating judgement implies a sentence of duty seems contradictory to Hume's famous rule which states the impossibility of deriving normative sentences from descriptive sentences. The rule is rarely questioned although some doubts do arise as to its original sense.[146] Two recent attempts to question it are worth mentioning.

M. Black presents the following instance of reasoning:

> Fisher wants to check-mate Botvinnik.
> The only way to check-mate Botvinnik is for Fischer to move the bishop.
> Therefore Fisher should move the bishop.[147]

This reasoning is an example of using the so called practical syllogism. As v. Wright claims, it is a logically correct formula which cannot be qualified within "regular" logic.[148] Cohesion of a practical syllogism seems to be based on an implied tautology, since "wants to" can be translated into: "is determined to do whatever is necessary to achieve the aim he wishes for". If Fischer did not make the move which he should make in order to check-mate Botvinnik, one would say that either he did not notice this possibility, or he did not want to check-mate his opponent. Fischer is obliged (to himself) to make the move with a bishop because, and only because,

---

146 Compare MacIntyre [1968] and Atkinson [1968].
147 Black [1964].
148 Wright [1963b: 167].

he wants to check-mate Botvinnik; it is a case of a norm imposed on one-self. This norm is already present in the word "wants", and not only in the word "should".

Yet, is its scope as wide as Kant claims, when he notes (discussing the notion of hypothetical imperative): "Whoever wills the end, so far as reason has decisive influence on his action, wills also the indispensably necessary means to it that lie in his power?".[149] Psychological observation does not support this statement, since one often wants to achieve a certain aim but does not accept the means necessary to achieve it. Therefore, although one's willingness logically imposes on one a certain obligation, one rejects it in favour of other reasons (social, moral, aesthetic, *etc.*), which may at times be a source of frustration.

Black's example does not falsify "Hume's guillotine" but it does limit the scope of its function, since it indicates that the verb "want", seemingly purely "descriptive", may include a normative element similar to the one which the words "should" and "ought to" contain. In other words, the fact of willing something may, at least in certain circumstances, oblige the willing person to obey certain rules of behaviour; it also seems to be the case with other verbs which describe intentions: "desire", "wish for something", "drive at something". Such an obligation is obviously an obligation undertaken by the subject himself and only referring to him.

John R. Searle presented another example of reasoning, based on the verb "promise".[150] Here as well we are dealing with an element of obligation encompassed in the meaning of a word other than "should". Yet, while Black's example includes "should" in the sense of obligation (towards oneself), Searle's example introduces "should" in the sense of requiring or expecting.

An essential difference between the three meanings is evident in examples:

"Fischer should (has an obligation towards his own willing) check--mate Botvinnik,

---

[149] Kant [1785: 45].
[150] Searle [1964].

but he should not (we require him not to) do it because a lost match would be the defeat of a lifetime for Botvinnik,

but he should not (we expect him not to) do it because he has a soft heart".

"John should (is obliged to) repay his debt to Stanley, but he should not (we do not require him to) do it, as Stanley is a cheat."

Jan Szewczyk, who interprets "should" as a requirement, also disagrees that norms can be derived from evaluating judgements, but he believes they can result from factual statements. As an example, he discusses the norm: "A soldier should be brave", which, as he claims, results from "the knowledge about what sort of work is generally required from a soldier" as well as "the knowledge about «necessary relationships» between the required process of activity and specific properties of its subject".[151] In this form, the quoted norm is still understood simply as a postulative definition of a soldier, analogous to "A ball should be round", "A runner should be able to run", *etc.* Such a definition may be based on factual statements; nevertheless, it does not mention any duty in the sense of obligations.

Imperativists do not reject Hume's rule; on the contrary, they always invoke it. Their statement that evaluating judgements imply sentences of duty is based on treating evaluating judgements as non-descriptive, or as utterances whose characteristic feature is the above mentioned normative implication. According to Hare, "initial principles" which guide one's evaluating reasoning have to "contain imperatives, explicitly or through implication".[152] These principles usually take on the form of evaluating judgements, whereas the imperative is implied in evaluating predicates. "Good" and similar pred-

---

[151] Szewczyk [1964: 151].
[152] Hare [1952: 39–40]. Contrary to MacIntyre's statement, who calls Hare "a pioneer of logical analysis of imperatives", [1966: 261] Hare's «logic of imperatives» is based on a principle which is an almost exact repetition of Dubislav's thesis, presented 15 years before. Dubislav [1937: 342]: "Die schliessenden Operationen lassen sich auf Forderungssätze in gewisser Weise übertragen. Dabei zeigt sich, dass man keinen vorderungssatz aus Foraussetzungen *sensu stricto* ableiten kann, die nicht selber mindestens einen Forderungssatz enthalten". [...] Hare [1966: 28]: "No imperative conclusion can be validly drawn from a set [of] premises which does not contain at least one imperative".

icates imply "should": that is the imperativists' fundamental thesis. It is supposed to apply mostly, or exclusively, to moral contexts.

Let us disregard for now the risk in separating the sphere of morality from all other spheres, which this conception leads to (compare §7 below). Do we always understand our judgement as one implying duty when we predicate on somebody or something that they are morally good? "Saint Francis was a good man"; should all or only some people (Why? Chosen on what grounds?) act as the monk from Assisi? One who devotes his life to raising orphans acts well; as well as one who does not have a family and devotes his life to creative work. There is no apparent contradiction between these evaluating judgements, although the directives of duty entailing from them would be contradictory. However, the theory of their entailment has questionable foundations and questionable usefulness, both philosophical and practical. This is even more apparent in the case of predicates whose evaluating quality is tied to particular values and ideals: heroic, steadfast, compliant, patient, gentle, *etc.* People who boast these features can be evaluated positively and even admired without simultaneously recommending an analogous method of behaviour. Imperativism seems to impose practical monism of moral ideas.

The theory of implied imperatives has yet another hidden flaw. One expects possibly concrete content of sentences of duty, since they have a direct practical function. Yet, the theory of implication partly deprives them from this concreteness of content, as it does not mention what kind of "should" is actually implied. As mentioned before, the word "should" can have three different meanings; moreover, within these meanings there is a lot of «clearance» which allow for the possibility of contradictory duty. What is the framework within which the duties which allegedly result from evaluating judgements fall? Is it within obligations which the descriptive part of an evaluating predicate imposes? Such a solution would be contradictory to the essence of imperativism, and moreover, it would not lead to acknowledging the implication, but rather to the investigation of cohesion of socially functioning systems of evaluation and behaviour. Or perhaps, is it within the requirements of the person uttering the judgement? This again leads to individualist-irrational understanding of axiological issues.

Evaluating judgements are utterances for which analysis poses a lot of difficulty, but the theory of the implication of imperatives, which is supposed to explain the essence of these judgements, explains *obscurum* through *obscurius*.

[4.] Just as it is characteristic to emotivism to obscure the difference between the uses of expressions and their meanings, it is symptomatic to imperativism to identify evaluating with uttering norms, dictates and recommendations. It is also typical for both not to differentiate between the motivational and theoretical systems of evaluation.

What is the nature of the relation of evaluating judgements, considered on the level of the theoretical system of evaluation, to sentences of duty, normative and imperative sentences?

Deducing a normative sentence from an evaluating judgement is practically impossible. Although the utterance: "*a* is good, so you should (or: one should) do *a*" sounds sensible, it is not the sensibility of inference, but rather sensibility of support by an argument whose acceptance or contestation depend on the decision of the person acting. Accepting or rejecting argumentation of the type: "You should, so do!" depends on a similar decision.

We are unable to discuss the immensely complex issue of reasoning which may bind evaluating judgements, normative sentences and imperatives. Let us only note that the manner of binding declarative sentences with normative ones with a practical syllogism, as mentioned above (§3), if used to bind evaluating judgements with sentences of duty, will also be based on the content of the verb "want" (or similar) rather than the content of evaluating predicates. For instance, the principle of value: "Honesty is good" can be bound with the norm: "One should be honest" with the aid of the condition: "if one wants": "If one wants to be good, one should be honest". The evaluating judgement: "John is truthful" can be bound with the sentence of duty: "You should act as John does" with the aid of "if you want to be truthful", or with the sentence: "You should be truthful" with the aid of: "if you want to be like John". *Mutatis mutandis*, the same applies to Kant's so called hypothetical imperative: "Killing is evil"; "If you do not want to be evil, do not kill!".

Without delving deeper into the issues of possible interconnections, let us point out the generally accepted DIRECTION of argumentation. It ascends from imperatives, through sentences of duty and normative sentences, to evaluating judgements and principles of value. The imperative: "Do not steal!" is supported by the norm: "One should not steal". In turn, this norm is supported by the principle: "Stealing is evil", or: "It is good to respect other people's property". However, the opposite direction of argumentation will not be regarded as sensible: "Lying is evil because one should not lie", or: "You are acting wrongly by not telling the truth because you should not lie". The only deviation from this "directional" rule will be reasoning such as: "Adam acted wrongly by acting cowardly because one should not be a coward". This deviation can be explained by the fact that general norms function as a replacement for principles of value. However, we would not say "Cowardice is bad because one should not act cowardly", but the other way around: "One should not act cowardly, because cowardice is bad".

Whatever the value is of the presented lines of argumentation, there seems to be no doubt as to its natural direction. This observation is contradictory to Hare's theory of imperatives, already included in «the initial principles» of our evaluating reasoning. Apparently, Hare was influenced by the motivational load of these initial principles. Besides, his theory, rather than reverse the natural direction of argumentation, blurs the differences between its elements, merging imperatives with principles of value, norms, sentences of duty and evaluating judgements, creating an almost homogenous whole. If we accepted Hare's theory, we would be forced to regard this variety of forms as redundant and apply Ockham's razor to it. However, the arguments accumulated above (let us also remember the issue of historical judgements) speak for such homogenization. Both the meaning and the function of evaluating judgements, normative sentences of duty and imperatives are different and at least partly separate.

[5.] Hare emphasizes the imperative «essence» of all evaluating and normative utterances, which is explained by the fact that he wishes to demonstrate the validity of certain common moral norms. In order to achieve it, he formulates "the universalizability principle", which states that "the meaning of the word "should" and other moral words is that the person who uses them is thus subordinated to a common rule".[153] In other words, if someone issues an ethical evaluating judgement or a normative sentence about an act, he *ipso facto* is obliged to issue the same judgement on all acts similar "in essential respects".[154]

The universalizability principle raises three reservations. Firstly, the decision as to which respects are in fact «essential» is in many cases a decision based on evaluation. The universalizability principle is based on a silent assumption that the situation and the objects undergoing evaluation are proportionally repetitive. Indeed, Hare proposes to assume as the criterion of significance the fact that we accept the feature as essential regardless of whether it is us or others who possess it.[155] Yet, this proposal does not have much in common with rules of proper reasoning, although it is an example of cunning persuasion.

Secondly, the universalizability principle silently assumes equality of men as well as convergence of their interests.[156] Unless we assume that people's rights, obligations and needs are equal, the attempt to apply the universalizability principle will get us entangled in a vicious circle of evaluation. Hare claims that the universalizability principle enables philosophical ethics "to play a role in moral decisions without losing neutrality".[157] Yet, this is not so. For instance, in medieval ethics a knight's duties were different from a henchman's duties, not to speak of a peasant; the differences in social position did not allow for «universalizability». The universalizability principle cannot be reconciled either with the morality of full achievement

---

[153] Hare [1966: 30].
[154] Hare [1966: 11].
[155] Hare [1966: 102–107].
[156] Comp. Hare [1966: 117]: "It is characteristic of moral thought in general to accord equal weight to the interests of all persona". The above sentence may be treated either (1) as a definition of morality, albeit very narrow and non-historical, or (2) as an empirical statement: explicitly false. It is true that more contemporary moralists usually (but not always: comp. Nietzsche) assume that people are "more or less equal" (Berlin [1955–1956: 304–305]; von Wright [1963b: 194]). Still, if the principle of equality is not considered as a tautology, then it is either a postulate or an evaluating axiomatic assumption, but certainly not a statement of empirical principle.
[157] Hare [1963: 80; comp. also 97].

of one's capabilities, characteristic to the Renaissance, or with 19th-century evolutionary morality. A hero who sacrifices himself for other people can do so under the assumption that he, braver and stronger than his companions, frees them from acting the same way. The interests of primitive and civilized people, weak and strong, healthy and ill differ and applying the universaliz-ability principle to them all would often be contradictory to prevalent moral intuitions. Revolutionary movements are examples of general rejection of the universalizability principle performed, paradoxically, in the name of the postulate of equality which is implied by this principle.

Thirdly, the universalizability principle, which is reminiscent of the «golden rule» known for centuries ("Treat others as you would like to be treated!"; "Do as you would be done by!"), as well as of Kant's categori-cal imperative, contains a flaw analogous to them both. Namely, according to this purely formal principle, one can proclaim and impose on others any principles if one agrees for them to be used in reference to himself.

More analogies to Kant's ethics are to be found in Hare's imperativism; further investigation reveals weak points of both of these theories. A silent assumption of proportional repetitiveness of moral situations corresponds to Kant's assumption that the shaping of human nature is perfectly purposeful, uniform for all and subject to general laws; one can also find in Kant's works the silent assumption of all people's convergence of interests.[158]

Thus, the universalizability principle is neither morally neutral, nor does it provide the basis to build a more solid moral program. While sneak-ing in some ethical assumptions, it leaves the rest to intuitions and individ-ual decisions; however, imperativism does not provide tools for analysis and discussion of the content of the decisions.[159]

[6.] Just as emotivists use the notion of "emotive meaning", impera-tivists use the notion of prescriptive, commendatory or imperative mean-ing. [...] Hare admits that in many cases we use evaluating predicates without imperative value.[160] His words may lead us to the conclusion that

---

[158] Kant [1785: 13, 37–38, 62–63].
[159] Comp. MacIntyre [1968: 261–262].
[160] Hare [1952: 124–125; 1963: 68, 190].

the presence of this meaning is always the question of intuition. The sup-position that this meaning is integral to evaluation cannot be upheld in the face of a simple observation that sentences which are clearly indicative--descriptive, for instance: "This snake is poisonous", "The mushrooms on your plate are poisonous", "They are selling cheap meat at the butcher's today", have a more distinct imperative function than, for instance: "John is a noble person".

Still, what remains to be considered is Hare's statement that «descrip-tive» meaning of evaluating expressions is «secondary» in relation to the imperative meaning.[161] In particular, this is supposed to concern the pred-icate "good". The thesis that secondary position of descriptive meaning can be interpreted in two following ways: (1) as referring to the genesis of the meaning and (2) as referring to the frequency and gravity of the mean-ing's occurrence.

(1) The etymology of the expression "good" is certainly not condu-cive to its "imperative" interpretation. The meaning of the Greek "*ag-athós*" is derived from "born free", or "noble". The Polish word "dobry" is etymologically connected to "worthy". The English "good" is derived from a word which means "relevant, adequate".[162] It can be stated with-out a doubt that the origins of the notion of "goodness" are not connected with encouraging exclamations, but rather with words which denote spe-cific objects or qualities which for some reason were regarded as valuable or worth possessing.

(2) If the fundamental meaning of the predicate "good" were imper-ative, the word would lose its close relationship with systems of evalu-ation and would become primarily an indication of preferences imposed on others. In order to prove his claim, Hare quotes, among others, the fol-lowing example:

Let us suppose that a missionary, armed with a grammar books, lands on a cannibal Island. The vocabulary of his grammar book gives him

---

[161] Hare [1952: 148].
[162] Liddell & Scott [1925]; Sławski [1956]; Skeat [1879].

the equivalent, in the cannibals' language, of the English word "good".
And let us suppose that, by a queer coincidence, the word is "good".
And let us suppose, also, that it really is the equivalent – that it is, as
the Oxford English Dictionary puts it, "the most general adjective of
commendation" in their language. If the missionary has mastered his
vocabulary, ha can, SO LONG AS HE USES THE WORD EVALUATIVELY AND NOT
DESCRIPTIVELY, communicate with them about morals quite happily.
They know that when he uses the word he is commending the person
or object that he applies it to. The only thing they will find odd is that
he applies it to such unexpected people, people who are meek end gentle and do not collect large quantities of scalps; whereas they themselves are accustomed to commend people who are bold and burly and
collect more scalps than the average.[163]

Hare's argumentation contains *petitio principii*: if we define "good"
as "the most general adjective of commendation", we do not have to prove
that it is mostly used to recommendation, and that its descriptive meaning
is secondary in relation to the imperative one, which is to be demonstrated
in the example.[164] Even if we deemed this question open, then: if cannibals
in fact understand "good" uttered by a missionary as a pure recommendation, the holy man would not have to exert himself and could simply smile
at the sight of gentle ones and gnash his teeth at the sight of scalps; his recommendations would then be expressed with equal clarity, albeit in a more
economical manner. But then, would we call his facial expressions "delivering moral information", as Hare calls them? Moral judgements are generally understood as more than mere expressions of personal recommendations, and the cannibals in Hare's story are treated to the latter.

[7.] One of the basic assumptions of imperativism is the conviction that
it is possible to isolate the sphere of moral considerations. This conviction

---

[163] Hare [1952: 148].

[164] This example is typical of Hare's whole method. He defines his basic notions so that
finding examples which might challenge his theory can be ruled out in advance. This
unsinkability of his theory leads to tautology and lack of testability. (Comp. Warnock
[1900: 127–129].)

constitutes a vital component of the whole imperativistic theory, as obviously, ascribing imperative meaning to predicates and evaluating utterances in contexts other than ethical would lead to absurdity. "It is good to be an athlete", "It is good to speak ten languages", "It is good to be able to assemble TV sets", "It is good to hike in the Himalayas": we readily agree with the content of these evaluations but we would deem it nonsensical to derive any general or specific norms from them.

We have already considered [...] [above] the possibility, or rather: the impossibility, of a sharp division between ethical evaluations and other types of evaluations. However, this notion, so vital for the evaluation of imperativistic conceptions, deserves some more attention.

When we discuss a moral issue, we usually take into consideration a lot of data outside of the sphere of morality, while not bothering to classify them. It is certainly impossible to settle once and for all the boundary between the significance of these extra-moral elements of reasoning and the "autonomous" area of moral considerations, if the latter exists at all. Let us exemplify this concept.

Suppose there is a certain amount of money and food to divide, allocated for the people of third-world countries. Let us assume that there is a choice between two bids: a primitive tribe which is dying out as a result of famine and disease, which will probably use our aid recklessly, increase birthrate and soon return to its present state of emaciation, and a nation which has at its disposal resources which are barely enough to survive on a low civilizational level, which our aid would definitely allow to develop culturally and achieve wellbeing. Nobody can call this example artificial; it is certain that moral decisions are at stake; but it is probably impossible to separate them from economic, social, cultural and other considerations. The issue of evaluation of various models of society certainly has ethical aspects, but it is hard to consider in «purely ethical» categories.

[8.] The imperativistic theory of evaluation equalizes semantic and functional differences between various kinds of utterances connected with evaluation, and most of all, between sentences which express value on the one hand and sentences which express duty or contain norms or dictates on the other.

The aim of the above criticism is not only to reveal the deficiency and vulnerability of the imperativistic theory, but also to build up a statement that, for the methodological point of view, it is more advantageous to treat the principles of value and evaluating judgements as basic; and normative sentences, sentences of duty and imperative sentences as based on the former in some way. This approach is represented in the philosophy of morality by, among others, Brentano and Moore (*Wertethik*), and by von Wright in the general philosophy of values. Certainly not the least significant advantage of assuming this view is the possibility of considering aesthetic issues in the wide scope of general axiology; the opposite standpoint which proclaims the primacy of norms over evaluating judgements (Kant's *Pflichtethik*) can only be applied to ethics, which is thus separated from other domains of evaluation.

Jerzy Kalinowski. Deontic logicians *avant la lettre*
[1972: 64–86]

Although the name *Deontik* was first used by E. Mally, who used it in relation to his logic of proper will, it was not until 1951 that the term "deontic logic" gained popularity and recognition. Therefore, those authors who continue to work on the logic of norms only deserve the name of "deontic logicians *avant la lettre*".[165]

At that time, the notion of a norm was neither obvious nor clarified. Norms and orders were usually confused; besides, that is still sometimes the case even at present. This mistake is rooted in legal positivism, which is strongly associated with voluntarism. This view is prevalent among lawyers and greatly affects a prominent number of philosophers, moralists and logicians who deal with the logic of norms. According to legal positivism, it is the lawgiver's will which is the ultimate source of law (at the same time, the lawgiver is the most effective, that is, able to ensure respect for the norms

---

[165] A list of their works can be found in: Conte [1961]. It was the first bibliography of logic of norms included in the bibliography of legal logic. Since then, there appeared numerous other bibliographical lists of the logic of norms, including Wright's [1968a: 97–107] and [1968b: 162–167] and Bernardo's [1969: 153–172].

settled by him, by using physical pressure). C. Cassio, H.N. Castañeda or the author of K_1 and K_2 systems, and others who claim, following Plato and Aristotle, the existence of practical knowledge and for whom ethics and law constitute the very knowledge of what a person should and/or can do, formulate their norms as normative sentences (sentences constructed with verbs: "should" and "can" or their synonyms).

Anti-cognitivists in this field (for instance, A. Ross[166]), who are at the same time positivists and voluntarists in the scope of legal norms, understand norms as orders and express them in the form of imperative sentences. Therefore, they also see the logic of norms as the logic of orders. Among the author we will consider at present, only W. Dubislav and R. Rand use a less precise, or a more general expression, namely: "demanding sentences" (*Forderungssätze*). All the other authors speak of the logic of orders or the logic of imperative sentences (A. Ledent[167]). Both groups agree that norms-orders do not fall into the category of truth or falsehood. This very issue poses a serious problem for them, described by A. Ross as "Jørgensen's dilemma". Indeed, the issue is a dilemma. Let us consider the following sets of utterances:

(1) *Love thy [your] neighbour.*
This is one of your neighbours.
Therefore, love him!

or:

(2) *Keep thy [your] promises!*
This is one of them.
Keep it!

Whatever attitude is assumed towards these systems, something which exists and requires respect is not taken into consideration, A. Ross and J. Jørgensen claim. If these systems are regarded as reasoning and logic whose theses would underlie their rules is developed, then the nature of logic is not respected; the logic which, according to the authors has only focused on

---

166 Ross [1933].
167 Ledent [1942].

the so called logical sentences, that is, true or false, since Aristotle's times. Yet, imperative sentences are neither true nor false and the very expression: "imperative logic" (in the meaning of "logic of orders"), if considered in its proper meaning, would be a common *contradictio in adiecto*. However, if as a result of this one relinquishes the whole concept of logic of orders, then one denies the existence of such systems of utterances as the ones presented above, which after all seem to possess the nature of a reasoning. In short, there are no grounds for the practice of the logic of orders and at the same time, no grounds for not practicing it. Therefore we face a true dilemma. What do we choose?

In fact, there is no dilemma at all, not only for those who claim, after Aristotle, Thomas Aquinas, Thomas Reid and more contemporary André Lalande, that norms are true or false, but also for those who accept [...] a broad understanding of logic and logical sentences [...], even when they deny norms their value of truth and falsehood and only grant them the value of validity. Yet, for the discussed authors this proved to be a real trap with only one way out, namely, constructing reasoning in the strict sense of the term, reasoning parallel to the discussed systems of imperative utterances. Understandably the term "imperative logic" was able to be retained with no damage to the logic constructed from laws which justify the rules of this parallel reasoning, as the logic's metonymic name. This idea is to be found in many papers by authors of this period, especially W. Dubislav, J. Jørgensen, A. Ledent and A. Ross. Also R.M. Hare can be included in this group.

It all starts in 1937 with the publication of W. Dubislav's article[168] which makes a distinction between a sentence which expresses a demand and a declarative sentence which refer to the object of the demand. "Nobody should commit murder" is an example of a sentence of the first kind, "For every x, if x is a person, there is no such person who should be killed by x" is an example of a sentence of the second kind. It is with this distinction that W. Dubislav defines quasi-inference of a sentence which expresses demand on the basis of another sentence of this kind. "A sentence which expresses a demand F can be derived from a sentence which expresses a demand E",

---

[168] Dubislav [1937].

writes Dubislav, "if a statement corresponding to F in the regular sense can be derived from the statement corresponding to E". J. Jørgensen develops W. Dubislav's theory of imperative sentence.[169] The elements he enriched it with influenced many other logicians, especially A. Ross, A. Ledent and R.M. Hare. In every imperative sentence, J. Jørgensen differentiates two elements: imperative and indicative, that is, descriptive. The former is common to all imperative sentences. In the terminology which seems the most proper, it constitutes an operator, connector or functor (which forms an imperative). The latter is specific to any imperative sentence considered separately, which in consequence means it can be different for individual imperative sentences. In "Peter, close the door!" the imperative factor, the manifestation of will and the order-giving attitude of the person who issues the order towards Peter is expressed through using the imperative form of the verb "to close". The factor which indicates the topic of the commission included in the considered order is presented in the indicative sentence: "Peter is closing the door". According to the author, this distinction allows for testing if the imperative sentence does or does not make sense. It is sensible if the indicative sentence (which describes the topic of the commission) itself makes sense. As we mentioned before, the distinction made by Jørgensen was adopted by many logicians, especially by A. Ross, A. Ledent and R.M. Hare.

For J. Jørgensen, just as for W. Dubislav, the logic of imperative sentences in the proper meaning of the word is implausible. Just as there exist syntactic rules which allow for the construction (in reference to every imperative sentence) of indicative sentences which describe the topics of its commission, there also exist syntactic rules which determine the manner in which sentences on this imperative are constructed (in reference to each imperative derived from a specific person), that is, sentences of the type: "Person so and so orders a given state of affairs to be created". In addition, J. Jørgensen considers expressions of the type: "Such and such state of affairs is to be created" as an abbreviation of the previous expression. This

---

[169] Jørgensen [1937–1938].

way, for instance by referring to (2), which is not actually an inference, one can construct a practical inference, namely:

(2*bis*) *All promises are fulfillable.*

Here is a promise.

Therefore it is fulfillable.

Referring to J. Jørgensen's statement, let us stress the fact that this is only possible when a given imperative comes from a giver of an order. What shall we do then when there is no giver of an order? This question was posed when the discussion on imperatives without an order giver was in progress. The answer presented by Jørgensen may not have been exhaustive. As A. Ross remarked in 1941, Jørgensen's reasoning forces us to return, at least on the metalinguistic level, to the field of theoretical logic and does not allow us to captivate any specificity of imperative quasi-reasoning. Thus, a more satisfactory solution was looked for, and finally, there emerged three proposals:

(a) the logic of satisfaction;

(b) the logic of validity;

and

(c) the principle of the dictive indifference of logic.

The logic of imperatives, called "the logic of satisfaction", was created by A. Hofstadter and J.C.C. McKinsey.[170] They assumed the notion of a declarative sentence which describes the topic of the commission of a given imperative, a concept invented by W. Dubislav. Such a sentence is true if the order corresponding to it is satisfied [*scil.* fulfilled]. Starting with this principle, the logicians mentioned above claim that imperative quasi-reasoning is conclusive when authentic reasoning, constructed from indicative sentences which describe the topics of commissions of imperatives is conclusive. Therefore we can work out a whole logic of imperatives analogous to the logic of sentences, that is, a whole imperative calculus analogous to sentential calculus. Satisfaction functions of the former would correspond to the truth functions of the latter and would be determined with the help of satisfaction charts, analogous to a truth matrix. For instance, the func-

---

[170] Hofstadter & McKinsey [1939].

tion of imperative implication '$C_1 > C_2$' would correspond to the function of propositional implication '$S_1 \supset S_2$' where 'C_1' and 'C_2' would be variables representing, respectively, any command (imperative), exactly the same as 'S_1' and 'S_2' are propositional variables which represent, respectively, any sentence. Similarly, the function '$S_1 \supset S_2$' is transformed into a false conditional sentence only when 'S_1' is replaced with a true sentence, and 'S_2' is replaced with a false sentence, just as the function '$C_1 > C_2$' results in an unsatisfactory formal imperative implication if 'C_1' is replaced with a fulfilled order, and 'C_2' is replaced with an unfulfilled order.

A. Hofstadter and J.C.C. McKinsey's logic of satisfaction is somewhat artificial, needlessly complicated and too limited. Its artificial character is apparent when, for instance, "Peter, close the door!" substitutes 'C_1' in '$C_1 > C_2$' and respectively, "Peter, get up!" replaces 'C_2'. Indeed, what results in this case is "If Peter close the door! then Peter get up!" which is a syntactically incorrect sentence and therefore not used. In order to obtain a correctly formulated expression one has to substitute the variables in the discussed function either with (a) sentences on orders, in this case: "The order: "Peter, close the door!"" is valid and "The order: "Peter, get up!"" is valid, as A. Ross does, or (b) norms or normative sentences, that is in this case: "Peter should close the door" and "Peter should get up".

If one uses imperatives, which as such do not fall into the categories of truth or falsehood, instead of taking into consideration norms which fall into these categories, he prevents himself from directly substituting variables of sentential calculus with the latter and imposes on himself a roundabout way of reaching the aim, through declarative sentences which describe topics of commissions, as well as through fulfilling or not fulfilling the latter, by reaching the analogates of theses of sentential calculus. Thus the logic of satisfaction turns out to be limited to these formulas, which deprives it of originality, since the rules of reasoning based on this logic's theses guide practical reasoning (in the Aristotelian meaning of the term), which are not at all specific and which are also not the most common. In this way, specific and the most common reasoning, like normative syllogistic reasoning, as well as reasoning which refers to the laws of opposition of norms, seem to have been entirely omitted.

Yet, the criticism of the logic of satisfaction undertaken by A. Ross[171] does not go in this direction. According to this author, A. Hofstadter and J.C.C. McKinsey's logic leads to unacceptable consequences; he attempts to demonstrate it with an example which is famously called "Ross's paradox" and which provoked a profusion of works. Let us take the imperative: "Send this letter!". The corresponding declarative sentence is: "This letter is sent". Let us now consider the thesis of sentential calculus:

(3) *CpApq*.

which is read as: "if *p*, then *p* or *q*". By substituting '*p*' with "This letter is sent" and '*q*' with "This letter is burnt", we obtain: "If this letter is sent, then this letter is sent or burnt". If a given antecedent of the expression ("This letter is sent") exists, then its consequent ("This letter is sent or this letter is burnt") can be detached, that is, regarded as a separate sentence. It is an alternative sentence and, as with any sentence of this kind, it is true when one of its elements is true. Therefore, it would be true if the letter it concerns was burned instead of being sent. The imperative which it corresponds to reads: "Send this letter or burn this letter!". In this context, it is a quasi-conclusion of the imperative: "Send this letter!" and, what is more, it would be fulfilled if the letter was burned, and this is exactly where the essence of the paradox lies.

This is exactly how the paradox can be described, if it can be called a paradox at all. For A. Ross and many other authors who wrote on the topic (among others, for G.H. von Wright lately[172]) it is clear that we are dealing with a paradox in the described case. However, our view on the matter is that there is no paradox here. When can the consequent: "This letter is sent or this letter is burnt", that is, an alternative sentence which corresponds to the alternative imperative: "Send this letter or burn this letter!" be detached from its antecedent: "This letter is sent" which corresponds to the imperative: "Send this letter!"? Only when the antecedent is true and the corresponding imperative is fulfilled. If this is the case, one has to be aware of that up until the end of the reasoning. One cannot change the assumption in the middle of the reasoning. In other words, having detached the consequent in question, one has

[171] Ross [1941].
[172] Wright [1967: 2] and Wright [1968a: 20 *et seq.*].

no right to claim that it is true, since the letter in question is burnt. It has been settled once and for all that the considered alternative sentence: "This letter is sent or this letter is burnt" is true because its first element ("This letter is sent") is true, and in consequence, according to the logic of satisfaction, the alternative imperative which the sentence corresponds to is fulfilled, since the letter has been sent. If during the reasoning one does not cross, in an unvindicated manner, from one assumption to another, then there is no paradox in the reasoning. The appearance of a paradox only exists in the eyes of someone whose reasoning is superficial, in the fact that "Send this letter or burn it!" is derived from "Send this letter!". Yet, the appearance is none the more pronounced in the case of dealing with imperatives that when we are dealing with theoretical sentences. It seems paradoxical to tell one's wife on receiving a letter with confirmation of one's promotion: "I got the promotion or I did not get a promotion". However, we realize this is only an apparent paradox when we become aware of the conditions on which one can derive "I got a promotion or I did not get a promotion" from "I got a promotion", or "Send this letter or burn it!" from "Send this letter!" Namely, it is necessary for "I got a promotion" in the first case and "This letter is sent" in the second to be true. Whatever remained paradoxical following this explanation is within the notion of alternative used in logic. Yet, from this point of view the logic of imperatives is not more paradoxical than the classic divalent logic of sentences, to name just the most basic theory of logic. Besides, it is not the notion of an alternative alone that is paradoxical in this sense among the notions of our logic. One could even conclude that all logic was paradoxical and requires inspection. R. Blanché seems to be of this opinion.[173] The question is whether a better logic can be devised. In any case, the classic divalent logic of sentences and the calculus at the base of it are still useful, and generally satisfactory, although some special cases might require special logic: modal, intuitive, or polyvalent.

Let us return to the drawbacks of the solution of Jørgensen's dilemma proposed by himself. A. Hofstadter and J.C.C. McKinsey replaced the solution with logic of satisfaction, whereas A. Ross deemed this logic paradoxical and suggested replacing it with logic of validity. According to Ross,

---

[173] Blanché [1967, particularly part II].

reasoning (authentic) parallel to imperative quasi-reasoning has to be constructed, not from declarative sentences which describe topics of commissions of corresponding imperatives, but from sentences of validity, that is, from sentences on imperatives (and therefore, meta-sentences) which state the validity of the imperatives which they concern. What the validity depends on is another story. It may depend on the fact of their issuing, on the fact of their acceptance by the person at whom the order was issued, or on some other factor. A. Ross does not deal with this issue; it remains open. (Is that not an overly nonchalant attitude towards a fairly serious issue? Since norms are confused with imperatives, it is obvious the issue concerns all rules, or directives, to mention Ross's favorite term, of one's behaviour.)

The Danish theoretician of law returned to work on the logic of imperatives 25 years after the publication of its first version, in the book entitled *Directives and Norms*,[174] changing the name to "deontic logic" under the influence of G.H. von Wright. In the years 1941–1944 (his article "Imperatives and Logic" was reprinted three years after its publication) A. Ross reproached (wrongly, as we believe) the logic of satisfaction for its paradoxes and felt obliged to replace it with logic of validity. The difference between the latter and logic of satisfaction (they can only be combined in the scope of negation) is reduced to differentiating between what the author calls "internal alternative and internal implication", which are characteristic to the logic of satisfaction, on the one hand, and on the other: "external alternative and external implication" which are characteristic to the logic of validity. Indeed, while the first alternative concerns alternative imperatives, like: "Send this letter or burn it!", the other encompasses only alternatives of sentences of validity, like: "The order: "Send this letter!" is valid or the order: "Burn this letter!" is valid", which practically eliminates (the supposed) Ross's paradox. It is similar in the case of implications. In 1968 Ross aimed at generalizing these results.

Indeed, he attempts to compile a deontic logic which would use internal as well as external deontic functors. Therefore he is forced to conduct a characteristic of both with the help of matrixes analogous to the truth tables of the logic of sentences, and in particular, internal and exter-

---

[174] Ross [1968].

nal negation, alternative, conjunction and implication. A. Ross presents a matrix for each of these functors. With the exception of the field of conjunction, internal matrixes differ from external matrixes. Unfortunately, as we attempt to prove in Kalinowski [1969a], all matrixes of internal deontic functors constructed by A. Ross are incorrect. In order to find it out, let us use as an example a matrix of a deontic internal alternative:

Op	Oq	O(p ∨ q)
V	V	I
I	V	I
V	I	I
I	I	I ∨ V

The expression 'Op', 'Oq' and 'O(p ∨ q)' are read, respectively: "IT IS VALID THAT p", " IT IS VALID THAT q" and " IT IS VALID THAT p OR q". The letters 'V' and 'I' symbolize, respectively, validity and invalidity of norms created through replacing the variables 'p' and 'q' with specific sentences which describe a state of affairs recognized as valid. In a formally correct matrix, functions written at the head of the first and the second column, as far as the characteristic of the functor of two arguments, are components of a function written at the top of the third column, as in the case of the matrix of a propositional alternative:

p	q	p ∨ q
1	1	1
0	1	1
1	0	1
0	0	0

where '1' and '0' symbolize, respectively, truthfulness and falsehood of sentences which replaced the variables 'p' and 'q' in the first, second and third column, as well as an alternative sentence in the third column obtained from the function '$p ∨ q$' as a result of the replacement. Thus we can see that 'p'

and 'q', the most basic functions of sentential calculus, are components of the alternative function '$p \lor q$'. Let us also note that 'Op' and 'Oq' from the previous matrix are not components of the function '$O(p \lor q)$'. This very fact is the reason why this matrix is incorrect. We will not attempt to discuss in more detail the deontic logic which A. Ross proposed in 1968 in place of his logic of imperatives from 1941.

The logic of satisfaction and logic of validity are not the only solutions proposed in place of Jørgensen's concept: R.M. Hare introduces a third proposal: the principle of the dictive neutrality of logic.[175] Inspired by Jørgensen's differentiation between the imperative and descriptive factors of any imperative, R.M. Hare subjects descriptive (theoretical) sentences to an analogous analysis and concludes that they also contain two elements: an indicative factor and a descriptive factor. A comparison of corresponding imperative sentences and descriptive sentences reveals that both types have the same descriptive factor ("descriptor" or "phrastic", in R.M. Hare's terminology), and the only difference is in the remaining factors: imperative in the first case and indicative in the second; factors called "dictors" or "neustics". R.M. Hare expresses an imperative dictor with the word "please" and an indicative dictor with the word "yes". Commencing from the same "stem", which is every descriptor, we either obtain an imperative sentence or a descriptive (declarative) sentence, regardless of whether the mentioned "stem" is accompanied with an imperative dictor or an indicative dictor. It is worth mentioning that instead of two kinds of logic: the logic of imperatives and the logic of descriptive sentences, there only exists one kind of logic, namely, the logic of descriptors. It is independent of dictors connected with descriptors. This is the sense of the principle of dictive neutrality of logic; a principle which – according to R.M. Hare – puts an end to the discussion of the relationship between imperatives and descriptive sentences on the one hand and the logic corresponding to them, wrongly believed to be discrete, on the other hand. The logic of imperatives would then only be a kind of quasi-logic or logic in the metonymic sense, whereas the only

---

[175] Hare [1949] and [1952: 17–31].

real logic would be the logic of descriptive sentences. This is clearly not the case: there is only one kind of logic, common to both.

Preoccupied with presenting the reactions caused by Jørgensen's dilemma, we stepped beyond the year 1951, which we determined as the boundary of the period of deontic logicians *avant la lettre*. Even so, this is because divisions of history into periods are never absolute: the phases which we distinguish by schematizing historical reality always overlap to a greater or lesser degree. Let us however return to the main topic [...]. Among deontic logicians *avant la lettre*, as the predecessors of the logic of norms, operating in the period between 1934 and 1951, are called, there is one more worth mentioning at this stage, that is: R. Rand.

What is the exact nature of the idea of the logic of sentences on commissions (*Forderungssätze*), as she calls them?[176] She claims that, on the one hand, axioms of the logic of (descriptive, declarative) sentences are used in the logic of sentences on commissions only through analogy, and on the other hand that deductive rules of substitution and detachment assumed by B. Russell for his system of logic of sentences are valid in the logic of sentences on commissions only in a metonymic sense. Is it therefore correct to conclude that R. Rand's logic of sentences on commissions is, just as W. Dubislav's, J. Jørgensen's, A. Ross's and R. Hare's logic of imperatives, logic only by metonymy?

Whatever is the view on the matter, axioms and theorems of sentential calculus have, according to this conception, an application analogous to that in the logic of sentences on commissions. Let us add for the sake of accuracy that R. Rand analyses only five theorems, whereas the remaining ones are omitted. Shall we conclude that the omission denotes that analogous use of these theorems in the scope of the logic of sentences on commissions is accepted and results from using axioms, which in turn contain all theorems, taking into consideration the metonymic validity of deductive rules? As for the axioms of sentential calculus, the author invokes B. Russell's system, which contains six axioms altogether, the first of which is formulated in natural language (as opposed to the remaining

---

[176] Rand [1939].

five, formulated in Russell's symbolic language), and the fifth one is not independent of the others, as was proved by J. Łukasiewicz, and then P. Bernays.[177] Therefore, R. Rand only takes into consideration the four remaining ones, which are as follows:

    *1.2. |-: $p \lor p. \supset .p$ Pp (the law of tautology).

    *1.3. |-: $q. \supset .p \lor q$ Pp (the law of addition).

    *1.4. |-: $p \lor p. \supset. q \lor p$ Pp (the law of alternation).

    *1.5. |-: $.q \supset r: \supset :p \lor q. \supset . p \lor r$ Pp (the law of attachment).[178]

"These axioms, writes R. Rand, can be accepted in the logic of sentences on commissions, in the axiological sense, if they turn out to be convenient for the operation on sentences on commissions." As for theorems, she only mentions the principle of non-contradiction, the principle of the excluded middle, the principle of double negation, *modus ponendo ponens* and *modus tollendo tollens.*

The principle of non-contradiction for sentences on commissions was formulated with the following words: "One cannot dictate something which would be in conflict or in contradiction with itself". As for whether one can issue contradictory commissions, one has to say that – alas! – it is possible. It is also not necessary to be the infamous sadist from the SS, who tore a cap off a prisoner's head and threw it over the barbed wire surrounding the camp, and then ordered the prisoner to pick it up, reminding him at the same time, even by his very presence, of the prohibition to leave the camp. It is sufficient to be a lawgiver to issue contradictory norms at times, to the great dismay of both a common citi-

---

[177] Łukasiewicz [1925]; Bernays [1926].

[178] 'Pp' (from *proposition première*, that is, "first proposition") indicates that formulas where this abbreviation is placed are axioms. These axioms read as follows: "If *p* or *p*, then *p*", "If *q*, then *p* or *q*" (a variant of J. Łukasiewicz's thesis 72 quoted in connection with Ross's paradox), "If *p* or *q*, then *q* or *p*" and "If [if] *q*, then *r*, then if *p* or *q*, then *p* or *r*". As opposed to what we did in the text, R. Rand does not copy these axioms literally, but quotes them in a meta-linguistic form, writing, for instance: (*1.2.): "It is true that if *p* or *p*, then *p*", which is a fairly common practice, but fundamentally incorrect and therefore inadvisable. Comp. Tarski [1943–1944: 15 – the text as well as footnotes 24, 25 and 26]. Let us add that for B. Russell, dots perform the function of brackets and curly brackets, punctuation marks in many logical symbolic notations.

zen and a lawyer. Still, there is no doubt that the principle of non-contradiction of sentences on commissions is a non-negotiable logical requirement, regardless of whether it is in fact complied with or not (complying
with this requirement is another issue). R. Rand would do better if she
pronounced this principle in objective language, proper both for imperative (normative) calculus and sentential calculus; this would let her avoid
the unfortunate "we cannot". Besides, she could have chosen, at her own
discretion, either natural or symbolic language. In the case of the latter
the principle of non-contradiction could have been formulated in the following manner:

(4) $\sim (!p. \sim !p)$.

where the formula's symbolic notation could, it seems, correspond to the author's intentions ('$!p$' denotes any imperative or any norm in this case,[179] or
in other words, any sentence on commissions, to use R. Rand's term), which
is a certain substitution of the thesis:

(5) $NKpNp$.

which reads: Not: BOTH p AND NOT-p, that is, the principle of non-contradiction for sentences, which is a part of the bivalent sentential calculus.
The formula (5) synthesizes all variations of the principle of non-contradiction for sentences on commissions, especially the three basic variants,
that is, the principles of non-contradiction valid for obligations to act, for
obligations not to act (prohibitions) as well as for bivalent permission. Indeed, the decision-making procedure, which is contained in the $\mathbf{K}_1$ system
enables one to prove that the following statements are theses of the logic
of norms: "Not: both x should do α and not: x should do α" (in the symbolic representation: '$NKSx\alpha NSx\alpha$'), "Not: both x should not do α and not:
x should not do α" (in the symbolic representation: '$NKLx\alpha NLx\alpha$'), and
"Not: both x can do α and not: x can do α" (in the symbolic representa-

---

[179] Norms can be divided [...] into dictative (which settle the obligation to perform
a certain activity), prohibitive and (bilaterally) permissive. Imperatives can be divided analogously, if we assume that the expression "x is willing to voluntarily do and
not do α!" means what can be called a seemingly paradoxical term of "a bilaterally
permissive imperative." It was already mentioned that the symbol "!p" which appears
in (4) – the same remark applies to formulas (7) and (8) – represents any norm or any
imperative.

tion: '*NKMxαNMxα*'). At the same time, this very method of verification shows that the expression: "Not: both *x* can do α and *x* can do not-α" (in the symbolic representation: '*NKMxαMxNα*') is not a thesis of the logic of norms, which is explained by the very nature of bilateral permission, which simultaneously enables the execution of a given action and enables failure to execute it, that is, according to $\mathbf{K_1}$ optics, it enables the execution of a given action and at the same time enables the execution of an action opposite to it.[180]

The principle of the excluded middle for sentences on commissions is formulated by R. Rand in the following manner: "What is valid is either an affirmative sentence on commissions or a negative sentence on commissions". Even if we disregard the issue of meta-language, the use of which is again improper, then the author's formula is still ambiguous. If we attempt to express, this time in objective language, R. Rand's idea with the formula:

(6) *ASxαLxα*.

which reads: "*x* should do *α* or *x* should do not-*α*", then the applied procedure of resolution reveals that formula (6) is not a thesis of the logic of norms, whereas the following formula is a thesis of this logic:

(6*bis*) *AASxαLxαMxα*.

We also suppose that R. Rand's actual idea should be expressed in the following formula:

(7) !*p* ∨ ~ !*p*.

which is a substitution of the principle of excluded middle of a bivalent sentential calculus:

(7*bis*) *ApNp*.

The formula (6) synthesizes all variants of the principle of excluded middle for sentences on commissions (just as formula (5) combines variants of the principle of non-contradiction for these sentences, and formula (8), which will be discussed later on, combines variants of the principle of

---

[180] The notion of opposite action [*opposée*] will be explained further on [...]; let us remark on the margin of this discussion on the law of non-contradiction for sentences on commissions that cohesion of normative systems is discussed, among others, in: Wright [1963a: 134–156].

double negation, also for these sentences), especially the three basic ones: "*x* should do *α* or not: *x* should do *α*" ('*ASxαNSxα*'), "*x* should not do *α* or not: *x* should not do *α*" ('*ALxαNLxα*') and "*x* can do *α* or not: x can do *α*" ('*AMxαNMxα*'). The method of verification of system **K**$_1$ proves that all of them are theses of the logic of norms. In view of the nature of divalent permission, a thesis of this logic is also the expression: "*x* can do *α* or *x* can do not-*α*" ('*AMxαMxNα*'), which is a consequence of the expression: "*x* can do *α* and *x* can do not-*α*" ('*KMxαMxNα*').

R. Rand's only remark on the principle of double negation for sentences on commissions is that the principle gives a doubly negated sentence on commissions the meaning of a positive sentence on commissions. In the symbolic notation, which the author would find suitable, the principle could be formulated like this:

(8) $!p \equiv {\sim}{\sim} !p$.

The determining procedure mentioned above proves that all variants of the principle of double negation for sentences on commissions virtually included in (8) are theses of the logic of norms, especially the three basic variants: "*x* should do *α* if and only if not: *x* should not do *α*" ('*ESxαNNSxα*'), "*x* should not do *α* if and only if not: *x* does not have to do *α*" ('*ELxαNNLxα*') and "*x* can do *α* if and only if not: *x* cannot do *α*" ('*EMαNNMxα*').

R. Rand moves on to construct two lines of reasoning on commissions: the first one is according to the rule based on the principle *modus ponendo ponens*, whereas the second one is based on the principle *modus tollendo tollens*. Here they are:

(9) If *A* should work, then *B* should also do it.

A should work.

Therefore, *B* should work.

(10) If crimes should be punished, then criminals should be locked up in prisons.

Criminals should not be locked up in prisons.

Therefore, crimes should not be punished.

The only remark which comes to mind here is that these two lines of reasoning demonstrate that R. Rand's sentences on commissions look as good in the form of normative sentences as in the form of imperative sentences. Therefore, we did not in fact go beyond her idea when we spoke both of norms and imperatives.

R. Rand is also one of those rare authors who are interested in imperative (normative) syllogistics. Indeed, the following lines of reasoning (examples of syllogistic normative reasoning) are found in her work:

(11) All citizens of this country should be honest.

All inhabitants of this island should be citizens of this country.

All inhabitants of this island should be honest.

(12) No citizen of this country should steal.

X is a citizen of this country.

X should not steal.

(13) No citizen of this country should steal.

Those who inhabit a given territory are citizens of this country.

Those who inhabit a given territory should not steal.

(14) You should not kill.

You possess given features as a person.

As a person who possesses given features, you should not kill.

These examples invoke the following remarks: (11) and (14) are incorrect. In the case of (11), as long as the inhabitants of the island in question should be citizens of a given country, and in fact are not, they are under no obligation to be honest. In order for the reasoning (11) to be correct, it should contain as a second premise the expression: "All inhabitants of this island are citizens of this country".[181] In the formula (14) it is claimed

---

[181] Systems of imperative or meta-imperative utterances, analogous to (11) and incorrect, like (11), are also found in other authors' works, for instance, by J. Jørgensen, A. Ross or K. Grue-Sørensen (comp. Jørgensen [1937–1938]; Grue-Sørensen [1939]; Ross [1941]). The first one constructs the following imperative pseudo-reasoning:
(a) *Love your neighbour as you love yourself!*
   Love yourself!
   Love your neighbour!
K. Grue-Sørensen writes:
(b) *Respect your neighbour as you respect yourself!*
   Respect your neighbour!
   Respect yourself!
thus, with the exception of one word, the same thing. In turn, Jørgensen makes the fol-

unjustifiably that the object of premises should not kill since he is a person endowed with certain features. The only conclusion which is vindicated by premises in (14) is the expression: "A person endowed with certain features should not kill". Systems (12) and (13) are correct, but they represent only two types of normative syllogisms. The system K_2, which will be discussed later, formalizes all kinds of them.[182]

Thus we can see how R. Rand perceives the deductive logic of sentences on commissions; the logic which she describes as being wholly a logic of statements applied through analogy. The examples are at times controversial, and even outright faulty. Yet, they draw an outline of the logic of norms which is sufficient to provide the author with one of the main positions among deontic logicians *avant la lettre*.

---

lowing system the equivalent of (a):
(c) *Your love towards [your] neighbour should be equal to your love towards yourself.*
   You should love yourself.
   You should love [your] neighbour.
presented in the language of sentences on imperatives [...]. It is hard to believe that (a), (b) and (c) can be accepted as reasoning, since their alleged conclusions do not result from their alleged premises. It is in vain that A. Ross replaces (a) with:
(d) *Love yourself!*
   If you love yourself, you should love your neighbour!
   Love your neighbour!
The only reasoning resembling the ideas which J. Jørgensen, A. Ross or K. Grue-Sørensen attempted to express are inferences of the following kind:
(e) *If you love your neighbour, you should love him as you love yourself.*
   You love your neighbour.
   Therefore, you should love him as you love yourself.
as well as:
(f) *If you should love your neighbour, then you should love him as you love yourself.*
   You should love your neighbour.
   Therefore, you should love him as you love yourself.
(Both (e) and (f) are lines of reasoning according to *modus ponendo ponens*.)
[182] With the exception of syllogisms, which we called, for want of a better term, "mereological syllogisms", like:
Peter should read Organon *by Aristotle.*
Reading Analytics *is a part of reading* Organon.
Therefore, Peter should read Analytics.
More on this subject: Kalinowski [1969b].

Zygmunt Ziembiński. Presuppositions of directives
[1972a: 15–19, 50–58, 142–143]

Undoubtedly, sentences in the logical sense have to be perceived as utterances which are possible to formulate in a given language, which state clearly that the situation is such and such, or is not such and such, and therefore, utterances which describe reality in some way (or possibly some «reality» imagined by someone). These utterances describe reality faithfully or not faithfully, and therefore they are true or false utterances. Naturally, descriptive utterances formulated by us are often only approximately an unequivocal description of reality. A sentence in the logical sense is therefore a sort of an ideal type, an idealization in relation to these descriptive utterances (which are usually incomplete and require conjectural complementation), which we actually formulate on a daily basis. Sentences in the logical sense which we definitely regard as true are described as our statements (which obviously does not mean that we are not wrong and that these statements are in fact true).

In our further discussion, we shall call evaluating utterances such utterances which, according to the semantic rules of a given language, even if they do not at present serve the purpose of expressing someone's approval or disapproval of a given state of affairs, they still are utterances with which one can express approval or disapproval of a given state of affairs. They can be utterances which have already been constructed or at least can be constructed in a given language. Such utterances should be distinguished from psychological sentences which state the fact that at a given moment one is experiencing a given evaluation, and from sentences which state that a given subject possesses certain objective features, of which one is prone *to approve* or disapprove (for instance, sentences which state that someone is truthful or honest, as these feature are usually generally approved). Utterances formulated in colloquial language often combine elements of a descriptive utterance (they state that it is or is not so) and evaluating (they express approval or disapproval of the fact). Since such an utterance describes some facts, either truthfully or mistakenly, it is a true or false utterance. An utterance which expresses exclusively evaluation and does not contain an element of description, cannot be described as true or false, unless one assumes the view of absolutism towards evaluations. According to this view, there is some (one by nature) non-relativized system of evaluations, that is, one that is not referred to the subject who performs the evaluation. Naturally, a standpoint which rejects the thesis of absolutism of evaluations and requires relativizing evaluations in relation to an evaluating subject, or at least one formulating the criteria of the manner of evaluation, is not at all equivalent to the standpoint which states indifference in evaluating, that is, a standpoint which states, in a colloquial speech, that anything can be evaluated in any way one pleases. The statement that some evaluations are allegedly commonly shared by people from a given environment cannot be identified with the statement that these evaluations are absolute, independent of evaluating subjects, just as a mass of stone is independent of a given subject who formulates a thought on it.

Finally, we shall call norms of behaviour such utterances constructed, or possible to construct, in a given language, which can be used according to the rules of this language to directly suggest (dictate or prohibit) a certain kind of behaviour to a subject. Norms of behaviour are treated as unequivocal, or practically unequivocal, utterances in this case.

Given that it is only reasonable to address someone with a dictate or a prohibition of performing an action in the cases when the addressee of the norm is able to act in various ways depending on the decision he had made, when speaking of norms we mean norms concerning someone's behaviour, that is, free behaviour. No one in their right mind will dictate to anyone to stop digesting the food they had swallowed, or prohibit someone from contracting his pupil in bright light. By using the term "norm" in the meaning of "norm of behaviour" we distance ourselves from many possible and frequent misunderstandings tied to substantially different meanings of the word "norm".

One can utter sentences on someone's behaviour without having evaluated, dictated or prohibited this behaviour; one can also evaluate someone's behaviour positively or negatively without formulating a norm which would dictate or prohibit it. Among other things, one can evaluate someone's past, present or future behaviour, whereas a norm of behaviour can be formulated in a reasonable way only in relation to future behaviour (even if it is very close future).

The assumed definition leads to the conclusion that the following are indispensable elements of an utterance considered as a norm of behaviour: (1) specifying an addressee of the norm, that is, a subject or subjects to whom the norm dictates or prohibits certain behaviour; (2) specifying the circumstances in which the dictated active or passive behaviour is to be realized (additionally, since there is no precise specification of these circumstances, we can infer that given behaviour is supposed to be realized by the addressees of the norm in any circumstances, as long as a given norm is valid); and (3) specification of behaviour the addressee of the norm is supposed to undertake in any circumstances or after the occurrence of some more clearly specified circumstances.

It is irrelevant and purely academic whether a norm will be formulated as, for instance, a conditional or unconditional utterance. What is significant is whether a given utterance contains definitions of basic elements which designate the content of the norm of behaviour, formulated explicitly or implicitly.

The scope of application of a norm is the category (set) of such situations, that is, simple or complex systems of circumstances, where subjects appointed in one way or another (addressees of the norm) are dictated or prohibited from undertaking the behaviour determined in the norm.

The scope of the normalizing of a norm of behaviour is a set of passive or active behaviours which the norm designates for the addressees to realize. It is irrelevant whether the norm is formulated as a prohibition or a dictate, since its scope of normalizing consists of two parts (subclasses) anyway: a positive part, that is, a class of behaviour dictated by a given norm, and a negative part, that is, a class of behaviour prohibited by a given norm (either prohibited directly or prohibited as interfering with dictated behaviour in some way.) The scope of normalizing is isolated by a norm from a class of future possible behaviours of the addressee of the norm, a class which otherwise consists of indifferent behaviours from the point of view of the discussed norm, that is, neither dictated nor prohibited by a given norm, though perhaps dictated or prohibited by some other norm. [...]

If we consider an act understood as causing a certain state of affairs by someone (semantic variant 2b[183]) through certain behaviour undertaken according to a given subject's decision (1b[184]), then settling norms which dictate or prohibit the execution of act interpreted in this way is a rational undertaking only when the act is "possible to execute". One has to assume that normally a rational codifier settles a norm which dictates to its addressee to fulfil or not to fulfil a given state of affairs because he wants a given state of affairs to occur through a given person's relevant behaviour. If he knew that fulfilling a given state of affairs is in some sense «impossible», he would act irrationally by settling a norm, unless he had a different aim in mind than causing the fulfilment of a given state of affairs. It is sometimes the case that someone settles a norm which dictates an act (2b) possible to be executed by a person competent in the field in order to prove that the addressee of the norm is not competent enough in the field. A malicious tyrant may dictate acts (2b) which are impossible to execute only to obtain a formal foundation to punish people for not executing them. Incidentally, this is the tyrant's rational behaviour if we consider his driving to humiliating and oppressing his subjects, although we consider such driving as despicable and wicked.

A special kind of such activity on the part of the codifier is settling norms which prohibit behaviour aiming towards obtaining what constitutes an essential minimum needed for an individual to exist, as Tadeusz Kotarbiński writes with bitter irony in his epigram from 1943 published in the book *Wesołe smutki (Merry Sorrows)*:

> You must not eat! – so they drank watered down food.
> You must not drink! – so they took a bath.
> Thus they managed to bypass every ban,
> Until an order was issued: You must not breathe!

---

[183] In this sense "*x*'s act" means the same as "*x*'s consecutive behaviour" and thus, as Ziembiński explains, "behaviour leading to retaining or changing some states of affairs, on the basis of assumed (appropriately or inappropriately) causal relationships between given behaviour and its consequences" [1972a: 32] [my footnote – JJ].

[184] In this sense "*x*'s act" means the same as "proceeding or proceedings" and thus "behaviour which is considered as guided by a given person's will to some degree, and therefore viewed as free behaviour" [1972a: 31] [my footnote – JJ].

> They breathed – so they were promptly executed.
> Was it right? Very right! Die, if you are a brawler.

However, if we disregard all sorts of special cases where the codifier who settles a norm attempts to achieve a different aim than fulfilling a given state of affairs appointed in the norm, with the help of the addressee of the norm, then the objects of normalizing are in principle acts which are «possible to fulfil» One should presume then that a rational codifier, settling a norm which dictates the state of affairs R to be fulfilled by a given addressee (or addressees,) assumes the following: (1) given future behaviour of the addressee of the norm could cause the occurrence of the state of affairs R; (2) the addressee of the norm is aware which behaviour on his part would cause the occurrence of the state of affairs R; and (3) he is able to make a decision which influences the choice of given behaviour. Only when all of the assumptions are fulfilled can we reasonably talk of "the possibility of the fulfilment of a given act" by the addressee of the norm. Still, in legal terms, not all elements which exclude "the possibility to fulfil a given act" are treated as equal.

In jurisprudence the following Latin adage is assumed: *Impossibilium nulla est obligatio* (There is no obligation to do the impossible). It expresses the idea that norms which are settled by a rational lawgiver (which is what lawyers assume a lawgiver to be) determine acts which are "possible to fulfil". If in some specific configuration of situations the dictated act turns out to be "impossible to fulfil", one should assume that the positive scope of normalizing of the settled norm was narrowed to a suitable degree for such situations, at least in the cases where "impossible" would consist in the fact that the first of the previously mentioned assumptions (that is, the assumption that given future behaviour of the addressee of the norm would be suitable to cause a given state of affairs) was false. There is often a different line of reasoning in the cases where «impossibility» is caused by the lack of relevant knowledge or the lack of skill in managing one's behaviour in a given field.

The impossibility of fulfilling the act (2b), reduced to the fact that it is false that the given behaviour of a given individual is suitable to cause the state of affairs indicated for execution, consists in some cases in conceptual impossibility, or purely logical impossibility. For instance, one cannot simultaneously, at the same moment, close a window and not close the same window (in the same, strictly specified meaning of the expression "close a window"), since one cannot cause a state of affairs whose description would create a self-contradictory sentence ("A given window is closed and is not closed at the moment"), even through very well advised behaviour. When we come across two radically contradictory norms in a legal system, then (in the absence of the collision rule which would repeal one of them) it is decided that the behaviour which the norms concern remains not standardized by the norms of a given system (which is sometimes called a logical gap in a legal system). Since in any situation which belongs to the uniform scope of use of contradictory norms, given behaviour is at the same time dictated and prohibited by the norms of the system, then in fact the norms of the system do not determine a given person's behaviour. However, such situations are unique in legal practice, as we assume a number of rules concerning accepting one of the mutually incompatible norms as legally invalid, or we assume a constricted scope of its use or standardization.

One might find more examples of settling norms which are incompatible with each other without one of them repealing the other (for instance, a guard in a concentration camp tells a prisoner to get over the fence to have a motive to shoot him in any case), but this is no place to discuss pathological phenomena in the organization of social life.

Probably the most frequent topic in legal considerations is "the impossibility to perform the act (2b)" of dynamic impossibility character. The most basic instances of dynamic inability simply concern the physical aspect of elements of a situation. One cannot trim the hair of a completely bald person, nor can one close a door which is closed at that moment, simply due to the lack of adequate material to perform the act. Similarly, one cannot break a stone with a bare hand or move a mountain with the power of one's muscles, or make a train accelerate by pushing the wall of a compartment. Any attempts of this kind on the part of an adult person would consist in some bizarre manipulations which would lead to doubts as to the person's sanity. The only tract of these manipulations would be perfectly irrelevant changes in the world, like turning mechanical energy into thermal energy, which is imperceptible and soon dispersed.

A dynamic possibility or impossibility of executing an act understood as causing a certain state of affairs by one's behaviour also has a mental aspect besides the physical aspect. A special phenomenon, considered from another point of view, is the fact that a given person, due to his retardation, mental illness or some disruption of mental activity, in unable to make the decision to perform a movement or refrain from movement which would be necessary to cause a given state of affairs in a given situation. In another case, someone might not possess sufficient knowledge of the connections between given behaviour and changes in the world caused by it, or he is intellectually disabled at that moment or does not notice certain elements of the situation. For instance, he had access to a pole which could have been used as a lever to dislodge beams which had crushed someone, but he is so mentally limited that he is not aware of the results which using the pole as a lever would bring about, or although he was aware of the properties of a lever, it did not occur to him as he was agitated at the sight of the accident, or he did not notice the pole lying about. The physical, dynamic possibility to provide assistance was eliminated by intellectual disability, just as in another case an intellectually able person may not have the possibility to provide assistance due to the lack of sufficient physical fitness needed to activate accessory devices, even very well designed ones.

One would probably have to indicate further, more complex examples of «impossibility to perform an act», especially those whose «impossibility» is connected to the intricate structure of social relations. There is no way for a poor person to pay a million dollar charge by check from his account, even if he had a bank account and the ability to write checks. However, an analysis of examples of this kind would extend beyond the narrow confines of the present work, although it is in such complex cases with «the impossibility to act» that the most interesting legal issues arise.

In some cases it is dynamically impossible for someone to perform a given act (2b); nevertheless, he undertakes behaviour which, in his understanding, aims at fulfilling the state of affairs which is supposed to be achieved through the act. It happens when he is unaware of the inefficiency of his behaviour in a given situation (inefficient attempt), or when there occurs a surprise intervention from factors which had not been taken into consideration (thwarted attempt). It may also be the case that one undertakes behaviour aiming at fulfilling a given state of affairs in an irrational way according to one's knowledge. It is obvious that a soldier of frail physical condition, and an inferior swimmer, will not swim across a wide river with a machine gun on his back. It is dynamically impossible due to the low physical efficiency of his muscles. However, out of obedience, following the order or out of fear, the soldier may walk into the water and make attempts to swim across the river, until he drowns in the river. This would be otherwise rational behaviour if we assume as chief and preferred over others the driving not to be disobedient to an order, to avoid being held captive, not to give one's gun over to the enemy, even though decisions of this sort are usually made on the spur of the moment rather than after reflecting upon the preferred driving and the choice of the means.

A series of a given person's acts, his complex behaviour (1b) aiming at fulfilling a given state of affairs according to the initial project is not always completed. This happens not only because the person loses the dynamic possibility to fulfil a given state of affairs with his behaviour, but because he simply does not withhold the project, forgot about it or got discouraged, or because he radically departed from his project, which may even result in undertaking activities aiming at preventing the intended state of affairs to occur.

In any case, it is worth mentioning that the same behaviour on the part of the subject can be considered as executing a certain act, if taken in conjunction with its effects (semantic variant 2b), or as being merely an attempt to execute another act. The person who attempted to perform an act called breaking into a warehouse, discouraged by the difficulty of having to saw the padlock, only executed an act called damaging the padlock.

However, it seems one has to differentiate between the notions of not fulfilling a given state of affairs through relevant activity or negligence and ascribing failure to execute a given act to a person as the basis for holding the person responsible. Ascribing failure to execute an act to somebody, we usually assume implicitly that the person had the necessary means to obtain dynamic possibility to fulfil a given state of affairs through his behaviour (either activity or negligence). If the considered case lacked any of the necessary elements, we would say that even though the person did not fulfil a given state of affairs, failing to execute an act consisting in causing the very state of affairs by his behaviour cannot be ascribed to him if it was dynamically, or otherwise, impossible.

The issue gets more complicated in the case of an act which was impossible to execute due to factors in the individual's psyche, the incapacity of his volition or intellect. Here we are prepared to refer to the state of knowledge of the mental properties of an average, normal person, rather than our knowledge of the mental properties of a given individual, and only if we confirm the existence of conspicuous anomalies in a given individual are we inclined to depart from such approach of the issue. Here again we encounter the problem of culpable or not culpable ignorance, except in a more complicated form. As mentioned before, it is not about knowledge or lack of knowledge about the effects of undertaken behaviour, but about knowledge or lack of knowledge of how to lead to the emergence of a given state of affairs dictated to be fulfilled through relevant behaviour. […]

Directives indicating what a given subject is supposed to do in order to perform a given conventional action (based in the assumed rules of sense) are teleological directives, specific as to their kind in the sense that they are not based on the knowledge of relationships of a naturalistic sort, but on social relationships occurring within a group which accepts these rules of sense for given actions. "If you push the button, the light will go off." "If you want the light to go off, then in view of the aforementioned causal relationship you should push the button." "If you toss a specific card into a specific box on a specific day, then according to the rules of sense which concern the rules for the act of voting in a given legal system, it will be interpreted as an elective act." "If you want to perform an elective act according to the rules of a given system, you should toss a specific card into a specific box on a specific day." Drawing up a handwritten act of disposing of one's property in the case of one's death, signed and dated, is supposed to be interpreted as making a (regular, handwritten) will, according to art. 949 §1 of *Civil Code*. The regulation reads: "The testator can draw up a will in the manner of handwriting it as a whole, signing it and writing the date". On the basis of this regulation and the rule of sense interpreted from it one can formulate the relevant teleological directive for someone who wants to draw up a valid handwritten will: "If you want to draw up a handwritten will, valid according to the *Polish Code of Law*, write by hand an act of disposing of your property in the case of your death, sign and date it". This directive can only be formulated with a conjectural antecedent: "A handwritten will must be drawn up individually, signed and dated".

In the latter form, the directive which determines how one should draw up a handwritten will seemingly has the same form as legal norms which dictate, for instance, to report for military service, to pay specific taxes, to exterminate Colorado beetle in one's field, to get vaccinated, not to take someone else's property, *etc*. Thus, conceptual confusion may arise.

Kazimierz Opałek. Directives
[1974: 25–48]

1. The problem of directive meaning is studied within ethics (in connection with philosophy and logic understood broadly, semiotics included) and within legal theory, both of which analyse such notions as "norm", "rule", and "directive". Since the semantic relations between these terms are not clear or distinct, there have been continuous attempts to define them, correlate them, and work out a terminology for classifying norms, rules, and directives.[185] For our aims, an in-depth discussion of these issues seems unnecessary. However, we do need to look into another terminological problem requiring an explanation: in the colloquial use of these terms it is not clear to what objects they are meant to refer – to statements[186] of a given shape, to the expressions (phrases) as the carriers of a given

---

[185] See: Wright [1963a: ch. I]; Black [1958: 100 *et seq*.]; Ross [1968: §§10–15].

[186] The term "wypowiedź" has been widely accepted within Polish literature as having a general meaning referring to all expressions in the shape of a sentence, thus serving as the common denominator of descriptive sentences, directives, evaluations, questions, *etc*. The term "statement" is used in English is a similar manner, as opposed to "utterance," which refers to a specific instance of saying something. The German "Aussage" seems a bit unsteady, sometimes having a meaning as broad as "wypowiedź" (as in "*normative Aussage*"), and sometimes having a narrow one, corresponding to "a logical proposition" (as in "*Aussagenlogik*").

meaning, or, finally, to the abstracted meanings themselves. It does seem that speaking about directives, norms, *etc.*, already presupposes climbing to the semantic and (or) pragmatic level, since, contrary to some opinions, it is not possible to distinguish them as specific syntactic formulations (even though there admittedly exist certain formulations typical for expressing norms and directives).[187] Terms such as "norms" and "directives" will be used synonymously with "directive statements", "normative statements", *etc.* (or "statements expressing directives, norms, *etc.*) as referring to the expressions together with their meanings. The semantic properties of such expressions will be referred to as "directive meaning," "normative meaning", *etc.*

Let us take the terms "directive" ("a directive statement") and "directive meaning" as the basis of our considerations. Within our linguistic intuition, these terms take precedence over not only such terms as "norm" (and "normative meaning") and "rule" (and "meaning of a rule"), but also over terms such as "order", "wish", "advice", "request", "recommendation", *etc.* (and, accordingly, to "meaning of an order", "of a wish", *etc.*).[188]

These introductory remarks concerning terminology already seem to justify the search for directive meaning, suggesting that it does exist despite the fact that its existence is sometimes completely negated.

2. Directive meaning can be examined together with evaluating meaning – there are certainly semantic and (or) pragmatic affinities between the two, and one can easily find examples of such studies.[189] Yet these two groups of statements do have certain specific logico-semantic properties that distinguish them from each other. Since research into these types of statements is still in its initial stages, it seems more reasonable to focus on directives in our analysis. This is not to say that this analysis cannot at the same time shed some light on the problem of evaluating meaning and the relations between directives and evaluations. It would of course also

---

[187] See: Lande [1959: 755 *et seq.*, 930 *et seq.*]; Weinberger [1964a: 214].
[188] See: Ross [1968: 8].
[189] *E.g.*, Carnap [1954: esp. 1001].

be possible to reverse the direction of the analysis and move from an examination of evaluations towards a study of directives and their relation to evaluations. The route chosen here is the result of the author's professional preferences.

It would be easier to fulfil the aims of this paper if there was more of a collaboration between metaethics and legal theory, which has been more closely connected to the study of directives (specifically, of norms). We must add that the connections between legal theory and philosophy, logic, and linguistics are not as well developed as in the case of metaethics, causing a certain lag in the research into directives.[190] The more practical focus of lawyers, as opposed to the distinctly philosophical focus of ethicists, must also be taken into account.

3. The view adopted in this paper is that the meaning of an expression is studied by semantics, understood as the study of the relationship between language and reality (where reality is the model of the language under investigation). Following this view, the only type of meaning that has been fully described is "cognitive" meaning. That is why we will start our investigation by confronting directives with the model of cognitive meaning. This seems advisable because most attempts at defining other types of meaning (directive, evaluating, *etc.*) do refer to this model in some way. Analyzing this model can help us make up our minds concerning both the means and the very possibility of defining directive meaning.

4. "Cognitive meaning" can be better defined through the terms "intension" and "extension" applied to the semantic analysis of sentences in the logical sense.[191] It needs to be kept in mind that such sentences seem analogous to directives where their semantic categories are concerned.

The intension of a sentence in the logical sense is the proposition expressed by it. Let us ignore, for now, the doubts concerning the ontological status of intension. The extension of such a sentence is the truth value of the proposition.

---

[190] It should be noted that recently some progress has been made by legal theorists. For an overview, see Woleński [1966].

[191] Carnap [1947: ch. I, esp. §6].

For example, the intension of the sentence "Peter is closing the door" is the proposition that Peter is closing the door. The extension of this sentence is the truth value of the proposition.

What can be said about the intension and extension in the case of a directive counterpart of the above sentence, *i.e.*, "Peter, close the door!" (or "Peter should close the door")?

Concerning the extension, we can say that such a statement has no truth value. It is not an empirical sentence, and as such it differs from the sentence "Peter is closing the door". But it is also not an analytical (or contradictory) sentence, such as the sentences of pure semantics concerning the meaning or the conditions of truthfulness of empirical sentences, or sentences explicating certain concepts (in this case, such directive concepts as "should"). Nonetheless, "It is true that Peter should close the door" is a meaningful statement, just as similar statements about evaluations would be. However, one might voice a reservation here and say that "It is true…" is ambiguous, either stating that a a dictate has been given, or accepting this dictate as sensible, right, or beneficial. Further, it needs to be noted that the statement "The directive «Peter should close the door» is true" does not seem meaningful, as opposed to the statement "The sentence "Peter is closing the door" is true", and to analogous statements about evaluations (*e.g.* "The evaluation «John is a good man» is true"). Yet according to certain views directives are logically related to empirical sentences: the former presuppose the latter (contain them as elements,) and thus directives can be assigned a truth value. We can, for example, say: "Peter should close the door as (because) it is cold and (or) windy". In our view, however, the empirical statement "It is cold and (or) windy" is not part of the sentence "Peter should close the door", but rather is associated (or can be in a given situation) with the fact of making such a statement.[192]

The above issue is connected with the question of the «reasons» behind directives (and evaluations). Apart from the strong thesis claiming that the relations between these «reasons» (empirical sentences) and directives are in fact logical relations in the proper sense, we can also come across,

---

[192] See: Carnap [1954: 999 *et seq.*].

perhaps even more frequently, weaker theses, stating that these relations are "logical" in some other, vague sense: the reasons would not be components of formal logical implications, but of the logic of colloquial language. However, these theses do not do much to elucidate the problem of the truth value of directives.[193]

Sometimes a great deal of emphasis is put on the difference between an order and a statement of duty. It has been stressed that it is impossible to meaningfully decide about the truthfulness (falsity) of an order: "It is true (false) that Peter, close the door" while it is indeed possible to do so with a statement of duty (as we have shown above). Far reaching conclusions have been drawn from this fact,[194] but in our opinion this difference is not of fundamental importance. It can only be found at the syntactic level, and not on the semantic one; it is based on the fact that deciding about the truthfulness (falsity) of declarative statements always appears to be meaningful ("Peter should close the door" is a statement in the indicative mood). AD-DITIONALLY, an order can be supported with reasons, just as a statement of duty can.

At first glance, things look hopeful where the intension of a directive is concerned. The "proposition" that Peter should close the door seems to be "an objective kind of thought",[195] just as the proposition that Peter is closing the door does. But what "kind of thought" is it exactly? Certainly not one suggesting that something is happening at the moment, but rather one suggesting that it should happen, *i.e.*, that this something has a special kind of relation to reality.[196] It is difficult to say that we are dealing here with a "type of thought" if we want to look at the problem in terms of cognition.

According to some views, which we shall return to later, the statements "Peter is closing the door" and "Peter should close the door" contain the same "phrase", which is "the closing of the door by Peter". The meaning of this

---

[193] See, *e.g.*, Weinberger [1970: ch. XIV], Wright [1971], Perelman [1968] – and their bibliographies.
[194] See: Elzenberg [1966: 113 *et seq.*], Wellman [1961: chs. IX, X and p. 290]. Weinberger [1958a] differs – *s. lin.*: "Der Imperativ erscheint uns schon als abgeleiteter Bergiff als Spezialfall des Sollsatzes".
[195] Ajdukiewicz [1931: 44].
[196] Ross [1968: 35].

phrase is called the "idea of a topic" or "primary conceptual content".[197] By combining the phrase with the operator "it is so" we get a sentence in the logical sense (with an intension and an extension), which is not what happens if we combine the phrase with the operator "it should be so". Thus it appears that this very operator is the key to the problem of directive meaning. At least our *prima facie* examination seems to reach an impasse at this point.

5. In the face of these difficulties the following views have been formulated concerning directive meaning, all of which take discussions of cognitive meaning as their point of departure:

- Directives can be reduced to statements with cognitive meaning.

- Directives do not have cognitive meaning *per se*, but they do have meaning analogous to it.

- Directives have no meaning at all.

5.1. The term "reduction" is often used in the sense also used above, but this use is not always precise. What is actually being referred to is an operation analogous to formulating an analytical definition. We can call this operation the analysis (of statements).[198] The *analysans* and the *analysandum* must be synonymous, thus making their *L*-equivalence a necessary condition. Both in the case of reduction of directives to logical sentences and in the case of their reduction to statements with some other type of meaning, the question arises of whether *L*-equivalence is possible here at all. It is sometimes pointed out that defining synonymy in terms of *L*-equivalence causes trouble in many situations, but even when we leave *L*-equivalence aside, the question of a criterion of synonymy for norms and logical sentences proves to be problematic. What is more, this issue seems secondary to the problem of meaning.

Since there is plentiful critical literature on the subject, we will only briefly discuss the reductionist views.[199]

Reducing directives to statements about objective duty requires one to make very strong speculative assumptions, both ontological and episte-

---

[197] *Ibid.*, §44. The term "primary conceptual content" was first introduced in: Brown *et al.* [1959: chs. 5 and 6].

[198] Rynin [1960: 234 *et seq.*].

[199] For Polish literature see Woleński [1966] and J. Wróblewski [1964: 254 *et seq.*].

mological.[200] Naturalistic approaches are quite common. Let us enumerate only the reduction of directives to sentences about the psychological experiences of the persons giving them, and the reduction applied within certain branches of legal theory, where directives become sentences about the possibility of sanctions, *i.e.* the so-called theory of prediction. Directives are replaced here with sentences lacking – according to widespread linguistic intuitions – an element actually crucial for directives, that of duty. This objection can be raised in relation to both the traditional and the modern versions of this view.[201] Reducing directives to evaluations (or to a conjunction of evaluations and empirical sentences) or to orders – when these evaluations and orders are treated as statements having certain meanings *sui generis* – remains unsatisfactory: the issue of meaning for these types of statements is no less problematic than directive meaning itself. If evaluations and orders were then, in turn, reduced to empirical sentences, the aforementioned objections would again come into play. Reducing directives to teleological rules leads, on the one hand, to the same difficulties we face when reducing directives to empirical sentences (when these rules are treated as variants of such sentences), and, on the other hand, to problems connected with reducing directives to evaluations (the issue of how these rules relate to specific evaluations).

5.2. Next, we have various attempts to define "directive meaning" as in some specific way analogous to cognitive meaning. These attempts focus either on the intension or the extension. In the first case, the expression "model of behaviour" is often introduced into the definition of "directive meaning" or "normative meaning". This term has been broadly used within the fields of sociology, social anthropology, and ethnology, which has impacted legal theory in turn.[202] The meaning of the term can be understood in a number of ways: the descriptive, strictly behaviouristic version states

---

[200] For a detailed critique, see, *e.g.*, Ross [1946: ch. II].

[201] Here we can apply Stevenson's remarks on defining ethical terms. See Stevenson [1963: 11 et seq.] Related to the theory of prediction is A.R. Anderson's conception in: Andersn [1958: 100 *et seq*.]; compare to Wright [1970: 90 *et seq*.].

[202] See, e.g., Frydman [1936: 143 *et seq*.]; Olivecrona [1939: ch. I]; Dias & Hughes [1957: 491 *et seq*.].

that "a model of behaviour" corresponds to the statistically dominant attitude of the members of a given population towards a specific type of situation; in the more «liberal» descriptive version "a model of behaviour"
corresponds to a sentence stating the expectations that members of the population have towards other members in a given type of situation (where the
basis of the expectations is the fact that the regular occurrence of a given
behaviour causes it to be treated as «normal»); in the descriptive version,
employing normative terminology, "a model of behaviour" corresponds to
a sentence stating that certain behaviours are treated within a given society
as fulfilling certain obligations or entitlements.[203] But this term is frequently
used in sociology in ways that leave its meaning far from clear, making it
an equivalent of both directives and evaluations, often without awareness
of the differences between such meanings and those we have pointed out
above. What also remains unclear is the boundary between understanding
the meaning of a model of behaviour as a proposition (see the descriptive
versions) and as "an idea of a topic" (of behaviour).

Some authors represent the viewpoint that the meaning of a directive
(norm) can be expressed with a formula consisting of the directive operator
'd' (let us for now skip the question of the number and type of directive operators) and a presentation of the "topic". That is as if someone was showing
a picture of a certain behaviour and saying "This is how it should be" ("This
is obligatory"). This is the view adopted by Wróblewski, who defines the
meaning of a norm as "a model of adequate behaviour".[204] Ross, on the other
hand, defines a directive (or directive meaning) as "an idea of a topic" (of
behaviour), understood as a model of behaviour.[205] Here the "model of behaviour" is defined directively as equivalent to the expression "understood
as real" ("happening at the moment"). These definitions do not resolve the
difficulties connected with the operator of duty. It seems that applying the
concept of a "model of behaviour" to the analysis of directive meaning is of
secondary importance in that it only makes it possible to point out the par-

---

[203] Studnicki [1961].
[204] Wróblewski [1964: 262 *et seq.*].
[205] Ross [1968: §9].

ticular features of the given topic (behaviour, activity). All in all, applying this term to the semantic analysis of directives is not advisable, as it presents more drawbacks than benefits: the advantage it gives is actually quite small in comparison to the difficulties caused by the ambiguity of its meaning. Even when we disambiguate it, it is difficult to see how it could become a component of the definition of "directive meaning".

Even more issues arise in connection with the formulas Ross adopts for directives (directive meaning) and logical propositions. The directive formula is '$d(T)$', where the directive operator 'd' is combined with the idea of a topic T; the formula for logical propositions is '$i(T)$' where the existential operator 'i' is combined with "the idea of a topic". The concerns are mainly about the logico-semantic status of the "idea of a topic" and the legitimacy of such a way of analysing directives and logical propositions. [...]

Out of the attempts focusing on extension, the conception of Aleksander Peczenik needs to be mentioned. This author attempts to create an analogue of extensions of sentences in the logical sense for directives (norms). Looking into the relations between language and reality, he treats logical propositions as qualified depending on the extralinguistic reality (as true or false), and norms as statements actually qualifying this reality. He writes that a semantic analysis of norms is possible, "because the relation of norms to reality, even though "turned" in the opposite direction, is as well defined as the relation of propositions to reality".[206] It seems that what we are dealing with here is a certain simplification of the relationship between language and reality (as the model of language). More importantly, however, qualifying reality (activities, behaviour) is equivalent to understanding behaviour as dictated (prohibited or allowed), which is a tautology. "Qualifying" is thus basically equivalent to intension as an immanent property of the content of the norm, a property independent of the relation between the norm and reality.[207]

Another of the extensional approaches to directive meaning is the conception of Franciszek Studnicki. His point of departure is the view that the

---

[206] Peczenik [1965: 50 *et seq.*]. See also Peczenik [1968: 117 *et seq.*].
[207] See Woleński [1966: 12 *et seq.*].

language of normative statements is richer than the language of descriptive statements. This is because the model of the language of normative statements includes normative states of affairs as its objects. This author introduces the idea of linguistic statements being "fulfilled" by states of affairs. The relation of truthfulness (or falsity) is a special case of being fulfilled. He writes that "only normative states of affairs can be the fulfilling (unfulfilling) states of affairs for normative statements".[208] Not getting into the particulars we can still say that, first of all, the problems with the ontological status of "normative states of affairs" are no lesser than with the "objective duty" found in more traditional views. And second of all, that the conception of "being fulfilled" can be reduced to a tautology, since it does not actually go beyond the intension (or rather, quasi-intension) of the norm, and it does this in a way similar to Peczenik's conception, as discussed above.

Carl Wellman took up a detailed analysis of "directive meaning" as compared to "descriptive meaning", as well as to other specific types of meaning. He stresses the descriptive components of directive meaning, but he finds the "dictate-prohibition" dimension to be most characteristic for this type of meaning, acknowledging, at the same time, the difficulties connected with the operator of duty. It must be added that Wellman places obligational propositions (mainly) within the so-called "critical meaning", which seems to produce results which run contradictory to our intuitions concerning directives (norms) and their meaning. After all, this approach erases what our intuitions tell us to be a distinctive feature of directive (normative) meaning.[209] This issue would in fact require further discussion.

5.3. The third view is that directives have no meaning. It is a well--known fact that this view was first formulated by representatives of logical empiricism in the early stages of its development, and that it was applied not only to directives (and norms among them), but also to evaluations. Directive and evaluating statements were thought to be «pure emotives», expressions of psychological experiences of the non-cognitive type.

---

[208] Studnicki [1968: 27 *et seq.*].
[209] Wellman [1961: chs. IX and X].

The main charge against this view boils down to the fact that it is based on a rather one-sided understanding of language and its function, and on a very narrow theory of meaning; that it basically does not take into account the role played within communication processes by statements other than those with a cognitive meaning, focusing only on the creation of a «pure» language of science.[210] In our view, these objections to the negative thesis of logical empiricism are too strong. On the one hand, analysing directives from the point of view of the model of cognitive meaning yields negative results, and on the other hand the attempts at constructing a broader theory of meaning, one that would make it possible to define different kinds of meaning (including directive) on a unified basis, have not been successful.

6. As presented above (§5), we seem to be dealing either with outright negation of directive meaning or with unsuccessful attempts at defining it, their failure only confirming the negation. But this raises the following objection: directives are, after all, meaningful expressions, quite different from what we call semantic nonsense. Within a specific social group, directives are understood in a certain typical and uniform way, because they do have some sense that is objective, not limited to the given subjective situation of having a mental experience, expressing it, and possibly influencing the addressee – the receiver of the directive. As in the case of legal norms, directives are often transmitted broadly and received with a neutral or quasi-cognitive attitude, rather than an emotional one. In this way directives are just as effective as a means of communication as statements clearly possessing cognitive meaning. The above statements partly touch upon the problems of pragmatics (functionality of directives as effective communication tools), but in other respects they concern issues more semantic in nature (objective sense of directives, the fact that they are typically and uniformly understood, which is exactly what makes them effective tools for communication.)

Overall, it does not seem justified to limit the discussion of directives to pragmatics only. This kind of restriction was typical for a number of views remaining under the influence of early logical empiricism. Basing

---

[210] See Brown *et al.* [1959: 121]; Alston [1964: 73 *et seg.*]; Wellman [1961: 16, 93 *et seq.*].

one's views on the theory of "pure emotives", one could not speak of any sort of meaning in connection with directives, but one could consider their pragmatic functions. Firstly, these functions could be discussed in their individual immediacy, as bound to specific expressions of mental experiences and their effects on the receivers. But secondly, they could be understood as conventional, and hence reducible to certain types, and this because of certain shared qualities of the mental experiences of the persons giving directives, and because of the commonality of the linguistic means for expressing those experiences, and of the reactions of the receivers. This does not explain, however, what properties of directives enable them to perform these functions, *i.e.*, to influence behaviour, to spur into activity, *etc.* Neither does it explain the basis for the uniform understanding of directives, a problem which emerges most clearly when dealing with "neutral" uses and understanding of directives (*e.g.* when a student is studying law for an exam).

7. At this point we should return to the question of intension. Directive meaning does seem to be a certain proposition, something «objective»; this objectivity comes across in the typical, uniform understanding of a directive within a given group. This view coincides with mentalistic theories of meaning, and even more with the behaviouristic theories formulated later, which take a more liberal stand when it comes to accepting the category of non-cognitive meaning. Let us focus here on just one version of the mentalistic theory, one which gives us roughly the following definition of meaning: "The linguistic meaning of expressions of the form W in language J is a type of thought T, where for two people speaking language J to use a W-expression without misunderstanding, it is necessary and sufficient for them to associate this expression with psychological meanings belonging to thoughts of type T".[211] At first it might seem that applying this or a similar definition to directive meaning is quite promising. But what remains enigmatic in the case of directives is the question of "type of thought", as well as of "understanding". The author of the above definition immediately applies relevant restrictions, important on account of those «questionable» types of thought, thus limiting meaning extensionally, to those expressions which comply

[211] Ajdukiewicz [1931: 44].

with the directives of sense formulated by him: axiomatic, deductive, or empirical; these directives settle the conditions for regarding expressions as true or false.[212] These conditions are not fulfilled by directives; they are fulfilled only by logical propositions.

These directives of sense for statements are formulated only for that part of colloquial language which consists in descriptive discourse and can be reconstructed in order to build a proper language of science. They do not take into account any other part of colloquial language, including directive discourse. But if the expressions of such discourse are meaningful, it seems that colloquial language must have also other directives of sense, apart from those for descriptive discourse. These directives are yet to be identified and specified.

8. Overall, the following can be said about directives: (a) their constituent parts include, on the one hand, expressions representing certain cognitive content (in our example, the depictions of Peter, the door, their closing,) and on the other hand, expressions that function as directive (normative) operators; (b) the combination of cognitive elements and directive (normative) elements does yield meaningful statements, corresponding to certain unidentified rules of sense of colloquial language – rules different from the directives of sense for propositions; (c) in directives we also come across some names created by combining cognitive (empirical) elements with directive (normative) ones, such as "judge", "normative act", or "limited liability company". Such names should be treated as the short forms of relevant directives (norms,) which define the directive (normative) qualifications of certain persons, teams of persons, acts, objects, *etc.*[213] Thus, what has been said in (b) applies to them; (d) directives have no intension, understood as a proposition that something is currently taking place. However, the thought expressed by a directive that something should take place does seem to be, analogically to an intension, an objective type of thought. As a linguistic expression, a directive is understood in a given social group in a typical, uniform manner. The experience of communication processes makes this statement self-evident, if not banal.

---

[212] Ajdukiewicz [1934].
[213] Compare Wróblewski [1959: 23 *et seq.*].

The nature of this understanding, however, is not so evident: people "understand" directives "perfectly", yet they cannot explain what it means that something should be, or the meaning of such terms as "obligation", "entitlement", *etc.* The same is also true of scholars, who in discussing these issues often invoke St. Augustine's "*Si rogas nescio, si non rogas scio*".[214] Here the explication (definition in the case of directive names, analysis in the case of directives) could consist in either replacing such expressions with expressions clearly possessing a cognitive meaning, or replacing them with directives whose meaning has already been explicated.[215] Since we do not have the latter, the former would seem the only way to go. Yet the arbitrary replacement of directive expressions with cognitive expressions must be excluded, since in light of linguistic intuition they are not suitable for explicating directives; (e) if we look at directives from the point of view of pragmatics, then there is no doubt that their basic function is influencing behaviour.

9. In discussing directive meaning we face two alternatives, and neither one of them seems to be satisfactory. The first consists in treating directives as logical propositions. If we apply this view consistently, we gain both an intension and an extension, but «duty» gets lost. The second consists in treating directives as statements *sui generis* – as "sentences of duty" in which «duty» is a primitive, irreducible term (and other directive terms are defined using it). A lot of the analytical discussions of directives (norms) accept this view, which, after all, is not quite satisfactory at the philosophical level. First of all, an ontological problem arises immediately: in our language we come across expressions which have no counterpart in the model of the language of descriptive statements. A «richer» language suggests a «richer» model, one that would include ideal objects of duty. And second of all, an epistemological problem arises as well: what type of thought corresponds to expressions of duty and how is duty recognized and understood? This often leads to accepting a kind of intuitive cognition when it comes to duty.

---

[214] See, *e.g.*, Baumgartner [1922: 642].
[215] See footnote 198 and Beth [1962: 64].

In both of the above cases we are dealing with a common tendency to understand duty cognitively, which can only be achieved through the extra-linguistic reality relation, or by accepting that duty has both a regular in-tension and an extension in relation to empirical reality, or by constructing a certain super-empirical reality only for «duty», which would allow it to fulfil the intension and extension conditions.

10. It seems that defining directive meaning from the point of view of the relation between language and reality (as something external, or «extra-linguistic». to which language refers), although highly tempting, is faulty. It is not the proper solution to artificially create a world for the sake of di-rective (normative) language, a world which would provide a model for that language by encompassing ideal objects or states of affairs. On the other hand, it is equally impossible for «duty» to correspond to objects and states of affairs of the real, empirical world. Generally speaking, one could say that directives are, in a sense, "auto-extensional" and "auto-intensional". These statements are not «reproductive» the way that statements with cognitive meaning are, *i.e.*, they are not groups of linguistic signs referring to some-thing external to themselves, but rather they are «productive» statements, which themselves create something through their meaning. The existence of statements with cognitive meaning comes down to linguistic signs taken together with the meaning ascribed to them; the existence of directives, on the other hand, comes down to signs whose meaning creates certain verbal objects – acts. In this sense we can say that directives are objects «independ-ent» of extra-linguistic reality.[216]

In other words, we can assume that directives connote and denote themselves. To put it succinctly, they mean what they are. Their «inten-sion» and «extension» are a unity. We are forced to simplify if we want to characterize this «intension» as linguistic meaning, understood as a typ-ical, uniform use of directives (and as a typical linguistic reaction to them),[217] and the «extension» as the self-denotation of standards of behav-iour created by the linguistic meaning of the statements under discussion.

---

[216] In connection with this see M. Black on "rules" [1958: esp. 98 *et seq.*].
[217] See: Quine [1960: ch. II].

This is our view of the semantic problem of the relation between language and reality in this case. [...]

11. As an act, a directive is a conventionalized verbal act capable of influencing human behaviour. Accordingly, from the point of view of linguistic pragmatics the main function of directives is the function of influencing. Directives do also have an informative function, which is crucial for their ability to influence behaviour. Let us add in passing that, analogically, statements whose main function is the informative function can also, to a certain extent, have the secondary function of influencing.[218] This function of influencing is fulfilled by directives thanks to the fact that they are «understood» – in the sense that people have certain typical, learnt ways of creating and reacting to directives.[219]

12. Independently of what has been said above about the semantic problem of the relation between language and reality, in the case of directives we should try and explain the fact that they do seem to somehow refer to the outer, extra-linguistic reality, thus also seeming to predicate something on it. Considering the fact that statements are distinguished depending on the mental experiences they express (have a tendency to express), we believe that the explanation needs to be sought at the level of psychology. For our aims let us adopt a general division into statements expressing cognitive experiences and those expressing non-cognitive ones.[220] Cognitive experiences are expressed through the describing of objects (states of affairs). Non-cognitive experiences are expressed by being «projected» onto external objects (states of affairs) through the use of directive (normative, but also other, *e.g.*, evaluating) expressions. Petrażycki called such expressions, devoid of cognitive meaning, "projected (or ideological) creations", or else "emotional phantasms".[221] Despite the diffi-

---

[218] However, it needs to be highlighted that the informative function of directives is a constant, while statements with cognitive meaning only sometimes fulfil an influencing function in certain specific situations.

[219] See: Black [1958: 121 *et seq.*].

[220] This distinction seems clearer than the one introduced by Stevenson [1963: ch. I] between "statements of conviction" and "statements of attitude".

[221] Petrażycki [1907a: I, 23 *et seq.*]. It would be interesting to compare these views with the theory formulated by Sören Halldén [1954: 41 *et seq.*].

culties in differentiating between the mental experiences that come into play here, it seems that when it comes to directives, we are mainly dealing with "projected creations" based on experiences of the volitional kind. These types of expressions get objectivized through experience and social adjustment, and in the end come to be thought of as having cognitive content. In some fields they become schematic, conventional means of influencing behaviour. And in this way, their uses also become quite diverse – form purely expressive ones to ones coming close to a large scale social control technique (*e.g.* law).

13. Directive meaning and the many complex issues connected with it do require further research. We believe that this research should branch out mainly in the following directions: (a) the direction pointed out by ordinary language philosophy – chiefly by J.L. Austin – where the issue of directive ways of using language is concerned; (b) the psychological direction delineated by the emotive theory; (c) the direction of logical analysis of directives from the point of view of modal models («possible worlds» models), A certain amount of hesitation has appeared when it comes to point (b), the psychological direction, and it might not be entirely unfounded – should we enter on this path if it does not have a solid foundation and is always burdened with inaccuracies? Despite such concerns, this type of investigation does look promising if we judge by the attempts of Petrażycki, Stevenson, or the Uppsala school led by Hägerström.

Zygmunt Ziembiński. Presuppositions of norms
[1977: 127, 129–133, 140]

Disputes, mostly of a verbal kind, as to whether normative utterances can be ascribed the logical value of truth or falsehood, often arise from the fact that the question of the logical value of a norm is identified with the question of the logical value of utterances expressing certain assumptions of the person settling a certain norm. Speaking of a person settling a norm, we mean a person who formulates a normative utterance «in earnest», thus demanding specific behaviour on the part of the addressee of the norm. At some point both K. Ajdukiewicz and J. Giedymin reflected on the assumptions of an utterance which demands specific behaviour.[222] Namely, they were interested in assumptions connected with the formulation of interrogative utterances, and interrogative utterances can be considered as a specific kind of normative utterances, that is, utterances which express, or at least can be used to express in a given language, a demand for specific verbal behaviour. [...]

If [...] interrogative sentences "can be used to communicate to others certain messages", they do not do so as utterances which are indicators of certain states of affairs which they describe. When a person who we perceive to be behaving rationally formulates a question, we treat this only as a sign of the fact that the person who poses the question believes, or is convinced of something.[223] [...]

It seems that the conceptions concerning the assumptions of interrogative utterances can be generalized for all kinds of utterances of directive or normative character, and also related to norms in the fundamental meaning of this term. A norm of behaviour as such, which is an utterance which dictates or prohibits specific behaviour to given subjects, or at least it is possible to use it in a given language to directly dictate or prohibit specific behaviour to given subjects through it, is not an utterance which describes reality. Since it does not describe reality, it cannot describe it truly or falsely.

The fact of settling a given norm in specific circumstances can be treated as a sign or symptom of the codifier's specific knowledge as well as a specific system of his preferences, provided that we are dealing with a rational codifier (which is usually presumed in case of the lack of grounds for assuming the opposite thesis). One may draw a conclusion on the state of reality from the fact that someone settled a given norm of behaviour, assuming the usually enthymematic premises, namely, that the act of settling a norm was a rational action on the grounds of the codifier's knowledge and preferences and that the knowledge he possesses is adequate in relation to reality. Naturally, drawing such conclusions may at times be risky, if only because of the poor justification of the enthymematic premises mentioned.

---

[222] Especially Ajdukiewicz [1965: part I, ch. VI, §30]; Giedymin [1964: part I].
[223] Ziembiński [1956: 130–131].

Leaving aside the assumptions of evaluating character, one may pose the question of what kind of knowledge can be ascribed to the codifier who is considered to be rational. It seems one ought to enumerate a couple types of assumptions which correspond to various fragments of the codifier's knowledge. Those would be assumptions connected to: (1) the codifier's logical knowledge, or more generally: logical and semiotic knowledge; (2) knowledge on the external systems of elements of the world, different from the person of the addressee of the norm; (3) knowledge on the personality of the addressees of the norms and the factors which influence the choices of the manner of behaviour.[224] Besides, the significance of these assumptions and their function in social practice might differ. [...]

Detecting the assumptions of the first kind is an essential matter in view of two practical issues.

Firstly, let us consider those assumptions in view of driving to eliminate from a given system of settled norms the norms which dictate acts whose characteristic would be formulated as internally contradictory sentences, or norms which would be logically incompatible with each other (contradictory or opposite).

Secondly, let us consider those assumptions in view of the conception of constructing a system of norms which makes us assume that if a codifier settled a norm N, then *ipso facto* he settled all the norms which should be recognized as consequences of the norm N on the basis of some clearly formulated, or only intuitively assumed, logic of norms. [...]

The most easily noticeable kind of assumptions which are connected to normative utterances formulated «in earnest», utterances through which a given norm of behaviour is settled, are assumptions as to the structure of the world and relationships between some behaviour of the addressee of the norm and relevant changes in the world (where, following G.H. von Wright, a "change" can also be considered as the preservation of the state of the world, which would undergo change within a given fragment in case of the lack of interference from a given subject).[225]

---

[224] See Nowak [1968a: 76–78]. This conception was modified in the author's later works.
[225] Wright [1963a: 29, 57].

Norms are probably more frequently formulated in such a way that they order to cause a given state of affairs through given behaviour (activity or negligence), rather than in such a way that they dictate to execute or refrain from executing given actions (movements).

If the latter, simpler case occurs, then the assumption of formulating a normative utterance is at least the fact that the addressee or addressees of the norm who the codifier addresses are able to perform specific movements in a given structure of the world.[226] [...]

Another kind of factual assumptions are assumptions as to the existence of the suitable subject for the activity, the material which is used to procure the product, or an object which is to be transformed. "Close the window if it rains!" is a norm in the form of an imperative, whose scope of use is clearly defined by the codifier and it refers to the future cases of rain occurring, but the factual element which determines the scope of use of the norm is also the fact that the window is open at that time, since it is impossible to close a closed window. If someone dictates: "Close the window now!" it signif–– that he is convinced the window is open, and if we assume that he is not mistaken, it also signifies that the window is open. "Boil the water!" is a dictate based on the assumption that an appropriate amount of water is available, that the water can be boiled with the help of means which are available and familiar to the addressee of the norm, and moreover, that the needed amount is not boiling at the moment. [...]

An equally significant issue from the point of view of social practice is the codifier's set of assumptions concerning the very person of the addressee of the settled norms, the nature of his reactions to the settled norms, and the possibilities of choosing specific behaviour. [...]

Without delving into these issues, we shall note that whoever addresses another person with a dictate or a prohibition of given behaviour he clearly assumes that he can influence the addressee's behaviour by settling a norm for him. [...]

Apart from the assumption that the addressee of the norm is able to choose the manner of behaviour in a given situation, which is connected in-

---

[226] Wright [1963a: 198 *et seq.*]; the author expands on other aspects of the problem.

directly to a series of previously discussed assumptions as to the real possibility of undertaking a given action by the addressee (lack of obstacles, appropriate physical strength, appropriate state of the material, *etc.*), further, often controversial questions come to mind, concerning the nature of the addressee's reaction to the fact of settling a norm for that addressee.

If the codifier settles a norm of behaviour for a given subject, then it is usually a certain sign that the settled norm of behaviour will cause the addressee's relevant behaviour in a great enough number of cases from the point of view of the codifier. The fact that someone settles a norm of behaviour for somebody is a sign (however unsure) that he has power over the addressee of the norm or at least that the codifier thinks (often mistakenly) that he has power over the addressee of the norm. […]

Indeed, one may earnestly discuss the true or false assumption of a normative utterance only when one considers a given utterance to be a norm settled by a subject acting upon specific knowledge and a system of preferences. When a poet says to his lover: "Extinguish all the stars in the sky!" [Polish "Zgaś teraz wszystkie gwiazdy na niebie!"] one may not decide on the true or false assumption of this norm, since its formulation is not linked with the actual state of the poetic «codifier's» knowledge. The utterance has a set normative meaning in Polish; its verbal form is suited to be a demand to extinguish all the stars in the sky, but in fact the «codifier» does not demand such an absurdity, but only pretends to demand it in the poetic game of the world where one can extinguish the stars in the sky as if they were candles in a Christmas tree. […]

This leads to the idea of the necessity to differentiate between objectively appropriate and inappropriate norms […] as well as norms which are only subjectively appropriate or ineffective based on the knowledge of the individual resolving the question. […] A norm may be objectively appropriate, all of its assumptions may be true, but subjectively it is inappropriate from the point of view of the person who regards some assumption as false. […]

One should also devote some space to evaluating assumptions which can usually be reasonably ascribed to the codifier. It is generally presumed that norms have some axiological justification in the codifier's evaluations, which are arranged into some sort of a system of preferences, naturally an imprecisely outlined one.

This sort of assumptions, besides factual assumptions, plays an important role in the legal exegesis of the content of laws, where – in the case of doubt as to the normative meaning of certain fragments of a legal text – such a meaning is ascribed to them that the norm of behaviour recreated on the basis of the text has the strongest axiological justification on the grounds of evaluations (and naturally: knowledge) ascribed to the codifier.

Eugeniusz Grodziński. Imperatives and performatives
[1980: 158, 175–177]

The communicative function of speech has an informative-reporting aspect. This means that thoughts which we communicate to other people through speech are always thoughts on something, on some objects of thought. Therefore, when we communicate our thoughts to other people, we thus inform them about these objects, or we report on the objects to them. The communicative function of speech can therefore be described also as an informative-reporting function, with the reservation that imperative and interrogative sentences also perform the function of reporting thoughts, although speaking of the informative-reporting function in relation to them does not seem suitable (unless we accept the fact that by asking a question we inform of our wish to obtain an answer to the question, and by ordering we inform about our wish to have the order executed). […]

Let us ask two significant questions for our topic: Can imperative and interrogative sentences perform the role of performative utterances? What is the relationship of these utterances to normative sentences?

The first question should be answered as follows: Imperative sentences, as well as interrogative sentences, can perform the role of performative utterances if, within a given system of these utterances, issuing an order entails the duty to execute it, whereas asking a question entails the obligation to give an answer to it, where failing to execute the order or failing to provide an answer to the question causes certain sanctions for the guilty party.

There are plenty of examples to illustrate and confirm this general thesis. The Military Code of Law in various countries provides various slight and severe penalties for soldiers who do not execute their superiors' orders. Codes of criminal and civil procedure provide penalties for witnesses who refuse to answer the questions of the judge without justified reasons. Fiscal codes of law provide penalties for people who refrain from answering the questions of the tax authorities concerning these people's revenue.

Yet, we can go beyond the framework set by these examples and ask if, for instance, parents' orders issued at their children in the form of imperative sentences in everyday life are performative utterances or not. Surely, they are not performative utterances of legal significance since no law provides for judging or punishing children who do not execute their parents' standard orders. However, are they not performative utterances of quasi-legal significance?

Performative utterances of quasi-legal significance is the name given to utterances which raise specific, sanctioned obligations for the author of the utterance or for other people, where these utterances derive their power from customary law in operation in a given environment to which the author of the utterance belongs. As for commissions given to children by their parents, the environment which usually accepts children's obligation to execute parents' orders is in this case the whole society (although if we speak of very small children, it is hard to speak of obligations at all).

Yet, there is some doubt in the case of sanctions, since probably none of the contemporary civilized societies agree unequivocally in the question of what sanctions should be applied to children who are disobedient or not always obedient to their parents, and whether to apply sanctions at all. Under these conditions the question of whether parents' orders issued at children are or are not performative utterances can be considered controversial. Let us add that we are not advocates of excessive expansion of the term PERFORMATIVE UTTERANCES, since we consider it purposeful to contrast these utterances very expressly with utterances which are not of a performative character.

However, there is no doubt that a commission issued in regular circumstances, for instance, by a friend to a friend (Bring me cigarettes!), is not a performative utterance of legal or quasi-legal significance. This is because neither state nor environmental regulations exist (perhaps with the exception of some environments with specific subculture) such that they impose an obligation of executing it on the person who received such a commission, under threat of sanctions prescribed in these laws.

Let us also add in the purely linguistic aspect that both imperative sentences and interrogative sentences can be replaced with declarative ones, and therefore, instead of "Drop your weapons!" – "I order you to drop your weapons", and instead of "What time is it?" – "I am asking you what time it is". The verbs "[I] order" and "[I] ask" belong to the group which Austin called explicit performatives.

The second question we have posed concerns the relationship between performative utterances and normative sentences. It will be easy to answer the question, especially when we take into consideration what concerns imperative and interrogative sentences in the same aspect. Naturally, performative utterances can be formulated as normative sentences. Rules and regulations of administrative law often assume such a form, for instance: "People who come to the city should fulfil the obligation to register" or "Caretakers should keep the yards and staircases clean". We often come across the term "I am obliged" (or in the third person: "He is obliged") in agreements, whose term is of normative character.

However, definitely not all normative sentences (just like not all imperative or interrogative sentences) are performative utterances. On the contrary, most of them are not of a performative character. When John says to Peter: "You should give me back the money you borrowed", it is not a performative utterance as it does not create any new rights or obligations, neither for John nor for Peter. Admittedly, John can demand the return of the debt from Peter, even in court, but this right (and Peter's obligation corresponding to this right) arose on the basis of the loan agreement they drew up rather than the quoted statement made by John.

Can we regard the sentence: "You should give me back the money you borrowed" as an informative utterance? It seems so. The utterance is supposed to be a reminder, and a reminder is also information in a broadened sense.

Even more so, John's utterance: "I should go to the doctor" is not a performative utterance of legal or quasi-legal significance. By saying so, John states the fact of his illness and the need to be cured but he does not impose on himself any obligations whose fulfilment could be executed by the state on the basis of the national *Code of Law*, or by some social group John belongs to – on the basis of customary law.

Jan Woleński. Adequacy of the logic of norms
[1980b: 60 – 64, 68 – 70, 89 – 97]

The issue of the logic of norms is best exemplified by the following line of argument, called Jørgensen's dilemma:

(1) according to the generally accepted meta-logical standards, only sentences in the logical sense are premises and conclusions of logical inferences;

(2) norms are not sentences in the logical sense;

(3) norms cannot appear as premises and conclusions in logical inferences;

(4) yet, there are examples of reasoning which cannot be denied intuitive validity, where norms appear as premises and conclusions, for instance: If you should tell the truth, then you must not tell lies.[227]

The dilemma, which has all the features of a «riddle» in Russell's meaning, consists in a conflict between thesis (3) which entails from (1), as well as thesis (2) and thesis (4). The latter contains in its formulation a provoking expression, "intuitive validity". It is difficult to avoid in this context, as in view of (1) and (2), the correctness of the reasoning whose inferential links are norms can be evaluated only from the intuitive point of view. Still, one may attempt to justify theoretically the bindingness of these normative inferences. Thus Jørgensen's dilemma leads to the problem of the logic of norms which has been widely discussed for over forty years, as the need arises to eliminate "intuitive validity" from (4) and to replace it with a more solid fundament.

Various ways to solve Jørgensen's dilemma present themselves here. The easiest one consists in questioning (2). Noticeably, the dilemma fails if

---

[227] Jørgensen [1937–1938].

the norms are true, *resp.* false. Rejecting (2) eradicates the whole problem, and the correctness of intriguing inferences can be evaluated with classic meta-logical criteria. The only question still left to be solved is the choice of relevant logical formalism – adequate to the normative sentence structures. This is no place to discuss the eternal problem of the truthfulness of norms.[228] Let me add just a few remarks. The notion of the propositional (propositional in the logical sense, not only grammatical) character of norms can be justified twofold. Firstly, one may present general arguments in the spirit of ethical realism or objectivism, arguments which are philosophical justification of that same view on the logic of norms.[229] Secondly, one may argue for the propositional character of norms, regardless of any philosophical assumptions, through an attempt to demonstrate that standard constructions of semantics of propositions in the logical sense also apply to norms. Let me add here for the sake of clarification that we are concerned with the so called proper norms, that is, utterances of the type: "It should be so and so" and not utterances of the type: "It should be so on so in view of the normative system *n*", since there is no serious doubt as to the truthfulness of the latter.[230] In both cases the effect is the same – complete implementation of applicability of the logic of sentences for normative reasoning.

Thus, Jørgensen's dilemma is an interesting issue and remains valid only if thesis (2) is accepted, which is equivalent to accepting the non-cognitive concept of norms. Further considerations will be conducted based on the assumption of the truthfulness of (2). This assumption implies the following significant consequence – norms are *sui generis* linguistic utterances whose properties are not reducible to the semantic properties of sentences in the logical sense; the category of norms is a discrete semantic category. This fact is of primary importance for any attempt to construct norms, since it prevents direct application of logic superstructured over semantics of truthfulness to normative reasoning. As a result, one needs to make the following remark of terminological nature. It concerns the relationship be-

---

[228] See Naess [1959]; Ossowska [1947]; Fritzhand [1966].
[229] Prior stresses the necessity of such argumentation for the truthfulness of norms [1971: 71].
[230] Kanger [1957]; Åquist [1973]; Wróblewski [1978].

tween the logic of norms and deontic logic. One may encounter the standpoint where the two terms: "the logic of norms" and "deontic logic" mean the same thing. Yet, this standpoint is wrong, at least from the non-cognitive point of view. Deontic sentences are true or false sentences and the so called deontic operators "it is dictated (prohibited, permitted) that…" are logical connectives with one argument, and they form sentences together with their arguments. On the other hand, the non-cognitive, norm-creating operators "it should (should not) be that…" form norms together with their arguments, and therefore expressions which belong to a different semantic category than sentences.[231] Therefore, deontic logic and the logic of norms can only be regarded as identical from the point of view of cognitivism. Still, it is sometimes the case that this thesis is also assumed by followers of non--cognitivism. As a terminological convention, such linguistic *usus* may not be of utmost importance, but at times it contributes to interpretative confusion. Therefore, from now on I will only discuss such constructions of the logic of norms which do not identify it with deontic logic.

Since we assumed the truthfulness of (2), the only possible solution of Jørgensen's dilemma seems to be questioning (1), or to be more precise, such generalization of meta-logic that the relationship of logical entailment can be reasonably defined on the set of norms. This is the idea behind the constructive trend in the logic of norms, as opposed to the nihilist trend, which accepts (1) and at the same time denies the possibility of the theoretical settlement of the logic of norms. I aim to prove that although there are solid grounds for nihilism towards the logic of norms, there is still a possibility to solve Jørgensen's dilemma in a manner completely independent from the logic of norms. In the above remarks, the term "logic of norms" denotes a specific division of formal logic. However, we ought to note that there is another conception of logic of normative utterances which is based on the idea of informal logic.[232] It occurs in two forms: informal logic of colloquial language in the spirit of […] Oxford philosophy, and Perelman's

---

[231] Here arises the problem of the character of utterances containing an operator of permission: this question will come up again in the present work.

[232] See Gregorowicz [1967]; Horovitz [1972]; Woleński [1978].

rhetoric. I shall not discuss the former version, as the essence of the logic of norms, treated as all relationships between the uses of normative utterances, seems fairly obvious on the basis of the remarks we had made. Yet, according to rhetorical logic, it is not the correctness of reasoning (correctness in the logical sense) that is evaluated but rather its effectiveness in the sense of persuasion. The aim of normative reasoning performed by judges, prosecutors, lawyers or any other people is to induce the opponent to accept a certain view and accordingly, the rationality of the argumentation cannot be evaluated from the theoretical point of view. It is easy to see that conceptions of informal logic eliminate Jørgensen's dilemma, since they provide justification for (4), independently of (1). Semiotic relationships as explained in the logic of informal language and praxeological aims of rhetoric argumentation guarantee (or not) the mentioned "intuitive validity" of reasoning whose links are norms.

Yet, Jørgensen himself, as well as most of those who later dealt with the logic of norms, meant to regard it as a part of formal logic, and therefore, a formal system which meets standard meta-logical expectations. These expectations are divided into the syntactic and semantic. Each system of formal logic has to be correct from the syntactic point of view, that is, it has to possess a precisely defined language (through a set of basic symbols and the rules of constructing complex formulas from basic symbols); it also has to be based on a specific set of axioms and inferential rules or solely on a set of inferential rules if it is constructed with the method of natural deduction. Early systems of the logic of norms were discussed mainly as syntactic entities, although in most cases the syntax was not precisely defined. The interpretation of such systems was considered to exemplify formalism through replacing the variables with utterances from legal or ethical language. It was not semantic interpretation in the contemporary understanding; even if we disregard the doubts which may arise in connection with Ajdukiewicz's remarks on the fact that replacing the variables in logical formulas with sentences taken from colloquial language is improper. A proper semantic interpretation consists in determining a model for a given formal system, which enables us to define the notion of tautology (that is, a statement in the semantic sense) and to compare the set of the logical consequences of axioms (that is, a set of statements in the syntactic sense) with the set of tautologies. The relationship between these two sets is crucial, since it concerns the issue of the completeness of formal systems – a formal system is deemed complete if and only if a set of statements in the semantic sense is identical with a set of statements in the syntactic sense.[233] Thus semantic interpretation enables us to solve, or at least pose the problem of completeness, and therefore constitutes a sort of criterion to evaluate the correctness of choosing this or that logical formalism.

Yet, such a meta-logical criterion of evaluation of a logical system is insufficient in view of the applications of logic, especially extra-mathematical applications.[234] Here arises a problem which may be called the issue of the pragmatic adequacy of calculus and its interpretation in relation to a given language whose formal representation is a given logic. It especially concerns logical systems which are constructed as intended formalizations of certain fragments of colloquial language, such as modal, temporal, assertive, normative discourse, *etc.*[235] Unfortunately, pragmatic adequacy is not something which can be defined clearly and precisely, and it requires referring to certain intuitions, which is connected to the fact that pragmatic adequacy concerns paraphrases of a logical system.

The logic of norms is undoubtedly one of the kinds of logic where the notion of adequacy is particularly significant. I propose the following condition which regulates the pragmatic adequacy of the logic of norms:

(CPA) The logic of norms is pragmatically adequate if and only if it formalizes a normative discourse which includes utterances containing operators of dictate, prohibition and permission. […]

Are we doomed to referring to vague justifications such as "intuitive obviousness" in the analysis of these [*scil.* normative] inferences? I do not believe so, but we are if we assume that deontic sentences, rather than norms, occur in these troublesome inferences. We are concerned with the semantic

---

[233] More precisely, the issue is the inclusion of a set of tautologies in a set of statements in the syntactic sense – the opposite inclusion is trivial.

[234] See Fraassen [1971: 2–3].

[235] Speaking of "fragments of natural language", I also mean fragments which have undergone regulatory manipulations.

characteristic of the language in which normative reasoning is conducted, and therefore: the characteristic of a normative discourse, or more precisely, its normative part, as normative discourse also contains sentences in the logical sense. Three possibilities arise here: (a) only norms are included in the normative discourse; (b) both norms and deontic sentences are included in the normative discourse; (c) exclusively deontic sentences are included in the normative discourse.

It is easy to notice that Jørgensen's dilemma assumes characteristic (a) or (b), and therefore its solution has to refer to characteristic (c). The view that normative discourse consists exclusively of norms is easy to refute, as it leads to the exclusion of utterances with an operator of permission from the discourse. Therefore, what remains is to prove that characteristic (c) is appropriate and should be assumed in place of characteristic (b), which seems to be widely accepted. [...]

I propose to choose another path which can justify characteristic (c). It consists in refuting the linguistic theory of norms, that is, the theory which claims that norms are utterances. Then all issues concerning logic and semantics of norms can be disregarded, as there is an assumption in the "deep structure" of Jørgensen's dilemma which states that norms are linguistic entities. It is worth adding that Jørgensen's dilemma is not the only puzzle in the subject of norms, although it is probably the most renowned one. If we assume that norms are utterances and we consider the statement that norms are obeyed, then we reach the not very intuitive consequence that obeying a norm is obeying an utterance.[236] What I believe is needed is a new conception of norms which manages to overcome this puzzle, that is, a non-linguistic theory.

A definition of a norm as an assignment of the type $\langle x_i, Z_i \rangle$ [where x_i is the act and Z_i is a set of postulated worlds assigned to the act x_i] can be regarded as the proper explication of the notion of a norm. In connection with the proposed explication, I wish to highlight the following two issues. I choose to regard norms as elements of real normalizing processes and therefore I mentioned elements of functions chosen as normalizing func-

[236] Black [1958].

tions in the first definition of a norm. Paraphrasing the presented explication of the notion of a norm in realistic language, one can say that a norm is a decision of a codifier, and the decision can be described formally as a set of pairs of the type $\langle x_i, Z_i \rangle$. A dictate is regarded as an element of the decision of choosing a given category of postulated worlds. I treat the notion of decision as primary, which can be explicated through suitable examples, for instance, taken from legislative practice. It seems more intuitive to explicate the notion of a norm through the notion of a decision than the other way around, for instance, that the codifier made a decision because he uttered a norm in the traditional understanding. Here the decision of the codifier is regarded as «a pragmatic marker» which determines the way language is used. Thus the present considerations can be included in formal pragmatics in Montague's definition.[237]

What is important is that regarding norms as decisions fulfils non-cognitivist intuitions; justifying the choice of a normalizing function does not consist in deducing sentences from the set O [*scil.* dictates] from some logical premises, nor does it consist in testing the sentences empirically. The justification process in question may refer to axiological or ideological reasons, as in the case of traditional non-cognitivist constructions. Normalizing is a sort of activity which appeals to «volition», if you permit me to use this traditional term, which does not mean it is totally voluntaristic, that is, devoid of any rational grounds.

A critic might remark that pairs of the type $\langle x_i, Z_i \rangle$ exist independent of real processes of normalizing. This is an appropriate remark. Such pairs can be called potential norms, and the difference between them and real norms is more or less like the difference between statements which express discovered laws of science and the so called law-like statements, whose differentiation occurs in the methodology of science.[238]

The second remark concerns the issue of the relationship of interpretation *de dicto* and *de re*. In fact, it is reduced to the relationship between the sentence Ox_i and the sentence $O[x_i]$. From the practical point of view, they

---

[237] Montague [1968]; Stalnaker [1972].
[238] Nagel [1961, ch. IV].

express the same idea, especially if one assumes the quite natural interpretation of the sentence Ox_i as the sentence: "The act described in sentence x_i is dictated". Regardless of how deontic sentences *de dicto* are interpreted, using them greatly facilitates purely logical considerations – logic works in the most efficient way on linguistic material. Even if we regard the sentence $O[x_i]$ as a concatenation of two symbols, it is not certain to which syntactic category (if any) the argument of the operator O belongs. This is supported by the fact that reading this sentence literally (that is, according to its syntax) leads to nonsense. "It is dictated that $[x]$" is not a correct expression in the English language, unless it denotes "Act x_i is dictated", which still does not correspond to the syntactic structure of the expression $O[x_i]$. These obstacles are probably possible to overcome somehow, for instance, with the help of a relevant algebra of acts, but a *de re* interpretation is undoubtedly more troublesome from the logical point of view.[239] At the same time, it is more natural – deontic sentences are sentences on acts, not about sentences. The same can be said of interpretations f_n. If 'x_i' in the couple $\langle x_i, Z_i \rangle$ is read as "act described in sentence x", then we almost get a *de re* interpretation, and the presence of the sentence in this couple can be explained with the fact that normalizing consists in communicating certain sentences. But the most intuitive explication of the notion of norm probably consists in recognizing it as a couple of the type $\langle [x_i], Z_i \rangle$, that is, a transformation of an act in the relevant deontic nucleus; naturally we mean a logical transformation, not a factual one, for instance: causal.

Still, regardless of whether we choose an interpretation *de dicto* or *de re*, it is vital to emphasize the fact that in neither of these interpretations are norms linguistic expressions, even in the interpretation *de dicto*. In order to repeal the possible dispute over what a norm is in the interpretation *de dicto*, I am inclined to accept the interpretation *de re* as basic.

This way «Jørgensen's riddle» can be considered solved – the logic of norms is not an obstacle, since norms are not linguistic utterances, and normative reasoning is *de facto* reasoning on deontic sentences and fall into

---

[239] Similar obstacles occur with interpretation of modal sentences about any kind of event or situation; see Suszko [1971: 69].

the schemes of deontic logic. Proponents of the logic of norms may present yet another argument, referring to the fact that normalizing can be contradictory, pleonastic, tautological, *etc.* Therefore, how can one settle such relationships since there is no logic of norms? On the other hand, it is said that the occurrence of deontic sentences in M^r [that is, in the real world], is a derivative of normalizing. Also this argument does not seem to contradict the proposed interpretation. A set of elements which belongs to a given normalizing function can be treated as a kind of algebra; operations on norms can be determined in it and thus, relations such as contradiction, *etc.*, can be formulated. For instance, if we normalize the couples: $\langle x_i, Y_i \rangle$ [*scil.* act x_i and a set of postulated worlds Y_i ascribed to the act x_i through the function of normalizing f], then the normalizing is undoubtedly contradictory. In this sense one can speak of the logic of norms as the algebra of norms – yet, it is not this meaning of the term "logic of norms" which is dealt with in conventional disputes.

Also «Black's riddle» can be solved easily. Since a norm is a decision, then it would be perfectly natural to say that obeying it is obeying a certain decision.

The fact that norms are not utterances does not at all mean that normalizing is not connected with using certain utterances. The choice of the function f is communicated by the codifier through the expression: "I herewith dictate (it is dictated) that…". One can assume that utterances of this type are linguistic correlates of a chosen normalizing function. At the same time, deontic sentences can be interpreted as equivalent, or even synonymous with sentences which describe the value of a normalizing function $f(x_i)$. Such an approach realizes two natural intuitions: the dependence of a deontic sentence on normalizing and the equivalence between Ox_i and $V(x_i, M_i)$ [*scil.* the value of the formula x_i in the possible world M_i] $= 1$, for each M_i, that $M^r R M_i$ [*scil.* M_i is a possible world available in view of the real world M^r). The relationship between "I dictate so and so" and Ox_i (and any other deontic sentence) obviously consists in a presupposition, except it should be noted that the sentence x_i does not have to be contained in "so and so".

The above considerations imply that we recognize that utterances of two kinds are parts of normative discourse: utterances which are correlates of normalizing functions and regular deontic sentences. There is no doubt that the latter are sentences in the logical sense – they describe the effects of normalizing, that is, postulated or anti-postulated worlds. What is at issue here is the interpretation of the sentences of the first type in view of their performative character. This is not the place for a detailed overview of the so called performative utterances.[240] The creator of the theory of imperatives – Austin – denied performative utterances the quality of sentences in the logical sense. The main reason for this is that performative utterances do not describe anything, but they do create certain states of affairs – they are activities with the help of language.[241] The utterance: "I herewith dictate it that so and so" is not a description of normalizing; it is a component of the action of normalizing. Yet, according to Austin and his followers, performative utterances can be "valid" or "invalid" depending on whether the activities with which they are conjugated fulfil certain, for instance procedural, conditions. These arguments do not seem entirely convincing. First of all, a performative utterance fulfils the convention (T). There is nothing unsuitable in assuming that the utterance "I herewith dictate so and so" is true if and only if the person uttering these words dictates so and so. Even if we assume that a characteristic feature of performative utterances is that uttering a given sentence (in the grammatical sense) or a word which is its substitute (for instance, the word "yes" during a wedding ceremony) is a necessary condition of the validity of a given action, then it is not an argument against the fact that performative utterances fulfil the convention (T). One could raise the argument against it which consists in indicating that the fulfilment of the convention (T) by a performative utterance is based only on the fact that the utterance has the grammatical structure of a declarative sentence, which is not a real logical structure; the superficial and deep structures of language are confused here. A justification of the above argument could be that the convention (T), if used according to grammatical criteria,

---

[240] See Opałek [1974: ch. VI]; Daniellson [1973]; Andersson [1975].
[241] See Austin; the creative character of performatives is well illustrated in some Polish terminological suggestions: "productive utterances" ("wypowiedzi produktywne") [Opałek (1974)], "performative utterances" ("wypowiedzi dokonawcze") [Studnicki 1969: 9].

can also be applied to norms as utterances, even though they are usually denied the character of sentences in the logical sense.[242] Naturally, the grammar of norms as utterances accepts the use of a semantic definition of truth; what raises doubts here is not the grammatical structure of a norm, but rather the nature of facts about which the norm is supposed to state something. Yet, performative utterances undoubtedly state something; when a codifier says "I herewith dictate it that so and so", he is making a statement that a certain fact is taking place – namely, normalizing, and the fact that normalizing occurs is a thoroughly empirical event. Therefore, a performative utterance contains information about an event and informs about the fact that the event is taking place.

I believe the proper stance on performatives is – in general terms – the following. One has to distinguish a performative from a performative utterance even assuming that an utterance is an element of a performative. Performatives are activities, so they can be called performative activities. The most significant element of performative activity is a decision; probably every decision is a performative activity, and the creative character of a performative consists in the very fact that it is a decision. If performative activity is to achieve something, then it has to be externalized somehow – therefore performatives are activities through language. As it seems, the «participation» of utterances in performatives is of instrumental character, which sometimes leads to using certain expressions in a ceremonial sense. At the same time, a performative utterance is information that a given fact (normalizing, promise, threat, *etc.*) is taking place. It seems that activities, rather than performative utterances, can be evaluated in the categories of validity. Let us call the conditions which determine the validity of a performative "a pragmatic background". Normalizing is normalizing if and only if the pragmatic background for this sort of activity, for instance, procedural conditions, is fulfilled. There is a clear connection between the truthfulness of a performative utterance and the validity of a performative activity. Therefore the following definition of truthfulness for performative

---

[242] This grammatical point of view towards norms and conventions (*T*) is assumed by J. Kalinowski [1977b].

utterances can be suggested: a performative utterance is true if and only if the performative activity to which it refers is valid.

The origin of the view that performative utterances are not sentences in the logical sense is probably the too-narrow notion of a description assumed by the standard conceptions of descriptive utterances. A description is usually understood as a set of sentences which indicate the features of objects. However, it seems that sentences which state that a given state of affairs occurs, even though they do not indicate the features of this state of affairs, are descriptive utterances and therefore there is no reason not to regard them as sentences in the logical sense.

In connection with the above explanation, we can finally (within the scope of the construction outlined in this chapter) answer the question of the proper characteristic of normative discourse. In its purely normative part, it consists of two kinds of sentences: performative utterances and deontic sentences, that is, utterances of the nature of sentences in the logical sense. In this manner the characteristic (c) was justified regardless of von Wright's thesis. It may seem questionable that deontic logic is applied to performative utterances. I believe this question is not justified – "I dictate it that..." can be treated as a special kind of a deontic operator which behaves in the same manner as a regular operator of dictate from the logical point of view.

Performative utterances and deontic sentences can be called normative utterances. They constitute variations of directive utterances in Opałek's definition.[243] I believe the construction used for normative utterances can also be used to analyse all kinds of directive utterances.[244] At this point I would like to note one significant result which can be derived from the analysis presented above.

The relationship between a deontic sentence and a performative utterance (presupposition) is in a sense the reduction of the former to the latter. It is a pragmatic, rather than a semantic, reduction – the user of a deontic sentence assumes the truthfulness of a performative utterance. This leads to the highly desirable construction: normativity, and more generally: directiv-

---

[243] Opałek [1974: ch. IV-V].
[244] Suggestions in this direction can be found in works by Åquist, especially [1972].

ity is a pragmatic rather than semantic feature of an utterance, since the latter is reduced to the notion of truth about a model. Normative utterances are sentences from a semantic point of view, just as non-normative utterances; they are true in some valuations which depend on the pragmatic context.

The conception of norms outlined here undoubtedly implies a certain ontology. As is known, there are two groups of ontological conceptions of norms: linguistic (a norm as an utterance or the meaning of an utterance) and realistic.[245] I will not discuss them here, but will only conduct a basic comparison. My theory is undoubtedly linguistic. Obviously, if someone wants to call normative utterances norms, they can do it – this convention is acceptable, although it broadens the meaning of the term "norm". I PREFER DIFFERENT TERMINOLOGY; NORMATIVE UTTERANCES EXPRESS NORMS, which is evident in the language of lawyers, who say that regulations, and therefore also utterances, express norms. Therefore, it seems that the nomenclature applied here is more concordant with colloquial intuitions, whereas the conception of norms as decisions which can be described with a certain formal schema is realistic; the decision of the codifier is, as I highlighted previously, an empirical fact in the full meaning of the word. It seems that hitherto most conceptions of norms got into the complex issue consisting in the basic fact that a norm is regarded as an utterance and then one has to work out what corresponds to this utterance in reality, especially if the norms are neither true nor false. Accepting a decision as the basic notion seems to let us avoid these troublesome issues. I am not claiming that my interpretation is absolutely novel; for instance, it is close to imperative theories of norms, except these usually treat an order as an utterance rather than an event.

The decisive conception of norms can be accused of preventing the explication of a norm as a model of the way one should behave. It seems natural to say that norms as decisions are expressed through performative utterances, whereas deontic sentences express models of the way one should behave. Let me demonstrate now that within the scope of deontic semantics a certain notion of a model of the way of adequate behaviour can

---

[245] See Opałek [1974: ch. VIII]; there are also other mixed conceptions which treat a norm as "a complex ontological structure" – I will not consider these here at all.

be explicated – a model which corresponds roughly to Wróblewski's approach.[246] It regards the model of the way of adequate behaviour as an equivalent of a proposition in the logical sense. Just as a proposition in the logical sense is the meaning of a sentence, also the model of the way of adequate behaviour is the meaning of a norm (as an utterance which is not a sentence in the logical sense). I criticized this analogy elsewhere – presently I believe there is a possibility for «rehabilitation» of the model of the way of adequate behaviour, even if it is not in the role of the meaning of a norm.[247] In modal semantics a proposition in the logical sense is identified with the subset of a set of possible worlds – namely, the one where a sentence corresponding to a given proposition is true. Analogously, one may speak of a proposition in the logical sense in view of a deontic sentence as a set of postulated worlds in view of this sentence, and even more – as the relevant deontic nucleus. Just as deontic sentences are derivatives of normalizing, models of the way of adequate behaviour are also generated by normalizing, or the decision of a codifier. In other words, a model of the way of adequate behaviour is a «fragment» of the value of a normalizing function.

There arises a question of whether one can assign an empirical interpretation to the model of the way of adequate behaviour as a formal construct. I believe so, although in this case the problem is more complicated than in the case of the interpretation of a normalizing function. But one may risk the view that the formal notion of the model of the way of adequate behaviour corresponds to individual or social acts of awareness which concern that which had been normalized, and thus, elements of individual or social consciousness.[248] There emerges a certain conceptual scheme which permits for a precise separation of the competences of a logician and a sociologist who deal with norms. A logician deals with language regarded as a formal entity and interpretations of this language, and so in the case of norms – performative utterances and deontic sentences from the point of view of their formal and semantic properties, whereas a sociologist is interested in norms as de-

---

[246] Wróblewski [1959: 20].

[247] Woleński [1972: ch. II].

[248] It is not an issue of logic to analyze the ontology of social awareness, therefore I consider this formulation to be merely a suggestion.

cisions and elements of social and individual consciousness. In the light of the linguistic theory a logician and a sociologist deal with the same issue, namely, norms as utterances, and I believe this view has to lead to «Black's riddle». I do not intend to protest against the statement that I make use of the dualistic conception of norms which distinguishes norms as abstract objects from norms as empirical facts. Even if this is so, then the advantage of the dualistic (in the above sense) construction of norms is reducing the issue of the relationship of norms as abstract entities and norms as empirical objects to a more general issue, that is, the relationship of «the world of logic» to «the world of empiricism». If compared to traditional dualistic concepts, the presented view differs in the fact that a norm is regarded as non-linguistic. Such an approach is more convenient from the semantic point of view and is more compatible with common intuitions.

The analysis of the notion of a model of the way of adequate behaviour raises a problem which is hard to ignore, namely, treating norms as intensions of performative utterances (formally specified normalizing functions) or deontic sentences (values of normalizing functions), and therefore, norms as meanings. I am not a proponent of intensionalism and I believe that adequate semantics can be built without the need to accept intensional entities, but in the present work, more so than in the previous ones, I recognize difficulties of purely extensional semantics.[249] Therefore, the issue of intesional analysis of meaning has to be considered open.[250] If we assume that norms are intensions, then the interpretation approaches all those conceptions which regard norms as meanings and use norm as an empirical category. One thing seems certain: if norms are supposed to be intensions, then they are intensions of sentences in the logical sense.

The decisional conception of norms regards the so called thetic norms as a paradigm (a model case).[251] But such norms are often regarded as

---

[249] Woleński [1972]; seemingly new perspectives for extensionalism are opened in the so called truth-value semantics – see Leblanc [1973] and [1976].
[250] I maintain my old view that intensionalism is undesirable from the philosophical point of view, at least for an empiricist and a materialist.
[251] In Znamierowski's understanding – see Znamierowski [1924] and Ziembiński [1963].

improper, because normative utterances (regardless of whether we assume that norms are utterances or that they are expressed through utterances) of a thetic character contain relativization to the codifier, the normative system, the act of settling, *etc.*[252] Yet, proper norms are supposed to be utterances devoid of any relativizing markers, for instance: "There should be no injustice" – it seems there are no other possibilities of interpretation of the so called proper norms in the traditional terminology. I believe the thetic paradigm can be expanded to encompass all kinds of normative utterances, so that they are always either a performative utterance or a deontic sentence. To prove this belief, let me refer to only one, albeit vital, factor. Let us assume that an utterance "It should be so and so" aims at becoming a proper norm.[253] Let us consider how it can function in an ethical discourse – proper norms are regarded as remittance of content, especially moral content. Someone who utters "It should be so and so", as far as he feels entitled to given reasons for moral normalizing, with the intention of settling a moral norm, uses "It should be so and so" as a performative utterance. If someone, knowing that "It should be so and so", expresses some moral content, regardless of whether he knows that they were settled by someone, or if he simply refers to these ideas, utters: "It should be so and so" with the intention of expressing his own convictions, then he uses the utterance as an expression of convictions accepted by him. But then he *de facto* understands "It should be so and so" as a short form of "I accept it that it should be so and so". Acceptance is a kind of a decision, a performative activity, and performs the role of a substitute of normalizing. Finally, if someone uses the utterance "It should be so and so" with reference to someone's (moral) settlement or someone's acceptance, then he understands it as a deontic sentence. Therefore, one may say that "It should be so and so" is always an abbreviation of a performative utterance or a deontic sentence in colloquial language. The sentence "It should be so and so" in the role of a norm proper occurs exclusively in the superficial structure of a language; only performative utterances or deontic

---

[252] See Åquist in this topic [1973].
[253] I based my further argumentation on the work mentioned in the previous footnote.

sentences occur in the deep structure of a language.[254] Therefore the whole conceptual apparatus developed for the thetic paradigm can be expanded to include utterances which have hitherto been considered as proper norms. The starting point for a uniform interpretation of a normative discourse, not only a thetic, is the assumption that every norm is settled by someone and for someone (settled in the broad sense which encompasses acceptance), and therefore consists in the choice of a normalizing function. I believe this is the only concept of norms compatible with empiricism and materialism, and each view which accepts norms as independent of the choice of normalizing functions is a kind of a reflection of a law of nature; one discovers norms just like laws of nature.

Władysław Wolter & Maria Lipczyńska. Norms and deontic logic
[1980b]

1. Imperative sentences *versus* sentences in the logical sense. Imperative sentences *versus* norms (normative sentences)

As it was ascertained before, sentences in the logical sense (which possess the logical value of truth or falsehood) are only – to use grammatical terminology – declarative sentences, whereas imperative sentences and interrogative sentences are not. Interrogative sentences are utterances which aim at obtaining certain information, whereas imperative sentences are utterances which indicate to someone (the addressee of the order) how one should or should not behave. Just as interrogative sentences, not being sentences in the logical sense, will necessarily remain within the scope of interest of lawyers, also – or even especially – imperative sentences are of interest to lawyers. Are the terms "imperative sentence", "normative sentence" and "norm" synonymous? The word "norm" is undoubtedly ambiguous, as these examples demonstrate: "He does not work out his designed norm", "His weight is higher than the norm", "The norm included in art. 183 of PC prohibits bigamy", "This norm has been valid since 1st January 1967". We

---

[254] I believe then only true or false utterances occur in the "deep structure" of language – it seems to result from the communicative function of language.

will be concerned with the meaning of the word "norm" as used in the last two sentences: a norm as an utterance which expresses an indication of certain behaviour to someone. The said behaviour can be an activity or negligence (passive behaviour). Logicians who are not lawyers are inclined to claim that utterances in the grammatical form of an imperative sentence are predominantly used to express a norm. When the addressee of the norm is a specific individual who is addressed directly by the person who settles the norm, an imperative sentence is indeed the usual form of the norm. (For instance: "Pass me your notebook!" or "Come back home before nine!" or "Come back in 7 days!", *etc.*) Various situations, various relationships between people, work, social or regional customs, determine various linguistic forms of imperative sentences ("Do it!" or "Would you do it?" or "Let comrade, colleague, citizen, private …do it!", *etc.*)

A lawyer will obviously notice that nowadays norms settled through legal acts do not usually take the form of imperative sentences. Contemporary codes of law do not include, for instance, simple prohibitions: "Do not kill!" or "Do not steal!". The duty to punish the perpetrator is usually expressed in the form: "Who kills a man, is subject to punishment …", *etc.* Notice that a clearly expression of duty ("should be punished…") was not used here and instead, the seemingly descriptive form ("is subject to punishment") indicates the duty to punish. Thus a norm can take on a form of an imperative sentence, expressing duty and seemingly descriptive. Let us remember to distinguish the fact of issuing a norm from the norm itself as a certain kind of utterance. Let us also distinguish norms from sentences on norms, for instance: sentences on validity, addressees, *etc.*, in which the norm is the object of an utterance, which entails truth or falsehood of such a sentence on a norm: for instance, the sentence stating that in the *Code of Law* of 1964 there is a norm which says that if someone is guilty of harming another person, he is obliged to repair the damage – is true.

An imperative sentence (to use the term "sentence" in its broader meaning, since it is not a sentence in the logical sense) is therefore not a synonym of a norm. The expressions "normative sentence" and "norm" will be regarded here as synonyms, with the reservation that the term "sentence" is used in its broader sense. On the other hand, one should also keep it in mind that an imperative sentence in the grammatical sense in not always a form of a (legal, moral or other) norm as it can also express a request ("Lend me 100 złotys!") or a wish ("Be happy!"), *etc.*

Finally, it is worth noting that sometimes, instead of the form of an imperative sentence, the so called rhetorical question form is used (instead of "Stop abusing our patience!" – "When will you stop abusing our patience?").

2. Individual and general norms

A norm has to determine (explicitly or implicitly) the addressee and the manner of behaviour which is dictated or prohibited. Some norms are directed at many addressees who are not individually determined, for instance, the norms of the *Code of Law*, although one should distinguish those among them which refer to all people (the prohibition of killing) and those which only refer to some people (for instance, regulations concerning offences of public officials).

When the court dictates to defendant X to pay plaintiff Y a given sum of money in a verdict, the verdict contains a norm whose addressees are only the defendant and the plaintiff in this case. The assumed form of the verdict formulates the norm in the following way: "The court dictates to the defendant to pay the plaintiff…" and so it is not in the form of an imperative sentence, which relatively rarely constitutes a vehicle for norms in legal language. The verdict dictates to the defendant to pay and entitles the plaintiff to execute his claim (naturally, in a legally specified manner).

In the example presented above the court created an individual norm through the verdict. Prohibitions included in the *Penal Code*, combined with dictates of imposing punishment for prohibited acts, or summoning men at a given age to appear before the Conscript Committee, or calling citizens of a given town to exchange their identity cards – constitute general norms.

A norm directed at one addressee (determined in any way) can be called individual, directed at more than one – general, and if the addressee does not exist – empty. For instance, a norm issued by the prosecutor calling witnesses of a crime to report to court immediately is an empty norm if there are no witnesses. One should also distinguish actual addressees of a norm (for instance, defendant NN is obliged by the court to pay a certain amount of money) from potential addressees ("Everybody who buys a radio transmitter is obliged to register it"). An individual norm can be common, for instance, included in a sentence for a couple of the accused, or unitary, when the only one person accused is sentenced. A general norm can be common and this is usually the case, but it can also be unitary (for instance, imposing a specific obligation on the winner of a competition in its regulations). […]

A legal norm expresses dictates, prohibitions and entitlements through functors "should", "has the right to", "can" (or their equivalents).

3. Validity of norms

A sentence in the logical sense is either true or false. One can state whether a norm is valid or not. Lawyers are mainly interested in the thetic justification of a norm (through referring to the fact that the legislator settled this norm and did not repeal it). If the justification refers to evaluations (*e.g.* moral) held by someone, we speak of an axiological justification of the norm. The validity of a norm or the lack of its validity is a sort of value of a norm, corresponding to the values of truth and falsehood in sentences in the logical sense.

The fact of a norm's validity is basically controlled based on the content of codes of law, regulations and other entities whose function is to produce information about a norm. It happens extremely rarely, especially in the period of great systemic changes, that a norm which had not been formally repealed ceases to be valid. […]

4. A legal regulation *versus* a legal norm

A legal norm is an utterance which indicates to given addressees a manner of behaviour. A legal regulation is defined as an item of legal text (an article, a section, a paragraph, or a point of an article) which contains one or more legal norms. There are also regulations whose task is solely to define or explain certain terms (interpretative regulations), for instance, the notions of "document", "the nearest relative" or "juvenile" (art. 120 *PC.*) There are also regulations which create certain legal organs (organizational regulations). Therefore, one cannot identify a legal norm with a legal regulation.

The language of legal regulations is specific, which concerns not only terminology of names but also of functors. For instance, in a procedural regulation, an expression of the type: "the court instructs", "the court proclaims" means that "the court is obliged to instruct", "the court is obliged to proclaim".

The acceptability to choose between certain kinds of behaviour has to be stressed with the expression "one can", or the equivalent.

5. The rule and exceptions

As the rules of Polish spelling teach us, the cluster "rz" follows consonants like "p" or "k", for instance: "przestępstwo", "krzak". However, "sz" is used in the words: "pszenica", "pszonak", "pszono", "pszczoła", as well as "kształt". Therefore, we say: "There is no rule without an exception", and when speaking of a rule, we mean most cases.

A similar phenomenon of «rule-exception» is also encountered in legal regulations, especially penal. For instance, if art. 48 § 1 *PC* states that "one who kills a person is punished", it does not mean that "everybody" who kills is punished. After all, there are some examples of killing which are not punishable by law, for instance, killing in self-defence or in the case of executing a lawful death penalty. Thus there occurs certain regularity (rule) and exceptions from it. However, if one cannot say of a regulation that the prohibition concerns most cases, but on the contrary, special cases, there is a certain dissonance in such coding of the situation. This is visible in the regulation of art. 165 § 1 *PC*, which states that "whoever deprives another person of their liberty is subject to the penalty… ‚etc.". What has to strike a reader is that "depriving a person of their freedom" is, after all, also punished with "depriving of freedom", where the cases of legally depriving someone of their freedom are highly superior to criminal cases of depriving someone of their freedom. From the logical point of view, the "rule-exception" scheme is reduced to a statistical majority of cases, and therefore, to some set of elements whose certain number, despite it equality with other elements, has been exempted for some reason. Let us also add that one cannot express the properties of a set in such manner that they encompass all the elements, without the need to refer to the exceptions.

Let us also add that prohibitions are formulated so that the exceptional situations which the prohibition does not concern are not exposed.

6. The logic of norms (deontic – the structure of the system)

Normative syllogism has been considered in works as early as Aristotle's. However, the logic of normative sentences generally developed slowly, so that its rise has not been observed until quite recently. Both logicians and theorists of law deal with this subject. Yet, the ambiguity of terms and the variety of assumptions still cause serious difficulties with regard to the attempts to build a theory of normative sentences.

Deontic logic is understood as a system of sentential formulas constructed with the help of the phrases:

"It is obligatory…" (*O*);

"It is allowed…" (*P*);

"It is prohibited…" (*F*).

A full deontic calculus was created by G.H. v. Wright (in 1951). It contains propositional variables ('*p*', '*q*', '*r*' …) in unlimited quantity, constants '*O*', '*P*', '*F*', conjunctions of propositional calculus (negation, logical conjunction, alternative, implication and equivalence), brackets. It is based on axioms of propositional calculus, the axiom of non-contradiction of validity '$\sim (Op \cdot O \sim p)$' and the axiom '$O\,(p \cdot q) \equiv (Op \cdot Oq)$'.

The logical analysis of the structure of a norm, the issue of entailment of norms from norms, the attempts to construct a theory of norms analogous to the theory of sentences in the logical sense offer a wide range of opportunities for research to lawyers and logicians alike. […]

Kazimierz Świrydowicz. Normative formula

[1981: 87–88]

An utterance which dictates to a given person directly, on the basis of the semantic rules of a given language, to undertake certain behaviour when specific circumstances (especially tautological) occur, shall be called a NORM OF BEHAVIOUR. […]

A norm shall be ascribed a certain formal character. Let us assume provisionally that a norm is an utterance whose structure follows the scheme:

(1) For any *x*: if *Z*, then let *x* realize *B*!

where '*Z*' is a certain sentence or propositional function which contains variable '*x*' (which can be a substitute for tautology), '*B*' is a certain general name (for instance paying taxes or returning an item), and '*x*' is a variable which represents individual names of persons. Using 'Re(*B*)' instead of "realize *B*" we can write scheme (1) in short as:

(1)' (x)[Z → x! Re(*B*)].

(such abbreviated notation will facilitate tracking the ever more complicated structure of a norm below).

If sentence *Z* represents only the description of the person *x* (addressee), that is, if the circumstance in which person *x* shall be *B*, can be described as a property of the person *x*, then scheme (1) can be written as:

(2) For any *x*: if *x* is *A*, then let *x* be the one realizing *B*!

In short:

(2)' (*x*)[*x* is *A* → *x*! Re(*B*)].

where '*A*' is a general name for a person (*e.g.* a citizen of Poland, the owner of a car, *etc.*), and *B* is a general name of the behaviour.

If sentence *Z*, besides the description of the person *x*, contains another sentence which does not belong to the description of the person *x* (for instance: "A fire breaks out"), the norm will be written in the following form:

(3) For any *x*: when *W* and *x* is *A*, then let *x* be the one realizing *B*!

(3)' (*x*)[*W* and *x* is *A* → *x*! Re(*B*)].

where '*W*' represents a sentence (propositional function.)

Let us also note that *A* and *B* can be nominal functions in particular (for instance, *y*'s father, paying in Polish złotys, *etc.*). Such variables shall be quantified similarly to variable *x* in examples (1)–(3).

The sentence situated between the word "when" and the word "then" in the formulation of a norm shall be called [...] the antecedent of the norm, whereas the clause following the word "then" shall be called the consequent of the norm. The functor "when... then..." is a special normalizing functor. Its first argument is a sentence, and the second – an imperative utterance (a dictate). Just as implication is distinguished from entailment in the logic of sentences, also here the functor should not be interpreted as a sign for the relationship of entailment, in this case: entailment of the «dictate» from the sentence, since any replacement in the schemes (1)–(3) will result in examples of norms which nobody has settled so far and probably never will, besides examples of norms which exist in the Polish law.[255]

Jan Woleński. Deontic operators
[1982]

Permission is probably the most complicated deontic notion – which is supported by the controversy over the so called permitting norms and over the relationship of the notion of permission to other deontic notions, such as dictate, prohibition, obligation and indifference.

As is well known, permission is commonly defined in the standard system of deontic logic as a non-prohibition.[256] Therefore, A is permitted if and only if it is false that A is prohibited.[257] According to many authors, this interpretation is incorrect as it does not allow for codifying in the language of deontic logic certain important intuitions connected to the use of words which express permission. We are concerned with two questions here: first, permission as a non-prohibition is not suitable to recreate the «normative» sense of permission (the problem of permitting norms); second, permission as a non-prohibition is not suitable for the analysis of permission in the situation of choice. Permission = non-prohibition is usually called weak permission and is contrasted with strong permission, a notion which has numerous interpretations: it is understood as either a substitute of permission in the normative sense or a substitute of permission in the situation of choice. I will omit the question of strong permission as a substitute of the mentioned normative permission connected with permitting norms; in this matter I con-

---

[255] Adopting the assumption that the first argument of the discussed functor is a sentence is a certain simplification of which the author is aware. Theorists of the law who deal with semiotics of norms present different views on this matter. Yet allowing for this simplifying assumption does not lead to contradiction or dangerous paradoxes, but rather it facilitates the discussion of the issues raised in the present article. These arguments seem to be sufficient justification for adopting this assumption for the aims of the present article.

[256] The system formulated by von Wright in 1951 is usually considered a standard system; see Wright [1951].

[257] Here I employ the predicative use of deontic terms, which is more convenient in informal considerations. Therefore the letters 'A', 'B' are nominal variables.

tinue to withhold my objections against the need to use a strong permission in this sense.[258] Instead, let me focus on the analysis of permission in the situation of choice, that is, the expression "*A* or *B* is permitted".

Von Wright, followed by other authors, claims that formalization of "*A* or *B* is permitted" should certainly satisfy the following condition:

(1) *A* or *B* is permitted if and only if *A* is permitted and *B* is permitted.

Weak permission does not satisfy condition (1), and moreover, attaching (1) to the standard deontic logic leads to contradiction, since it is claimed in this logic that:

(2) For every *A*, *A* or not-*A* is permitted.

But (1) and (2) together lead to the conclusion:

(3) For every *A*, *A* is permitted.

and therefore to a conclusion which is impossible to accept: that everything is permitted in the face of any normative system.[259] This factor renders the fulfilment of condition (1) by weak permission. However, since it is thought that weak permission is intuitively uninteresting since it does not fulfil the natural (from the point of view of linguistic practice) condition (1), then it is no wonder that there emerged attempts to build other deontic formalisms, namely, such that permission fulfils condition (1).[260] Yet, there emerges another line of argument, in which it is possible to introduce to standard deontic logic a permission which fulfils condition (1) without causing contradiction.

Føllesdal and Hilpinen propose the following definition (hereinafter, weak permission will be called "permission$_1$," whereas permission with choice will be called "permission$_2$"):

(4) *A* or *B* is permitted$_2$ if and only if *A* is permitted$_1$ and *B* is permitted$_1$.[261]

(4) is not a statement of deontic logic: it is a kind of a terminological postulate. It does not lead to a paradoxical consequence (conclusion (3)) as

[258] See Opałek & Woleński [1974].
[259] Wright [1968a.] The reasoning which demonstrates that condition (1) leads to unwanted consequences in the standard system was drawn from Benthem's work [1979: 38].
[260] Wright [1968a: 24 *et seq.*].
[261] Føllesdal & Hilpinen [1971: 23].

statement (2) does not occur for permission$_2$. However, the terminological postulate (4) does not seem entirely compatible with intuitions. The following statement occurs in deontic logic:

(5) For every *A, A* is dictated or prohibited or indifferent (= not dictated and not prohibited).

It results from (5) that permission$_1$ = dictate or indifference, that is, *A* is permitted$_1$ if and only if *A* is dictated or indifferent. Let us assume that a certain *A* is dictated and a certain *B* is indifferent. From statement (5) we have:

(6) *A* is permitted$_1$ and *B* is permitted$_1$,

and from (4) we get:

(7) *A* or *B* is permitted$_2$.

The notion that *A* or *B* is permitted$_2$ in the situation where *A* is dictated is not in the least incorrect from the logical point of view. Still, it seems counterintuitive to state that *A* or *B* is permitted with the right to choose when it is obvious that *A* is dictated.

I believe that permission$_2$ requires a stronger condition and should fulfil the following intuition:

(8) *A* or *B* is permitted$_2$ if and only if *A* is permitted$_1$ and not-*A* is permitted$_1$, as well as *B* is permitted$_1$ and not-*B* is permitted$_1$.

Through the definition of indifference (*A* is indifferent if and only if *A* is permitted$_1$ and not-*A* is permitted$_1$) postulate (8) leads to:

(9) *A* or *B* is permitted$_2$ if and only if *A* is indifferent and *B* is indifferent.

According to (8) and (9), *A* or *B* is permitted with the right to choose if and only if one can do *A*, do not-*A*, do *B* and do not-*B*. (9,) as well as (4), is not a statement but a terminological postulate. Statement (2) does not occur for permission$_2$ which fulfils condition (9); it is not true that for every *A, A* or not-*A* is permitted. The difference between permission which fulfils condition (4) and permission$_2$ which fulfils condition (9) is that if *A* (*resp.* *B*) is dictated, and *B* (*resp. A*) is indifferent, then in the light of condition (9) *A* or *B* is not permitted$_2$, but it is dictated – this is because since *A* is dictated, then *A* or *B* is also dictated; this statement belongs to deontic logic. It is worth noting here that this statement, known as Alf Ross's paradox, leads to an entirely intuitive result in this case.

However, it appears that an even stronger notion of permission with a choice can be introduced. From the fact that A or B is permitted$_2$ it does not entail that A or B is permitted, or even permitted$_1$. Undoubtedly (in the light of the Polish law), being intoxicated or driving a car is permitted$_2$ in the sense of condition (9), but being intoxicated and driving a car is prohibited.

In connection to the above, the following condition can be postulated:

(10) A or B is permitted$_3$ if and only if A or B is permitted$_2$ as well as A and B are permitted$_1$.

In the light of (10), A or B (for instance, going to the cinema or theatre) is permitted$_3$ if and only if one can do A, do not-A, do B, do not-B, and do A and B.

It is easy to see that permission$_2$ and permission$_3$ require relativization to a given normative system – strictly speaking, we should put it "A or B is permitted$_2$ (permitted$_3$) in relationship to the normative system N". Condition (9) is in a certain sense a minimal condition for permission with the right to choose, as it states that such permission only occurs when elements of the disjunction are indifferent; however, whether they are indifferent depends on the content of some N in relation to which one considers what is permitted. Condition (10) adds another reservation to the minimal condition, that is, condition (9), which consists in the fact that A and B are permitted$_1$. It is clear that permission$_3$ implies permission$_2$ in the sense that if A or B is permitted$_3$, then A or B is permitted$_2$. However, it may be the case that there occurs the following situation: A or B is permitted$_3$, but not-A and not-B are prohibited; for instance, let us substitute A with being sober, and B – with not driving a car. To relativize it to the Polish law: A or B is permitted$_3$, but not-A (being drunk) and not-B (driving a car) is prohibited. The above observation suggests a condition for permission with maximal choice:

(11) A or B is maximally permitted if and only if A and B are permitted$_1$, as well as not-A and B are permitted$_1$, as well as A and not-B are permitted$_1$, as well as not-A and not-B are permitted$_1$.

Thus maximal permission denotes that for specified A and B, in the light of a given normative system, any (two-piece) combination of A, B and their negations is permitted$_1$. It is obviously the case that maximal permission implies permission$_3$. Permission$_1$ was used in the record of conditions (10) and

(11), which might seem too weak a formulation at first glance; yet, it is out
of the question that A and B are dictated. If A and B were dictated, then also
A would be dictated and B would be dictated, since deontic logic states that
if A and B are dictated, then A is dictated and B is dictated. But since it additionally results from conditions (10) and (11) that A is indifferent and B is
indifferent, therefore A and B cannot be dictated; in fact, in both cases per-
mission₁ is limited to indifference for purely logical reasons.

The above analysis suggests several conclusions, which I aim to present.
Firstly, standard deontic logic is not as deficient in means of expression as is
commonly thought. It appeared that several notions of permission can be presented in standard deontic language, that is, weak permission and (at least)
three versions of permission with choice.[262] I am not attempting to claim that
in the language I used the uses of the following phrases can be expressed:
"be permitted", "can" (in the normative sense), "have the right to", *etc.*[263] Besides, it can be assumed that no deontic formalism is able to provide analytical
means to fully reproduce the use of respective normative or deontic terms, just
as propositional calculus is insufficient to explain all meanings of inter-prop-
ositional conjunctions. I am only claiming that one should not discard standard deontic logic in haste for the so called dyadic systems where expressions
of the following type are considered: "A is permitted in view of B". While I
do not deny the need for the analysis of such expressions, I believe certain
doubts may arise as to whether dyadic deontic logic is more intuitive from
its standard version. Secondly, the above analysis indicates the important role
of the underestimated notion of indifference in deontic description. I believe
indifference deserves to be called strong permission; it seems entirely intuitive to me to say: "A is strongly permitted if and only if A is weakly permitted and not-A is weakly permitted", as well as the phrase: "A or B is permitted with the right to choose as long as (at least) A is strongly permitted and B
is strongly permitted". Finally, possibly the most important conclusion from
the point of view of the theory of law is that the presented analysis undoubt-

---

[262] At least, as there exist more possibilities within maximal and minimal concepts of
permission with choice.
[263] For instance, it is hard to express conditional permission, that is, an expression of the
type: "As long as conditions w are fulfilled, A is permitted".

edly implies that the notion of permission is derivative of the notion of obligation (= dictate or prohibition). This is already true for the relation to weak permission and to indifference, as well as various versions of permission with choice. In any case, when speaking of permission one must assume the existence of a domain of obligation determined by the repertory of dictates and prohibitions of a given normative system. This factor implies a certain course of the analysis of legal notions traditionally connected with permission, for instance, entitlement or competence, so that the analysis consists in eliminating permission for the benefit of dictates and prohibitions as well as their various relationships.[264] Such a suggestion is programmatic in its nature and cannot be evaluated *a priori*, although in my view certain circumstances of logical nature strongly testify to the fact. W. Lang presented the following objection to the reductionist analysis: it cannot be applied to preferential entitlements, for instance, the right to one's own, normatively preferred behaviour correlated with other subjects' obligations to neglect interference with the domain of freedom determined by the law.[265] Yet it seems to me that the objection can be reconciled with the program of semantic elimination of permission which does not have to lead to the conclusion that "permission terms" are completely useless in legal language; it is actually quite obvious that from the pragmatic point of view normative preferences can be delivered more efficiently with entitlement than with obligation. Both theses can be accepted at the same time: permission is logically derived from obligations, and permission is pragmatically indispensable to deliver normative preferences. I believe this matter requires further analysis and discussion.

Tomasz Gizbert-Studnicki. Formulating directives
[1983]

It is only in the last few decades that we have observed more considerable interest in the issues of directival discourse in the fields of the philosophy of language, logical semiotics and linguistics. The boundary between

---

[264] See Świrydowicz *et al.* [1975].
[265] Lang, Wróblewski & Zawadzki [1979: 342 et seq.]

these fields, manifested in dissimilarities in its issues, methods and results, hitherto distinct, is becoming more and more blurred. The integration of the philosophy of language, logical semiotics and linguistics is particularly vividly manifested in the theory of directival discourse.

The boundaries of directival discourse are blurred. The following types of utterances within the discourse are mentioned: norm, principle, rule, order, encouragement, wish, suggestion, proposal, request, begging, advice, warning, recommendation, guideline, hint and admonition. This list is probably not exhaustive. Moreover, the scopes of some of these terms overlap or are included in one another, and thus the list cannot be identified with the classification of directives [Opałek 1974: 134]. One should also note that most of the mentioned terms are fundamentally ambiguous. This ambiguity consists in the terms denoting either an utterance (that is, a text or a sequence of sounds), or an act of using the utterance. For the purposes of this study it is more convenient to understand directives as utterances rather than acts.

Directival discourse includes a wide scope of utterances which are syntactically, semantically and pragmatically varied. Thus regulatory attempts to define the term "directive" encounter obstacles which are hard to overcome. The present paper does not require setting the boundaries of directival discourse. Only those utterances will be discussed here which are considered to be directives according to all semantic intuitions connected with this term, and especially those utterances for which the use of is an act of issuing an order (commission) or submitting a request.

Directives appear in various grammatical forms:

(1) *I order you to close the window.* (performative form)

(2) *Close the window!* (imperative from)

(3) *You should close the window.* (modal form)

(4) *I want you to close the window.* (declarative form)

(5) *Can you close the window?* (interrogative form)

(6) *You shall close the window.* (prognostic form)

The above list is not exhaustive. Directives also occur in other grammatical forms which, however, will not be discussed here [Opałek 1974: 50].

The performative and imperative forms of directives are visibly different from all the others. The grammatical form of utterances like (1) and

(2) determines the fact that these utterances are not directives, that is, us-ing these utterances is an act of issuing an order (request). Utterances in this form are therefore clearly directival, whereas utterances in modal, de-clarative, interrogative and prognostic forms are not unequivocally direc-tive, since using each of these types of utterances can be, respectively, mak-ing a statement, asking a question, formulating a prediction. The ambiguity of utterance (3) is the consequence of lexical ambiguity of the modal verb "should". Only when deontic meaning is ascribed to a verb can utterance (3) be a directive. The ambiguity of the utterance in the declarative, inter-rogative and prognostic forms is not a consequence of lexical ambiguity of the components of these utterances. One of this sort of utterances will be considered here.

Meta-ethical and theoretical-legal considerations concerning the struc-ture of directives focus on utterances in a clearly directival form. It is usu-ally only claimed of utterances in different forms that ascribing the meaning of directives to them is dependent on the context, and therefore this issue belongs to the field of the pragmatics of language. This view is unsatisfac-tory. If one takes into account the dependence of acts of speech on the con-text, it occurs that practically every utterance can be used to perform very many different acts of speech, including orders, requests and commissions [Downes 1977: 94]. For instance, let us consider the utterance:

(7) *It got cold.*

In certain contexts using this utterance is a statement, in others – a warn-ing, and in others still – issuing an order or a commission. In the latter con-texts utterance (7) can be used to issue very varied orders, including: "Bring me a sweater!" or "Close the window!" or "Turn on the heating!". The re-lationship between utterance (7) and acts of speech performed through us-ing it cannot be explained systematically, that is, by referring to the rules of a language, as (a) the utterance is suitable to perform various acts of speech in various situational contexts; (b) even when the utterance is used to issue an order (a commission), the content of the order is not determined by lin-guistic meaning (7). Being familiar with the context in which (7) was used allows for the interpretation of the utterance. Since there is an infinite num-ber of possible situational contexts, it is impossible to formulate rules which would let us determine *ex ante* what act of speech will be performed by using (7) in any situational context.

The issue of utterances in the prognostic, declarative and interrogative form is another matter. For instance, let us consider utterance (5). It is not obviously directival since it can be used both to issue an order (request) and to ask a question. Still it should be noted that, unlike in the case of utterance (7), whenever (5) is used to issue an order, the content of the order is determined by the linguistic meaning of (5). Thus (5) can only be used to formulate a directive which concerns closing the window by the addressee of the utterance. The content of the directive formulated by uttering (5) is independent of the situational context (which still indicates which window is meant and who is the addressee of the directive). This remark refers to all utterances in the form of (4), (5) and (6). The fact that these utterances can be used to formulate directives whose content is determined by their linguistic meaning requires explanation.

There arises the question of whether this explanation should refer to grammar (that is, the syntax and semantics of a language), or to pragmatics. The answer to this question largely depends on how we determine the border between grammar and pragmatics. There is a widespread belief that the issue of acts of speech belongs to the realm of pragmatics. Thus, according to Stalnaker's popular statement [1972: 283], "pragmatics is the study of acts of speech and the contexts in which they are performed". This view determines the fact that the issue raised here is of a purely pragmatic character, since the notion of directives is determined by referring to the notion of the act of speech, and moreover, the directival interpretation of an utterance in the declarative, interrogative and prognostic form depends on the context.

It is quite another matter when one treats the distinction between grammar and pragmatics as correlate to the distinction between linguistic competence and linguistic performance. In this approach grammar shapes the linguistic competence of a native user of the language, that is, it recreates the rules which generate all sentences of the language, and only those sentences. Linguistic competence of a native speaker of a language is the knowledge which allows him to formulate and interpret an infinite number of sentences in the language and to recognize various syntactic and semantic properties of utterances, and especially: recognizing ungrammatical sentences and utterances, ambiguous and unambiguous utterances, self-contradictory sentences, sentences which entail from one another, *etc.* Grammar is to explain the reactions of a native speaker of a language by recreating the rules which cause these reactions. On the other hand, pragmatics concerns linguistic performance, that is, actual behaviour of specific language users in various situational contexts. Indeed, language performance may differ from linguistic competence. These differences may consist in the fact that users of a language sometimes ascribe a meaning to certain utterances which is different from their grammatical meaning, they accept ungrammatical utterances or regard utterances which were generated by the rules of grammar as unacceptable. These reactions of specific users of a language are due to various cultural and situational factors as well as certain psychological limitations (limitations of memory, mistakes, *etc.*). These factors lead to the fact that actual behaviour of language users does not realize linguistic competence in a perfect manner. Grammar abstracts from these factors and refers to the idealizational notion of a native user of a language.

Since grammar models a native language user's linguistic competence, then *eo ipso* the question of the role of situational context in the creation and interpretation of utterances is excluded from the scope of its interest. Yet the question arises whether the issue of acts of speech lies entirely beyond the scope of grammar.

Which act of speech is performed by using an utterance depends both on linguistic meaning of the utterance and on various situational factors. Linguistic competence of a given language includes, among other things, the knowledge that the utterance (2) *Close the window!* can be used to issue an order, whereas utterance

(8) *John closed the window.*

can be used to make a statement, regardless of the situational context where the utterances will be used. Since grammar is to model linguistic competence of a native speaker of a language, it should take into account the relationships between certain forms of utterances and acts of speech performed by using them. Thus grammar ought to answer the question: to what degree does semantic and syntactic structure determine the illocutionary force of an utterance? [Katz 1977: 9]. The illocutionary force of an utterance is understood as its property which consists in the fact that it can be used to perform an act of speech of a specified kind [Austin 1962: 93]. In this scope the issue of acts of speech lies within the domain of grammar.

The conviction that the dependence of directival interpretation of utterances like (4), (5) and (6) from the context determines the pragmatic character of the issue stated above is inappropriate. Admittedly, utterance (5) is interpreted as a directive in certain contexts and a question in other contexts can be presented as a purely grammatical phenomenon. We can accept that utterance (5) is grammatically ambiguous.

Thus there are two possible explanations of the fact that utterances in declarative, interrogative and prognostic form are interpreted as directives in certain contexts: (a) explanations based on the assumption that these utterances are grammatically ambiguous and the context updates one of their grammatical meanings; (b) explanations based on the assumption that these utterances are grammatically unambiguous (and therefore, for instance, (5) is a question) and the context changes their meaning.

Each of these explanations is based on distinguishing the grammatical meaning of an utterance from its pragmatic meaning. Grammatical meaning is interpreted as the meaning which is granted to an utterance, regardless of the situational context in which the utterance was delivered. Pragmatic meaning, on the other hand, is the meaning which is granted to an utterance in a given situational context in which the utterance was delivered. The pragmatic meaning of an utterance may differ from its grammatical meaning. The task of pragmatics is, among other things, to explain the mechanisms which cause it that in some contexts utterances are ascribed meanings which are different from their grammatical meanings.

In other words, the grammatical meaning of an utterance is the meaning which a native speaker of a language ascribes to it when he does not have any information as to the context in which the utterance was given. Such a situation is described as zero context [Katz 1977: 15]. The notion of zero context, just as the notion of a native user of a language, is of idealizational character.

Explanations which belong to the first of the presented kinds are based on the assumption that utterances like (4), (5) and (6) are ambiguous in zero context. This assumption requires recreation of grammatical rules which ascribe double meaning to these utterances.

One of the tasks of pragmatics is to answer the question of which properties of contexts cause these utterances to be ascribed the meaning of directives, statements, questions or prognosis as pragmatic meanings. In this approach, the pragmatic meaning of each of these utterances is an update of one of the grammatical meanings.

Explanations which belong to the second type are based on the assumption that utterances like (4), (5) and (6) are unambiguous in zero contexts (and therefore, for instance, (5) is a question). In some non-zero contexts their pragmatic meaning differs from their grammatical meaning, and moreover, the meaning of directives is ascribed to them. Therefore, context changes the meaning of these utterances. This assumption requires reproducing pragmatic mechanisms which cause this change of meaning.

It seems a convincing justification of any of the two alternative answers to the question of whether utterances like (4), (5) and (6) are ambiguous or unambiguous in zero contexts is extremely complicated. These complications are the consequence of the idealizational character of the notion of zero context and the notion of a native user of a language. Answering this question would require examining the meaning of these utterances in a pure zero context, and therefore, leaving behind all our convictions concerning the conditions in which communication with language occurs. Conducting such a thought experiment is impeded, among other things, by the fact that the distinction between linguistic competence and extra-linguistic knowledge is unclear, as we do not realize fully which of our convictions come from the knowledge of the language and which are of objective (extra-linguistic) character. Therefore, it seems that resolving the controversy between the presented types of utterances should consist in researching the appropriateness of the consequences from which they arise rather than researching the appropriateness of the assumptions on which they are based; in particular, which of these explanations allows for more appropriate predictions of various linguistic facts.

The explanations which belong to the first of the presented types can be described as grammatical conceptions, whereas the explanations of the second type are pragmatic conceptions. The following discussion concerns certain conceptions selected from those which have been discussed in other works. The discussion does not claim to be exhaustive, as its aim is not to analyse certain conceptions thoroughly, but rather to present general properties of grammatical and pragmatic conceptions.

As for grammatical conceptions, there are two kinds of them. According to the first one, the ambiguity of utterances in the declarative, interrogative and prognostic form is a regular grammatical ambiguity. According to the second one, the ambiguity of these utterances is the consequence of the idiomatic character of some of their components. Katz and Postal [1964: 74] discuss utterances like (6) *You shall close the window* [Polish *Zamkniesz okno*]. They work on the assumption that utterance (6) is grammatically ambiguous. In one of its meanings it is a paraphrase of (2) *Close the window!* and has the meaning of a directive, whereas in the second meaning (6) is a prognostic sentence. The ambiguity of (6) is not a consequence of the ambiguity of any morpheme occurring in the superficial structure. Katz and Postal explain the ambiguity through assuming that (6) is derived from two different deep structures, wherein one of these structures is identical with the deep structure of (2). The structure [for Polish version] is represented by the following phrasal marker:

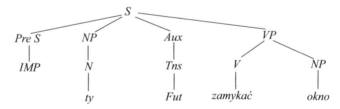

Therefore an abstract morpheme *IMP*, not realized in the superficial structure, occurs in the deep structure of directives. This morpheme cannot be identified with any lexical entity.

Postulating the morpheme *IMP* in the deep structure of directives allows for the explanation of various linguistic facts, according to Katz and Postal. This explanation refers to selective limitations which exclude the coexistence of various types of verbs, adverbs, *etc.*, with this morpheme. Thus, the ungrammatical form:

(9) **Be able to swim!*

is a consequence of selective limitations which exclude the coexistence of the morpheme *IMP* with the so called stative verbs (verbs which denote states independent of human will). Referring to other selective limitations lets us explain the unambiguity of utterances like:

(10) *You will probably close the window.*

and especially the fact that this utterance does not have the meaning of a directive. The same selective limitation explains the ungrammaticality of the following utterance:

(11) **Probably close the window!*

Postulating the morpheme *Fut* in the deep structure of the morpheme lets us explain the ungrammaticality of utterances like:

(12) **Close the window yesterday!*

as well as the unambiguity of the utterance:

(13) *You closed the window yesterday.*

Therefore Katz and Postal treat ambiguity (6) as a regular grammatical ambiguity.

Katz and Postal's conception refers directly to utterances in prognostic form. Expanding it to utterances in declarative and interrogative form presents serious technical difficulties. Although it is easy to reconstruct the transformations which lead to the deep structure presented in the [above] scheme […] to the superficial structure of the utterance (6), it is difficult to recreate the transformational rules which derive utterances such as (4), (5) and (6) from this structure, mainly because there occur in these utterances such lexical items ("want", "be able to") which are not announced by the deep structure. Thus there comes the question of whether the ambiguity of an utterance in the declarative or interrogative form is also of a grammatical character [Downes 1977: 77].

Irrespective of this technical difficulty, the statement that the ambiguity of an utterance in prognostic form is a regular grammatical phenomenon leads to predictions contradictory to linguistic facts. For instance, according to the discussed conception, the utterance:

(14) *You will marry and you will have three children.*
should be grammatically ambiguous. In one of the meanings, the utterance should be a prognostic sentence, analogously with (6), and in the other – a directive equivalent to (15):

(15) *Marry and have three children!*

Yet, utterance (14) is unambiguous, and moreover, meaning (15) is not ascribed to it. Katz and Postal's conception does not allow for an explanation why such utterances as (14) are not ambiguous in the same way as (6). This proves that the ambiguity of utterances in prognostic form cannot be regarded as a regular grammatical phenomenon.

According to the second type of grammatical conceptions, the ambiguity of such utterances as (4), (5) and (6) is the consequence of the idiomatic character of some of their components, which is especially true for utterances in the interrogative form. The phrase "can you" in these utterances is ascribed idiomatic character. It should be noted here that a certain specific sense of idiomatic character is meant here. An idiom is defined as a linguistic construct of at least two words whose meaning cannot be derived from the meanings of individual words in this structure [Urbańczyk 1978: 123]. It is stressed that in many respects idioms require the same treatment as lexical items. Still, the phrase "can you", considered as idiom, is not a lexical item. The idiomatic character of this phrase is visible only on the level of a sentence, and thus the idiomatic character lies in syntax, rather than lexis.

The thesis about the idiomatic character of the phrase *can you* is supported with the following arguments [Bogusławski 1979: 312]. Firstly, replacing the modal verb "can" with any synonym in this phrase leads to the fact that utterance (5) loses its character of a directive. For instance:

(16) *Will you manage to [(are you able to)] close the window?*
[…] is not interpreted as a directive. A feature of idiomatic constructions is that certain words cannot be replaced with their synonyms. Secondly, an utterance in the interrogative form has the meaning of a directive only if the modal verb "can" is used in the second person singular or plural. Using any other form of conjugation makes the utterance take on the meaning of a question, for instance:

(17) *Can he close the window?*

(18) *Can we close the window?*

Thirdly, it is claimed that utterances in the interrogative form have the meaning of directives only if they are uttered without interrogative intonation and the word "can" is not stressed, or even only if the intonation is the same as in imperative mood [Green 1973: 67]. The first of the quoted arguments is unquestionably the most significant. Before it is considered more thoroughly, one has to decide whether phrases like "manage to" or "be able to" are exact synonyms of the word "can". This problem will be discussed later on.

The second argument is not convincing. The fact that the meaning of a directive is ascribed to utterances in interrogative form only when the modal verb "can" is used in the second person is a consequence of pragmatic properties of directives. The considered directives have the listener as the addressee, and one addresses the listener in the second person. Therefore, we deal with the second person in pragmatic, rather than grammatical, understanding. For instance, in Polish the following utterance can be a directive:

(19) *Can you close the window [Mr Smith]?*

Grammatically, the modal verb "can" occurs in (19) in the third person.

The following arguments are against ascribing idiomatic character to the phrase "can you". If the phrase is treated as an idiom, then it is claimed that two different meanings are inherent to it: literal meaning and idiomatic meaning. When the phrase occurs in an utterance in its idiomatic meaning, then it is not entitled to literal meaning in this utterance. It would result from this view that when utterance (5) is a directive (that is, when the phrase "can you" has idiomatic meaning), the utterance is not a question. Yet, this consequence is incompatible with the observation that utterance (5), also when it occurs in the meaning of a directive, allows (or even sometimes requires) a literal response, and therefore acts like a question [Searle 1976: 970]. The answer is as follows:

(20) *Of course (I am afraid I cannot).*

Moreover, if the phrase *can you* were an idiom every utterance containing this phrase would be potentially ambiguous. This is incompatible with the observation that certain phrases containing this phrase are never interpreted as directives, for instance:

(21) *Can you learn infinitesimal calculus in a week?*

It seems that the conception which attempts to explain the directive character of utterances in the interrogative form when ascribing the phrase "can you" idiomatic character cannot account for the differences between (5) and (21). The explanation of these differences has to refer to pragmatic notions, for instance: the fact that a positive answer to (5) interpreted as a question is obvious in most contexts. Let us also add that the fact that utterance (5) retains its directive character when translated literally into most other languages speaks against interpreting the phrase "can you" as an idiom. Idioms are usually untranslatable.

The above remarks reveal certain limitations of all grammatical (that is, intra-linguistic) attempts to explain the directive character of such utterances as (4), (5) and (6). The first limitation is that these attempts concern only one of the discussed forms of directives. Extending it to other forms of directives encounters problems which are difficult to overcome (for instance, it raises the question of which element of an utterance in prognostic form has the character of an idiom). Thus, these explanations give an *ad hoc* impression.

The second of the mentioned limitations is that treating the ambiguity of an utterance in declarative, interrogative and prognostic form as grammatical ambiguity inevitably leads to the following consequence: when these utterances have the meaning of directives, they are not ascribed the meaning of, respectively, a declarative sentence, a question, or a prognosis. This consequence is incompatible with the observation that, for instance, utterance (5) has the properties of both a directive and a question.

The third limitation of the discussed conceptions is that they are unable to account for the fact that the ambiguity of utterances like (4), (5) and (6) is not only the consequence of their syntactic structure and lexical content, but it also depends on certain pragmatic properties of these utterances. This is evidenced by the differences occurring between (5) and (21) as well as (6) and (14) mentioned above.

These limitations connected with attempts of explaining the directive character of utterances in the declarative, interrogative and prognostic form through grammar (intra-linguistically) encourage seeking an adequate explanation in the field of the pragmatics of language. Such an explanation is needed which would avoid the mistake of *ad hoc* explanations, that is, an explanation which refers to more general statements concerning communicating through language.

It seems that a convenient theoretical basis of such an explanation can be the so called theory of conversational implicatures. The aim of this theory, formulated by H.P. Grice [1975: 41], is to explain pragmatic mechanisms allowing for delivering information not included in the linguistic meaning of a given utterance by the speaker and receiving it by the listener. For instance, in regular contexts, the utterance:

(22) *I tried to communicate with John yesterday.*

implies conversationally:

(23) *I did not communicate with John yesterday.*

although (23) does not result analogously from (22).

Grice's theory is based on the statement that conversation does not consist in exchanging pieces of information which are unconnected and independent of each other, but is characterized by a certain degree of cooperation between the interlocutors. This cooperation is manifested in the participants of the conversation accepting certain rules of maintaining it. These rules are formulated by Grice in the following conversational maxims:

Maxims of quantity:

(I) Make your contribution to the conversation as informative as necessary.

(II) Do not make your contribution to the conversation more informative than necessary.

Maxims of quality:

(III) Do not say what you believe to be false.

(IV) Do not say that for which you lack adequate evidence.

Maxim of relation:

(V) Be relevant.

Maxim of manner:

(VI) Avoid obscurity and ambiguity.

Grice is not claiming that participants of every conversation always abide by these maxims. He does not consider the conversational maxims to be recommendations of how conversation should be held. On the other hand, he believes that the interpretation of utterances formulated in the course of conversation is based on the assumption that the interlocutors abide by these maxims. In particular, referring to this very assumption lets the receiver of an utterance catch the information which is implied as well as the information which is included in the linguistic meaning of the utterance. The notion of conversational implicature is defined by Grice as follows: "A man who, by (in, when) saying (or making as if to say) that *p* has implicated *q*, may be said to have conversationally implicated that *q*, PROVIDED THAT (1) he is to be presumed to observing the conversational maxims, or at least the cooperative principle; (2) the supposition that he is aware that, or thinks that, *q* is required in order to make his saying or making as if to say *p* (or doing so in THOSE terms) consistent with this presumption; and (3) the speaker thinks (and would expect the hearer to think that the speaker thinks) that it is within the competence of the hearer to work out, or grasp intuitively, that the supposition mentioned in (2) IS required" [Grice 1975: 47]. This definition can be illustrated with the following example. The aim of the conversation of persons *A* and *B* is to plan a journey together. *A* knows that *B* wants to visit person *C* during the journey. *A* asks: *Where does C live? B* answers: *Somewhere on the coast. B*'s utterance violates the maxim of quantity, as it contains too little information to realize the aim of the conversation. *A*, thinking that *B* does not want to violate conversational maxims on purpose, explains the violation of the maxim of quantity by assuming that *B* does not know where exactly *C* lives. Thus *B*, by saying *C lives somewhere on the coast* implies conversationally: *I do not know where exactly C lives.*

This example demonstrates that conversational implicatures of an utterance are not a part of its linguistic meaning. Moreover, conversational implicatures are strongly dependent on the aim of the conversation and the factual situation in which the conversation occurs.

In the above example, *B*'s utterance would not have an implicature if the aim of the conversation was different. The assumption that the interlocutors obey the conversational maxims seems to be a consequence of the more general assumption concerning the interpretation of all cultural actions, namely, the assumption that subjects performing these actions act rationally. The reconstruction of conversational maxims conducted by Grice is based on the assumption that the aim of a conversation is maximally effective exchange of information. Such an approach seems too limited since it does not include other possible aims of a conversation (Larkin & O'Malley [1973: 117]; Martinich [1980: 215]). Thus, the maxim of relation in reference to questions asked in the course of a conversation will probably take the following form: (Va) Ask relevant questions, that is, do not ask questions you know the answers to, or questions the answers to which do not contribute to the realization of the aim of the conversation.

Let us note now that in regular contexts delivering such utterances as: (4) *I want you to close the window*, (5) *Can you close the window?* and (6) *You shall close the window* cannot be reconciled with the assumption that the speaker obeys conversational maxims. Thus for instance delivering utterance (5) violates the maxim of relation, as it is obvious in regular contexts that the listener can perform the action mentioned in the question. Similarly, utterance (4) is irrelevant when the topic of the conversation is not the speaker's present mental experience. On the other hand, utterance (6) violates the maxim of quality in such contexts where there are no grounds for the speaker to predict the speaker's future behaviour. The incompatibility of these utterances with conversational maxims occurs in a certain kind of contexts. However, there are some situational contexts in which these utterances do not violate conversational maxims (*e.g.* utterance (5) delivered by a doctor examining a patient's motor skills).

According to Grice's theory, the incompatibility of utterances with conversational maxims in some contexts is a signal that the speaker's intention is to communicate a certain conversational implicature. Yet, a question arises of how conversational implicatures of utterances (4), (5) and (6) should be re-created, and especially, why these utterances imply directives.

The statement that participants of a conversation obey conversational maxims is a consequence of a more general assumption that participants of a conversation act rationally. Addressing the above problem requires a reconstruction of the conditions of rationality of such acts of speech as an order, a request or a commission (of directival acts of speech). A full reconstruction of the conditions of rationality of acts of speech is a very complex task (Searle [1969: 73]; Ziembiński [1977: 127]). Without engaging in an attempt at full reconstruction, one can assume that since the person performing such an act aims to induce certain behaviour, the act is rational when:

(a) the speaker wants the addressee to act in a manner determined in the directive;

(b) the speaker believes that the addressee can behave in this manner;

(c) the speaker believes that in the normal course of action (that is, if the act of speech was not performed) the addressee would not behave in this manner.

Thus a fundamental convergence is noticeable between the conditions of the rationality of directival acts of speech formulated in the above way and utterances in declarative, interrogative and prognostic forms [Gordon & Lakoff 1971: 83]. In particular, utterance (4) states that the first condition has been fulfilled, utterance (5) is a question whether the second condition has been fulfilled, and utterance (6) is a prognostic sentence which is contradictory to the third condition. This convergence leads to the following generalization: a directive can be communicated as a conversational implicature through stating that the first condition of rationality of directival acts of speech has been fulfilled, through asking whether the second condition has been fulfilled, or through formulating a prognostic sentence which is contradictory to the third condition.

Still, the sole generalization does not explain why utterances (4), (5) and (6) have conversational implicatures which are directives. This explanation can be twofold. Firstly, it may be based on the statement that certain rules of conversational implication hold in a language whose status is analogous with that of rules of grammar. Secondly, the explanation can consist in reconstructing the reasoning which leads the addressee of utterances like (4), (5) or (6) to interpret them as directives.

An example of an explanation of the first kind is the conception formulated by Gordon & Lakoff [1971: 83]. They claim that certain rules of conversational implicature (conversational postulates) are in operation in a language:

(I) *A* states that *A* wants *B* to do *d** → *A* asks (orders) *B* to do *d*;

(II) *A* asks if *B* can do *d** → *A* asks (orders) *B* to do *d*.

A list of these conversational postulates can be broadened by referring to other conditions of the rationality of directival acts of speech. Gordon & Lakoff claim that a directive is communicated by delivering utterances (4) and (5) as a conversational implicature only when the intention of the speaker is not to communicate the literal meaning of these utterances and when the listener has the grounds to ascribe this very intention to the speaker. Such «weakening» of the relationship between antecedents and consequents of conversational postulates is noted with an asterisk occurring after the antecedents.

Since ascribing the relevant intention to the speaker is based on the situational context in which the utterance was delivered, the utterance has certain conversational implicatures only in this context (or contexts which belong to a certain group). According to Gordon & Lakoff, taking this dependence of conversational implicature on contexts into account allows for identifying the relationship of conversational implicature with the relationship of logical entailment, and in particular, for the formulation of the following definition:

L conversationally implies *P* in context *Con*₁ if and only if *P* entails from *L* in the context of *Con*₁ on the grounds of conversational postulates.

Gordon & Lakoff claim that conversational postulates are grammatical rules when they govern the distribution of morphemes. The acceptability of certain transformations of utterances is not only dependent on their literal meaning, but also on what these utterances imply conversationally. For instance, the phrases *please* and *would you be so kind* can be added to utterance (5) only when the utterance conversationally implies a directive. The utterance:

(5a) *Would you be so kind as to close the window?*

taken literally, is ungrammatical.

Clearly, identifying conversational postulates with grammatical rules leads to far-reaching consequences in determining relationships between pragmatics and grammar. Yet, this question will be ignored here.

Gordon & Lakoff's conception, which assumes the validity of the rules of conversational implicature in a language, raises certain reservations. The first one concerns identifying the relationship of conversational implicature with the relationship of logical entailment. Naturally, we cannot mean the relationship of logical entailment which occurs, for instance, between a question and a directive. Therefore, what Gordon & Lakoff probably have in mind is that from a sentence which states that a given person asked a question there entails the sentence that the person issued a directive, in a given class of contexts and based on conversational postulates. But even this approach raises serious objections. One could speak of entailment if delivering utterance (5) in contexts which belong to a certain class of utterances invariably and inevitably led to issuing a directive. Even if one disregards the difficulties connected with attempts to determine the class of contexts where (5) conversationally implies a directive more accurately, one notes that a context which would determine it that (5) has to be interpreted as a directive does not exist. In other words, there is no such context in which one cannot utter (5) without the intention to communicate a directive [Morgan 1977: 277]. One can at most state that in some contexts it is more probable, and in others – less probable, that utterance (5) was delivered with the intention to communicate a directive. Therefore, it is inappropriate to claim that from a statement that a given person delivered utterance (5) in a given context there logically entails, based on conversational postulates, that the person issued a directive. The second issue which raises objections is Gordon and Lakoff's statement that a directive as conversational implicature is communicated when the intention of the speaker is not to communicate the literal meaning of utterances (4), (5) or (6). Thus, according to them, it is not the case that one communicates both a question and a directive when delivering utterance (5). This statement prevents the explanation of the differences between (5) and (2) mentioned above, and among other things, the fact that (5), unlike (2), requires a verbal response, and therefore acts like a question.

It seems these shortcomings of Gordon & Lakoff's theory are consequences of their "paragramatic" approach to the rules of conversational implication. In this approach, conversational implicatures seem to automatically result from a given utterance in a specific context, based on conversational postulates. This approach remains at odds with the observation that the relationship between an utterance and its conversational implicatures is much looser, and no context prejudges specific implicatures. This loose relationship makes it impossible to speak of rules of conversational implicature.

The explanation of why utterances like (4), (5) and (6) have implicatures which are directives should therefore consist in the reconstruction of reasoning which leads the addressee of these utterances to such interpretation [Searle 1975: 73]. One can immediately assume that the loose character of the relationship between an utterance and its implicature is a consequence of the fact that such reasoning is not deductive.

The first stage of such reasoning was presented above. In particular, this stage ends with the conclusion that ascribing to utterances (4), (5) and (6) a meaning which does not extend beyond their literal meaning is in a given context incompatible with the assumption that the speaker obeys conversational maxims. Thus maintaining the latter claim requires the assumption that the intention of the speaker is to communicate a certain conversational implicature. Further stages of reasoning have to be considered separately for every utterance.

Utterance (4) is stating the fulfilment of one of the conditions of rationality of directive acts of speech. The situational context is the basis for the claim that the remaining conditions are fulfilled (that is, the listener can perform an action consisting in closing the window, and it is clear that he would not perform the action without the speaker's intervention). In this context maintaining the assumption that the speaker obeys conversational maxims requires the assumption that his intention was to communicate a directive, and the direct function of (4) is to direct the listener's attention towards fulfilling one of the conditions of rationality.

In the contexts where a positive answer to (5) is obvious both for the listener and for the speaker, the function of the utterance is to direct the listener's attention towards fulfilling the second condition of rationality of directive acts of speech. If these contexts provide a basis to assume that all the remaining conditions have been fulfilled, then he will maintain the assumption that the speaker obeys conversational maxims, assuming that the intention of the speaker is to communicate the directive as a conversational implicature. Ascribing another intention to the speaker would force the listener to repeal this assumption.

Similarly, utterance (6) conversationally implies a directive only in such contexts where it is obvious for the listener that the speaker has no grounds to predict the listener's future behaviour. Thus, in such contexts the third condition of rationality of directival acts of speech is fulfilled. If the context provides grounds to assume that the remaining conditions are fulfilled, the listener will maintain the assumption that the speaker obeys conversational maxims, assuming that his intention is to communicate a directive.

Reasoning which leads to ascribing relevant conversational implicatures to such utterances as (4), (5) and (6) are highly complex. The premises for this reasoning include an assumption that the speaker obeys conversational maxims, statements concerning situational context and suppositions concerning the intentions of the speaker based on these statements, statements about fulfilling the conditions of rationality of directival acts of speech [Searle 1975: 63]. One should note that the conclusions of this kind of reasoning cannot be accepted with absolute certainty, both because the premises of this reasoning cannot be accepted with absolute certainty (for instance, suppositions concerning the speaker's intentions), and because the reasoning is not deductive reasoning in terms of formal structure. Thus conversational implicature of an utterance, contrary to Gordon & Lakoff's claim [1971: 83], is not a logical consequence of this utterance on the basis of a certain set of rules. Recreating a conversational implicature consists in the reconstruction of the speaker's supposed intentions. Moreover, it is not the case that a receiver of such utterances as (4), (5) and (6) *de facto* conducts the reasoning reconstructed above in its basic form. Ascribing the relevant conversational implicatures to them occurs automatically in some measure, without the need for reflection. As it seems, this can be explained by the fact that the assumption that the speaker obeys conversational maxims does not allow for ascribing the intention of communicating only the literal meaning of utterances (4), (5) or (6) in regular contexts. Only special situational contexts provide an idea that the intention of the speaker does not go beyond communicating the literal meaning of the utterance. Thus the above reconstruction of reasoning cannot aspire to psychological reality.

In the approach presented above, unlike Gordon & Lakoff's conception, conversational implicature is information which is attached to information included in the linguistic meaning of a given utterance rather than information which replaces (displaces) the linguistic meaning of the utterance. Thus a person delivering utterance (5) in the relevant situational context does not only issue a directive (as conversational implicature), but also asks a question. Therefore, this approach lets us explain why (5) retains certain properties of a question even if it was uttered with the intention to issue a directive. However, the presented approach encounters a serious difficulty. The pragmatic character of this approach, manifested in the fact that explaining the directive interpretation of an utterance in declarative, interrogative and prognostic forms refers to conversational maxims, conditions of rationality of acts of speech and situational contexts, leads to the conclusion that conversational implicatures of an utterance are independent of its syntactic form and linguistic content. In particular, two synonymous utterances should have identical conversational implicatures [Green 1973: 72]. However, it occurs that the consequence of the presented approach is incompatible with observation. Let us consider the utterances:

(5) *Can you close the window?*

(16) *Are you able to close the window?*

The modal verb *can* is lexically ambiguous. In utterance (5) it occurs in the sense of "be able to". Therefore, (5) and (16) are linguistically synonymous. Yet, in regular contexts only utterance (5) is ascribed a directive as conversational implicature. Moreover, the following utterance is unacceptable:

(16a) **Are you able to be so kind as to close the window?*

although the utterance:

(5a) *Would you be so kind as to close the window?*

is perfectly acceptable.

As for the last remark, it seems that the distribution of such utterances as "be so kind as" can be explained only by referring to pragmatic properties of utterances in view of the polite character of these utterances [Leech

1977: 142]. In particular, it is not true that the acceptability of including this phrase can be regarded as a test for the directive character of an utterance, as for instance the following utterance is unacceptable:

(24) **Attention, if you would be so kind!*

The difference between (5) and (16) does not consist in the fact that (5) conversationally implies a directive in any context whereas (16) does not imply it in any context. The difference is reduced only to the fact that a directive as conversational implicature is ascribed to utterance (5) automatically so to say, without the need for reflection. This presumption of directivity does not concern utterance (16). Ascribing conversational implicature to this utterance requires some reflection. Moreover, if the listener does not possess sufficient information concerning the situational context (for instance, he does not know whether all the conditions of rationality of directival acts of speech are fulfilled), then he will be inclined to ascribe only literal meaning to utterance (16). Thus the difference between (5) and (16) is visible only when these utterances are discussed regardless of situational context. In a specific situational context they have identical conversational implicatures (that is, either both imply a directive or neither of them implies it).

Another obstacle which the present approach faces concerns the conditions for the acceptability of a conjunction. It is claimed that a conjunction of a question and a statement is linguistically unacceptable, for instance:

(25) **Are you going to watch TV and I will read a book?*

Yet, the conjunction of a directive and a statement is acceptable in certain conditions [Sadock 1974: 112]:

(26) *Watch TV and I will read a book.*

The statement that utterance (5) remains a question from the grammatical point of view results in the fact that the conjunction of (5) with any statement should be unacceptable. Still, the utterance:

(27) *Can you close the window, and I will turn on the heating?*
seems grammatical.

This argument is based on unstable intuitions concerning the grammaticality of such utterances as (25). Even if one regards this utterance as ungrammatical, then the grammaticality of utterance (27) only proves that the ability of the utterance to be in conjunction with other utterances does not only depend on its linguistic meaning but also on which conversational implicatures it has in a given situational context, and so it also depends on pragmatic factors.

Besides, it seems one has to approach the issue of the consistency of conjunctions in the same manner as the issue of consistency of a multi-sentence text, and it is clear that the consistency of a multi-sentence text is by and large pragmatically determined.

The conducted review of possible versions of explaining why utterances in declarative, interrogative and prognostic forms are interpreted as directives leads to the conclusion that a satisfactory explanation should refer to the pragmatics of language.

At the same time it is worth noting that, contrary to the openly proclaimed or silently accepted conviction that pragmatic phenomena are of irregular and incidental nature, it may be presumed that these phenomena are governed by important regularities. A further exploration of the problem of conversational implicatures and acts of speech will probably allow for the explanation of many phenomena which hitherto have not been satisfactorily accounted for.

Jan Woleński. Semantics of norms
[1983]

The validity (or lack of validity) of norms is often treated as an analogon of truthfulness (falsity) of sentences in the logical sense. This view is based on the assumption that norms are neither true nor false, and therefore they are not sentences in the logical sense and they belong to a specific semantic category. Thus validity and lack of validity are to serve as a basis for the semantics of norms, just as truthfulness and falsity determine the semantics of sentences. As a result, analogies between validity (lack of validity) and truthfulness (falsity), if they occur at all, can be of formal character at most. The content of the notion of truthfulness (falsity) is different from the content of the notion of validity (lack of validity), whereas "the logic of truth" and "the logic of validity" are analogous. Some authors, like Castañeda, believe the analogy to be complete; others, for instance Rudziński, believe that it is limited.[266] According to

---

[266] Castañeda [1975: 131 *et seq.*]; Rudziński [1947: *passim*].

Rudziński, a complete analogy does not occur as certain laws of logic, important in semantics of truthfulness, are not crucial in semantics of validity, *e.g.*
the law of contradiction and the law of excluded middle.[267] I will return to
this issue in the second part of this article.

Rudziński claims, or assumes, that applying the notion of validity to sentences is devoid of sense. The canonical formula which, according to him, can
be analysed is in the following form: "Norm *N* is valid". This assumption does
not seem appropriate. There is nothing unsuitable in the following statement:

(1) It is valid that it is dictated that citizens with higher incomes pay
higher taxes.

The part of (1) following the phrase "it is valid that" is a sentence, and
more precisely: a deontic sentence. Generally speaking, deontic sentences
are sentences on acts, relativized to norms.[268] Deontic sentences are true or
false and they state that certain acts are dictated, prohibited, permitted or
indifferent. Assuming that *A* represents a sentence which describes an act,
the following formulas symbolize respective deontic sentences: O*A* – it is
dictated that *A*; F*A* – it is prohibited that *A*; P*A* – it is permitted that *A*; I*A* –
it is indifferent that *A*. The following definitional relationships occur: $FA = O\neg A$, $OA = F\neg A$, $PA = \neg FA$, $IA = \neg OA \wedge \neg FA = P\neg A \wedge PA$.

It is disputable whether the above list of kinds of deontic sentences is
exhaustive. A distinction between a weak permission (permitted = not prohibited) and a strong permission (permitted = clearly permitted) is often
proposed. As for this issue, I harbour the view that there is no need to make
a distinction of weak and strong permission. I shall not justify this view here
as it is not crucial in the light of further discussion.[269]

---

[267] A precise formulation of this argument requires a reservation that the semantics of
norms is compared with the semantics of classical logic because, for instance, the law
of excluded middle does not occur in intuitive logic.

[268] That is, to a non-empty (especially singleton) set of norms. I shall not define the notion of validity here as it seems to me that it is quite clear in practice, even though there
are at least as many theories of validity as theories of truth. Even if my judgement on
the clarity of the notion of validity (in practice) is inappropriate, then one can conduct
a logical analysis of validity, or actually: its logical function, without engaging into disputes over the notion of validity – as it is done with the logical analysis of the function
of the notion of truth.

[269] See Opałek & Woleński [1973b] and [1974]; Woleński [1980c] and [1982] on this

Since (1) is an acceptable context, the formula V(D) means "It is valid that D", where D represents any deontic sentence.[270] Thus also sentences which express indifference are valid. It might seem counterintuitive at first sight, as statements of the kind: V(P*A*) or V(I*A*) are the result of the statement that certain prohibitions or dictates are not valid. I believe the counterintuitive feeling is caused by the silent assumption that there is a sphere of freedom with respect to which no prohibitions or dictates are valid. Still, this assumption is questionable. From the point of view of any normative system (even one consisting of one prohibition), every act is either dictated, prohibited or indifferent. Naturally, the sphere of indifference is not autonomous and it changes together with the change of the repertoire of dictates and prohibitions – in this sense the sphere of indifference is derived from a given normative system. But since a system (*e.g.* legal) does not prohibit going to the cinema but also does not dictate it, one can say: it is valid that going to the cinema is indifferent. Metaphorically speaking, a normative system is possessive, that is, it regulates *implicite* a whole universe of acts, even though it accomplishes it by only regulating a part of its own universe.[271] The tendency to refer validity only to prohibitions and dictates expressed *explicite* is psychologically understandable but is not grounded in logic; «the possessiveness» of normative regulation leads to «the possessiveness» of validity.

Deontic sentences: O*A*, F*A*, P*A* and P¬*A* form the following logical square:

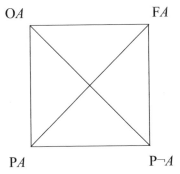

$$\text{O}A \qquad\qquad\qquad \text{F}A$$

$$\text{P}A \qquad\qquad\qquad \text{P}\neg A$$

question; see also Opałek & Woleński [1986] and [1991.] These papers contain information on opposite views.

[270] If (1) seems stylistically jarring, one may use the utterance: "It is valid that paying a higher tax by citizens with higher incomes is dictated".

[271] See Opałek & Woleński [1986].

In formal terms the above square is isomorphic with the renowned logical square which settles the relationships between categorical sentences: *SaP* (every *S* is *P*), *SeP* (no *S* is *P*), *SiP* (some *S* is *P*) and *SoP* (some *S* is not *P*); *IA* is a formal equivalent of the conjunction *SiP* and *SoP* (only some *S* is *P*).[272] This analogy leads to the following findings: sentences *OA* and *FA* (= O¬*A*) are opposite (cannot be true simultaneously, but can be simultaneously false), sentences *PA* and P¬*A* are complimentary (they cannot both be false but they can be true), sentences *OA* and P¬*A* (*FA* and *PA*) are contradictory (they have contrary logical values), the sentence *OA* (*FA*) is superior to sentence *PA* (P¬*A*), that is, if the first one is true then the second one cannot be false.

In the above discussion nothing will change structurally if "truthfulness" is replaced with "validity" and on this basis one can develop a logical theory of validity which would be fully analogous with the theory of the logical square for categorical sentences. Here are a few examples of statements: $V(OA) \Rightarrow \neg V(FA)$, $V(OA) \Leftrightarrow \neg V(OA) \land \neg V(FA)$, $V(FA) \Rightarrow \neg V(IA)$. This and other statements are based on the following general rules:

(a) from the validity of sentences *OA* or *FA* one can conclude the validity (lack of validity) of the remaining sentences;

(b) from the lack of validity of sentences *OA* or *FA* one can conclude exclusively the validity of contradictory sentences («diagonal reasoning»);

(c) from the lack of validity of sentences *PA* or P¬*A* one can conclude the validity (lack of validity) of all the remaining sentences;

(d) from the validity of sentences *PA* or P¬*A* one can conclude exclusively diagonally.

The presented construction can be generalized to the abstract system of V-logic (the logic of validity) which is an expansion on the standard deontic logic.[273]

---

[272] Moreover, the square of deontic sentences is analogous to the square of modal sentences (it is necessary that *A*, *etc.*). The square of deontic sentences can be expanded to the form of a hexagon which will also include sentences *OA* v *FA* (obligation) as well as *IA*; see Ziembiński [1966b: 104] on this subject.

[273] See *e.g.* Chellas [1980: 190–203] on standard deontic logic. I am using this system as it is the simplest and perfectly sufficient for my aims, but one can obviously use any other system as long as it is well formalized and is an expansion on the standard propositional calculus.

The dictionary of the language of V-logic consists of propositional variables, constants of propositional calculus (negation, conjunction, *etc.*), symbols O, F, P, I, V, and brackets.

The simple formula of V-logic (assuming that the definition of a formula of propositional calculus and a formula of deontic logic is provided) is any expression of the type $V(D,)$ where D is any deontic formula; examples of simple formulas are expressions: $V(Op,)$ $V(Op \lor Oq,)$ $V(P \neg p,)$ whereas expressions $Fp \land V(Op,)$ $V(Pq) \Rightarrow V(Fp)$ do not meet the definition of a simple formula. Expression X is a formula of V-logic if and only if (a) X is a simple formula or if (b) $X = \neg Y$ or $X = Y \land Z$ or $X = Y \lor Z$ or $X = Y \Rightarrow Z$ or $X = Y \Leftrightarrow Z$ or $X = V(Z,)$ where Y and Z are formulas of V-logic; the definition of a formula permits for the iteration of the operator V and thus the formula of V-logic is expression $VV(Op)$.

Formula X is a statement of V-logic if and only if it fulfils one of the following conditions:

(I) X resulted from a statement of propositional calculus in such a way that propositional variables occurring in this statement were replaced with formulas of V-logic;

(II) X resulted from a statement of deontic logic in such a way that every occurrence of a deontic operator in this statement was preceded with the symbol V;

(III) X falls under one of the following schemes (Y, Z – formulas of V-logic):[274]

(A1) $V(\neg Y) \Leftrightarrow \neg V(Y)$,

(A2) $V(Y \land Z) \Leftrightarrow V(Y) \land V(Z)$.

(A3) $V\neg(Y \land Z) \Leftrightarrow V(Y) \land \neg V(Z) \lor \neg V(Z) \land V(Z) \lor \neg V(Z) \land \neg V(Z)$;

(A4) $V\neg V(Y) \Leftrightarrow \neg V(Y)$.

(IV) $X = VY$, where Y is a statement of V-logic.

(V) $X = Z$, where $Y \Rightarrow Z$ and Y are statements of V-logic.

The following formulas are examples of statements of V-logic: $V(Op)$ $\lor \neg V(Op)$ – by virtue of (I), $V(Ip) \Leftrightarrow V(I\neg p)$ – by virtue of (II), $V(Op \land Oq)$

---

[274] V-logic is modeled on the system of the logic of truth by von Wright; see Wright [1973].

⇔ V(O*p*) ∧ V(O*q*) – by virtue of (A2), ¬V(V(O*p*) ∧ ¬ V(O*p*)) – by virtue of (I), (A1), (IV) and (V). Yet, the formula V(O*p*) ∨ V(O¬*p*) is not a statement, as O*p* and O¬*p* are a pair of opposite, rather than contradictory, sentences.

V-logic can be treated as an explanation of logical relationships occurring in a coherent normative system. By this I mean the following. Let us assume that we are dealing with a coherent system of norms.[275] The content of this system can always be represented by a relevant set of deontic sentences.[276] If the considered system is valid, the validity is automatically transferred to certain deontic sentences and the lack of validity – to other deontic sentences. In this sense V-logic codifies the relationships between validity (lack of validity) of deontic sentences which reproduce the content of a given system; V-logic also adheres to incoherent systems, since it is easy to demonstrate that the validity of contradictory deontic sentences leads to the conclusion that any deontic sentence is valid.

I do not intend to deny that the construction of V-logic is trivial, as what lies at its basis is replacing "truthfulness" with "validity". Still, this replacement leads to an important conclusion: validity has formal properties which are fully analogous to the properties of truth.[277] I would like to reinforce this conclusion further with the construction of an equivalent of the liar paradox for the notion of validity.

Let '*s*' be the abbreviation of "The sentence printed under number (2) on the current page". Let us consider the sentence:

(2) *s* is not valid.

By virtue of (A4) we have the equivalence:

(3) It is valid that '*s*' is not valid if and only if *s* is not valid.

From the agreement concerning *s* there entails:

(4) *s* is not valid if and only if *s* is valid,

---

[275] The notion of coherence is used here in the intuitive sense where a coherent normative system does not contain rules which simultaneously dictate and prohibit the same act.
[276] See Wright [1963a: 100].
[277] I am inclined to defend the stronger thesis which states that "validity" and "truthfulness" in the field of deontic sentences mean the same. See Woleński [1980a: ch. 4] on this subject.

and therefore: a contradiction.[278] It occurs that a self-reflexive application of the notion of validity leads to paradox, just as a self-reflexive application of the notion of truth does. It seems to me that this fact significantly strengthens the theory of analogy of these two notions.

In von Wright's T-logic [...] there occurs the axiom (A) $T(\neg A) \Rightarrow \neg T(A)$, where T denotes truth, and A denotes any propositional formula (of propositional calculus). Von Wright distinguishes context "A is false" ($T(\neg A)$) and context "It is not true that A" ($\neg T(A)$). The first statement is stronger that the second one, as from the fact that A is false there entails that A is not true, and not the other way around. T-logic permits sentences devoid of sense, and as long as A is devoid of sense, then it is not true, but A is not false then, but, rather, also devoid of sense. This leads to a suggestion of applying von Wright's idea to V-logic and thus realizing the intuition of attempting to limit the applicability of the notion of validity exclusively to dictates and prohibitions. Therefore let us assume the sample axiom:

(A1') $(V(\neg Y) \Rightarrow \neg V(Y)$.

leaving the rest unchanged.

Since the implication opposite to (A1') does not occur, then for instance, from $\neg V(Fp)$ there does not entail $V(Pp)$. Yet, it is easy to demonstrate that the aim was only partly achieved, as *e.g.* by virtue of (A1') from $V(\neg Fp)$ there entails $\neg V(Fp)$, and thus from $V(Pp)$ there entails $\neg V(Pp)$. Thus weakening (A1) does not provide applicability of validity exclusively to dictates and prohibitions. A further modification may consist in an attempt to limit V-logic exclusively to O-formulas with the reservation that operator O cannot be preceded by the symbol of negation (naturally, F-formulas are O-formulas in view of the definition $FA = O\neg A$); definitional equivalents of dictates and prohibitions with the help of operator P are also O-formulas.

The following axiom system realizes the above intuitions – Y and Z represent expressions in which only O-formulas occur.[279]

(A1") $V(OA) \Rightarrow \neg V(O\neg A)$.

---

[278] Naturally, this reasoning is a repetition of the famous version of the liar paradox by Łukasiewicz and Tarski. (A4) permits for the omission of quotation marks in (3).
[279] Naturally, the definition of formula and the definition of statement must be changed (narrowed down) for V"-logic.

(A2") = (A2).

(A3") = (A3).

(A4") = (A4).

Adopting (A")-axioms results in the need to distinguish validity and truthfulness. All deontic sentences can be true or false, all of them may not be valid, but only some can be preceded with the operator V. Thus there is no further analogy with von Wright's ideas and there may not be, as P-sentences and I-sentences are not similar to sentences devoid of sense; a negation of a sentence which cannot be preceded with the symbol V can be valid; such a negation is, for instance: $\neg PA$, that is, FA. In V-logic without any restrictions the formula V($D \vee \neg D$) is a statement, as well as the equivalent formula V(D) $\vee$ V($\neg D$). It is different in the case of V''-logic, as negations of valid sentences are not valid under the assumption. V(PA) is therefore always false, and V($\neg$PA) can be false in connection with the shape of the normative system, and in consequence V(PA) $\vee$ V($\neg$PA) can be false. Still, this does not violate the rule of the excluded middle, as the formula V(D) $\vee$ $\neg$V(D) is a statement of V''-logic. Let us then assume that someone wishes to treat OA i O$\neg A$ as mutual negations – naturally, it is possible if negation is interpreted in a non-standard way. In V''-logic the formula V(OA) $\vee$ ~V(OA,) where '~' is a symbol of this new negation, is not a statement. Also this example does not violate the rule of the excluded middle, since the new negation expresses only the fact that there occurs a relationship of opposition between OA and FA.

From a certain point of view, V''-logic seems to correspond to certain intuitions, especially legal ones. Lawyers usually assume "a constructive standpoint" on validity, which consists in predicating on validity based on finding a relevant rule in a legal text, and since such a rule does not exist, the notion of validity is not used – this is true in the case of P-sentences and I-sentences which may be logical consequences of O-sentences but are not valid. This constructivism leads to the fact that one never rules on the validity of dictates and prohibitions from the lack of validity of P-sentences and I-sentences, as it makes no sense to search the sphere of indifference in order to rule on dictated and prohibited acts based on this. Even more so, it cannot be done as settling this sphere assumes a previous search in normative texts. Finally, a constructive point of view leads to aversion towards alternative conclusions. In V-logic, from the fact that $\neg V(OA)$, there entails that $V(FA \lor IA)$; a rule which would lead to an unambiguous normative conclusion is desirable. In spite of these arguments, I believe V"-logic to be an artificial and formally inelegant construct. A constructive point of view can be reconciled with V-logic with the simple observation that not all schemes of V-logic are used in practical reasoning which concerns validity, and on the other hand, all reasoning which refers to the notion of logical entailment can be formalized in this logic. Therefore, it seems that distinguishing truthfulness from validity is not necessary, and the conclusion on a formal analogy between both of these notions is fully justified.

I began this article stating that validity refers to norms, but in fact I have focused on deontic sentences. Therefore an objection can be raised that I did not in fact comment on the fundamental topic of validity of norms. At the same time, it is possible that the analogies between truthfulness and validity, easy to settle when referring validity to deontic sentences, fail with respect to norms. Indeed, they do fail, but for different reasons than expected; *e.g.* not because the semantics of norms of validity falsifies the rule of the excluded middle or the rule of contradiction, as Rudziński claimed.

Rudziński's arguments are the following. Let us consider the norm:

(5) To smoke or not to smoke.

assuming that smoking is indifferent. If this is the case, then neither the dictate nor the prohibition to smoke is valid. Neither of the parts of (5) is valid, and therefore the whole alternative, which is a «normative equivalent» of the rule of the excluded middle, is not valid. Thus validity does not behave like truth.

Yet, (5) can be interpreted in three ways. Firstly, as:

(6) It is the case that you should (smoke or not smoke),

which can be written as $O!(p \lor \neg p,)$ where the symbol O! represents the normative (rather than deontic) operator.

The second interpretation leads to:

(7) It is the case that you should smoke or it is the case that you should not smoke ($O!p \lor \neg O!p$).

Finally, the third possibility is:

(8) It is the case that you should smoke or it is not true that it is the case that you should smoke (O!p v ¬O!p).

Rudziński permits the interpretation within the meaning of (8) but he discards it – I will return to this matter later. Thus what remains is the choice between (6) and (7). (6) can be treated as analogous to the law of deontic logic O(p v ¬p,) except this is clearly not «the deontic law of excluded middle». In standard deontic logic the formula O(p v ¬p) is often accepted axiomatically, but this axiom has recently faced some criticism – for instance, von Wright accepts the axiom P(p v ¬p).[280] The reasons for dismissing O(p v ¬p) as an axiom are the following. This formula is equivalent to Ot, where 't' represents any tautology. From this we can immediately conclude that there is such p that p is dictated. Yet, logical statements should not lead to existential consequences – the existence of dictates is a random fact from the point of view of logic. If O(p v ¬p) is read as "There is such p that p is dictated", then ¬O(p v ¬p) means "For every p, p is indifferent, and therefore Ot is not universally valid and is not true in the «non-normalized world».[281] Let us apply these remarks to (6). It seems that the formula O!(p v ¬p) shares the fate of its equivalent. All the same, (6) does not occur if everything, not only smoking, is indifferent. (7) is not valid, as in this case O!p and O! ¬p remain in opposition to each other and do not have to be valid simultaneously, and in consequence their alternative does not have to be valid – thus (7) is not a logical tautology. At the same time, (7) is obviously not the law of excluded middle – the deontic equivalent to (7) has been discussed above when discussing V- and V''-logic.

Rudziński claimed that (5) expresses two norms, which seems to indicate (7) as the official interpretation of his views: (6) is an alternative norm and (7) is an alternative to norms. If the above interpretative speculation is right, it leads to the question of why Rudziński assumed (7) as the expres-

---

[280] Wright [1981].
[281] This issue still requires further discussion. "Existential" interpretation of Ot is conducted in meta-language. On the other hand, Ot fulfils the condition of tautology in the so called semantics of possible worlds. Thus either the "existential" interpretation is wrong, or the definition of valuation in Kripke's deontic structures has to change – the discussion of this issue is beyond the scope of the present article.

sion of "the normative law of excluded middle". It seems to me that it was determined by a grammatical suggestion in view of which "it is not the case that you should" appears to be a negation of "it is the case that you should". However, such a view is unacceptable.

Beyond doubt:

(9) It is not the case that you should = you must not.

If in (9) the word "not" occurred on both sides of the equation in the same meaning, we would have:

(10) it is the case that you should = you are permitted.

which is obviously absurd. Grammatical custom of colloquial speech, which suggests that a dictate is a negation of a prohibition (and *vice versa*), constitutes an obvious logical deviation. The context of "it is not the case that you should" should be treated as a whole equivalent to "you should not".

I assumed that (7) is the interpretation of (5) Rudziński had in mind and I demonstrated that he considered (7) to be "the law of excluded middle", thus following a grammatical illusion. From remarks on (6) there results that also in this case "the law of excluded middle" is not violated. Let me also add that Rudziński demonstrated great intuition by attaching the validity of (6) to the question of indifference. This is why his forgotten work is worth recollecting.[282]

What remains is discussing (8). Rudziński claims that the utterance cannot be interpreted as "the law of excluded middle" in the field of norms. This is because (8) is not a norm at all. The second part of the alternative is equivalent to:

(11) It is not the case that you should (= you must not) smoke or you are permitted (= it is indifferent) to smoke.

(11) is a sentence, and therefore (8) does not have an unambiguous normative content, because "it is not the case that" in (8) is a negation which leads to a sentence. As a result, the proper notation for (8) is the formula:

(12) $O!p \lor (Fp \lor Ip)$.

and therefore something which expresses a normative-deontic context.

It is perfectly natural to pose the question of whether the contexts which (12) exemplifies make sense at all since they contain parts which by

---

[282] See Woleński [1980d].

definition belong to different semantic categories. I strongly believe a negative answer is justified here. In consequence, for (8) to "make some sense" it has to be written as the formula:

(13) Op ∨ Fp ∨ Ip.

(13) is equivalent to the law of excluded middle, but in the field of deontic sentences.

At this point we reach the fundamental question: Can a normative equivalent of the law of excluded middle be formulated at all? The answer is obviously connected with the question of the negation of norms. It results from previous discussion that "you should not" is not a negation of "you should", and "(you should) not" does not have normative sense. Then what can perform the function of the negation of a norm? Using the analogy with deontic sentences, one could propose that the negation of O!A is a sentence of the type D!$\neg A$, and the negation of F!A is a sentence of the type D!A, and therefore, permission treated as a norm. Without the normative interpretation of permission the whole construction loses its meaning. I am inclined to disregard such an option entirely, as in the case of "strong deontic permission" – besides, it is easy to see that strong permission in deontic interpretation is closely related to strong permission in normative interpretation.[283] In other words, I assume that utterances with operators of permission are always deontic sentences if permission is interpreted as $\neg FA$. Since utterances with operators of permission are always deontic sentences, rather than norms, then the issue of the law of excluded middle in the field of norms is immediately clear. This law cannot be formulated at all since there is no such thing as a negation of a norm, and (13) does not and cannot have a normative interpretation. The same reasoning concerns the law of contradiction.

Rudziński assumed that the rules of standard logic are violated "in the field of norms, as from the lack of validity of a dictate (prohibition) there does not entail the validity of the opposite norm".[284] The entailment obviously cannot take place because, since "an opposite norm" = "a contradictory norm", then it cannot be verbalized at all, and if the pair of "opposite norms" is a dic-

---

[283] See works quoted in footnote 269.
[284] See also Lemmon [1965: 52 *et seq.*].

tate and a prohibition, then the relationship between them is governed by the relationship of opposition which permits for inference from validity on lack of validity but not *vice versa*, which is in accordance with the standard rules.

Indeed, the notion of validity is not used with reference to norms, just as in the case of deontic sentences. Yet, this does not result from defects of semantics of validity, but rather, from logical "defects" of norms. Let me repeat that the issue is not that certain laws of standard logic fail in the field of norms, but that they cannot be reasonably formulated. I do not mean exclusively the law of excluded middle and the law of contradiction: in the language of norms indifference cannot be expressed at all, even when the language is enriched with some interpretation of a strong permission. Therefore, one could state that the power of expression of deontic language is greater than the power of expression of the language of norms.

Various conclusions can be drawn from the present situation. One could attempt to «improve» the logic and semantics of norms, or rather attempt to create it, as there is nothing to «improve» as yet. In my opinion, it is more reasonable to assume a radically sceptical stance on the logic of norms as a possible formal construction based on solid semantics.[285] Let me remind that the content of every normative system can be recreated with a properly selected set of deontic sentences, which will permits for the supposition that all reasoning which is important for the so called normative discourse can be reconstructed in deontic language. The author of these words is not familiar with any counterexample.

The final conclusion concerning validity and truthfulness is the following: in the field of deontic sentences both notions are of equivalent scope, and if they differ, then only in that validity is a certain kind of truthfulness: the truthfulness of deontic sentences as relativized to norms. In the field of norms validity and truthfulness cannot be compared at all as the validity of norms is not their semantic property. The answer to the question of what the validity of norms is exceeds the scope of the present work.[286]

---

[285] See Woleński [1980a: ch. 3] on this subject. There I present the so called non-linguistic theory of norms, which states that norms are not «linguistic entities» at all. This view eliminates the problem of the logic and semantics of norms.

[286] See Woleński [1980a: ch. 4], where I outline the conception of validity in accordance

Zdzisław Ziemba. The code of norms
[1983: 58–60, 222–232]

[1.] Dictate, addressee of dictate, implementation of dictate

We shall precede the introduction of deontic terms with a crucial distinction between a dictate (a norm) and a deontic sentence. In some discussions devoted to deontic logic this distinction is not taken into account and deontic sentences are called norms. In the following analyses deontic sentences are not only distinguished from norms, but also deontic sentences are relativized to a finite, non-empty set of dictates called a code. An example of norms considered here is:

(1) Let everybody who is at a gas station at this very moment be a non--smoker!

In colloquial language, such a dictate is obviously interpreted as: any person in any moment of his life is not supposed to smoke at a gas station. Such a norm will be adapted as follows:

(2) For any x, t: if x in time t is person at a gas station, then let x in time t be a non-smoker!

Naturally, the expression "for any" is not a quantifier from predicate calculus, because norms are not logical sentences, and the scheme "if x in time t is a person at a gas station, then let x in time t be a non-smoker!" is not a propositional formula. (2) is interpreted as a transcription (paraphrase) of the whole norm (1) rather than an expression consisting of the scheme "if x in time t…" and the quantifier "for any". Norm (2) will be presented schematically as:

$\bigwedge x,t\ [A(x,t)!B(x,t)]$.

We should always keep it in mind that this is a scheme of a dictate which orders for every individual who in any moment, albeit from the individual's span of existence, is A, to be B at that very moment.

We will not introduce the distinction between dictating and prohibitive norms. We are in favour of the idea that prohibitive norms are only a special case of dictating norms, or they are equivalent in meaning to the corre-

---

with the non-linguistic theory of norms.

sponding dictating norms. If a norm in the following form is called a prohibitive norm:

$\wedge x,t\ [A(x,t)!{\sim}B(x,t)]$.

then it is only a special case of a dictating norm. If an expression in the following form is called a prohibitive norm:

For any x, t: if x in time t is A, then let x in time t not to be B!

then instead of this norm an equivalent norm can be used:

For any x, t: if x in time t is A, then let x in time t be not-B!

The latter norm is a dictating norm. Thus we still use the term "dictate",
which encompasses both norms called dictating and norms called prohibitive (in a certain form).

When norm n is a norm $\wedge\alpha,\tau\ [\Phi(\alpha,\tau)!\Psi(\alpha,\tau)]$ and x,t fulfil the expression α **est**$_\tau$ Φ in place of variables α,τ respectively, then x in time t is the addressee of prescription n. Thus John is the addressee of the dictate in time t:

(3) For any x,t: if x in time t crosses the road, then let x in time t keep
his hand raised!

provided that John is crossing the road in time t.

When norm n is a norm $\wedge\alpha,\tau\ [\Phi(\alpha,\tau)!\Psi(\alpha,\tau)]$ and x,t fulfil the expression α **est**$_\tau$ Φ in place of variables α,τ respectively, then x in time t fulfils
norm n. As you can see, one can fulfil a norm even if one is not its addressee.

Thus John fulfils dictate (3) in time t when John keeps his hand raised
in time t, even if he is not crossing the road at this very moment.

Let us introduce suitable abbreviations. Instead of the expression "the
addressee of a dictate from the set of dictates K" we will write '**Ad**(K)'. Instead of "fulfilling jointly all of the dictates from the set of dictates K which
x is the addressee of in time t" we will write '**Re**(K,x,t)'. These formulas
will be classified as predicative formulas, where expressions '**Ad**' and '**Re**'
are constants. [...]

[2.] Deontic logic, the logic of norms, "inferring norms from norms"

Various authors use the term "the logic of norms" and at the same time
lament the absence of such a construct.

Naturally, deontic logic is not at all logic of norms as it uses propositional formulas rather than formulas of norms (dictates). It is not entirely
clear what such logic of norms would be. One may encounter a view claim-

ing it to be a set of statements on the occurrence of "entailment" between specific norms. An example of such a statement would undoubtedly be:

From the norm "Let any *A* be *B* and *C*!" there entails the norm "Let any *A* be *B*!".

From the norm "Let any *A* or *B* be *C*!" there entails the norm "Let any *A* be *C*!".

As was mentioned before when discussing A. Ross's paradox, various definitions of entailment occurring between orders can be designed, but from such a definition alone it does not entail that the validity of norms is heredi-tary with respect to the relationship of entailment. Yet, if this property of en-tailment between norms is not demonstrated, there is doubt as to the aim of ascertaining the occurrence of entailment between given norms. Probably as-certaining that a given norm entails from another is actually needed to de-rive the validity of the second norm based on ascertaining the validity of the first one. But then the task of formulating a definition of entailment between norms would be secondary to ascertaining the relationships between validi-ties. Only with the knowledge of the relationships can one formulate defini-tions of entailment between norms. But if these relationships were settled, ascertaining the occurrence of entailment between norms would not be nec-essary any more. We represent the view that calling for the logic of norms is making unnecessary noise.

When distinguishing norms and deontic sentences some attention should be paid to a certain absurdity encountered in legal works. "Infer-ring a norm from a norm" is a construct which appears with great fre-quency there. Logical methodology only mentions inferring a sentence from a sentence, which is defined as accepting a certain sentence (partly or fully) due to accepting the previous sentence (partly or fully). Accept-ing a sentence is the conviction that it is like the sentence claims. The conviction can be harboured in connection to sentences (true or false) but not to orders or norms which are not sentences and which ascertain noth-ing. It seems that sometimes one can be convinced that promises should be kept. If this utterance is given the form of a commission: "Keep your promises!" then it becomes clear that it cannot be accepted, since one can-not be convinced that keep your promises! It is not unnatural to say "I am convinced that I should keep my promises" because after the phrase "I am convinced" there occurs a grammatical indicative sentence. But if it predicates on something, it is not a norm, and therefore, it is not a commission but a logical sentence, and one may contemplate the meaning of this sentence. Let us suppose that there is an utterance in the form of a grammatical sentence in the code:

If someone harmed someone else through a fault of their own, that person is obliged to repair the damage.

But it does not entail from it that it is a logical sentence, whether true or false. It is hard to agree with the notion that if the *Civil Code* will be proclaimed by the Parliament in the appropriate manner then the quoted utterance is true, and if not – then the quoted utterance is false. The truthfulness of sentences does not depend on whether they were proclaimed. Besides, lawyers themselves admit that statutory utterances are grammatical, rather than logical, sentences and that they are neither true nor false. After appropriate transformation, they can become commissions. Thus a norm cannot be accepted in the same way a logical sentence is accepted. In consequence, one also cannot infer a norm from a norm, unless we are dealing with some special kind of mental activity, but lawyers do not explain what it would consist of. Similarly, one cannot infer a norm from a norm and some logical sentence. In certain naïve discussions, judging is presented as inferring, where for instance from the norm:

If someone harmed someone else through a fault of their own, that person is obliged to repair the damage.

and the sentence:

John harmed Peter through a fault of his own.

the norm is derived:

John is obliged to repair the damage done to Peter.

Naturally, the utterance on the validity of a norm is a logical sentence and it can occur as a premise or a conclusion. The above «reasoning» can be reconstructed as follows:

In a given place and a given time the following norm is valid: "If someone harmed someone else through a fault of their own, that person is obliged to repair the damage".

John harmed Peter and therefore in a given place and time the following norm is valid: "John is obliged to repair the damage done to Peter".

Except this reasoning is not justified by standard logic, in spite of what some lawyers who claim that a judge's reasoning proceeds according to "a syllogism". Yet, the above reasoning does not even roughly follow a syllogism:

Every A is B.

Every B is C.

Therefore every A is C.

as some seem to believe. The scheme of the reasoning has the following form:

The norm "Let every A be B!" is valid.

X is A.

The norm "Let X be B!" is valid.

Naturally, this scheme does not fall under standard logic where the term "is valid" does not occur.[287]

It seems the considered reasoning can be reconstructed as reasoning from a deontic sentence and a certain other sentence on a deontic sentence, rather than reasoning on the validity of a norm, and even more so: reasoning on a norm from a norm.[288] For instance, instead of reasoning the sentence:

In time t the norm $\bigwedge x,t\ [(A)(x,t)!C(x,t)]$ is valid.

from the sentence:

In time t the norm $\bigwedge x,t\ [(A \vee B)(x,t)!C(x,t)]$ is valid.

one can reason from the sentence:

(1) $x\ \textbf{est}_t\ A \vee B \rightarrow x\textbf{OB}_{...(K,t)}C.$

the sentence:

(2) $x\ \textbf{est}_t\ A \rightarrow x\textbf{OB}_{...(K,t)}C.$

where it is not necessary for the following relationship to occur:

If in time t a norm in the form $\bigwedge x,t\ [(A \vee B)(x,t)!C(x,t)]$ is valid, then in time t $\bigwedge x,t\ [(A)(x,t)!C(x,t)]$ is valid.

---

[287] See Ziembiński [1972b: 211].
[288] Ziembiński formulated such a postulate [1972b: 204].

Reasoning sentence (2) from sentence (1) we only learn that the person who is A but is not C in time t inevitably violates a norm from a given set of norms. We learn the same thing when, based on the norm in the form of:

$\wedge x,t \, [(A \vee B)(x,t)!C(x,t)].$

to the set K we accept the sentence:

$x \, \mathbf{est}_t \, A \vee B \rightarrow x\mathbf{OB}_{...(K,t)}C.$

and from it we reason the sentence:

$x \, \mathbf{est}_t \, A \vee B \rightarrow x\mathbf{OB}_{...(K,t)}C.$

Also those who call "reasoning norms from norms according to the laws of logic" a logical interpretation should be warned that there is no reasoning of norms from norms, and especially, that it cannot fall under the laws of logic. Instead, reasoning can be proposed which consists in accepting a deontic sentence based on accepting a deontic sentence, which seems to correspond more closely to what in fact occurs in the alleged reasoning of norms from norms.

Ultimately, what we are after is knowledge on how to behave so as not to violate any norm from a given set of norms. Such information can not only be provided with the sentence: "In time t a norm in the form: $\wedge x,t$ $[(A \vee B)(x,t)!C(x,t)]$ is valid", but also with the sentence in the form: $\wedge x,t$ $[x \, \mathbf{est}_t \, A \rightarrow x\mathbf{OB}_{...(K,t)}B]$. Additionally, reasoning on a deontic sentence from a deontic sentence can be applied even when norms are not valid in any sense (weak understanding of deontic functors), and moreover, no relationship between the validity of given norms has to be assumed. To sum up, it seems that some legal reasoning is more in line with reasoning on a deontic conclusion from a deontic premise than with reasoning on the validity of a norm from a sentence on the validity of another norm. Besides, if we took into account exclusively the reasoning on the validity of a given norm from a sentence on the validity of another norm, we would not be able to conduct the reasoning where the premise or the conclusion is a sentence on permission, in the meaning of a negation of a prohibition. For instance, we can reason:

$\wedge x,t \, [x \, \mathbf{est}_t \, A \rightarrow x\mathbf{per}_{1(K,t)}B \cdot C].$

And therefore $\wedge x,t \, [x \, \mathbf{est}_t \, A \rightarrow x\mathbf{per}_{1(K,t)}B].$

This reasoning cannot be replaced with the following reasoning:

The norm $\bigwedge x, t$ $[(A)(x,t)!$ $(B \cdot C)$ $(x,t)]$ is not valid.

Therefore the norm $\bigwedge x, t$ $[(A)(x,t)!$ (B) $(x,t)]$ is not valid.

as it is clear that the scheme of this reasoning is defective. The sentence "The norm $\bigwedge x, t$ $[(A)(x,t)!$ (B) $(x,t)]$ is not valid" is not equivalent to the sentence "$\bigwedge x, t$ $[x \ \mathbf{est}_t A \rightarrow x \mathbf{per}_{1(K,t)} B]$".

When the following norm is not valid:

For every x, t: if x in time t is a person, then x, in view of K, is allowed to smoke.

(Smoking at a gas station is prohibited.)

Thus there are numerous arguments in favour of reconstructing some legal reasoning as reasoning in which a deontic sentence is accepted based on a deontic sentence or both deontic sentences and, if need be, some sentences which are not deontic. The so called «judge's syllogism» can be reconstructed in the form:

$\bigwedge x, t$ $(x \ \mathbf{est}_t A \rightarrow x\mathbf{OB}_{...(K,t)} B).$
$x \ \mathbf{est}_t A.$

Therefore $x\mathbf{OB}_{...(K,t)} B.$

The infallibility of this scheme is based on the relevant statement of standard logic.

[3.] Conclusion

It seems to us that previous discussion allows the conclusion that statements of deontic logic do not allow for the implementation of such reasoning which would lead to some sensationally insightful conclusions.

The relationships these statements form are too simple to hope that further acquaintance with them would be useful to disperse the doubts as to whether a given conclusion results from given premises. It is different in the case of standard propositional calculus, when conducting a proof of a proposition and mere «intuition» is not enough to decide whether a given proof step is correct. In such cases, it is often «not visible» whether a given sentence entails logically from another sentence or sentences without properly realizing whether a given formula is a tautology of propositional calculus. So far, deontic logic cannot boast such statements.

Then what is the use of presenting existing outcomes of deontic logic, besides merely satisfying one's curiosity?

It seems that so far the main advantage of the outcomes of deontic logic consists in developing a network of concepts, where formal methods which ensure coherence of the set of these concepts are used in the course of the analysis of deontic concepts. Due to the outcomes of deontic logic it is possible to emphasize, or even indicate, certain notional distinctions, for instance, between strong and weak understanding of deontic functors, between permission and indifference, entitlement, competence, explicit permission, and entitlement which is a correlate of obligation.

One must be aware that when deontic concepts are inferred definitionally, they may not have exactly the same meaning as they had outside the language of deontic logic. This could be the consequence of the fact that terms of colloquial language tend to be imprecise and any clarification of the scope of such a concept would entail partial departure form colloquial language. However, there is no proof that colloquial language is the best of all possible languages. For instance, material implication from the classical propositional calculus does not have the same meaning as a conditional sentence from colloquial language. But then, the meaning of material implication is clearly defined, whereas the meaning of a conditional sentence is not entirely clear, cannot be easily defined, and in consequence, it is not even possible to prove the validity of a hypothetical syllogism, which we all use all too often, for a conditional sentence. Naturally, not all we have to say can be formulated using material implication instead of a conditional sentence. However, the scope of use of material implication is wide (for instance, mathematics) and within that scope one can resign from using conditional sentences, thus not only gaining precision of formulating statements, but also the possibility of formulating the rules of inference more accurately. Therefore, it would not matter greatly if deontic functors in deontic logic did not mean exactly the same as, for instance, in legal language, as long as one understands the meaning and is able to use the functors of deontic logic. Whet remains then is the question whether this language developed in deontic logic is at all useful for theoreticians of the law or meta-ethicist. A theoretician of the law, or a meta-ethicist, is interested in analysing certain concepts, regardless of whether any practical consequences result from it. Characteristically, little attention is devoted to deontic concepts by theoreticians of the law, as if the meaning of these concepts was «obvious» and did not require further explanation. Deontic logic can be rejected as useless in a specific field, claiming that it includes meanings of deontic functors which are very different from the meanings they assume in that field. But now one cannot start analysing these notions "on one's own", without any previous knowledge of the results of deontic logic, especially since there are various systems of deontic logic and, contrary to some naïve beliefs, it is not necessary to wait for logicians to «agree on» which deontic logic is «appropriate». All of them are appropriate just like both Euclidean geometry and Łobaczewski's geometry are appropriate. Deontic functors are simply understood differently, and deontic sentences are written differently in various systems, and this is how it should be so that various representatives of other fields had plenty to choose from, just like physicists can choose between Euclidean geometry and Riemann's geometry.

It is particularly important to discover that specific understanding of deontic constants entails such relationships between deontic sentences whose existence we cannot guess. Our «intuitions» tend to be incompatible there. For instance, when accepting the instrumental understanding of obligation we may be surprised that the following relationship has to occur:

$$x\mathbf{ob}_{1(K,t)}A \rightarrow x\mathbf{ob}_{1(K,t)}A \vee B.$$

and we do not notice that we fall into contradiction when we reject this relationship. It is not usually recognized that the solemnly proclaimed principle "What is not prohibited is allowed", with permission understood as a negation of a prohibition, is merely a tautology and in fact means the same as "What is not prohibited is not prohibited". If "allowed" has another meaning in this principle that "not prohibited", then the question is how to prove such a principle.

We do not believe jurisprudence is an exception among various branches of research – an exception in which statements claimed in jurisprudence do not have to be justified (unless they cannot be justified at all).

The distinction introduced between norms and deontic sentences in deontic logic allows for a more precise description of certain legal procedures and prevents absurdities like "Such and such a norm entails logically from such and such a norm" from being uttered. The contradiction between norms can be distinguished, as well as the fact that a given person is the addressee of a contradictory norm, or contradictory norms can be distinguished from the fact that a sentence in the form "$xob_{...(K,t)}A \cdot \sim A$" or "$x\textbf{OB}_{...(K,t)}A \cdot \sim A$" is true about a given person. Even such obvious ideas are critically considered as the one that the following equivalence is valid:

$$X\textbf{ob}_{...(K,t)}A \cdot B \leftrightarrow (x\textbf{ob}_{...(K,t)}A \cdot x\textbf{ob}_{...(K,t)}B).$$

No linguistic custom is sacred for deontic logic. Even if no solution provided by deontic logic can satisfy a theoretician of the law or a meta-ethicist, then at least research on deontic logic can provide an incentive to seek other, better solutions which enable researchers to avoid traps detected by deontic logic itself.

Maciej Zieliński & Zygmunt Ziembiński. The ontic status of norms
[1988: 146–150, 167]

Two kinds of issues have to be clearly distinguished: whether the issue is to justify the statement that a given norm «exists» (is real) in the sense that it is socially effective, and thus – a statement on a fairly complex social fact, or the issue is to justify (vindicate) a norm by indicating that there are certain arguments in support of the fact that the norm should be obeyed by its addressees. These are two fundamentally different issues. A norm can be perfectly justified with numerous divine and human arguments and still not be obeyed by most of its addressees, even if this fact fills them with shame and pangs of conscience. Another norm may be widely obeyed and its violation may be socially sanctioned although it would actually be hard to point out arguments in favour of obeying it, for instance, the norm which prohibits eating fish with a knife or one which dictates covering or uncovering one's head in certain circumstances. Indicating the fact that a given norm is commonly obeyed performs the function of justifying the norm as long as one silently accepts the assumption that one must act like others do.

Therefore, what remains is a seemingly ontological issue of a norm's «existence» induced by confusing a norm as a specific kind of directival expression or utterance with the fact of social influence of such kind of an utterance. A norm of behaviour as an utterance «exists» in the sense that its material substrate exists in circumstances when someone accepts semantic rules (with such a material substrate) which require the involvement of a relevant directival meaning. Still, thusly interpreted «existence» of a norm is a vastly complex issue, and the material existence of a substrate of a norm is only a necessary condition for the «existence» of a norm, rather than a sufficient condition.[289]

Yet, when we consider the «existence» of a norm as the social fact that a given norm is socially real as an utterance which influences people's behaviour, then a number of divergent conceptions is formed as to what is meant by a norm being real, which refer to various criteria of «real» validity of the norm.

The minimal requirement is that the addressees of the norm are aware of its meaning as a directival utterance and that the utterance influences their consciousness to some degree, arousing in them a sense of duty to act in the manner indicated by a given norm. The stronger condition states that a norm «exists» if its influence upon the addressees' behaviour is formally effective, that is, if there is an appropriately high (although usually unspecified) probability that the addressees will act in the manner indicated to them. The requirement of real efficiency, that is, the idea that the addressees' behaviour which is according to the norm should cause the state of affairs intended by the codifier, is more rarely raised. At other times the assumed criterion of the «existence» (validity) of a norm is whether there is a sufficiently high probability that violating the norm will entail a specific sanction on the part of the society, whether it is a focused and formalized sanction or a scattered, informal sanction of social condemnation (for instance, in order for the sanctioning norm to be ef-

---

[289] Besides, the fact of formulating a specific directival utterance can be regarded as unimportant (see Weinberger [1980: 437–438]) if "the existence of a norm" is interpreted as its validity.

fective when it is applied).[290] There also emerge various combinations of referring to the efficiency of a sanctioned and sanctioning norm. It is usually assumed, which is quite another matter, that the considered norm or norms will be applied in some cases – claiming that a norm which will never find application is a «dead» norm, and thus, «non-existent» in a certain specific sense.

Identifying the «existence» (validity) of a norm with its efficiency is troublesome as, among other things, the criteria of the efficiency of a norm are usually unclear and do not provide an operative method to resolve whether a given norm is or is not valid in a given system in a given time. We will return to this issue further on.

The statement that a given norm «exists» (is valid) in a given social system, understood as stating its efficiency as, for instance, a standard of morals, is therefore possible in an indisputably justified way only in reference to particularly conspicuous cases where the universality of certain praxis of behaviour in the manner dictated by the norm is clearly visible, and where it is not important whether 90% or 95% of its potential addressees follow the norm. It is enough to be out in the street on Christmas Eve to decide that Poles respect the norm which dictates spending this evening at home. In other cases such resolution is hard to reach in the absence of objective criteria. Thus, as will be discussed further on, it is difficult to ascertain the binding force of a valid customary norm, for instance in Juridical Relations, if we do not introduce a criterion consisting in relying on the decision of a decision-maker equipped with adequate competence.

If «existence»-efficiency is a notion which releases the discussion on the validity of norms from «philosophical speculation», then this conception is only seemingly useful from this point of view. Identifying the validity of a norm with its efficiency is silently based on a number of additional assumptions which are not decidable in a purely empirical manner.

Viewed from a different perspective than has hitherto been discussed, the validity of a norm is reduced to the possibility to indicate for that norm

---

[290] See Ross [1958: 40 *et seq.*].

an axiological justification in the form of approval of acts dictated by it (or disapproval of acts prohibited by it) from the point of view of a given system of values – or is reduced to demonstrating the fact of the settlement of this norm by a subject whose acts of settlement are regarding as binding for its addressees for certain reasons, that is, it is reduced to indicating a thetic justification for a given norm.[291] In particular, the axiological justification may refer to the system of evaluations regarded as absolute, and the thetic justification – to acts of settlement of the subject who was granted the position of an absolute codifier. [...]

Referring to «changing» of the norm, rather than repealing the old one and settling a new one, is used in practice in order to demonstrate that a certain norm has been valid for a long time, except that it was «changed» at some point. This convenient shorthand may otherwise cause various kinds of misunderstanding connected with a hypostatic approach to a norm as an entity which emerges, transforms, and withers. If a norm of behaviour is understood as an utterance which clearly dictates or prohibits given behaviour to given addressees in given circumstances, then a norm in this understanding cannot undergo changes, just like a sentence in the logical sense does not undergo changes, which is an utterance describing a given state of affairs explicitly. A «change» of a norm consists in repealing the previously valid norm and settling a new norm which has only some portion of such addressees, circumstances of application, and the positive and negative scope of normalizing as the norm which was valid before. Yet in colloquial language the boundary between the notion of «change» and the notion of settling a new norm is notoriously elusive.

Maciej Zieliński & Zygmunt Ziembiński. The logic of norms *versus* deontic logic [1988: 281–283]

The assumptions on the rationality of the lawgiver may [...] sometimes interfere with each other [....]

---

[291] See Znamierowski [1924: 27].

Thus there emerges the necessity to refer to a systematized set of inference rules, or at least, to rules based on formal relationships between norms, and especially such a relationship which is referred to as "logical entailment of norms", although it irritates some logicians.[292] Therefore, there emerges the need to refer to some kind of a formal conception of the logic of norms, which still (although what prevails today the intuition that formal logic does not end with descriptive utterances[293]) causes numerous complications of a philosophical nature connected to the concept of extra-descriptive utterances.[294] As is well known, these difficulties can be pertly overcome by building a logic of deontic sentences which predicate on estimating a given kind of people's acts in view of a given norm or an internally consistent set of norms. Deontic sentences remain in certain formal relationships analogous to the relationships between regular modal sentences, which may constitute a starting point for building deontic logic *sensu stricto*, albeit with only limited use, that is, use in legal reasoning.[295] These are specialized issues which are difficult to discuss merely on the margin of a discussion of a more general nature.

If one assumes the possibility to build the logic of norms in the strict meaning of the term, which would provide the basis for formulating inference rules on accepting certain norms as valid in a given system in view of having accepted other norms, then there are two available conceptions of how to construct such logic.[296] On the one hand, one may begin by accepting certain intuitive assumptions and then, after having determined the axioms, definitions and construction rules of the system, one can conduct acceptable formal operations in the hope that at least some of the obtained statements will be interesting from the point of view of practice of reasoning. This starting point is characteristic for expert authors – formal logicians, who are more interested in the very art of building a formal system on the previ-

---

[292] Ziemba [1983: 232].

[293] For the discussion of J. Jørgensen's dilemma see Weinberger [1972: 321–322].

[294] "There is always certain risk in overusing the term "logic" in order to justify extralogical theses, as then the term is used persuasively" – Wróblewski [1979: 217].

[295] Ziemba [1983: 299 *et seq.*] Otherwise – Weinberger [1984: 565–566].

[296] See Ziemba [1969: 7–87] for the discussion of the most important systems of deontic logic.

ously unexploited ground than in the practical applicability of the obtained results. On the other hand, one may encounter such a way of constructing systems of the logic of norms that practically useful statements can possibly be derived from the systems quickly, even from counterintuitive axioms. At the same time, they are derived in such a way as to avoid paradoxes troublesome for the practice of legal or ethical reasoning, and simultaneously, to give the paradoxes a harmless interpretation. Both of these ways have their advantages and disadvantages; still, one has to take into account the fact that, when attempting to refer to the existing colloquial intuitions, one may discover that some elements of the intuitions are incoherent,[297] which is admittedly a useful consequence for the progress of legal thought, but not very pleasant for lawyers as it arouses resentment for the discussion of the «stiff and formal» logic of norms.

In any case, the logic of norms is an outcome of certain mental constructs which can be accepted or rejected by lawyers.[298] By accepting reasonable logic of norms and rejecting unreasonable logic of norms one obtains the basis for determining the set of valid legal norms in a practically useful manner; otherwise one obtains a defective set from the point of view of praxeology. Yet, it does not have to be true that the notion of a set of valid legal norms is equivalent to the notion of a well systematized set of legal norms, that is: a system. The actual lawgiver's mistakes cannot always be eliminated by assuming the rationality of the lawgiver.

In order to protect the system of legal norms from negative consequences of internal incoherence, legal doctrine created traditional collision rules which, however, are hard to formalize, and thus – to connect with a system of logic of norms in a manner which would be useful for the purpose of practical legal reasoning.

One should note here that even if the logic of norms were the only basis for constructing a legal system, the starting point for the construction of such a system would not be a small system of carefully chosen norms-axioms, but a great number of norms settled by various state authorities based

---

[297] Ziemba [1983: 6].
[298] Ziemba & Ziembiński [1964: 113].

on legislative competences vested in them.[299] Thus, despite the assumption idealizing the rationality of a lawgiver which is usually assumed, it would be difficult to make an assumption so strong that the «lawgiver» settles the norms in such a measured way that their consequences do not prove formally or praxeologically incompatible.

Jerzy Kalinowski. The logic of norms
[1990: 352–356]

The relationship between legal logic [...] and the logic of norms has already been indicated. Namely, the theses of the logic of norms are treated as laws which provide a logical basis for rules and schemes of reasoning which are used in legal practice in the indicated broad meaning of the latter term. These are such inferential rules which are given binding force by the laws of logic, and schemes which these laws make conclusive, which is granted to any reasoning based on such a scheme.

Logic-knowledge (as this is the one taken into consideration in relation to legal logic, attempting to discover the logical grounds for real, rather than imaginary – and constructed in this meaning – legal discursive thought) is, despite its formal character, knowledge of reality, referring to real situations, possible if not actual, rather than intentional objects such as notions or judgements in the logical sense or their linguistic symbols. When a logician utters:

(1) p or not-p.

he speaks about reality and states that a situation described by the propositional utterance symbolized by p or a situation described by the propositional utterance symbolized by not-p occurs. Similarly, if he utters:

(2) [If x should do a, then x is allowed to do a.]

as a thesis of the logic of norms, then he also speaks about reality; in this case: about normative relationships actually occurring between the subject x and his act symbolized with a. These two statements, namely: (1) and (2),

---

[299] More on this subject see Opałek & Woleński [1973a: 12–14]. Let us add that validation rules of a system can be "loosened" (W. Zakrzewski's term). Another issue which cannot go unnoticed is the case of violating the rule of law in the legislative process; more on this – see Ziembiński [1982: *et seq.*].

are of general character: it is always so. Thus they are scientific laws just as laws formulated with any other nomological science.

The laws of science, whatever they are, enable us to obtain practical knowledge by providing theoretical knowledge of the reality. This knowledge, just like any other knowledge, refers to reality, and in this case: it refers to human act as such, which should or can be performed or not performed. Norms which state this (as they are statements from the grammatical point of view) stand out as obvious in the light of the relevant scientific laws with the force of *a posteriori* obviousness (obviousness is analytical when it is derived *ex terminis*; moreover, it is obviousness *a posteriori* if the denotation and the designates of the considered terms are determined in connection with previous, or at least contemporary knowledge of reality, rather than *a priori*, that is, independently of the reality and the knowledge of it).[300] In view of the fact that science states that in certain conditions water boils at 100°C, it is analytically obvious *a posteriori* that any person who wants to boil water in such conditions should heat it to the temperature of 100°C. Similarly, in view of the fact that a logician states that in all cases, if x should do a, then x is allowed to do a, it is analytically obvious *a posteriori* that whoever accepts the utterance "x should do a" is also obliged to accept the utterance "x is allowed to do a".

The expression:

(3) Whoever accepts an utterance of the type "x should do a" is obliged to accept an utterance of the type "x is allowed to do a" (naturally, respectively with the same transposition to variables),

is an inferential rule. The bindingness of this rule is based on (2) which is the logical basis for the rule.

Each inferential rule determines the method of reasoning consistent with it. The result of a mental action dictated by an inferential rule is called "reasoning" if it does not contain free variables (not bound with a quantifier) or "the scheme of reasoning" if the premise or premises as well as the conclusion contain at least one free variable. For instance:

(4) x should do a, therefore x is allowed to do a.

---

[300] See Kalinowski [1983b] on the issue of analytical obviousness *a posteriori*.

is a scheme of reasoning, whereas:

(5) Peter should do military service, therefore Peter is allowed to do military service.

is a specific reasoning.

It is easy to see why legal logic in the conception I assumed needs the logic of norms and why it is sufficient as long as it is logic-knowledge which takes into account the binding force of norms. Deontic logic *sensu stricto*, unless it goes beyond the normative syntactic structure of the discussed utterances, remains only a mental construct.

This could be accepted as the conclusion of our discussion. However, the conclusion should also contain a few remarks on legal logic practised according to conceptions other than the one I have described in the present discussion.

Logical basis indicated for legal reasoning discussed so far demonstrate that the formal structure of legal reasoning is usually very simple (if certain works by I. Tammelo suggest the opposite view, it is because the author consciously complicated the structure, wishing to broaden the scope of legal logic, adding the methods to check if reasoning is conclusive, which are used in the modal and non-modal logic of sentences, and even in the logic of predicates to a certain degree).[301] Also members of Juridical Relations usually reason correctly without instruction in the art of reasoning, just as Molière's Jourdain in the art of speaking in prose. Their natural predispositions in this field, usually inherent to every person, developed and perfected in life, prove to be sufficient.

On the other hand, what poses a problem is the choice of premises. Legal discussions never concern inferential rules and schemes which are supposed to be used, but accept the premises which are convenient for drawing conclusions. This is why some entrust legal logic with the task of justifying the choice of premises for legal reasoning, that is, accepting the premises. For instance, the late Chaim Perelman wrote:

> The role of formal logic consists in coordinating conclusions with premises, and the role of legal logic is to demonstrate that these prem-

---

[301] See Kalinowski [1983a: 7 and other]; see *e.g.* Tammelo & Moens [1976].

ises can be accepted. The possibility of acceptance results from the confrontation of the evidence with arguments and values confronting each other in a court dispute; if the judge wants to make a decision and justify the verdict, he should mediate between them.[302]

The choice of premises is often conducted in the course of a court dispute, or any other kind, whose protagonists argue in favour of their viewpoint. In some cases, and using a properly chosen chain of reasoning, one of them is able to demonstrate that the premises submitted by them naturally impose themselves as the only ones. Perelman calls it "convincing" in court. It is rare that one convinces somebody. One is usually limited to persuasion, that is, obtaining acceptance from the majority in a given auditorium through more or less appropriate arguments. Both in the case of convincing and persuading there is a reference to reasoning, which can be of different kinds. Yet, one should always indicate the logical grounds for the reasoning one is conducting, attempting to justify the accepted premises and convince the opponent that the premises are appropriate. Thus emerges the second conception of legal logic, which, for all its differences with respect to the first one, does not exclude it: they complement each other, which I stressed on several occasions.[303]

Apart from these two complimentary conceptions there is a third, which supplements both and does not exclude either of the former, and is historically the earliest. It occurs *implicite* in a rudimentary form in Cicero's *Ad Trebatium Topica* and always finds its advocates: for instance, A. Bayart.[304] At some point it was the primary conception of Leibniz's legal logic, until he turned towards the conception presented here as our basic concept, becoming its precursor.[305] According to the conception which is discussed as the third here, although historically it is first, legal logic is a set of rules of interpretation of the law, mostly the interpretation conducted from the point of view of the application of law. A typical example is the 1615 work by Martinus Schickhardus entitled *Logical iuridica* which, if I am not mis-

---

[302] Perelman [1976: 176] [...].
[303] Especially: Kalinowski [1982: 288 *et seq.*]; Kalinowski [1983a: 16 *et seg.*].
[304] See Bayart [1966].
[305] Kalinowski [1977a].

taken, uses the term "legal logic" for the first time.[306] Interpreters draw a major premise of their normative reasoning in the field of interpretation from this set of rules. The interpretation is conducted either in the course of study and teaching of the law, or in the course of application of the law. Yet at the same time the choice of a rule of interpretation as a premise is made mostly, if not always, in terms of the choice of such reasoning for which one could find logical grounds, according to the first conception of legal logic, for which I advocate. Again, these conceptions compliment each other rather than exclude each other. [...]

We were to determine the relationship of legal logic to deontic logic. However, this required preliminary specification of the understanding of legal logic. We considered it advisable to take into consideration primarily the conception of legal logic as the knowledge of the logical basis of legislative reasoning; a conception whose most significant precursor was Leibniz. Nevertheless, we also presented two other conceptions which were successfully complimented by it. The kind of normative reasoning common among legal reasoning is one whose logical bases constitute proper theses of deontic logic understood as the logic of norms.

In turn, we stated about deontic logic as the logic of utterances on norms that it will be connected with legal logic in the basic meaning if it is logic-knowledge which takes into consideration the binding force of norms. On the other hand, the logic of utterances on norms, putting aside their binding force and focusing on examining the syntactic structures of the examined normative utterances, is not tied to legal logic in the interpretation settled at the beginning of this work, and thus is devoid of any significance.

Kazimierz Opałek. Normative formulas
[1990: 313–314, 317–318]

In order to correct the shortcomings of Kelsen's analysis one should start with reconstructing the utterances discussed here.

1. Let us assume as the formula of a norm:

---

[306] Schickhardus [1615].

$N(p)$.

The operator N (which should be read as "is settled as adequate") is connected to the sentence in the subjunctive mood, (p), which should be read: "that someone behaves so and so"; for instance: "It is dictated that the owner register his car".[307]

2. The formula of the optative is:

U *(utinam) p*.[308]

U (may) is again connected with a sentence in the subjunctive mood, for instance: "May it be sunny tomorrow!".

3. The subject of norms can be only (adequate) behaviour, and optatives – (wished) behaviour or another event. The subject of evaluation can be behaviour (which occurred or was intended to occur), another event or thing. We assume that also people belong to the latter category. In Kelsen's work evaluations of people are reduced to evaluations of behaviour [...].

4. Evaluations of things have the following structure:[309]

S is W^+ (positive value).

S is W^- (negative value).

S symbolizes the name of a thing and evaluating expressions have the character of predicates, for instance: "This painting is beautiful", "This law is unfair".

5. Evaluations of behaviour and other events have the structure:

W^+p.

W^-p.

Evaluating expressions occur here as operators, connected to p with sentences of descriptive character; for instance: "It is good that the son helps his parents", "It is bad that Peter did not get the job". This reconstruction of evaluations of behaviour and other events is particularly important as in colloquial speech one often comes across formulations which use names of

---

[307] A notation which is simplified in comparison with the previously used (Opałek [1974: chapter III *et passim*]): (p), unlike p, denotes the subjunctive character of a sentence, in contrast to the former (ut p).

[308] Derived from Carnap [1954: 1001 *et seq.*].

[309] Also the changed notation: W^+ as a positive value (instead of Wp), W^- as negative value (instead of Wn); see Opałek [1974: 90].

behaviour or events or infinitives instead of *p* (sentences), which may obscure the analysis, for instance: "Helping one's parents is good", "Stealing is bad", "*Dulce et decorum est pro patria mori*". [...]

We should now consider what the nature is of the discussed relationship of correspondence/lack of correspondence, or fulfilment/lack of fulfilment of a norm, by behaviour or event – according to my view. This issue is only seemingly simple. In order to resolve it, Kelsen uses the conception of modally neutral substrate. We will not duplicate our critique of this conception presented in another study.[310] It suffices to present Kelsen's motives for this resolution. Kelsen was aware that if this relationship was presented as a semantic relationship of fulfilment / lack of fulfilment of a norm through behaviour, the norm would have to be a sentence in the logical sense, or it would have to contain such a sentence, as claimed by the authors he criticized. Kelsen rejects the conception of fulfilment / lack of fulfilment with regard to norms. He argues: "Only an utterance which is true or false can be declarative or theoretical; yet a norm, which is neither true nor false, is not such an utterance".[311] The solution he assumes is that the discussed relationship occurs between modally neutral substrates of duty and being.

One has to agree with Kelsen in that in the case of norms (but also of optatives) there is no question of a semantic relationship of fulfilment / lack of fulfilment. However, even if we disregard the problem of the modally neutral substrate, Kelsen's argumentation obscures the issue, as on the one hand, he recognizes norms as extra-linguistic entities (admittedly, ideal), but on the other hand, he often sees them as utterances with a set meaning.[312] Naturally, this impedes the explanation of the relationship: norm – behaviour. In my opinion, one should state clearly that in this case the issue is not the relationship between an utterance and the extra-linguistic reality, but the relationship between two empirical facts, namely: between a norm as a verbal act of influencing behaviour, and the behaviour, or between a wish as an optative verbal act – and behaviour or an event.

---

[310] Opałek [1980: 25 *et seq.*].
[311] Kelsen [1979: 48].
[312] Kelsen [1979: 131 *et seq.*].

Contrary to appearances, one could follow this direction in the interpretation of Kelsen's view in *General Theory of Norms* (interpreting norms as "the empirical sense of the act of will", which is difficult to reconcile with the idea that the ideal expression of a norm is supposed to be its validity).[313] Yet, we will not discuss this issue further, as our aim is solely to highlight the nature of the discussed relationship as a relationship between two empirical objects. It is a relationship of pragmatic fulfilment / lack of fulfilment, a relationship between an empirical act of demanding specific behaviour and a corresponding or not corresponding demand for behaviour, or the relationship between the empirical act of wishing certain behaviour or an event to occur and a corresponding or not corresponding wish for behaviour or an event. The settlement of this relationship occurs through understanding, which should be achieved as in every society there are certain standard ways to create normative and optative acts and to understand the conditions and situations of their fulfilment or lack of fulfilment. In the case of a normative act, this relationship should be distinguished from the relationship of efficiency/inefficiency of the motivational influence of this act on behaviour.[314] In any case, this manner of solving the problem seems simpler than Kelsen's solution, since adopting a modally neutral substrate entails problems of semantic nature – not to mention more far-reaching philosophical difficulties.

> Maciej Zieliński. Methods of verbalizing norms
> [1992]

1. Norms communicated through non-verbal behaviour

Someone who is responsible for the condition of the lawns in a given estate might react in a variety of ways to people continuously treading paths in them.

He may take the most reasonable course of action, namely: after having discovered which ways people really want or need to use, he could aban-

---

[313] Kelsen [1979: 2, 21 *et seq.*]. See Weinberger [1981: 127 *et seq.*].
[314] Opałek [1974: 120].

don his attachment to the previously designed superfluous paths, eliminate them and provide people with the possibility to walk safely in the places they themselves chose, which would also take care of the lawns.

However, if he prefers imperious behaviour in such situations (which is sadly more probable), he can choose one of the following solutions, for instance, he can watch the lawn nonstop and admonish people, or put up a notice informing of the prohibition of treading on the lawns, or he can fence off the unwelcome paths. According to one legal conception, the last case would denote that he performed "settlement through physical creations",[315] and thus in a way indirectly "informed" others of the validity of a given norm. This conception has not been widely accepted in jurisprudence.

Yet it is indisputable that in practical human activity it is possible, and actually often done, to communicate norms of behaviour in a PARALINGUISTIC manner, with the help of all kinds of non-verbal signs, for instance: maritime signal flags, commissions issued at a race track, *etc.* Using this form of expression of norms of behaviour is often necessary due to the low efficiency or total inefficiency of using utterances of the standard verbal communication, for instance, due to the impossibility of hearing or seeing the substrates of verbal signs because of great distance, speed or noise, *etc.*

2. The imperative form of a norm of behaviour

It is often thought, especially in circles unconnected to legislature, that the basic and most proper way to express norms of behaviour is formulating them as an IMPERATIVE utterance that is, one containing a verb in the imperative mood as well as bearing the proper punctuation mark: the exclamation mark. Yet one should note that such a manner of formulating norms is not free of flaws, or at least drawbacks.

Firstly – an utterance in imperative mood does not have to perform the suggestive role, but by performing the EXPRESSIVE role it can simply be used to EXPRESS someone's emotional state or to BE FREED FROM the state of emotional tension. It is not a suggestion of any kind if someone utters: "Damn you to hell!" (as it is difficult to issue orders towards hell) but also: "Go to hell!" (even if the utterance is directed at a person).

---

[315] Znamierowski [1924].

Secondly – not every norm of behaviour can be formulated in the imperative form, for instance: it is impossible to do in the case of settling norms for oneself, mostly because there is no form in the imperative mood which would correspond to the first person singular. The claim of a three--year-old that "HE ISSUES ORDERS TOWARDS HIMSELF" is naturally an ambitious manifestation of rebellion rather than taking a position in linguistic issues.

Thirdly – using the imperative mood does not prejudge the firm character of a given utterance. People use this mood also to indicate some behaviour to someone, without speaking from the position of authority. This is true for the case of expressing begging, a request or encouragement, as in the utterances "Give me one more smile" or "Buy only in Pewex shops", *etc.*

Fourthly – in principle, the imperative mood is used in settlement only in the cases where someone settles norms for other people with the people physically present, and the idea is for the act of settlement to carry a particularly powerful suggestive load in order to ensure immediate execution – for instance, when the commander of a platoon attempts to make his terrified and tired subordinates charge, by shouting: "Forward!". Due to this very feature of imperative utterances – they are not used to formulate legal texts.

Fifthly – dictating, and even settling norms for someone in his absence can be done in many ways, and the form of an imperative utterance is not actually necessary or sufficient, and it is frequently downright INEFFECTIVE. Those who doubt the inefficiency of imperative utterances have obviously never tried to dictate something to an adolescent in the imperative form.

3. The obligative («of duty») form of a norm

The "OBLIGATIVE" form of a norm is indicated as the most proper one even more often than the imperative form. The former is sometimes considered as the classic form of a norm in legal or ethical discussion. The use of this form consists in formulating an utterance which states that someone SHOULD act (behave) so and so in given circumstances.

Traditionally this form assumes two different forms: «categorical» and «hypothetical».

According to the first one, the norm «of duty» has the following form: "X which has the characteristics of A, in circumstances O, should do Z", and after adding quantification: "Every A which has the characteristics of A, in circumstances O, should do Z". This form is particularly suitable for deter-mining behaviour in the situation where the obligation should concern the behaviour of any subject in any circumstances, as then the norm can take assume the form: "X should do Z in any case".

In the «hypothetical» form the norm assumes the following form: "If subject X which has the characteristics of A finds himself in circumstances O, he should do Z". This form is very convenient in the cases where it is im-portant for someone to clearly separate in the structure of the utterance the elements which define the scope of use (that is, the features of the addressee and the circumstances) from the elements which define the scope of normal-izing of a given norm (determining behaviour). Such a form is sometimes assumed in order to construct various kinds of calculus of norms. Then, also sometimes,[316] the different character of the elements of a given utterance is recognized: what can be called the antecedent of a «hypothetically» formu-lated norm is regarded as a descriptive sentence, whereas only the conse-quent is regarded as a normative utterance (a norm). In order to escape the deficiencies of the above form (for instance: certain syntactic incompatibil-ity), among other things, we often assume such a structure of norms in dis-cussions in the field of semiotics and the logic of norms which the descrip-tion of a subject's given behaviour in given circumstances (not necessarily in the hypothetical form) is preceded by the normative operator "it should be so that", for instance: "It should be so that if a subject purchases a motor vehicle, he registers it".[317]

While distinguishing the «categorical» and «hypothetical» form of norms one has to take into consideration the following remarks.

Firstly – utterances formulated in these forms are mutually translata-ble, and accepting any of them is determined by practical reasons: scien-tific (*e.g.* for certain analyses), substantive (*e.g.* to emphasize that the scope

---

[316] See for instance Weinberger [1958b].
[317] This structure allows for a relatively simple distinction between a norm and a sen-tence, depending on whether one uses the norm-creating operator "it should be so that" or the logical operator "it is so that" at the beginning. See Zieliński & Ziembiński [1988: 69–70].

of addressees is limited), or even simply a habit of the person formulating the norms.

Secondly – mutual translatability of the «categorical» and «hypothetical» utterances constitutes a vital argument in favour of acknowledging the fact that the dispute of what the scope is of the «hypothesis» and what the scope is of the «disposition»,[318] which sometimes occurs in jurisprudence, is practically pointless, just as the dispute over what falls under the characteristics of the addressee and what belongs to the characteristics of the circumstances. It is equally correct and adequate in terms of content to say: "*X* which has the properties of *A*, which is in the circumstances *O*" as "*X* which has the properties of being in circumstances *O*" or "In the circumstances where there is *A* conditions *O* occur", *etc.*

Thirdly – in the case of distinguishing these two types of formulation the issue is in fact the «conditional» or «non-conditional» way of the very STRUCTURE of the utterance, rather than the fundamental substantive difference which, for instance, could have been meant by Kant when he formulated the distinction between categorical and hypothetical imperatives,[319] which can ultimately be reduced to the distinction between norms and teleological directives.

Practical use of this form (relatively common in theoretical discussion) involves many opportunities for confusion, as the phrase "should" can be interpreted in at least five different ways, and then three additional ones within one of them («descriptive»), which gives a total of seven various meanings, and thus, seven reasons for confusion.

The meanings we are dealing with are: normative, directival, teleological, evaluating, prognostic and descriptive.

An utterance containing the phrase "should" in its NORMATIVE meaning is equivalent to an utterance through which someone directly dictates or prohibits something. In this situation, the utterance «of duty» "John should study systematically", or "It should be so that John studies systematically"

---

[318] Śmiałkowski, Lang & Delorme [1961: 104 *et seq.*].
[319] See Ossowska [1947: 112].

is equivalent to the expression "It is dictated that John studies systematically", or more emphatically "It is dictated, let John study systematically".

The utterance in which the phrase "should" is used in the DIRECTIVAL (TELEOLOGICAL) meaning is an utterance through which it is advised, recommended, *etc.* how one should behave in order to achieve a given aim. For instance, the utterance "John should put bait on the hook if he wants to catch any fish" is equivalent to the utterance "It is advised (recommended) to John to put bait on the hook if he wants to catch any fish".

An utterance contains the phrase "should" used in the EVALUATING sense when it directly expresses approval for a given state A or disapproval for a given state non-A. If this is the use of the phrase "should" in the utterance "John should study systematically", then it is equivalent to the utterance "It is good when John studies systematically".

In turn, in the case of PROGNOSTIC use, the utterance «of duty» is equivalent to the utterance which directly expresses someone's conviction that, in view of certain knowledge concerning relationships between certain facts, the fact that when one of them occurs, the occurrence of the other one will be according to expectations (which obviously can be based on adequate or inadequate knowledge). For instance, if the expression "should" was used in the prognostic meaning in the utterance "If the groundhog sees its shadow on Groundhog Day, there should be 6 more weeks of winter", then the utterance is equivalent to the utterance "If it is sunny on 2nd February, then it will be according to expectations that the winter will last until the middle of March". In this case, the utterance "If someone's application meets formal requirements, it should be considered" is in this case equivalent to the utterance "If someone's application meets formal requirements, then it will be according to expectations that it will be considered".

Finally, in the DESCRIPTIVE meaning the utterance «of duty» "X should do Z" can be equivalent to the following utterances: (1) In view of the validity of a given norm, X is dictated to do Z; (2) I estimate that it would be good if X did Z (it would be bad if X did not do Z); (3) I advise (advised) to X to do Z if he wants to achieve the aim C.

This great ambiguity of the phrase "should" may be the cause of many practical drawbacks, and especially: misunderstandings. It is especially inconvenient that normative, evaluating and descriptive meanings can be so entangled with each other that one could basically say that the phrase "should" is a hybrid, and individual elements of this hybrid gain certain advantage over the remaining elements only in different circumstances. Yet, sometimes there are only such practical situations in which some of the meanings can be eliminated without doubt. For instance, if the utterance states that "It should rain tomorrow", it can be assumed that it is not the normative sense that is meant here. Still, it can just as well be prognostic as evaluating, and moreover, one has to realize that in this case the normative sense is not eliminated automatically, but rather on the basis of the (admittedly, banal) ASSUMPTION that the author of a given utterance is a rational subject.

It seems that the easiest way to avoid misunderstanding connected with using phrases «of duty» is to accept some general assumptions which determine given meaning of these phrases in a given field, assumptions similar to the general assumption on THE NORMATIVE CHARACTER OF LEGAL TEXT.

Yet, it should be noted that the legal assumption concerns the normative character of WHOLE compound expressions rather than the normative character of individual components. Moreover, the normative character of an utterance in a legal text does not only concern utterances which contain the phrase "should", but all complex signs of the text. For these reasons the fact that an utterance «of duty» in a legal text is of normative character does not prejudge the normative character of the phrase «of duty» itself. This is the case only when the phrase "should" acts as the main functor in the utterance. In other cases it can even have descriptive meaning. For instance, in art. 3 §2 of the *Family and Guardianship Code* ("If obtaining the document which should be submitted to the head of the registry office one encounters obstacles which are difficult to overcome, the court may exempt one of the obligation to submit the document") the whole expression is of NORMATIVE character, whereas the phrase "should" was used descriptively instead of the phrase "the submission of which has been dictated" (or "the submission of which is necessary").

What is significant here is that even in the cases where the phrase "should" is definitely used normatively rather than descriptively (or performs the role of a main functor) it is sometimes regarded in judicial practice as the mildest of the directival forms (for instance, more as an expression of a recommendation than a dictate) rather than a form of absolute dictate.[320] This constitutes a symptom, though luckily a marginal one, of a discrepancy between theoretical conceptions and legal practice.

Even if the phrase "should" occurs in legal texts as the operator of dictate rather than in the «descriptive» sense, recognizing its normative function may entail certain difficulties.

The issue is relatively simple when the phrase refers to people, like for instance in the law of art.183 §1 sentence 1 of the *Civil Code*: "Whoever finds a lost item should immediately notify a person authorized to receive such items". It is easily recognizable as a norm of behaviour (with a clear indication of the addressee, the circumstances and the behaviour).

It is much more complicated to reconstruct a norm in the cases where the phrase "should": (1) is used impersonally (*e.g.* in art. 305 §1 of *Penal Code*: "At least 7 days should elapse between delivering the notification and the date of the hearing") or (2) refers to things or states of affairs (*e.g.* the sentence in art. 2 sentence 1 of *Family and Guardianship Code*: "Marriage should take place before the head of the registry office in the place of residence of one of the parties").[321] [....]

4. The «modal» form of a norm of behaviour

The method which is very similar to the one «of duty», and often identified with it, or at least regarded as a special form of the method «of duty», can be called "modal" due to the use of the modal phrase "must" in normative utterances. According to this method of formulating norms, a normative utterance has the following form: "X must execute behaviour Z in circumstances O".

Unfortunately, it is again necessary to note the disadvantages of using this phrase, as the term "must" (or more precisely: "must be A") has at least

---

[320] See art. 74 §4 of *Executive Penal Code*: "Before issuing a decision in the question of prescription of the execution of a suspended sentence, the court SHOULD (my highlight – MZ) hear the accused and his defender, and the presence of the prosecutor during the hearing is obligatory".

[321] More in this subject: Zieliński [1972: 50].

five significantly different meanings, four of which are of a DESCRIPTIVE character and only one – NORMATIVE.

It is usually outlined that descriptive meanings of this phrase can assume four different INTERPRETATIONS. These are: (1) LOGICAL interpretation, (2) DYNAMIC interpretation, (3) AXIOLOGICAL interpretation, and (4) PSYCHOLOGICAL interpretation.

In the LOGICAL interpretation the phrase "Must be A" means the same as "There occurs a sentence among (some, someone's) sentences of knowledge which states that it is (was, will be) A". In this case the utterance "A triangle must have three sides" is equivalent to the utterance "In (*e.g.* the speaker's) knowledge, a sentence (*e.g.* the definition of a triangle) is included from which it results that a (any – if one adds quantification) triangle has three sides".

In the DYNAMIC interpretation the phrase "Must be A" means the same as "There are such factors in the existing set of circumstances which inevitably lead to the fact that the state A will be realized". Such interpretation of the phrase "must" makes the utterance "Milk bottles exposed to temperatures of minus thirty degrees (Celsius) must burst" mean the same as "There are such factors (*e.g.* expansion of fluids in low temperatures and fragility of glass) which inevitably lead to the fact that milk bottles exposed to temperatures of minus thirty degrees will burst".

In the AXIOLOGICAL interpretation the phrase "Must be A" refers to someone's evaluations and is equivalent to the utterance "According to evaluations (of some subject or subjects), it would be good if it was A" (or "it would be bad if it was not A"). For instance, the utterance "Students must study diligently", interpreted axiologically, means the same as "According to evaluations (*e.g.* of the person formulating the utterance), it would be good (for students, or in general) if students studied diligently".

In the PSYCHOLOGICAL interpretation the phrase "Must be A" used in an utterance causes it to be equivalent to the expression "I (that is, the subject uttering) am absolutely convinced that it is (will be) A". For instance, the sentence uttered by someone after having finished a cycle of courses preparing for the exam: "I must pass this exam", is equivalent to the sentence "I am absolutely convinced (on some basis, for instance, because I am well prepared) that I will pass the approaching exam (that is, get a positive result)" in the psychological sense. Naturally, the basis of this confident attitude may be very diverse, and in particular, it may be a justification included in another interpretation of the phrase "must" (*e.g.* "I am convinced that a triangle has three sides", "I am convinced that milk bottles exposed to temperatures of minus thirty degrees will burst").

In the NORMATIVE interpretation the phrase has two meanings: weak and strong. In the former (normative-WEAK) the phrase "Must be *A*" means: "A norm (*e.g.* norm *N*) dictates the realization of *A*", whereas in the latter (normative-STRONG) the phrase means: "A norm (*e.g.* norm *N*) is VALID which dictates the realization of *A*". In this case the phrase "Students must go to classes" would mean in the weak interpretation: "A norm dictates it that students must go to classes", whereas in the strong interpretation it would also take into account the fact of a given norm being valid and would mean "A norm is valid which dictates it that students must go to classes".

Naturally, one cannot draw far-reaching conclusions from the fact that it is possible to settle the meaning of the phrase in question in the presented examples relatively easily due to the meaning of the other elements (that is, the context of the phrase "must"). As a matter of fact, the utterance "Students must study diligently" can be just as legitimately interpreted as corresponding to (true or false, which is another matter) sentences: "In knowledge *W* there is a sentence from which it entails that students study diligently", "There are factors which inevitably lead to it that students study diligently", "A norm dictates to students to study diligently", "A norm is valid which dictates to students to study diligently", "According to someone's evaluation, it would be good if students studied diligently", "I am absolutely convinced that students study diligently". In any [...] case, apart from axiological interpretation, this phrase can also have a normative interpretation (*e.g.* as one expressing at least an axiological norm, if not a thetic norm).

Thus using the modal phrase "must" does not determine the normative character of an utterance, all the more so that it can also be used in teleological directives; for instance, one may encounter the directive: "If you want to turn on the light, you must flip the switch".

For the reasons indicated above, this phrase does not provide even the broadest directival character of the utterance.

5. A seemingly descriptive form of norms of behaviour

In the practice of formulating norms of behaviour, especially in the practice of the textual formulation of norms, and definitely in the practice of formulating norms in legal texts, a descriptive form is the most commonly used. It is used when IT IS KNOWN (for instance, from the context or an official assumption) that a given utterance expresses norms of behaviour, and at the same time it contains a verb in the indicative mood which performs the function of a logical connective (regardless of the tense, aspect, personal or impersonal use, *etc.*).

Expressions of this kind constitute a numerous and greatly varied group. They usually proclaim that: (a) a given subject behaves in a given manner at a given time, or will behave like that in the future (performs, recognizes, commences, will issue, will draw); (b) something is happening (or something will happen) to a person or an object (is subject to penalty, is on probation); (c) someone or something has certain specific features or belongs to a given class (is responsible, is limited, is a prosecutor, is included, is entitled, is invalid); (d) something is done or something is happening (is returned, is commenced, is delivered, is divided); (e) an action causes a certain state (amortization causes, entails, has an effect); (f) someone is held responsible for something; (g) someone has... (has the ability, has entitlement, has an obligation); (h) someone can do something (or cannot do something); (i) something may happen to something; (j) something should (must) be done with something; (k) something can be done; (l) doing something is (is not) allowed; (m) something is used to do something, *etc.*[322]

Admittedly, the normative character of these kinds of utterances is acceptable in colloquial speech to some degree, but in an exceptionally weak and marginal way, definitely peripheral. The issue that comes to the fore is undoubtedly their descriptive interpretation, and this is how they function unless additional conditions are created in which their normative meaning will obviously be allowed, or even more so, accepted as

---

[322] More on this subject: Zieliński [1972: 50 *et seq.*].

the only adequate one. The obviousness and power of these additional conditions has to change together with and match the smaller probability of a given normative utterance assuming a normative character. As it is relatively easy to proceed to the normative interpretation of phrases in which it is said: "Someone is performing", that "he is doing something", but without any strong assumptions it would be hard to encounter a norm in utterances stating that "Someone is allowed to do something", or that "Someone can do something" or that "he is entitled", *etc.*; and indeed, proceeding to norms in the last few cases is accomplished in a particularly complicated manner. [....]

In connection with the assumption on the normative character of legal texts, there occurs in legal language a radical reversal of normative probability and the descriptive meaning of respective utterances in comparison with the proportions in colloquial language indicated above.

Thanks to this assumption, normative sense comes to the fore in legal texts, and ascribing descriptive character to some phrases requires fulfilling additional conditions or making certain explanations, similarly as in the case of the phrase "should" in art. 3 §2 of *Family and Guardianship Code* described above. […].

6. «Deontic» manner of formulating norms

Another way to formulate norms of behaviour can be called the DEONTIC manner. It is connected with the use of certain declarative sentences in order to formulate a norm (thus in this meaning it is a subgenus of the «descriptive» form) which has the character of a modal sentence (and in this sense it is also a specific subgenus of the «modal» kind of formulating norms). However, we are not concerned here with using alethic modal sentences, stating that it "must" ("can") be so and so in the real world, but rather DEONTIC sentences which state the qualification of a given person's given act in view of a given norm (thus indicating normative modality).

These sentences may characterize a given act in six different ways: dictated, prohibited, allowed, facultative, indifferent or obligatory. However, not all of these cases can be used to express a norm.

The most useful ones in this respect can be those deontic sentences which characterize a given act as DICTATED or PROHIBITED. On the other hand, characterizing an act as optional, or facultative, would require a particularly complicated translation (besides, it would only be possible to a limited degree, with a negative form: not-allowed or not-facultative) into sentences on dictate or prohibition which would be contradictory to these characteristics. Characterizing an act as obligatory would not determine the specific content of the norm at all, and ascribing indifference to the action would only constitute a description of a given situation.

The limitations of the use of the «deontic» manner of formulating norms, even if the characteristics of dictate or prohibition are used, are connected to the fact that using these characteristics in order to formulate a norm is basically only possible if one uses somewhat deficient deontic sentences, and more precisely: incomplete deontic utterances.

Full deontic sentences have a clearly DESCRIPTIVE sense. For instance, a sentence concerning a dictate has the following form: "Person X's act C is dictated in view of the validity of norm N" (in short: N_{ncx}), and one concerning a prohibition has the form: "Person X's act C is prohibited in view of the validity of norm N" (Z_{ncx}). The descriptive character of these utterances is unlikely to raise any doubts, all the more as that normative character is only referred to, as the norm which determines the dictate or prohibition is in a way outside the sentence.

Normative character can at most be ascribed to an utterance of the type "Act C is dictated to person X" as it is an incomplete utterance, and therefore, not very clearly descriptive. But for the same reason one cannot exclude the descriptive character of this utterance. The fact that using this utterance can lead to misunderstanding probably does not require any argumentation, especially if such an utterance is encountered in other circumstances than in a legal text, for instance, uttered by someone who can just as well act as a commentator or one realizing his entitlements (*e.g.* teacher).

7. The performative form of a norm of behaviour

In methodological texts the properties of performative utterances are often ascribed to norms through the formulation in which someone performs a cultural action of at least the second order (since every utterance is a cultural action of at least the first order) or the uttering of that which is a necessary condition for performing the cultural action in a given situation.[323] In this sense the performative character of a norm is manifested in the fact that through its formulation in a given social system a cultural action of dictating given behaviour in given circumstances to someone is performed.

The easiest way to provide a norm with a clear performative function would be to equip it in an initial phrase which is commonly accepted as determining performative character: "herewith…". Thus a perfectly constructed performative norm would have the following form: "Herewith it is dictated that X does Z in circumstances O". However, normative utterances constructed in such a way are uncommon in practice. The most common are abbreviated utterances which usually omit the phrase "herewith", *e.g.* "It is dictated that X does Z in circumstances O". Unfortunately, this utterance does not have a clear performative or normative character. The phrase "it is dictated" (or more common in practice: "it is prohibited") can be interpreted descriptively as well as normatively.

It has also been postulated at times that the normative, and in consequence: also performative, character should be ascribed to utterances by using the phrase "let".[324] Yet, also this phrase does not ensure an unambiguous normative character as it may express an optative as well as a dictate, like for instance in the utterance: "Let heaven help you" ("May heaven help you"), or the approval of someone's behaviour (*e.g.* "Let it be as you wish"). Thus it was proposed that a complex phrase "it is dictated let" should be used, which eliminates the respective ambiguity of both components ("it is dictated" + "let"), thanks to which it certainly has a strictly normative character.[325] Yet, this phrase was only adopted to a limited extent in theoretical discussions, and is not at all used in practice.

8. Direct and indirect formulation of norms

The characteristic of the manners of constructing normative utterances, encountered both in the practice of theoretical discussion and in the practice of common activity, presented in this chapter probably leads to a fairly

---

[323] Nowak [1968b: 155 *et seq.*].
[324] Ziemba [1969: *passim*].
[325] Zieliński [1972: 19, footnote 31].

explicit conclusion that practically none of these manners verbalize norms directly since none provide explicit normative properties to these utterances. In itself, not one of them explicitly verbalizes a dictate or a prohibition of given behaviour, perhaps except for the most radical forms of the «performative» manner, but these in turn are not encountered in the practice of formulating normative utterances. It can only be postulated that, at least in theoretical discussion which requires particular subtlety and precision, these forms should be used. Yet, the value of this postulate is limited to a degree as the performative character of normative utterances is not commonly acknowledged.

At the same time, all other structural forms only verbalize norms in an indirect way, as: (a) they require the consideration of certain additional, extra-linguistic circumstances, especially certain assumptions as to the semiotic character of given utterances; and (b) after considering these additional circumstances, they still require specific TRANSLATION of the actually formulated utterances into some ideal (which do not raise doubts as to the semiotic status and certain meaning) expressions which are undoubtedly norms.

Thus it is necessary to REALIZE in practice complete advantages of the socio-linguistic situation in which a given utterance is formulated, and to develop a certain SKILL of using the knowledge on the utterance itself and the situation accompanying it, in order to perform an adequate TRANSLATION of utterances which are in fact formulated with the intention of ascribing a normative character to them – into utterances which in fact obviously have such a character. This should occur regardless of whether this translation requires any special technique or is done automatically.

Roman Laskowski. The category of a mood
[1998]

1. Modality of a sentence *versus* morphological category of a mood

Uttering a sentence, a speaker may find different ways to determine the relationship between a propositional expression uttered by him and the content of this expression (and the extra-linguistic situation in question), as well as his attitude to the content of the propositional expression uttered by him.

He could simply state the existence (in the present, past, or [...] in the future) of the situation described by the propositional expression, without any reservations, taking full responsibility for the truthfulness of the uttered sentence (*e.g. It is snowing*). However, he can also impose certain restrictions on the truthfulness of the uttered sentence, thus partly or wholly removing the responsibility for the sentence's correspondence to reality (its truthfulness), *e.g.* only indicating the degree of objective probability of truthfulness of the sentence (*The water is probably boiling*), or expressing the power of his own conviction (belief) about the truthfulness of the sentence (*I believe it is / Presumably it is boiling*). Finally, the speaker may completely repudiate the attempt to state the truthfulness of the sentence, demanding the statement on the truthfulness/falsity of the sentence from the listener (in interrogative sentences: *Is the water boiling?*), or demanding the listener to perform the necessary actions in order to make the sentence true (in orders and requests, *e.g. Boil the water!* – "Make the water boil"). Such differences in meaning between sentences are called DIFFERENCES IN MODALITY of a sentence. Let us note that, except for the first type of sentences (which state the existence of certain events), all the other types mentioned here are non-factive sentences [...], where the condition for issuing an order (expressing a request or a wish) in a reasonable manner is the NON-EXISTENCE of a situation constituting the content of the order (requests, wishes [...]) in the moment of its utterance. All types of non-factive modality are MARKED modalities.

Polish (just as other languages) has at its disposal special means to express marked modalities. These could be lexical means (*definitely, probably, presumably, surely, I suppose that, whether, let, may, ...*), prosodic (see the intonation of Polish interrogative sentences and orders of the type: *Are you going home?, You'll come back at four!*), syntactic (see word order in some languages, *e.g.* the word order of an interrogative sentence in English), or finally, morphological means which are of interest to us here. A morphological mean to express the modality of a sentence is the category of a mood.

In Polish, mood is used to express two types of modality: (1) the so called DEONTIC (volitive) MODALITY – signalling the desired action; the function of a morphological indicator of deontic modality is performed by

IMPERATIVE MOOD (lexical means to express it are: *must, can, is allowed, should,* ..., as well as *let, may, if only*); (2) EPISTEMIC (truthful) MODALITY – signalling the degree of conviction of the person speaking on the truthfulness of the sentence uttered by him; the indicator of this modality is the SUBJUNCTIVE MOOD (lexical indicators are: *probably, perhaps, possibly, surely, I doubt that,* ...; see Bralczyk 1978; see Lyons 1977, book II on the terms and their meaning).

> The line between epistemic modality and ALETIC MODALITY (the modality of objective probability, see above) is not always easy to draw. Primarily, the subjunctive mood is used in epistemic modality, but it can also be the indicator of the modality of objective probability, *e.g.* in conditional sentences.

An unmarked element of morphological opposition within the category of mood is INDICATIVE MOOD, which is the basic morphological indicator of neutral, unmarked modality.

2. Indicative mood

The fundamental function of the indicative mood is its use in ASSERTORIC SENTENCES – in statements of existence of certain extra-linguistic situations. By using a sentence in the indicative mood the speaker takes unlimited responsibility for its truthfulness (as long as such limits are not indicated by extra-morphological indicators of modality present in a given sentence). This also concerns sentences in the future tense despite their lack of non-factivity: for instance, by saying *The water will boil in five minutes* the speaker states his full responsibility for the truthfulness of this sentence, and in a way guarantees the occurrence of the adequate situation in the specified moment in time in the future.

> Let us note the difference in meaning between the above sentence and the sentence: *The water will most certainly boil in five minutes*, which contains an indicator of epistemic modality which informs of the highest possible degree of conviction of the truthfulness of the sentence on the part of the speaker. In this last sentence, besides the information

on the mentioned future fact, the listener is presented with the reservation that it is only the speaker's conviction which the listener may or may not share. The latter sentence is a sentence about the speaker and his conviction rather than the fact of boiling water. Thus even if the water does not boil in the indicated time, one cannot accuse of the speaker of lying. On the other hand, in the case of the first sentence, the objection that it is false is fully entitled after the indicated time (five minutes) elapse.

Since it is unmarked, the indicative mood finds its secondary use in functions primarily fulfilled by both marked moods: imperative [...] or subjunctive. This situation commonly occurs in propositional expressions with lexical indicators of marked modality.

3. Imperative mood

A component of the grammatical category of mood marked due to deontic (volitive) modality is the imperative mood, used to express the intentions of the speaker, in order to make the listener lead to the occurrence of the situation expressed by a given sentence. Deontic modality expressed through the imperative mood is of specific kind: here the sphere of the validity of a DEONTIC NORM is limited to the participants of the act of speech, where the source of the norm is the person speaking, and the subject subordinate to the norm is the listener. Therefore, expressions in the imperative mood are a grammatically specific subtype of directival acts of speech. Correct use of a directival act of speech (including imperative acts) requires direct involvement in the act of communication between the person speaking and the listener; thus the components of a directive (including imperative) act of speech are: the Speaker, the Listener and the directive (of the Speaker to the Listener), where: (a) the Listener can be collective (*Come back in a week!*); (b) in the case of a collective Listener the Speaker can be included in the Listener's sphere (*Let's go for a walk!*).

In expressions of the type: *Let Kate go shopping*, where the directive is addressed to a person who is not the Listener, we are dealing with indirect directival acts of speech. Their meaning can be described in the following manner: 'The Speaker demands from (asks) the Listener that the Listener tells the Third Party that the Speaker demands from (asks) the Third Party that he executes the indicated action' ('I demand from (ask) you to tell Kate that I am telling her *Go shopping*'). The use of indirect directival acts of speech is specific in the case of the individualization of a collective Listener: *You both go shopping!*, *Let Jerry buy the vegetables and let Mary buy bread and milk!* Seemingly, we are dealing with the use of the expression *let +3rd person form of the verb*, and thus, an indirect directival act of speech, in the function of a direct directive. Yet, in fact, in such cases a direct directive is expressed with the personal pronoun YOU: *You buy the vegetables and you buy bread and milk!* with an accompanying gesture of indicating the direct listener. In the above type of sentences with *let* we are in fact still dealing with an indirect directive, directed at an individual listener *via* a collective listener. However, there is a type of sentences with *let* which are direct directives, namely, sentences which contain expressions of the type *Sir* (*Madam*, *Sirs*) in the function of a polite (or contemptuous) pronoun in the 2nd person: *Let Sir* (*the colleague, citizen, private*) *bring some water!*

The semantics of the imperative mood consist of several components which are not equivalent with respect to their communicative status. What is directly communicated is the will of the Speaker to stimulate the Listener to take activity directed at achieving a certain situation *p* desired by the Speaker: "The Speaker wants it that *p*; the Speaker issues a directive towards the Listener (the Speaker aims at stimulating the Listener) so that he will take activity which leads to the occurrence of *p*". In a typical situation where an imperative act of speech is used, there occurs a presupposition that at the time of speaking *t,* situation *p* does not exist (see below on the uses of the imperative when it comes to continuing the existing situation). Moreover, there are certain conditions of correct use of an imperative (directival) act of speech: (1) The Listener is able to execute activity needed to achieve *p*; (2) The Speaker knows that (1). Moreover, correct use of the imperative (directival) act of speech requires a specific distribution of social roles of the

Speaker and the Listener, which depends on the character of the directive. Thus issuing an order/prohibition, or expressing a demand, requires the social authority of the Speaker over the Listener, whereas giving advice does not require such a hierarchy of roles, and a request assumes a converse social hierarchy of the participants of the act of communication.

The scope of use and the function of the imperative mood depends on the lexical meaning of the verb, its aspect, and the occurrence/lack of occurrence of negation in an imperative expression. The standard meaning for the imperative mood is, as was stated above, the directival function. However, the directival function is possible only for verbs which denote controlled actions (that is actions, acts and states which can be controlled by the subject: *sit, crouch, dwell, etc.* [...]): in order for a directive to be executed it has to be feasible, that is, the addressee of the directive (Listener) has to have the possibility of controlling the course of action which is the content of the directive.

Let us introduce the notion of A POSITIVE DIRECTIVE (order/wish/request/advice that *p* is executed) and A NEGATIVE DIRECTIVE (a prohibition of executing *p*/wish/request/advice not to execute *p*). In Polish, the fundamental morphological means to express a positive directive are forms of the imperative mood of perfective verbs: *Przynieś mi wody!* [*Bring me some water!*], *Poczekajcie!* [*Wait!*], *Przeczytaj ten artykuł!* [*Read this article!*], *Zjedzmy obiad!* [*Let us have lunch!*], *Zmień żarówkę!* [*Change the light bulb!*]. On the other hand, a negative directive is expressed in a typical way, with a negative form of the imperative of AN IMPERFECTIVE verb: *Nie przynoś wody!* [*Do not bring any water!*], *Nie czytaj tego artykułu!* [*Do not read this article!*], *Nie jedzmy obiadu!* [*Let us not have lunch!*], *Nie zmieniaj żarówki!* [*Do not change the light bulb!*]. The difference in Polish is justified with the meaning of the aspect and in the directival function of the imperative. The proper essence of a positive directive is to give rise to the situation desired by the Speaker (as a result of the Listener's activity): what is significant is that the water is brought and the light bulb is changed; thus it is the result of the Listener's activity that is significant, rather than the activity itself. Thus a natural way to express a positive directive is the perfective aspect which presents situations as a result of certain action (action, process [...]). On the other hand, the content of a negative directive is the desire to prevent a situation which is undesirable on the part of the Speaker; preventing the action leading to the occurrence of such a situation prevents its occurrence in an effective way, hence the typical use of the imperfective aspect in the case of a negative directive.

> The opposition: the perfective form of imperative to express a positive directive *versus* the imperfective form of imperative to express a negative directive in a pure form is possible only in the case of verbs (denoting controlled actions) which form pairs of aspects (that is, in verbs denoting activities [...]): *uśpij – nie usypiaj, pomaluj – nie maluj, zbuduj – nie buduj, naucz – nie ucz, rozbij – nie rozbijaj, zbliż się – nie zbliżaj się, wbij gwóźdź – nie wbijaj gwoździa, siądź – nie siadaj* [*put to sleep – do not put to sleep, paint – do not paint, build – do not build, teach – do not teach, break – do not break, approach – do not approach, drive a nail – do not drive a nail, sit – do not sit*]. In the case of verbs denoting controlled states and activities, that is, *tantum imperfective*, the function of the opposition part which expresses a positive directive is performed by forms of the imperative of relevant perfective verbs denoting acts (indicating the occurrence of a situation named through the relevant verb of state or through a verb of activity which is the derivative basis of a given inceptive verb): *zamieszkaj u niego – nie mieszkaj u niego, zamilcz – nie milcz, zatańcz z nią – nie tańcz z nią, zawołaj ich – nie wołaj ich* [*stay with him – do not stay with him, be silent – do not be silent, dance with her – do not dance with her, call them – do not call them*].

Apart from imperative expressions of the type mentioned above, negative forms of imperative of perfective verbs (*Nie przeczytaj tego artykułu!* [*Do not read this article!*], *Nie zmieniaj żarówki!* [*Do not change the light bulb!*] are also in use, as well as non-negated forms of the imperative mood of imperfective verbs (*Jedz obiad!* [*Have lunch!*], *Zmieniaj żarówkę!* [*Change the light bulb!*]). Yet, imperative expressions of this type are semantically marked and vary semantically from standard directives.

Let us first analyse the possible functions of non-negated imperatives in the IMPERFECTIVE aspect. Here one can distinguish several functions of non-negated expressions with an imperative form of an imperfective verb:

(1) A directive to continue action – a presupposition of non-existence in the moment of speaking t_i (in the moment of issuing the directive) in situation p which is the content of the directive is not valid with such kinds of uses of the imperative. On the contrary, in these strongly situationally conditioned uses, the situation which the directive encourages to continue is observed directly by the Listener and the Speaker. Language has specific means at its disposal to express the directive of continuation. A typical way is reduplication (doubling) of the imperative: *Pisz, pisz!* [*Write, write!*], *Naprawiaj, naprawiaj!* [*Fix, fix!*].The continuational character of a directive can also be indicated by the language context (see the expressions characteristic to this type of directival uses of the imperative: *Nie przeszkadzaj sobie, siedź!* [*Do not bother to get up!*], *Czytaj dalej* [*Read on!*], *Odpoczywaj sobie!* [*Czytaj dalej!*].

(2) A directive concerning action of an outdated course: iterative (repetitive), habitual or having the character of a common norm – *Pisz do mnie jak najczęściej/ręcznie!* [*Write to me as often as possible / by hand!*], *Mleko pij tylko przegotowane!* [*Drink only cooked milk!*]. The outdated character of a directive is usually indicated linguistically (it concerns especially iterative actions).

(3) A directive of the immediate execution of an action (which often assumes the character of a reinforced directive) – such uses are normally situationally conditioned and, like directives of continuation, refer to a situation which is observed directly in the moment of uttering the directive: *(No) Otwieraj!* [*(Well) Open up!*] (to a person hesitating by the door), *Płyń do brzegu!* [*Swim to the shore!*] (to a person swimming), *Wodzu, prowadź!* [*Lead, commander!*].

(4) The Speaker emphasizes the action itself (*Odrabiaj lekcje do piątej, a potem możesz iść się pobawić!* [*Do your homework until five, and then you can go play!*]) or the manner of executing it (in this case the action itself is already taking place: *Czytaj uważnie!* [*Read carefully!*], *Siedź prosto!* [*Sit up!*]) rather than the effect of the Listener's action.

Negative forms of the imperative of PERFECTIVE verbs denoting controlled actions can be negative directives: *Nie wypij mleka!* [*Do not drink the milk!*] (see the difference in Polish between *Nie pij mleka!* [*Do not drink milk!*] – a general recommendation, and *Nie wypij mleka!* [*Do not drink the milk!*] – a specific prohibition concerning specific milk, or a specific portion of milk), although this is a rarely encountered function of these norms (see the oddity of the directives: *Nie przeczytaj tego artykułu!* [*Do not read this article!*], *Nie zbuduj domu!* [*Do not build a house!*]). On the other hand, there is another typical function – the PREVENTIVE function of negative perfective forms of the imperative as an expression denoting warning against the occurrence of a given situation undesired by the Speaker, rather than a directive; see *e.g. Nie przewróć się!, Nie złam sobie nogi!, Nie zgub kluczy!, Nie przezięb się!* [*Do not fall!, Do not break your leg!, Do not lose your keys!, Do not catch cold!*] Although the meaning of the non-negated perfective forms of the imperative (*Rozbij szklankę!* [*Break the glass!*]) – can be described as "Act in such a way that effect *p* occurs" and the negated perfective forms of the imperative (*Nie rozbijaj szklanki!* [*Do not break the glass!*]) as "Do not do *p*", the discussed imperative expressions (*Nie rozbij szklanki!* [*Do not break the glass!*]) can be ascribed the meaning of "Be careful! (= control your behaviour) and act in such a way that effect *p* does not occur". Expressions of this type contain the presupposition that the Listener's activity (behaviour) may cause the situation *p* undesired by the Speaker. Thus the semantic ingredients of the preventively used imperative can be described in the following way:

presupposition   What you do / The way you behave (are going to do / act) may cause the occurrence of the situation *p*; I do not want *p* to occur.

assertion   I want you to act in such a way that your behaviour does not lead to the occurrence of the situation *p*.

Since the meaning of the forms of the imperative mood used in such a way does not encompass a directive of activity (that is, executing a given action controlled by the Listener – executor), imperative expressions of this

kind are also derived from perfective verbs which denote uncontrolled actions (incidents; see the above examples). The latter have an exclusively
cautionary meaning. There are non-obligatory lexical indicators of the preventive (cautionary) use of the imperative mood: *tylko* [*just*], *przypadkiem*
[*by any chance*], *uważaj!* [*careful!*], the expressive *mi* [*me*]; they may occur in an utterance together or in any combinations: *Uważaj!*, *Tylko mi się*
przypadkiem nie przezięb!, *Tylko się nie zakochaj!*, *Nie pomaluj przypadk-*
iem furtki! [*Careful!*, *Do not catch a cold by any chance!*, *Just do not fall in*
love!, *Just do not paint the gate!*].

On the difference between the prohibitive (denoting a negative directive) and preventive (denoting warning) use of the imperative mood – see
Chrakovskij [1990.]

As is evident, directival meaning does not exhaust the possible functions of the imperative, nor does it encompass all verbs. Therefore, for all
imperfective verbs which denote uncontrolled actions (states, processes,
incidents [...]) directival meaning of the imperative is semantically impossible (one cannot require execution of an action over whose course the
executor has no control); still, forms of the imperative mood are possible
in the case of these verbs, although not commonly used in texts. However,
these forms have OPTATIVE rather than directival meaning (they do not express the will of the speaker but rather his wish for the situation *p* to occur): *Zdrowiej!*, "*Obyś wyzdrowiał(a)!*", *Płyń, łódko moja!*, *Kręć się, kręć,*
wrzeciono! [*Get well!*, "*I wish you will get well!*", *Sail, my boat!*, *Spin,*
my spindle, spin!].

Such uses of the imperative may assume the character of a spell
(they are used in the magic of language: *Rośnij, kwiecie, wysoko, jak*
pan leży głęboko! [*Grow, flower, grow as high as he is lying low!*]
[A. Mickiewicz], *Nie umieraj!* [*Do not die!*]). With such uses of the
imperative the Speaker usurps the right (and believes it is possible)
to take control over a situation which does not objectively succumb
to control. Yet, unlike the standard, directival uses of the imperative,
where the Listener, the direct addressee, exercises direct control over
the course of action, the Speaker puts himself in the position of one

exercising direct control over the situation in the magical uses of the imperative. Also semantic limitations imposed on the addressee of a directive ("an animate being, able to understand the directive and undertake activity") are not respected in the magical use of the imperative (*Mówię tej nocy – nie dzwoń złotem gwiazd!* [*I said to the night – do not tinkle with golden stars!*] [H. Poświatowska]).

There is another specific, non-directival function of the imperative mood of verbs which denote mental states (intellectual and emotional), and thus, internal states which are not controlled. Verbs denoting cognitive states do not have the imperative form at all (a lexical exception: *Know!* "I want you to know that *p*; I am telling you that *p*"). For the verbs of conjecture (*suppose, imagine, believe*$_2$ ("suppose"), *think* "suppose", *claim*$_2$ "suppose; judge as"*, assume*$_2$ *that..., presume, conjecture, expect*, but also *wonder, hesitate*) as well as for verbs denoting emotional states (*fear, enjoy, sulk, be nervous, be angry, be worried, get impatient, be offended, get angry*), imperative forms are possible.

Here the function of negated imperative is PERSUASIVE rather than directival. See examples of such use of verbs of conjecture: *Nie myśl, że ci wszystko wolno!, Nie sądź, że uda się to załatwić!* [*Do not presume that you are allowed anything!, Do not think this can be done!*]. In utterances of this kind the Speaker does not demand any activity from the Listener, but he directly attempts to change the state of his mind.

The meaning of these utterances can be described as follows:

presupposition   The Speaker knows (believes) that the Listener is convinced that *p*.

The Speaker knows (believes) that not *p*.

assertion   I want you to know that not *p*.

Negated forms of the imperative of verbs which denote emotional states have a similar function: see *Nie bój się!, Nie gniewaj się!, Nie ciesz się, że to już koniec!* [*Do not be afraid!, Do not be angry!, Do not be glad it is over!*]. The speaker attempts to influence the Listener's emotional state by suggesting that there is no reason for such a state. The meaning of these expressions can be presented as follows:

presupposition   The speaker knows the listener is (can be) in the emotional state *p*.

The speaker knows (believes) there are reasons for the Listener to be in the state *p*.

assertion   I want you to know that there are reasons for you to be in the state *p*.

Not negated forms of the imperative of this kind of verbs *Myśl, co chcesz, ale ja i tak wiem swoje* [*Think what you will but I know what I know*], *Ciesz się, póki możesz* [*Be happy while you can*], *Gniewaj się, ale i tak Ci muszę to powiedzieć* [*You can get angry but I have to tell you this anyway*] denote forced (or resigned) permission on the part of the Speaker to the Listener's state of mind (emotional state) indicated by the verb.

A lexical exception is *be ashamed* (*wstydzić się*) with the form of non-negated imperative: *You should be ashamed* (*wstydź się*) 'I want you to be ashamed'.

The INFLECTIVE PARADIGM of the imperative mood is composed of three forms in Polish: *idź-idźmy-idźcie* [*let's go*]. The fundamental functional opposition between the forms of the imperative mood *idź-idźmy-idźcie* is not the category of person but number – the juxtaposition: Listener-Listener and accompanying persons, that is, the juxtaposition of forms of the type: *idź* – on the one hand (appeal to the Listener – the natural addressee of the appeal) and *idźcie, idźmy* on the other hand (appeal to the listener + additional information about the multitude of listeners or about the fact that other people apart from the listener should be taken into account). Within the forms of the plural of the imperative, forms of the type *idźcie* which mean "YOU + other people" are a functionally unmarked part and are juxtaposed with forms of the type *idźmy* "YOU + ME (+ other people)": thus, contrary to the forms of the type *idźcie,* they INCLUDE the Speaker into the addressees of the appeal. The forms of the imperative of the first type shall be called EXCLUSIVE forms of the plural form of the imperative, whereas the forms of the second type shall be called INCLUSIVE forms of the plural form of the imperative.

> The situation where the exclusive form of the imperative is an appeal directed at a group of listeners (that is, when the meaning 'YOU + others' included in it is realized as "$YOU_1 + YOU_2 + ...$") is a special case, which does not occur all too often in the real act of communicating anyway.

4. The subjunctive mood

The morphological indicator of marked epistemic (truthful) modality is the subjunctive mood which determines HYPOTHETICAL situations. The Speaker using the subjunctive mood does not claim that the situation described in a given sentence in fact exists (or will exist) but only informs of the POSSIBILITY of the occurrence of the situation. The said possibility can only be theoretical, not realized in practice. Thus the subjunctive mood is used to present conjectures, hypotheses, and suppositions of the speaker on the extra-linguistic reality. The subjunctive mood, non-factual – just like the future tense of the indicative mood but unlike it in that it carries information that the speaker does not accept responsibility for concerning the truthfulness of the uttered sentence. As long as the world (reality) on which one can predicate truthfully or falsely with the help of sentences in the future tense is limited to the future (in relationship to the moment of speaking or – in the case of relative use of the future tense – in relationship to some moment in time determined by the context), then the reality (the world) which is the subject of the sentences in the subjunctive mood does not contain such a limitation. It could be, *e.g.*, the world of expectations (*Oby było ciepło!* [*May it be warm!*], wishes (*Niechby się to skończyło!* [*Let it end!*]), but predominantly, it is the world in which some conditions (formulated openly) have to be fulfilled, *e.g. Przyjechałby, gdyby miał czas* [*He would come if he had time*].

Within the subjunctive mood there are no temporal positions: the difference between the forms of the so called "present tense" and the so called "past tense" (*he will come – he would come*) concerns modality rather than the category of tense. Forms of the type *he would come* always express an unfulfilled possibility, a hypothetical situation about which the speaker knows that it did not in fact take place; thus these forms have A COUNTER-FACTIVE character. Forms of this type will still be described according to their function, as FORMS OF THE UNREAL SUBJUNCTIVE MOOD. Forms of the type *he will come* have a NON-FACTIVE character; they also speak of hypothetical situations, but they do not contain information about failure to realize the hypothetical possibility. In the modal opposition within the category of mood they constitute an unmarked part and can be used both in reference to hypothetical situations which are potentially possible and in reference to impossible situations. We shall call them FORMS OF THE POTENTIAL SUBJUNCTIVE MOOD. See, for instance, the clearly counter-factive meaning of sentences of the type: *He would finish his study long ago, I would call you tomorrow*, as well as sentences with an unreal (unfulfilled) condition: *If you had known about it, you would have done otherwise*. Contrary to the sentence: *If you had known about it, you would have done otherwise*, which does not exclude the idea that the listener in fact 'behaves otherwise' knowing about 'it', the preceding sentence excludes this possibility.

In Polish, sentences with the inflective form of the verb ending with-*t* used after a conjunction or a particle ending with-*by*, like *Gdybym wiedziała, Obyś miał rację* [*If I only knew, If only you were right*]) are problematic from the point of view of the category of mood. They are sometimes regarded as forms of the subjunctive mood and sometimes as forms of the indicative mood. Contrary to J. Puzynina (1971), and according to the tradition, forms of verbs which occur in propositional expressions of this type are considered to be contextually conditioned variants of forms of the subjunctive mood. This interpretation is supported with (1) the fact that the meaning of future tense inherent to the forms of the indicative mood ending with -*l* does not occur in the discussed type of propositional expressions; (2) the discussed forms ending with -*l* regularly express the modal opposition POTENTIAL ACTION – UNREAL ACTION; see: *If I only knew – If only you were right.* For semantic reasons, this opposition is not possible in purposive sentences like *He highlighted the most vital fragments so that she would think about them,* as the notion of purpose excludes the idea of the speaker accepting the assumption about the impossibility of its realization.

The potential subjunctive mood, unmarked in view of its deontic (volitive) modality, is sometimes used in the function of a polite request or a weakened order, and thus, in the function which is primarily performed by the imperative mood; see: *Wpadłabyś do mnie jutro!* [*You could come by tomorrow!*].

For semantic reasons (the counter-factive character which remains in opposition to expecting the request or the order to be fulfilled), forms of the unreal mood cannot be used in this function.

Bibliography

Adler, Mortimer Jerome
[1931] Legal Certainty. *Law and the Modern Mind: A Symposium. Columbia Law Review* vol. XXXI, p. 91–108.

Ajdukiewicz, Kazimierz
[1931] O znaczeniu wyrażeń [On the Meaning of Expressions]. [In:] *Księga* [1931: 31–77].
[1934] Sprache und Sinn. *Erkenntnis* vol. IV, p. 100–138.
[1948] *Propedeutyka filozofii dla liceów ogólnokształcących* [*Introduction to Philosophy for Secondary Schools*]. Wrocław-Warszawa (4th ed.), Książnica-Atlas.
[1955] *Zarys logiki* [*Outline of Logic*]. Warszawa, PZWS.
[1965] *Logika pragmatyczna* [*Pragmatic Logic*]. Warszawa, PWN.

Alston, William Payne
[1964] *Philosophy of Language. Foundations of Philosophy.* Englewood Cliffs (N.J.), Prentice-Hall.

Anderson, Alan Ross
[1958] A Reduction of Deontic Logic to Alethic Modal Logic. *Mind* vol. LXVII, p. 100–103.

Andersson, Jan
[1975] *How to Define "Performative".* Uppsala, Philosophical Studies, University of Uppsala.

Åquist, Lennart
[1972] *Performatives and Verifiability by the Use of Language.* Uppsala, University of Uppsala.
[1973] The Emotive Theory of Ethics in the Light of Recent Developments in Formal Semantics and Pragmatics. [In:] *Modality* [1973: 130–141].

Atkinson, Ronald F.
[1961] Hume On "Is" and "Ought": A Replay to Mr MacIntyre. [In:] Chappell (ed.) [1968: 265–277].

Austin, John Langshaw
[1961a] Performative Utterances. [In:] Austin [1961b: 220–239].
[1961b] *Philosophical Papers.* Oxford, Clarendon Press.
[1962] *How to Do Things with Words.* Oxford, Clarendon Press.

Baier, Kurt
[1958] *The Moral Point of View.* Ithaca (N.Y.), Cornell University Press.

Barzykowski, Tadeusz & Jaroszyński, Jan
[1928] *Podręcznik fotografii* [*Handbook of Photography*]. Warszawa, Wydawnictwo M. Arcta.

Baumgartner, Arthur
[1922] *Die Wissenschaft vom Recht und ihre Methode.* Vol. II–III. Tübingen, Verlag Mohr.

Bautro, Eugeniusz
[1934] *De iurisprudentia symbolica.* Cz. I. Prolegomena do logistyki prawniczej [Part I. Preliminaries to Legal Logistics]. Lwów-Kraków, Księgarnia Leona Frommera.

Bayart, Arnould
[1966] Leibniz et les antinomies en droit. *Revue Internationale de Philosophie* vol. XX, p. 257–263.

Benthem, Johan [Johannes Franciscus Abraham Karel] van
[1979] Minimal Deontic Logic. *Bulletin of the Section of Logic.* Polish Academy of Science vol. VIII, No. 1, p. 36–42.

Bergström, Lars
[1962] Comments on Castañeda's Semantics of Prescriptive Discours. *Theoria* vol. XXVIII, No. 1, p. 70–72.

Berlin, Isaiah
[1955–1956] Equality. *Proceedings of the Aristotelian Society.* New Series vol. LVI, p. 281–326.

Bernardo, Giuliano di
[1969] *Logica, norme, azione.* Trento, Instituto Superiore di Scienze Sociali.

Bernays, Paul
[1926] Axiomatische Untersuchung des Aussagenkalküls der *Principia mathematica*. *Mathematische Zeitschrift* vol XXV, p. 305–320.

Beth, Evert Willem
[1962] Extension and Intension. [In:] *Logic* [1962: 64–68].

Bierling, Ernst Rudolf
[1883] *Zur Kritik der juristischen Grundbegriffe*. Band II. Gotha, Perthes.
[1894] *Juristische Principienlehre*. Band I. Freiburg i.B. and Leipzig, Mohr.

Binding, Karl
[1877] *Die Normen und ihre Übertretung*. B. II. Leipzig, W. Engelmann.

Black, Max
[1958] Notes on the Meaning of "Rule". *Theoria* vol. XXIV, I.2 & 3, p. 107–136, 139–161.
[1963] Austin on Performatives. *Philosophy* vol. XXXVIII, No. 145, p. 217–226.
[1964] The Gap Between "Is" and "Should". *The Philosophical Review* vol. LXXIII, No. 2, p. 165–181.

Blanché, Robert
[1967] *Raison et discours*. Paris, J. Vrin.

Bogusławski, Andrzej
[1979] Performatives of Metatextual Comments? On the Cognitive and Non-Cognitive Linguistic Conventions. *Kwartalnik Neofilologiczny* vol. XXVI, No. 3, p. 301–326.

Bondarko, Aleksandr V. *et al.* (ed.)
[1990] *Теория функциональной грамматики. Темпоральность. Модальность* [*Theory of Functional Grammar. Temporality. Modality*]. Ленинград, Наука.

Borowski, Marian
[1923] O składnikach czynu [On the Elements of Acts]. *Przegląd Filozoficzny* vol. XXVI, No. 3–4, p. 144–159.
[1924] O rodzajach czynu [On the Types of Acts]. *Przegląd Filozoficzny* vol. XXVII, No. 1–2, p. 37–64.

Bralczyk, Jerzy
[1978] *O leksykalnych wyznacznikach prawdziwościowej oceny sądów* [*On Lexical Determinants of Truthful-Evaluation of Judgements*]. Katowice, Uniwersytet Śląski.

Brown, Roger W. *et al.*
[1959] *Language, Thought & Culture.* Ann Arbor, University of Michigan.

Brożek, Anna
[2007] *Pytania i odpowiedzi. Tło filozoficzne, teoria i zastosowania praktyczne* [*Questions and Answers. The Philosophical Background, Theory and Practical Applications*]. Warszawa, Wydawnictwo Naukowe *Semper.*

Brożek, Bartosz & Stelmach, Jerzy
[2004] *Metody prawnicze* [*Legal Methods*]. Kraków, *Zakamycze.*

Cardozo, Benjamin Nathan
[1921] *The Nature of the Judical Process.* Yale, Yale University Press.

Carnap, Rudolf
[1929] *Abriss der Logistik.* Wien, J. Springer.
[1935] *Filozofia jako analiza języka nauki* [*Philosophy as an Analysis of the Scientific Language*]. Warszawa 1969, PWN.
[1947] *Meaning and Necessity.* Chicago 1958, University of Chicago Press.
[1954] Abraham Kaplan on Value Judgments. [In:] Schilpp [1963: 999–1013].

Castañeda, Héctor-Neri
[1957] Some Nonformal "Logical" Relations. *Philosophical Studies* vol. VIII, No. 6, p. 89–91.
[1962] The Semantics of Prescriptive Discourse (A Reply to Lars Bergstöm). *Theoria* vol. XXVIII, No. 1, p. 72–78.
[1975] *Thinking and Doing.* Dordrecht, Reidel.

Chappell, Vere Claiborne (ed.)
[1968] *Hume. Modern Studies in Philosophy.* London, Macmillan.

Cheliński, Stanisław
[1925] Pojęcie rozkazu w świetle ogólnej teorii norm [The Notion of the Order in the Light of the General Theory of the Norms]. [In:] Jaworski (ed.) [1925: 89–147].

Chellas, Brian F.
[1980] *Modal Logic*. Cambridge, Cambridge University Press.

Chrakovskij, Victor S.
[1990] Повелительность [*Domineeringness*]. [In:] Bondarko *et al.* (ed.)
    [1990: 185–238].

Chwistek, Leon
[1936] Rola zasady konsekwencji w zagadnieniu sprawiedliwości społecznej
    [The Role of the Principle of Consequence in the Matters of Social Jus-
    tice]. *Przegląd Filozoficzny* vol. XXXIX, No. 4, p. 494–498.

Cole, Peter & Morgan, Jerry L. (ed.)
[1977] *Syntax and Semantics*. Vol. III. New York-San Franciso-London (2nd
    ed.), Academic Press.

Conte, Amadeo Gustavo
[1961] Bibliografia di logica giuridica. *Rivista Internazionale di Filosofia
    del Diritto* vol. XXXVI, p. 120–141.
[1962] *Saggio sulla completezza degli ordinamenti giuridici*. Torino, Gi-
    appichelli.

Conte, Amadeo Gustavo *et al.* (ed.)
[1977] *Deontische Logik und Semantik*. Wiesbaden, Akademische Ver-
    lagsgesellschaft Athenaion.

Czeżowski, Tadeusz
[1946] *Główne zasady nauk filozoficznych* [*Main Principles of Philosophi-
    cal Sciences*]. Wrocław 1959 (2nd ed.), *Ossolineum*.
[1964a] Czym są wartości [What are the Values]. [In:] Czeżowski [1964c:
    106–109].
[1964b] Dwojakie normy [Double Norms]. [In:] Czeżowski [1989: 144–149].
[1964c] *Filozofia na rozdrożu* [*Philosophy at the Crossroads*]. Warszawa,
    Wydawnictwo Naukowe UMK.
[1970] Aksjologiczne i deontyczne normy moralne [Axiological and Deon-
    tic Moral Norms]. [In:] Czeżowski [1989: 150–156].
[1989] *Pisma z etyki i teorii wartości* [*Writings on Ethics and Theory of Va-
    lues*]. Wrocław, *Ossolineum*.

Czeżowski, Tadeusz *et al.* (ed.)
[1967] *Fragmenty filozoficzne. Seria trzecia* [*Philosophical Fragments. Se-
    ries Three*]. Warszawa, PWN.

Daniellson, Sven
[1973] *Some Conceptions of Performativity*. Uppsala, Filosofiska Studier.

Davidson, Donald & Harman Gilbert (ed.)
[1972] *Semantics of Natural Language*. Dordrecht, D. Reidel.

Davis, John W. *et al.* (ed.)
[1970] *Philosophical Logic*. Dordrecht, D. Reidel.

Dąmbska, Izydora
[1938] Z semantyki zdań warunkowych [On the Semantics of Conditional
    Sentences]. *Przegląd Filozoficzny* vol. XLI, No. 3, p. 241–267.

Dias, Reginald Walter Michael & Hughes, Graham Beynon John
[1957] *Jurisprudence*. London, Butterworth.

Downes, William
[1977] The Imperative and Pragmatics. *Journal of Linguistics* vol. XIII, No.
    1, p. 77–97.

Dubislav, Walter
[1937] Zur Unbegründbarkeit der Forderungssätze. *Theoria* vol. III, I. 2–3,
    p. 330–342.

Ehrlich, Eugen
[1913] *Grundlegung der Soziologie des Rechts*. München u. Lepzig,
    Duncker & Humblot.

Elzenberg, Henryk
[1933] O różnicy między „pięknem" a „dobrem" [On the Difference be-
    tween "Beauty" and "Goodness"]. [In:] Elzenberg 1999, p. 7–20.
[1935] Les idées de valeur et d'obligation. *Sprawozdania z posiedzeń To-
    warzystwa Naukowego Warszawskiego*. Wydział II. 1934 vol. XXVII,
    No. 1–6, p. 66–74. Fragment w „przekładzie własnym i częściowej
    przeróbce" jako: Pojęcie wartości perfekcyjnej. Fragment komunikatu:
    O pojęciach wartości i powinności [A fragment in „my own translation
    and partial reconstruction" as: The Notion of a Perfect Value. A Frag-
    ment of an Announcement: On the Notions of Values and Duty]. [In:]
    Elzenberg 1999, p. 3–6.
[1938] Powinność i rozkaz [Duty and Order]. *Przegląd Filozoficzny* vol.
    XLI, No. 1, p. 85–91.

[1966] *Wartość i człowiek* [*Value and Humankind*]. Toruń, Towarzystwo Naukowe w Toruniu.
[1999] *Pisma estetyczne* [*Aesthetic Writings*]. Lublin, Wydawnictwo UMC-S.

Føllesdal, Dagfinn & Hilpinen, Risto
[1971] Deontic Logic: An Introduction. [In:] Hilpinen (ed.) [1971: 1–35].

Fraassen, Bas van
[1971] *Formal Semantics and Logic*. New York, Macmillan.

Frank, Jerome
[1931] *Law and the Modern Mind.* New York, Bretano's.

Fritzhand, Marek
[1966] Zagadnienie prawdy w etyce [The Notion of Truth in Ethics]. *Studia Filozoficzne* No. 2, p. 11–34.

Frydman, Sawa [*vel* Nowiński, Czesław]
[1936] Dogmatyka prawa w świetle socjologii [Legal Dogmas from the Viewpoint of Sociology]. [In:] Wróblewski (ed.) [1936: 141–316].

Gabryl, Franciszek
[1905/1906] Władysław Witwicki, *Analiza psychologiczna objawów woli* [*A Psychological Analysis of Symptoms of Will*] (rev.). *Przegląd Polski* vol. XL, t. 1, No. 1–3, p. 127–134.

Giedymin, Jerzy
[1964] *Problemy, założenia, rozstrzygnięcia* [*Problems, Assumptions, Decisions*]. Poznań, PWN.

Gizbert-Studnicki, Tomasz
[1983] O sposobach formułowania dyrektyw [On the Methods for the Formulation of Directives]. *Studia Semiotyczne* vol. XIII, p. 91–109.

Gordon, David & Lakoff, George
[1971] Conversational Postulates. [In:] Cole & Morgan (ed.) [1977: 83–106].

Grice, Herbert Paul
[1975] Logic and Conversation. [In:] Cole & Morgan (ed.) [1977: 41–58].

Green, Georgia M.
[1973] How to Get People to Do Things with Words? [In:] Shuy (ed.) [1973:
    51–81].

Gregorowicz, Jan
[1967] Dwie koncepcje logiki prawniczej [Two Conceptions of the Legal
    Logic]. [In:] Czeżowski *et al.* (ed.) [1967: 237–243].

Grodziński, Eugeniusz
[1980] Wypowiedzi performatywne o doniosłości prawnej lub *quasi-*
    prawnej [Performative Utterances of Legal or *Quasi*-Legal Impor-
    tance]. [In:] Schaff (ed.) [1980: 157–180].

Grue-Sørensen, Knud
[1939] Imperativsätze und Logik. Begegnung einer Kritik. *Theoria* vol. V,
    I. 2, p. 195–202.

Grzegorczykowa, Renata *et al.* (ed.)
[1998] *Gramatyka współczesnego języka polskiego. Morfologia* [*Grammar
    of Contemporary Polish Language. Morphology*]. Warszawa, Wydaw-
    nictwo Naukowe PWN.

Grzybowski, Stefan
[1961] *Wypowiedź normatywna oraz jej struktura formalna* [*A Normative
    Utterance and its Formal Structure*]. Kraków, UJ.

Halldén, Sören
[1954] *Emotive Propositions.* Stockholm, Almquist & Wiksell.

Hare, Richard Mervyn
[1949] Imperative Sentences. *Mind* vol. LVIII, p. 21–39.
[1952] *The Language of Morals.* Oxford, Oxford University Press.
[1963] *Freedom and Reason.* Oxford, Oxford University Press.

Hedenius, Ingemar
[1963] Performatives. *Theoria* vol. XXIX, i. 2, p. 115–136.

Hilpinen, Risto (ed.)
[1971] *Deontic Logic: Introductory and Systematic Readings.* Dordrecht,
    D. Reidel.
[1983] *New Studies in Deontic Logic.* Dordrecht, D. Reidel.

Hobhouse, Leonard Trelawny
[1906] *Morals in Evolution: A Study in Comparative Ethics.* London 1915,
Chapman & Hall.

Hofstadter, Albert & McKinsey, John C.C.
[1939] On the Logic of Imperatives. *Philosophy of Science* vol. VI, No. 4,
p. 446–457.

Horovitz, Joseph
[1972] *Law and Logic.* Wien-New York, Springer-Verlag.

Ingarden, Roman
[1948] Uwagi o względności wartości [Notes on Relativity of Values].
Przegląd Filozoficzny vol. XLIV, No. 1–3, p. 82–94.

Interpretacje
[1966] *Naturalistyczne i antynaturalistyczne interpretacje humanistyki*
[*Naturalistic and Antinaturalistic Interpretations of the Humanities*].
Poznań, Wydawnictwo UAM.

Jevons, Wiliam Stanley
[1870] *Logika [Logic].* Warszawa 1921, Trzaska, Evert & Michalski.

Jørgensen, Jørgen
[1937–1938] Imperatives and Logic. *Erkenntnis* vol. VII, p. 288–296.

Kalinowski, Jerzy
[1953] Teoria zdań normatywnych [Theory of Normative Sentences]. *Studia Logica* vol. I, p. 113–146.
[1963] *Introduction à la logique juridique.* Paris, Presses Universitaires de
France.
[1969a] Note critique sur la logique déontique d'Alf Ross. *Archiv für Rechts- und Sozialphilosophie* vol. LV, p. 41–68.
[1969b] Des syllogismes méréologiques. [In:] *Rozprawy* [1969: 119–125].
[1972] *Logika norm [Logic of the Norms].* Lublin, Instytut Wydawniczy
Daimonion.
[1977a] Le logique de Leibniz. *Studia Leibnitiana* vol. XI, No. 2,
p. 168–189.
[1977b] Über die Bedeutung der Deontik für Ethik und Rechtsphilosophie.
[In:] Conte *et al.* (ed.) [1977: 101–129].
[1982] La logique juridique et son histoire. *Archives de Philosophie du Droit* t. XXVII, 275–289.

[1983a] La genèse d'un système de logique des normes. *Informatic e Diritto* vol. II, No. 2, p. 251–267.
[1983b] Logique juridique. Conceptions et recherches. *Rechtstheorie* vol. XIV, No. 1, p. 1–17.
[1990] Logika prawnicza a logika deontyczna [Legal *versus* Deontic Logic]. [In:] Wronkowska & Zieliński (ed.) [1990: 345–357].

Kanger, Stig
[1957] *New Foundations of Ethical Theory.* Stockholm, Stockholm University Press.

Kant, Immanuel
[1785] *Uzasadnienie metafizyki moralności* [*Groundwork for the Metaphysics of Morals*]. Warszawa 1971 (2nd ed.), PWN.

Katz, Jerrold J.
[1977] *Propositional Structure and Illocutionary Force.* New York, The Harvester Press.

Katz, Jerrold J. & Postal, Paul M.
[1964] *An Integrated Theory of Linguistic Description.* Cambridge (Mass.), MIT Press.

Kaufmann, Felix
[1922] *Logik und Rechtswissenschaft. Grundriss eines Systems der reinen Rechtslehre.* Tübingen, J.C.B. Mohr.

Kelsen, Hans
[1945] *General Theory of Law and State.* Cambridge (Mass.), Harvard University Press.
[1979] *Allgemeine Theorie der Normen.* Wien, K. Ringhofer & T. Walter.

Klibansky, Raymond (ed.)
[1968] *La philosophie contemporaine. Chroniques / Contemporary Philosophy. A Survey.* Vol. I. Firenze, La Nuova Italia Editrice.

Kotarbiński, Tadeusz
[1929] *Elementy teorii poznania, logiki formalnej i metodologii nauk* [*Elements of the Theory of Cognition, Formal Logic and Methodology of Sciences*]. Wrocław 1961, *Ossolineum.*
[1931] Czesław Znamierowski: *Prolegomena do nauki o państwie* [*Preliminaries to Civic Studies*] (rev.). [In:] Kotarbiński [1957: 398–421].

[1934] Ideały [Ideals]. [In:] Kotarbiński 1957, p. 450–482.

[1947] *Kurs logiki dla prawników* [*A Course of Logic for Lawyers*]. Warszawa 1963, PWN.

[1957] *Wybór pism*. T. I. *Myśli o działaniu* [*Chosen Writings*. Vol. I. *Thoughts on Activity*]. Warszawa, PWN.

[1966] Zagadnienie racjonalności rozumowań rozkaźnikowych [The Problem of Rationality of Imperative Reasonings]. *Studia Filozoficzne* No. 2, p. 53–60.

Krawietz, Werner *et al.* (ed.)

[1984a] *Theorie der Normen*. Berlin, Duncker & Humblot.

[1984b] *Objektivierung des Rechtsdenkens*. Berlin, Duncker & Humblot.

Księga

[1931] *Księga pamiątkowa Polskiego Towarzystwa Filozoficznego we Lwowie* [*The Commemorative Book of Polish Philosophical Society in Lvov*]. Lwów, PTF.

Lande, Jerzy

[1925a] [Głos w dyskusji:] Narady nad teorią prawa [[Expressing opinion:] Discussions on the Theory of Law]. [In:] Jaworski (ed.) [1925: 61–75].

[1925b] Norma a zjawisko prawne [Norm *versus* Legal Phenomenon]. [In:] Jaworski (ed.) [1925: 235–348].

[1948] O ocenach. Uwagi dyskusyjne [On Evaluations. Comments to the Discussion]. *Kwartalnik Filozoficzny* vol. XVII, No. 3–4, p. 241–315.

[1956] *Nauka o normie prawnej* [*Theory of Legal Norms*]. Lublin, Wydawnictwo UMC-S.

[1959] *Studia z filozofii prawa* [*Studies in Philosophy of Law*]. Warszawa, PWN.

Lang, Wiesław

[1960] Obowiązywanie normy prawnej w czasie w świetle logiki norm [The Validity of Legal Norm in Time in the Light of the Logic of Norms]. *Zeszyty Naukowe UJ* No. 31. *Prace Prawnicze* No. 7, p. 47–88.

[1962] *Obowiązywanie prawa* [*The Validity of Law*]. Warszawa, PWN.

Lang, Wiesław & Delorme, Andrzej

[1957] Z zagadnień tzw. swobodnego uznania (w związku z projektem wprowadzenia sądowej kontroli administracji) [On Problems of the So-Called Free Acceptation (in Connection with the Project of Introducing Legal Control of Administration)]. *Państwo i Prawo* vol. XII, No. 4–5, p. 729–751.

Lang, Wiesław, Wróblewski, Jerzy & Zawadzki, Sylwester
[1979] *Teoria państwa i prawa* [*Legal and Civic Theory*]. Warszawa, PWN.

Larkin, Don & O'Malley, Michael H.
[1973] Declarative Sentences and the Rule-of-Conversation Hypothesis. [In:] Nawrocka-Fisiak (ed.) [1976: 117–130].

Laskowski, Roman
[1998] Tryb [The Mood]. [In:] Grzegorczykowa *et al.* (ed.) [1998: 178–187].

Leblanc, Hugues
[1973] On Dispensing with Things and Worlds. [In:] Munitz (ed.) [1973: 241–259].
[1976] *Truth-Value Semantics.* Amsterdam, North Holland.

Ledent, Adrien
[1942] Le statut logique des propositions imperatives. *Theoria* vol. VIII, I. 3, p. 262–271.

Leech, Geoffrey
[1977] J. Sadock, *Toward a Linguistic Theory of Speech Acts.* Cole & Morgan (ed.), *Syntax and Semantics.* Vol. II (rev.). *Journal of Linguistics* vol. XIII, No. 2, p. 133–145.

Lemmon, Edward John
[1965] Deontic Logic and the Logic of Imperatives. *Logique et Analyse* vol. VIII, s. 39–71.

Liddell, Henry George & Scott, Robert
[1925] *A Greek-English Lexicon.* Vol. I-X. Oxford 1925–1940, Clarendon Press.

Logic
[1962] *Logic and Language. Studies Dedicated to Professor Rudolf Carnap.* Dordrecht, D. Reidel.

Logika
[1980] *Logika i jej nauczanie w dziejach Uniwersytetu Jagiellońskiego* [*Logic, and Teaching of Logic, at the Jagiellonian University through the Ages*]. Kraków, Wydawnictwo UJ.

Löhrich, Rolf
[1937] Über Unverbindlichkeit, Verbindlichkeit und Wahrheit einer Normlehre, bezw. Normwissenschaft. *Actualités Scientifiques et Industrielles* c. XI, p. 71–77.

Łukasiewicz, Jan
[1925] Démonstration dela compatibilité des axiomes de la théorie de la déduction. *Annales de la Société Polonaise de Mathématiques* vol. III, p. 149.

MacIntyre, Alasdair Chalmers
[1966] *A Short History of Ethics.* New York-London 1966, Macmillan – Routledge.
[1968] Hume on „Is" and „Ought". [In:] Chappel (ed.) [1968: 240–264].

Martinich, Aloysius P.
[1980] Conversational Maxims and Some Philosophical Problems. *The Philosophical Quarterly* vol. CXX, No. 3, p. 215–228.

Modality
[1973] *Modality, Morality and Other Problems of Sense and Nonsense. Essays dedicated to Sören Halldén.* Lund, Greelus.

Montague, Richard
[1968] Pragmatic. [In:] Klibansky (ed.) [1972: 102–122].

Morgan, Jerry L.
[1977] Conversational Postulates Revisited. *Language* vol. LIII, No. 2, p. 277–284.

Munitz, Milton Karl (ed.)
[1973] *Logic and Ontology.* New York, New York University Press.

Naess, Arne
[1959] Do We Know that Basic Norms Connot Be True of False. *Theoria* vol. XXV, I. 1, p. 31–53.

Nagel, Ernest
[1961] *The Structure of Science.* New York, Harcourt, Brace and World, Inc.

Najder, Zdzisław
[1971] *Wartości i oceny* [*Values and Evaluations*]. Warszawa, PWN.

Nawrocka-Fisiak, Jadwiga (ed.)
[1976] *Readings in Generative Semantics.* Poznań, Wydawnictwo Naukowe UAM.

Nowak, Leszek
[1968a] *Próba metodologicznej charakterystyki prawoznawstwa* [*An Attempt of a Methodological Characteristic of Jurisprudence*]. Poznań, Wydawnictwo Naukowe UAM.
[1968b] Performatywy a język prawny i etyczny [Performatives *versus* Legal and Ethic Language]. *Etyka* vol. III, p. 147–158.

Nuckowski, Jan
[1903] *Początki logiki dla szkół średnich* [*Basic Logic for Secondary Schools*]. Kraków 1920 (3rd ed.), J. Czernecki.

Olivecrona, Karl
[1939] *Law as Fact.* Copenhagen-London, Einar Munksgaard-Humphrey Milford.

Opałek, Kazimierz
[1974] *Z teorii dyrektyw i norm* [*From the Theory of Directives and Norms*]. Warszawa, PWN.
[1990] Wartości i oceny w świetle dwóch teorii norm [Values and Evaluations from the Viewpoint of Two Theories of Norms]. [In:] Wronkowska & Zieliński (ed.) [1990: 307–321].

Opałek, Kazimierz & Woleński, Jan
[1973a] Problem aksjomatyzacji prawa [The Problem of Axiomatisation of Law]. *Państwo i Prawo* vol. XXVIII, No. 1, p. 3–14.
[1973b] On Weak and Strong Permissions. *Rechtstheorie* B. IV, H. 2, p. 369–384.
[1974] O tzw. słabych i mocnych dozwoleniach [On the So-Called Weak and Strong Permissions]. *Studia Filozoficzne* No. 8(105), p. 115–124.
[1980] *Überlegungen zu Hans Kelsens "Allgemeine Theorie der Normen".* Wien, Manz.
[1986] On Weak and Strong Permissions Once More. *Rechtstheorie* B. XVII, H. 1, p. 83–88.
[1991] Normative Systems, Permission and Deontic Logic. *Ratio Iuris* vol. IV, p. 334–348.

Ossowska, Maria
[1946] O dwóch rodzajach ocen [On Two Types of Evaluations]. *Kwartalnik Filozoficzny* t. XVII, No. 2-4, p. 279–292.

[1947] *Podstawy nauki o moralności* [*Foundations of the Theory of Morality*]. Warszawa 1963, PWN.

Peczenik, Aleksander
[1965] Problemy prawoznawstwa a logika norm [Problems of Jurisprudence *versus* Logic of Norms]. *Państwo i Prawo* t. V, p. 47–55.
[1968] Norms and Reality. *Theoria* vol. III, I. 2, p. 117–133.

Pelc, Jerzy
[1971] *O użyciu wyrażeń* [*On the Usage of Expressions*]. Wrocław, *Ossolineum.*

Perelman, Chaim
[1968] Le raisonnement pratique. [In:] Klibansky (ed.) [1968: 168–176].
[1976] *Logique juridique. Nouvelle réthorique.* Paris, Dalloz.

Petrażycki, Leon
[1905] *Введение в изучение права и нравственности. Эмоциональная психология* [*Introduction to the Theory of Law and Morality. Foundations of Emotional Psychology*]. С.-Петербург 1907, Типография Ю.Н. Эрлиха. Przekład polski: *Wstęp do nauki prawa i moralności. Podstawy psychologii emocjonalnej.* Warszawa 1959, PWN.
[1907a] *Теория права и государства в связи с теорией нравственности* [*Legal and Civic Theory in Relation with the Theory of Morality*]. Т. I-II. С.-Петербург 1910, Типография товариства "Екатериновское Печатное Дело". Przekład polski: *Teoria prawa i państwa w związku z teorią moralności.* Vol. I–II. Warszawa 1959–1960, PWN.
[1907b] *O pobudkach postępowania i o istocie moralnosci i prawa* [*On Motives of Behaviour and on the Essence of Morality and Law*]. Warszawa 1924, Księgarnia K. Wojnara.
[1907c] O normach moralnych i prawnych i sposobach ich wyrażania [On Legal and Moral Norms and Methods for Expressing Them]. [In:] Petrażycki [1985: 249–253].
[1939] *Nowe podstawy logiki i klasyfikacja umiejętności* [*New Foundations of Logic and Classification of Sciences*]. Warszawa, Towarzystwo im. Leona Petrażyckiego.
[1985] *O nauce, prawie i moralności* [*On Science, Law, and Morality*]. Warszawa, PWN.

Piotrowski, Mariusz
[1978] O rodzajach i odmianach niezgodności norm [Of Types and Variants of Norm Incompatibilities]. *Studia Filozoficzne* No. 11, p. 93–103.

Prior, Arthur Norman
[1971] *Objects of Thought*. Oxford, Oxford University Press.

Puzynina, Jadwiga
[1971] Jeden tryb czy dwa tryby? (Problem form trybu przypuszczającego
       w języku polskim) [One Mood or Two Moods? (The Problem of Forms
       of Conjectural Mood in Polish)]. *Biuletyn Polskiego Towarzystwa
       Językoznawczego* vol. XIX, p. 131–139.

Quine, Willard van Orman
[1960] *Word and Object*. Cambridge (Mass.), MIT Press.

Rand, Rose
[1936] Die Logik der verschiedenen Arten von Sätzen. *Przegląd Filozo-
       ficzny* vol. XXXIX, No. 4, p. 438.
[1939] Logik der Forderungssätze. *Revue Internationale de la Théorie du
       Droit – Zeitschrift für die Theorie des Rechts* vol. I, p. 308–322.

Reinach, Adolf
[1913] Die apriorischen Grundlagen des bürgerlichen Rechtes. [In:] *Jahr-
       buch für Philosophie und Phänomenologische Forschung*. Band I,
       p. 685–847.

Ross, Alf
[1933] *Kritik der sogenannten praktischen Erkenntnis*. Kopenhagen – Leip-
       zig, Levin & Munksgaard – Felix Meinor.
[1941] Imperatives and Logic. *Theoria* vol. VII, I. 1, p. 53–71.
[1946] *Towards a Realistic Jurisprudence. A Criticism of the Dualism in
       Law*. Copenhagen, Einar Munksgaard.
[1958] *On Law and Justice*. London, Stevens and Sons.
[1968] *Directives and Norms*. London, Routledge and Kegan Paul.

Rozprawy
[1964] *Rozprawy logiczne. Księga pamiątkowa ku czci profesora Kazimie-
       rza Ajdukiewicza* [*Logical Treatises. A Commemorative Book in Ho-
       nour of Professor Kazimierz Ajdukiewicz*]. Warszawa, PWN.
[1969] *Rozprawy filozoficzne. Księga pamiątkowa dla uczczenia 80. rocz-
       nicy urodzin T. Czeżowskiego* [*Philosophical Treatises. A Commemo-
       rative Book on T. Czeżowski's 80th Birthday*]. Toruń, Towarzystwo Na-
       ukowe w Toruniu.

Rudziński, Aleksander Witold (*vel* Steinberg, Witold)
[1947] *Z logiki norm* [*From the Logic of Norms*]. Kraków, Polska Akademia
    Umiejętności.

Russell, Bertrand
[1924] *Einführung in die mathematische Philosophie*. München, Drei
    Masken.

Rynin, David
[1960] Non-Cognitive Synonymy and the Definability of "Good". [In:]
    Logic [1962: 234–241].

Sadock, Jerrold M.
[1974] *Toward a Linguistic Theory of Speech Acts*. New York-San Franciso-
    London, Academic Press.

Schaff, Adam (ed.)
[1980] *Zagadnienia socjo- i psycholingwistyki* [*Problems of socio- and psy-
    cholinguistics*]. Wrocław, *Ossolineum*.

Schickhardus, Martinus
[1615] *Logica iuridica*. Herbornae Nassoviorum.

Schilpp, Paul Arthur (ed.)
[1963] *The Philosophy of Rudolf Carnap*. La Salle-London, Open Court.

Schopenhauer, Arthur
[1841] *Die beiden Grundprobleme der Ethik*. Frankfurt am Main, Hermann.

Searle, John Rogers
[1964] How to Derive "Ought" from "Is". *The Philosophical Review* vol.
    LXXIII, No. 1, p. 43–48.
[1969] *Speach Acts. An Essay in the Philosophy of Language*. Cambridge
    1975, Cambridge University Press.
[1976] J.M. Sadock, *Toward a Linguistic Theory of Speach Acts* (rev.). *Lan-
    guage* vol. LII, p. 966–971.

Shuy, Roger W. (ed.)
[1973] *Some New Directions in Linguistics*. Washington, Georgetown Uni-
    versity Press.

Sigwart, Christoph
[1879] Der Begriff des Wollens und sein Verhältnis zum Begriff der Ur-
    sache. [In:] *Kleine Schriften. Zweite Reihe.* Band 2, Freiburg i. Br. 1889,
    J.C. Mohr, p. 115–211.

Skeat, Walter William
[1879] *An Etymological Dictionary of the English Language.* Parts I–IV.
    Oxford 1879–1882, Clarendon Press.

Sleszyński, Jan
[1925] *Teoria dowodu* [*Proof Theory*]. Tom I. Kraków, Nakładem Kółka
    Matematyczno-Fizycznego UJ.

Sławski, Franciszek
[1956] *Słownik etymologiczny języka polskiego* [*The Etymological Diction-
    ary of Polish*]. Vol. I–V, Kraków 1952–1982, Towarzystwo Miłośników
    Języka Polskiego.

Somló, Felix
[1917] *Juristische Grundlehre.* Leipzig, Felix Meiner.

Spiegelberg, Herbert
[1935] *Gesetz und Sittengesetz.* Zürich und Leipzig, Max Niehans Verlag.

Stalnaker, Robert
[1972] Pragmatics. [In:] Davidson & Harman (ed.) [1972: 169–218].

Stevenson, Charles Leslie
[1944] *Ethics and Language.* New Haven, Yale University Press.
[1963] *Facts and Values.* New Haven, Yale University Press.

Stróżewski, Władysław (ed.)
[1978] *Studia z teorii poznania i teorii wartości* [*Studies in the Theory of
    Cognition and the Theory of Values*]. Kraków, Wydawnictwo PTF.

Studnicki, Franciszek
[1961] Wzór zachowania się, wzór postępowania i norma [Models of Be-
    haviour and Norm]. *Zeszyty Naukowe UJ. Prace Prawnicze* vol. VIII,
    p. 5–29.
[1967] O prawniczych rozumowaniach subsumpcyjnych [On Legal
    Subsumptive Reasonings]. *Studia Filozoficzne* 1967, No. 1(48), p.
    121–134.

[1968] Znaki drogowe [Road Signs]. *Studia Cywilistyczne* vol. XI, p. 177–211.
[1969] O wypowiedziach dokonawczych [On Performative Utterances]. *Studia Cywilistyczne* vol. XIII–XIV, p. 343–354.

Suszko, Roman
[1971] Reifikacja sytuacji [Reification of Situation]. *Studia Filozoficzne* No. 2, p. 65–82.

Szewczyk, Jan
[1964] Zagadnienie zależności wzajemnej ocen i norm [The Interdependence of Evaluations and Norms]. *Studia Filozoficzne* No. 4, p. 123–140.

Sztykgold, Jerzy
[1936] Negacja normy [Negation of the Norm]. *Przegląd Filozoficzny* vol. XXXIX, No. 4, p. 492–494.

Śmiałowski, Jerzy, Lang, Wiesław & Delorme, Andrzej
[1961] *Z zagadnień nauki o normie prawnej* [*Problems of Legal Norm Theory*]. Warszawa, PWN.

Świrydowicz, Kazimierz
[1981] W sprawie pojęcia obowiązku [On the Notion of Obligation]. *Ruch Prawniczy, Ekonomiczny i Socjologiczny* vol. XLIII, No. 1, p. 87–100.

Świrydowicz, Kazimierz *et al.*
[1975] O nieporozumieniach dotyczących tzw. "norm zezwalających" [On Misunderstandings Regarding the So-Called "Permitting Norms"]. *Państwo i Prawo* No. 7(353), p. 57–64.

Tammelo, Ilmar & Moens, Gabriël
[1976] *Logische Verfahren der juristischen Begründung.* Wien-New York, Springer-Verlag.

Tarski, Alfred
[1943–1944] The Semantic Conception of Truth and the Foundations of Semantics. *Philosophy and Phenomenological Research* vol. IV, p. 341–376.

Tatarkiewicz, Władysław
[1919] *O bezwzględności dobra* [*On the Absolute Value of Goodness*]. Warszawa, Gebethner i Wolff.

[1966] Obrachunek i nakazy, uczciwość i dobroć [Calculation and Dictates, Honesty and Goodness]. [In:] Tatarkiewicz [1971: 297–311].

[1971] *„Droga do filozofii" i inne rozprawy filozoficzne* [*„ The Road to Philosophy" and other Philosophical Treatises*]. Warszawa, PWN.

Twardowski, Kazimierz

[1901] *Zasadnicze pojęcia dydaktyki i logiki* [*Basic Notions of Didactics and Logic*]. Lwów, Nakładem Towarzystwa Pedagogicznego.

[1904] Psychologia pożądań i woli [Psychology of Desires and Will]. [In:] Twardowski [1992: 203–248].

[1905/1906] O zadaniach etyki naukowej [On the Tasks of Scientific Ethics]. *Etyka* vol. XII (1973), p. 135–137.

[1992] *Wybór pism psychologicznych i pedagogicznych* [*Selected Writings in Psychology and Pedagogics*]. Warszawa, WSiP.

Urbańczyk, Stanisław (ed.)

[1978] *Encyklopedia wiedzy o języku polskim* [*Encyclopaedia of the Knowledge on Polish Language*]. Wrocław, *Ossolineum*.

Wallis-Walfisz, Mieczysław

[1937] Les énoncé des appréciations et des normes. *Studia Philosophica* vol. II, p. 421–437.

Warnock, Mary

[1900] *Ethics Since 1900*. London, Oxford University Press.

Weber, Max

[1920] *Gesammelte Aufsätze zur Religionssoziologie*. Bd. I. Tübingen, Mohr.

Weinberger, Ota

[1958a] Die Sollsatzproblematik in der modernen Logik. *Rozpravy Československé Akademie Věd* vol. LXVIII, No. 9, p. 1–124.

[1958b] Können Sollsätze (Imperative) als Wahr Bezeichnet Werden. *Rozpravy Československé Akademie Věd* vol. LXVIII, No. 9, p. 145–160.

[1960] Studie k logice normativnich vět [Studies on the Logic of Norms]. *Rozpravy Československé Akademie Věd* vol. LXX, z. 1, p. 23–44.

[1964a] Einige Betrachtungen über die Rechtsnorm vom Standpunkt der Logik und der Semantik. *Logique et Analyse* vol. VII, p. 212–232.

[1964b] Philosophische Studien zur Logik. *Rozpravy Československé Akademie Věd* vol. LXXIV, No. 5, p. 24–49.

[1970] *Rechtslogik.* Wien – New York, Springer Verlag.

[1972] Fundamental Problems of the Theory of Legal Reasoning. *Archiv für Rechts- und Sozialphilosophie* Bd. LVIII, H. 3, p. 305–336.

[1980] Das Recht als institutionelle Tatsache. *Rechtstheorie* Bd. XI, H. 4. 427–442.

[1981] *Normentheorie als Grundlage der Jurisprudenz und Ethik. Eine Auseinandersetzung mit Hans Kelsens Theorie der Normen.* Berlin, Duncker & Humblot.

[1984] Logik und Objektivität der juristischen Argumentation. [In:] Krawietz *et al.* (ed.) [1984b: 557–568].

Wellman, Carl

[1961] *The Language of Ethics.* Cambridge (Mass.)-London, Harvard University Press.

Whitehead, Alfred North & Russell, Bertrand

[1910] *Principia matematica.* Vol. I. Cambridge 1935, Cambridge University Press.

Wilkosz, Witold

[1925] [Głos w dyskusji:] Narady nad teorią prawa [[Expressing Opinion:] Discussions on the Theory of Law]. [In:] Jaworski (ed.) [1925: 45–51].

Witwicki, Władysław

[1904] *Analiza psychologiczna objawów woli* [*Psychological Analysis of Symptoms of Will*]. Lwów, Towarzystwo dla Popierania Nauki Polskiej [*Archiwum Naukowe. Wydawnictwo TPNP.* Section I, vol. I, No. 2, p. 1(261)–127(387)].

Woleński, Jan

[1966] Spór o «znaczenie normatywne» [Controversy on «Normative Meaning»]. [In:] *Interpretacje* [1966: 3–14].

[1972] *Logiczne problemy wykładni prawa* [*Logical Problems of Law Interpretation*]. Kraków, UJ.

[1978] Filozoficzne aspekty sporu o logikę prawniczą [Philosophical Aspects of the Controversy on Legal Logic]. [In:] Stróżewski (ed.) [1978: 33–40].

[1980a] Logika, semantyka, normy [Logic, Semantics, Norms]. [In:] Woleński [1980a: 60–97].

[1980b] *Z zagadnień analitycznej filozofii prawa* [*Problems of Analytical Legal Philosophy*]. Warszawa-Kraków, PWN.

[1980c] Note on Free-Choice Permissions. *Archiv für Rechts- und Sozjal-philosophie* B. LXVI, p. 507–510.

[1980d] Z historii logiki zdań normatywnych: W. Wilkosz i A.W. Rudziński [From the History of Logic of Normative Sentences: W. Wilkosz and A.W. Rudziński]. [In:] *Logika* [1980: 61–77].

[1982] Przyczynek do analizy pojęcia dozwolenia [A Contribution to the Analysis of the Notion of Permission]. *Państwo i Prawo* vol. XXXVII, No. 1–2, p. 61–64.

[1983] Obowiązywanie i prawdziwość [Validity and Truthfulness]. *Studia Filozoficzne* No. 10, p. 15–25.

Wolter, Władysław & Lipczyńska, Maria

[1980a] Zdanie normatywne (norma) i logika deontyczna [Normative Sentence (Norm) and Deontic Logic]. [In:] Wolter & Lipczyńska [1980b: 220–225].

[1980b] *Elementy logiki. Wykład dla prawników* [*Elements of Logic. Lectures for Lawyers*]. Warszawa-Wrocław (3rd ed.), PWN.

Wright, Georg Henrik von

[1951] Deontic Logic. *Mind* vol. LX, No. 237, p. 1–15.

[1957] *Logical Studies.* London, Routledge & Kegan Paul.

[1963a] *Norm and Action.* London, Routledge & Kegan Paul.

[1963b] *The Varieties of Goodness.* London, Routledge & Kegan Paul.

[1964] A New System of Deontic Logic. *Danish Yearbook of Philosophy* vol. I, p. 173–182.

[1967] Deontic Logics. *American Philosophical Quarterly* vol. IV, p. 1–18.

[1968a] *An Essay in Deontic Logic and the General Theory of Action.* Amsterdam, North Holland.

[1968b] The Logic of Practical Discourse. [In:] Klibansky (ed.) [1968: 141–167].

[1970] On the Logic and Ontology of Norms. [In:] Davis *et al.* (ed.) [1970: 89–107].

[1971] On So-Called Practical Inference. *Acta Sociologica* vol. XV, No. 1, p. 39–53.

[1973] Truth as Modality. [In:] *Modality* [1973: 142-150].

[1981] On the Logic of Norms and Actions. [In:] Hilpinen (ed.) [1983: 3–35].

Wronkowska, Sławomira & Zieliński, Maciej (ed.)

[1990] *Szkice z teorii prawa i szczegółowych nauk prawniczych* [*Essays on Legal Theory and Legal Particular Sciences*]. Poznań, Wydawnictwo UAM.

Wróblewski, Bronisław (ed.)
[1936] *Ogólna nauka o prawie*. T. I. [*General Theory of Law*. Vol. I]. Wilno, Koło Filozoficzne Studentów USB.

Wróblewski, Jerzy
[1959] *Zagadnienie teorii wykładni prawa ludowego* [*Theory of People's Law Interpretation*]. Warszawa, Wydawnictwo Prawnicze.
[1964] The Problem of the Meaning of the Legal Norm. *Österreichische Zeitschrift für öffentliches Recht* Bd. XIV, H. 3–4, p. 253–266.
[1978] Zwroty zrelatywizowane systemowo [Systemically Relativized Phrases]. *Studia Filozoficzne* No. 3, p. 143–159.
[1979] Struktury logiczne a system prawa pozytywnego [Logical Structures *versus* the Positive Law System] (rev. of L. Villanova's Work *As estructuras lógicas e o sistema do direito positivo*). *Studia Prawno-Ekonomiczne* vol. XXI, p. 211–217.
[1984] Negation in Law. [In:] Krawietz *et al.* (ed.) [1984a: 457–471].

Zieliński, Maciej
[1972] *Interpretacja jako proces dekodowania tekstu prawnego* [*Interpretation as the Process of Decoding of a Legal Text*]. Poznań, Wydawnictwo UAM.
[1992] Formy przekazywania norm postępowania [Forms of Sharing the Norms of Behaviour]. [In:] Ziembiński & Zieliński [1992: 79–90].

Zieliński, Maciej & Ziembiński, Zygmunt
[1988] *Uzasadnianie twierdzeń, ocen i norm w prawoznawstwie* [*Justification of Statements, Evaluations, and Norms in Jurisprudence*]. Warszawa, PWN.

Ziemba, Zdzisław
[1957] Logika formalna w myśleniu prawniczym [Formal Logic in Legal Thought]. *Państwo i Prawo* vol. XII, No. 2, p. 265–283.
[1968] Paradoksy logiki deontycznej [Paradoxes of Deontic Logic]. *Państwo i Prawo* vol. XXIII, No. 1, p. 45–56.
[1969] *Logika deontyczna jako formalizacja rozumowań deontycznych* [*Deontic Logic as Formalisation of Deontic Reasonings*]. Warszawa, PWN.
[1983] *Analityczna teoria obowiązku* [*Analytic Theory of Obligation*]. Warszawa, PWN.

Ziemba, Zdzisław & Ziembiński, Zygmunt
[1964] Uwagi o wynikaniu norm prawnych [Notes on Entailment of Legal Norms]. *Studia Filozoficzne* No. 4, p. 111–122.

Ziembiński, Zygmunt

[1956] *Logika praktyczna* [*Practical Logic*]. Warszawa 1994, Wydawnictwo Naukowe PWN.

[1963] Normy tetyczne a normy aksjologiczne w koncepcji Cz. Znamierowskiego [Thetic Norms and Axiological Norms in Cz. Znamierowski's Conception]. *Studia Filozoficzne* No. 2, p. 87–112.

[1964] O wynikaniu norm z norm [On Entailment of Norms from Norms]. [In:] *Rozprawy* [1964: 241–245].

[1966a] La logique et la jurisprudence de demain. *Archives de Philosophie du Droit*, t. XI. *La Logique du Droit*, p. 221–225.

[1966b] *Logiczne podstawy prawoznawstwa* [*Logical Foundations of Jurisprudence*]. Warszawa, Wydawnictwo Prawnicze.

[1972a] *Analiza pojęcia czynu* [*Analysis of the Notion of Act*]. Warszawa, *Wiedza Powszechna*.

[1972b] O warunkach zastosowania logiki deontycznej we wnioskowaniach prawniczych. [On Conditions for Using Deontic Logic in Legal Reasoning]. *Studia Filozoficzne* No. 2, p. 201–215.

[1977] Założenia faktyczne wypowiedzi normatywnych [Factual Assumptions behind Normative Utterances]. *Etyka* vol. XV, p. 127–141.

[1982] Typologia naruszeń praworządności [A Typology of Law Violation]. *Państwo i Prawo* vol. XXXVII, No. 8, p. 20–32.

[1984] Kinds of Discordance of Norms. [In:] Krawietz *et al.* (ed.) [1984a: 473–484].

Ziembiński, Zygmunt & Zieliński, Maciej

[1992] *Dyrektywy i sposób ich wypowiadania* [*Directives and How They are Uttered*]. Warszawa, Polskie Towarzystwo Semiotyczne.

Znamierowski, Czesław

[1924] *Podstawowe pojęcia prawa. Cz. I. Układ prawny i norma prawna* [*Basic Notions of Law. Part I. Legal System and Legal Norm*]. Poznań 1934 (2nd ed.), Górski i Tetzlaw.

[1925] [Dyskusja z Witoldem Wilkoszem w:] [A Discussion with Witold Wilkosz in:] *Przegląd Filozoficzny* vol. XXVIII, No. 3–4, p. 252–257.

[1930] *Prolegomena do nauki o państwie* [*Preliminaries to Civic Theory*]. Poznań 1947 (2nd ed.), Księgarnia Zdzisława Gutowskiego.

[1957] *Oceny i normy* [*Evaluations and Norms*]. Warszawa, PWN.

Index of names